Speaking the Incomprehensible God

Gregory P. Rocca, O.P.

Speaking the Incomprehensible God

Thomas Aquinas on the Interplay of

Positive and Negative Theology

The Catholic University of America Press

Washington, D.C.

Library of Congress Cataloging-in-Publication Data
Rocca, Gregory P., 1949–
   Speaking the incomprehensible God : Thomas Aquinas on the interplay of
      positive and negative theology / Gregory P. Rocca. — 1st ed.
      p. cm.
   Includes bibliographical references and indexes.
    ISBN 0-8132-1367-3 (alk. paper) ISBN 978-0-8132-1574-7 (pbk)
    1. Thomas, Aquinas, Saint, 1225?–1274. 2. God—Knowableness—History of
doctrines—Middle Ages, 600–1500. 3. Knowledge, Theory of (Religion)—
History of doctrines—Middle Ages, 600–1500. I. Title.
  BT98.R57 2004
  230'.2'092—dc21
                              2003011997

To my parents
Aldo and Irena Rocca

Contents

If God has spoken to us, then must it not be the case that we can speak of him? If he searches us out and indeed desires to be near us, then must it not be possible for us to encounter him, and know him, and converse with him? If the Word of God has taken flesh, can we not rely on him to provide the words we need to participate in a conversation that God himself has initiated?

Notwithstanding the resoundingly affirmative response which the Christian faith must give to these questions, it remains true that, upon closer examination, things are not quite as simple as they seem. The God who has spoken to us is the Creator of the universe, and we are his creatures. We do not have a direct experiential knowledge of him comparable to our experience and knowledge of the world around us. Even when we know him—as we surely do in faith—we cannot comprehend him. Only God knows himself truly and, as Aquinas says, our knowledge of him is but a kind of participation in the knowledge he has of himself. The language we use to speak of him—even when it is legitimated by the authority and usage of Scripture itself—is nonetheless language drawn from our experience of the world around us. It is not clear precisely how successful this language is in its endeavor to speak about the Creator of the universe.

Almost from the beginning, the Christian theological tradition has found it unavoidable to ponder the questions raised by, on the one hand, an absolute assurance that the triune God has spoken to us, and, on the other, the fundamental difficulties that arise when human beings attempt to speak about him. It has by no means been unusual for Christian theologians and mystics to describe God as incomprehensible and ineffable, or unknowable and unspeakable. In doing so, they have not meant to deny the most basic convictions of our faith in the incarnation and redemption, in the sending and indwelling of the Holy Spirit—in other words, in God's awesome nearness to us. But they have been unable to avoid the utter mystery surrounding our knowledge of God and our discourse about him, and unable to avoid wondering what we really can know or speak about the unknowable and unspeakable God.

There has been a temptation—which some Christian thinkers have found hard to resist—to allow reflection concerning the difficulties posed by our knowing and speaking about God to go forward independently of the conviction, based in faith, that he has spoken to us in his Word and that, in a real sense, the words to speak about him are already his gift to us. In this way, inquiries into what came to be called the possibility of "God-talk" in the last century often drifted into dreary byways of practical skepticism and agnosticism, far from the confident liturgical and pastoral discourse of the Church. Certainly, in the Catholic tradition, an authentic "theological epistemology"—as this sub-field of theology has come to be known—needs to be firmly grounded in faith in the freely bestowed grace of God's nearness to us in his Son and in the Holy Spirit. Theological epistemology must, in other words, retain its distinctive theological identity as an inquiry seeking the intelligibility of the faith.

Although the theological epistemology of St. Thomas Aquinas has often been read in ways that detach that enterprise from its properly theological moorings, Gregory Rocca's remarkable book avoids this pitfall. What is more, readers will find here an account of Aquinas's theological epistemology that fully locates it within his overall theological enterprise and provides the most comprehensive analysis of this aspect of the Angelic Doctor's thought that is currently available. I know of no comparable work that demonstrates such a complete mastery of Aquinas's writings and of the relevant secondary literature in this area. It is a particular pleasure to be able to introduce to readers a work that not only presents a thoroughgoing recovery of Aquinas's theological epistemology but also shows at various points how this account relates to a range of current theological debates about "God-talk" and more broadly about the central issues of philosophical theology.

Rocca shows that, for Aquinas and other Christian theologians, we can know and speak about God, finally, because he has known and spoken to us.

Preface

The present work is an extensive investigation into St. Thomas Aquinas' theological epistemology, an investigation attempted for its own sake and also in the hope that a synthetic retrieval of his thought might serve as a helpful resource for the contemporary dialogue concerning how we ought to think and speak about God. Aquinas' theological epistemology (an expression he himself does not use) is his theory about the manner in which humans are able to know and speak about God. He often casts his theological epistemology as a discussion of the knowledge and predication of the divine names, which include elements of negative and positive theology, and analogy, which lies at the heart of his positive theology. A thorough understanding of his theological epistemology, then, is largely a matter of grasping how these three elements interrelate and condition one another. Difficult problems face those who would try to comprehend these issues, for they all partake of that great and ultimate Mystery, God, who is implicated in each of them. Nevertheless, this study will be successful as a retrieval of Aquinas' theological epistemology only if it is able to reach these deep and intertwined roots of his thought.

Very often, writers who delve into the riddle of how we can know and talk about God will give a nod, and sometimes more than a nod, toward Aquinas' thought on the subject, for he is generally recognized as one of the great classical theologians, but rarely can they devote enough space to the kind of detailed treatment of his views that may discover the full intricacy of his thought and also preserve it from being too easily capsulized in familiar slogans. A nuanced and comprehensive treatment of the interplay of his positive and negative theology, therefore, should prove helpful to contemporary discussions.

This book aims to show that Aquinas' theological epistemology is a combination of negative and positive theology and that his positive theology is rooted in an analogy subsisting in judgments, including the judgments of faith; it also discovers the ultimate unity of his theological analogy in judgment instead of concept, so that his theological epistemology gives precedence to truth over meaning. In the last thirty or forty years, a few writers have mentioned the role of judgment in Aquinas' doctrine of analogy, and the present work underscores the consequences of viewing analogy as such. This study also relates Thomistic analogy to the truths of faith, though Thomas himself treats of analogy in what have often been considered the more strictly philosophical sections of his doctrine on God. Finally, this work details how Thomas' theological epistemology, as a second-order reflection, is directly grounded in the first-order judgments of his doctrine about God and creation. It is especially important to underline that Thomas' teaching on our knowing and naming of God is thoroughly grounded in a few crucial theological truths, especially his understanding of God as Creator.

Hoping to shed new light on the fragile though fruitful unity of Aquinas' positive and negative theology, a unity based on the truths about God he holds dear, I have divided the book into four parts: the incomprehensibility of God and negative theology in Aquinas, analogy and the web of judgment, Aquinas' crucial theological truths, and his theology of the divine names. Part One begins with a chapter devoted to the Greek tradition on apophatic theology, which will permit the reader to grasp how deeply Thomas is indebted to the Greeks, especially Pseudo-Dionysius, for his own negative theology, while also permitting the reader to understand how Thomas has transformed what he has imbibed from them, both in the overall context as well as the comparatively less radical nature of his negative theology. Likewise, Part Two begins with a chapter about analogy in Aristotle, since Thomas continually hearkens to the one he calls the Philosopher for much of his theory, language, and examples concerning analogy.

This study is a work of interpretation, for in no single place does Thomas divulge, with all its connecting arrows, the total synthetic or genetic makeup of his theological epistemology. It can be gleaned, nevertheless, from many places and indications in his works, and interpreted as an intelligible whole. One of the central supporting pillars of this interpretation is that Thomas weaves his negative and positive theology together, precisely because *only that interweaving* can do justice to the fact that the church must speak and praise, must invoke and love and follow the God *who just is* the Mysterious and Incomprehensible One who ever escapes and is never caught by our ideational and conceptual schemes.

The method I have followed involves a close intertextual reading of all the pertinent passages in Thomas' works—from his commentaries, compendia, summas, expert opinions, occasional works, and letters—both his lesser known as well as his more famous works. The method is also analytic, synthetic, and genetic. It is synthetic in that it attempts to understand, through their relations and internal connections, all the principles required for a proper appraisal of Aquinas' theological epistemology, though no well-founded synthesis can occur without a preceding analysis that is sufficiently detailed and comprehensive. The method is also genetic in that it desires to hazard a reasonable supposition as to how Aquinas' theological epistemology was built up in his own mind, as to how it was grounded and justified in his own thought.

My translation of Aquinas' relatively simple Latin aims to be rather exact, and I will note any difficulties or ambiguities of translation, or any terms of special philological, philosophical, or theological significance. As regards two important English words used to render two rich Latin terms frequently used by Thomas: *meaning* and *being* usually translate *ratio* and *esse*, respectively, unless another Latin term is noted in parentheses, though of course these Latin words are not restricted to those translations. All translations from other foreign languages are also my own, unless otherwise noted.

Aquinas' works will be cited in text and notes in an abbreviated form (please refer to the list of Abbreviations). The sections within each work are separated by periods and follow the normal order of progression for the published Latin text mentioned in the Bibliography (please consult its prefatory note). For example, *Meta.* 6.1.1144 refers to Thomas' commentary on Aristotle's *Metaphysics*, book 6, lecture 1, number 1144; *SS* 2.33.2.2 ad3 signifies his commentary on Peter Lombard's *Sentences*, book 2, distinction 33, question 2, article 2, response to the third objection; *Quod.* 8.4.2 ad1 means *Quaestiones Quodlibetales*, eighth quodlibet, question 4, article 2, response to the first objection. Sometimes a page and/or line number from the appropriate Latin edition named in the Bibliography will be added to the citation. In the notes, *same* means that the ensuing references from Thomas' works refer to passages that are nearly exact replicas, with only minor variations, of the thought and structure of the principal text cited. In a series of citations from his works, items lacking titles are to be referred back to the most recent title.

A book cannot come into existence without the help of many, to all of whom I am very grateful. My thanks to J. Augustine Di Noia, O.P., for encouraging me to publish and for graciously consenting to write the Foreword, and to David Burrell, C.S.C., and James LeGrys for also playing supportive roles in the eventual outcome of this book; to my faculty colleague Professor Mark Delp for his useful suggestions about the Greek tradition of negative theology; and to Fred Hinnebusch, O.P., for his help with Leonine Commission editions of Aquinas' works.

My thanks to the Governors and Trustees of the Dominican School of Philosophy and Theology, who granted me a much-needed sabbatical; to Patrick Finley, the Chair of the Board of Trustees, who energetically encouraged my book project; to Antoninus Wall, O.P., who took over for me as Acting President and has never wavered in his support for me and this book; and to Scott Connolly, the School's Dean of Students/Registrar, who helped Fr. Wall in his duties, making sure everything ran smoothly in my absence, and has continued to act as my technical expert.

My thanks to the Dominican community at St. Thomas More Parish serving the University of Oregon, especially Michael Fones, for their warm welcome and brotherly care during my sabbatical, and for creating space in their lives for my longish disquisitions and other odd antics born of too much intense intellectual labor.

My thanks to three of my Dominican confreres who provided timely boosts for this book at crucial points—Fergus Kerr, Kurt Pritzl, and John Vidmar; and to those who in their own ways have bolstered me and my project over the past few years: Dominican brothers and sisters— Raymond Bertheaux, Luke Buckles, Maria Goretti Eder, John Paul Forte, Hilary Martin, John Mellein, Michael Morris, Mary Nolan, Fabian Parmisano, Anthony Rosevear, Michael Sherwin, and Martin Walsh—and other friends, especially Maureen Baldwin and Jason Escalante, Gayle Emery, James and Kay Jezek, Andrew Porter, Helen and Armando Rendon, and Margie and Pete Wilkinson.

My thanks to Brian Shanley, O.P., for permission to use in revised form in chapter 11 an article that originally appeared in *The Thomist*.

My thanks to Dr. David McGonagle, Director of the Catholic University of America Press, for his ever valuable assistance and cooperation; to Susan Needham, Managing Editor at the Press, for her competent guidance and detailed oversight of the whole editorial process; to Elizabeth Benevides, Marketing Manager at the Press, for helping to promote the use of the captivating photo on the dust cover; to Carol Kennedy, for her expert and meticulous copyediting of the text and for her preparation of the indexes of names and of texts of Aquinas; and to Kathleen Pluth, for her preparation of the index of subjects.

My final word of thanks goes to my wonderful family, who have twined me into their lives with lavished love, and especially to my parents, Aldo and Irena, who have made so many good things possible for me and to whom this book is dedicated with heartfelt gratitude.

GREGORY ROCCA, O.P.
Berkeley, California
March, 2003

Abbreviations

I. Works by Thomas Aquinas

Anima	Sententia libri De anima
Ave	Collationes super Ave Maria
BDH	Expositio libri Boetii De hebdomadibus
BDT	Super Boetium De Trinitate
Caelo	Sententia super libros De caelo et mundo
CEG	Contra errores Graecorum
Credo	Collationes super Credo in Deum
CT	Compendium theologiae ad fratrem Raynaldum
DA	Quaestio disputata De anima
DC	Quaestio disputata De caritate
DDN	Super librum Dionysii De divinis nominibus
DE	De ente et essentia
De aetern.	De aeternitate mundi
De articulis	De articulis fidei et ecclesiae sacramentis ad Archiepiscopum Panormitanum
Decretalem	Expositio super primam et secundam Decretalem ad Archidiaconum Tudertinum
De perfec.	De perfectione spiritualis vitae

De prin.	*De principiis naturae*
De ration.	*De rationibus fidei ad Cantorem Antiochenum*
De unitate	*De unitate intellectus contra Averroistas*
DM	*Quaestiones disputatae De malo*
DP	*Quaestiones disputatae De potentia*
DS	*Quaestio disputata De spe*
DSC	*Quaestio disputata De spiritualibus creaturis*
DSS	*De substantiis separatis ad fratrem Raynaldum*
DV	*Quaestiones disputatae De veritate*
Ethic.	*Sententia libri Ethicorum*
Gener.	*Sententia super libros De generatione et corruptione*
Herm.	*Expositio libri Peri hermenias*
Isa.	*Expositio super Isaiam ad litteram*
Job	*Expositio super Job ad litteram*
John	*Lectura super Joannem*
Matt.	*Lectura super Matthaeum*
Memoria	*Sententia libri De memoria et reminiscentia*
Meta.	*Sententia super Metaphysicam*
Meteor.	*Sententia super Meteora*
Pater	*Collationes super Pater Noster*
Phys.	*Sententia super Physicam*
Post.	*Expositio libri Posteriorum*
Praeceptis	*Collationes in decem praeceptis*
Psalm	*Postilla super Psalmos*
Quod.	*Quaestiones de quodlibet I–XII*
R36	*Responsio ad Lectorem Venetum de 36 articulis*
R43	*Responsio ad Magistrum Joannem de Vercellis de 43 articulis*
R108	*Responsio ad Magistrum Joannem de Vercellis de 108 articulis*
Rom., etc.	*Expositio et Lectura super Epistolas Pauli Apostoli*
SCG	*Summa contra Gentiles*

SDC	*Super librum De causis*
Sensu	*Sententia libri De sensu et sensato*
SS	*Scriptum super libros Sententiarum*
ST	*Summa theologiae*

II. Journals and Other Abbreviations

ACPQ	*American Catholic Philosophical Quarterly*
ACR	*Australasian Catholic Record*
AFP	*Archivum Fratrum Praedicatorum*
AHDLMA	*Archives d'histoire doctrinale et littéraire du moyen âge*
AJP	*American Journal of Philology*
AP	*Archives de philosophie*
BibThom	Bibliothèque Thomiste
BT	*Bulletin thomiste*
CS	*Cistercian Studies*
CUA	Catholic University of America
DC	*Doctor communis*
DN	Pseudo-Dionysius' *On the Divine Names*
DR	*Downside Review*
DTP	*Divus Thomas* (Piacenza)
ETL	*Ephemerides theologicae Lovanienses*
EvT	*Evangelische Theologie*
FC	Fathers of the Church, Washington, D.C.
FP	*Faith and Philosophy*
FS	*Franciscan Studies*
FSt	*Franziskanische Studien*
FZPT	*Freiburger Zeitschrift für Philosophie und Theologie*
HJ	*Heythrop Journal*
IPQ	*International Philosophical Quarterly*
ITQ	*Irish Theological Quarterly*
JJS	*Journal of Jewish Studies*

JTS	*Journal of Theological Studies*
LC	Leonine Commission (Rome/Paris, 1882–)
LTK	*Lexicon für Theologie und Kirche,* 2nd edition
LTP	*Laval théologique et philosophique*
MS	*Medieval Studies*
MSch	*Modern Schoolman*
MT	Pseudo-Dionysius' *Mystical Theology*
NCE	*New Catholic Encyclopedia*
NS	*New Scholasticism*
NV	*Nova et vetera*
NZST	*Neue Zeitschrift für systematische Theologie und Religionsphilosophie*
PACPA	*Proceedings of the American Catholic Philosophical Association*
PG	Patrologia Graeca
PIMS	Pontifical Institute of Mediaeval Studies
PJ	*Philosophisches Jahrbuch*
PL	Patrologia Latina
PQ	*Philosophical Quarterly*
PS	*Philosophical Studies*
RevSR	*Revue des sciences religieuses*
RFNS	*Rivista di filosofia neo-scolastica*
RLT	*Rassegna di letteratura tomistica*
RM	*Review of Metaphysics*
RNP	*Revue néoscholastique de philosophie*
RP	*Revue de philosophie*
RPL	*Revue philosophique de Louvain*
RS	*Religious Studies*
RSPT	*Revue des sciences philosophiques et théologiques*
RSR	*Recherches de science religieuse*
RT	*Revue thomiste*
RTAM	*Recherches de théologie ancienne et médiévale*

RUO	*Revue de l'université d'Ottawa*
SE	*Science et esprit*
SJP	*Salzburger Jahrbuch für Philosophie*
SJT	*Scottish Journal of Theology*
SP	*Studia Patristica*
SUNY	State University of New York
SVTQ	*St. Vladimir's Theological Quarterly*
ThPh	*Theologie und Philosophie*
TLZ	*Theologische Literaturzeitung*
TP	*Tijdschrift voor Philosophie*
TRE	*Theologische Realenzyklopädie*
TS	*Theological Studies*
UND	University of Notre Dame
USQR	*Union Seminary Quarterly Review*
VC	*Vigiliae Christianae*

Part One. God the Incomprehensible and Negative Theology

1. A Brief Survey of Negative Theology in the Hellenistic and Patristic Traditions

Since Aquinas' chief source for his understanding of negative theology and God's incomprehensibility in the Christian tradition is indisputably Pseudo-Dionysius the Areopagite—with John Damascene playing a supporting role—and since these two writers, as well as the earlier authors that paved the way for them, both Christian and non-Christian, come largely from the Hellenistic world on the border between East and West, it is important to become familiar with the terminology and traits of that world's understanding of God's incomprehensibility and negative theology. The intention is not to be exhaustive but to give enough background so that Aquinas' position on negative theology can be better appreciated.

The two most significant formal terms for the Greek system of negative theology are *aphairesis* (Latin: *remotio/abstractio*) and *apophasis* (Latin: *negatio*). *Aphairesis* means a taking away or removing: it could mean subtraction in a mathematical context, abstraction in a logical context, or even amputation in a medical context. It remained a core word for negative theology from its beginnings in Albinus right on into medieval theology with its "way of removal." Etymologically, *apophasis* signifies "a saying from," that is, a denying or negating, from which we derive the term *apophatic* to refer to "negative" theology. Although *apophasis* does not in itself have the same meaning as *aphairesis*, in later writers it makes its appearance with a signification indistinguishable from that of *aphairesis*.[1] A third term, *analysis* (Latin: *resolutio*), meaning a loosing or dissolving, was also sometimes used as a synonym for *aphairesis*.

The apophatic or "aphairetic" way of understanding God, however, was actually only one of three interlinking paths woven into a comprehensive threefold method of coming to know God; the other two ways are *analogia* (Latin: *analogia*) and *hyperochē/epochē* (Latin: *eminentia/excellentia*). *Analogia* etymologically means a "reckoning up"; *synthesis* (Latin: *compositio*), meaning a putting or placing together, was at times used as a synonym for *analogia*. *Hyperochē*, meaning supereminence, preeminence, or transcendence, has its etymological roots in *hyperechein* (to rise or project above).

Nevertheless, the so-called "negative way" *(via negativa)* and negative, apophatic theology, though closely related, are not exactly the same. Negative theology often refers to a theory about how the divine predicates signify in the discipline of theology, even academically understood; and while *via negativa* can sometimes function as a synonym for negative theology so understood, it can also refer to a spiritual way or method by which one lives and thinks in order to arrive at union with God, and in this case it is not merely of academic interest but amounts to a life program with ascetical, moral, mystical, and spiritual elements. This latter sense is the one we find in authors such as Clement of Alexandria, Plotinus, and Pseudo-Dionysius.[2]

---

1. According to Raoul Mortley ("The Fundamentals of the *Via Negativa*," *AJP* 103 [1982]: 436–38), *aphairesis* as distinct from *apophasis* is connected, in the earlier Platonists, with the ancient Greek theory of reality as being fully formed by a process of gradual accretion, probably based on the Pythagorean view that reality is formed from numbers, beginning from a single unit. *Aphairesis*, then, would be a process of removing outer layers so as to come to an inner, essential core.

2. Raoul Mortley and David Dockrill, eds., *The Via Negativa*, Papers from the *Via Negativa* conference held at the University of Sydney in 1981 (n.p.: *Prudentia*, 1981). Christian Guérard even attempts to distinguish between what he calls the apophatism and the negative theology of the Greeks ("La théologie négative dans l'apophatisme grec," *RSPT* 68 [1984]: 183–200). After a lifetime of studying the *via negativa*, Vladimir Lossky recognized that apophasis is not coterminous with mysticism and that the use of apophasis by Christian writers varies, since it may be used speculatively or mystically, as a full-blown theory or only incidentally (R. G. Williams, "The *Via Negativa* and the Foundations of Theology: An

If we turn our attention to the material terms employed by negative theology to deny various attributes of God, it is clear they all begin with an *alpha (a)*, which is sometimes followed by a *nu (n)* if the original word root begins with a vowel. This is the celebrated "alpha privative," the normal means by which Greek signifies negation. As the pre-Christian passed into the Christian era, there was a proliferation of alpha privatives in theological language, from the Hermetic Corpus to the Nag Hammadi documents, and the negative adjectives thus formed show "a tendency to magnify the mystery of God."[3]

Jean Daniélou designates the chief sources of the negative names of apophatic theology as Hellenistic Judaism, Middle Platonism, and Gnosticism, recognizing that all of these are themselves partial developments out of certain oriental and Platonic influences, and that some negative terms find their provenance in more than one source.[4] He sees three items as coming from Hellenistic Judaism, which as a general tradition aims to express God's transcendence. Certain terms stress God's unapproachability and transcendence, and may originate from a Hellenistic Jewish gnosis that is itself based on Palestinian apocalyptic: examples of such terms may be found in the Pauline texts discussed below. Another set of terms, found principally in the apologists and Clement of Alexandria, stem from the Helleno-Judaic polemic against idols, wherein God's spiritual and uncreated nature is emphasized: *atheatos* (invisible); *aoratos* (invisible), also found in St. Paul; *achōrētos* (uncontainable); *agenētos* (uncreated); *anendeēs* (not needy), also found in Greek philosophy. The final set comes from Philo, the first theologian to treat fully of the divine transcendence while combating philosophical rationalism: *aperigraphos* (uncir-

---

Introduction to the Thought of V. N. Lossky," in *New Studies in Theology*, no. 1, ed. S. Sykes and D. Holmes [London: Duckworth, 1980], pp. 96–99). Mortley ("Fundamentals," pp. 438–39) remarks that the *via abstractiva* will be more or less radical depending on whether the *aphairesis* is aiming at a Neoplatonic and quasi-pantheistic, or a Christian and transcendent God.

3. Mortley, "Fundamentals," pp. 432–33.

4. Jean Daniélou, "L'incompréhensibilité de Dieu d'après saint Jean Chrysostome," *RSR* 37 (1950): 178–79; *A History of Early Christian Doctrine before the Council of Nicea*, vol. 2: *Gospel Message and Hellenistic Culture*, trans. and ed. J. A. Baker (London/Philadelphia: Westminster, 1973), chap. 15.

cumscribed); *aperinoētos* (incomprehensible); *anōnomastos/akatonomas-tos* (unnameable); *akatalēptos* (incomprehensible). This latter, not found in the Hebrew scriptures, eventually becomes, in the fourth century, the technical term for God's transcendent incomprehensibility.[5]

Middle Platonism (Albinus, Celsus, Maximus of Tyre), which stresses that God transcends all definition and delimitation, is a source for the following terms: *anarchos* (without beginning); *agennētos* (unbegotten); *anōlethros* (indestructible); *aphthartos* (incorruptible); *aoratos* (invisible), also found in Jewish anti-idol apologetic; *anaphēs* (intangible); *amorphos, aschēmatistos, aneideos* (all bespeaking God's formlessness and lack of shape); *arrētos* (ineffable), though found in Paul, in Philo, and elsewhere, is still a technical term deriving from Albinus and his school since it is not found in Plato as a predicate for God.[6] Certain words from Greek philosophy, like *asōmatos* (incorporeal) and *analloiōtos* (unchangeable), though generally used by the Greeks to signify God's bodilessness, were later used by Philo and others after him to express the biblical notion of God's transcendence.

Gnosticism, underscoring above all God's absolute unknowability, invested some terms taken from Judaism and Middle Platonism with a more radical sense of God's inconceivability, and possessed others more proper to itself: *anousios* (without essence), forerunner of the Neoplatonic *hyperousios*; *anennoētos* (inconceivable), exclusive to Gnosticism; *agnōstos* (unknown), a term used in a nontechnical sense by others before Gnosticism but denoting for the latter the absolute unknowability of the supreme God. The most common term of Gnostic negative theology is *akatalēptos*,

5. For Philo, see *De sacrif.* 59.124; *De somn.* 1.67; *De mut.* 15; *De fug.* 41. Daniélou writes that it is likely that *akatalēptos* "passed into archaic Christian apologetic" through Philo, and that "the fact that Justin and Tatian do not employ it suggests that it does not come from the language of Middle Platonism" (*Gospel Message*, p. 327). The first instance of *akatalēptos* in Christian literature, about the year 95, is from *1 Clement* 33 (PG 1:273A), who writes that God established the heavens by his almighty power and adorned them by his incomprehensible intelligence.

6. For a typical passage from Middle Platonism, see Clement, *Strom.* 5.12. Daniélou claims *anekphrastos* (inexpressible) comes from Clement of Alexandria, and *aphatos* (ineffable) from Plotinus, since neither Philo nor Clement uses this latter ("L'incompréhensibilité," pp. 178–79).

and Gnostics were pioneers of the technical sense it was to gain in the fourth century: the word (and its abstract cousin *akatalēpsis*) denies that God is *kataleptos,* a term denoting the capacity for something's being grasped or seized, or comprehended by the mind; *akataleptos* thus denies that God can be comprehended by the mind.

Daniélou relates the three sources instructively:

> For a Jew, to say that God is transcendent is to say that he cannot be measured by any created thing, and is therefore incomprehensible to the creaturely mind; but at the same time it is to assert that his existence can be known. For the Platonist, to say that God is ineffable is to say that he surpasses any conception of him that the mind can form in terms of the sensible world; but it is also to affirm that, if only the mind can shake itself free from all conceptions of that kind, it will be able to grasp his essence. For the Gnostic, however, the matter goes far deeper. God is unknown absolutely, both in his essence and in his existence; he is the one of whom, in the strictest sense, nothing is known, and this situation can be overcome only through the Gnosis.[7]

The same terminology may mean different things for different systems, and context plays a role in determining content.

1. Authors before Pseudo-Dionysius

Since Jewish and patristic writers sometimes refer to the Hebrew and Christian scriptures as they formulate their views about negative theology, we begin with scripture, which presents us with statements that might justify the view that God is incomprehensible, although it does not make use of *akatalēpsis* or propound a theory about how God is known and named. For the Old Testament, God's ways are unsearchable, his greatness without limit (Ps. 145:3; Job 5:9; 9:10; 11:7; 36:26; Is. 40:28); God is exalted on high (Ps. 148:13; Is. 2:11, 17; 12:4; 33:5); we cannot discern his ways or works (Eccl. 3:11; 8:17), for God is far from us (Ps. 10:1; 22:2; Eccl. 7:24); indeed, the angel of the Lord (=God) will not tell Manoah his name, for it is mysterious (Jgs. 13:18), and Yahweh's name "I am" (Ex. 3:14) can be interpreted as an ironic denial of name.

7. *Gospel Message,* pp. 335–36.

The spirit of apophatic theology also finds a foundation in the life and teachings of Jesus Christ[8] and in the following negative terminology employed by the Pauline tradition:

• *aoratos* (invisible), from Romans 1:20, where Paul states that the invisible things of God are known from the visible things of creation; the same word appears in Colossians 1:15, where Christ is said to be the image of the invisible God

• *arrētos* (ineffable), from 2 Corinthians 12:4, where Paul describes how he was caught up in rapture to paradise and heard ineffable words

• *anekdiēgētos* (indescribable), from 2 Corinthians 9:15, where Paul praises God for his indescribable gift of grace

• *anexereunētos* (unsearchable), from Romans 11:33, which is a doxological statement declaring to be unsearchable the judgments of God concerning the fall and eventual restoration of Israel

• *anexichniastos* (untraceable or uninvestigable), from Romans 11:33, occurring as a general synonym for *anexereunētos;* it also occurs in Ephesians 3:8, which mentions the privilege of preaching to the Gentiles the gospel of the uninvestigable riches of Christ

• *athanasia* (immortality), from 1 Timothy 6:16, a doxology claiming that God alone has immortality

• *aprositos* (inaccessible), from 1 Timothy 6:16, a doxology stating that God dwells in light inaccessible.

Seven passages from the Pauline tradition, therefore, account for seven different negative predicates; three of the passages (Rom. 11:33; 2 Cor. 9:15; 1 Tim. 6:16), which account for five of the terms, are clearly doxological in character, and Colossians 1:15, utilizing a sixth term, is thought by many to be a remnant of an ancient Christian hymn exalting the divine status of Christ. Only two of the terms *(athanasia* and *aoratos)* are applied directly to God. Finally, although Christ is the explicit subject only once (Eph. 3:8),

8. Denis Edwards writes that "negative theology, with all its borrowing from Neoplatonism, is, nevertheless, a providential historical phenomenon which has kept the Church in touch with something that is a central concern of the historical Jesus," namely, Jesus' constant pointing to the mystery of God and his surrendering in trust unto God ("Negative Theology and the Historical Jesus," *ACR* 60 [1983]: 184–85).

since God's mysterious decree for our salvation centers on Christ (1 Cor. 2), since the indescribable gift of grace only happens in Christ (2 Cor. 9:15), and since the immediate contexts of the doxologies of Romans 11:33 and 1 Timothy 6:16 are Christological, the scriptural negative predicates clearly possess a Christological foundation, the only exceptions being *aoratos* and *arrētos*.

Philo Judaeus (d. ca. A.D. 50) is an essential link between the Jewish scriptures, Greek philosophy, and later Christian writers. He distinguishes between knowing that God exists and knowing what God's essence is,[9] and calls God "the most generic," meaning that God lacks any genus or species and thus is indefinable.[10] God's essence is unknown to any creature, and God is called incomprehensible to the human mind, unnameable, ineffable.[11] H. A. Wolfson claims that Philo is the first to propound God as incomprehensible to the mind, since earlier Greek philosophers thought of God as incomprehensible only to the senses. Wolfson reconstructs the path Philo took to such a conception.[12] On the basis of his philosophical sources he is ready to grant that God is incorporeal, simple, and indivisible, but this alone would not exclude the distinction of genus and species in God and thus God's indefinability. But in scripture Philo found statements that God did not reveal the divine name during apparitions (Ex. 3:14; 6:3), and also laws prohibiting the mentioning of God's proper name or the treating lightly of any name of God (Ex. 20:7; 33:27; Lv. 24:15–16; Dt. 5:11). In scripture, God's unnameability is taught; but this leads logically to God's indefinability and incomprehensibility, and Philo finds corroboration for God's incomprehensibility in the scriptural verses about Moses walking into the thick darkness where God was appearing on Sinai (Ex. 20:21) and not seeing God's face (Ex. 33:23).

Although Philo taught God's incomprehensibility and used negative descriptions of God based on the scriptural record, he never espoused an explicit *via negativa*. But Albinus (2nd century) does expound such a neg-

---

9. *De specialibus legibus,* 1.6–8.

10. *Legum allegoria,* 2.21.

11. Harry Wolfson, *Philo,* 2 vols. (Cambridge: Harvard, 1947), 2:111.

12. Ibid., pp. 111–27. For Philo's influence in this matter upon later thought, see pp. 149–60.

ative way, along with two other paths to God.[13] We first arrive at God by the *aphairesis* of all sensible predicates, just as we conceive a point by abstracting from the sensible, for first we conceive surface, then line, then point. Albinus is here referring to Euclidean geometry's negative definition of the point as that which is indivisible and without dimensions. Just as the point is isolated by successively abstracting the three dimensions we normally experience, so God is arrived at and described by means of the successive removal of sensible predicates.[14]

The second way to God is that of *analogia:* here Albinus coordinates the sun, sight, and the objects of sight with the First Mind, our mind, and the objects of our mind, all of which is obviously a variation of the Platonic theme of the comparison between the Good and the sun in *Republic* 6.508–9. This way aids us in understanding God's existence, for just as the sun is the cause of visibility for sight, so God or First Mind is the cause of understanding for our mind. *Analogia* does not merely express proportion but also announces the causal relation between God and the world.

The third path is an ascent unto God that begins by beholding the beautiful in bodies, progresses by grasping the beauty in souls, penetrates even further by rising to the beauty that exists in morals and laws—and thence to the vast sea of the beautiful and the good and the lovable themselves—and finally culminates in the forming of a conception of God in our minds on account of his exalted dignity *(dia tēn en tō timiō hyperochēn)*. This process is patterned on Plato's description in *Symposium* 210–12, a process that is noetic but with mystical overtones. This third way is one of gradual noetic ascent unto God based more on exemplarity than causality and leading to our conceiving God by means of supereminence.

---

13. For a good treatment of Albinus, see Harry Wolfson, *Studies in the History of Philosophy and Religion*, ed. I. Twersky and G. H. Williams, 2 vols. (Cambridge: Harvard, 1973–77), vol. 1, chap. 6. He thinks that neither Plato nor Aristotle had any *via negativa* or theory of God's incomprehensibility (vol. 1, chap. 5), although Anton-Hermann Chroust detects in Aristotle *(On the Heavens* 1.9.279a18–35, a fragment of his dialogue *On Philosophy;* and *On Prayer)* a sense of God's ineffability, inasmuch as God is beyond sensibility, time and eternity, and even mind ("Some Comments on Aristotle, *De caelo* 279a18–35," *DTP* 53 [1976]: 263–64). See Albinus, *Ep. (Didaskalikos)* 10.5–6, ed. Dübner, vol. 3, *Platonis opera,* 1873.

14. Wolfson thinks Albinus was the first to formulate the negative interpretation of divine attributes (*Studies,* 2:500).

Albinus names the three ways as *aphairesis, analogia* and *hyperochē*, and in that order.[15]

Plotinus (205–70)[16] speaks in two passages (*Enneads* 5.3.14; 6.7.36) of a threefold way, with yet again a different order: in the first passage the order seems to be *aphairesis,* ascent, and *analogia,* whereas in the second it is *analogia, aphairesis,* and ascent. Moreover, in the second passage the threefold way is situated within a context that underscores the need for virtue and purification in order to reach the Good, which demonstrates that for Plotinus the three paths are part of an ascetical, mystical philosophy bent on attaining union with the Good.

Plotinus, like Albinus before him, also begins to associate *aphairesis* with apophatic predications about God. For example, the *aphairesis* of *Enneads* 6.7.36 seems to be the same as the process of saying what the One is not in *Enneads* 5.3.14.[17] After Plotinus, *aphairesis* and *apophasis* are often used equivalently in philosophical and theological literature.[18] Wolfson writes: "In medieval Latin philosophy, the term *remotio,* used in the sense of *negatio,* in the expression *via remotionis,* is a translation of the Greek *aphairesis.*"[19]

15. Two other Middle Platonists, Maximus of Tyre and Celsus, also mention the threefold way, but their terminology and order are different. Maximus puts *hyperochē* first, then *analogia,* and finally *aphairesis;* Celsus uses *analysis* for *aphairesis,* and *synthesis* for *hyperochē,* and his order is *synthesis, analysis, analogia.* None of the three agree on the third position, Albinus placing *hyperochē* there, Maximus *aphairesis,* and Celsus *analogia.* Of special interest is Celsus' use of *synthesis* to signify the way of preeminence, and the fact that both Maximus and Celsus place it first. See Daniélou, *Gospel Message,* pp. 340–41.

16. Wolfson, *Studies,* vol. 1, chap. 6; Raoul Mortley, "Negative Theology and Abstraction in Plotinus," *AJP* 96 (1975): 363–77.

17. Wolfson, *Studies,* 1:129–30. "Both Albinus and Plotinus use the term *aphairesis* in the technical sense of Aristotle's *apophasis*" (ibid., p. 121). Mortley argues that Plotinus construes *aphairesis* in its more traditional sense of abstraction, since abstraction is more purifying and refining than mere negation: negating a line results in mere non-line, whereas abstracting from it results in the point ("Negative Theology," p. 376). However, although *aphairesis* had its first home in the mathematical sphere, its actual use by Albinus and Plotinus for divine predications shows that it can also be conceived negatively. A mathematical term with the general meaning of "taking away," once transported to the logical arena, can easily be extended to mean a negative predication.

18. For example, Gregory of Nyssa, *De anima et resurrectione* (PG 46:40B); Pseudo-Dionysius, *DN* 2.4 (PG 3:641A); *MT* 2 (PG 3:1000B); John Damascene, *De fid. orth.* 1.4 (PG 94:800BC).

19. Wolfson, *Studies* 1:130.

Plotinus also uses the negative proposition called *aphairesis* to express God's grandeur. This proposition may be negative both in form and meaning ("God is not temporal"); positive in form but with a negative predicate and thus a negative meaning ("God is timeless"); or even positive in form with a seemingly positive predicate ("God is simple"), though the actual meaning of the predicate is negative ("God is not composite"). Since Plotinus also claims that God is neither good nor not-good (*Enneads* 5.5.13), presumably because God is *hyperagathon* (above the good, *Enneads* 6.9.6), these negations also signify that God transcends the categories and predicates in question.[20]

The Greek apologists of the second century[21] took their negative theology and its terminology from Daniélou's three sources outlined above, although they have no formal *via negativa* and do not advocate an abstractive method of successively eliminating positive attributes. Their negative theology is mainly polemical and apologetic,[22] combating pagan notions of divinity and thus hearkening back to the critique by Xenophanes of the Homeric and Hesiodic gods because of their vices and anthropomorphism. Justin Martyr, the first among the Fathers to emphasize divine ineffability, says anyone who would want to name the inexpressible God suffers from an incurable madness.[23] Aristides describes God as incomprehensible, unbegotten, uncreated, and immortal, deploying these negations in his attack against the blasphemous conceptions of deity among the Greeks.[24] For Theophilus of Antioch, God is ineffable and inexpressible,

20. Wolfson, *Studies* 1:131–39. For Albinus and Plotinus, "the negation of any predicate of God . . . means the exclusion of God from the universe of discourse of the predicate in question" (ibid., 1:132).

21. D. W. Palmer, "Atheism, Apologetic, and Negative Theology in the Greek Apologists of the Second Century," *VC* 37 (1983): 234–59.

22. "The atheism of the Christian apologists with respect to the pagan gods is expressed in criticism on various grounds, while the Christian God is defined in negative terms in opposition to the concepts so criticized. At the same time the definition of God in negative terms allows the apologists to reject the charge of atheism against the Christians" (ibid., p. 252).

23. *1 Apology* 61 (PG 6:421B); cf. *2 Apology* 6 (PG 6:453A).

24. See his *Apology*, chaps. 1 and 13. For much of the same, see Tatian, *Oratio ad Graec.* 4 (PG 6:813). Athenagoras of Antioch calls God incomprehensible, invisible, eternal, and impassible (*Legatio pro christianis* 10 [PG 6:908B]).

incomprehensible in greatness, unthinkable in sublimity, inimitable in goodness. He argues from one negative attribute to another: God is without beginning because unborn, unchangeable because immortal.[25] Arguing with pagans who deemed they were looking upon God in their idols, he accentuates God's invisibility to human eyes, claiming that God cannot be seen by eyes of flesh since he is uncontainable.[26]

Clement of Alexandria (150–215),[27] after reminding his readers that the anthropomorphic names of scripture are to be taken only allegorically, acknowledges other names that are to be taken negatively and delineates a process, similar to Albinus', by which one arrives at the "primary concept" of oneness by way of resolution *(analysis)*, that is, by abstracting the three dimensions until we arrive at the point, and finally by abstracting the very position in space held by the point until we are left with unity, the primary concept. Applying this method to God, he encourages us, after we have abstracted qualities belonging to bodies and to incorporeal realities, to throw ourselves into the greatness of Christ that thereby we may progress into the abyss by holiness and somehow reach the Almighty with our minds, not knowing what he is but what he is not, for the First Cause is above place, time, name, and conception *(noēseōs)*.[28] Clement's language, the mention of holiness, and his passing remark that the purgative way occurs through confession but the contemplative way through resolution, show that his negative theology is firmly set within the encompassing matrix of an ascetical and spiritual outlook and purpose.

Gregory of Nyssa (330–94), availing himself of some forty expressions to denote God's incomprehensibility, is the first Christian writer to rest that incomprehensibility squarely upon the divine infinity.[29] He interprets

25. *Ad Autolycum* 1.3–4 (PG 6:1028BC–1029A).

26. Ibid., 1.5 (PG 6:1032A).

27. For a general treatment of Alexandrian negative theology, see Joseph C. McLelland, *God the Anonymous: A Study in Alexandrian Philosophical Theology*, Patristic Monograph Series 4 (Cambridge, MA: Philadelphia Patristic Foundation, 1976).

28. *Stromata* 5.11 (PG 9:104A–109A).

29. Thus Ekkehard Mühlenberg, *Die Unendlichkeit Gottes bei Gregor von Nyssa* (Göttingen: Vandenhoeck & Ruprecht, 1966), pp. 147–205. He considers Gregory's theology to be purely rational/theological and anti-mystical, entirely beyond the pale of traditional

privative divine predicates in a negative fashion: for example, *incorruptible* said of God signifies that corruption is not present in God.[30] Moreover, he makes the way of negation a function of the way of preeminence: "In order that the transcendent *(hyperkeimenē)* nature may not appear to have any connaturality with things below, as regards the divine nature we have made use of notions and words which separate that nature from them"— for example, as being above the ages, God is said to be before the ages; and as beyond beginning *(hyperarchēn)*, God is said to be without beginning *(anarchon)*.[31] Negation is at the service of expressing God's transcendence.

At Antioch during the years 386–87, John Chrysostom (d. 407) preached five homilies on the incomprehensible nature of God against the rationalistic positions of Eunomius and his followers.[32] *Akatalēptos* and cognate forms and expressions occur constantly as he attempts to prove the incomprehensibility of the divine essence. Do you say that God's wisdom is declared incomprehensible in the psalms, Chrysostom asks, but that his essence is comprehensible to us? "But is not this clearly madness? His greatness has no bounds and yet you claim to circumscribe his essence?"[33] He proves God's essential incomprehensibility by showing from the scriptures that God's judgments are unsearchable, his paths untraceable, his peace surpassing every understanding, his gifts inexpressible; and then he asks rhetorically, can all these divine qualities be incomprehensible and yet the divine essence alone be comprehensible? Of course not. His aim is to make clear that the divine essence is incomprehensible to every creature.[34]

---

negative theology. Charles Kannengiesser, while agreeing with Mühlenberg's primary contention, nevertheless thinks that he has not realized that Christian negative theology is not necessarily opposed to divine infinity and that there is a Christian form of mystical union with God which escapes the problems of Neoplatonic monistic pantheism ("L'infinité divine chez Grégoire de Nysse," *RSR* 55 [1967]: 63–65).

30. *Contra Eunomius* 12 (PG 45:953BC); see also ibid., PG 45:1105A.

31. Ibid., PG 45:1104D–1105A. For Athanasius of Alexandria (d. 373), God "transcends *(hyperekeina)* every essence and human thought" (*Contra gentes* 2 [PG 25:5C]).

32. PG 48:701–48. These are actually the first five of twelve homilies *Against the Anomoeans*. See Adhémar d'Alès, "De Incomprehensibili," *RSR* 23 (1933): 306–9; Jean Daniélou, "L'incompréhensibilité de Dieu d'après saint Jean Chrysostome," *RSR* 37 (1950): 176–94.

33. Homily 1.4–5 (PG 48:705–6).

34. Homily 4.4 (PG 48:732). Augustine of Hippo (354–430) offers an instructive contrast

ii. Pseudo-Dionysius and John Damascene

Pseudo-Dionysius the Areopagite (fl. ca. 500), most likely a Syrian author who took the pseudonym of Paul's famous convert at Athens (Acts 17:34), thereby gaining almost apostolic authority for his writings through the sixteenth century, attempted to combine Neoplatonism with Christianity throughout his work, and the synthesis he wrought wielded enormous influence upon Thomas Aquinas.[35] Three topics will hold our inter-

---

to the Greek tradition of negative theology and divine incomprehensibility. He is more concerned to deny any mutability or temporality of God's substance than to promote a Plotinian type of apophatic theology that would exalt God above being and substance (Vladimir Lossky, "Elements of 'Negative Theology' in the Thought of St. Augustine," trans. T. E. Bird, *SVTQ* 21 [1977]: 67–75). Nor does he have a theory of the *via negativa*, though he does speak of God as the one "who is known better by not knowing" (*De ordine* 16 [PL 32:1015]; cf. 18.47 [PL 32:1017]). Indeed, God cannot be comprehended: "We speak about God, and what wonder if you do not comprehend? For if you comprehend, it is not God" (*Sermo* 117.3.5 [PL 38:663]). However, God can be "contacted" or "touched" by the mind somehow (ibid.; cf. *De doc. chris.* 1.7 [PL 34:22]), and Augustine gives one description of how this occurred when he relates the famous discussion he had with his mother at Ostia: after traversing the various grades of the material world and after entering our own souls and transcending even them, he writes, we barely touched *(attingere)* the eternal wisdom in an instant of thought (*Confessions* 9.10.24–25 [PL 32:774]). Even if the heart's pure eye can touch God, however, it can never comprehend the divine essence (*Sermo* 117.3.5 [PL 38:664]), and even in prayer we must be ready not to identify any thought with God, so that as we pray there is in us a "learned ignorance," an ignorance "learned in the Spirit of God, who helps our infirmity" (*Letter 130 to Proba* 14.27; 15.28 [PL 33:505]; Lossky affirms that Nicholas of Cusa took his *docta ignorantia* from Augustine's *Letter to Proba* ["Elements," p. 71, n. 6]). Augustine is familiar with God's incomprehensibility, but his negative theology is not part of a speculative threefold way, nor is it a mysticism which plunges into God by an act of supreme unknowing.

35. For two English translations, see *The Divine Names and Mystical Theology,* trans. with introduction by John D. Jones (Milwaukee: Marquette, 1980); *The Complete Works,* trans. Colm Luibheid, with foreword, preface, introduction, and notes by various authors; Classics of Western Spirituality (New York: Paulist, 1987). In the text, *DN* and *MT* refer, respectively, to *The Divine Names* and *Mystical Theology,* and the numbers within brackets or parentheses refer to the columns of PG, vol. 3, which contains the Pseudo-Dionysian corpus. Other literature on Pseudo-Dionysius: Vladimir Lossky, "La théologie négative dans la doctrine de Denys l'Aréopagite," *RSPT* 28 (1939): 204–21; René Roques, *L'Univers Dionysien: Structure hiérarchique du monde selon pseudo-Denys* (Paris: Aubier, 1954); Walther Völker, *Kontemplation und Ekstase bei Pseudo-Dionysius Areopagita* (Wiesbaden: Franz Steiner, 1958); Jean Vanneste, *Le mystère de Dieu: Essai sur la structure rationnelle de la doctrine mystique du pseudo-Denys l'Aréopagite,* Museum Lessianum, section philosophique, no. 45 (Brussels: Desclée de Brouwer, 1959); Walter M. Neidl, *Thearchia. Die Frage nach dem Sinn von Gott bei*

est: Pseudo-Dionysius' view of God's incomprehensibility, the nature of his negative theology, and the "ways" to God that he envisages. As a prelude, it should be noted that he sometimes equates *aphairesis* and *apophasis:* the former term, like the latter, can refer to negative propositions, or to affirmative propositions using predicates prefixed by the alpha privative (e.g., *MT* 4 [1040D] and *DN* 1.1–2 [588BC]); moreover, a text like *MT* 1.2 (1000B) can say that we should not assume that "the negations *(apophaseis)* are simply the opposites of the affirmations *(kataphaseis)*, but rather that the cause of all is considerably prior to this, beyond privations, beyond every denial *(aphairesis)*, beyond every assertion *(thesis)*."[36]

As to God's incomprehensibility, for Pseudo-Dionysius (hereafter Dionysius) God is not one of the beings (*DN* 7.3 [872A]); the essence-surpassing God is also thereby the God removed from our knowledge, inaccessible to mind and speech and sight (*DN* 1.4 [593A]); God is the unnameable (*DN* 1.6 [596A]). The scriptures call "the much-praised and the many-named One ineffable and nameless, and the One present to all and found by all they call incomprehensible and unsearchable" (*DN* 7.1 [865C]). But this presents a problem for Dionysius: if God is the unnamed One, based on the *Egō eimi ho ōn* (I am who am) of Sinai, and yet we sing his

---

Pseudo-Dionysius Areopagita und Thomas von Aquin (Regensburg: Habbel, 1976); John D. Jones, "The Character of the Negative (Mystical) Theology for Pseudo-Dionysius Areopagite," *PACPA* 51 (1977): 66–74; Salvatore Lilla, "The Notion of Infinitude in Pseudo-Dionysius Areopagita," *JTS* 31 (1980): 93–103; Paul Rorem, "The Place of the *Mystical Theology* in the Pseudo-Dionysian Corpus," *Dionysius* 4 (1980): 87–97; idem, *Biblical and Liturgical Symbols within the Pseudo-Dionysian Synthesis* (Toronto: PIMS, 1984); idem, *Pseudo-Dionysius: A Commentary on the Texts and an Introduction to Their Influence* (New York: Oxford, 1993); Michel Corbin, "Négation et transcendance dans l'oeuvre de Denys," *RSPT* 69 (1985): 41–76; Andrew Louth, *Denys the Areopagite* (London/Wilton, CT: Chapman/Morehouse-Barlow, 1989); Fran O'Rourke, *Pseudo-Dionysius and the Metaphysics of Aquinas* (Leiden: Brill, 1992); Denys Turner, *The Darkness of God: Negativity in Christian Mysticism* (Cambridge: Cambridge University, 1995), pp. 19–49; Janet Williams, "The Apophatic Theology of Dionysius the Pseudo-Areopagite," *DR* 117 (1999): 157–72, 235–50.

36. Luibheid trans., p. 136. Janet Williams (pp. 167–69) disagrees with this reading of *MT* 1.2, holding that in it Pseudo-Dionysius makes a clear *linguistic* distinction between "aphairetic" and "apophatic" negations. But her interpretation does not discount the other passages mentioned above, and although I agree with her that Pseudo-Dionysius acknowledges at least two kinds of negation, I do not think he makes such a sharp linguistic separation between *apophasis* and *aphairesis*.

praises with all sorts of names, how can we sing and name the praises of the unnameable One (*DN* 1.6 [596ABC])? He tries to overcome the dilemma by exactly balancing positives and negatives, theses and denials, so that he may be true both to the scriptural praises and to the ultimate unknowability of the Nameless One. In a passage remarkable for the beautiful exactitude of its Greek rhetoric and the mystic fervor that inspires it, he writes:

God is known in all and separate from all; God is known through knowledge and through unknowing, and of him there is understanding, reason, knowledge, apprehension, perception, opinion, imagination, and name and all other things—and yet he is neither understood nor spoken nor named; he is not any of the beings nor in any of the beings is he known; he is all in all and nothing in anything; he is known to all from all, and to no one from anything. (*DN* 7.3 [872A])[37]

The second topic examines the nature of Dionysius' negative theology. Should it be identified with a global mystical unknowing? Or does it involve rather the theological denials that form a dialectic with the affirmations of cataphatic theology? Or is it instead a combination of mystical unknowing and theological denials? Various interpretations are possible given that Dionysius never totally unifies his system, for although in *MT* 3 and elsewhere he distinguishes affirmative theology from global mystical unknowing, in the *Divine Names* we often discover a mixture of positive assertions and negative denials *within* rational theological discourse.[38]

37. Lossky claims that Dionysius can deny that God is an object of either knowledge or ignorance, and can join affirmations and negations the way he does, because for him God already possesses divine unions and distinctions within the divine nature, and processions or powers that go forth from him and that creatures can participate in—and while the former can never be known, the latter ground our knowledge of God as cause of all ("Théologie négative," pp. 204–11). Lilla (pp. 101–3) offers some texts where Dionysius links God's incomprehensibility with the divine infinity, detecting in their association the influence of Gregory of Nyssa.

38. Lossky thinks that the Dionysian negative way is not only a journey toward ecstatic union with God but also a "dogmatic speculation on divine transcendence" ("Elements," p. 67). Vanneste sees Dionysius' negative way as comprising three moments: the abandonment of affirmation and the logic of successive negations *(aphairesis)*, unknowing *(agnōsia)*, and final union *(henōsis)* with God. The negative theology of the first moment possesses a primarily logical value of successive negations evolving at the level of knowledge and heading toward the Unknown, since it is not yet a personal mystical experience *(Mystère*, pp. 70–81). Jones delineates two negative theologies: one that, based on God as cause, functions within an affirmative theology in order to express God's transcendence; and another that is a

Although there are texts in the *Divine Names*, to be discussed under the next topic below, that mention a way of negation within an overall context of affirmative and conceptual theology, at the conclusion of that work Dionysius mentions the scriptural writers' (and presumably his) preference for "the way up through negations," which "guides the soul through all the divine notions, notions which are themselves transcended by that which is far beyond every name, all reason and all knowledge."[39] Here he seems to single out another negative way, a path of ascent through negations that

---

mystical unknowing, whose final non-word is the dark silence of ecstasy. The first begins with God and works its way down through creatures, and the second is a mystical ascent that commences by denying the least of creatures and continues the denials, even of divinity and Trinity ultimately, until union with God is achieved (introduction to *Divine Names*, pp. 15–26, 89–103; cf. also "Character," p. 67). Affirmative theology gives rise to both affirmation and the first type of negation, but the second type of negation requires the cessation of all intellectual activity and affirmation altogether (*Divine Names*, p. 25, n. 34). Louth also recognizes in Dionysius both the dialectical interplay between affirmative and negative theology, as well as the distinction between negative theology, which is a matter of human understanding, and a correlative mystical theology, which is "a matter of surrender to the dark ray of divine light, a matter of a 'theopathic state' . . . of loving surrender to God" (*Denys the Areopagite*, pp. 87–88, 107). Rorem notes that "the climax of the Dionysian method is not simply the negation of some concept about God, but the negation of the concept of negation itself" (*Pseudo-Dionysius: A Commentary*, pp. 11–12). Turner distinguishes in Dionysius between the negative proposition or image, which occurs in an environing cataphatic context and is termed by Turner the "Aristotelian negation," and the genuine "self-subverting" apophatic utterance, which negates the very attempt to name God by any image or proposition whatsoever, whether affirmative or negative (*Darkness of God*, pp. 33–46). Dionysius is clear about these two kinds of negative theology in practice, as is evident in his two quite different works, *Divine Names* and *Mystical Theology*, but he "lacks the conceptual and logical tools in which to state the grounds on which the distinction is to be made" (*Darkness of God*, p. 35). Turner also notes that Dionysian apophaticism "presupposes the cataphatic 'dialectically' in the sense that the silence of the negative way is the silence achieved only at the point at which talk about God has been exhausted" ("Apophaticism, Idolatry, and the Claims of Reason," in *Silence and the Word: Negative Theology and Incarnation*, ed. Oliver Davies and Denys Turner [Cambridge: Cambridge University, 2002], p. 18).

39. *DN* 13.3 (981AB); Luibheid trans., p. 130. This passage and many others (*Dn* 1.1 [588AB]; 7.3 [872AB]; *Celestial Hierarchy*, 2.3 [141A]; *Letter* 9.1 [1105CD]; *MT* 3 [1032D–1033D]) display the superiority, in Dionysius' eyes, of the mystical way of negation. Lossky has some fine words on the Dionysian mystical way of *agnōsia* (unknowing), which requires spiritual detachment, purgation, and the continual denial of predicates in order to prepare for ecstasy, *henōsis* (union), and finally *theōsis* (divinization—"Théologie négative," pp. 211–18).

eventually applies its scalpel to excise from God even the most revered names of Trinity, Unity, and Goodness (13.3 [980B–981B]).

In a passage describing the dual components of the scriptural tradition, Dionysius clearly distinguishes the mystical from the notional and philosophical:

> Theological tradition has a dual aspect, the ineffable and mysterious on the one hand, the open and more evident on the other. The one resorts to symbolism and involves initiation. The other is philosophic and employs the method of demonstration. (Further, the inexpressible is bound up with what can be articulated.) The one uses persuasion and imposes the truthfulness of what is asserted. The other acts and, by means of a mystery which cannot be taught, puts souls firmly in the presence of God.[40]

The deeper, mystical way is based on initiation into the mystery of God. The statement between parentheses also seems to imply that the mystical way, which strives to make us cognizant of God's inexpressibility, is always "bound up" with the articulate way of theology or scripture. And so, perhaps the way of mystic negation is never entirely absent from the affirmations of the *Divine Names*.

It will be worth the effort to summarize the brief *Mystical Theology*, for both this and the next topic.[41] Chapter 1 opens by encouraging Timothy to relinquish sense and intellect in order to contemplate in the rays of divine darkness, warning him not to disclose anything to the uninitiated (1000A). For although one can affirm of God all the divine predicates, since he is cause of all, these predicates are more properly denied of God, since God is superessentially beyond all. Purification is needed, however, in order to ascend the divine summits and enter the divine darkness. He adduces the example of Moses on Mount Sinai, who separated himself from the impure multitude and with the sacred elect mounted the summit. But even Moses did not then see God, but only the place of God. However, abandoning seers and seen, Moses then enters the "truly mystical darkness of

---

40. *Letter* 9.1 (1105D); Luibheid trans., p. 283. In *Divine Names* 2.9 (648B) Dionysius mentions Blessed Hierotheus, his teacher, who was taught (the passive form of *muein* means to be initiated into the mysteries) by divine inspiration, not only learning but also suffering divine things *(ou monon mathōn alla kai pathōn ta theia)*.

41. It is in PG 3, cols. 997–1048.

unknowing," where all knowledge is excluded and where he is most perfectly united to the That-Beyond-All, and where, by knowing nothing, he knows beyond mind (1001A).[42] In chapter 1, then, we recognize the division between exoteric and esoteric knowledge—the latter type requiring special purification and initiation—the superiority of the negative unknowing beyond mind, and the way of negation as based on God's transcendent superessentiality.

Chapter 2 describes mystical negation—which aims at that Beyond-Being and Beyond-Light which is darkness and which is hidden by beings and light—as an ascent that begins with the least of beings and by successive removals *(aphairesis)* mounts to the Beyond-Being; whereas the way of *thesis* begins with the first of beings and descends through the middle regions to the least of beings. The process is similar to sculpting a statue by removing what hinders and obstructs the beautiful image within from manifesting itself.[43] This chapter explains mystical negation as an ascent that involves a successive removal of realities increasingly close to the Beyond-Being.

Chapter 3 describes the ways of ascent and descent more closely. In his *Outlines of Theology,* Dionysius says, he treated of God as one and triune and of Jesus incarnate in human nature; in the *Divine Names* he celebrated the intelligible divine names *(noētē theōnymia);* and in the *Symbolic Theology* he discussed names transferred from physically sensible realities to the divine.[44] Now, however, entering the darkness beyond mind, there is to be a complete lack of reason and intelligibility *(alogia, anoēsia).* After the ascent, reason will be totally soundless and totally united to the unsayable. Unlike the divine theses, which begin with the first beings and proceed to the last, the divine denials begin with what is farthest from the Beyond-Every-Removal. For as regards the theses, is it not truer that the

42. Louth remarks that "Denys's account of the ascent of Moses into the Divine Darkness has many parallels with Gregory of Nyssa's much more extended treatment in the second part of his *Life of Moses,* and it seems certain that Denys has drawn on it" (*Denys the Areopagite,* pp. 100–101).

43. Col. 1025; See Vanneste, pp. 66–67, for the sculpture image in Plotinus and Gregory of Nyssa as possible sources for Dionysius.

44. Cols. 1032D–1033A; cf. *DN* 1.4 (589D–592B).

Beyond is more life and goodness than air and stone? And as regards the denials, is it not likewise truer that the Beyond is more removed from drunkenness and anger than from being spoken and understood (1033CD)? In this chapter the "way of negation" is hardly a theo-*logy* at all since the negative ascent concludes in total unknowing.

Chapter 4 commences the way of negative ascent by denying the names treated of in the *Symbolic Theology:* those that imply sensate or material reality and are the farthest from God: body, form, figure, and the like (1040D). But at this point the Cause of all still possesses essence, life, mind, and *logos.*

Chapter 5 continues the ascent by denying some fifty of God's intelligible names, those that are closer to the Cause: intellect, *logos,* being/essence *(ousia),* life, eternity, truth, one, unity, divinity, goodness, spirit, sonhood, fatherhood. These are the names treated of in the *Divine Names* and *Outlines of Theology,* and the last group (from unity through fatherhood) is an exact reversal of the order of theses and names of the latter work; thus the beginning of all affirmative theology *(Outlines)* is the summit of the negative ascent, beyond which there is only the Unsayable, the Unknowable, the Beyond-All.

It is hard to escape the conclusion that to some degree Dionysius recognizes two kinds of negative theology: one is exoteric and forms a dialectic with the assertions of affirmative theology, while the other is an esoteric mystical unknowing based on the dark ascents. This second type is not a part of discursive theology at all since its primary act is silence and its object is the God beyond reason. But are these two kinds of negative theology entirely separate from one another in Dionysius' thought, or are they connected? I think that they are connected and that the negative theology which is uppermost in Dionysius' mind and heart is the darkness of mystical unknowing, for it is both the underlying cause and the ultimate motivation for his symbolic and conceptual types of negative theology. In this view, the symbolic or conceptual negative theology contained in the three cataphatic treatises mentioned in *MT* 3 is a corrective offered to those still entwined in sensation and reason, written by one who has already tasted of the absolute unknowing and who is making the absolute negations as intelligible as possible within symbolic and notional contexts for those who are still beginners, until they can finally forsake the way of affirmation altogether and begin their own direct ascent unto unknowing and union with God. According to this interpretation, then, Dionysius' negative theology is primarily mystical and nonconceptual; and when it occurs as an element within affirmative theology it appears as a gift from a higher region and takes in affirmative theology the form it does due to the constraints of the imaginative or notional context, and as a concession to human weakness.

The third topic concerns the number of paths to God that Dionysius teaches. By Aquinas' time the standard interpretation, with which Thomas concurred, saw in Dionysius a threefold path to God, with the customary order of causality, negation, and preeminence. We begin by noting how closely Dionysius associates the paths of negation and preeminence or transcendence. At the very beginning of the *Divine Names* he writes that God is the cause of being for all but is not a being *(on)*, since God transcends *(epekeina)* every essence *(DN* 1.1 [588B]). Transcendence is the reason for the negation; note also what looks like an incipient threefold way: God is *cause* of being, but *not* a being, because of *transcendence.* In the *Mystical Theology* we read that though one can affirm predicates of God as the cause of all, these predicates are more properly denied of God since God is superessentially beyond all.[45] Again we see negation based on supereminence, although this time there appears to be more of a twofold way: affirmation based on God as Cause, and negation based on God as transcendent Beyond. The dependence of negation upon preeminence is indisputable in a few phrases used by Dionysius where either negation as a noun is modified by preeminence as an adjective, or negation as a verb is modified by transcendence as an adverb: thus he speaks of a "preeminent negation" *(hyperochikē aphairesis)*[46] and of God as "transcendently removed from all" and "supersubstantially taken away from all" *(DN* 1.5 [593C]).[47] And a twofold way seems to be indicated when he says that ulti-

---

45. *MT* 1.2 (1000B); for the same idea, see *DN* 2.4 (641A).

46. *DN* 2.3 (640B); he is here referring to transcendent names such as supergood and superliving, and distinguishing them from causal names.

47. Vanneste (pp. 101–11) notes the connection between negation and eminence and asks

mately there is neither affirmation nor denial of God, "since beyond every positing is the complete and unitary Cause of all, and beyond every negating the preeminence *(hyperochē)* of that One which is absolutely detached from all and beyond the whole."[48] There seem to be two basic ways to God as regards both their ultimate reasons (cause and supereminence) and their results (affirmation and negation).

Two more texts from the *Divine Names* remain to be discussed. In the first (*DN* 1.5–8), Dionysius begins by questioning how the divine names can be predicated of the nameless and unutterable one and responds by asserting that when Godlike minds become united with the divine light, so that their natural powers cease, they sing God's praises most perfectly by removing *(aphairesis)* from God all things that exist. In 1.5 (593C) he writes that due to their supernatural illumination and blessed union with God such minds learn that although God is the "cause of all beings, he is himself no-thing since he is superessentially removed from all" *(pantōn men esti tōn ontōn aition, auto de ouden hōs pantōn hyperousiōs exērēmenon)*. But because the Deity is the very subsistence of goodness, it is the cause of all and ought to be praised from the things that have been caused (1.5 [593D]). The theologians thus praise the Deity with every name and yet call it nameless; it has many names drawn from all the things that are caused; it is all of the beings and yet none of the beings. Here Dionysius furnishes us with a plethora of scriptural names, both intelligible and sensible, which are treated in the *Divine Names* and *Symbolic Theology* respectively (1.6 [596ABC]), as we know from elsewhere.[49] Since the Deity is an all-creative

---

whether the negation is a means of attaining or of expressing God's eminence. The second alternative is closer to the mark: the Dionysian seeker of God already knows by faith and grace the numinous supereminence of God, which leads to the negative ascent, which itself leads to a mystical enjoyment of and union with the Beyond, known in the beginning only by faith but not yet by experience.

48. *MT* 5 (1048B); cf. *Celestial Hierarchy* 2.3 (141A). Corbin considers the way of eminence to be the most important in Dionysius, since it holds together and at the same time relativizes the ways of affirmation and negation. René Roques states that "negative theology presents itself as a theology of eminence . . . as the true theology of Transcendence" (*La "Hiérarchie Céleste"* [Paris: Cerf, 1970], p. xxvii, cited and translated by Thomas Hibbs, *Dialectic and Narrative in Aquinas: An Interpretation of the "Summa contra gentiles"* [Notre Dame: UND, 1995], p. 47).

49. *MT* 3 (1032D–1033D); *DN* 4.5 (700C); 1.8 (597C); 9.5 (913B).

Providence that has grasped all things beforehand in a simple and unlimited fashion, the scriptural writers praise it and give it names derived from all of creation (1.7 [596C–597A]).

In the second text (*DN* 7.3 [869D–872B]) Dionysius remarks that we cannot know God from the divine nature, for that is unknown and exceeds every thought and mind. But "from the disposition of all beings, as determined by God and as possessing certain images and similitudes of the divine exemplars, we ascend according to our ability by an orderly path unto the Transcendent over all, by the removal of and preeminence over all things, and by the cause of all things" *(en tē pantōn aphairesei kai hyperochē kai en tē pantōn aitia)*. The syntactic structure of the Greek grammatically displays the close association in Dionysius' mind between negation and transcendence: the *aphairesis* and *hyperochē* are related as a unit to the first *pantōn* and *tē*, while the second *kai* relates *aitia* by itself to the second *pantōn* and *tē*. Thus the syntax of the passage suggests a twofold path to God.[50]

Another indication of a twofold path occurs a little later in the same passage when Dionysius claims that the most perfect divine knowledge is that which occurs in unknowing, "according to the union that is beyond mind, when the mind, standing aloof from all beings and then even deserting itself, is united to the transcendently radiant beams and then to the unsearchable depths of the shining wisdom," although, he adds, this wisdom is also known from all things, as scripture says, because it is creative *(poiētikē)* of all things (*Dn* 7.3 [872AB]). The *via negativa* is here not merely a logical stratagem in a fundamentally positive theology but rather, as in the *Mystical Theology*, a mystical way that amounts to a global denial of all affirmative theology.

Three points can summarize our interpretation of Dionysius' thought. First, for Dionysius, God is absolutely unknowable in conceptual, notional, or rational terms.

Second, while the negative way, for him, is at its purest level a mystical, nonconceptual, and esoteric path of ascent unto the silent darkness of

50. O'Rourke, *Pseudo-Dionysius* (pp. 14–18, 33–35) remarks that Aquinas sees a threefold pattern in Dionysius' basically twofold path.

God, it can also take in cataphatic contexts the form of symbolic or conceptual denials, which it does as a concession to human weakness, though in its deepest reality it is the polar opposite of all rational affirmation *and* denial.

Third, the Dionysian path to God is fundamentally twofold: the way of negation and the way of affirmation, or more precisely, negation based on God as the transcendent Beyond and affirmation based on God as Cause of all things.

As we shall see, Aquinas will often interpret the Dionysian maxim about God's absolute unknowability to mean something quite different from what Dionysius originally intended. Aquinas will also elicit a threefold path from the statements of Dionysius, and he will tend to emphasize a domesticated version of the Dionysian *via negativa,* inasmuch as in his hands it becomes a "way" comfortably at ease within the contours of his positive theology.[51]

We conclude this chapter with a brief look at John Damascene (d. ca. 750), the synthesizer of the whole Eastern tradition in theology who also exercised some influence on Thomas Aquinas. Damascene also uses *aphairesis* and *apophasis* as synonyms,[52] and the predicates formed from alpha privatives are clearly to be taken as negations, for they show what God is not—for example, *aoratos* means "God is not seen."[53]

De fide orthodoxa 1.4[54] gives us a synoptic view of his negative theology. That God exists is clear, but what God is in essence and nature is "incomprehensible" and "totally unknown" *(akatalēpton, pantelōs agnōston).* Terms such as *unbegotten* and *incorruptible* do not signify what God is but what he is not, and thus they are not indicative of the divine essence, since whoever declares the essence says what something is and not what something is not. Since we cannot declare God's essence, it is better to speak of God by removing all things from God. We will find again in Thomas the Damascenean notion that essential knowledge means a definitional

51. For Thomas' fundamental indebtedness to Dionysius for his teaching on how we know God, see O'Rourke, pp. 3–61.

52. *De fide orthodoxa* 1.4 (PG 94:800B); 1.12 (PG 94:845C).

53. Ibid., 1.9 (PG 94:837AB).

54. PG 94:797–800; for an English translation, see FC 37:170–72.

knowledge of the essence, though Thomas will distinguish a definitional knowledge of God's essence from predicating something of God substantially.

John Damascene shows how negative theology is rooted in God's positive transcendence: God is not one of the beings, not because he does not exist but because he is above all beings and even being itself *(hyper panta ta onta kai hyper auto to einai ōn)*.[55] Some affirmative assertions, like "God is darkness," really have the force of a "transcendent negation" *(hyperochikēs apophaseōs)*:[56] for we do not mean that darkness is in God but that he is not light since he is beyond light *(hyper to phōs)*; and the same holds for "God is light": this means God is not darkness because he is beyond darkness. The negation depends upon and attempts to express the divine preeminence and transcendence.

---

55. Cf. ibid., 1.12 (PG 94:845CD, 848B).

56. In another passage, things said *apophatikōs* (like *unessential* or *timeless*) are said to "manifest the supersubstantial" (ibid., 1.12 [PG 94:845C]). The phrasing and the dependence of negation upon preeminence are reminiscent of Dionysius.

2. God's Dual Incomprehensibility in Aquinas

Chapters 2 and 3 will examine the nature and tenor of Thomas Aquinas' negative, apophatic theology.[1] This chapter will show that Aquinas' stance on God's incomprehensibility—supplemented by some expressions that designate God, in genuine Dionysian fashion, as a preeminent darkness— can be summarized in two theses: no created intellect naturally possesses a

1. Among the interpreters of Aquinas, A. Sertillanges is noted for his forceful expression of Aquinas' extreme negative theology ("Agnosticisme ou anthropomorphisme," *RP* 8 [1906]: 129–65), though he offers a more balanced view in *Les grandes thèses de la philosophie thomiste* (Paris: Bloud, 1928), pp. 67–80. Other exponents of Aquinas' negative theology are Étienne Gilson (*The Christian Philosophy of St. Thomas Aquinas*, trans. L. K. Shook [New York: Random, 1956], pp. 108–10; *The Elements of Christian Philosophy* [New York: New American Library, 1963], pp. 113–21, 149–58); and Anton Pegis, who affirms that for Aquinas the most we can know about God is that we do not know what God is, but that this is a positive unknowing rather than mere ignorance: "When St. Thomas said that God was utterly unknown, what was he saying but that man should seek the divine transcendence by a total unknowing?" (*"Penitus Manet Ignotum," MS* 27 [1965]: 226). Victor Preller (*Divine Science and the Science of God: A Reformulation of Thomas Aquinas* [Princeton: Princeton University, 1967], pp. 266–71) underlines Aquinas' negative theology from the standpoint of linguistic analysis. For an understanding based in part on Preller, see David Burrell, *Aquinas: God and Action* (Notre Dame: UND Press, 1979), chap. 2; and *Knowing the Unknowable God: Ibn-Sina, Maimonides, Aquinas* (Notre Dame: UND Press, 1986), chap. 4. For other accounts stressing Aquinas' negative theology, see Victor White, *God the Unknown* (New York: Harper, 1956), pp. 16–25; Battista Mondin, *The Principle of Analogy in Protestant and Catholic Theology*, 2nd ed. (The Hague: Nijhoff, 1968), pp. 99–100; James Doig, *Aquinas on Metaphysics* (The Hague: Nijhoff, 1972), pp. 376–81; Isaac Franck, "Maimonides and Aquinas on Man's Knowledge of God: A Twentieth Century Perspective," *RM* 38 (1985): 591–615.

quidditative knowledge of God's essence; and no created intellect can ever possess, in principle, a comprehensive knowledge of God's essence.

1. God as Supereminent Darkness

Knowing God according to the "way of reason" is generally a difficult task,[2] and even at its end we are left in darkness since, as Dionysius says, we are united to God as to one unknown, which Thomas interprets to mean that although we know what God is not, what God is "remains totally unknown";[3] and in order to show that Moses did not know what God is, "it is said of Moses (Ex. 20:21) that 'he approached the darkness in which God is'" (SCG 3.49.2270). In another passage Thomas claims, with Dionysius, that we are best joined to God in this life according to a certain ignorance, "and this [ignorance] is a kind of darkness, in which God is said to dwell."[4]

Thomas shows a tendency to explain as referring merely to our imperfect knowledge of God certain statements that would be taken in a more

2. There are many prerequisites to such a knowledge, "since almost all of philosophy is ordained to the knowledge of the divine" (SS 3.24.1.3.1).

3. *Penitus manet ignotum* (SCG 3.49.2270). "There is something about God which is totally unknown to humans in this life, namely, what God is; thus Paul found at Athens an altar inscribed to the *Unknown God*" (Rom. 1.6.114). Cf. CT 2.8.50–54; 2.9. Thomas explains the inscription according to his own theory of God's unknowability, although its meaning in the polytheistic pagan context was entirely different. See also BDT 1.2 ad1; SCG 1.5.30; DDN 7.4.731. Pegis comments on the phrase at the head of this note in *"Penitus Manet Ignotum,"* pp. 212–26. He finds that Thomas uses the expression as his own paraphrase for *omnino autem ignoto*, which he would have read in the Latin translations of Dionysius by John Scotus Erigena or Michael Sarrazin, who employed the phrase to translate the *pantelōs de agnōstō* of MT 1.3 (PG 3:1001A); however, after William of Moerbeke's translation of Proclus' *Elements of Theology* in 1268 (a few years after the *Summa contra Gentiles* was finished), Thomas could have read *penitus ignotum* as Moerbeke's Latin translation of Proclus' *pantelōs agnōston* (pp. 212–16). Pegis stresses the wide gulf between the Proclean and Thomistic understandings of *penitus ignotum*.

4. SS 1.8.1.1 ad4. Joseph Owens comments on the "darkness of ignorance" in this text in "Aquinas—'Darkness of Ignorance' in the Most Refined Notion of God," in *Bonaventure and Aquinas: Enduring Philosophers*, ed. R. W. Shahan and F. J. Kovach (Norman: University of Oklahoma, 1976), pp. 69–86. He sees the darkness as signifying for Aquinas our nonconceptual knowledge of God, where there is "privation of both intuitional and conceptual light" (p. 86).

radically negative fashion by Dionysius and others. He interprets Dionysius' calling the Deity unnameable to mean either that no one can explain
God's being with perfect knowledge (not that no names at all apply to God
[*DDN* 1.1.30]); or that God is unnameable insofar as existing over all (but
not insofar as being the cause of all [1.3.98]). Thomas also explains the Dionysian maxim that we know God through our ignorance as meaning that
we truly know God only when we know that we are ignorant of God's
essence (7.4.731)—which makes Dionysian ignorance part of a "knowing
unknowing." God's ways in Romans 11:33 are said to be "not investigable"
because we cannot comprehend them to the full, not because we cannot in
any way arrive at them through creatures (*SS* 1.3.2.1 ad1). The Augustinian
axiom that God eludes our intellect does not mean that no form can represent God at all but that no form does so perfectly (*DV* 2.1 ad10).

Thomas closely connects our noncomprehensive knowledge of God to
our sense of God's transcendence. "God's reality surpasses our intellect . . .
exceeds our intellect."[5] God "is understood to be above intellect" insofar as
we understand that the divine goodness is above that which we conceive
about God (*SS* 1.2.1.3 ad2). It is because of God's boundlessness that the divine substance exceeds every concept of the intellect,[6] and the divine truth
transcends our knowledge because "God is greater than our hearts" (*John*
7.3.1063, quoting 1 John 3:20). God is said to be hidden because the divine
essence is beyond all that the created mind can excogitate,[7] and the ultimate in human knowledge of God occurs when someone "knows that he
knows not God, insofar as he recognizes that what God is exceeds everything that we understand of him."[8] God dwells in a supereminent darkness, and the human darkness of unknowing is a direct consequence of
God's excessive, dazzling light.

---

5. *SS* 1.2.1.3, pp. 69–70; also: *DV* 2.1; cf. *SS* 1.34.3.1; 4.49.2.7. God "exceeds every natural
faculty and capacity" (*SS* 4.49.2.6), and every category or class (*DV* 10.11.178–79).

6. *SCG* 1.14.116–17; cf. 1.30.278.

7. *DDN* 13.3.993; neither simple name nor complex proposition can fully express God's
essence.

8. *DP* 7.5 ad14; cf. *SDC* 6.160, *DDN* 7.4.731. The unknowing arises when we become
cognizant that God exceeds all that we understand, although we are not told how we become cognizant of God's transcendence.

11. Our Nonquidditative Knowledge of God

Quiddity (whatness or essence) is the English transliteration of the medieval Latin *quidditas*, which is itself a somewhat artificial, abstract form of the interrogative pronoun *quid*. The quiddity of something is broadly synonymous with a thing's essence or nature, given in response to the query, What is it *(quid est)?*

Thomas frequently says that during our earthly life we can know that God exists but not what God is.[9] We cannot grasp God's essence but only "what God is not and how other things are related to him" (*SCG* 1.30.278). Not even the wise can give a detailed exposition of God's essence (*Job* 36.264–68), and our knowledge of God is not by essence but "obscure, as in a mirror and from afar" (*John* 1.11.211). Just as we do not know God's essence, so we do not know the depths of the divine existence that is identical to the divine essence, though we do know *that* God exists.[10]

What is Aquinas' view of quidditative knowledge? The quiddity of something is what something is.[11] The definition is the intelligible meaning *(ratio)* that manifests or signifies the quiddity of something, revealing that thing's essence;[12] and the definition is not just any meaning but the essential, categorical meaning specific to the entity in question.[13] A lapidary sentence provides a summary statement: "A thing's definition is the meaning which the name signifies" (*Meta.* 4.16.733). Quidditative knowledge, then, is essential, specific, definitional knowledge.

9. *SS* 1.8.1.1; *SCG* 1.11.66, 69.

10. *DP* 7.2 ad1; cf. 7.2 ad11; *SCG* 1.12.78.

11. *Post.* 2.7.477; *Meta.* 1.12.183 and 7.9.1469 equate something's quiddity with the *quod quid est* (the Latin equivalent, lacking the definite article, of Aristotle's *to ti estin,* "the what it is") and the *forma totius* (the form of the whole essence), which in material realities comprises substantial form *(forma partis)* and matter.

12. *Post.* 1.33.279; 2.2.421, 424, 427; 2.4.447; 2.6.465; 2.8.484; *Meta.* 7.4.1351, 1355; 7.5.1378; 7.12.1537. In the texts cited from his *Sententia super Metaphysicam,* and elsewhere, Thomas generally equates the *quod quid est* and the *quod quid erat esse* (the Latin equivalent of Aristotle's *to ti ēn einai,* "the what it was to be" [*Metaphysics* 7.5.1031a12]), although Aristotle distinguishes the *to ti ēn einai* and the *to ti estin* as the specific from the generic (Joseph Owens, *The Doctrine of Being in the Aristotelian "Metaphysics,"* 3rd ed., preface by E. Gilson [Toronto: PIMS, 1978], pp. 180–88).

13. *Meta.* 7.3.1325, 1328; 7.4.1342.

More pertinently, Thomas views nonquidditative knowledge of God as nondefinitional, nonrepresentational, nonintuitional, and noncomprehensive. We are told that God cannot be defined since God does not belong to any category or class, for every definition places its object in a category.[14] Moreover, what we conceive with our intellect fails to represent God.[15] The language of sight, physical or mental, must not be associated with God, and so we are refused the capacity during this life to fix our mind's eye upon God by means of an essential intuition.[16]

Aquinas also denies that we can grasp or comprehend God. When the human intellect, for example, comprehends anything (e.g., stone or triangle), it knows the essence in such a way that none of the intelligible factors of the entity in question exceed the human faculty of knowing; but this is not the case with the divine essence (*SCG* 1.3.16–17). Again, "every intelligible form through which the quiddity or essence of something is understood comprehends that thing in representing it, and thus we call the statements signifying the quiddity . . . definitions" (3.49.2268). Another text asserts that our nonquidditative names for God are neither defining, circumscriptive, equalizing, nor comprehending (*DP* 7.5 ad1, 5, 6, 9). Nonquidditative knowledge, therefore, means knowledge that is nondefini-

---

14. *SS* 1.2.1.3; *CT* 1.26; *SCG* 1.25.233–34; *ST* 1.3.5.

15. "Whatever our intellect conceives of God fails to represent him, and thus the divine essence always remains hidden from us" (*DV* 2.1 ad9); and: 8.1 ad8; 10.11.178–85; *ST* 1.12.2. Material realities, the native objects of human knowledge, are not capable of representing the divine essence (*Rom.* 1.6.114), and no created form can represent the divine essence as it is (*John* 1.11.211).

16. In this life we are not able to see God by fixing an intuitive gaze (*intuitum*) or fastening the mind's eye upon the divine essence (*SS* 3.35.2.2.2). Thomas is denying an immediate, representational view of God's essence. He distinguishes between knowing and seeing God, for the intellect, when it considers some creature as a likeness of God, "immediately thinks about God although it does not immediately see God" (*SS* 4.49.2.7 ad8). God also escapes what Aquinas calls our *formatio intellectus* (*SS* 3.24.1.2.1; cf. 4.10.1.4.5; 4.49.2.1 ad3); *formatio* is the Latin translation of an Arabic term referring to the definitional grasp of essence or quiddity (cf. *SS* 3.24.1.1.2) and probably signifies the mind's representing an essence to itself by forming or constructing it. To say that God escapes our *formatio intellectus*, then, means that our knowledge of God is neither intuitional nor representational. For the historical background on *formatio intellectus*, see M.-D. Chenu, "Un vestige du stoicisme," *RSPT* 27 (1938): 63–68; Joseph Owens, *St. Thomas Aquinas on the Existence of God*, ed. J. R. Catan (Albany, NY: SUNY, 1980), pp. 24, 43; 239, n. 10; 242, n. 21.

tional, nonrepresentational, nonintuitional, noncomprehensive, and even nonessential.[17]

A. No Intellect Sees God by Its Natural Powers

Thomas undergirds his thesis about our nonquidditative knowledge of God by showing that no created intellect by dint of its own natural powers can see God's essence, even if helped by faith or revelation.[18] Marshaling texts from Romans 6:23 (the grace of God is life eternal) and John 17:3 (life eternal is to know the one true God), his faith teaches him from the outset that seeing God's essence belongs to eternity and is a matter of grace rather than nature. Since the divine essence "exceeds every natural faculty and capacity," in order to see God the light of glory is required, which is "above nature."[19] For "the divine essence is not the native intelligible form of the created intellect," and thus "neither human nor angel is able from purely natural powers to attain to the vision of God's essence" (DV 8.3).

After Aquinas' early works, the identity of God's being and essence, and the infinity this implies, become the primary reason why God remains in-

17. John Wippel (*Metaphysical Themes in Thomas Aquinas* [Washington, DC: CUA, 1984], pp. 238–41) asserts that from the very beginning of his career Thomas taught that we have no quidditative knowledge of God in this life, and that when Thomas says that what God is remains unknown to us completely, he is taking *quid est* knowledge strictly, as meaning comprehensive, defining knowledge. Wippel gives a more detailed treatment of the same issues in *The Metaphysical Thought of Thomas Aquinas: From Finite Being to Uncreated Being* (Washington, DC: CUA, 2000), pp. 502–43, where he describes Thomas as denying to us in this life not only comprehensive knowledge of God, "but any knowledge of God's essence which would enable us to grasp that essence as it is in itself in the way we can grasp the essence of something such as a human being and define it" (p. 536). In *Metaphysical Themes* (p. 232, n. 56; p. 240, n. 79) it is unclear whether Wippel would also see Thomas as disallowing even an imperfect and nondefining positive concept of God's essence, as Thomas does allow, for example, in those cases where we understand various material realities in a direct and positive way though with less than essential or definitive knowledge. In *Metaphysical Thought* (p. 543), however, Wippel more clearly states that "when Thomas denies that we can in this life know 'what God is', he is recognizing a greater limitation in our knowledge of God than any which applies to our knowledge of purely corporeal entities," even for those cases where we possess at best a nondefinitive and merely descriptive knowledge of certain material realities based on their accidental qualities. For another interesting treatment of Thomas' position about our nonquidditative knowledge of God, see Brian Davies, "Aquinas on What God Is Not," *Revue internationale de philosophie* 52 (1998): 207–25.

18. SS 4.49.2.6; same: *Isa.* 1.74–103; *DV* 8.3; cf. *SCG* 3.52; *ST* 1.12.4; *Quod.* 7.1.1.

19. SS 4.49.2.6; same: *DV* 10.11.178–85.

tuitionally unknown in this life. "Every act of knowing arrives at something which exists, i.e., at some nature which participates in being; but God is the unparticipated act of being itself and therefore is unknown" (*Col.* 1.4.30). Since the proper object of every created intellect is essence as distinct from being, "that which surpasses the essence exceeds the capacity of every intellect; in God, however, being is not other than essence" (*1 Tim.* 6.3.269). To know Subsistent Being Itself "is connatural to the divine intellect alone" and "is above the natural faculty of any created intellect, since no creature is its own being but possesses a participated being" (*ST* 1.12.4).

In several places Aquinas manages a complicated discussion about the three media of intellectual vision and concludes that while on earth we know God through concepts and as in a mirror, in heaven there remains only the first medium, the light of glory.[20] Since "the totality of creatures is for us a sort of mirror," "insofar as we know the invisible things of God through creatures, we are said to see through a mirror, but insofar as those invisible things are hidden from us, we see in obscurity."[21]

Even the knowledge garnered through faith does not possess an intuitional vision of God, since the divine truth is proposed to faith clothed in words and images that originate in sensation and thus fail to express and represent that divine truth fully; faith's knowledge also occurs in a mirror and obscurely.[22] Faith is not the sight of something present but the assent to something heard even though it is absent.[23] Since even in revelation we continue to know in a normal fashion rooted in sensation, our knowledge of immaterial realities is always nondefinitional, "whether it occurs through natural reason based on the effects of creatures or through revelation by means of images taken from material reality" (*BDT* 6.3).

20. *Quod.* 7.1.1; 10.8.1; *DV* 8.3 ad17; 18.1 ad1; *1 Cor.* 13.4.800–801; *ST* 1.56.3.

21. *1 Cor.* 13.4.800–801; *SCG* 3.47.2245 speaks of "this mirror which is the human mind." Manlio Brunetti ("La conoscenza *speculare* di Dio in S. Tommaso d'Aquino," *Divinitas* 1 [1957]: 528–49) places knowledge *per speculum* (in a mirror) somewhere in the middle between intuitive and discursive knowledge and sees creation as the mirror that imperfectly and analogically reflects the glory of God. But Thomas tends to equate knowledge *per speculum* with the discursive knowledge of a cause through its effect.

22. *SS* 3.24.1.2.3; cf. *ST* 1.12.13 ad3; 2-2.1.5 ad1.

23. *SS* 3.24.1.2.3 ad4; also: *DV* 10.11 ad11.

Sometimes Thomas singles out angels[24] or Adam (*DV* 18.1) in order to deny of them any natural essential knowledge of God. Quidditative knowledge of God can occur only when there is a perfect agreement between God and the image or likeness by which God is known; but the likeness of God received in any created intellect can be only analogical, "and thus the knowledge which would occur through such a similitude would not be of God's essence and in fact would be much more imperfect than if a substance were known through the likeness of an accident" (*DV* 8.1).

B. The Graced Vision of God's Essence

For all his insistence on the impossibility of any creature's seeing God by dint of its own natural powers, Thomas is just as sure, on account of his faith, that the blessed, both human and angelic, enjoy an essential, beatifying vision of God in heaven. He tries to establish four closely interconnected theses:

1. That no created intellect possesses a natural essential knowledge of God
2. That it is not *in principle* impossible for a created intellect to see God
3. That grace enables us to have a beatific vision of God in heaven
4. That this vision occurs only through the light of glory and when God becomes both the object of an intellectual intuition and the intelligible means by which that intuition is accomplished.[25]

Whatever the order of these theses in any given passage, the pattern of dependence is fairly evident: the third thesis, which states Aquinas' Christian faith, is paramount and primary, guiding the others; the second is a consequence of the third, for whatever faith promises must be possible, and although one may not be able directly to prove the content of faith's assertion, one can show that the arguments purporting to prove its impossibility are not in fact probative; the first derives partially from the

24. *DV* 8.1; 8.3; *ST* 1.56.3.
25. These theses can be seen, with varying sequence and emphases, in *SCG* 3.38–54 and *ST* 1.12.

third (for if the vision of God is a matter of grace, then it cannot be a naturally attainable goal) and partially from that sense of God's mysterious
eminence that lies behind Thomas' negative theology; the fourth tries to
give a reasoned account of the nature of the beatific vision, granted that it
does occur through grace. For Aquinas, the thesis about our natural nonquidditative knowledge of God, in the context of eschatology, serves to
emphasize that the beatific vision is a matter of God's free grace, just as the
same thesis in other contexts is used to accentuate God's mysterious transcendence.[26]

Thomas quotes scripture (1 Cor. 13:12; John 14:21) to prove that we will
see the essence of God and argues that in the beatific vision "the intellect
is able through the divine essence to see the divine essence itself."[27] Besides
utilizing these and other scriptural texts (Matt. 5:8; 1 John 3:2) to substan-
tiate faith's belief in the beatific vision, he also realizes that other texts
seem to prove the opposite (John 1:18; 1 John 4:12; Ex. 33:20; 1 Tim. 6:16),
although he interprets them as merely establishing that we do not have a
bodily or imaginative vision of God, or a vision of God in this mortal life
(barring the exception of Saint Paul), or a comprehensive intellectual vision of God.[28]

26. In Rahner's eyes, Thomas' view of God's incomprehensibility "is a statement of faith
which is to be found in the witness of Scripture and tradition," and that incomprehensibility "must always be considered in relation to the possibility of the direct vision of God, which
is only made known to us through revelation" ("An Investigation of the Incomprehensibility of God in St. Thomas Aquinas," in *Theological Investigations,* trans. D. Morland [New
York: Seabury, 1979], 16:246). Rahner speaks of his own theology as stressing the "holy inconceivability" of God ("The Experience of a Catholic Theologian," trans. P. Verhalen,
Communio 11 [1984]: 406). Cf. Paul Wess, "Die Inkomprehensibilität Gottes und ihre Konsequenzen für die Gotteserkenntnis bei Thomas von Aquin und Karl Rahner" (doctoral dissertation, University of Innsbruck, 1969); idem, *Wie von Gott Sprechen? Eine Auseinandersetzung mit Karl Rahner* (Graz: Styria, 1970).

27. *SS* 4.49.2.1. Paradoxically, "although man is naturally inclined towards the ultimate
end, he is nevertheless not able naturally but only through grace to obtain it" (*BDT* 6.4 ad5).
DV 8.1 calls heretical the position that no created intellect can ever see the divine essence
and also arrives at the conclusion that God must be both the object and the means of that
vision.

28. *John* 1.11.210, 213–14; 6.5.947; *Matt.* 5.434; 1 *Tim.* 6.3.270. Basing himself on 2 Corinthians 12:3 and Augustine's authority, Aquinas claims, by way of exception, that the light of glory was given miraculously, though only temporarily, to Saint Paul during his earthly existence, so that he possessed a kind of temporary beatific vision (*SS* 4.49.2.7; *DV* 10.11; 13.2–3;

C. Finite Intellectual Creatures and God's Infinity

Aquinas supplies two basic warrants to support his contention that humans lack a natural ability to see God's essence in this life: (1) God is immaterial, whereas all human intuitional knowing of essences involves abstracting material images from the data of the senses; (2) God is infinite, unparticipated being, whereas humans are finite participants in being. The second warrant is the more fundamental and searching, for it rests, on the one hand, on the divine infinity that is unique to God, and on the other, on the finitude that is proper to every creature as such; but the first warrant is perhaps more accessible and understandable, since it is proper to humans as humans and deals with matter rather than finitude, and knowing rather than being. Moreover, Aquinas employs the first, properly human warrant to demonstrate that humans also lack a natural ability to see an angel's essence in this life, for angels too are immaterial. Finally, although the second warrant is more basic and more theologically rich, the first receives a good deal of attention for two pedagogical reasons: it is more comprehensible since it discusses the characteristically human way of knowing, and it allows Aquinas to treat of the divine and angelic natures together as immaterial objects of the human intellect.

As to his first warrant, in *BDT* 1.2 Thomas provides three reasons for our natural inability to see God's essence in this life: two are taken from our natural mode of knowing, in which we make use of images garnered from material reality;[29] the other is based on God's epistemic infinity which transcends any created intelligible principle of knowledge, even one that bypasses our natural way of knowing and is impressed directly by God on our intellect.

In *SCG* 1.3.16 we read that those realities not falling directly under the senses cannot be grasped by the human intellect unless such knowledge can be collected from sense data; but sense data cannot lead us to see the

---

18.1 ad13; *SCG* 3.47.2239; *Rom.* 1.6.117; *1 Cor.* 13.4.802; *2 Cor.* 12.1.451–57; *John* 1.11.211–213; *Quod.* 1.1.1; *ST* 1.12.11; 2-2.175.3; 2-2.180.5).

29. *BDT* 6.3 states that we have no immediate insight into God's essence because our intellect in this life has immediate insight only into images rooted in sense data. *ST* 1.12.4 also refers to the sensate origin of human knowledge.

divine essence, for the former are "effects which are not equal to the power of their cause," although from them we can be led to know that God exists "and other things of this sort which must be attributed to the first principle."

In *SCG* 3.41–46 Aquinas is concerned to show that in this life we have no intuitional knowledge of what he calls "separate substances"—by which he means immaterial angels separated from the realm of matter—so that in chapter 47 he can argue, a fortiori, that we have no essential knowledge of God either. His basic argument is a form of the first warrant: since angels do not exist in matter, no human knowledge based on images taken from sense data can know them essentially, for sense data is not powerful enough for such a knowledge of immaterial realities (3.41). After some complicated corollaries to the first warrant, he must then reinterpret the revered Augustine, who had written (*De trin.* 9.3) that the mind knows itself through itself, since it is incorporeal, and that by understanding itself it also understands separate substances. Thomas argues, however, that our soul does not understand its own essence through an act of intense introspection, as in Augustine's theory, but rather that it knows its own activity and its epistemic objects only in and through knowing the realities of the material world; even the soul's knowledge of itself, then, based as it is on sensation and imagination, will not be sufficiently powerful to reveal the essence of angelic substances (3.46).[30] And if such is the case with angels, then "much less in this life can we see the divine essence which transcends all separate substances" (3.47.2239).[31]

As to the second warrant, we begin with *SCG* 3.49,[32] where Thomas asks whether angels and the soul separated from its body possess a quidditative knowledge of God. For three reasons he responds in the negative. First, knowing God from one's own essence (which is how angels and the separated soul know God) is like knowing a cause from its effect; but a cause's essence can be known from its effect only if the effect is equal to the cause,

---

30. Cf. *SS* 4.49.2.7; Aquinas does affirm that metaphysics or theology can know that angels exist with certain attributes, such as intellectuality and incorruptibility (*BDT* 6.4; *Post.* 1.41.363).

31. Cf. *DA* 16–17; *Heb.* 4.2.228; *ST* 1.12.11; 1.50.2; *SDC* 7.180–81; *Meta.* 2.1.285.

32. Cf. *SS* 2.23.2.1; *DDN* 13.3.996; *DV* 8.3; *ST* 1.12.13 ad1; 1.56.3.

so that the cause's total power is expressed in the effect; but no created intellect is an effect equal to the unlimited power of God, and thus no created intellect can possess an intuitional knowledge of God's essence.[33] Second, every separated substance or soul belongs to a determinate category of being, whereas God belongs to no category and is infinite; but no created substance that is "terminated" and belongs to a determinate category of being can be a fully adequate likeness of God, who is indeterminate and infinite.[34] Third, since the being of any creature is other than its essence, but God's essence is identical with his being, no created essence can be a sufficient medium by which to see God's essence.[35] In one way or another, whether implicitly or explicitly, all three of these reasons accentuate God's infinity.

In the *Summa theologiae*, likewise, Thomas maintains that God cannot be seen by means of any created likeness since no creature whose essence and being are distinct can represent the God whose being and essence are identical, for every created likeness is limited to some partial aspect of reality and thus cannot represent God's very supereminence and status as the One who is unlimited and uncircumscribed (1.12.2); and no created intellect, whose existence is participated, can by its own natural powers see the essence of God, who is Subsistent Being Itself (1.12.4).

In the late *Super librum De causis*, Thomas notes that all understanding pertains to beings *(entia)*, so that "whatever does not possess the *ratio entis* [which may mean the 'nature of being' or the 'meaning of being'] is not graspable by the intellect" (6.174); and so, if the First Cause transcends the *ratio entis*, then the intellect cannot grasp it. The First Cause does transcend the *ratio entis*, he asserts, but not for the reasons tendered by the Platonists; rather,

The First Cause is above being *(ens)* insofar as it is the infinite act of being itself *(ipsum esse infinitum)*. That which finitely participates the act of being *(esse)*, however, is called a being *(ens)*, and this is commensurate with our intellect, whose ob-

---

33. *SCG* 3.49.2265; same: *SCG* 1.3.17.

34. *SCG* 3.49.2266–68; references to an essence's "termination" originally stem from a Neoplatonic context, where the plenitude of the One is successively and increasingly terminated (i.e., limited, bounded, or finitized) at each lower level of the hierarchy of being.

35. *SCG* 3.49.2269; same: *1 Tim.* 6.3.269.

ject is an essence *(quod quid est)*. Thus, only something that possesses an essence which participates in the act of being *(esse)* is graspable by our intellect; but God's essence is God's very act of being, and thus God transcends understanding.[36]

God's infinity *means* the subsistent act of being unparticipated by an essence distinct from that being: and God's infinity is why God transcends all creaturely acts of understanding.

For Aquinas, the divine infinity is the most proper, profound, and theologically rich warrant in support of the contention that no creature by dint of its own natural powers can possess a quidditative insight into God.[37] Only this warrant rests on what is totally unique to God, and only this warrant looks to the creature as creature and not merely to the human qua human, although Aquinas for certain pedagogical reasons also uses the warrant based on the specifically human mode of knowing. Divine infinity, however, also raises a conundrum: How can the blessed in heaven, according to Aquinas, see the infinite God face to face without, by that very fact, also comprehending the infinite God as much as God is able to be comprehended—that is, infinitely—something that, as we shall see, Thomas is unwilling to permit?[38] How can the same divine infinity be

---

36. *SDC* 6.175; cf. *DDN* 1.2.74–75; 2.4.180; 11.2.897. The First Cause is distinguished from angels by being *esse subsistens* and is called "supersubstantial and absolutely untellable *(inenarrabilis)*" (*SDC* 7.180–82); cf. *Post.* 1.30.254; *ST* 1.88.2 ad4.

37. God's infinity is in reality the same as the divine *ipsum esse subsistens*, but expressed differently. Gilson writes that "the whole negative theology of Thomas Aquinas is tied up with his notion of *esse* conceived as the act of being" (*Elements of Christian Philosophy*, p. 255). Pierre Faucon underlines that Thomas' apophatism is different from that of Dionysius because Thomas replaces the Good of Neoplatonism with the *ipsum esse* of the Mosaic revelation (*Aspects néoplatoniciens de la doctrine de saint Thomas d'Aquin*, [Paris/Lille: Champion/University III, 1975], pp. 635–45).

38. H.-F. Dondaine, in a little article replete with rich historical data ("Cognoscere de Deo 'quid est,'" *RTAM* 22 [1955]: 72–78), manifests Thomas' originality both in denying any knowledge of God's quiddity in this life and in distinguishing a quidditative knowledge of God from a comprehensive knowledge of God. There were two tendencies among his contemporaries: those of Augustinian bent easily granted to the saints—even to those on earth—a knowledge of God's essence, however imperfect; those more imbued with Dionysian propensities refused a knowledge of God's quiddity even to the blessed of heaven. Thus, on the one hand, the *Summa fratris Alexandri* taught that God's essence could be known imperfectly through grace in this life and perfectly through glory in heaven, and Bonaventure thought that God's essence could be known through grace by those on earth; on the other hand, Albert the Great identified knowing God's quiddity with having a

quidditatively comprehended without being *ipso facto* infinitely comprehended, unless God's essence is to be severed into parts? We will look at this enigma below.

III. *Our Noncomprehensive Knowledge of God*

God's incomprehensibility means for Aquinas that God always exceeds every kind of knowledge.[39] Often he mentions this incomprehensibility when commenting upon scriptural texts that treat of the inscrutability of God's will and wisdom. "Humans are not able to comprehend the reason of the divine judgments because they are hidden in the wisdom of God," nor are God's ways "perfectly traceable by humans."[40] God's judgments are incomprehensible because of the even more profound incomprehensibility of the divine will, which no one can plumb (*Job* 23.209–17). God's infinite wisdom and love, from which the mysteries of Christ are said to radiate, are incomprehensible to thought, exceeding "every created intellect and all knowledge" (*Eph.* 3.5.176–78). God is incomprehensible because God transcends everything that is comprehensible, and every comprehension (*1 Tim.* 6.3.268). Thomas' sense of the numinous depths of God and of the religious awe in which we hold them is evident from a remark of his in which he utilizes a text from Hilary of Poitiers' *De Trinitate:*

Though he who pursues the infinite with reverence will never finally reach the end, yet he will always progress by pressing onward. But do not intrude yourself into the divine secret, do not, presuming to comprehend the sum total of intelligence, plunge yourself into the mystery of the unending nativity; rather, understand that these things are incomprehensible. (*SCG* 1.8.50)

---

comprehensive definition of it and found this to be impossible, and thus would not grant a quidditative knowledge of God even to the blessed in heaven. Thomas, however, asserts that while there is no knowledge of God's quiddity in this life (against the Augustinians), there will be such a knowledge in heaven (against Albert). Severing the knot Albert had tied between quidditative and comprehensive knowledge, Aquinas teaches that the saints will see God's essence in heaven without comprehending it fully.

39. *ST* 1.12.1 ad1, 3; 1.12.7 ad2.

40. *Rom.* 11.5.937; the dispositions of divine providence are unknown to us, especially in their minute details (*Job* 11.59–74).

In these texts God's incomprehensibility, acknowledged by the religious awe and reverence felt in the face of the divine preeminence, possesses a general meaning bound up, dynamically, with God's will, wisdom, love, judgments, and providential ways.

Instructed by the words of the Latin Vulgate, Aquinas sometimes differentiates *comprehendere* as meaning inclusion or containment from *comprehendere* as signifying a holding or attaining. He notes that Philippians 3:12 uses *comprehendere* to signify the attainment of our ultimate good,[41] but adds that this cannot imply that God is enclosed or contained in anything; the word refers, rather, to a certain "taking hold of" *(tentio)*, for when we see God in eternity "we will possess *(tenere)* him in ourselves."[42] When commenting on the same scriptural locus in his exposition of Paul's epistles, he remarks that *comprehendere* can mean to contain, "as a house contains us," and in this sense God is always incomprehensible; or it may mean to attain *(attingere)*[43] or hold *(tenere*—he quotes Song of Songs 3:4, "Tenui eum" [I held him]), in which sense God is not incomprehensible.[44] He interprets the *comprehendere* of 1 Corinthians 9:24 to mean the possession of something sought after.[45] God cannot be comprehended as being contained in something greater but can be comprehended (grasped) as an object present to the intellectual sight of the blessed.

41. The Latin reads: "Sequor autem, si quomodo comprehendam in quo et comprehensus sum a Christo Jesu." Paul follows his course in order to grasp the prize for which he has already been grasped by Jesus Christ.

42. *CT* 2.9.335–63; cf. *De perfect.* 4–5.

43. Sometimes *attingere* is opposed to *comprehendere* and refers to grasping God quidditatively. Commenting on Matthew 11:27, "No one knows the Father except the Son," Thomas notes that the saints know God not by comprehending but by attaining *(attingere)* or by faith *(Matt.* 11.965), in which *attingere* probably refers to how the saints grasp God in heaven, while faith is their means of knowing God on earth. In *1 Tim.* 6.3.269 and *Phil.* 3.2.127, the context clearly shows that *attingere* refers to heaven's intuitional grasp of God. In some texts *(SS* 1.3.1.1 ad4; 1.34.3.1), however, *attingere* does not refer to a quidditative grasp but simply to any knowledge at all of God.

44. *Phil.* 3.2.127; same: *ST* 1.12.7 ad1.

45. *ST* 1-2.4.3, and ad1; same: *De articulis* 2.389–91; cf. *Eph.* 3.5.176; *2 Cor.* 6.3.240; *John* 1.3.112. Cf. *ST* 1.12.7 ad1. The Latin: "Nescitis quod ii, qui in stadio currunt, omnes quidem currunt, sed unus accipit bravium? Sic currite ut comprehendatis" (Do you not know that all the runners in the stadium run to win, but only one receives the prize? So run in order that you may grasp [the prize]).

When Aquinas speaks of the knowledge of God's essence as a "comprehensive knowledge" (*DDN* 1.1.32), we realize he is doing so on the authority of the scriptural loci we have just seen; his usual practice, however, is to distinguish comprehensive from essential knowledge of God (*DDN* 1.1.34), or conversely, God's *incomprehensibilia* from God's *incontemplabilia*.[46] Indeed, heaven's essential knowledge of God cannot be a comprehensive knowledge of God.[47]

In an article for which the point at issue is whether the soul of Christ comprehended the Word by seeing it,[48] Thomas clearly demonstrates that comprehending God requires something more than merely seeing God. "Something is truly comprehended when it is attained by the intellect according to the whole range *(tota ratio)* of its knowability," and thus God is said to comprehend himself because he knows himself "according to every aspect *(ratio)* by which he is knowable." The intellect requires two things in order to understand: an intellectual light, by which it is able to understand, and the intelligible likeness of the reality known, by which it is equipped to know the reality. If either of these is exceeded by the being of the reality in question, then the intellect will not comprehend that reality. However, a distinction needs to be made: if the reality exceeds the intelligible likeness by which the intellect knows the reality, then the intellect will not attain to seeing the reality's essence, as the essence of the human would not be seen if the intelligible form of the human represented only the sensate and not the rational side of the human; if the reality exceeds the very intellectual light itself but not the intelligible form by which the reality is known, then although the essence will be seen it will not be seen in as perfect a manner as it is knowable, for "one's intellectual light determines one's strength of understanding." The intellect sees the essence of God when that very essence is joined to it as the intelligible form by which it knows, as happens in the blessed. But because the intellectual light by

---

46. *DDN* 1.1.26–27; cf. 1.2.72, 74. Dionysius, in the passage Thomas is commenting upon, uses these two words as rough equivalents. For Aquinas, in this life God's essence is not able to be contemplated, that is, cannot be known quidditatively.

47. *SS* 4.49.2.3 ad5; same: *DP* 7.3 ad5.

48. *SS* 3.14.1.2.1; same: *DV* 8.1 ad9; parallel texts may be found in *DV* 20.4–5; *CT* 1.216; 1 *Tim.* 6.3.268–69; *John* 1.11.219; 7.3.1065; *ST* 3.10.1.

which any creature knows is received from God and "falls short of the divine being," even when the creature sees God's essence it does not see it in a perfect manner. "On this account no created intellect can be given the capacity to comprehend God." Thus even Christ's soul cannot comprehend the Word of God. Clearly, in this passage, although a creature may fail to comprehend God for two different reasons, the more basic reason, the one that establishes the strictest and most profound meaning of God's incomprehensibility, is the creature's lack of intellectual power, which cannot be rectified or changed by God since it is an element of creaturehood as such, although the lack of an adequate likeness or intelligible form may be overcome by God with the grace of the beatific vision.[49]

What, then, are the warrants by which Aquinas establishes the strict meaning of God's incomprehensibility? For he claims it is impossible that the conception of any created intellect should "represent the total perfection of the divine essence,"[50] whereby God would be comprehended by being known as perfectly as he knows himself.[51]

In the *Sentences* and *De veritate* Aquinas advances as the reason for God's incomprehensibility the transcendence of God's power. SS 4.49.2.3 remarks that something is comprehended by an intellect when the knowable object does not exceed the capacity of the intellect, but that the intellect lacks comprehension whenever the intelligible object is more powerful or knowable than the intellect's capacity to know. But the truth of the divine essence "exceeds" the light of any created intellect and thus cannot be comprehended by such an intellect. Similarly, DV 8.2 remarks that "the power of the divine essence, by which it is intelligible," and "the truth of the divine essence, by which it is knowable," "exceeds" the light of every created intellect, so that no created intellect comprehends God, "not because it is ignorant of some part of God but because it is not able to attain

---

49. *John* 1.11.211–13 displays a similar procedural order: although no "created form" can represent the divine essence since no finite can represent the infinite (211), scripture nevertheless promises the vision of God to humanity (212); still, no creature can ever comprehend God because of God's infinite being and knowability (213).

50. SS 1.2.1.3, p. 70; the only conception that perfectly represents God is the uncreated Word (ibid.); same: DV 2.1.

51. SS 1.3.1.1; same: *Isa.* 6.115–17; DV 8.1 ad1.

to the perfect mode of the knowledge of God." The reason for God's in-comprehensibility, therefore, is the transcendence of the divine power over every created intellect.[52]

This transcendence of divine power becomes, in the *Summa contra Gentiles* and later texts, the infinity of the divine substance itself. *SCG* 3.55 aims to prove that no created intellect can comprehend the divine sub-stance:[53] for no finite power can "adequately correspond to an infinite ob-ject," and since the divine substance is infinite while every created intellect is "limited to a certain species," no such intellect can comprehend the di-vine essence (3.55.2320).[54] The same divine infinity which here in chapter 55 keeps God from being comprehended also prevents God, in chapter 49, from being seen quidditatively by methods natural to creatures. However, God may be seen essentially if the light of glory is supplied in the beatific vision (3.54.2316). Thus, although the same divine infinity can be used as a reason against either a quidditative or a comprehensive vision of God, it is not a hindrance to God's being seen essentially if God chooses to bestow grace, but it does remain a bar to God's being comprehended, even in ce-lestial beatitude. Thomas writes that even if in the beatific vision the di-vine essence "becomes the intelligible form of the created intellect, not nevertheless does the created intellect grasp it according to its whole ca-pacity *(totum posse)*."[55]

---

52. *SS* 4.49.2.3 ad6 mentions God's infinity in passing, but it is not the primary warrant offered by the article; cf. *SS* 1.3.1.1 ad4. However, God's power as infinitely exceeding its ef-fects is sometimes given as the reason for God's incomprehensibility (*Job* 11.51–58, 125–30; 37.356–58; *De ration.* 6.85–96); "What means can be adopted in order to know the power of God inasmuch as it exceeds every creature?" (*Job* 11.146–48).

53. For parallel texts see *SS* 3.14.1.2.1; 3.27.3.2; 4.49.2.3; *Decretalem* 1.227–38; *DDN* 13.3.992; 13.4.1000; *John* 1.11.213; *Eph.* 5.3.280; *DV* 8.2; 20.5; *DC* 10 ad5; *ST* 1.12.7; 1-2.4.3; 2-2.27.5; *CT* 1.106; 2.9.335–63.

54. *CT* 2.9.339–51 says a creature cannot comprehend God since that would mean in-cluding and containing God *totum et totaliter*, which a creature cannot do since God is infi-nitely visible "according to the clarity of his truth which is infinite." For *1 Tim.* 6.3.269 God is infinitely comprehensible on account of the infinity of divine entity and light; *Phil.* 3.2.127 mentions God's infinite light and truth.

55. *SCG* 3.55.2321. *ST* 1.12.7 argues it is impossible for created intellect to know God as far as he is capable of being known—that is, infinitely—since the created light of glory is never infinite. Other texts linking infinity and incomprehensibility: *ST* 1.62.9; 3.10.3 ad1–2; *DV* 20.4; *DDN* 1.2.72–75; 5.1.641; *R43* 16.

Aquinas expresses this difference between seeing and comprehending God by the interplay and distinction between the adjective *totus* (whole or total) and the adverb *totaliter* (wholly or totally). If to comprehend something is to contain and include it as a whole and wholly (*totum et totaliter*—CT 2.9.335–45), then no intellect can comprehend God, for "no created intellect can see the essence of God totally, since its power of understanding is not as great as the truth or clarity of the divine essence."[56] In the beatific vision the *whole* created intellect will see God, and the *whole* essence of God will be seen, but the vision will not take place in a fashion *wholly* comprehensive of God, since its mode of knowing will not be as perfect as God's intrinsic knowability.[57] Another pithy sentence reads: "The very boundlessness *(immensitas)* of God will be seen but it will not be seen boundlessly *(immense)*: for [God's] total measure *(totus modus)* will be seen but not totally *(totaliter).*"[58] Thomas allows the adjective *totus* to modify God, who is seen by the blessed as a single, simple whole; but he rejects the adverb *totaliter* as it modifies the creaturely power of understanding, for no finite power can extend its capacity in an intensively infinite manner into the boundless depths of the infinite God. But the paradox is one that stretches faith and reason to the limit: Infinity as such will be seen but never infinitely.

In the *Summa theologiae* Aquinas sees the problem clearly and attempts an illuminative comparison (1.12.7 ad3). The objection asserts that if one sees the *total* essence of God with one's *whole* intellect, then one sees God *totally*. Aquinas responds:

Whoever sees God in essence, sees that which in God infinitely exists and is infinitely knowable, but this infinite mode does not belong to the one seeing such that he himself should know infinitely; just as someone can know with probability that

---

56. *SS* 3.14.1.2.1 ad2; same: *DV* 2.2 ad5; 20.4 ad4; *SCG* 3.55.2323; *CT* 1.106; 2.9.335–45; *John* 1.11.213; *DDN* 2.3.161; 5.1.609.

57. *DV* 8.2 ad2; also: *DV* 2.1 ad3; 8.4 ad11; *SS* 4.49.2.3 ad3.

58. *DV* 8.2 ad6; cf. *DV* 8.4 ad6; *DP* 7.1 ad2. Thomas answers a cognate question, Can God be totally loved? in a similar fashion, asserting that *everything* in the creaturely lover can love God and that the *whole* God can be loved by the creature, but that no creature can love God *totally*, as much as God is infinitely lovable (*ST* 2-2.27.5; *DC* 10 ad5; *SS* 3.27.3.2; *De perfect.* 4–5).

some proposition is demonstrable although he himself does not know it demon-stratively.[59]

The comparison he is suggesting is this: just as someone can know with probability that a proposition is demonstrable without knowing that demonstrable proposition demonstratively, so the saints in heaven can know in a finite manner the God who is infinite without knowing that infinite God infinitely. The "demonstrable/demonstratively" and "infinite/infinitely" couplets are clearly variations on the theme of the *totus/totaliter* dyad and help us come to grips with the subtleties of the problem.

Still, the comparison itself limps somewhat, as all comparisons must, in illuminating the paradox involved in claiming that the saints in heaven possess a noncomprehensive though essential knowledge of God. For one can know *with probability* that a proposition is demonstrable only if one has *not already* demonstrated it for oneself, for in that case one would have demonstrative knowledge that the proposition is demonstrable (demon-strating a proposition is ipso facto proof that it is also demonstrable). In fact, the situation where one knows only with probability that a proposi-tion is demonstrable can come about from only two sources: either the ex-terior witness of others who do have demonstrative knowledge of the proposition or the lack of full insight into the principles and parameters of the problem at hand that could form the basis for a demonstration of the proposition. If this is so, then the disanalogies between Thomas' example and the case of the graced vision of God stand out sharply: the blessed see the interior riches of the infinite God as fully and perfectly as each is capa-ble of; their quidditative, essential knowledge of God is neither based on

59. "Qui igitur videt Deum per essentiam, videt hoc in eo, quod infinite existit, et infinite cognoscibilis est: sed hic infinitus modus non competit ei, ut scilicet ipse infinite cognoscat: sicut aliquis probabiliter scire potest aliquam propositionem esse demonstrabilem, licet ipse eam demonstrative non cognoscat." The *quod* may be either a conjunction meaning "that" or a relative pronoun meaning "which." While the general context of the beatific vision fa-vors "which" over "that," since to see an essence directly is much more perfect than merely to judge *that* an essence possesses some quality, the comparison Thomas uses only works with a "that" understood: for the example does not claim that one knows with probability a proposition, which just happens to be demonstrable, but that one knows with probability *that* a proposition is demonstrable.

an exterior report by witnesses nor due to a lack of full awareness of the divine being; otherwise, by definition, they would *not* be enjoying a genuine quidditative knowledge of God. Thomas' comparison lags insofar as the conditions that make the example of the demonstrable proposition viable cannot be translated to the situation of the beatific vision without implicitly denying the stupendous reality of the saints' essential knowledge of God. In the end, the paradox of a noncomprehensive yet quidditative knowledge of God is sui generis and resists the formation of illuminating comparisons. How the finite creature can finitely know the infinite being of God must remain as mysterious as the Infinite Mystery itself.[60]

iv. Conclusion

The following conclusions are warranted at this stage of our investigation into Aquinas' negative theology.

First, Thomas softens the negative theology of Dionysius and his followers, for Thomas' negative theology is not an *agnōsia* total and supreme. While no stranger to the biblical and patristic interpretation of God's incomprehensibility as rooted in the dynamic and mysterious working out of God's will and wisdom in history, he ultimately encapsulates his view of that incomprehensibility in two theses: no creature (especially the human in this life) by its own natural forces can possess a quidditative grasp of God's essence, knowing at best only that God exists and what God is not; and no creature can ever possess a comprehensive, infinite grasp of the divine essence. Although a quidditative knowledge of God is possible in heaven due to God's grace, a comprehensive knowledge of God by the

---

60. Rahner realizes the problem Thomas has in proposing a direct vision of God, especially when we remember that God is seen as a simple whole and *as* incomprehensible: "The assertion of the direct vision of God and assertion of his incomprehensibility are related for us here and now in a mysterious and paradoxical dialectic" ("Incomprehensibility of God," p. 247). A. N. Williams also has some illuminating words on how Thomas resolutely grasps both sides of the paradox that the blessed possess an essential though noncomprehensive vision of God, and remarks that it is by this paradox that he protects God's unfathomable transcendence—the same transcendence that Gregory Palamas tries to secure by his distinction between God's essence and energies (*The Ground of Union: Deification in Aquinas and Palamas* [New York: Oxford, 1999], p. 47).

creature is never possible, not even by God's grace. The second thesis states Aquinas' most profound and fundamental sense of God's incomprehensibility, for it holds even in eternity and rests on the basic distinction between Creator and creature. However, the problem of how to reconcile the saints' noncomprehensive though essential knowledge of God perdures.

Second, Thomas' negative theology is grounded in a sense of God's transcendence and preeminence: the negatives are attempting to evoke, in an indirect manner, a sense of God's utter beyondness. In this, Thomas is a devoted disciple of Dionysius. Moreover, the most fundamental reason adduced in support of both senses of God's incomprehensibility is the divine infinity, and in this Thomas is a continuator of the tradition originating with Gregory of Nyssa. In fact, the divine infinity is simply another way of stating that God is Subsistent Being Itself. If we want to know how Thomas knows that God is incomprehensible, we must ask how he knows that God is infinite, supereminent, and Subsistent Being Itself. Is it by rational proof, faith, religious feeling? We will return to this issue in Part Three.

3. *Aquinas'* Via Negativa

In addition to his discussion of God's incomprehensibility, Aquinas' negative theology includes his treatment of the *via negativa,* the negative path to God. In order to understand this negative path we need to see how it is situated within the overall structure of the threefold way to God.

1. The Threefold Way to God

For Aquinas the threefold way is primarily a human method of arriving at the knowledge of God;[1] angels, however, are said to practice it even more perfectly than humans (*SCG* 3.49.2271–74), and its object can be anything that transcends our sensate mode of knowing, whether God, angels, celestial bodies, or the mathematical point.[2] The terminology of the threefold way is quite fluid in Aquinas. The way of causality is expressed by *causa* (cause), *causalitas,* and infrequently *habitudo* (relation); the way of preeminence is signified by *excessus* (excess), *eminentia* (eminence or preeminence), *excellentia* (excellence), and the prefix *super*[3] (above); and the

1. See Rolf Schönberger, *Nomina divina: zur theologischen Semantik bei Thomas von Aquin,* Europäische Hochschulschriften XX/72 (Frankfurt/Bern: Lang, 1981), pp. 44–52, 82–89.
2. *DA* 16; *Anima* 3.5.183–92; *ST* 1.84.7 ad3; 1.88.2 ad2.
3. Harry Wolfson shows how Thomas substitutes *eminentia* and *excellentia* for the *excessus* that appeared in contemporary Latin translations of Dionysius, how these terms all

way of negation is denoted by *ablatio* and *privatio* (removal), *separatio* and *segregatio* (separation), *abnegatio* (denial), *remotio* (removal), and *negatio* (negation)—the last two being the most frequently used terms.[4]

The sequential ordering of each individual way within the general triple pattern is also highly flexible. Using the following abbreviations—C for causality, N for negation, and E for eminence—there are only six possibilities: CNE, CEN, NCE, NEC, ECN, and ENC. I have found instances in Thomas' works of every combination except ENC, and the first two combinations account for the majority of them.[5] As the citations show, he espouses no conventional or set pattern for the threefold way, and the combinations tend to be spread throughout his works, though triads beginning with negation do not extend beyond the *De potentia* and *De divinis nominibus*. While triads beginning with causality are numerically dominant, there is no clear victor between CNE and CEN, even though his commentators, when they mention or explain the threefold way, most often have the CNE combination in mind.[6]

We begin with the two triads whose first member is the way of causali-

---

translate *hyperochē* or *hyperochikē* in Dionysius and John Damascene, and how the prefix *hyper* (*super* in Latin) is the normal manner for Dionysius, Plotinus, and Proclus to express this eminence (*Studies in the History of Philosophy and Religion*, ed. I. Twersky and G. H. Williams, 2 vols. [Cambridge: Harvard, 1973–77], 2:506–7).

4. Thomas clearly uses the last three terms as synonyms, as the following texts demonstrate: *DDN* 1.3.104; 7.1.702; *John* 1.11.211; *ST* 1.11.3 ad2. *Negatio* and *remotio* translate, respectively, the Greek *apophasis* and *aphairesis*, which, as we have seen already, were also used synonymously by Albinus, Plotinus, Dionysius, and John Damascene. Wolfson explains how Thomas came to substitute *remotio* for the *ablatio* that was the translation of *aphairesis* in the Latin versions of Dionysius and John Damascene that he employed (*Studies* 2:497–500).

5. CNE: *SS* 1.3, division of the first part of the text; 1.4.2.1 ad2; *DP* 7.5 ad2; *DDN* 1.3.83; 1.3.98; *ST* 1.12.12; CEN: *BDT* 1.2; 6.2; *SCG* 3.49.2270; *DDN* 5.2.661–62; *DA* 16; *Rom.* 1.6.115; *ST* 1.13.10 ad5; 1.84.7 ad3; 2-2.27.4; NCE: *SS* 1.35.1.1; *BDT* 6.3; *DP* 9.7; NEC: *DDN* 7.4.729–31; ECN: *ST* 1.13.8 ad2.

6. Charles Journet, *The Dark Knowledge of God*, trans. J. F. Anderson (London: Sheed and Ward, 1948), pp. 6, 72; J. H. Nicolas, *Dieu connu comme inconnu* (Paris: Desclée, 1966), pp. 255–58; Klaus Riesenhuber, "Partizipation als Strukturprinzip der Namen Gottes bei Thomas von Aquin," in Miscellanea Mediaevalia, vol. 13/2, *Sprache und Erkenntnis im Mittelalter* (Berlin/New York: de Gruyter, 1981), pp. 969–70; Michael Ewbank, "Diverse Orderings of Dionysius' *Triplex Via* by St. Thomas Aquinas," *MS* 52 (1990): 83–109. Fran O'Rourke also underscores the variety of sequences Thomas uses in his explication of the threefold way (*Pseudo-Dionysius and the Metaphysics of Aquinas* [Leiden: Brill, 1992], pp. 35–41).

ty. The earliest mention of the threefold path to God is from Thomas' commentary on the *Sentences*,[7] where he attempts to explain the Lombard's proofs for the existence of God by reference to the Dionysian ways. Dionysius says we reach God from creatures by three ways *(modus)*: causality, removal, and preeminence. For the creature's existence is derived from another, and thus we are led to the cause by which the creature exists—the way of causality; but we can also be led to God by the creature's very mode of receiving perfections, which is imperfect: and here we have two ways: removal, by which that imperfection is removed from God, and preeminence, by which we realize that what is received in the creature is in the Creator more perfectly and nobly. Thomas then tries to line up the four proofs for God's existence the Lombard gives with the three Dionysian ways, allotting different proofs to different ways.[8] Clearly Thomas views the ways as a means of arriving at God's existence, not as a method of extrapolating from that existence to other divine characteristics; he also sees the ways as individually competent to arrive at God's existence and not as an integral whole with three component parts; and since the context is the proofs for God's existence, which require that causality be paramount, he puts causality first in the combination CNE, although his reference from Dionysius (*DN* 7.3 [PL 3:872A]) has the order of removal/eminence followed by causality, and his own commentary on this passage years later preserves that Dionysian order (*DDN* 7.4.729–31). He obviously does not shy away from molding the threefold way to his own purposes.

Other instances of the combination CNE have to do not with God's existence but with other divine attributes, and the way of eminence is often the foundation for the way of negation. For example, God is said to be both wise and not wise, but also superwise, since wisdom is not denied of God on the grounds of deficiency but because God possesses it supereminently.[9] God is the cause of all existents but is nothing in any of

---

7. *SS* 1.3, division of the first part of the text (pp. 88–89); cf. 1.3.1.3.

8. Leo Elders ("Les cinq voies et leur place dans la philosophie de saint Thomas," in *Quinque Sunt Viae*, Studi Tomistici 9 [Vatican City, 1980], pp. 142–43) also tries to parcel out the five proofs for God's existence in the *Summa theologiae* among the three ways, but in an artificial and unconvincing fashion.

9. *DP* 7.5 ad2; cf. *SS* 1.4.2.1 ad2.

them, not as deficient in being but as supereminently separated from all beings.[10]

The other combination that begins with causality, CEN, sometimes acknowledges the second element as the basis for the third, sometimes not.[11] In *SCG* 3.49.2270 Thomas asserts that humans and angels know that God exists and that he is the cause of all, eminent over all, and removed from all. The threefold way in this passage rests squarely upon reason's grasp of God through effects. In *Rom.* 1.6.115 the way of causality is said to be the means by which we know whether God exists, though the latter two ways are not so described; and in a somewhat contrived fashion similar to what we saw with respect to God's existence in the passage from his commentary on the *Sentences,* Thomas distributes the three attributes of God mentioned in Romans 1:20 among the three ways: the invisible things of God are known through negation, God's eternal power through causality, and God's divinity through the way of excellence (1.6.117). Once again, Thomas displays a tendency, when it suits his purpose, to see the various ways as individually competent to arrive at particular attributes of God, or to view the way of causality as part of the proof for God's existence.

Triads that begin with negation are in general more consonant with the Dionysian pattern. Aquinas uses the schema NEC when he comments on *DN* 7.3, which is the primary Dionysian locus he cites in his other works with respect to the threefold way. Whereas, however, he changes the order of the ways in *SS* 1.3 to CNE, here he preserves the Dionysian order of NEC. God exists and is known in all things by the way of causality, but exists and is known as separate from all things by the ways of negation and excess.[12] God's excess is again the basis for the negation even though it appears in the second position; Thomas makes a threefold way out of the basic Dionysian twofold way but still respects the manner in which Dionysius closely joins the ways of negation and excess.

BDT 6.3 and *SS* 1.35.1.1 are two instances of the combination NCE in

---

10. *DDN* 1.3.83; 1.3.98; *ST* 1.12.12.
11. Such acknowledgment occurs in *DDN* 5.2.661–62, *DA* 16, and *Rom.* 1.6.115, but not in the following texts: *BDT* 1.2; 6.2; *SCG* 3.49.2270; *ST* 1.13.10 ad5; 1.84.7 ad3; 2-2.27.4.
12. *DDN* 7.4.729–31; cf. 8.3.770.

Aquinas' works. In *BDT* 6.3 he argues that we know that God and angels exist, whether by reason or revelation, "and instead of knowing what they are we have knowledge of them through negation, through causality, and through transcendence." In *SS* 1.35.1.1 he raises the question whether knowledge belongs to God and, taking each Dionysian way individually, uses it to prove that there must be knowledge in God. The first way, through removal, leads us to realize that God is free from all potency and materiality and that as a subsistent form is per se intelligent. The second way of causality is used to demonstrate that God, as the first agent, acts for an end not by necessity of nature but by knowledge and will. He associates the third way of preeminence with the Neoplatonic process of mounting up through degrees of perfection to maximal perfection itself, in order to demonstrate that God possesses the most noble cognition of all intelligent beings. He views the three ways, taken individually, as independent means of arriving at truths about the knowledge of God.

DDN 1.3, which is Thomas' commentary on *DN* 1.5–8, offers us a unique exposition of the threefold way found nowhere else in his works. As we remember, in *DN* 1.5–8, a notoriously difficult text, Dionysius first speaks of the way of negation *(aphairesis)* as the sweetest fruit of a mystical contemplation akin to a dark night, but then immediately mentions a basic twofold way, in which God is said to be the cause of all beings but also nothing in any of them since he is "superessentially removed" *(hyperousiōs exērēmenon)* from them (1.5). Dionysius thus concentrates on negation (superessentially caused) in most of 1.5, begins his treatment of God as cause in the same section, and continues with it in 1.6–7; in these latter two sections he treats mainly the intelligible names of God based on things that are caused, though in 1.6 we also discover material names such as sun, star, or rock; finally, in 1.8 he distinguishes the scriptural names for God based on God's all-creative providence from the scriptural names that are symbolic and based on images received in prophetic visions. What is unclear in the text is whether Dionysius is making the treatment of scriptural symbolic names in 1.8 a part of the overall treatment of God by way of causality in 1.5–7 (in effect subdividing the scriptural names based on causality into those that derive from God's providence and those that derive from prophetic visions), or is expounding yet another way founded on names taken from the images of prophetic visions.

Thomas sees in the foregoing passage a threefold way of naming God by removal, by causality, and by material images received in divine visions. The first way is dependent upon the fact that God is "supereminently segregated from all things," "above all things," and "exceeds our knowledge" (*DDN* 1.3.83–84); the second way, using scriptural loci that name God as cause (1.3.98), praises God not univocally but supereminently (1.3.85–90); the third way occurs when holy theologians name God on the basis of the material images and forms by which God is revealed in divine apparitions. While Dionysius' *Symbolic Theology* treats of the names based on material images received in divine visions, his *Divine Names* discusses intellectual names (such as *being* and *living*) taken "from intelligible perfections proceeding from [God] into creatures."[13] Thomas concludes by apportioning the three ways of naming God to three different books from the Dionysian corpus: the way of removal is treated in the *Mystical Theology;* the way based on intelligible perfections is found in the *Divine Names;* and the way based on material likenesses is discussed in the *Symbolic Theology* (1.3.104). Thomas has interpreted the three ways as able to stand on their own individually, has linked each one with a single work of Dionysius (*Symbolic Theology* has been lost, however, if Dionysius ever wrote such a work), has seemingly identified the way of causality with the way based on the intelligible perfections of God in creatures, and has quietly marked the presence of supereminence at the heart of the first two ways even though it is not acknowledged as an independent path to God.

Aquinas' exposition of *DN* 1.5–8 is a possible interpretation of that refractory text, especially if 1.8 can be read as adding yet another way instead of as subdividing the way of causality (this latter alternative, however, seems more probable). However, the exclusive apportionment of the ways among the three Dionysian works seems somewhat forced, for as we have already seen, the *Mystical Theology* is not so much an epistemological discussion of the negative divine names as a complete repudiation of all divine knowledge whatsoever, and the *Divine Names* uses causality and

---

13. *DDN* 1.3.102, 104; same: 4.4.322; 9.2.827; 13.4.999, 1007; cf. *DM* 16.8 ad3.

negation together in many of its pericopes, not simply causality alone. The interesting point is that Thomas draws from the basic twofold way of Dionysius (negation/eminence and cause/affirmation) a threefold path that in this text possesses the unique configuration of removal, causality, and sensible similitudes originating in prophetic visions.

I have found only one passage where Aquinas employs the threefold schema with preeminence as the first element (ECN). The word *Deus* is said to signify the divine nature through eminence, causality, and negation, for it is used to denote something existing above all reality, which is the principle of all reality and removed from all reality (*ST* 1.13.8 ad2). The immediate feeling of awe toward the divine transcendence that the name *Deus* evokes is very likely the reason why eminence holds its lead position in this example of the threefold way.

The triple way to God, in Thomas' hands, displays a great variety in terminology, order of components, and contexts in which it is used. The combinations that begin with negation are less numerous than those that begin with causality (for causality is paramount in Aquinas' philosophical theology). Sometimes the individual ways of the triple schema are used independently of one another as a means of reasoning toward or referring to particular, predetermined goals, which may be as diverse as God's existence (*SS* 1.3), God's knowledge (*SS* 1.35.1.1), the three divine attributes mentioned in Romans 1:20 (*Rom.* 1.6.115), or the different books of the Dionysian corpus (*DDN* 1.3.104); and whereas Dionysius himself does not look upon his twofold way, especially with respect to the path of negation/transcendence, as a means of establishing positive truths about God within the limits of an affirmative theology, Thomas, inspired by his natural ingenuity, invests the threefold way with an artful plasticity that can serve manifold purposes. Sometimes the threefold way can also be utilized as an integral whole, most especially in those contexts where a positive quality such as wisdom is affirmed of God, then denied, and then immediately reaffirmed in a supereminent fashion (*SS* 1.4.2.1 ad2; *DP* 7.5 ad2).[14]

---

14. "And so through that triple way of speaking according to which God is said to be wise, Dionysius offers a complete understanding of how such names are to be attributed to God" (*DP* 7.5 ad2).

II. The Via Negativa

Aquinas shows himself a worthy heir of the Dionysian tradition when he writes that holy minds are united to God through the way of negation *(remotio)* and that since the ultimate knowledge of God in this life is that God surpasses everything that can be thought, the naming of God through negation is "especially proper" (*DDN* 1.3.83). Our most perfect knowledge of God is this very consciousness of God's epistemic transcendence: "We know God most perfectly in the present life when we realize him to be above all that our intellect can conceive; and thus we are joined to him as to one unknown" (*SS* 4.49.2.1 ad3). The reverential realization of the divine superiority demands that our minds be united in this life to an unknown God, and this is the heart of Dionysian mysticism. But if God is to remain unknown to us, then we must deny of him any creature that comes under our earthly purview, and thus the negative way becomes the most perfect manner of knowing God.[15] Our sense of God's transcendence requires that the *via negativa* be our method of choice whenever we attempt to discourse about the mysteries of God. We can also practice the ordered sequence of negations in order to experience (or reexperience) an intellectual, mystical union with the transcendent, dark Unknown. As Aquinas affirms, the negations leave us in a certain confusion, and once even existence, as it is found in creatures, is removed from God, our understanding "remains in a certain darkness of ignorance according to which, in this present state of life, we are best united to God, as Dionysius says, and this is a sort of thick fog in which God is said to dwell."[16] More than any other,

15. *John* 1.11.211 speaks of the "negation *(privatio)* of all creatures" as the most perfect mode of knowing God in this life. Cf. *SCG* 3.49.2270; *DP* 7.5 ad14.

16. *SS* 1.8.1.1 ad4; for an exegesis of the text, see Joseph Owens, "Aquinas—'Darkness of Ignorance' in the Most Refined Notion of God," in *Bonaventure and Aquinas: Enduring Philosophers*, ed. R. W. Shahan and F. J. Kovach (Norman: University of Oklahoma, 1976), pp. 69–86. Cf. *1 Tim.* 6.3.270; *SCG* 3.49.2270. Denys Turner writes that, for Aquinas, "so 'other' is God," that the normal concept of otherness we recognize in creatures no longer holds as regards God, which means we do not really know "how 'other' God is," but only realize that "God must be thought of as off *every* scale of sameness and difference" ("Apophaticism, Idolatry, and the Claims of Reason," in *Silence and the Word: Negative Theology and Incarnation*, ed. Oliver Davies and Denys Turner [Cambridge: Cambridge University, 2002], p. 29).

this text demonstrates the mystical strains that, due mainly to the influence of Dionysius, lie at the heart of Thomas' *via negativa*.[17]

Nevertheless, Thomas does not accentuate in his overall doctrine the mystical lineage of the *via negativa* but rather deploys it within the cognitive contours of an academic theology. Without adverting to it consciously, he uses three basic grammatical forms for the expression of his *via negativa* or negative theology: negative propositions that use predicates positive in form and meaning ("God is not a body"); affirmative propositions that use predicates negative in form and meaning ("God is incorporeal");[18] affirmative propositions that use predicates positive in form but negative in meaning ("God is simple").[19] Our next task is to specify the different types of negative theology that can be discerned in Aquinas, realizing that they will always be expressed grammatically by one or more of the forms just mentioned.

17. M. Waldmann ("Thomas von Aquin und die *Mystische Theologie* des Pseudodionysius," *Geist und Leben* 22 [1949]: 121–45) is wide of the mark when he claims that Aquinas rejects the mysticism of Dionysius on account of its negativity and occultism. In reality, Thomas reinterprets some of the more extreme negativity so that it does not exclude proper predication of God's positive names, but he does not deny the mysticism that spawned the *via negativa*. Laura Westra ("The Soul's Noetic Ascent to the One in Plotinus and to God in Aquinas," *NS* 58 [1984]: 99–126) asserts that for Thomas, as distinct from Plotinus, the soul's noetic assent to the unknown God has no mystical or ethical components but is a matter strictly of cognition alone. It would seem to be a matter of emphasis: Thomas does not stress the mystical and ethical to the degree that Plotinus does, though the texts we have just seen do display the mystical themes at the base of his *via negativa;* moreover, the ethical requirements for our cognitive ascent to God are not unknown to him, especially in his scriptural commentaries and in part 2-2 of the *Summa theologiae*. For more on the character of Thomas' negative theology, see T.-D. Humbrecht, "La théologie négative chez saint Thomas d'Aquin," *RT* 93 (1993): 535–66; J. B. M. Wissink, "Aquinas: The Theologian of Negative Theology—A Reading of *ST* I, qq. 14–26," *Jaarboek 1993* (Utrecht: Thomas Instituut, 1994): 15–83.

18. The *in* makes the predicate morphologically negative, with a meaning denying corporeality.

19. With no morphological sign of negation, *simple* nevertheless means, in Thomas' eyes, the denial of composition. At times he can understand certain words in a negative fashion though they appear quite positive morphologically: *unity* (*Quod.* 10.1.1); *intelligible* (*BDT* 1.2 ad4); *intelligent* (*SCG* 1.44.376); *perfect* (*DV* 2.3 ad13).

A. Three Types of Negative Theology

Although Aquinas does not formally delineate three different kinds of theological negation, one can detect in his works the three types, which we may call qualitative, objective modal, and subjective modal. A qualitative negation is a total and absolute denial of a quality, property, or characteristic to God, excising from God the whole universe of discourse connected with the predicate in question; for example, "God is immaterial" means that God has nothing to do with matter and should not be thought or spoken of in material terms; a predicate denied by qualitative negation cannot be affirmed of God in any manner whatsoever, even supereminently. An objective modal negation denies the creaturely objective mode of a perfection to God, while the perfection itself as such, according to the divine mode of supereminence, is still able to be affirmed of God. A subjective modal negation denies of God the usual ways humans tend to think of and express the divine attributes, due to the manner in which humans inevitably understand and signify by means of propositions.

When Thomas states that the way of negation removes from spiritual realities the "way" found in corporeal realities (*SS* 3.35.2.2.2), he is thinking of the negation in a qualitative sense, for the characteristics and properties of bodies are being totally removed from the realm of spiritual reality. Materiality and temporality are removed from God in such fashion (*DV* 7.1 ad3), and so God is said to be immobile and infinite (*Rom.* 1.6.115).[20]

Thomas also uses examples of objective modal negations. Agreeing with Augustine, he writes that "if we should remove all aspects of particularity *(rationes particulationis)* from goodness itself, there will remain in our understanding a goodness that is integral and full, which is the divine goodness" (*SS* 1.19.5.2 ad3). Goodness itself is not removed from God but rather all "aspects of particularity," which presumably constrict and contract the divine goodness to a creaturely mode. Further, God does not exist as creatures do, for in God "the nature of entity exists eminently" (*SS* 1.3.1.1 ad1); even being must be removed from God "as regards the mode in

20. God's infinity is a special case, as I will discuss below, since it is not so much a qualitative denial as the paradigmatic and primary instance of objective modal denial.

which it is suitable to creatures," for God did not exist in the past, will not exist in the future, and cannot even be said to exist in the present, "since his being is not measured by time" (*DDN* 5.1.630). Knowledge may also be denied of God by an objective modal negation:

Whenever knowledge or understanding or anything pertaining to perfection is re-moved from God, this must be understood according to transcendence *(excessus)* and not according to defect. . . . If it is denied, then, that the name *understanding* is properly suitable to God, this is because God does not understand according to the creature's mode but more eminently. (*SS* 1.35.1.1 ad1)

He continues, "Whatever is said of God should always be understood by way of preeminence, so that anything implying imperfection is removed"; thus God's knowledge does not include the discourse of inquiring reason, which is imperfect, but simply the "correct view about the thing known."[21] Because of the divine transcendence, objective modal negation separates from God not the perfection as such but any creaturely limitation or im-perfection that the perfection entails in its created realizations. The divine mode beyond the creaturely mode, unconstricted and nonparticularized and transcendent, is really no mode at all but the infinite absence of mode, for infinity understood as a perfection is that which "is in no way finite" (*SS* 1.3.1.1 ad4), and God does not exist "in a certain way," that is, "accord-ing to any finite and limited mode," but possesses the whole of being "uni-versally and infinitely" (*DDN* 5.1.629). God's transcendent, preeminent mode, therefore, is in reality infinite modelessness.

We also have examples of subjective modal negation, which, while closely connected with objective modal negation, is nevertheless distinct from it. Consider the following quote:

Every name fails to signify the divine act of being on account of the fact that no name simultaneously signifies something perfect and simple, for abstract names do not signify a being subsisting in itself, and concrete names signify a composite being; . . . rejecting whatever is imperfect, we use each kind of name in divine predication: abstract names on account of their simplicity and concrete names on account of their perfection. (*SS* 1.4.1.2)

---

21. *SS* 1.35.1.1 ad5. "If we attribute to God something found in creatures, we must separate [from God] all that pertains to imperfection so that only the elements of perfection remain, since the creature imitates God only according to this perfection" (*DV* 2.1 ad4).

Aquinas is warning us about the temptation to impute to God the imperfections of composition and nonsubsistence that are ineluctably *connoted* whenever we form predications using concrete or abstract terms. This is a temptation precisely because of the mode of signifying proper to human subjects, for the divine perfection is not denied, but only those aspects of imperfection accruing to it by reason of our human mode of signification.[22] Since all names predicated of God signify in the mode by which our intellect automatically thinks and judges, the connotations engendered by the cognitive processes of the human subject must be consciously denied of God: to truthfully deny that God is wise, for example, as an instance of subjective modal negation, means that wisdom does not reside in God as a nonsubstantive quality in a subject—though our inborn manner of thinking and signifying would lead one to think so—since wisdom exists in God in a more noble way than can be signified by the name as employed by us (*SS* 1.4.2.1 ad2). Our predications can never do justice to God since they always signify "some definite form" (*DP* 7.5 ad2), whereas God possesses no definite form of anything. Succinctly and summarily: "All things affirmed of God are also able to be denied of God since they do not belong to God as they are found in created things and as they are understood and signified by us" (*DDN* 5.3.673).

The distinction between qualitative and objective modal negations is clear. Describing a process of successive negations, Thomas states that first we deny bodily realities of God, then we negate spiritual realities (like goodness and wisdom) and even existence itself "as they are found in creatures" (*SS* 1.8.1.1 ad4). The first denial is an absolute qualitative negation, while the latter two are objective modal negations modified by the phrase "as in creatures." In another place he remarks that while nothing said of God should be understood as it is found in creatures, it is more obviously the case that bodily reality ought to be removed from God (*SS* 1.34.3.1). Another text asserts that spiritual perfections are to be removed from God because he has them in a more excellent manner than our mind can grasp,

---

22. A subjective modal negation is in effect when Thomas says that even with regard to positive perfections such as goodness the mode of signifying must still be denied of God (*SCG* 1.30.277).

but material dispositions "are to be totally removed from God" (*DP* 9.7); and while "in the removal of certain things from God their predication of God through eminence and causality ought to be understood at the same time, there are certain realities which should only be denied and in no way predicated of God, as when it is said, 'God is not a body'" (*DP* 9.7 ad2).

The distinction between qualitative and subjective modal negations is also in evidence, perhaps especially in those passages where Thomas propounds his appreciative interpretation of a putative enigmatic statement by Dionysius that "negations in divine matters are true but affirmations loose *(incompactae)*."[23] Two things can be considered in a theological predication, he maintains: the reality signified and the mode of signifying. Whereas both may be truthfully denied of God, only the former may be truthfully affirmed of God. That is, a negation may be true either because a certain reality does not belong to God at all ("God is not corporeal," a qualitative negation) or because our mode of signifying does not belong to God ("God is not wise," a subjective modal negation), but an affirmation is only true as regards the reality signified (wisdom) and not as regards the mode of signifying (for the contradictory of the affirmation, i.e., "God is not wise," a subjective modal negation, is always capable of a true interpretation). A negation, if true of God, is actually truer than a true affirmation, for a true affirmation can never be true as a whole, since in the case of God an affirmation is true only as regards the reality signified and not as regards the mode of signifying. Since God's mode is always higher than humans can signify, there can never be a perfect modal match in any theological affirmation between God the subject and the divine predicate, and thus in every theological affirmation the subject and predicate are but

23. *DP* 7.5 obj. 2; cf. *SS* 1.4.2.1 ad2; 1.22.1.2 ad1; *BDT* 1.2 ad4; *SCG* 1.30.277; *DP* 9.7; *ST* 1.13.12 ad1; *SDC* 6.161. In the last two passages cited, to the usual assertion that negations are *incompactae* (from the translation of John Scotus Erigena) Thomas adds *vel inconvenientes* ([unfitting], from John the Saracen's translation). Dionysius had actually written that while in divine matters negations are true, affirmations are *anarmostoi* (*Celestial Hierarchy* 2.3 [PG 3:141A]). This Greek word means ill-fitting, disharmonious, or incongruous, and is suitably translated by *inconveniens; incompactus,* however, means loose or vague. Perhaps Erigena confused *anarmostos* with the similar-looking term *anarmos,* which means without joints, unarticulated, or loose, for which *incompactus* is an appropriate translation.

loosely connected.[24] It is important to note for our purposes here that Aquinas' whole treatment of the Dionysian phrase turns on the true theological affirmation's capacity to be truthfully denied by a subjective modal negation without also being subject to a truthful denial by a qualitative negation.

Qualitative negations are absolute denials, while modal negations are relative denials; objective modal negations remove the finite mode of the creature from God, while subjective modal negations refuse to assert of God those imperfections arising from our human manner of understanding and signifying. Qualitative negations are true due to an inherent imperfection in the attribute denied of God, whereas modal negations are true on account of God's transcendence. Qualitative negations principally remove from God matter and material conditions, while objective modal negations principally remove the creaturely mode as such. Just as the creature's mode is essentially the same as its finitude, so God's "mode" is actually the divine infinite modelessness. The assertion of God's infinity, then, which is the same as the absolute denial of God's finitude, is a unique case of negation, for it acts as an absolute qualitative negation though it also concerns God's "mode." For if we isolate that finitude which defines the creature as such, then that finitude must be denied always and absolutely of God, since God is not a creature, even though we may with some grain of truth predicate of God certain perfections that among creatures are nevertheless tied up with finitude in both their realization and their understanding. After all, it is the very purpose of the modal negations to focus on the finite human and creaturely elements present in every theological affirmation and to admonish us not to think that *these* can ever be truthfully predicated of God.[25]

24. *SS* 1.22.1.2 ad1; *DP* 7.5 ad2. Aquinas is at his valiant (and brilliant) best here in tendering a plausible interpretation for a hopelessly muddled Latin text, an interpretation that in the end also does justice to Dionysius' original statement.

25. Contemporary feminist theology has found a strong ally in the *via negativa* and the doctrine of divine incomprehensibility. Mary Collins, "Naming God in Public Prayer," *Worship* 59 (1985): 291–304; Elizabeth Johnson, "The Incomprehensibility of God and the Image of God Male and Female," *TS* 45 (1984): 441–65; idem, *She Who Is: The Mystery of God in Feminist Theological Discourse* (New York: Crossroad, 1992), pp. 104–12; Catherine Mowry LaCugna, "God in Communion with Us: The Trinity," in *Freeing Theology: The Essentials of*

B. Growth and Progress of Negative Theology

There are three contexts in Aquinas where growth and progress in our knowledge of God occur through the practice of negative theology: one has to do with qualitative negations, another with the two modal negations, and the third culminates in the darkness of mystical unknowing.

We can never know the essence of God in this life, but we can approach that knowledge, Aquinas teaches, through the successive addition of qualitative negations. In *SCG* 1.14 he discusses God's attributes by using the way of negation, for we can know what God is not and obtain a clearer knowledge of the divine substance to the degree that we can remove more and more realities from it. Whereas our knowledge of the objects of this world begins by placing them in a general category and then makes that category more specific by adding successively narrower differences, we can distinguish God from all other beings only by successive negations, since God belongs to no category whatsoever. Just as affirmative differences contract one another as they descend from more general to less general categories, so too do theological negations constrict one another: if God is first aligned with substances by having all qualities and other predicamental accidents denied of him, he is further distinguished from material substances by the denial of corporeality; and further demonstrations of qual-

Theology in Feminist Perspective, ed. C. LaCugna (San Francisco: HarperCollins, 1993), pp. 102–3. Feminist theologians have reminded us that the apophatic approach of the *via negativa* says what God is not and is able to negate any positive statement we make about God. Although God's incomprehensibility should not lead to agnosticism, it does entail that "since God's mystery cannot be fully captured in any single metaphor, we are licensed to use an array of images and metaphors, feminine as well as masculine" (LaCugna, "God in Communion," p. 103). Elizabeth Johnson also argues that due to God's incomprehensibility, "absolutizing any particular expression as if it were adequate to divine reality is tantamount to a diminishment of truth about God," and that "made in the image and likeness of God, women participate in the fire of divine being and signify the excellence of the Creator in a creaturely way. Correlatively, God can be pointed to in symbols shaped by women's reality as well as in imagery taken from the world of nature and of men. Not doing so has allowed one set of images to become a block to remembrance of the incomprehensible mystery of God. Doing so, on the other hand, has the immediate effect of bringing to light the true nature of language about divine mystery in male terms, namely, that it is as legitimate and inadequate as female and cosmic terms to express what is ultimately inexpressible" (*She Who Is*, p. 112).

itative negations, which prove God to be immobile[26] and eternal, lacking any composition or division, and so forth, will help gradually distinguish God from all that God is not.[27] Our knowledge of God will be most proper and exact when God is known as distinct from all other beings, but such knowledge cannot be perfect, for "when specific *(propria)* knowledge of a reality is gained through affirmations, one knows what the reality is and how it is separated from other realities; but when specific knowledge of a reality is obtained through negations, although one knows that it is distinct from other realities, what it is remains unknown."[28]

For the sake of his theological project Thomas requires a specific knowledge of God as close to essential knowledge as possible, and the strategy of successive qualitative negations serves that end.[29] If all negations are rooted in some basic affirmation, however, and if the successive qualitative negations cannot be based on an intuitional insight into God, then they must be grounded upon some other basic affirmations and judgments. Indeed, as we shall see in Part Three, Thomas does base the negations upon some primary affirmations which assert that God is pure act and infinite subsistent being; in various ways he claims that God is the infinite positivity of being without knowing *what* that pure positivity is or how it *is* God. Yet, it is from these affirmations that his negative theology lives and moves and has its being.

26. *SCG* 1.14.119 and *CT* 1.4 make the primary principle of negative theology the fact that "God is totally immobile." For Thomas' doctrine on the closely related topic of divine immutability, see the fine study by Michael Dodds, *The Unchanging God of Love*, Studia Friburgensia, N.S. 66 (Fribourg, Switzerland: University of Fribourg, 1986).

27. *SCG* 1.14.118; for how we also know angels by successive negations, see *BDT* 6.3 and *CT* 2.9.184–212. See Anton Pegis ("*Penitus Manet Ignotum*," *MS* 27 [1965]: 216–19) for some thoughts on the progression of successive negations in Aquinas. Norman Kretzmann discusses the successive qualitative negations of what he calls Thomas' "eliminative method" in *SCG* 1.15–28 (*The Metaphysics of Theism: Aquinas' Natural Theology in "Summa contra gentiles" I* [Oxford: Clarendon, 1997], pp. 113–38). See also John Wippel, *The Metaphysical Thought of Thomas Aquinas: From Finite Being to Uncreated Being* (Washington, DC: CUA, 2000), pp. 516, 530–32.

28. *SCG* 3.39.2167; cf. *SCG* 3.46.2232. Thomas states that by successive negations our intellect is guided in knowing the simple realities of God (*SS* 1.8.2.1 ad1).

29. "For whoever knows something as distinct from all other things approaches the knowledge by which its essence is known" (*DV* 10.12 ad7 of 2nd series). And although theology cannot rest upon knowing what God is, it can rest upon knowing what God is not (*BDT* 2.2 ad2).

The second kind of progress occurs through the two modal negations of God's positive perfections. In this situation, which is implied in Thomas' works but not taught formally as a method, the intention is not to heap up negations so as to gain as specific a knowledge of God as possible, but to explain all the ways in which the positive perfections *cannot* be said of God and thus to act as a constant, purifying corrective to the theses of affirmative theology. While there are no texts espousing such a program, every time he amends an understanding or rectifies a misunderstanding of some perfection as predicated of God, progress in our knowledge of God is taking place through modal negations.

Finally, Thomas authors a text imbued with mysticism, where the negations do not merely help us to progress within the bounds of academic, affirmative theology but in fact burst the confines of all noetic pursuits and lead us into the darkness of ignorance.

When we proceed into God through the way of negation *(remotio)*, first we deny of him all corporeal realities; and next, even intellectual realities as they are found in creatures, like goodness and wisdom, and then there remains in our understanding only that God exists and nothing further, so that it suffers a kind of confusion. Lastly, however, we even remove from him his very existence, as it is in creatures, and then our understanding remains in a certain darkness of ignorance according to which, in this present state of life, we are best united to God, as Dionysius says, and this is a sort of thick fog *(caligo)* in which God is said to dwell.[30]

The first denial is a qualitative negation and the last two are modal negations, but the first does not attempt to procure a quasi-essential knowledge of God nor do the other two attempt to correct some affirmation so that theology may continue with more affirmations. Rather, all three are merely steps preliminary to the final leap of the mind into the darkness of mystical union with God. Seldom do Thomas' negations draw so mightily on

30. *SS* 1.8.1.1 ad4. In Thomas' commentary on the *Divine Names* of Dionysius, to whom he is indebted for his outlook on the process of mystical negations, he describes a similar procedure (*DDN* 13.3.996): first our soul rises from material things that are connatural to it, when we understand that God is nothing sensible or material or bodily; then we hasten through all the orders of angels, denying that God belongs to them; then we ascend by negation and are joined to God at the very boundaries of creaturehood, where the most universal and excellent creatures are; and finally our union with God is perfected as far as possible in this life, when we come to know God as transcending even these most excellent creatures.

the mystical inspirations of Dionysius, and although this text is more mystical than most that describe the progress of our negative knowledge of God, we must not let ourselves suppose that the saintly theologian ever forgot, even as he labored over the propositions and arguments of his theology, that the ultimate goal of all negations is the mind's union with the Mystery of God, in the tenebrous mists of unknowing.

C. Negation and Preeminence

Aquinas often relates negation and preeminence closely, which is not surprising, since for Dionysius, his teacher in these matters, they are really only two sides of one path to God.

At a basic level, affirmation is naturally prior to negation as regards speech, understanding, and reality.[31] Every negation is founded upon something existing in reality: the truth of the assertion "A human is not a donkey," for example, is based on the real natures of humans and donkeys (SS 1.35.1.1 ad2). Since every negative is proved through an affirmative,[32] "unless the human intellect knew something affirmative about God, it would not be able to deny anything of God; it would not know anything at all of God, however, unless something predicated of God were verified of God affirmatively" (DP 7.5). Eventually, if we take the arguments by which Thomas proves negative conclusions about God and reduce them to their primary premises, we discover the foundational affirmations of his theology. For example, in the *Summa theologiae* he proves God's simplicity, that is, God's noncomposite nature, by means of premises which assert that God is being in act, being itself, first being, and pure act.[33] Every negation is in general connected with some affirmation, but there is also a special manner in which for Aquinas some theological negations are closely bound up with a sense of God's transcendence.

Consciousness of God's preeminence is the primary source of theological negations in Aquinas' eyes. "Through his eminence" God escapes any form that our intellect can conceive (SS 1.22.1.1), and we know that the di-

---

31. *Herm.* 1.8.90; cf. 1.1.10; 1.5.61.

32. *SS* 1.19.5.1 ad1; *Meta.* 4.8.644. A negative conclusion must have one affirmation and one negation among its premises.

33. *ST* 1.3.1–2, 4, 6–7. Parallels can be found in *SCG* 1.16–27; *CT* 1.9–17.

vine essence must remain hidden since God is above every possible representation of our intellect.[34] God is said to be "separated by reason of a certain eminence" (*DDN* 5.3.673) and "supereminently segregated from all."[35] God's *excessus* and *eminentia* lead to the removal of every imperfection in divine predication (*SS* 1.35.1.1 ad1, 5). Because we know God as a transcendent *(excellens)* cause, we know that he does not have the same entitative status as his effects do (*DA* 16).

As a disciple of Dionysius, Thomas enunciates the general rule that transcendence *(excessus)* leads to negation: for names are often removed from God not because God is lacking in the perfections they signify but because he is above and exceeds all creatures.[36] Negation by way of eminence applies to spiritual perfections that are attributed to God, but material conditions are said to be "totally removed" from God and "in no way" predicated of him.[37] Thus, divine wisdom seems to be foolish because of its superiority over human wisdom (*1 Cor.* 1.4.62); God can be called nonexistent, not as failing in existence but as transcending all existents;[38] and God is called irrational because above reason, and imperfect because "perfect above all and before all" (*DDN* 7.3.721).

Sometimes Aquinas gives as the warrant for qualitative negations the intrinsic imperfection of the quality denied of God, but he also mentions the divine preeminence as the basis for qualitative negations. Potency and materiality are removed from God by dint of God's being pure act (*SS* 1.35.1.1)—which is ultimately identical with God's preeminence; God as transcendent cause is the reason why we call God immobile and infinite (*Rom.* 1.6.115). Further,

---

34. *DV* 8.1 ad8; 10.11 ad4, 5. Karl Rahner writes that "for Thomas the incomprehensibility of God is present in an 'excessus', in an 'excedere'. This 'excessus' should not simply be identified with the 'via eminentiae', even though it is the latter's ultimate foundation" ("An Investigation of the Incomprehensibility of God in St. Thomas Aquinas," *Theological Investigations,* trans. D. Morland [New York: Seabury, 1979], 16:253–54).

35. *DDN* 1.3.83; also: 2.1.126.

36. *DDN* 1.1.29–30; 1.3.83–84, 98; 2.1.126; 4.2.297–98; 4.5.355; 4.8.392; 4.14.478; 7.2.708; 7.4.729; 8.3.770; 11.2.897; 13.3.990, 993. God is also said to "superexceed" (*ST* 1.12.12).

37. *DP* 9.7 and ad2; 7.5.ad2; *SS* 1.35.1.1 ad1. By implication, the material dispositions would seem to be denied of God because they are beneath the divine dignity.

38. *DDN* 4.13.463; *ST* 1.12.1 ad3.

It is usual in the divine scriptures for those things it says privatively of God to be attributed to God on account of his transcendence: as when God who is the clearest light is called invisible; and he who is laudable and nameable from all things is called ineffable and unnameable; and he who is present to all is called incomprehensible as if absent to all; and he who can be found in all reality is called untraceable—and all of this on account of God's transcendence. (*DDN* 7.1.702)

Clearly, God's preeminence is a source for all three types of theological negation.

However, the divine eminence is also the goal of theological negations in the sense that they serve to express and highlight it. God's eminence is more clearly displayed by removing those attributes that do not belong to God (*SS* 1.34.3.1). God is called eternal, immeasurable, immutable, omnipotent, incomprehensible, and ineffable in order to express the "excellence of the divine nature or essence"; for example, God is called infinite *(immensus)* since he "incomparably exceeds every creature's magnitude," and so on for the rest.[39] Thomas associates negative names (eternal and infinite) with names that positively signify God's transcendence (omnipotent, first cause, highest good) and that, by expressing the supreme divine mode along with the perfection in question, are said of God alone (*SCG* 1.30.278). The theological negations do not themselves attempt to prove or make us know for the first time, but rather help to exhibit and recommunicate from different perspectives that divine preeminence which is known from elsewhere. In those texts, nevertheless, where he imitates Dionysius and treats of the "ascent by negations" unto God, one's religious sense of the divine transcendence appears to be the result rather than the cause of the divine negations (*DDN* 13.3.996).

III. *The Way of Preeminence*

The divine preeminence is often stated in terms of our epistemic inability to grasp God conceptually. The divine goodness is "above that which is conceived," "above understanding" (*SS* 1.2.1.3 ad2); our mind has

39. *Decretalem* 1.178–243. The thick mist in which God was veiled on Mount Sinai signifies the divine excellence, for "excessive light dulls the eye and thus obscures the one who dwells in light inaccessible" (*Heb.* 12.4.699); cf. *1 Tim.* 6.3.270.

progressed furthest in knowledge when it knows God's essence "to be above everything that can be apprehended in the present life."[40] God transcends the ways of knowledge based on sense perception but even more fundamentally "exceeds without measure" any type of knowledge (*SCG* 4.1.3340–42). God's epistemic transcendence is rooted in the divine preeminence: "God transcends human cognition through his own preeminence (*excellentia*)."[41] How does Thomas describe God's own transcendence?

In one place, God's transcendence means that God has nothing added to his essence, that his sublimity is essential and immobile, and that his glory and goodness are infinite.[42] In another text, God's eminence of perfection comprises three things: universality, because God has all perfections joined together, which are not collated in any creature; plenitude, because his perfections are without any defect, which is not the case with creatures; and unity, for those perfections that are diverse in creatures are one in God.[43]

To characterize God as infinite is another way to describe the divine preeminence. God is above "every definition and distinction, above the boundaries of any nature" (*DDN* 9.3.832). God is compared to all transcendently since he does not belong to any category whatsoever (*ST* 1.6.2 ad3), which occurs because the divine essence and being do not really differ (*ST* 1.3.5), a state of affairs tantamount to calling God Subsistent Being Itself, which is infinite (*ST* 1.7.1). God's eminence is thus identified with the divine infinity. Another gnomic, lapidary text: "The first cause is above being (*supra ens*) insofar as it is infinite Being Itself (*ipsum esse infinitum*). . . . God's essence is Being Itself and thus is above understanding."[44] God's epistemic transcendence is based upon God's ontological transcendence, which is equated with the infinity of divine being and with the fact that God's essence and being are the same in reality.

---

40. *BDT* 1.2 ad1; same: *DV* 2.1 ad9; *DDN* 1.3.83–84; 13.3.996.

41. *Job* 36.280–86; cf. 37.296–99, 352–55, 364–67.

42. *Job* 40.46–105; cf. 11.70–72; 37.361.

43. *SS* 1.2.1.3, p. 68. Cf. Battista Mondin, *The Principle of Analogy in Protestant and Catholic Theology*, 2nd ed. (The Hague: Nijhoff, 1968), p. 99.

44. *SDC* 6.175. Harry Wolfson writes that "predicates which St. Thomas interprets in the excellent or eminent sense mean predicates which are applied to God in an infinite sense" (*Studies*, 2:508).

At this point a question imposes itself: How does Thomas come to know the divine preeminence, by faith or by reason? He certainly evinces how his faith and reading of scripture help to generate a lively sense of God's preeminence. "God is superior to humanity . . . by the authority of his majesty" (*Job* 9.700–702). Recognizing the divine excellence comes from knowing that God is greater than our heart (citing 1 John 3:20) and from realizing that however much we glorify and serve God it is not enough, since "God is greater than our praise" (quoting Sir. 43:32–33).[45] Quoting Job 36:26, "Behold the great God who conquers our knowledge," he speaks of "the divine sublimity transcending all things, even human desire and understanding, so that whatever is able to be thought or desired is less than God."[46] However, in the very same text he can on the one hand speak of God as "that most excellent substance" and quote scripture (Job 11:7; 36:2; 1 Cor. 13:9) to the effect that God exceeds our knowledge, and yet can on the other hand also quote Aristotle's *Metaphysics* (2.1.993b9–11) on how our intellect is like the owl's eye to the sun when it comes to knowing the first beings, and argue that neither we nor angels can see God's essence since the realities from which a creature's knowledge is taken are effects that do not equal the power of their cause (*SCG* 1.3.16–19).

This last reason, a favorite of Thomas', concludes to God's preeminence on the grounds of a more general philosophical principle: "Every effect is in its cause in a more excellent fashion according to its power, and thus in the first cause of all, which is God, all things must exist more eminently than they do in themselves."[47] This principle does not hold for univocal causes, which possess the same nature as their effects, but only for nonunivocal or equivocal causes.[48] And since whatever perfection is found in

45. *Praeceptis,* p. 32.

46. *Pater* 1040; same: *Credo* 1.864.

47. *DSS* 14.76–85; also: 15.51–55; *DDN* 7.2.708. "Something belongs more eminently to the cause than to the caused" (*SDC* 1.23); cf. *DDN* 8.3.770.

48. The proper, univocal cause is distinguished from the common, transcendent cause, God's excellence being tied to the latter (*Rom.* 1.6.115); the form of the effect is in nonunivocal agents not according to the same nature but "in a certain higher and more universal manner" (*Phys.* 8.10.1053); also: *DP* 7.5. God is most transcendent *(excellentissimus)* because he is an equivocal cause of goodness (*ST* 1.6.2).

creatures cannot be found in God univocally, according to the same definition, but only supereminently, God is not praised by divine names univocally but rather supereminently (*DDN* 1.3.90). Thomas' widespread use of the philosophical principle concerning causes and effects suggests that reason also has a role in helping us come to a consciousness of God's preeminence.[49]

This supposition is corroborated by other texts where reason leads us to acknowledge God's preeminence. From the order, goodness, and magnitude of the realities caused by God we come to know the divine wisdom, goodness, and eminence (*1 Cor.* 13.4.800). *ST* 1.12.12 says that through natural reason based on God's effects we are able to know whether God exists and "those things which must belong to him inasmuch as he is the first cause of all things, surpassing all the things caused by him." Commenting on Romans 1:19, Aquinas states that the knowledge of God was made available to the Gentiles through the interior light of reason:

Humans are able from creatures of this kind to know God in three ways, as Dionysius says. One way is through causality, for since creatures of this sort are changeable and imperfect, it is necessary for them to be led back to some immobile and perfect principle, and in this way we know whether God exists. A second way is through excellence, for all things are not led back to a first principle as to a proper and univocal cause (as a human generates a human) but as to a general and transcendent cause, and in this way we know that God is above all things. . . . They [the Gentiles] had this sort of knowledge implanted in them through the light of reason.[50]

The threefold way is here depicted as indebted to reason's light, and the same process of thought that concludes to the existence of God is simply extended, along the same line, in order to arrive at the transcendence of God. He summarizes his position concisely when he affirms that humans,

---

49. *Isa.* 40.178–85 interprets God's transcendence in terms of the doctrine of participation. Although in *Credo* 1.882 Thomas rests God's eminent status upon the fact that God is the maker of all things, he also thinks that God as Creator can be proved, as we shall see later. In *SCG* 1.5.30 he asserts that we truly know God only when we believe *(credere)* that God is above all that can be thought by humans, but it is unclear from the context whether *credere* denotes an act of saving faith or, more secularly, a person's viewpoint based on reason.

50. *Rom.* 1.6.115; cf. 1.7.127.

through effects, and angels, through their own essence, know that God exists, and that he is cause of all, eminent over all, and removed from all (*SCG* 3.49.2270). If preeminence is the source of negation, and if causality recognized through reason is the source of preeminence, then the efforts of reason lie behind the entire threefold way, though texts are not lacking that also exhibit faith's influence in helping us come to a consciousness of God's preeminence. A crucial question is whether knowledge of God's existence is identical with the knowledge of God as transcendent Creator, an inquiry we must take up in a subsequent chapter.

iv. Conclusion

First, Aquinas' *via negativa* is not, as with Dionysius, primarily a step beyond the boundaries of rational theology but a moment within it serving to correct the oversights and deficiencies of affirmative theology and doing the best it can to construct a negative theology of the One who cannot be known essentially. Aquinas' *via negativa* is certainly rational and noetic, but it also remains imbued with that dark and denying mysticism whose inspiration and beautiful expression derive primarily from Dionysius. While Aquinas' *via negativa* places God above and beyond being *(ens)*, it also defers to his theology's fundamental claim that God *is* Subsistent Being *(esse)* Itself.[51] Affirmation and infinite positivity are the fecund roots of all subsequent negations.[52]

Second, unlike Dionysius' use of a basic twofold way, Thomas expounds a threefold way with a varying terminology and order of elements. In various contexts he employs particular ways in order to establish particular goals, but he also uses the threefold way as an integral whole in those situ-

51. Vladimir Lossky notes that apophatic theology can be either mystical or speculative and that it may exalt God's transcendence as beyond being, or not. "If Thomas Aquinas was able to impart to Dionysian apophasis a new sense which would not involve transcending existence, it is because the usage of negations required by the idea of a transcendent God is not an exclusive characteristic of those who exalt God beyond being" ("Elements of 'Negative Theology' in the Thought of St. Augustine," trans. T. E. Bird, *SVTQ* 21 [1977]: 67).

52. Cf. Mark Johnson, "Apophatic Theology's Cataphatic Dependencies," *Thomist* 62 (1998): 519–31.

ations where a positive predicate is first affirmed of God, then denied, and finally affirmed once again in a supereminent fashion. No positive perfection can be predicated of God appropriately and truthfully unless it has first been filtered through the corrective lenses of the threefold way.

Third, there are three types of theological negation in Aquinas, unannounced as a formal grouping but present nevertheless: qualitative, objective modal, and subjective modal. Qualitative negations may be more fundamental in the sense that they absolutely deny of God realities that are far from the purity of the divine nature and thus are more obviously to be removed from God (e.g., material reality with all its consequences). Modal negations, however, which look to deny of God a perfection's creaturely and finite aspects, are just as basic in the sense that they are at the heart of any affirmation about God and are necessary in order to curtail the mind's propensity to attribute perfections univocally to God.

Fourth, as in Dionysius, the cause and goal of theological negations is the divine preeminence, which Thomas identifies with God's infinite act of subsistent being.

As we conclude the first part of this study we should remind ourselves that Thomas also possesses a positive, affirmative theology based on analogy.[53] Part Two contains a brief exposé of analogy in Aristotle and a de-

---

53. Charles Journet claims that Aquinas' theology is "primarily and essentially affirmative, cataphatic, and secondarily negative, apophatic" (*Dark Knowledge of God*, p. 71); Denis Edwards sees Aquinas' theology as "basically cataphatic" with "an important apophatic stream" ("Negative Theology and the Historical Jesus," *ACR* 60 [1983]: 172). Denys Turner points out Aquinas' "fundamental confidence in theological speech, a trust that our ordinary ways of talking about God are fundamentally *in order*, needing only to be subordinated to a governing apophaticism, expressed as an epistemological principle" ("Apophaticism," p. 32). However, some detect a contradiction between Aquinas' positive and negative theology, which is often due to not grasping Aquinas' distinction between a defining knowledge *of* God's essence and the knowledge of a truth *about* God's essence (B. Bonansea, "The Human Mind and the Knowledge of God: Reflections on a Scholastic Controversy," *FS* 40 [1980]: 8). For example, Walter Kasper thinks that Aquinas' thesis that we are united to God "as to one unknown" "is at odds with the many passages in which he makes statements about the being of God" (*The God of Jesus Christ*, trans. M. J. O'Connell [New York: Crossroad, 1984], pp. 63–64). But see Klaus Riesenhuber, "Partizipation," p. 970. Sometimes the putative contradiction is based on the conflation of concept and judgment, as in J. H. Nicolas, "Affirmation de Dieu et connaissance," *RT* 64 (1964): 200–204, 221–22; and Paul Wess,

tailed discussion of those elements of Thomas' doctrine of analogy that are relevant to an understanding of his positive theology. The treatment of analogy will have to address an insistent question implicitly raised by the use of modal negations, which remove creaturely modes from the divine perfections without our ever being able to cleanly separate the creaturely mode from the perfection itself in our concepts. How can one judge to be true what one cannot conceive?

Wie von Gott Sprechen? Eine Auseinandersetzung mit Karl Rahner (Graz: Styria, 1970), p. 107. But see Denis Bradley, "Thomistic Theology and the Hegelian Critique of Religious Imagination," *NS* 59 (1985): 77–78. Gerard Hughes offers a balanced and correctly nuanced account of the genuine agnostic moments of Aquinas' positive analogical knowledge of God in "Aquinas and the Limits of Agnosticism," in *The Philosophical Assessment of Theology* (Washington, DC: Georgetown University, 1987), pp. 37–52.

Part Two. Analogy and the Web of Judgment

4. Analogy in Aristotle

This chapter focuses chiefly on Aristotle, Aquinas' primary source on analogy, with much briefer treatments of Plato and Neoplatonism, some of Aristotle's commentators, and a few medievals.

Analogy commences its career in the Presocratics as mathematical or geometrical proportionality, a meaning it continues to have in Plato, Aristotle, and the rest of the Western philosophical tradition.[1] Having received a tradition on analogy limited to the religious, artistic, and mathematical domains, Plato perceived the unrestricted potential of analogy and transposed it to the properly philosophical plane, detecting in it, as a "similitude of rapports" and "resemblance mixed with dissimilarity," the law of knowledge, being, and action within an ontological and epistemological framework.[2] In the *Timaeus* (31C) we read that "the most beautiful of all bonds is analogy" *(desmōn kallistos analogia)*. Overstepping the Pythagorean beginnings of *analogia* in mathematical proportion, Plato viewed it

1. Eberhard Jüngel's *Zum Ursprung der Analogie bei Parmenides und Heraklit* (Berlin: de Gruyter, 1964) is still helpful despite its somewhat contrived etymologies and German word-plays. For some informative pages on the Presocratics and Plato, see Hampus Lyttkens, *The Analogy between God and the World,* trans. A. Poignant (Uppsala: Almqvist and Wiksells, 1952), pp. 15–28.

2. Paul Grenet, *Les origines de l'analogie philosophique dans les dialogues de Platon* (Paris: Boivin, 1948), pp. 16, 229–38. James F. Anderson discusses this work in "Analogy in Plato," *RM* 4 (1950): 111–28.

epistemologically as an instrument for identifying diverse realities and discovering new ones,[3] and ontologically as the condition for unifying the many, since being itself is neither pure unity nor pure plurality but an ensemble of the relations between different realities harmoniously converging through both a vertical and a horizontal order.[4]

Staying close to its technical meaning in mathematics, Aristotle also uses *analogia* to mean a similarity of relations, or proportionality, especially in the field of biology.[5] In the *Posterior Analytics* (2.17.99a7–16), *analogon* and *kat' analogian* mean "proportional" or "according to proportion," and are distinguished from both equivocal and generic predication. In the *Nicomachean Ethics* (5.3.1131a30–b8), that which is just is said to be a species of *analogia*, for *analogia* is an equality of ratios *(logōn)* requiring at least four terms,[6] and justice is that which preserves the equality of the proportion A:B :: C:D. While arguing earlier in the same work against the Platonic notion of the separate Good in itself, Aristotle remarks that wisdom, honor and pleasure are not all good in the same way and that therefore the Good is not something common "according to one idea" *(kata*

---

3. Some examples of the analogy of proportionality as an instrument of discovery: as wisdom, courage, and temperance are in those who have these virtues, so are *x, y* and *z* in the state which as a whole is wise, courageous, and temperate—and after much debate the variables turn out to be the guardians, the warriors, and the general citizenry (*Republic* 428–32); as governors, warriors, and the citizenry are to the state, so are *x, y* and *z* to the individual—and these are discovered to be mind, will, and appetite (ibid., 441C–443B); just as the vision of things by sight is conditioned by light, which is caused by the sun, so the understanding of the Forms by the mind is conditioned by *x,* which is caused by *y*—where *x* is found to be the truth and *y* the Good (ibid., 506E–509C); see also *Republic* 478; 576C–588B; *Philebus* 29–30. Erhard Platzeck asserts that analogy as a method of reasoning in Socrates and Plato was the forerunner of the Aristotelian syllogism and the driving force in the development of Greek logic (*Von der Analogie zum Syllogismus* [Paderborn: Schöningh, 1954], esp. p. 104). David Burrell sees analogy in Plato as the way of dialectical inquiry, where answers to ultimate questions cannot be clear, concise or definitive (*Analogy and Philosophical Language* [New Haven: Yale, 1973], pp. 37–67).

4. Grenet, *Origins,* chaps. 5–7, 11, 13. Peter Cataldo argues that Plato's *Sophist* also has a doctrine of being based on equivocity by reference to something one ("Plato, Aristotle, and *pros hen* Equivocity," *MSch* 61 [1984]: 237–47).

5. For Aristotle's use of *analogia* in biology, ethics, physics, and metaphysics, see Lyttkens, *Analogy,* pp. 29–58. Mary Hesse ("Aristotle's Logic of Analogy," *PQ* 15 [1965]: 328–40) sees Aristotelian *analogia* as an instrument chiefly for expressing biological homologies and for devising poetic metaphors.

6. Cf. *Metaphysics* 5.6.1016b34–35.

mian idean), that is, univocally, but also that it is not predicated as a pure equivocal *(apo tychēs,* "by chance") either; rather, things exist and are called good either by being derived from one good *(aph' henos),* by being related to one good *(pros hen),* or according to proportion *(kat' analogian):* for example, just as sight is in the body, so is mind in the soul.[7]

Analogia is a way of expressing the likenesses of things belonging to different categories: for example, as knowledge is related to the object of knowledge, so is sensation related to the object of sensation; as calm is in the ocean, so is windlessness in the air.[8] Sometimes, Aristotle reduces to a yet higher category the various lower genera structured by a four-term proportionality. Thus, the ocean's calmness and the air's windlessness possess the common genus of stillness *(hēsuchia)*;[9] and although there is no common name for the fish's spine, the cuttlefish's calcified shell, and the vertebrate's bone (which are biological homologies able to be expressed *kata to analogon*), their common properties imply that they partake, as it were *(hōsper),* of a single and more general nature.[10] *Analogia,* then, is a tool for gathering common characteristics across genera and

---

7. *Nicomachean Ethics* 1.4.1096b14–29 (the passage is in book 1, chapter 6 of the McKeon translation and edition). Cf. *Topics* 1.17.108a12. For a rich compilation of texts on *analogia* and *analogon,* see M.-Dominique Philippe, "*Analogon* and *Analogia* in the Philosophy of Aristotle," *Thomist* 33 (1969): 1–74.

8. *Topics* 1.17.108a7–13.

9. Ibid., 1.18.108b25–26. At b26–29 the point and the number one are said to be the same insofar as each is a beginning *(archē).*

10. *Posterior Analytics* 2.14.98a20–23. Nevertheless, at 2.17.99a7–16, Aristotle distinguishes things one in genus but different in species, things one by equivocity, and things one according to *analogia.* Thomas inherits this ambiguity in Aristotle. After identifying *analogon* with *proportio,* Thomas states that things which are analogous cannot be the same either specifically or generically, but then to sustain his interpretation he must accentuate the "as it were" (implying that Aristotle did not want to be taken seriously) in Aristotle's suggestion of a single nature underlying the fish's spine and the vertebrate's bone (*Post.* 2.17.563). Two chapters later, moreover (*Post.* 2.19.577), Thomas mentions the rainbow and the echo as examples of things that agree "according to *analogia,*" even though at 2.17.563 he had already stated they were species of reverberation, which simply repeats Aristotle's view (*Posterior Analytics* 2.15.98a24–29) that an echo, a reflection, and a rainbow, though different specifically, all belong to the one genus of reverberation *(anaklasis).* Two factors are at work here: Thomas picks up Aristotle's suggestion that *analogia* as four-term proportionality can be reduced to generic predication, but at the same time he unconsciously conflates *analogia* as proportionality with *analogia* as equivocal predication—and of course analogy in this latter sense must be resolutely preserved from the univocity of generic predication.

species, and at times may itself be synthesized under a yet more inclusive category.

In an important remark from his *Physics* (1.7.191a7–12) Aristotle informs us that *analogia* does not prove the existence of the realities structured by the four-term proportionality; rather, once the realities are known to exist through other means, it helps us to understand more clearly the nature of one of them by placing it within the context of the other three. His example is the nature of what he calls the primary substratum or subject of all substantial change, which he says is known "according to proportion," for just as bronze is to the statue, wood to the bed, or the formless to that which has form, so is the nature of the basic substrate to the singular existent essence; he goes on to tell us how he first showed that a primary substratum was necessary and then later elucidated its nature. First comes the recognition of the existence of a primary substratum and then a clarification of its nature through *analogia* as proportionality. Aristotle's comments about the primary substratum of substantial change also hold for the other examples we have seen of *analogia* as proportionality, for in each case the left and right couplets are already known in some way independently of each other (e.g., recognition of a still night does not depend on previously knowing a tranquil ocean, or vice versa) before they are happily juxtaposed so that their similarities may bear fruit for understanding.

Aristotle also discusses what will become two other very influential themes—equivocal predication in general and the equivocal predication of being[11]—both of which remain quite distinct in his thought from the treatment of *analogia* as proportionality.[12] Nowhere does he provide an overarching theory to tie these three strands of thought together, but later

11. A third theme is Aristotle's use of the word *amphibolos* (ambiguous), especially as he employs it in chapters 4 and 19 of his *On Sophistical Refutations* to name some fallacies that deal with the ambiguous use of language. The term will reappear in some of his commentators in connection with the two themes mentioned in the text.

12. A perusal of G. L. Muskens, *De vocis analogias significatione ac usu apud Aristotelem* (Groningen: Wolters, 1943), shows that Aristotle never invokes *analogia* with reference to being; cf. Thomas M. Olshewsky, "Aristotle's use of *Analogia*," *Apeiron* 2 (1968): 1–10. Philippe attempts to harmonize *analogia* and *pros hen* equivocity, seeing the similarity of relations as their common core and thinking that he detects *pros hen* equivocity as referring to the division between substance and accident, and *analogia* as referring to the division between act

commentators and authors, including Aquinas, will show a tendency to blend and systematize them, even to the point that *analogia* will come to serve as the preferred term for designating the equivocal predication of being. We will note below how these three separate currents from the Aristotelian fountainhead find their confluence in the writings of his commentators.

The classic text for equivocal predication in general is from *Categories* 1.1a1–12, at the very beginning of all Aristotle's logical treatises. He remarks that things are equivocally *(homōnyma)* named when they have only the name in common, while the definitions for the realities themselves are different. For example, both a human and a portrait can be properly called a *zōon* (in ancient Greek *zōon* could mean both animal, and picture or artistic representation in general, not simply the picture of an animal), but this is obviously an equivocal predication since, though the name is the same, the definitions for a human and a portrait are quite different. Things are univocally *(synōnyma)* named when they bear the same name with the same meaning. For example, a human and an ox are univocally called a *zōon*, for the identical name also carries an identical meaning in each case.

Is Aristotle speaking here of pure, random equivocation or of a more intelligibly meaningful equivocation? If *zōon* is taken to name a portrait insofar as it represents the figure of an animal, then the second alternative is to be preferred, since the lifeless representation of an animate being is not called an animal simply by the luck of the alphabetic draw but because there is at least a likeness of superficial form. Thomas favors this second alternative when he writes that Aristotle is not speaking of "pure" equivocation but of equivocation "broadly understood" as even including analogicals.[13] But if *zōon* means any artistic representation of any object, then the

---

and potency ("*Analogon* and *Analogia*," pp. 30–32, 44, 56, 64–68, and n. 193). Despite their ingenuity these points do not correspond to the text of Aristotle, who never equates *analogia* as proportionality with the equivocal predication of being or attempts to combine them within a higher synthesis.

13. *ST* 1.13.10 ad4. Thomas implies that this broad equivocation is rooted in the fact that the real animal and the pictured animal bear "a certain likeness" to each other (*Phys.* 7.8.947); however, in an earlier text (*DV* 2.11 ad8) he had held that an object and its superficial resemblance in a picture can only with pure equivocation be called by the same name.

first alternative is to be preferred. Aristotle demonstrates a shrewd pedagogy in keeping *zōon* as his example for both equivocal and univocal predication, for his point is that the bare predicate itself is neither univocal nor equivocal but must be seen in relation to its possible subjects before a decision can be rendered. In any case, he establishes the limpid distinction between the equivocal (of either kind) and the univocal.

In *Physics* 7.4.249a23–25, Aristotle envisions three meanings for equivocity: when equivocal terms are applied to things far removed from one another; when there is a certain likeness or resemblance between the things meant by equivocal terms;[14] and when equivocal terms are applied to things that are close to one another either generically or by *analogia*, so that they appear not to be equivocal at all. The commentator Simplicius says that in the first case the meanings arise "by chance" *(apo tuchēs)*,[15] and Porphyry offers the example of *Alexander* said of both Priam's and Philip of Macedonia's sons. In explanation of the second category, Simplicius says that Aristotle has in mind the way images are related to their prototypes. When Thomas wants to distinguish analogy, univocity, and equivocity, however, he always has in mind the "purely equivocal," or the "equivocal by chance,"[16] and his usual example of the pure or chance equivocal is *dog* said of the celestial star and the barking animal.[17]

Other texts also show how Aristotle can oscillate between pure and broad equivocity. In *Topics* 2.3.110b16–111a7, he speaks of terms that are said "in many ways" *(pollachōs)*—and thus cannot be univocal—but that at the same time are also not said equivocally *(kath' homōnymian)*. Here he is proposing a way of predication intermediate between univocity and pure equivocity. This is very similar to other texts where being is said to be predicated in many ways, but not equivocally;[18] or neither equivocally nor

---

14. This brings to mind another text asserting that *man* said of a living and a dead body, and *hand* said of a real hand and a bronze or wooden hand, are predicated equivocally (*On the Parts of Animals* 1.1.640b33–641a1).

15. In *Nicomachean Ethics* 1.6.1096b26–27, Aristotle uses the same phrase.

16. *ST* 1.13.5; *CT* 1.27.

17. *Meta.* 4.1.535. For background detail and documentation for Simplicius and Porphyry, see Harry Wolfson, *Studies in the History of Philosophy and Religion*, ed. I. Twersky and G. H. Williams, 2 vols. (Cambridge: Harvard, 1973–77), 2:510–12.

18. *Metaphysics* 4.2.1003a33–35.

univocally (*kath' hen*—"in one way"), but with a reference to one *(pros hen)*.[19] These texts would naturally lead one to distinguish pure equivocity from a term's being said "in many ways." However, because he elsewhere distinguishes terms said in many ways from those said univocally *(monachōs)*, and then, after offering *beautiful* and *loving* as examples of terms said in many ways, calls them equivocal,[20] it is clear he can also associate equivocity with a term's being predicated in many ways.[21]

In his commentary on Aristotle's *Topics,* Alexander of Aphrodisias states that terms predicated "in many ways" are also called "equivocal" and "ambiguous" *(amphibola)*.[22] Although Aristotle never associated *amphibola* with terms predicated in many ways, as we have just seen he did recognize a mean between univocity and pure equivocity and did connect the broad sense of equivocity with such terms. Grounded in Aristotle and inspired by Alexander's commentary, Alfarabi, Avicenna, Algazali, Averroes, and Maimonides all proposed a threefold classification of predication—univocal, equivocal, and ambiguous—placing under the latter one or more of the types mentioned by Aristotle in *Topics* 2.3.110b16–111a7, and often employing his very examples.[23]

The discussion of a term's "being said in many ways" (*legesthai pollachōs*—often translated below by "multivocal" and "multivocity") especially flourishes in the soil of Aristotle's *Metaphysics* with its thinking about being, since the multivocity of being functions as a mean between univocity and pure equivocity.[24] He often provides the same three examples of multivocal predication: healthy, medical, and being.[25] In all three cases

19. Ibid., 7.4.1030a32–b4.

20. *Topics* 1.15.106a9, 22–23; b3–4.

21. In another text (*Physics* 7.4.248b6–249a8) he informs us that a pen, wine, and a note of the musical scale cannot be compared by a common measure as to sharpness, since *sharp* is used equivocally in these instances; other equivocal terms are *quick, much, equal, one,* and *two.*

22. Ed. Wallies (1891), p. 97, lines 22–23.

23. For a detailed account of this process from Alexander through Maimonides, see Wolfson, *Studies,* vol. 1, chap. 22. He writes that in St. Thomas "'analogy' has absorbed what in Arabic philosophy is called 'ambiguous'" (p. 477).

24. *Metaphysics* 4.2.1003a33–34; 7.4.1030b1–3; 11.3.1060b31–34; cf. *Topics* 2.3.110b16–17.

25. *Metaphysics* 4.2.1003a33–b15; 7.1.1028a1–10; 7.4.1030a35–b3; 11.3.1060b31–1061a12; *Topics* 2.3.110b17–19.

there is always a reference to some one thing, to a singular reality that bestows unity upon the various multivocal senses. Thus, health in the body, and the physician's medical skill, are the focal points for the various significations of *healthy* and *medical* respectively: hence, urine is called healthy only insofar as it is a sign of bodily health, while a diet is called healthy only insofar as it contributes to bodily health; likewise, the scalpel is called a medical tool only insofar as it serves the doctor's skill in surgery.

The one focal point is not itself a concept or meaning (though it can of course be signified by the multivocal term) but a single reality to which all the multivocal predications must bear reference. This becomes clear if we lay out the terminology Aristotle uses in the *Metaphysics* for describing what he calls "being said in many ways by reference (or relation) to one" *(legesthai pollachōs pros hen)*. We find "by reference to one and the same thing" *(pros to auto men kai hen)*,[26] "by reference to something one and common" *(pros hen ti kai koinon)*, "by reference to a certain single nature" *(pros mian tina physin)*, and "by reference to one principle" *(pros mian archēn)*.[27] The mention of "nature," "principle," "something," and "one thing" should help us appreciate the fact that Aristotle is thinking of a certain single nature or reality to serve as the focal point of unity for multivocal predication, so that when he mentions "the common" *(to koinon)* in reference to multivocal terms,[28] he is not proposing a common univocal concept but an individual reality that is common insofar as it is that to which all the different multivocal senses of a particular term must somehow refer if they are to attain and preserve their own nuanced meanings.

Another point of terminology regards the distinction or equivalence of *pros hen* and *kath' hen*. Often terms predicated univocally *(kath' hen)* are distinguished from those predicated by reference to one nature or thing *(pros mian physin* or *pros hen)*;[29] however, in one text terms predicated *pros*

---

26. *Metaphysics* 7.4.1030b1; at b1–3 the *pros hen* is depicted as a mean between pure equivocity *(homōnymōs)* and strict univocity *(to auto de kai hen* and *kath' hen); pros to auto* also occurs at 11.3.1061a3.

27. For these last three phrases, respectively, see *Metaphysics* 11.3.1061a10–11; 4.2.1003a33–34; and 4.2.1003b6.

28. Being is said "according to something common" *(kata ti koinon)*—ibid., 11.3.1060b32–33; note the *ti* (something) here and at 1061a10–11.

29. Ibid., 4.2.1003b12–14; 7.4.1030b3.

mian physin are also said "in a certain way" to be predicated *kath' hen*;[30] moreover, within a single chapter Aristotle can claim that being is predicated "by reference *(pros)* to something one and common" and also that "it is said in many ways according to something one and common" *(kath' hen ti kai koinon legetai pollachōs)*.[31] From these texts we may infer that for Aristotle *kath' hen* need not always refer to strict univocity but may at times be associated with *pros hen* multivocity; nevertheless, as *kath' hen* normally signifies univocity, he finds it necessary to add "in a certain way," which is quite understandable in our interpretation of his outlook on multivocal predication, for in the case of univocity the *hen* and the *koinon* refer to a single but common concept, whereas in multivocal predication they signify a single nature or reality that is common insofar as it is the focal point of all reference.

In the *Metaphysics*, therefore, being is predicated by reference to one nature, which turns out to be *ousia*, or entity (also substance or essence). And as Joseph Owens shows, Aristotle eventually demonstrates that the primary instance of entity is that divine nature which in 12.6–7 is found to be the separate and final cause of all things, so that the focal entity referred to by all the senses of the term *being* cannot in Aristotle's philosophical system be merely a concept or universal.[32] Being is said primarily, simply, and absolutely, of *ousia*, and secondarily, or relatively, of all other things, which are but modifications, qualifications, quantifications, or the like, of *ousia*.[33]

For Aristotle, entity is primary in both knowledge and existence. In chapter 12 of his *Categories* he furnishes five meanings of the word *prior (proteron)*: (1) the prior in time; (2) the prior in existence, such that when the existential sequence of two things cannot run both ways (e.g., the number one may exist without the number two but not vice versa), the

---

30. Ibid., 4.2.1003b14–15.

31. Ibid., 11.3.1061a10–11 and 1061b10–12.

32. Joseph Owens, *The Doctrine of Being in the Aristotelian "Metaphysics,"* 3rd ed., preface by E. Gilson (Toronto: PIMS, 1978). This is one of the principal theses of the book.

33. *Metaphysics* 4.2.1003b5–11; 7.1.1028a10–20. Being is said of *ousia prōtōs* (primarily) and *haplōs* (absolutely—7.1.1028a30–31); being belongs to all things, but to one *prōtōs* and to the rest *hepomenōs* (secondarily—7.4.1030a22–24); *haplōs* and *prōtōs* are opposed to *pōs* (in a certain sense) and *eita* (afterwards—7.4.1030a23–24, 30–31; 1030b5–6; 11.3.1061a7–10).

prior will be the thing that must come first; (3) the prior in any order or sequence; (4) the prior in honor or goodness. On further reflection he adds a fifth possibility, which is really a modification of the second category: (5) the prior in causality even when the existential sequence is mutually interdependent, that is, when each reality mutually implies and necessitates the other, and yet one is the cause of the other and not vice versa (e.g., the fact that a human exists requires the truth of the proposition that a human exists, and vice versa, but the former causes the latter and not the other way around).

Moreover, *Metaphysics* 7.1.1028a31–b3 explains that since *ousia* is the only category of being that can be separate *(chōriston)*, it is therefore predominant in the three principal meanings of the term *prōton* (primary): entity is primary in definition since the definition of every other reality must include entity, primary in knowledge since we think we know something best when we know its entity, and primary in time. At 4.2.1003b16–19 we also read: "In all cases knowledge is chiefly concerned with what is primary, i.e., with that upon which other things depend *(ērtētai)* and on account of which they are named. . . . *ousia* is this primary reality"; and at 12.7.1072a30–33 we are told that the primary reality in the class of *ousia* is that entity which is absolute and exists actually. But Aristotle's ultimate final cause, his god, is actuality and life without potentiality, is separate from matter and the corruptive influence of time, and is the principle upon which the heavens and nature depend.[34] In other words, the separate divine entity is that principle upon which the heavens and our world causally depend, and also that reality from which all other beings are named as beings; for all these reasons, entity is what the term *being* primarily (in the three senses of *primary* and most if not all of the five senses of *prior*) names and signifies.[35] For Aristotle, then, the *pros hen* multivoci-

---

34. Ibid., 12.7.1072b13–15, 25–30; 1073a4–5.

35. Giovanni Reale warns us about calling Aristotle's multivocity of being an analogy of being (*Aristotele, "La Metafisica,"* trans. in 2 vols., with introduction and commentary, Filosofi Antichi 1–2 [Naples: Loffredo, 1968], 1:322, n. 2); cf. 1:430, n. 32. Joseph Owens (*Doctrine*, pp. 107–35, 264–75) has some fine pages on *pros hen* equivocity in Aristotle, also advising us not to confuse equivocals by reference with equivocals by analogy. *Pros hen* equivocity (by reference) "may be expected to *characterize* the Aristotelian metaphysics" (p. 287).

ty of being is ultimately grounded in the fact that the term *being* primarily signifies the one (realm or sphere of) divine entity or essence.

Later writers in the Western philosophical tradition will combine and mix in various permutations the original Aristotelian terminology, often used in separate contexts, of *analogia, homōnyma, amphibola,* and *legesthai pollachōs.* Boethius, for example, synthesizes Aristotelian texts on analogy, equivocity, and multivocity, placing them all under a twofold division of equivocity. His Commentary on Aristotle's *Categories*[36] divides equivocal terms into those that occur by chance and those that happen by design, and then subdivides the latter class into four types easily recognizable as having their source in various texts of Aristotle: equivocal terms "according to likeness" (the real person and the person in the picture);[37] terms "according to proportion" (as the number one is at the beginning of the number series, so the point is at the beginning of a line);[38] terms that "derive from one" (a scalpel or a drug derive their capacity to be called medical from the "one medical skill"); terms that "are referred to one" (as food or riding is called healthy by reference to bodily health).[39] As we have also seen, some other authors, following a suggestion of Alexander of Aphrodisias, funnel Aristotle's terminology into the three categories of univocity, equivocity, and ambiguity, placing under the last the various types of multivocity described by Aristotle in *Topics* 2.3.110b16–111a7.[40]

Aristotle's multivocity thus passes into the amphibology/ambiguity of Alexander and other commentators, and thence into Aquinas' analogy. For while Aquinas does not use the term *ambiguous* in connection with analogy, his multivocal analogy is definitely a middle, "ambiguous" ground between univocity and pure equivocity. Further, unlike various Aristotelian

36. PL 64:166BC.

37. From *Categories* 1.1 and *Physics* 7.4.249a23–25.

38. From *Topics* 1.18.108b25–26 and *Physics* 7.4.249a23–25.

39. These last two types are from *Ethics* 1.6.1096b26–30 and *Metaphysics* 4.2.1003a33–b5; 11.3.1061a1–7.

40. See Wolfson, *Studies,* vol. 1, chap. 22, for details. Johannes Hirschberger ("Paronymie und Analogie bei Aristoteles," *PJ* 68 [1960]: 191–203) argues that another current in the development of thought on analogy is the Aristotelian paronym from the beginning of the *Categories,* as developed by certain Neoplatonic commentators and applied to the *pros hen* type of attribution from his *Metaphysics.*

commentators and Maimonides, who restricted *analogia* to its original
meaning of proportion, Thomas may mean by it either proportionality or
multivocal equivocity. In one text he weaves, somewhat like Boethius, the
Aristotelian themes of multivocity, equivocity, and analogy.[41] The exact
generational line from Aristotelian multivocity/equivocity to Thomistic
analogy remains unclear, but perhaps similitude is the common thread: if
analogia as proportion can denote a likeness or similitude of relations,
then it is not inconceivable that Thomas could see the term as also relevant
to a theological epistemology that wants to explain the way things are
named and known once they are recognized as similar by reason of God's
transcendent causality. In any case, Thomas will employ the Latin *analogia*
(on loan from the Greek) to mean either proportional analogy or multi-
vocal/referential analogy.

For Aristotle, multivocal predication is common, not by enveloping
everything within a common concept as in univocal predication, but by always maintaining some reference to a particular reality (which of course
may be signified by some concept) that can serve as the focal point for the
various predications. Whereas proportional analogy helps us to learn
more about the nature of some reality by juxtaposing various elements
that can mutually enlighten one another, multivocal analogy is more inherently involved in coming to any knowledge at all of the realities in
question, for reference must somehow be made to the primary reality if
there is to be any genuine knowledge and naming of the total reality clus-
ter, and if there is to be a properly appreciated employment of the common term.[42] In sum, multivocal analogy occurs whenever there is a genuine knowledge and naming of the relevant realities by means of the
common term understood in various ways. Aristotle does not explain his

---

41. *ST* 1.13.10 ad4; cf. *Meta.* 4.1.535. For some thoughts on possible reasons for the mixture and change of terminology, see Wolfson, *Studies,* 2:516–18.

42. For example, we have no way of knowing that (or why) the many things we call
healthy—urine, blood, diet, exercise, medicine, and medical procedure—really are healthy
and ought to be called so, unless we relate them all to an understanding of what it means for
the human body to be and to be called healthy. *Some* reference must be made to bodily
health, whether verbally or mentally.

epistemology of multivocal or referential predication, but we may suspect that judgment is involved.[43]

After Aristotle, the Neoplatonists were the ones who used *analogia* most frequently, and mainly in three ways, as shown by Hampus Lyttkens.[44] First, analogy was used in the sense of Aristotle's referential *(pros hen* or *aph' henos)* multivocity but with a decidedly ontological cast, that is, to express the fact that all being has originated from *(aph')* and is on the way back to *(pros)* the One, the divine substance. Analogy means the likeness of the image-effect to the prototype-cause: something in the effect, which is secondary, corresponds to something in the primary cause, and thus analogy carries an ontological import based on causality.[45]

Second, analogy was utilized as an ethical and cosmic principle of distribution: the world is synthesized from top to bottom according to analogy, and any characteristic is realized in different ways according to the nature of each subject. Cosmic being and ethical rewards are proportioned, respectively, to ontic levels and ethical behavior.[46]

Third, analogy was the manner in which different spheres of reality were linked by knowledge. Middle Platonists and Neoplatonists began to use analogy as an aid to knowing God, a usage that appears similar to Pla-

---

43. A series of judgments is implied in such texts as *Topics* 1.15.106a9–b4 and *Physics* 7.4.248b6–249a8. Burrell argues that the *pros hen* equivocal term is a matter of grasping similarity-in-difference across a range of uses; responsibly used equivocal terms are based on the judgments themselves (*Analogy*, pp. 68–91).

44. *Analogy*, pp. 58–110.

45. Wolfhart Pannenberg sees the Neoplatonic worldview as applying analogy, for the first time, to the God-world relationship ("Analogie und Offenbarung: Eine kritische Untersuchung der Geschichte des Analogiebegriffs in der Gotteserkenntnis" [Habilitationsschrift, Heidelberg, 1955], pp. 43–51).

46. See Wolfgang Marcus ("Zur religiösen philosophischen Analogie in der frühen Patristik," *PJ* 67 [1959]: 143–70) on the analogies of the pre-Arian fathers by which they related the inner-divine and cosmological economies. Raoul Mortley ("*Analogia* chez Clément d'Alexandrie," *Revue des études grecques* 84 [1971]: 80–93) explains how analogy in Clement of Alexandria can bear a mathematical, cosmic and moral sense, in which the moral sense arises from the cosmic, an idea based on Plato's *Timaeus*, where God uses analogy to care for the cosmos. But analogy also grounds our knowledge since it assures us of an identity between things: we can compare ideas on the worldly level, as well as between the visible and invisible, because of the bond between things.

to's invocation of the analogy of the Sun in order to explain the Good, but that is even more so than in Plato a causal analogy that bestows a name on God because of the divine effects.

Despite the thoroughgoing apophatism that is his preferred way to God, Dionysius speaks of rising by stages to God, the universal cause of all beings, through the order of all things, which is instituted by God and which contains images and likenesses of the divine models. We speak correctly about God when the divine praises are sung "according to the proportion *(analogia)* of all the things of which he is the cause." This *analogia* is a matter of God's causative action over all things, which harmonizes all and causes their indissoluble unity and order, making sure that the ends of the first beings touch the beginnings of the secondary beings, and working beautifully so as to bring about the agreement (literally, the "breathing-together") and harmony of the whole.[47] Here *analogia* signifies a hierarchical grade or order according to which various divine characteristics, diminishing as their distance from the primal source becomes greater, are received in proportion to each level's capacity. The *analogia* of Dionysius thus carries an ontological emphasis rooted in the divine causality and exemplarism, and is intimately connected with the hierarchical levels of being distinctive of the Neoplatonic worldview. *Analogia,* however, is also a path of knowledge *(gnōsis analogikē)*[48] lying at the heart of his affirmative way based on causality, by which we are led back up to the Cause of all.[49]

According to Pannenberg, Averroes was the first to make analogy a mean between univocity and pure equivocity, identifying *analogia* in its

47. *DN* 7.3 (PG 3:869C–872B).

48. Ibid., 5.3 (PG 825A).

49. Vladimir Lossky ("La notion des 'Analogies' chez Denys le Pseudo-Aréopagite," *AHDLMA* 5 [1930]: 279–309) expounds how *analogia* in Dionysius nearly always refers to the relation between God and creature, both the relation of creatures to God (by love and desire for deification) and the relation of God to creatures (in the divine ideas and theophanies). The "analogies" of creatures determine their place in the hierarchical orders of being and are the capacities creatures have for participating in God's powers. The "analogies" in God are the divine ideas insofar as they are the goals predetermined and set by God for each created being. The divine analogies/ideas are manifested by the analogies of creatures: God can be known as the cause of beings inasmuch as all beings are images of the divine ideas.

older meaning of *proportio* with the Aristotelian *pros hen* equivocity, which entails a term's being predicated *per prius et posterius* by means of a relation of dependence.[50]

Although Augustine did not expound a theory of analogy, he still influenced medieval thought on the subject through his doctrines of exemplarism, the divine ideas and their images in creation, participation, illuminationism, and the psychological analogies for the Trinity. We can detect this influence at work in Alexander of Hales, Bonaventure, and Albert the Great,[51] Aquinas' fellow Scholastics. If Alexander is perhaps the first to synthesize the Augustinian doctrine of participation with the Aristotelian notion of analogy/proportion (an idea followed by many of the great Scholastics contemporary with Aquinas), so that analogy signifies the indefinite likeness or proportion which, because of participation, holds between God and creation,[52] he stands nevertheless solidly within the Augustinian tradition, teaching an innate knowledge of God as well as a knowledge from God's effects, and viewing analogy not as a path to God but rather as a means of binding God, from above, to creation. Analogy in Bonaventure is ontologically grounded in the imitation that the creaturely image has for its divine archetype, where the creature is conformed to God through God's idea of it; analogy betrays the likeness of creation and the soul to God, and proportional analogy is used to show the soul's likeness to the Trinity.[53] Nevertheless, even though Bonaventure says that we know God from below by reason of his effects, in the end he is idealistic and Augustinian since he holds that only divine illumination—the perfect, inner way to God—permits the soul to see the divine perfections mirrored in nature. Finally, while Albert the Great makes use of the Neoplatonic participation analogy and analogy of proportionality in order to speak of the angelic hierarchy and of the soul as the image of God, he does not allow

50. "Analogie," pp. 77–82.

51. For extensive discussions of Augustine and the others, see Lyttkens, *Analogy*, pp. 110–21, 123–63; and Pannenberg, "Analogie," pp. 83–105.

52. On this point, see Jan Walgrave, *Selected Writings*, ed. G. de Schrijver and J. Kelly, Bibliotheca Ephemeridum Theologicarum Lovaniensium 57 (Louvain: University Press, 1982), pp. 20–25.

53. For this latter point, see *In Sententiis*, 1.3.1.1–3.

any intrinsic likeness between creatures and God, since for him analogy is a matter of extrinsic denomination.[54]

With an emphasis on Aristotle, this chapter has described some of the historical precedents for and influences upon Thomas' understanding of analogy, many of which will be met again as we discuss that understanding in the next three chapters. As we will see, he uses the word *analogia* to signify a wide range of realities—logical, semantic, epistemological, and ontological—which, though kept more or less distinct by Aristotle, were blended by later authors who influenced Thomas. He discusses analogy within a general Aristotelian epistemological framework, unlike many of his contemporaries who followed Augustine's illuminationism. As we will see, analogy for him can carry ontological import, as in Neoplatonism, though unlike the Neoplatonists, his ontology is based on the transcendent God's freedom in creation rather than on the necessary emanations of the immanent One; and unlike his own teacher Albert, he will not restrict analogy merely to the semantics and logic of extrinsic denomination.

54. For these last points, see Pannenberg, "Analogie," pp. 100–105.

5. The Various Meanings of Analogy in Aquinas

1. Critique of Analogy

Before we begin our treatment of analogy in Aquinas, it would be remiss not to acknowledge that various critiques have been directed at analogy, one of the most devastating of which sees analogy as blasphemously derogating from God's transcendence on the grounds that analogy is ultimately reducible to a univocal common being shared by God and creatures. Karl Barth and Wolfhart Pannenberg are two of the most prominent names identified with this philosophical and theological critique against analogy. We begin with Barth, who probably had the Jesuit scholar Erich Przywara in mind when he aimed his criticism at analogy.

Przywara's *Analogia entis*,[1] a phrase probably taken from the Dominican scholar Cardinal Cajetan de Vio, is a dense and difficult book that reveals the Catholicism at the heart of Przywara's philosophy. His is a meta-

---

1. *Analogia entis: Metaphysik, Ur-Struktur und All-Rhythmus, Schriften,* vol. 3 (Einsiedeln: Johannes, 1962). The first part of the original work was published in 1932 as *Analogia entis: Metaphysik I, Prinzip.* For more on Przywara, see André Favre, "La philosophie de Przywara: métaphysique de créature," *RNP* 37 (1934): 65–87; B. Gertz, *Glaubenswelt als Analogie: Die theologische Analogielehre Erich Przywaras und ihre Ort in der Auseinandersetzung um die Analogia fidei* (Düsseldorf: Patmos, 1968); James Zeitz, "Erich Przywara: Visionary Theologian," *Thought* 58 (1983): 145–57; idem, "Reflections on Erich Przywara and Eberhard Jüngel," *Communio* 12 (1985): 158–72; Thomas O'Meara, *Erich Przywara, S.J.: His Theology and His World* (Notre Dame: UND, 2002).

physics of the rational creature who is full of transcendence and obedien-tial potency toward God, and it touches on the relation between the natu-ral and the supernatural. He develops his philosophy from the concrete re-ality of the Christian revelation, which proposes supernatural mysteries as the solution for problems naturally insoluble. *Analogia entis* is the meta-physics of created beings and engenders the analogical cast of thought. He sees it as the exclusive principle of metaphysical ontology and epistemolo-gy; it is positive and negative, evincing at first "such a great similarity" but then more and more "an even greater dissimilarity."[2] He demonstrates, first, that any true metaphysics will have to coincide with a metaphysics of the creature, who is a being opened toward mystery; second, that only analogy can be the principle of a metaphysics of the creature, for analogy is the expression of the creature's movement and rhythm; and third, by means of a historical investigation, that the great metaphysical tradition of the West has always been dominated by analogy.[3] Analogy remains an in-dictment of the creature's impotence and yet also indicates the creature's need to progress toward mystery.

Karl Barth, in his monumental *Church Dogmatics,*[4] fires an opposing salvo. God is hidden, incomprehensible, ineffable, but in his revelation in Jesus Christ, God has made himself apprehensible (2/1:179–204). God is known only through God, by revelation and faith, and it is by the divine choice that our speech corresponds to God. Thus there is no knowledge of God outside revelation and faith. Our concepts and words apply only to creatures but can apply to God because God, as creator of our words and their normal objects, permits or orders us to apply them to him, and be-

2. The phrases are reminiscent of Lateran IV (*DS* 806); cf. Favre, "Philosophie," pp. 68–69, 78, n. 23.

3. Zeitz, "Visionary Theologian," says Przywara came to *analogia entis* as the core of his thought around 1924 and worked it out in a series of ascending polarities in a deeply spiri-tual vision of reality. *Analogia entis* is a matter of rhythm, of oscillation between polarities and tensions; it is the basic dynamism within creation, between creature and God, and with-in the Trinity (cf. Przywara, *Schriften,* 3:210).

4. *Church Dogmatics,* trans. G. T. Thompson et al., 5 vols (Edinburgh: T. and T. Clark, 1936–77). All parenthetical numerical references in the text are to the volumes and pages of this work. For German literature relating to the debate between Barth and Catholics over the *analogia entis,* see Walter Kasper, *The God of Jesus Christ,* trans. M. J. O'Connell (New York: Crossroad, 1984), p. 343, nn. 84–88.

cause God is by right both their first and their ultimate object. But we cannot lead our words back to God, and only the grace of revelation makes them analogously true, for the believer only speaks analogies that God has given.[5]

Barth then asks, Could the veracity of our knowledge of God be a matter of analogy? Examining the analogy theory of Johann Andreas Quenstedt (d. 1688), the classical Lutheran theologian (2/1:237–43), Barth finds him ultimately advocating, after all his verbal distinctions, a "being which is without question identical in God and in us" (2/1:241). Barth sees this theory as

in fact identical with the cardinal dogma of Roman Catholicism, namely, with the doctrine of the *analogia entis*, . . . this doctrine of analogy means a return to the flesh-pots of Egypt. . . . We shall ask [Catholics] whether their doctrine of the *analogia entis* has any claim at all to justification as a decision demanded by Holy Scripture and how far it can be justified from this source. Our contention is that so far as we can see this is quite impossible. (2/1:243)

This is reminiscent of Barth's most famous statement about the *analogia entis:*

I regard the *analogia entis* as the invention of Antichrist, and think that because of it one cannot become Catholic. Whereupon I at the same time allow myself to regard all other possible reasons for not becoming Catholic, as shortsighted and lacking in seriousness. (1/1:x)[6]

Later in the first volume, however, Barth notes that to apprehend the word of God, in faith, requires not a deification but a conformity of the

5. Roger White considers Barth's "most profound single contribution" to theology to be the insight that it is only from God's self-revelation in Jesus Christ that we truly learn the primary import of love, power, kingship, etc., and that we discover in God-talk, from God's revelation, a "homecoming of concepts" ("Notes on Analogical Predication and Speaking about God," in *The Philosophical Frontiers of Christian Theology,* ed. B. Hebblethwaite and S. Sutherland [Cambridge: Cambridge University, 1982], pp. 224–25).

6. Barth rarely if ever explicitly connects Przywara with the notion of *analogia entis,* though he must have been aware of his thought and in fact quotes a text from him employing the expression (1/2:144). Barth's early *Epistle to the Romans* (trans. E. C. Hoskyns [London, 1950], p. 296, cited in Rüdiger Safranski, *Martin Heidegger: Between Good and Evil,* trans. E. Osers [Cambridge, MA: Harvard, 1998], p. 111) castigates the cultural appropriation of God that delights in acknowledging the "overflowing, bubbling life in which we think we can discover a continuity of existence between us and God."

human with God. "Apprehension of the word of God could not take place, were there not in and along with this event something in common between God who speaks and man who hears, an analogy, a similarity, for all the dissimilarity involved in the difference between God and man, a 'point of contact' . . . between God and man" (1/1:273). This point of contact is the human image of God, but it is only real within faith, for before faith everything in humanity is null and lost, even the image. Thus Barth's "analogy of faith" is a human decision of faith corresponding to God's decision of grace. He indeed realizes that this talk of image and similarity seems close to the Catholic *analogia entis* but then offers a reason for why this is not really the case: the Catholic theory bespeaks a possession by the creature of a being that is common to creature and God, whereas his theory rests on a decision in faith. Still, he can detect a glimmer of truth even in *analogia entis:* a similarity, even in spite of greater dissimilarity (1/1:274).

Barth also disputes with Catholicism over the natural knowability of God (2/1:79–84). But he notes with approval some articles of G. Söhngen that subordinate the analogy of being to the analogy of faith, so that the "participation in being" cannot be opposed to the "participation in faith," for human nature is assumed in the personal Word of God. God works the analogy of being through Jesus Christ, who allows the analogy of faith to heal and elevate the analogy of being.

If there is a real analogy between God and man—an analogy which is a true analogy of being on both sides, an analogy in and with which the knowledge of God will in fact be given—what other analogy can it be than the analogy of being which is posited and created by the work and action of God himself, the analogy which has its actuality from God and from God alone, and therefore in faith and in faith alone? (2/1:83)

And if Söhngen's understanding is a correct interpretation of the Catholic doctrine of *analogia entis,*

then naturally I must withdraw my earlier statement that I regard the *analogia entis* as "the invention of anti-Christ." And if this is what that doctrine has to say to our thesis, then we can only observe that there is every justification for the warning that participation in being is grounded in the grace of God and therefore in faith, and that substance and actuality must be brought into this right relationship. (2/1:82)

But Barth does not think this is the usual Catholic interpretation of the analogy of being, and so he must remain against it.

Barth, then, will only permit an analogy of being that is previously rooted in an analogy of faith, faith in Jesus Christ as the Word of God. His analogy is both fideistic and Christic. The problem, as he sees it, with almost every variety of the analogy of being is the unavoidable positing of a being shared in common between God and creatures, which is simply unacceptable for a scripturally based theologian. His own preferred analogy of faith requires that the ontology and epistemology of any purported analogy between God and creatures be based on faith in Jesus Christ.[7]

Hans Urs von Balthasar and Henri Bouillard attempted to reconcile Barth's position on analogy with the classical tradition best exemplified in Aquinas. Von Balthasar discusses Barth's shift, from the dialectics of the two editions of his commentary on Paul's Letter to the Romans to the *analogia fidei* of the *Church Dogmatics*, which is based and centered on faith, Christ, creation, and covenant. The analogy of faith and the centrality of Christ grow in importance with each succeeding volume of the later work.[8] Von Balthasar, affirming that it was the *analogia entis*—as described

7. Other Protestant theologians have come to conclusions very similar to Barth's. Rudolf Bultmann, under the influence of Marburg Neo-Kantians and Luther's "by grace and faith alone," agrees with Barth in an actualism of faith and a positivism of our knowledge about God, asserting that objective knowledge of God is sinful knowledge, since it tries to master and control God from our standpoint outside God ("What Sense Is There to Speak of God?" in *Religious Language and the Problem of Religious Knowledge*, ed. R. Santoni [Bloomington: Indiana University, 1968], pp. 186–97; cf. Houston Craighead, "Rudolph Bultmann and the Impossibility of Godtalk," *FP* 1 [1984]: 203–15). For Jürgen Moltmann, the Lutheran "crucified God" and a genuine "theology of the cross" destroy any hope for a peaceful, pure theory of analogical knowledge of God. The cross and Luther's "by grace and faith alone" condemn even the desire to know God according to analogy's comfortable and serene continuities (*The Crucified God*, trans. R. A. Wilson and J. Bowden [New York: Harper and Row, 1974], pp. 65–75). Eberhard Jüngel contends that in Christ the world gains a correspondence to God, for in Christ, God's ever greater dissimilarity is taken up into an even greater similarity; however, there can still be no analogy outside of Christ and faith (*God as the Mystery of the World*, trans. D. L. Guder [Grand Rapids: Eerdmans, 1983], pp. 261–98; cf. John Webster, "Eberhard Jüngel on the Language of Faith," *Modern Theology* 1 [1985]: 253–76).

8. Hans Urs von Balthasar, *The Theology of Karl Barth*, trans. J. Drury (New York: Holt, Rinehart and Winston, 1971), pp. 73–150. The first German edition was published in 1952. For two studies on von Balthasar's own theory of analogy, see J. Schmid, *Im Ausstrahl der Schön-*

and explained by Erich Przywara—that Barth focused on as the cardinal tenet of Catholicism,[9] states that

in order to justify the Reformation's charge against Catholicism, Barth was forced to ground Catholic theology on a *mistaken* notion of the analogy of being and then develop a proper counternotion. We have tried to show that the supposed opposition is an illusory one. . . . Barth's way of understanding God's revelation in Christ (the analogy of faith) includes within itself the analogy of being; in the Catholic Christocentric approach presented here, the analogy of being becomes concrete and real only within the more all-embracing analogy of faith.[10]

Von Balthasar agrees with Barth as to the primacy of Christ and the analogy of faith, but insists that the attempt to set up a real opposition between the analogy of being and the analogy of faith is no longer meaningful.[11]

Henri Bouillard stresses that Aquinas never used the expression *analogia entis* and never spoke of a common being shared by God and creation, that he in fact, no less than Barth, rejected a *tertium quid* common to God and creature, and that his analogy is judgmental, whereas Barth is reacting to an analogy that is representational and conceptualist.[12] Can Barth save the analogy of faith by imposing on our words a meaning bestowed by revelation and received in faith? Perhaps this is no more than superimposing "on a natural equivocity a univocity gained from grace."[13] But Barth's real purpose in rejecting the *analogia entis* is "to validate the *sola gratia*

---

heit Gottes: Die Bedeutung der Analogie in "Herrlichkeit" bei Hans Urs von Balthasar (Münsterschwarzach: Vier-Türme, 1982); Georges de Schrijver, *Le merveilleux accord de l'homme et de Dieu: Étude de l'analogie de l'être chez Hans Urs von Balthasar*, Bibliotheca Ephemeridum Theologicarum Lovaniensium 63 (Louvain: University Press, 1983). Eugene Rogers Jr. has recently argued very persuasively, contrary to the expectations of many, that Aquinas and Barth also show an astonishing convergence in their exegesis of Romans 1:20 and thus in their views of humanity's natural knowledge of God (*Thomas Aquinas and Karl Barth: Sacred Doctrine and the Natural Knowledge of God* [Notre Dame: UND, 1995]).

9. Von Balthasar, *Karl Barth*, pp. 29–32.

10. Ibid., pp. 286–87.

11. Ibid., pp. 295–96; 311, n. 9 (this note, which also serves as part of von Balthasar's response to an article by Pannenberg taking him to task over analogy, belongs to the foreword of the second German edition, which becomes part of the epilogue in the English translation).

12. Henri Bouillard, *The Knowledge of God*, trans. S. D. Femiano (New York: Herder and Herder, 1968), pp. 104–18.

13. Ibid., p. 118.

against the principle of natural theology."[14] If Przywara reacted to Barth's dialectics with his *analogia entis,* and Barth answered in kind with his *analogia fidei,* we must relate the two in the broader type of perspective[15] that von Balthasar offers:

Whereas in classical theology analogy is opposed to univocity and equivocity, in von Balthasar's terminology it is opposed to dialectic, . . . It designates, in short, the proper consistency and relative autonomy of the creature at the very heart of his relationship with God. It is called *analogia fidei* when the author wishes to indicate that this consistency has been placed there by God within the heart of the Christic order. It is called *analogia entis* when it envisages the internal constitution of the creature as such.[16]

14. Ibid., p. 122.

15. For other authors who compare analogy and dialectic, Hegel is often the dialogue partner of Aquinas. For the theological importance of the two traditions of analogy and dialectic, see Pierre Gisel and Philibert Secretan, eds., *Analogie et dialectique* (Geneva: Labor et Fides, 1982). For the confrontation between analogy and dialectic, see Bernhard Lakebrink, "Analektik und Dialektik: Zur Methode des Thomistischen und Hegelschen Denkens," in *St. Thomas Aquinas, 1274–1974: Commemorative Studies,* 2 vols. (Toronto: PIMS, 1974) 2:459–87; Erich Heintel, "Transzendenz und Analogie," in *Wirklichkeit und Reflexion,* Festschrift Walter Schulz, ed. H. Fahrenbach (Pfüllingen: Neske, 1973), pp. 267–90. David Tracy, in chapters 5 and 10 of *The Analogical Imagination* (New York: Crossroad, 1981), tries to show the complementarity of analogy and dialectic: just as analogy (based on manifestation) without its own negative moment becomes wooden univocity, so dialectic (based on proclamation) left to itself becomes equivocity and destruction. Colman O'Neill ("Analogy, Dialectic, and Inter-Confessional Theology," *Thomist* 47 [1983]: 43–54, 62–65) sees a moment of negativity at the heart of analogy and considers analogy to be the fundamental matrix within which dialectic can find a place, for dialectic itself cannot be fundamental; see also his "La prédication analogique: l'élément négatif," in *Analogie et dialectique,* ed. Gisel and Secretan, pp. 81–91. For feminist theologian Elizabeth Johnson, it is because of the "complexity of analogy including its negating moment" that analogy can function "as a wheel on which [women] can spin out emancipatory language in fidelity to the mystery of God and their own good mystery which participates in that fire" (*She Who Is: The Mystery of God in Feminist Theological Discourse* [New York: Crossroad, 1992], pp. 116–17).

16. Bouillard, *Knowledge,* p. 126. Cf. Henry Chavannes, *L'Analogie entre Dieu et la monde selon Thomas d'Aquin et selon Karl Barth* (Paris: Cerf, 1969). Marcel Reding distinguishes the logician's analogy of names from the theologian's analogy of divine names and from the metaphysician's analogy of being, and by severing the alleged necessary connection between the last two would encourage Barth to accept an analogy of the divine names (*"Analogia entis* und *analogia nominum,"* *EvT* 23 [1963]: 225–44). K. Surin detects a reconciliation between the analogy of being and the analogy of faith in Aquinas' revealed theology of creation: "Barth gives us the eschatological dimension essential to a proper understanding of Aquinas' analogy of being, while the 'ontological' analogy theory of Aquinas gives us the requisite ontological foundations for Barth's analogy of faith. Or to put it even more briefly:

However, Wolfhart Pannenberg has argued forcefully that the analogy of being and the analogy of faith, Aquinas and Barth, cannot be so easily reconciled.[17] His first published article argued that Barth had granted too much by allowing a similarity between God and creation, for this is an implicit admission of the Neoplatonic "common logos" which Pannenberg impugns.[18]

In his *Habilitationsschrift* Pannenberg marshals his forces against analogy by means of a historical investigation.[19] From its very beginnings, all analogy somehow involves similarity, but similarity always announces a moment of partial identity—otherwise it would be an empty concept—and this partial identity is univocity. Basically, analogy never recovers from this "core of univocity" present in every similarity, from this "common logos." He makes three points: first, even Aristotle and Averroes, with their *pros hen* equivocity, are still adhering to the common logos of the older Greek concept of analogy as a "comparison of similarities"; second, Christian Neoplatonic analogy destroys the uniqueness of God's self-revelation in Christ, dilutes sin's radical break with God, and does not permit the radically new in history; and third, scholastic analogy logically presupposes the univocal core of meaning and theologically compromises God's transcendence.[20] Elizabeth Johnson summarizes Pannenberg's conclusion:

analogy from the perspective of God is analogy of being, analogy from the perspective of man is analogy of faith, and the two are complementary because man has his being, through God's work of creation, in the being of God (the *imago Dei*)" ("Creation, Revelation, and the Analogy Theory," *JTS* 32 [1981]: 420).

17. See his following works: "Zur Bedeutung des Analogiegedankens bei Karl Barth," *TLZ* 78 (1953): 18–23; "Analogie und Offenbarung: Eine kritische Untersuchung der Geschichte des Analogiebegriffs in der Gotteserkenntnis" (Habilitationsschrift, Heidelberg, 1955); "Möglichkeiten und Grenzen der Anwendung des Analogieprinzips in der evangelischen Theologie," *TLZ* 85 (1960): 225–28; "Analogy and Doxology," in *Basic Questions in Theology,* trans. G. H. Kehm, 2 vols. (Philadelphia: Westminster, 1970), 1:211–38. For two studies of Pannenberg's thought, see Barbara Alpern, "The Logic of Doxological Language: A Reinterpretation of Aquinas and Pannenberg on Analogy and Doxology" (Ph.D. dissertation, University of Pittsburgh, 1980); Elizabeth Johnson, "The Right Way to Speak about God? Pannenberg on Analogy," *TS* 43 (1982): 673–92.

18. Pannenberg, "Zur Bedeutung des Analogiegedankens"; cf. Johnson, "Pannenberg on Analogy," pp. 686–87.

19. This paragraph relies heavily on Johnson's "Pannenberg on Analogy."

20. Ibid., pp. 676–85.

Analogy is a relation requiring a logos common to both analogates. The structure of analogy understood in this way held good from primitive human thought to the Neoplatonic causal schema, and no subsequent concept of analogy, whether early Christian, medieval, or modern, has ever broken through the confines of that Neoplatonic schema and its presuppositions. . . . If one is opposed to univocity, however slight, existing in the essential characteristics of Creator and creature, one must oppose analogy.[21]

She chides him, however, for not hearkening to the negation at the heart of analogy and for being too conceptualist; moreover, at the root of his uneasiness about analogy lies "a fundamentally different vision of reality," the dialectical.[22]

For Pannenberg, analogy only connects us to God as nature, necessity, essence, or generality, and by intrinsic attribution it argues from God's effects to God as cause. But the biblical idea of God is based on historical encounter, not causal inference, and it sees God as concrete, personal, and free. The only way to God is by faith and doxology.[23]

Indeed, doxology becomes Pannenberg's central counterconcept to analogy.[24] Doxology speaks of God in adoration on the basis of the divine works, whereas analogy infers God's attributes from the divine effects. Since adoration surrenders both the ego and conceptual univocity, if there is any analogy it is only at the level of a movement from everyday language to doxological language—but this is not the analogy that knows God's very being. Doxology arises from a specific experience of a divine act, and it speaks on the basis of that act. Can doxology be true? Yes, but it is equivocal, gaining its truth not from present actuality but from the future revelation of God.

At the place where the old doctrine of analogy asserted a correspondence of the word used to name God with God himself, there stands, in our view, the concept of revelation. This is connected with the opposition between the Greek under-

21. Ibid., p. 687.
22. Ibid., pp. 690–91.
23. Pannenberg, *Basic Questions*, 2:171–73. Walter Kasper also does not ground analogy in classical ontology but in salvation history and God's freedom (*God of Jesus Christ*, pp. 94–99).
24. Pannenberg, *Basic Questions*, vol. 1, chap. 7.

standing of the divine as the ground of the present world, and the biblical conviction that the creation is still underway to its proper reality and that the essences of all things will finally be decided simultaneously with the final end by which God will be definitively revealed. . . . [God] makes our metaphorical speech his own through his revelation, and thereby for the first time gives our words of praise their ultimately valid content. The correspondence of our words to God himself has not already been decided, but is yet to be decided. This temporal difference between our speech about God and its fulfillment by God himself cannot be expressed by means of the concept of analogy. Judged from our standpoint, the concepts by which we praise God's essence become equivocal in the act of the sacrifice of praise.[25]

Pannenberg's substitution of doxology for analogy is bound up with his own preference for the future and for doxological equivocity. He critiques theological analogy for reducing God and creatures to a univocal core of identity,[26] which destroys God's transcendence and takes away God's ability to do the radically new in history's future. For this reason, analogy must be rejected and be replaced by doxology.

Barth's and Pannenberg's critiques of analogy must be taken seriously, and any theory of analogy that lacks an answer for them cannot remain viable.[27] However, at various points in chapters 5 through 8 we will have oc-

25. Ibid., 1:237–38.

26. Similarly, William Lane Craig asserts that "analogical predication without some univocal, conceptual content cannot be regarded as anything more than metaphor" ("The Eternal Present and Stump-Kretzmann Eternity," *ACPQ* 73 [1999]: 535), whereas Janice Thomas contends that we must remain agnostic as to whether positive terms that denote both human qualities and God's attributes are univocal or equivocal ("Univocity and Understanding God's Nature," in *The Philosophical Assessment of Theology,* ed. Gerard Hughes [Washington, DC: Georgetown University, 1987], pp. 85–100. David Burrell speaks of philosophers and philosophy possessing an "inertial tendency" toward the "default position" of univocal language concerning God ("Analogy, Creation, and Theological Language," *PACPA* 74 [2000]: 40, 48), and argues that even Christian philosophers will tend to do the same unless they keep in mind the ineradicable distinction between creature and Creator ("Creation, Metaphysics, and Ethics," *FP* 18 [2001]: 204–21).

27. More recently, William Alston, following a Scotist and functionalist interpretation of theological language, contends that Thomas' philosophical theology implicitly relies on the supposition that at least a few general and abstract perfection terms are predicated univocally of God and creatures ("Aquinas on Theological Predication: A Look Backward and a Look Forward," in *Reasoned Faith: Essays in Philosophical Theology in Honor of Norman Kretzmann,* ed. Eleonore Stump [Ithaca: Cornell, 1993], pp. 145–78). He says that Thomas' treatment of analogy "attempted to hold together more themes than can comfortably exist

casion to remark how Aquinas escapes from the net of objections deployed
by Barth and Pannenberg: this chapter and the next will show that the
commonality evident in Aquinas' analogy is not the same as the hidden
univocal core of Greek/Neoplatonic analogy, that is, that his analogy does
not posit a common being shared in differentially by God and creatures;
chapters 7 and 8 will emphasize the judgmental rather than conceptualist
nature of analogy in Aquinas, discuss the relation between faith and analogy in his thought, and also argue that Neoplatonic participation in the
One, based on emanation, is not the same as Thomistic participation in
the Creator, based on creation. With the critique of analogy never far from
consciousness, therefore, we begin our treatment of analogy in Thomas
Aquinas.

II. Analogy as Proportion and Proportionality

In the Latin translations of Aristotle current in the time of Aquinas, the
Greek *analogia* is sometimes transliterated into the Latin *analogia,* sometimes rendered by *similitudo* (likeness) or *proportionalitas* (proportionality), but most often translated by *proportio* (proportion or relation), which
is also the term most favored by Aquinas himself.[28] In general, a pro-

---

in a single coherent account" (p. 145), and that as regards "pure perfection terms" Thomas
"lacks any sound reason for denying that they can be univocally applied across the divine-
creature gap," for "we may be able in some cases to use terms univocally of God and creature so far as the *res significata* is concerned, even though the mode of signification will mis-
represent the divine being" (p. 178). Alston argues that our process of concept-formation
can at times arrive at such a general and abstract notion of perfection that it transcends the
differences between Creator and creature and thus can be predicated univocally of them.
His criticism is inspired by Duns Scotus and thus conceptualist in flavor, but according to
this and the next two chapters, conceptualism misses the mark as to what Thomas actually
understands by analogy, even though Alston is right to assume conceptualist presuppositions in most previous interpretations of Thomas' theory of analogy (even Cajetan and Scotus shared a common conceptualist view of analogy), and even though, as we shall see in
chapter 7, Thomas' standard theory of concept-formation cannot do justice to what is going
on in the judgments that give rise to analogy.

28. Harry A. Wolfson, *Studies in the History of Philosophy and Religion,* ed. I. Twersky and
G. H. Williams, 2 vols. (Cambridge: Harvard, 1973–77), 2:514–15 and nn. 138–41. Thus, although at *Physics* 7.4.249a23–25, Aristotle differentiates between *homoiotēta* (similitude) and
analogia, Thomas' commentary (*Phys.* 7.8.947) is forced to mention *similitudo* twice since

portion is "a relation of two things compared with each other in some respect, whether by agreement or difference" (*BDT* 1.2 ad3), and typically requires at least two terms (*SS* 4.16.3.1.1). There are two types of proportion.

Narrowly speaking, proportion denotes a relation of one definite quantity to another, so that one exceeds or falls short of the other by a determinate, defined amount;[29] or things may be in proportion if they are at a fixed distance from or possess a fixed relation to each other, so that an exact, definite measure of their relationship can always be given (*DV* 2.11). This meaning obviously owes much to the traditional sense of Greek *analogia* as mathematical proportion.

This narrow sense can be broadened, however, so that proportion comes to signify a "relation of order" (*SS* 3.1.1.1 ad3) or *any* relation of one thing to another.[30] That proportion can mean any relation at all is shown by the many texts in which two obviously correlative realities are said to be "proportioned" *(proportionatus)* to one another: form and matter, agent and patient, knower and known, moved and mover, our intellect and the divine essence, maker and made, cause and ef-

---

the translation before him most probably used it to construe both of the Greek words. In his Aristotelian commentaries we find Thomas using *proportio* most frequently to construe Aristotle's *analogia* or *analogon*: *Caelo* 2.11.398; *Meteor.* 1.3.21; *Phys.* 1.10.81; 1.13.118; 1.15.138; 4.12.529; 7.9.957; *Post.* 2.19.577; *Ethic.* 5.5, passim; 9.1.29–30; *Meta.* 9.5.1826–29. In *ST* 1.13.5 he explicitly identifies *analogia* with *proportio*. But Greek *analogia* is rendered by *proportionalitas* at *Ethic.* 5.5.23–24, 105–6; and by the third and fourth occurrences of *similitudo* at *Phys.* 7.8.947. In *ST* 1.1.10 ad2, *analogia* is mentioned twice in reference to the interpretation of scripture: in Romans 12:6, St. Paul bids the person with the gift of prophecy to use it in proportion to faith *(kata tēn analogian tēs pisteōs)*; in *De utilitate credendi* 3.5 (PL 42:68), Augustine hearkens back to this text and asserts that a scriptural passage from the Old Testament is interpreted "according to analogy" when it is shown that the two testaments are not opposed to each other, and thus *analogia fidei,* or just *analogia,* can mean agreement or harmony of faith and its expressions. Nevertheless, Aquinas does not use *analogia* as a direct transliteration of Paul's *analogia,* for the Vulgate's rendering of the Greek word was *ratio,* and thus we find *secundum rationem fidei* when he is commenting directly upon the text from Romans (*ST* 2-2.172.5, 3rd objection).

29. *SS* 3.1.1.1 ad3; 4.49.2.1 ad6; *DV* 2.3 ad4; 3.1 ad7; 8.1 ad7; 23.7 ad9; *Post.* 1.12.105; *Ethic.* 5.5.26–27; *ST* 1.12.1 ad4.

30. *SS* 4.49.2.1 ad6; *DV* 8.1 ad6; 23.7 ad9; *Quod.* 10.8.1 ad1; *BDT* 1.2 ad3; *SCG* 3.54.2317; *DP* 7.10 ad9; *ST* 1.12.1 ad4.

fect, act and actor, potency and act, and creature and God.[31] Likewise, matter is said to be known by analogy, that is, by its direct relation, to form.[32]

Aquinas can also understand *analogia* as a four-term proportionality. Proportionality is a "likeness of proportions" with at least four terms, where two are compared with another two in the same "relation of proportions,"[33] which may also be called an "agreement of proportions" (*DV* 2.11 ad4), "combination of two proportions" (*Post.* 1.12.105), or "equality of proportion."[34] He makes use of proportionality in the following five areas: (1) as a way of comparing similar proportions or functions;[35] (2) as a way of showing how the principles of all things are proportionately the same;[36] (3) as a way of comparing and connecting the finite creature with the infinite God;[37] (4) as a way of explaining metaphor; and (5) as a means of understanding the Trinity.[38] These latter two require more comment.

First, the likeness between two things based either on a common participation in the same form or on analogy is distinguished from the "likeness of proportionality" that occurs whenever metaphorical characteristics are predicated of God.[39] However, the metaphorical predication of divine qualities may also be differentiated from both proportion and proportion-

31. *SS* 3.1.1.1 ad3; 4.49.2.1 ad6; *BDT* 2.1 ad3; *DV* 8.1 ad6; *Quod.* 10.8.1 ad1; *SCG* 3.54; *ST* 1.12.1 ad4; 1.12.3; 1.21.4; 1.23.1; 1.23.7 ad3; 1.25.6 ad3; 1.46.1 ad6; 1.84.7; 1.97.1. Matter is proportioned to form and vice versa, because the being that form can give, matter can receive (*SS* 3.1.1.1 ad3). In the case of God, the creature is proportioned to God but not vice versa, for God exceeds the proportion of every creature (*Quod.* 10.8.1 ad1; *ST* 1.12.1 ad4; 1.23.1; cf. *SCG* 4.1.3340; *Job* 11.70–72). In *Psalm* 8.1 God is said to "transcend without proportion."

32. *SS* 2.17.1.1 ad4; *BDT* 4.2; *DV* 10.4.90–101.

33. *SS* 1.34.3.1 ad2; *DV* 2.3 ad4; 2.11; 23.7 ad9; *Meta.* 7.4.1334.

34. *Ethic.* 5.5.23–24, 105–6; 5.6.26–28; 5.8.104–6; cf. *SS* 2.16.1.1 ad4. In his *Nicomachean Ethics* (5.3.1131a31) Aristotle had written that "proportion is an equality of ratios" *(hē gar analogia isotēs esti logōn)*, which the Old Latin translation that Aquinas likely knew rendered *proportionalitas enim aequalitas est proportionis* (Wolfson, *Studies*, 2:519).

35. *DV* 2.11; *Quod.* 1.10.2 ad1; *Phys.* 7.8.947; *Meta.* 5.8.879; 9.5.1828–29; *Ethic.* 1.7.96; *Post.* 1.12.105; 2.19.577. Cf. *ST* 1.14.3 ad2; 1.91.3 ad3; 1-2.3.5 ad1.

36. *BDT* 5.4; *Meta.* 3.10.465; 12.4.2477, 2480, 2485–86.

37. *DV* 23.7 ad9; cf. *ST* 1-2.3.5 ad1.

38. See George Klubertanz, *St. Thomas Aquinas on Analogy: A Textual Analysis and Systematic Synthesis* (Chicago: Loyola, 1960), pp. 80–86.

39. *SS* 1.34.3.1 ad2; 1.45.1.4; 2.13.1.2; 2.16.1.2 ad5; 4.45.1.1.1 ad2.

ality (*DV* 2.11). Hence, proportionality and metaphor are not coextensive for Thomas, though metaphor may always be explained through proportionality. Terms expressing a transfer or change of meaning from one realm to another—*transferre, transumptio, translative, metaphorice*—designate metaphorical predication, for the metaphor involves a transfer of meaning from the bodily to the spiritual sphere in order to signify spiritual characteristics by corporeal qualities.[40]

Second, seeking whether the image of the Trinity is found in our minds insofar as we know temporal or eternal things, Aquinas follows Augustine and discovers three levels of likeness. It is in the middle level, where the mind knows itself, that the representation of the Trinity occurs "according to analogy," for just as the mind, knowing itself, gives birth to a word, with love then proceeding from both, so the Father begets the Son from eternity, with the Holy Spirit proceeding from both (*DV* 10.7). This Trinitarian *analogia*, which is unique in Thomas' works, is obviously a matter of proportionality.[41]

Probably due to the Latin translation that he knew, which could render Greek *analogia* by either *proportio* or *proportionalitas*, Thomas sometimes does not clearly distinguish the two and even makes them virtual synonyms.[42] Infrequently, he mentions the term *proportionalitas* but then goes on to explain it by means of a two-term proportion (*SS* 4.49.2.1 ad7); more often, he mentions *analogia* or *proportio* and then explicates these by offering a four-term proportionality:[43] for example, to say that matter is known by "analogy" or "proportion" to form means that just as prime matter is related to substantial forms, so are material realities related to ac-

---

40. *SS* 2.13.1.2; 2.16.1.2 ad5. Other texts dealing with metaphor as proportionality: *SS* 3.2.1.1.1 ad3; 4.1.1.1.5 ad3; *ST* 1.13.6. Texts such as these in the last two notes led Cardinal Cajetan to propose his famous distinction between proper and improper proportionality, though Thomas never announced one.

41. The parallels to *DV* 10.7 (*SS* 1.3.4.4; *ST* 1.93.8) do not use *analogia*. Other expressions of the Trinitarian proportionality: *SS* 2.16.1.1 ad4; *SCG* 4.2–3; 4.11; *Decretalem* 1.337–64.

42. For texts in the Commentary on the *Sentences* where Aquinas uses them as synonyms, see Battista Mondin, "L'analogia di proporzione e di proporzionalità nel Commento alle Sentenze" (*RFNS* 66 [1974]: 585).

43. *De prin.* 6.78–81; *SS* 3.1.1.1; 4.1.1.4.4; *Post.* 2.19.577; *Ethic.* 1.7.206–9; *Meta.* 5.8.879; 9.5.1828–29.

cidental forms.[44] At other times, however, proportion is clearly distinguished from proportionality, especially in those texts defining proportionality as a likeness or relation of proportions.[45]

In summary, by *analogia* Thomas sometimes means four-term proportionality (the traditional sense in Greek philosophy) and sometimes two-term proportion (in either its narrow or broad senses), and in practice may either blend or differentiate them.

III. Analogy as Referential Multivocity

Aquinas also sees *analogia* as a multiple predication of one name to many things, based on reference, attribution, or proportion to some one reality, in which *proportio* generally carries its broad meaning of any relation at all, though at times its narrow sense is underlined.[46] He can say that analogy is proportion (*ST* 1.13.5), or more exactly, "proportion with a reference to one" (*proportio ad unum*).[47] In the four texts that follow, we may observe the unobtrusive manner in which he insinuates his own interpretation of analogy as multivocal predication in those contexts where *analo-*

---

44. *Phys.* 1.15.138; also, 1.13.118, where Thomas is commenting on the famous text of *Physics* 1.7.191a7–12. Nevertheless, he can also understand *analogia* as a two-term direct relation, as when he claims that matter is known through its relation to form, as the curved nose is known through its very curvature (*DV* 10.4.90–101; cf. *SS* 2.17.1.1 ad4). Another text combines the two interpretations (*BDT* 4.2).

45. *SS* 4.49.2.1 ad6; *DV* 2.3 ad4; 2.11; 3.1 ad7; 23.7 ad9; *Post.* 1.12.105. He knows the distinction between arithmetic proportion and geometric proportionality (*SS* 3.33.1.3.2; 3.36.1.4; 4.15.1.2; 4.32.1.3).

46. Joseph Owens ("Analogy as a Thomistic Approach to Being," *MS* 24 [1962]: 303–22) would divide all predication into univocal and equivocal, and then subdivide the equivocal into equivocal by chance, equivocal by proportion (for which *analogy*, in its traditional Greek meaning of proportionality, ought to be reserved), and equivocal by reference (thus analogy of attribution ought to be called predication by reference and not analogy at all). Our practice follows that of Aquinas, however, and uses *analogy* with various significations, for *analogy* is itself a rich example of a multivocally analogous term whose various meanings must be gathered from its use and context. On analogy as itself analogous, see Ralph McInerny, *Studies in Analogy* (The Hague: Nijhoff, 1968), chap. 4; Mortimer Adler, "The Equivocal Use of the Word 'Analogical,'" *NS* 48 (1974): 4–18.

47. *CT* 1.27; *ad unum* translates Aristotle's celebrated *pros hen*. Healthy, medical, and being are analogous predicates because they are "proportioned to one" (*Meta.* 11.3.2197).

gia is either absent or also carries its customary meaning of four-term proportionality.

1. *De Principiis Naturae* 6. In this very early work, Thomas notes that a term may be predicated of many subjects in three ways: univocally, equivocally, and analogically. Analogical predicates, which correspond by proportion or comparison, are attributed *(attribuere)* either to one goal (as the predicate *healthy* has its meaning eventually referred to the one goal of health); to one agency (as all the various possible meanings of *medical* are ultimately ascribed to the one agency of medical skill); or to one subject (as the highest categories of being may be called such due to the fact that they are attributed to substance, which is the subject of the others). One may say, therefore, that substance and quantity are "the same according to analogy." At this point in the chapter, *analogia* for Thomas must refer to a two-term proportion, for the different meanings of an analogical predicate retain their harmony only because they each carry some direct relation or attribution to something one and the same for all of them. But he continues, remarking that things which agree only in analogy or proportion have principles that are the same only in analogy or proportion: for example, as the matter of a substance is related to the substance, so is the matter of a quantity to the quantity. At this point, however, he has bestowed upon *analogia* its traditional signification of four-term proportionality.

In this early work, then, three points should be noted: the joining of *proportio* and referential, *ad unum* predication;[48] two senses of *analogia*—proportionality and multivocal predication; and the mention of attribution in a context that implies the making of many judgments and the knowledge of the truth of those judgments (for when the judgments "urine is healthy" and "medicine is healthy" are made, and the different meanings of *healthy* in each case noted, the validity and truth of each judgment can be recognized only on the grounds that *healthy* in each case has a different but related meaning because it signifies a diverse relation to that actual bodily health which is one and the same).[49]

---

48. See *Meta.* 4.1.534, which also speaks of analogy in terms of predication.

49. In this text, forms of *attribuere* are found five times and seem to make special reference to "the one and same thing" that is the sole source of analogy's unity. There are a few

2. *Sententia super Metaphysicam 4.1.535–39*. This late text comments on Aristotle's *Metaphysics* 4.2.1003a33–b10, where Aristotle is making the case that being is said in many ways *(legesthai pollachōs)* but always with reference to some one nature, offering as examples of this type of predication the ways in which *healthy* and *medical* are said of various things. Reading *dicitur multipliciter* as his text's able translation of *legesthai pollachōs*, Aquinas equates a term's being said in many ways with something's being predicated analogically *(analogice)*, though Aristotle does not mention *analogia*, and then explains *analogice* by *proportionaliter*, though this latter word does not mean four-term proportionality but rather proportion in its broad sense as signifying any relation (no. 535). When he reiterates Aristotle's examples of healthy, medical, and being, he also adds some points Aristotle left out: *healthy* is predicated by reference to one end, *medical* by reference to one efficient principle, and *being* by reference to one subject (nos. 537–39). This text is close to the earlier one from the *De principiis naturae*, although *attribuere* is not mentioned. One can also perceive the Aristotelian origin of the examples Aquinas uses throughout his career for multivocal, referential analogy.

3. *Sententia super Metaphysicam 5.8.879*. This late text comments on Aristotle's *Metaphysics* 5.6.1016b31–35, which states that things analogically one are related to each other as a third thing is to a fourth. Thomas writes:

Things which are one by proportion or analogy are in accord with one another because they are related to each other as a third thing is to a fourth. But this may be understood in two ways: either two things have different relations *(habitudo)* to

---

other places where Thomas uses *attribuere* in explaining analogy, and these texts seem to understand the term as a synonym for predication (*Quod.* 9.2.2; *SCG* 1.33.291; *CT* 1.27.18–23; cf. *DDN* 11.2.897). Bernard Montagnes (*La doctrine de l'analogie de l'être d'après saint Thomas d'Aquin*, Philosophes Médiévaux 6 [Louvain/Paris: Publications Universitaires/Béatrice-Nauwelaerts, 1963], pp. 32, n. 16; 174–80) tells us that after the *De principiis naturae*, *attributio* is never again used with the same sense in Thomas' works. He borrowed his vocabulary from the Arabic-Latin translation of Aristotle's *Metaphysics (Metaphysica Nova)*, particularly *comparatio* and *attributio* (this latter translating the Greek preposition *pros*), while the details of his exposition closely followed Averroes' Commentary on Aristotle's *Metaphysics* IV, c. 2. For more interesting comparative details on Aquinas' use of Averroes, see John Wippel, *The Metaphysical Thought of Thomas Aquinas: From Finite Being to Uncreated Being* (Washington, DC: CUA, 2000), p. 76, n. 44.

something one (as *healthy* said of urine signifies the relation of the sign of health, and *healthy* said of medicine signifies the relation of the cause of health); or there is the same proportion of two things to two different things (as tranquillity to the ocean and serenity to the air, for tranquillity is the ocean's calm and the air's serenity).

He preserves Aristotle's original sense of proportionality both in the opening general statement and in the second member of the ensuing division, but he also slips in analogy as a two-term *proportio* based on a direct relation, all the while purporting to describe two types of four-term proportionality. But clearly the two types of proportionality are very diverse, for the ways urine and medicine are related to health do not keep the same proportion, whereas the same proportion is preserved in the example about the ocean and the air. Thomas has rather artificially forced the inclusion of the first member of the division under the rubric of proportionality, whose proper meaning does require that sameness of proportion be kept within each set of terms.[50]

4. *Sententia Libri Ethicorum* 1.7.168–213. This late text comments on *Nicomachean Ethics* 1.4.1096b14–29,[51] where Aristotle asks how the good is meant. Surely not like things purely equivocal in meaning; rather, things are good by being from one *(aph' henos)*, or by doing all in relation to one *(pros hen)*, or still more, according to analogy, for as sight is in the body so mind is in the soul. He gives an example of his third type but not of the first two.

Aquinas comments:

One name is said of many according to meanings not totally diverse but agreeing in something one. Sometimes, because they are referred *(referre)* to one principle, as something is called military either because it is a soldier's weapon (as a sword), or part of his armor (as a breastplate), or because it is his means of transport (as a horse). Sometimes, because they are referred to one end, as medicine is called healthy because it fosters health, diet because it preserves health, and urine because it signifies health. Sometimes, according to different relations *(proportio)* to the same subject, as quality is called a being because it is a per se disposition of being, i.e., of substance, and quantity because it measures substance, and so on for

---

50. For another instance where proportionality and proportion alternate as meanings of *analogia*, see *Meta.* 9.5.1826–29.

51. Chapter 6 in the McKeon edition.

the rest; or according to one relation to different subjects, for sight has the same relation to the body as intellect has to the soul, and hence as sight is a power of a bodily organ, so is intellect a power of the soul without the body's participation.

Thomas fleshes out Aristotle's first two types with his own examples and preserves Aristotle's only example for his own fourth type. We can now appreciate Aristotle's influence upon Thomas' division of analogy, even as far back as the *De principiis naturae.* In the present text, *referre* plays the same role as *attribuere* did in the *De principiis,* which shows that both denote the necessary reference all multivocal analogical meanings must bear toward some one real thing; and it is clear the *proportio* of the third type must mean relation, for the parallel text above from *Meta.* 5.8.879 uses *habitudo* (relation) in place of *proportio.* Most importantly, although Aristotle offers only a threefold division, and Thomas recognizes the fact by only repeating *sometimes* thrice, he nevertheless subdivides the third Aristotelian type into two members, and not too cleanly, for the first member of his third type talks about "*different* relations *(proportio)* to the same subject" (á la multivocal analogy), whereas a few lines after the long quote from above he himself acknowledges that *analogia* (understand: analogy of proportionality) means "the same proportion." Once again, Thomas has managed to slip in his own meaning of analogy as "multivocal reference to one," appearing all the while as if he were offering just another subtype of the category of analogy of proportionality.

These four texts demonstrate the remarkable unity of Thomas' thought from the very beginning to almost the very end of his career. The *attribuere* of text 1 is synonymous with the *referre* of text 4, as is the *habitudo* of text 3 with the *proportio* of text 4. The fourth text gives him two of the three terms for his threefold division of multivocal analogy by reference to one (principle *[aph' henos],* and end *[pros hen]*), to which he adds the relation to one subject;[52] while the second text presents him with his most frequent examples (healthy, medical, and being). He can use the threefold division on his own (text 1), or identify it with *analogia* in the course of a commentary even when Aristotle does not use the word (text

52. Aquinas received the third member, subject, from his reading of Averroes' commentary on the *Metaphysics* (Montagnes, *Doctrine,* pp. 178–80).

2). He must perform a little intellectual gymnastics in order to include his "different proportions to one" as one of the types of an analogy/proportionality that always comprises the "same proportion" of two things to two others (texts 3 and 4). Thus, *proportio* retains its uncanny ability to mean either a two-term direct relation or a four-term proportionality, the senses lying side by side in his expositions due to Aristotle's authority. Thomas divides analogy into those terms that keep the same proportion when two are related to another two, and those terms that signify different relations to something one; he will then subdivide the second member according to what the "one" is: end, principle, or subject.

IV. *Analogy of Attribution, Proper Proportionality, and Cajetan's Interpretation*

Even though there is no intention of reploughing thoroughly furrowed earth, we can no longer ignore the looming figure of Cardinal Cajetan de Vio (1469–1534), the eminent Dominican scholastic and Augsburg debater of Martin Luther, and we must briefly explicate his interpretation of Aquinas' theory of analogy, which until about forty years ago wielded enormous influence within Thomistic circles.[53] For two reasons this is not simply a historical exercise. First, the position of Cajetan and his followers on analogy of attribution versus analogy of proper proportionality is contrary to the stance of the present study and calls for some response. Second, at this point in our exposition of the various meanings of analogy in Aquinas, the treatment of Cajetan as commentator on Aquinas will also provide the added benefit of throwing further light upon two of the topics already discussed in this chapter: the nature of analogy as referential mul-

---

53. For more on Cajetan's interpretation and influence, see Hampus Lyttkens, *The Analogy between God and the World*, trans. A. Poignant (Uppsala: Almqvist and Wiksells, 1952), pp. 205–25; Montagnes, *Doctrine*, pp. 126–50; Klubertanz, *Aquinas on Analogy*, pp. 461–62; Henry Chavannes, *L'Analogie*, pp. 73–90; William Hill, *Knowing the Unknown God* (New York: Philosophical Library, 1971), pp. 1–29; Ralph McInerny, *The Logic of Analogy: An Interpretation of St. Thomas* (The Hague: Nijhoff, 1961), pp. 3–23; in *Aquinas and Analogy* (Washington, DC: CUA, 1996), McInerny gives a more concise and updated version of some of the same themes from *Logic of Analogy* and *Studies in Analogy*.

tivocity, which Cajetan calls analogy of attribution; and Aquinas' use of the broad meaning of *proportio*, which is what ultimately empowers his understanding of analogy as direct rapport, even in contexts dealing with the relationship between God and creatures.

Cajetan wrote his highly consequential *De nominum analogia* in 1498.[54] Basing his interpretation upon a few of Thomas' early texts (*SS* 1.19.5.2 ad1, and a few early passages from the *De veritate*, especially 2.11) and one later text (*Ethic.* 1.7.198–213), Cajetan offers a fourfold division of analogy and reduces all intrinsically predicated analogous terms to the so-called analogy of proper proportionality, thus permitting only an *extrinsic* analogy of attribution. In essence, he combines *SS* 1.19.5.2 ad1, which discusses the distinction between extrinsic and intrinsic naming and tenders a threefold division of analogy, with several texts from the *De veritate*, which permit the relation between creature and Creator to be expressed only according to a four-term proportionality. On the basis of this combination he announces the general principle that all intrinsic analogous predication is by way of proper proportionality.

In the first chapter, Cajetan divides analogy into the three types Thomas lays out in *SS* 1.19.5.2 ad1: analogy according to being *(esse)* but not according to understanding *(intentio)*; analogy according to understanding but not according to being; and analogy according to being and understanding. Cajetan calls the first type the analogy of inequality, though he does not consider it a true analogy since it holds for all genera vis-à-vis their species.[55] It plays a minor role in Thomas' thought and shall not detain us further.

The second chapter discusses the second type, the analogy of attribu-

---

54. *De nominum analogia et de conceptu entis,* ed. P. N. Zammit (Rome: Angelicum, 1934); English translation in *The Analogy of Names and the Concept of Being,* trans. E. A. Bushinski and H. J. Koren, with annotations, Duquesne Studies, Philosophical Series, no. 4 (Pittsburgh: Duquesne University, 1953).

55. Armand Maurer, offering a modern rendition of Cajetan's first type ("St. Thomas and the Analogy of Genus," *NS* 29 [1955]: 127–44), thinks Thomas means that, at the level of existential participation, every generic meaning is shared in unequally by its species. Maurer differs from Cajetan in that he thinks the analogy of genus is a genuine analogy. Agreeing with the Maurer/Cajetan position are Cornelio Fabro (*La nozione metafisica di partecipazione secondo S. Tommaso d'Aquino,* 2nd ed. [Turin: Società editrice internazionale,

tion, where the perfection really exists only in the prime analogate but is attributed to the secondary analogates by reason of some extrinsic relation (cause, sign, etc.). This type of analogy always involves extrinsic predication in the secondary analogates. Cajetan's examples of extrinsic attribution are Aristotle's famous *healthy* and *medical.* Analogy of attribution involves a common word that implies an identical reality referred to diversely.

Linking the third type of analogy mentioned in *SS* 1.19.5.2 ad1 with the proportionality discussed in *DV* 2.11 and elsewhere, chapter 3 names this third type the analogy of proportionality. Since this type of analogy predicates inherent perfections of each analogate, it is the most useful one for metaphysics. Cajetan divides it into proper and metaphorical proportionality. There are, then, four kinds of analogy: inequality, attribution, metaphorical proportionality, and proper proportionality, although only the last is genuine analogy, as the Greeks by their use of *analogia* have taught us.

In the rest of his work (chapters 4–11) Cajetan will attempt to show how the analogous concept in proper proportionality is one, how it is neither univocal nor equivocal, and how all the analogates are intrinsic and primary. Analogy of proper proportionality involves a term that transcends all the analogates, possesses a unified meaning proportionally the same, and abstracts from the proper concepts of the analogates. The unity of the analogical concept keeps it from being used equivocally (chap. 10). What is this unity? George Klubertanz writes:

First, there is a clear concept that perfectly represents the relation in one of the analogates and imperfectly represents the others; this concept is simply many concepts and only proportionately one concept. Secondly, there is a "confused" concept which only imperfectly represents the relation in the analogates and so is simply one concept, though it is proportionately many. The clear multiple concepts become the common concept by a special abstraction in which the particular modes are run together (con-fused); the single, common but confused concept becomes one of the clear concepts by way of fuller expression.[56]

1950], pp. 168–78) and Bernard Montagnes, *Doctrine,* p. 61, n. 100. Disagreeing with the analogy-as-genus position are George Klubertanz, *Aquinas on Analogy,* pp. 100–103, 108–9; and Ralph McInerny, *Logic of Analogy,* pp. 98–122.

56. Klubertanz, *Aquinas on Analogy,* p. 462.

For the next four and a half centuries, Cajetan's theory of analogy received almost universal adulation in Scholastic circles and was enthroned as the correct interpretation of Aquinas on analogy.[57] Cajetan's adherents in the middle third of the twentieth century included Antonin Sertillanges, Maurilio Penido, Gerald Phelan, Charles Journet, Eric Mascall, James Anderson, and Jacques Maritain.[58] Their theory of analogy is generally highly conceptualist and beholden to the characteristically Cajetanian interpretation of those few early texts of Aquinas. James Ross presents an interesting contrast in that at various stages of his intellectual evolution he is either a party to or a corrector of the Cajetanian tradition.[59] Whereas his earlier work follows Cajetan's views on the analogies of attribution and proper proportionality, his *Portraying Analogy*, criticizing both Aquinas and Cajetan for their linguistic atomism, can still agree with Cajetan about the centrality of the analogy of proper proportionality while also disagreeing with his insistence that the analogy of attribution is only extrinsic.[60]

While the break from Cajetan may have begun as early as the 1920s,[61] it did not get up a full head of steam until the 1950s–60s. In 1952–53, Hampus Lyttkens and Santiago Ramírez[62] began to question the equivalence

---

57. There were a few exceptions, such as Francisco Suarez (1548–1617), who contends that analogy of proportionality is always metaphorical and that analogy of attribution may be either intrinsic or extrinsic. See Lyttkens, *Analogy*, pp. 234–41; Chavannes, *L'Analogie*, pp. 100–105.

58. A. Sertillanges, *Les grandes thèses de la philosophie thomiste* (Paris: Bloud, 1928), pp. 48–49, 70–72; M. Penido, *Le rôle de l'analogie en théologie dogmatique*, BibThom 15 (Paris: Vrin, 1931); Gerald Phelan, *Saint Thomas and Analogy*, Aquinas Lecture 1941 (Milwaukee: Marquette, 1941); Charles Journet, *The Dark Knowledge of God*, trans. J. F. Anderson (London: Sheed and Ward, 1948), pp. 5–7, 22, n. 10; Eric Mascall, *Existence and Analogy* (London: Longmans, 1949); James Anderson, *The Bond of Being* (St. Louis: Herder, 1949); Jacques Maritain, *The Degrees of Knowledge*, trans. under the supervision of G. B. Phelan from 4th French ed. (New York: Scribner, 1959), pp. 418–21.

59. "A Critical Analysis of the Theory of Analogy of St. Thomas Aquinas" (Ph.D. dissertation, Brown University, 1958); "Analogy as a Rule of Meaning for Religious Language," *IPQ* 1 (1961): 468–502; Review of *The Logic of Analogy*, by Ralph McInerny, *IPQ* 2 (1962): 633–42; "Reply of Professor Ross," *IPQ* 2 (1962): 658–62; "A New Theory of Analogy," *PACPA* 44 (1970): 70–85; *Portraying Analogy* (Cambridge: Cambridge University, 1981).

60. James Ross, *Portraying Analogy*, pp. 124–33, 164–65.

61. So Klubertanz, *Aquinas on Analogy*, p. 462.

62. Lyttkens, *Analogy* (1952), pp. 270–71, 296–97; Ramírez, *De analogia*, vol. 2 (in four parts) of *Edición de las obras completas de Santiago Ramírez, O.P.*, ed. V. Rodriguez (Madrid:

Cajetan had postulated between *SS* 1.19.5.2 ad1 and *DV* 2.11 in order to arrive at his fourfold division of analogy, and found that the two texts are not parallel. Lyttkens also devised the most telling objections against proper proportionality, showing that it is neither primary nor free of internal problems. It is not primary because it is only due to the causal analogy that there is anything really interesting in it, and a direct analogy of proportion must lie behind every analogy of proper proportionality, for the two terms dealing with God on one side of the proportionality are themselves analogous, and there can only be an infinite regress if proportionality itself attempts to establish their analogicity. The most devastating internal problem of proper proportionality is its conceptual unity, which is highly suspect.[63]

The critique of Cajetan continued into the 1960s. Klubertanz contended that after 1256–57 Thomas totally abandoned proportionality because he must have realized that it either leads to agnosticism about one of the analogates or can make only trivial assertions while simply reformulating previous knowledge of the analogates. The proportionality of the *De veritate* was a temporary and isolated position to which Thomas never returned.[64] Ralph McInerny marshaled trenchant reasons against Cajetan's insistence that all analogy of attribution is extrinsic, proving that analogy for Thomas, formally as such, is quite neutral with regard to whether the

---

Instituto de Filosofia "Luis Vives," 1970–72), 2/4:1811–50; the original article was from *Sapientia* 8 (1953): 166–92.

63. Lyttkens, *Analogy*, pp. 49–54, 63–74. Other voices were also raised against Cajetan in the 1950s. Pannenberg argues against him that analogy of attribution is basic in Thomas and undergirds the analogy of proper proportionality ("Analogie und Offenbarung: Eine kritische Untersuchung der Geschichte des Analogiebegriffs in der Gotteserkenntnis" [Habilitationsschrift, Heidelberg, 1955], pp. 105–31). Sister Thomas Flanigan ("The Use of Analogy in the *Summa contra gentiles,*" *MSch* 35 [1957]: 21–37) and Ralph Masiello ("The Analogy of Proportion according to the Metaphysics of St. Thomas," *MSch* 35 [1958]: 91–105) show how, in the works they study, Thomas gives priority to analogy of proportion over analogy of proportionality.

64. *Aquinas on Analogy* (1960), pp. 27, 86–100, 109–10. Although Cornelio Fabro thinks that proportionality in Thomas is purely formal and posterior to attribution and proportion, he still believes that it remained an important part of his teaching on analogy (*Participation et causalité selon S. Thomas d'Aquin,* preface by L. De Raeymaeker, Chaire Cardinal Mercier 2 [Paris/Louvain: Béatrice-Nauwelaerts/Publications Universitaires, 1961], pp. 510, 527, 636–37).

attribute in question belongs intrinsically to the subject or not.[65] Bernard Montagnes was in accord with Klubertanz that Thomas accepted proportionality early on in his career and later abandoned it, but he gave another reason for the switch. In the *De veritate*, where Thomas identified every multivocal, referential analogy with a determinate relation that would allow us to know God perfectly, and where he saw the analogy of direct rapport as suppressing the infinite distance that separates creatures from God, he had recourse to proportionality in order to preserve God's transcendence both noetically and ontologically. In his later works, however, where he understood God as pure act and as the productive cause at the heart of being, God could create other beings that might be directly related to him without loss of the divine transcendence, and thus proportionality was no longer necessary.[66]

Without denying the reasons put forth by Klubertanz and Montagnes, it is time to delve more closely into the diachronic pattern[67] of Aquinas'

65. *Logic of Analogy* (1961), chap. 1 (and throughout his more recent *Aquinas and Analogy*).

66. *Doctrine* (1963), pp. 7–10, 65–66, 75–93. On p. 93 he also gives one of Klubertanz's reasons: that Thomas must have realized that the ultimate effect of proportionality is agnosticism. For other literature on the Cajetanian problematic, see M. S. O'Neill, "Some Remarks on the Analogy of God and Creatures in St. Thomas Aquinas," *MS* 23 (1961): 206–15; Battista Mondin, *The Principle of Analogy in Protestant and Catholic Theology*, 2nd ed. (The Hague: Nijhoff, 1968), pp. 35–51, 100–102; Robert Meagher, "Thomas Aquinas and Analogy: A Textual Analysis," *Thomist* 34 (1970): 230–53; David Burrell, *Analogy and Philosophical Language* (New Haven: Yale, 1973), pp. 119–24; Tobias Chapman, "Analogy," *Thomist* 39 (1975): 127–41; Harry Wolfson, *Studies*, 2:518–22; Paul Kuntz, "The Analogy of Degrees of Being: A Critique of Cajetan's *Analogy of Names*," *NS* 56 (1982): 51–79; Paul Tirot, "Autour du debat sur l'analogie de proportionnalité propre chez saint Thomas d'Aquin," *Angelicum* 63 (1986): 90–125. Cf. Albert Patfoort, "La place de l'analogie dans la pensée de S. Thomas d'Aquin," *RSPT* 76 (1992): 235–54. In a recent summarizing statement as to where Cajetan went wrong, Wippel writes that he "has unfortunately joined two members of Thomas's threefold division of analogy as found in *In I Sent.*, d. 19, q. 5, a. 2, ad 1—analogy *secundum intentionem tantum et non secundum esse* and analogy *secundum intentionem et secundum esse*—with the analogy of proportion (attribution) and analogy of proportionality distinguished in the troublesome text from *De veritate*, q. 2, a. 11. He has then used this artificial schema to control his understanding of Thomas's many other discussions of analogy" (*Metaphysical Thought*, p. 90, n. 87; cf. pp. 548–55).

67. According to Edward Schillebeeckx, Aquinas early on described the relation of creature to creator by *proportio*, and then in *SS* 3.1.1.1 ad3 and 4.49.2.1 ad6, as well as a few early questions of the *De Veritate*, used *proportionalitas* to describe the same relation; after

understanding of *proportio* as yet another reason for his switch between proportion and proportionality. This review will conclude our discussion of Cajetan as well as underscore the crucial importance of *proportio* for Aquinas' view of analogy. We will discuss in their probable chronological order nine of the texts most crucial for resolving part of the issue about analogy as attribution versus analogy as proportionality: two from the *Sentences*, five from the *De veritate*, one from the quodlibetal disputations, and one from the commentary on Aristotle's *Nicomachean Ethics*.

1. *Scriptum super Libros Sententiarum* 3.1.1.1 ad3. In this text from around 1254–55, an objection is raised against God and humanity's being able to be united in the Incarnation on the grounds that there can be no proportion between God and creature. Thomas distinguishes *proportio* as the exact measurement of two quantities (which can happen only between two finite quantities) from *proportio* as the "relation of order." In this latter sense, matter and form, mover and moved, and agent and patient are said to be proportional *(proportionalis)* according to a certain proportionality *(proportionalitas)*.[68] In the same way, such a proportion, and even a union, can obtain between God and creature, even though they are infinitely distant.

---

resorting to both terms in *DV* 23.7 ad9, he afterward dropped *proportionalitas* altogether ("The Non-Conceptual Intellectual Dimension in Our Knowledge of God according to Aquinas," in *Revelation and Theology*, trans. N. D. Smith, 2 vols. [New York: Sheed and Ward, 1968], 2:181–93). According to Klubertanz, however (*Aquinas on Analogy*, table on p. 21), *proportio* did not make an appearance in the first book of Thomas' *Sentences*. Acknowledging that *proportio* is not used in the first two books of the Sentences, Montagnes argues (*Doctrine*, pp. 71–81) that in several texts from those two books (*SS* 1.prol.1.2 ad2; 1.35.1.4; 1.48.1.1; 2.16.1.1 ad3) Aquinas still preserves the meaning of analogy as a direct proportion or relation to God wherein the creature imperfectly participates and imitates what God perfectly and essentially is, and that after rejecting *proportio* and retaining *proportionalitas* in *DV* 2.11 and elsewhere, in later writings (*SCG* 1.34; *DP* 7.7; *ST* 1.13.5) he returns to the basic position he took in the *Sentences* but now with a terminology of *proportio* based on God's efficient causality rather than *imitatio* based on exemplarism. For positions similar to that of Montagnes, see Pierre Faucon, *Aspects néoplatoniciens de la doctrine de saint Thomas d'Aquin* (Paris/Lille: Champion/University III, 1975), pp. 622–31, who sees Thomas as having later changed back to the more metaphysical, Neoplatonic approach of direct rapport; and Jan Walgrave, *Selected Writings*, ed. G. de Schrijver and J. Kelly, Bibliotheca Ephemeridum Theologicarum Lovaniensium 57 (Louvain: University Press, 1982), pp. 25–35.

68. It does not make any great difference if one chooses the alternative readings *proportionabilia* and *proportionabilitas* instead.

This also may be a very rare instance where *proportionalitas* does not mean a four-term proportionality or likeness of proportions, for Thomas explains the terminology by saying that just as an agent is able to cause an effect so a patient is able to receive that same effect. While the grammar looks like a four-term proportionality, the "same proportion" always supposed to be expressed by such a proportionality is not in evidence, for the agent's causing is not the same as the patient's receiving. In this text, *proportionalitas* seems to furnish Thomas a manner of expressing, from different though correlative standpoints, the direct relation or *proportio* between the entities in question.

2. *Scriptum super Libros Sententiarum* 4.49.2.1 ad6. The objection states that we cannot see God's essence in the beatific vision since the finite and the infinite cannot be proportioned.[69] Two replies are offered. First, there cannot be any *proportio* between the infinite and finite, because "the amount by which the infinite exceeds the finite is not determinate"; but there can be *proportionalitas*, for the finite is equated to the finite as the infinite to the infinite. Second, our intellect can be proportioned to God (as matter is *proportionata* to form), if *proportio* is extended, beyond signifying a relation of finite quantities, to mean "any relation of one thing to another." Thomas offers two solutions but does not decisively settle for either. He mentions standard four-term proportionality and both the broad and narrow senses of proportion, and would seemingly opt for proportionality if the only other option were the narrow sense of proportion. However, in the very next response (ad7) it seems that *proportionalitas* and *proportionatus* are synonymous, which is a situation similar to that in text 1 above. At this stage in his thought, Thomas' vocabulary of *proportio* and *proportionalitas* is fluid and oscillating.

3. *De Veritate* 2.3 ad4. The question is whether God can know anything other than himself, and the objection turns once again on the lack of proportion between the finite and the infinite. Thomas distinguishes only the

---

69. The reason given is based on a saying of Aristotle (*On the Heavens* 1.7.275a11–14); see *Caelo* 1.14.139. Thomas announces the same viewpoint elsewhere: if two things are proportioned, then they can measure one another; but God exceeds every creature infinitely and thus "there is no commensuration or proportion of any creature to him" (*Decretalem* 1.191–207; cf. 2.273–76).

narrow sense of proportion from proportionality, realizes that such proportion cannot obtain between God and creature, and thus opts for proportionality, in which the infinite can equal the infinite just as the finite can equal the finite. Surprisingly, he has come down solidly on the side of proportionality in a text written considerably less than a year after text 2,[70] where he furnished two solutions but did not decide firmly for either one.

4. *De Veritate* 2.11. The article asks whether knowledge can be predicated analogically of God and ourselves. Thomas distinguishes proportion in its narrow sense from proportionality, remarking that since the former, but not the latter, implies a "determinate relation," names such as *being* and *goodness* are said of God and creature only according to the analogy of proportionality, "because no creature has such a relation to God that through it the divine perfection may be delimited."

5. *De Veritate* 3.1 ad7. The article asks whether ideas exist in God, and this short response simply repeats the seemingly exhaustive division between proportion in its narrow sense and proportionality.

6. *De Veritate* 8.1 ad6. Around mid 1257 this response takes up once again the objection against the created intellect's capacity to see God based on the familiar problematic of the mutual lack of proportion between finitude and infinity. It delineates between the strict and broad senses of proportion and claims, on the basis of the second meaning, that the creature is proportioned to see God, although "in terms of the level of power there can be no proportion on account of the infinite distance." So soon after texts 3 through 5, and barely a year after text 2, proportionality is nowhere to be seen.

7. *Quaestio de Quodlibet* 10.8.1 ad1. This response faces the same objection as in text 2 and was disputed no later than three years after it.[71] Thom-

---

70. *De veritate* was written from 1256 to 1259, which means questions two and three are probably from fall–winter of 1256, or at least winter of 1257, if we assume Thomas wrote the questions in the sequence of their final redaction. Also, as *SS* 4.49 is almost at the end of the *Sentences*, it was likely written in the summer or fall of 1256 (assuming the same as with the *De veritate*), since the writing of the *Sentences* flowed over into the beginning of Thomas' term as master at Paris, which began in Spring of 1256 (Jean-Pierre Torrell, *Saint Thomas Aquinas*, vol. 1, *The Person and His Work*, trans. Robert Royal [Washington, DC: CUA, 1996], p. 45 and n. 35).

71. Since most scholars agree *Quod.* 10 was written sometime during Thomas' first mas-

as forsakes proportionality entirely, simply differentiating the narrow from the broad meaning of proportion and opting for the latter.

8. *De Veritate* 23.7 ad9. Probably written in early to mid 1259, the question asks whether our will should be conformed to the divine will, and the objection is the familiar one based on infinity. As he did in text 2, Thomas here presents us with two solutions without showing any strong preference for either. In the first solution, he avers that while we cannot be "proportioned" to God according to the narrow meaning of proportion, we can be proportioned when the word means any relation of one thing to another, since we are related to God inasmuch as we have been made by God and are subject to God. To help us grasp what he means by *proportio*, he gives an example of what he calls a "likeness of proportions: as the ruler is related to the city, so is the pilot to the ship." Although at first blush it looks like he is explaining *proportio* by an example of proportionality, he is actually pointing out that when we call a four-term proportionality a likeness of two-term proportions, then each two-member unit is itself a direct relation or rapport of one thing to another (the ruler is related to the city, etc.), and that this is the way we are related to God as our maker and ruler. The second solution hinges on proportionality, for although the finite and the infinite cannot be directly proportioned, they can be made proportionable through a four-term proportionality. Thus, as the infinite is equal to the infinite, so is the finite equal to the finite; and as God is related to the realities that belong to him, so is the creature related to the realities that belong to it *(propria).*[72]

Let us pause and harvest some results from these eight texts before proceeding to the ninth. First, there are three different divisions in them pertaining to *proportio* and *proportionalitas:* a twofold division, between the

---

tership at Paris (1256–59), it can be no later than summer/fall of 1259 (Torrell, *Thomas Aquinas,* 1:208–11). R.-A. Gauthier, the editor of the critical Leonine edition of the *Quaestiones de quodlibet* (vol. 25, Paris, 1996), places it sometime in 1258, but the dating of individual questions is uncertain.

72. This is Cajetan's "proper proportionality," infrequently used in practice by Thomas. For another example, see *ST* 1-2.3.5 ad1. *BDT* 1.2 ad3, written not more than about two years before *DV* 23.7, asks whether the human mind can know God and, abandoning proportionality altogether, declares that the creature is directly related to God as the caused is to the cause and the knower to the knowable.

narrow and broad senses of *proportio* (texts 1, 6, and 7); a twofold division, between the narrow sense of *proportio* and *proportionalitas* (texts 3–5); and a threefold division, comprising both senses of *proportio* and *proportionalitas* (texts 2 and 8). It is crucial to observe that Thomas decisively chooses proportionality *only* when it appears in the texts of the middle division above, where he is struggling with the problem of God's infinity while *simultaneously* ignoring the broad sense of *proportio*.[73]

Second, the chronology is somewhat as follows. Text 1 is the first time *proportio* appears in Aquinas' works as the basis for the solution to the problem of how to relate the finite and the infinite. Four-term proportionality is first proposed in text 2 (second half of 1256) as one of two possible solutions to the problem, but it is not until texts 3–5 (from fall 1256 through winter 1257), which leave out the broad meaning of proportion entirely, that proportionality is enshrined as the only option for a successful solution. Nevertheless, texts 6 and 7 (mid 1257 for 6 and sometime between 1256 and 1259 for 7) reinstate the broad meaning of proportion and disenfranchise proportionality. And then in text 8 (mid 1259) proportionality regains the position it had in text 2 as one of two possible solutions—and after that disappears. Thus, only from mid 1256 to mid 1259 was proportionality even suggested as a possible solution to the problem of relating the finite and the infinite, and only for a few months (however long it took Thomas to write fourteen articles of the *De veritate*, from 2.3 to 3.1) was it put forward as the only solution.[74]

Third, how can we explain the changes we have just seen? Montagnes contends that the final solution had to wait until Aquinas' philosophy and

73. Montagnes is incorrect, then, when he states that in the texts from the *De veritate* Thomas is opposing proportionality to *proportio* in both its strict and broad senses (*Doctrine*, p. 77, n. 23), for Thomas has only the narrow sense in mind in texts 3–5.

74. This chronology assumes, once again, that Thomas wrote the articles in the order they appear in our present editions. Further, if we could somehow push *DV* 23 back in time closer to *SS* 4.49, it would make the sequence of changes more comprehensible: Thomas would have chosen *proportio* as the solution in the earliest text (1), then tentatively put forward both *proportio* and *proportionalitas* as possible solutions in the next two texts (2 and 8), then opted for *proportionalitas* alone in the next three (3–5) before returning to his earliest answer in the last two texts (6–7). Alas, our present state of historical knowledge renders *DV* 23 resistant to easy explanation.

theology were profound enough to handle the tough enigma of divine infinity and finitude's relation to it; but we find him, as early as *SS* 3.1 in 1254–55, coming up with what turns out to be his ultimate solution, and returning to it sometime between 1256 and 1259 after a brief interlude when he lost his way—and all of this happened presumably before his metaphysics and ontology had fully matured. What our analysis has shown is that what Aquinas' ultimate solution hinges on, even in its earliest stages, is his ability to retool and expand the meaning of *proportio*, which from its infancy in Greek philosophy had been closely tied to finding the exact ratios between finite numbers, and to be comfortable enough with its extended sense not to forget it when confronted with God's infinity, for as we have seen, he only decides for proportionality when he also ignores the broad sense of proportion. This broad sense of *proportio* as "direct relation" is the bridge that allows theological attributes to cross from us to God and, more generally, is the philosopher's stone Aquinas utilizes to transmute *analogia* as four-term proportionality into *analogia* as referential multivocity.

9. *Sententia Libri Ethicorum* 1.7.198–213. Thomas is commenting in this text upon Aristotle's attempt to answer the question, How is the good meant? The context of the question is the latter's argument against the Platonic separate Good, or Good in itself. Thomas follows Aristotle in finding three ways in which things may be called good (by reference to one principle, by reference to one end, and by preserving the same proportion in a proportionality), but also slips in a fourth member without warning, as part of the third Aristotelian type, namely, when things have different relations to the same subject (the example is substance and the other categories). He continues:

[Aristotle] states that the good is said about many things . . . insofar as all things depend upon a first principle of goodness, or insofar as they are ordained to one end; for Aristotle did not want to make the separate good the Idea and meaning of all goods, but their principle and end. Or, things are called good even more according to analogy, i.e., according to the same proportion, as sight is the good of the body and intellect the good of the soul. He prefers this third way since it is understood according to a goodness inherent in things, whereas the first two ways are understood according to a separate goodness by which something is not so properly named.

Thomas remarks that Aristotle realizes his first two ways of predicating the good play right into the hands of the Platonists, with their separate, extrinsic Good, even if he insists that the separate good is an efficient and final rather than formal cause of goodness. But the way of analogy as four-term proportionality ensures that goodness will be inherent in things, and that is why it is preferred by Aristotle.

Cajetan, in turn, will see this passage as another proof of Thomas' putative view that all intrinsic attribution is a matter of proper proportionality. But Thomas says that Aristotle prefers the third way, *not* because it is a matter of proportionality (although it happens to be so), but because it involves the intrinsic predication of goodness, as opposed to the extrinsic naming of his first two ways. And Thomas also added his fourth type, not because he viewed it as an instance of proper proportionality but because it was, along with Aristotle's third type, another kind of intrinsic attribution. Thomas is not trying, *pace* Cajetan, to suggest that all intrinsic attribution happens by way of proportionality, or else he would not have included the example of substance and accident under Aristotle's *analogia,* for as Thomas states, being is *not* said of substance and accident by keeping the same proportion (which is required for all proportionality) but by signifying different proportions or relations with respect to the same subject.[75]

In conclusion, there is no good reason to suppose that Aquinas reduces all intrinsic analogous predication to the structures of four-term proportionality. Indeed, there may be warrant for proposing just the reverse, that analogy as proportionality is ultimately grounded in the properties of analogy as referential multivocity, also known as analogy of attribution.

v. The Primacy of Analogy as Referential Multivocity

Aquinas does not discuss in any *ex professo* fashion the primacy of analogy as referential multivocity vis-à-vis analogy as proportionality, but two

---

75. This is a wonderful example of Thomas' wizardry in transmuting *proportio* from one realm to another: *proportio* in the realm of Greek philosophy means a finite, rational ratio involving two numbers, but in Thomas' hands it has metamorphosed into meaning any direct rapport as it crosses the semantic boundary into referential multivocity.

kinds of data may be sufficient for a reasonable interpretation of his thought to draw out his implicit position.

First, there are certain proportionalities whose terms seem to share, according to Aquinas, a common genus or quasi-genus, and thus are ultimately grounded in univocity. In the proportionality "spines are to fish as bones are to animals," he notes it is "as if" the spines and the bones agreed in a single generic or specific nature, namely, that of "being covered with flesh" (*Post.* 2.17.563). Lines and numbers also share the same genus, for they are both augmented in such fashion that they can be put into proportionalities where the proportions alternate (ibid., 2.19.577). In one text, echoes, images, and rainbows are said to be different species of the same genus, reverberation, while in another text they are said to "agree according to analogy," where the context shows analogy of proportionality is meant.[76] This seems anomalous, unless we suppose that sharing a univocal genus is compatible with at least *some* instances of analogy as proportionality. But any such instances of analogy of proportionality sharing a generically common notion must themselves be eventually grounded in the multivocal analogy of direct rapport, for in one of his later works Thomas asserts, quite universally and boldly, that "all univocal terms are reduced to one primary term, not univocal but analogical, which is being" (*ST* 1.13.5 ad1); and being is fundamentally predicated of things according to direct rapport or relation, by which being is said primarily of substance as "that which is" and of all else in relation to substance. If, infrequently, Aquinas does make use of proportionality as regards substance and the nine categorical accidents, this must be understood as a secondary formulation.[77]

Second, if we examine the way Aquinas uses the analogy of proportionality in his treatment of various subjects dealing with God and creation, it

76. *Post.* 2.17.564 and 2.19.577; cf. 1.37.328.

77. He says, for example, that the ten ultimate categories of being participate in essence according to proportionality: as animal is of the essence of humans, so is color of the essence of whiteness, and number of the essence of twoness (*Meta.* 7.4.1334). Nevertheless, in each case the most inclusive essence (substance for humans, quality for whiteness, and quantity for twoness) is already analogical in a more direct, fundamental sense, for just a few lines later he also says that essence is predicated of substance and the nine categorical accidents by reference to one reality, for it is predicated of every accident in relation to substance (*Meta.* 7.4.1337). For two other examples dealing with the ultimate categories of predication,

becomes clear that the analogy of proportionality rests and depends upon a previous kind of knowledge that it itself cannot provide. When he employs proportionality in his treatment of the Trinity, for example, it always serves as a way of trying to understand the nature of the mysterious divine generation and procession, and it always comes after he has already proven, through faith and scripture, that the Trinity exists with certain characteristics.[78] Again, the way the body is united to the soul is a suitable exemplum for how the human is united to the divine in Christ; and the example of bodily life with its needs can be put into a proportionality with the sacraments in order better to understand their nature and function.[79] But we do not first come to realize the actual existence of the incarnation or the sacraments in and through these proportionalities.

Consider some of the other instances of proper proportionality Aquinas employs with respect to God and creation: the infinite is equal to the infinite just as the finite is to the finite (*DV* 23.7 ad9); as our finite understanding grasps finite things so does God's infinite understanding grasp infinite things (*SCG* 1.69.580); as our practical intellect is to what it knows so is God to what he knows (*ST* 1–2.3.5 ad1); just as humans distribute human goods so does God distribute all the goods of the universe, and just as human justice is related to the city or home so does God's justice deal with the whole universe (*SCG* 1.93.790); just as God is related to the things that belong to him so is the creature related to the things that belong to it (*DV* 23.7 ad9). These only work for our instruction insofar as we *already* know certain truths about God and have some inkling of what they might mean for God—which is the preserve of the analogy of referential multivocity.[80]

---

see *De prin.* 6.78–81 and *SS* 3.1.1.1. Montagnes (*Doctrine*, pp. 40–41) and Wippel (*Metaphysical Thought*, pp. 82–86) both contend that, at the level of being and the ten categories, Aquinas' analogy of referential multivocity (called by Wippel "analogy by reference to a first") is more basic than his analogy of proportionality. Wippel (pp. 84–86) also gives a plausible explanation for a seeming counterexample from Aquinas' Commentary on the first book of Aristotle's *Nicomachean Ethics*. See also McInerny, *Aquinas and Analogy*, pp. 105–11.

78. *SCG* 4.2–3 proves through scripture that there are Trinitarian relations, and then 4.11 searches for a deeper way of understanding them. Cf. *Decretalem* 1.337–64.

79. See *De ration.* 6.109–31 for the first and *De articulis* 2.25–69 for the second example.

80. See Günther Pöltner, "Die Repräsentation als Grundlage analogen Sprechens von Gott im Denken des Thomas von Aquin," *SJP* 21–22 (1976–77): 37–43.

What analogy of proportionality can do is help us understand better the nature of the divine attributes by comparing them to various human or creaturely qualities and characteristics that we comprehend more fully.

This interpretation of Aquinas proposes that for him the analogy of proportionality, in the two ways described, is secondary to and dependent upon the analogy of referential multivocity.

vi. The Logical Status of Multivocal Analogy

For Aquinas the analogy of referential multivocity is primarily a logical mean between univocity and pure equivocity and as such is neutral as regards the ontological question of whether a subject possesses an analogous predicate intrinsically or not. That being said, however, it is also true, as a kind of corollary to our main thesis, that Aquinas grounds the analogous predication of the divine attributes in the real similarity between creatures and the Creator-God, and also uses the notion of analogy to refer not merely to logical realities but also to metaphysical structures of causality within the real world.[81]

81. Scholars debate whether Aquinas' understanding of analogy is logical, ontological, or both. Reacting to what he perceives as the Thomistic tradition's overly metaphysical interpretation of analogy, McInerny sees Cajetan as having laid the foundation for such an interpretation by importing foreign metaphysical conclusions into his commentary on Thomas' purely logical doctrine of analogy, where analogy, formally as such, is neither intrinsic nor extrinsic. This metaphysical neutrality of analogy is one of the chief theses of McInerny's *Logic of Analogy*, a position he strongly confirms in *Aquinas and Analogy*. William Hill (*Knowing the Unknown God*, pp. 127–28, 255, n. 40) and David Burrell (*Analogy*, pp. 203, 208) second McInerny's interpretation. But others fault Cajetan for forgetting the ontological foundations that underlie Thomistic analogy. Montagnes writes: "We would address Cajetan with the inverse reproach to that which [McInerny] blames him with, and we would critique him for having excessively separated the logic of analogy from its metaphysical foundation" (*Doctrine*, p. 22, n. 21; cf. pp. 10–11, 150–58); Fabro takes a similar stance (*Participation et causalité*, p. 515); and Wippel also agrees with Montagnes (*Metaphysical Thought*, p. 87, n. 79). For others, however, including the present author, logic and metaphysics go hand in hand in Aquinas' doctrine of analogy. Klubertanz writes: "Analogy arises only when the mind and things both enter into the picture" (*Aquinas on Analogy*, p. 114; cf. pp. 120–23). For Mondin, although analogy is basically a matter of logic and semantics, it cannot be divorced in Thomas' thought from its epistemological and ontologiocal presuppositions (*Principle of Analogy*, pp. 53–84). Colman O'Neill asserts that theological analogy belongs to the linguistic expression of our knowledge of God, but its inspiration is "always ontological" ("Prédication analogique," pp. 81–82).

When Aquinas describes multivocal analogy as a mean between uni-vocity and equivocity, he is obviously taking equivocity in its strict or pure sense, for equivocity broadly taken is the same as multivocal analogy.[82] Pure equivocity is also called equivocity by fortune or chance, for the chance equivocal is predicated of several specifically different realities that, although they bear the same name due to some historical accident or lin-guistic quirk, do not actually possess any common intelligible relation or bond.[83] However, both strict and broad equivocity are opposed to univoc-ity, for the latter always involves the "same meaning," whereas no equivo-cal term of any kind involves the same meaning in all its various uses.[84] Aquinas often calls certain predications equivocal and leaves it to the read-er to decide which kind of equivocity is meant.[85]

In one of his earliest works, the *De principiis naturae* (6.19–41), Aquinas explains how analogy stakes out a middle ground between univocity and pure equivocity. A univocal name is what is predicated of different things according to the same name and the same meaning or definition; an equivocal name is predicated according to the same name but with a dif-ferent signification or definition; and an analogical name is predicated of various subjects according to different meanings that are referred to some-thing one and the same. All three kinds of predication involve the same name being predicated of different subjects; but whereas the univocal term always carries the exact same meaning, and the purely equivocal term bears a completely different meaning as applied to different subjects, the analogical term involves different meanings with a reference to something

82. Pure equivocity is opposed to equivocity understood broadly, which Aquinas identi-fies with the type of analogy (*Meta.* 9.1.1780) by which being (*ens*), for example, can be said to be predicated equivocally (*ST* 1.13.10 ad4). Although purely equivocal terms are reduced to univocal terms, the latter are themselves grounded in the broadly equivocal predication of being (*ST* 1.13.5 ad1). Cf. E. J. Ashworth, "Analogy and Equivocation in Thirteenth-Cen-tury Logic: Aquinas in Context," *MS* 54 (1992): 94–135.

83. *Meta.* 1.14.223; cf. *SCG* 1.42.344; *Herm.* 1.2.21, 1.5.70, 1.9.116; *Post.* 1.19.166; *Ethic.* 1.7.172–201.

84. *Phys.* 7.7.934–37; *Quod.* 3.2.2; *Post.* 1.37.329–30. The univocal term involves "one meaning" and "signifies absolutely the same thing" (*Meta.* 4.7.616; 7.4.1335, 1351).

85. *Herm.* 1.10.124; *Ethic.* 1.7.172–81; *Phys.* 7.8.947; *Meta.* 7.9.1480–81; *DSC* 1; 2; 4; 9 ad9; *DA* 1; 6; 9; 10; *Anima* 2.2.81–104; *Quod.* 3.2.2; 3.8.1; *DE* 4.152–58; *BDT* 5.4 ad3; 6.3; *SS* 2.3.1.1; *DSS* 7–8; *ST* 1.50.2 ad3.

one. Terms predicated analogically have a partial identity and a partial diversity of meaning.[86]

In the *Summa theologiae* we read that analogical predication

is a mean between pure equivocity and simple univocity. For in those things which are said analogically there is neither one meaning, as is the case with univocal names, nor a totally different meaning, as happens with equivocal names; but the name which is said analogically of many signifies different relations to something one: as *healthy* said of urine signifies a sign of animal health, but said of medicine signifies a cause of the same health.[87]

He is even clearer in a passage from a few years later:

Something is predicated of different things in various ways: sometimes according to a meaning totally the same, and then it is said to be predicated of them univocally, as animal of horse and cow; sometimes according to meanings totally diverse, and then it is said to be predicated equivocally of them, as dog of the star and the animal; and sometimes according to meanings which are partly different and partly not different—different inasmuch as they imply different relations, one insofar as those different relations are referred to something one and the same—and then it is said to be predicated analogically, i.e., proportionally, as everything according to its own relation is referred to that one thing.[88]

For Aquinas, analogy formally understood as such is also a logical entity that is neutral as regards the ontological question of whether a subject possesses an analogous predicate intrinsically or not. This ontological neutrality is clear from the manner in which he employs his few stock examples of analogy, since the point he is making in each case is often blind to the metaphysical status of the example and sometimes actually opposed to it.[89] For starters, he uses the substance/accident and health examples, without making any ontological commitments, simply to show that analogy is a matter of primary and secondary meanings with a reference to one reality.[90] Nevertheless, he certainly realizes that the substance/accident ex-

---

86. "Aliquid habet de identitate rationis et aliquid de diversitate" (*SS* 1.21.1.1.2; cf. *SS* 1.22.1.3 ad2, 2.42.1.3).

87. *ST* 1.13.5; same: *ST* 1.13.10.

88. *Meta.* 4.1.535; same: *Meta.* 7.4.1337.

89. For texts demonstrating that material conditions are irrelevant to analogy formally as such, see William Meissner ("Some Notes on a Figure in St. Thomas," *NS* 31 [1957] 68–84), who shows how Thomas can use the same example for different types of analogy.

90. *DE* 6; *SS* 3.33.1.1.2 ad1; 3.33.2.1.1 ad2; *ST* 1.13.6; 3.60.1.

ample is an instance of intrinsic naming,[91] and he is certainly not unaware that the health example is an instance of extrinsic naming.[92] The fact that he can use these examples neutrally without adverting to their ontological status, though he is not ignorant of that status, is a prima facie indication

91. *SS* 1.19.5.2 ad1; *ST* 1.45.4; 1.90.2; 1-2.26.4. Because *being (ens)* principally signifies "the one reality which is substance," and because a predicamental accident is not substance, an accident cannot be being absolutely, but that does not mean it is totally nonbeing either (*Phys.* 1.7.51). Also, being is divided into the ten ultimate categories according to "the diverse modes of being" (*Phys.* 3.5.322; *Quod.* 2.2.1), which implies that each category shares in being. Wippel argues that in addition to holding that being is said analogically of substance and the nine predicamental accidents, Thomas also thinks that being is predicated analogically of the different kinds of finite substances themselves, and even of the individuals within in one and the same species of substance (*Metaphysical Thought*, pp. 90–93).

92. *SS* 1.19.5.2 ad1; *DV* 1.2. Neither food nor urine is called healthy because they possess the inherent form of human bodily health but because they are referred to that health as to a form extrinsic to themselves (*DV* 1.4; 21.4 ad2), for genuine health does not exist except in the animal body (*ST* 1.16.6). Let us quote this latter text more fully, as it brings up an important issue often misunderstood. "When something is predicated univocally of many things, it is found in all of them according to its proper meaning *(ratio propria)*, as animal is found in any species of animal. But when something is said analogically of many things, it is found according to its proper meaning in only one of them, from which the others are named—as healthy is said of animal, urine and medicine; not that health exists except in the animal alone, but from the animal's health the medicine is called healthy insofar as it produces that health, and the urine insofar as it signifies that health. Although health does not exist in either medicine or urine, nevertheless, in each there is something through which the former produces health and the latter signifies it" (*ST* 1.16.6; same: *ST* 1.16.7). Two points are in order. First, extrinsic naming is eventually reduced to some type of intrinsic naming: for example, although neither medicine nor urine (nor food: see *DV* 1.4.200–209) is intrinsically healthy, each possesses *some* inherent quality by which it can be named intrinsically by some other predicate (e.g., ibuprofen may be called "anti-inflammatory" intrinsically because of the nature of its internal chemical structure); and this intrinsic quality is the reason the medicine or urine can be called healthy by an extrinsic name, for the intrinsic quality engenders some kind of intelligible relation as regards the actual bodily health of the animal (e.g., the ibuprofen's inherent anti-inflammatory quality is what permits it to be helpful in promoting bodily health and thus to be called a healthy medicine). Second, *ratio propria* refers to the fullest, the most basic, and the most characteristic meaning of the predicate in question, *not* to the intrinsic possession of the predicate by the subject. Since, in the article just quoted, the term *healthy* as predicated of medicine and urine involves extrinsic naming, some have been led to believe that all so-called analogy of attribution is a matter of extrinsic predication; but the article actually requires an example of extrinsic naming in order to elucidate its main point—that truth is said intrinsically of intellect and extrinsically of other things. Nevertheless, the statement about analogy's *ratio propria* is quite neutral and would hold even for the intrinsic examples of substance and accident: for both substance and accident are quite obviously beings in an intrinsic sense, and yet *being* in its fullest, most basic, and most characteristic meaning is only predicated of substance (*BDH* 2.63–65; *Quod.* 9.2.2; *DSS* 8.109–16; *DDN* 4.9.404).

that their formal structures, and not their ontological content, is what interests him when he invokes them to exemplify multivocal analogy as such.

Furthermore, he sometimes invokes an example of extrinsic naming in order to elucidate the predication of some quality that is quite obviously intrinsic to the subject. Thus, the health example is called upon to explain the fact that every created reality, insofar as it exists, is good (*BDH* 4.125–45); and the same example is employed in contexts where predicates such as *wise* and *good* are meant to apply intrinsically to both God and creatures.[93] He would not use examples of extrinsic naming to clarify points involving intrinsic naming, however, unless the formal structures of analogy and not the ontological content of the examples were what mattered.

One final indication of analogy's metaphysical neutrality is Aquinas' propensity, when discussing the nature of analogy, to line up side by side examples of both intrinsic and extrinsic analogical naming without the slightest hint that they differ as examples of analogy's nature.[94]

Aquinas is not oblivious to the fact that certain material elements in the examples he uses may lead readers astray and is especially solicitous to forestall any misunderstandings whenever he is discussing the perfection terms that apply intrinsically to God and creatures. To an objection attempting to equate the manner in which a creature is called good by relation to the Creator, with the manner in which urine is called healthy by relation to the healthy animal, he responds with the Scholastic's weapon of choice, a distinction:

Something is named by reference to another in two ways. First, when the relation itself is the very meaning of the name, and thus urine is called healthy by relation to the animal's health, for the meaning of healthy as predicated of urine is to be the sign of the animal's health; in such cases, what is named by relation to another is not named by reason of some form inherent to it but from something extrinsic, to which it is referred. Second, when the relation is not the very meaning of the name but its cause. . . . And in this way the creature is called good through its relation to God.[95]

93. *DP* 7.7; *ST* 1.13.5. Similarly, in *Meta.* 7.4.1337, the medical example is summoned in order to help explain the case of substance and accident.

94. *De prin.* 6.36–62; *DV* 2.11; *SCG* 1.34.297–98; *Meta.* 4.1.535–39; 11.3.2196–97; *ST* 1.13.10.

95. *DV* 21.4 ad2. For an interesting commentary on this passage, see James Ross, *Portraying Analogy*, pp. 124–26.

In this manner he preserves both the creature's relation to God and its intrinsic possession of perfection predicates, two things whose concurrence was threatened by the material elements of the health example. Similarly, to an objection arguing that just as *healthy* is said secondarily of medicine because it causes health, so for the same reason should the divine names be said secondarily of the God who causes being, Aquinas answers that the objection would hold if the divine names were said of God only because of the divine causality (as *healthy* is said of medicine because medicine causes health) and not also essentially.[96]

However, Aquinas also grounds the analogous predication of the divine attributes in the real similarity that obtains between creatures and the Creator-God. In his commentary on the *Sentences* he calls the similarity between God and creature a "community of analogy," which occurs because the creature imitates God as much as it can (*SS* 1.24.1.1 ad4). This ontological imitation is the basis for the creature's names: "The creature does not possess being *(esse)* except insofar as it descends from the first being *(ens)*, nor is it named a being *(ens)* except insofar as it imitates the first being; and the case is similar with wisdom and all the other things said of the creature."[97] Thus is the logic of analogical names rooted in the creature's ontological imitation of the divine nature and properties.

Moreover, Thomas also uses the notion of analogy to refer not merely to logical realities but also to metaphysical structures of causality within the real world. He provides us with either a twofold or a threefold division of the efficient or agent cause, in which terms taken originally from the realm of logical predication are applied to real causes in the world. Less frequently, we find three kinds of agent cause: the equivocal cause, in which cause and effect do not agree in either name or meaning (as the sun enkindles the heat of the sublunar world without itself being hot);[98] the

---

96. *ST* 1.13.6; cf. 1.16.1 ad3.

97. *SS* 1.prol.1.2 ad2; "a creature is called wise insofar as it imitates the divine wisdom" (*SS* 1.2.1.2).

98. In the physics Thomas was conversant with, the sun was thought to be an equivocal or nonunivocal cause producing a heat in the sublunary world that is essentially different from what it is as the cause of that heat (*SCG* 1.29.270; 1.31.280; *DM* 1.3; *Phys.* 2.11.242; 8.10.1053; *DDN* 4.3.312; *ST* 1.4.2). Thus the sun cannot be called hot intrinsically but only as an efficient cause (*SS* 2.14.1.2 ad3), that is, heat is said of the sun only as a cause of heat in

univocal cause, in which cause and effect agree in name and meaning (as humans generate humans); and the analogical cause, in which cause and effect agree according to an order of primary and secondary meanings (as God causes the being of creatures).[99]

More often, we find two types of agent cause: the univocal agent, which brings about a form of the same species and "is proportionate to the thing receiving its effect"; and the equivocal agent, which is not proportionate to its effect, so that the effect only attains to some likeness of it (the example of the sun appears again).[100] The twofold schema also appears in the *Summa theologiae* as a division between the univocal and the nonunivocal agent,[101] the latter also called the universal or analogical agent (*ST* 1.13.5 ad1). If we join the two versions of the twofold schema, we find that the universal, nonunivocal, analogical, and equivocal agent all amount to the same thing, if *equivocal* is understood broadly, for nothing is ever predicated purely equivocally of a cause and what it causes, inasmuch as what is caused always bears some likeness to the cause.[102]

Sometimes Thomas even mentions in one breath both realms where analogy functions. In some texts he notes that whereas pure logical equivocity presupposes some univocity, univocal generation in the real world presupposes equivocal generation.[103] But in *ST* 1.13.5 ad1 he notices an iso-

---

other things (*SDC* 12.279). The sun is not "the hottest thing there is," which is fire, but rather something "even greater than the hottest thing" (*Meta.* 2.2.293).

99. *SS* 1.8.1.2; same: 4.1.1.4.4. In *SS* 1.2.1.2 God is, as the exemplar form of things, neither a wholly equivocal, nor a univocal, but rather an analogical cause. *SS* 1.3.1.3 teaches that the creature proceeds from God as from an analogically similar cause because (in the variant from the Parma edition) "every creature imitates him according to the capacity of its nature." In *Meta.* 7.8.1444–47, Thomas bows to the requirements of Aristotle's text and offers a threefold division, unique in his works, between univocal generation, generation that is partly univocal and partly equivocal, and generation that is not at all univocal. For more on the analogical cause, see McInerny, *Logic of Analogy*, pp. 126–35; Norman Kretzmann, *The Metaphysics of Theism: Aquinas' Natural Theology in "Summa contra gentiles" I* (Oxford: Clarendon, 1997), pp. 144–57.

100. *SS* 2.1.2.2; same: *SS* 4.1.1.4.1 ad4; 4.41.1.1.5; *DV* 4.6; *DP* 7.1 ad8; 7.5; 7.6; 7.10; *CT* 1.43; *DDN* 1.3.89; *Meta.* 12.3.2444; *ST* 1.4.2. Cf. Montagnes, *Doctrine*, pp. 47–49, and n. 62.

101. *ST* 1.13.5 ad1; 1.25.2 ad2; 1.45.8 ad3; 1-2.60.1; 3.62.3.

102. *DP* 7.7. "In equivocal generations there must be some likeness between the generator and the generated" (*Meta.* 9.7.1849).

103. *DV* 10.13 ad3; also: *BDT* 1.4 ad4. In these texts and elsewhere (*SCG* 2.21.973; *DP* 7.7 ad7; *ST* 1.13.5 ad1; 1.104.1) he explains that the univocal generator, which causes individuals

morphism between the ontological and logical realms: after acknowledging that purely equivocal terms must be reduced to univocal terms, which is contrary to the situation in causal actions where the nonunivocal agent must precede the univocal agent, he also claims that in predications, as in causal actions, all univocal terms are reduced to a primary analogical term, which is being.[104] He recognizes a close connection between causal actions and logical predications, for just as nonunivocal agents must precede univocal agents in the realm of action, so is the analogical meaning prior to the univocal meaning in the preserve of logic.

In conclusion, multivocal analogy is for Aquinas primarily a logical entity most at home in the domain of words and meanings. But other truths in his metaphysics and theology form the ontological infrastructure that supports and justifies the processes of analogical naming and predication. And in an instructive example of analogy's semantic range and virtuosity, he is able to transfer one of analogy's own analogous senses from the land of logic to the real world's structures of causality.

---

in the species but not the species itself (or else it would have to cause itself), must be reduced to the equivocal generator that causes the species itself.

104. Cf. Klubertanz, *Aquinas on Analogy*, pp. 24–26.

6. The Unity and Diversity of Analogy as a Web of Predication

This chapter delves a little more into the finer though extremely crucial points of Aquinas' analogy of referential multivocity,[1] especially as regards its ordered series of meanings with a reference to one, and its unity and diversity.

1. Primary and Secondary Meanings

Throughout his career Aquinas uses the phrase *per prius et posterius*[2] to denote how analogous names signify according to an interwoven web of primary and secondary meanings. It is absolutely critical to note, moreover, that for him one of the significations of an analogous name (the primary one) is always included in all of the name's other meanings (the secondary ones). For example, substance, which is the primary meaning of the noun *being*, since a substance is a being that exists independently on its own, is included in the definition of that kind of being which is an accident, which is a secondary meaning of *being*, since a categorical accident is

1. Hereafter just "analogy" and its associated grammatical forms, unless otherwise specified.
2. Literally, "through the prior and posterior," that is, through the first and second, or more genially to the ears of English speakers, "primarily and secondarily."

a being that exists in and through a substance;[3] in another of his examples, the adjective *healthy* as predicated of the animal's body is placed in the definition of healthy insofar as it is predicated of urine or medicine, for healthy urine and healthy medicine are called such because they are, respectively, either a sign of or productive of the healthy animal's body.[4] What Aquinas is carefully pointing out is that whenever an analogous term is predicated of different subjects with different meanings (the physician in her office says to the man, "You are healthy"; and the lab assistant a few days later confirms her judgment by saying, "He has healthy urine"), the one meaning of the analogous term that is thought to be basic or primary (for Aquinas, *healthy*'s native home or primary context is presumably the physical wellness of an animal's body) is always referred to or adverted to, at least implicitly, in all the other secondary meanings of the term (no one thinks healthy urine might jump for joy as a healthy calf might, but the *healthy* in "healthy urine" possesses an easily recognizable meaning obtained only by referring to the man's physical health as somehow evidenced by his urine).[5]

Aquinas' most frequent example of analogical names predicated *per prius et posterius* is *being* as predicated of substance and the nine predicamental accidents.[6] But other examples include: *evil* as said primarily of fault and secondarily of punishment (*SS* 2.37.3.2); *potential infinite* as said primarily of quantity and secondarily of motion and time;[7] *health* as said primarily of the healthy person and secondarily of the causes of health (*DP* 7.6); *heaven* as meaning first the supreme outer sphere and secondly other things insofar as they are contained under the supreme sphere (*Caelo* 1.20.199); *one* as said principally of simple realities and secondarily of

3. Substance is "primarily being," and from it are derived all the other categories of accidents, which are only called being insofar as they happen to substance (*Ethic.* 1.6.105–23); accidents are not being absolutely but rather "beings of a being" (*Meta.* 12.1.2419).

4. *ST* 1.13.10; cf. *SS* 3.33.1.1.2 ad1; *SCG* 1.32.289.

5. *ST* 1.13.10 even shows how Christians may predicate the word *God* of different subjects in different contexts, but always with a reference to the one true God, the primary meaning (for Christians, in Aquinas' eyes) of the word *God.*

6. *DE* 6.133–38; *De prin.* 6.56–57; *Meta.* 4.1.539, 543; 4.3.568; 7.4; *Herm.* 1.5.70; 1.8.107; *ST* 1-2.88.1 ad1.

7. *Meta.* 11.10.2354; cf. *Phys.* 3.12.397.

composite realities (*Herm.* 1.10.127); *goodness* as predicated primarily of the virtues and secondarily of what is pleasant or useful;[8] *truth* as predicated principally of intellect and secondarily of things in comparison to intellect (*ST* 1.16.1); *sin* as said primarily of mortal and secondarily of venial sin (*ST* 1–2.88.1 ad1); *sacrament* as primarily meaning a sacred or mysterious reality *(res sacra)* and secondarily an oath or one of the seven sacraments (*ST* 3.60.1 ad3).

We have seen that one of the meanings is called primary because it must be included in all of the other secondary meanings. From other texts it is also clear that by *prius* Thomas is referring to what he variously calls the perfect, total, proper, or complete meaning, which is predicated absolutely and primarily, whereas by *posterius* he is referring to the imperfect meaning, which is predicated relatively and secondarily. In *Metaphysics* 7.5.1031a12–13, Aristotle contends that essence or being belongs to substance most of all, that is, primarily and simply. Thomas picks up on this terminology and remarks that whatever is said *per prius* is said absolutely, and whatever is said *per posterius* is said relatively.[9] The common analogical term is predicated of one thing according to its perfect meaning, and of other things only imperfectly and relatively.[10] A common analogous term is predicated *per prius* of that subject in which the full meaning of the term is found to be true.[11] A name is predicated *per prius* of that reality in which the total meaning of the name is perfectly realized, not of that reality in which the meaning is only partially realized (*ST* 1.33.3). When something is said of many subjects analogically, "it is found according to its proper meaning in only one of them, from which the others are named."[12]

But how are we to detect *which* meaning in an analogical grouping is the proper, complete and perfect one? Although Thomas is silent on the

8. *ST* 1.5.6 ad3. Goodness is also said to be predicated primarily of substance and secondarily of the accidents of substance (*Ethic.* 1.6.105–23).

9. *Meta.* 7.4.1331–33, 1338, 1355.

10. *SS* 2.42.1.3; cf. *SS* 3.33.2.1.1 ad2.

11. ". . . Illud in quo est primo ratio illius communis completa" (*DV* 1.2.49–52). Thomas does not tell us how we know which subject possesses the full meaning.

12. *ST* 1.16.6; whatever is said of things *per prius et posterius* "more properly belongs to that of which it is said primarily" (*SS* 1.22.1.2, *sed contra*).

general question, it is possible from his customary description of the process of analogical naming, and from certain examples such as *healthy* and *medical,* to garner the idea, in more contemporary terms, of something like a web of predication, whose primary meaning is the central thread teased out for various reasons, some of which we recognize today (consider some of the examples from the previous paragraph) as temporally and culturally conditioned. It is plausible he would hold universally that, by observing and analyzing how the predications employing an analogous term actually work—that is, by reflecting upon our intelligent use of language—we can trace the web's connections and intelligibilities back until we spot the central anchoring thread from which the spokes radiate. For him, the primary meaning would be the thread that always tends to show up as connecting or surrounding the others, and it should always be possible to discern it. For example, we see him deciding, on the basis of such an analysis (though it is hardly exhasutive), that the primary meaning of *healthy* is the physical wellness of an animal's body, on the grounds that the intelligible semantic vectors from the other predications of *healthy* all converge upon and transect one another at the point of an animal's bodily health, such that only by reference to that health do the predications involving the secondary meanings of *healthy* partake of intelligibility and truth.[13]

Thomas also tenders a few examples which hint that the primary and secondary meanings of at least some analogous terms are also implicated by the objective truths concerning the relevant realities meant by those terms. *Herm.* 1.8.93 offers the predication of being *(ens)* as an example of how analogical terms participate according to priority and posteriority in the common analogical meaning, "since in the very meaning of being, substance, which is per se being, has priority as regards accident, which is being through another and in another." This priority is ontological, for whereas substance has an absolute essence not dependent on anything

---

13. Thomas' analysis is rudimentary and raises questions about the ease with which he decides the primary meaning. What would he say, for example, about calling a plant healthy? Is this a proper or metaphorical use of *healthy?* If the former, then the animal's body is not a broad enough locus for the primary meaning of *healthy.*

else, an accident depends for its being on its subject, for accidents do not possess being except by existing in a substance (*Meta.* 7.4.1352). The priority of substance in receiving the predication of *being* rests on its ontological independence, just as the posteriority of accident in receiving the same predication is rooted in its real dependence upon substance.[14] A second example of basing predication *per prius* upon ontological priority is found in the case of God, for since the divine being *(esse)* is not received but subsists through itself, God most truly and primarily receives the predication of *being* (*ens*—*SS* 2.37.1.2).

The process of analogical naming, together with the examples we have just seen, suggests that, for Aquinas, the web of primary and secondary meanings only makes sense within a matrix of intelligibly connected predications and, in some cases, of true judgments about the relevant realities. The notion of a web of predication is perhaps quite congenial to many thinkers today, especially those imbued with a lively sense of language's central role in understanding, but for several other reasons many contemporary theorists would be quite reserved about Aquinas' ease at deciding primary meanings and about his reliance upon various objective truths in determining some of those meanings. Nevertheless, the question about *how* to decide primary and secondary meanings need not detract from the validity of viewing analogy as a web of intertwined and interconnected predications.

II. *Reference to an Individual Reality or Nature*

All analogical predication occurs "according to an order or reference *(respectus)* to something one."[15] This "one" is not specifically or conceptually one, but one as an individual reality or nature is one. For example, medicine's or urine's "health" is derived from the health that is in the animal's body, "and the health of the medicine and urine is not other than the health of the animal, which medicine produces and urine signifies" (*ST* 1–2.20.3 ad3). Whenever *healthy* is used as a predicate, then, the same, con-

---

14. For the ontological priority of substance, see *Meta.* 5.13.950–51.
15. *SCG* 1.34.297; same: *CT* 1.27; *Caelo* 1.20.199; cf. *De prin.* 6.33–35.

crete health of the animal is referred to, and thus Thomas can assert that the health of the medicine or urine is really the same as the animal's health. The various meanings of an analogical term are one insofar as the different relations signified are referred "to something one and the same."[16] Again, he is not talking of something one in essence or meaning *(unum ratione)*, as occurs in univocal predicates, but of something "which is one thing as one certain nature."[17]

The individual "one" is what receives the primary signification of an analogical term. For example, all the varied meanings of being are reduced to one first meaning, which is the per se existing, primary subject of other beings: substance.[18] More universally,

All analogous names predicated of many subjects are all necessarily predicated by relation to one thing: and thus that one must be placed in the definition of all. And since the meaning that the name signifies is the definition . . . the analogous name must be predicated primarily of that which is placed in the definition of the others, and secondarily of the others. (*ST* 1.13.6)

---

16. *Meta.* 4.1.535. This reference to something one and the same *(ad unum aliquid et idem)* hearkens back to Aristotle's *pros hen kai mian tina physin* (*Metaphysics* 4.2.1003a33–34).

17. *Meta.* 4.1.536; cf. 537–39; 9.1.1780. In 7.4.1337 he explains that *medical* is said of various things neither equivocally (because equivocals have no relation to something one), nor univocally (since univocals share one meaning), but analogically, through relation to one medical art. This one art remains the same even as the meanings of *medical* vary with respect to the subjects of which it is predicated.

18. *Meta.* 5.13.951; same: 7.4.1331; 11.3.2197. "Being *(ens)* signifies principally the one which is substance" (*Phys.* 1.7.51). In *Meta.* 4.4.584, the various meanings of *ens* are reduced immediately to the one reality of substance without first being led back to one primary meaning. In *SCG* 2.15.923, the analogical predication of *ens* is reduced to an individual reality, which the context of the chapter shows is God. This means that the true primary signification of *being* is not really substance but God, though in our knowledge and naming its first meaning refers to creaturely substance. Bernard Montagnes (*La doctrine de l'analogie de l'être d'après saint Thomas d'Aquin*, Philosophes Médiévaux 6 [Louvain/Paris: Publications Universitaires/Béatrice-Nauwelaerts, 1963], pp. 23, 60–63) thinks that Thomas' teaching on analogy unites the Aristotelian theme of unity of order by reference to a first with the Platonic theme of participation, the former component appearing early on and remaining constant throughout his career. Both predicamental and transcendental analogy became universally a "relation to one," the "one" being either substance or God; and once accident has been referred to substance, both together as creatures—and thus the whole horizontal order—are referred to God.

Analogical names, therefore, are predicated *per prius et posterius* through reference to an individual reality or nature. By speaking this way, and by describing the "one" as an individual reality or nature, in contrast to the noetic, abstract unity of the generic or specific concept characteristic of univocity, Thomas is taking great pains to protect the peculiar logical status of analogy from the depredations of conceptualist or univocist misinterpretations.

III. *God and Creatures*

Aquinas is constantly on the lookout to defend God's transcendence whenever he is discussing our knowledge of God. Some samples of this diligence occur in the first book of his commentary on the *Sentences*, where he is chary of using the phrase *per prius et posterius* to describe the analogical relationship between creatures and God. After acknowledging that creature and Creator agree analogically, he denies that they do so by partaking of some third reality *per prius et posterius;* rather, they harmonize analogically because the creature receives being directly from God and is named a being insofar as it imitates God.[19] But in several other texts from the same work he employs the phrase in a positive manner to describe the analogy between creature and Creator.[20] He rejects the phrase when it appears to imply that God and creature share unequally in a common perfection distinct from and prior to both of them, and accepts it when it can be incorporated into a context where analogy is a direct relation or rapport between the creature and God.[21] He will use the phrase without qualm after the first book of his commentary, but in order to dispel ambiguity he will also distinguish analogy as the relation of "one to

19. *SS* 1.prol.1.2 ad2; 1.35.1.4.

20. *SS* 1.8.1.2; 1.8.4.3 ad1; 1.22.1.2 ad3; 1.25.1.2.

21. George Klubertanz (*St. Thomas Aquinas on Analogy: A Textual Analysis and Systematic Synthesis* [Chicago: Loyola, 1960], pp. 29–31) shows how *per prius et posterius* is neutral until placed in the context of an unequal sharing of a common perfection, or the context of a direct rapport. Thomas' wholesale acceptance of the phrase after the first book of his commentary on the *Sentences* proves that he quickly came to see it exclusively in the context of a direct rapport between God and creation.

one" or "one to another" from analogy as the relation of "many to one" or "two to a third," employing *per prius et posterius* as an explanatory device only for the former types.

Aquinas first mentions the distinction between analogy as a relation of "one to one" versus "two to a third" in *SS* 2.16.1.1 ad3, where he notes that whereas God and creature cannot share in a third reality beyond them, God can be called a being *(ens)* insofar as he is his own act of being *(esse)*, and the creature can be called *ens* insofar as it participates in God's *esse*.[22]

In *SCG* 1.34.297 analogy is presented as happening in two ways: either "many have a relation to something one," for which the example of health is given; or two things are directly related to each other, "as *being* is said of substance and accident insofar as accident has a relation to substance, not insofar as substance and accident are referred to a third thing." Names are not said analogically of God and other things according to the first way, "since we would have to posit something prior to God," but according to the second. Now while Thomas denies that anything can be predicated *per prius* of God as regards the first way, he is not averse, two chapters earlier (*SCG* 1.32.289), to using the full technical expression in a positive sense: "Nothing is predicated of God and other things as if they were of the same order, but according to priority and posteriority *(secundum prius et posterius)*."

DP 7.7 once again lays out a twofold manner of analogical predication:

In one way something is predicated of two things through a relation to yet a third thing, as *being* is predicated of quality and quantity through their relation to substance. Another way is that by which something is predicated of two things through the relation of one to the other, as *being* is predicated of substance and quantity. In the first way, moreover, the third thing, to which the other two things have a relation, must be prior to both of them, as substance is prior to quantity and quality; in the second way this is not so, however, but one must be prior to the other. And thus, since nothing is prior to God but he himself is prior to the creature, the second mode of analogy is appropriate for divine predication and not the first.

22. Cf. *SS* 2.37.1.2. "All things are predicated essentially of God . . . but predications about other things occur through participation" (*SCG* 1.32.289). For similar thoughts from Albert the Great on the type of analogy that obtains between creatures and God, see Francis Ruello, *Les "noms divins" et leur "raisons" selon saint Albert le Grand, commentateur du "De divinis nominibus,"* BibThom 35 (Paris: Vrin, 1963), pp. 82–83 and nn. 36–37.

Noteworthy here is the fact that Aquinas makes use of the same example for both types of analogical predication.[23]

What can never be doubted is Thomas' desire to defend the divine transcendence. In those early texts where he rejects the phrase *per prius et posterius,* he is clearly aligning it with the analogy of two to a third, which must be avoided in the interests of divine transcendence since it makes God derivative and posterior to something else. Whereas he accepts or rejects the phrase according to its context, he is unwavering in his dismissal of any kind of analogy that he thinks will compromise God's excellence and superiority.[24] He will arrive at his final solution once he comes to understand transcendental analogy as a direct relation of one to another, a relation of the creature to God that is indeterminate and immeasurable.

---

23. *ST* 1.13.5 offers another instance where the same example serves to illustrate both kinds of predication: analogy can be a relation of many to one (*healthy* said of medicine and urine insofar as both have a relation to the animal's health) or one to another (*healthy* said of medicine and animal). Montagnes (*Doctrine,* pp. 72–73) sees in Aquinas the gradual triumph of analogy as the relation of "one to another": whereas in some texts of the *Sentences* predicamental analogy (accident vis-à-vis substance) is described as an analogy of two to a third while transcendental analogy (creature vis-à-vis God) is explained as an analogy of one to another (and Thomas seems to be following Albert the Great very closely here), in *SCG* 1.34 both are described in exactly the same terms as analogies of direct rapport between one thing and another, which greatly unifies his teaching on analogy. We might note, however, that already in *DV* 2.11 Thomas can view predicamental analogy as a relation of one to another, and in *DP* 7.7 use it as an example for the analogy of two to a third as well, which demonstrates how easily Thomas can slide from one use to another to suit his needs. The analogy of two to a third is hardly of independent value, immediately reducible as it is to the analogy of one to another.

24. Montagnes (*Doctrine,* p. 71, n. 16, and pp. 73–80) shows how Thomas upheld God's transcendence by always eschewing descriptive expressions for analogy such as "many to one," "two to a third," and "two to one." The rejection of these phrases remains constant even though he may swing between a negative and a positive appraisal of *per prius et posterius.* For more on the difference between the analogy of "many to one" and the analogy of "one to another," at both the predicamental and transcendental levels, see John Wippel, *The Metaphysical Thought of Thomas Aquinas: From Finite Being to Uncreated Being* (Washington, DC: CUA, 2000), pp. 82–84, 568–70. Wippel shows how Thomas uses both types of analogy for the predicamental level of being, although he only permits the analogy of one to another for the transcendental level between God and creatures; and even at the predicamental level, the analogy of many to one is reducible to the more fundamental analogy of one to another.

iv. *The Analogical Community*

The community or unity of analogy in Aquinas is a crucial topic for this study, for the decision whether or not he reduces analogy to a common core of univocity—an accusation analogy is commonly charged with—will largely hinge on the manner in which he treats it. As far as possible in the rest of this chapter we will attempt to present a diachronic account of his position on this topic, and for the terms most critical to the discussion we will use as much of his own language as possible.

In the *De principiis* (6.42–44) Aquinas speaks of analogy as a kind of agreement or harmony *(convenientia)* and says that things agree according to analogy *(convenire secundum analogiam).*[25] In the *Sentences,* however, analogical *convenientia* may be denied between creatures and God if he understands it as their sharing in a third reality beyond them, for in that case it must be rejected just as univocity is;[26] or it may be allowed if he makes a distinction between univocal and analogical agreement, for in that case the *convenientia analogiae* between God and creatures means that creatures participate as much as they are able in the being of God, who is his own very Being.[27] In later texts, certain physical or logical realities are also said to *convenire secundum analogiam:* the matter of a heavenly body and the matter of the elements (*ST* 1.66.2); the principles of all natural things (*Phys.* 1.10.81); and logical middle terms dealing with diverse realities (*Post.* 2.19.577).[28]

---

25. In *DV* 2.11 analogy is termed a *convenientia* and a *communitas.*

26. *SS* 1.35.1.4. For univocals are also said "to agree in something one," which cannot be accepted in God's case since something would then be prior to and simpler than God; thus, God and creature "do not agree in something one according to any mode of agreement," but they do have a "community of analogy" (*SS* 1.24.1.1 ad4). In this text, then, *convenientia* is opposed to the *communitas* of analogy. The reason for the rejection is the same one Aquinas offers for the few times he disallows the *per prius et posterius* in the *Sentences,* as we have seen above.

27. *SS* 2.16.1.1 ad3. This is how we ought to understand Aquinas, then, when he states that life and wisdom "agree analogically in God and creatures" (*SS* 2.16.1.2 ad5). In *DV* 8.1 we are told that any likeness of the divine essence received in our mind can possess only an analogical agreement with the divine essence itself.

28. In these last two texts, *convenire secundum analogiam* carries the sense of a four-term proportionality.

For Aquinas, *convenientia* signals that analogy is some sort of harmony, suitability, or agreement of terms, meanings, or things. He does not use the word often and does not seem in his later works to apply it to the analogy between creatures and God. Even in the *Sentences* he allows it to be used of creatures and God only when there is no danger of compromising the divine transcendence and simplicity, and in those cases it is clear that *convenientia analogiae* implies no univocal sharing in a common quality but rather the creature's participation in God's act of being.

Communitas analogiae and *communitas secundum analogiam* are employed more frequently than the *convenientia/convenire* couplet mentioned above. Often they are used of analogy in reference to metaphysical or ethical subjects. Being is analogically common to all other realities,[29] and certain things are distinguished as common analogues, according to priority and posteriority: sin,[30] virtue (*SS* 3.33.2.1.1 ad2), and vows (*SS* 4.38.1.2.1). Community of analogy can also mean a four-term proportionality.[31]

Creature and Creator can also share a community of analogy, not as though participating in some third reality but insofar as the creature receives being from and imitates the first being, God.[32] In his earlier Trinitarian theology, following the lead of Basil of Caesarea, he writes that "to receive from the Father is common to the Son and every creature by a community of analogy."[33] Knowledge, life, and being are, according to a community of analogy, extended from God even to animals, plants, and stones (*SS* 4.49.3.1.2 ad3).

As one can see, Thomas' use of *communitas analogiae* extends throughout his works but is confined to the *Sentences* and the *De veritate* as regards God and creatures, though in *ST* 1.13.5 he does refer to names being said analogically of God and creatures as a *modus communitatis*. As was the

---

29. *Phys.* 3.1.281; *Meta.* 11.1.2170; *ST* 1-2.61.1 ad1.

30. *DM* 7.1 ad1; *SS* 2.42.1.3.

31. *Post.* 2.17.563; cf. *SS* 2.13.1.2; 3.9.2.1 ad1.

32. *SS* 1.prol.1.2 ad2; same: *SS* 1.35.1.4. Cf. *SS* 1.24.1.1 ad4; 1.29.1.2.1; *DV* 2.11; *ST* 1.13.5.

33. *SS* 1.44.1.1 ad2. Also: *SS* 3.11.1.1 ad3; *DV* 29.4.207–12. In the parallel Trinitarian text from *ST* 1.33.3 ad2, he writes that to receive from the Father is common to a creature and the Son, not by univocity but "according to a certain remote likeness."

case with *convenientia analogiae,* moreover, he permits *communitas analo-giae* to describe the relation between creatures and God only in environments where he can ensure God's supereminence.

v. Analogy's "Common Meaning" and "Different Meanings"

The question concerning the viability of Thomistic analogy as a way of characterizing our knowledge and speech about God and creatures comes down ultimately to the significance of the distinction between analogy's "common meaning" and "different meanings."

For Aquinas, the noun *ratio* is a richly polysemic word that can signify the faculty of reason or a process of reasoning, a meaning or definition, the form or nature of something, a mathematical proportion, and any aspect of a thing's intelligibility.[34] *Ratio* generally signifies "meaning" in the phrase *ratio communis,* but it may also denote "nature"; nor are the two senses mutually exclusive, for substance and accident are said to participate in the *ratio communis* of being,[35] and the nature of entity across all realities is said to participate in one *ratio* according to analogy (*SS* 2.1.1.1). The various meanings of an analogical term are also said to participate in an *intentio communis.*[36]

Ratio communis is employed in the context of the relationship between God and creatures. The name *goodness,* according to the analogical *ratio communis* of that perfection, is common to God and creatures, that is, "common both to the communicating principle and all the participants."[37] Aquinas sees Anselm attempting to find a *ratio communis* of free will in God, angels and humans, according to a certain "most common analogy" (*DV* 24.10 ad18). Various things concerning God and creatures are said to be "of one *ratio,*" not univocally but analogically: God's knowledge and

34. Form: *Anima* 2.7.183–87; 2.24.73, 94; proportion: ibid., 2.24.94, 103; definition: ibid., 2.24.87–88; "Ratio, quam significat nomen, est definitio" ("the meaning which a name signifies is the definition"—*Herm.* 1.2.20; *Meta.* 4.16.733).

35. *SS* 3.33.2.1.1 ad2; *DM* 7.1 ad1; *ST* 1-2.61.1 ad1; *Herm.* 1.8.93.

36. *SS* 3.33.2.1.1 ad2 *(intentio* here is a synonym for *ratio);* cf. *DM* 7.1 ad1. *Herm.* 1.8.93 speaks of analogous terms with their various meanings participating in the *ratio communis.* *SS* 1.19.5.2 ad1 mentions a *natura communis* with respect to analogical terms.

37. *SS* 1.19.2.1 ad3; cf. 1.29.1.2.1.

ours (*SS* 1.35.1.4 ad2); Christ's eternal and temporal nativity (*SS* 3.8.1.4.1 ad3); Christ's predestination and ours (*SS* 3.10.3.1.2); the truth of things in the Word and in themselves (*DV* 4.6 ad5); the eternal procession of the Holy Spirit in God and the Spirit's temporal mission in the justified.[38] The latest example from his works is *DP* 2.5 ad6, where Thomas states that the generation of the Son and the production of creatures are of one *ratio* analogically.

Two more texts are noteworthy because of the different manner in which Thomas handles them when he treats of the same issues in the *Summa theologiae*. First, fatherhood in God and creatures has the same meaning *(eadem ratio)* analogically, which implies that in such a *ratio* there are elements of both identity and diversity (*SS* 1.21.1.1.2). Second, in the course of arguing that the noun *person* is said of God and creatures not equivocally but analogically, he writes that "the meaning *(ratio)* of person implies distinction in general and hence is abstracted *(abstrahere)* from every mode of distinction; thus there can be one meaning *(una ratio)* analogically in those things which are distinguished in different ways."[39] Read on their own, these texts, especially the latter, could easily give the impression that Thomas is falling back into an unguarded univocity or into Cajetan's theory of "imperfect abstraction," for he seems to say that *person* can be predicated of God and rational creatures on the grounds that the analogically common meaning abstracts from the different modes by which God and creatures are persons.

If we take a look at the two parallel texts from the *Summa theologiae*, we can detect, due to important omissions, a possible change in Thomas' outlook. In *ST* 1.31.3 ad3 he concludes the same as in *SS* 1.21.1.1.2 above and asserts that paternity is found in various realities analogically, though he makes no mention of any *eadem ratio*. In *ST* 1.29.4 he takes up the same issue as in *SS* 1.25.1.2 ad5 above, and although a person is defined, in general, as an individual substance of a rational nature who is distinct from others, there is no mention of *una ratio* or *abstrahere;* and he also is at pains to point out in response to the fourth objection that the *communis defini-*

38. *SS* 1.14.1.2 ad6; cf. *SS* 1.22.1.2 ad3; 1.22.1.3 ad4.
39. *SS* 1.25.1.2 ad5; same: 1.24.2.1 ad3.

tio of univocity cannot apply to the relation between God and creatures. Between the *Sentences* and the *Summa* the *ratio communis* seems to have fallen silently out of favor, at least as regards the analogy between God and creatures.

Instead, Thomas' attention in his later works has begun to focus more on the *diversae rationes* (different meanings) that enable analogy's semantic multiplicity, though the phrase shows up as early as the *De principiis naturae* (6.34–35). *ST* 1.13.5 presents his mature position in a nutshell: "In those things which are predicated analogically, there is a meaning *(ratio)* which is neither one, as in univocals, nor totally different, as in equivocals, but a name that is predicated in such manifold and various ways signifies different relations *(proportiones)* to something one."[40] In this passage, though he is willing to use the word *ratio* in reference to analogical names, he is wary of calling it either simply one or totally diverse and wrestles to chisel out the formula we have seen elsewhere: analogy's *ratio* is both one and diverse because the analogical term, when used in various contexts and predications, signifies different relations to something one. In another text composed around five years later we read that as regards the ten ultimate categories of being (which we already know are predicated analogically) there is no *una ratio communis* whatsoever, "for nothing is predicated univocally of them."[41] Here, the *una ratio communis* is clearly viewed as the exclusive prerogative of univocity.

It is in Thomas' commentary on Aristotle's *Metaphysics* that we detect the Stagirite's inspiration for Thomas' switch to an emphasis on analogy's multitude of different meanings. Besides the assertion "being is said in many ways," which we studied in the last chapter, it is there we also find the phrases *multiplicitas analogiae* and *multiplicitas entis*,[42] which hardly exist in his earlier works and thus display his later sensitivity, under the tutelage of Aristotle, to the multiple predications at the heart of any analogical grouping.[43] Aristotle had said that being is predicated in many ways

40. The same position is in *ST* 1.13.10.
41. *Ethic.* 1.6.130–48; cf. ibid., 1.7.167.
42. *Meta.* 1.14.224; 9.1.1773, 1780; 11.3.2194, 2197; 12.1.2419.
43. The *multiplicitas* of the noun *principium* is also mentioned in *SS* 1.31.2.1 ad2.

(pollachōs) but with respect to something one, to some one nature (pros hen kai mian tina physin).[44] Thomas writes that a term is analogically predicated "according to meanings (rationes) which are partly different and partly not different: different inasmuch as they imply different relations (habitudines) but one inasmuch as those different relations are referred to something one and the same" (Meta. 4.1.535).[45] He asserts that "in analogical terms, that 'one' to which the different relations are referred is one in number, and not only one in meaning (ratio) as is that 'one' which is designated through the univocal name"; indeed, the analogical "one" is not a unity of meaning (ratione unum) but is one as a certain nature is one (unum sicut una quaedam natura—Meta. 4.1.536).

A few paragraphs later we deduce that the strict and proper sense of una ratio can only belong to univocity. In the text Thomas comments upon, Aristotle has been essaying to establish the unity of metaphysics, reasoning that it belongs to one science to investigate not only "things predicated according to one [notion]" (ta kath' hen legomena) but also "things predicated in relation to one nature" (ta pros mian legomena physin).[46] Thomas comments that it belongs to one science to investigate not only those things predicated secundum unum ("according to one," a literal translation of kath' hen), "i.e., according to one reason totally, but also those things predicated through relation to one nature [the last five words are a literal translation of pros mian physin] according to different relations," for the unity of the one nature is sufficient for the unity of a science (Meta. 4.1.544). Two lectures later, following Aristotle, who has economized his language to the point that he can simply oppose the kath' hen to the pros hen,[47] Thomas remarks that univocal predication is secundum unum, that is, according to una ratio, whereas analogical predication occurs when different things are referred to one thing by means of a ratio diversa (Meta. 4.3.568). Una ratio, it would seem, is a natural citizen of the land of univocity, and in order to travel to the country of analogy it re-

---

44. Aristotle, Metaphysics 4.2.1003a33–34.
45. The habitudines of this text are synonymous with the proportiones of ST 1.13.5.
46. Aristotle, Metaphysics 4.2.1003b12–15.
47. Ibid., 4.2.1004a24–25.

quires a passport and identification papers that mark it as a stranger in that place. The "one" proper to univocity is a *ratio*, a meaning, but the "one" characteristic of analogy is a nature or even an *aliquid*, a something. This is clear from his example of the word *medical*, which, although it is predicated analogically of many things by means of "a relation to something one and the same," namely, medical skill, "does not nevertheless signify something one and the same for all the things of which it is said"; and thus its meanings are not univocal since they do not possess one meaning *(una ratio)*, "for *medical* does not have the same meaning *(eadem ratio)* when it is predicated of what medical skill uses and of what medical skill produces."[48]

Aquinas takes up our problem once more in the eleventh book of the same commentary. In the text he is interpreting, Aristotle is again discussing the unity of metaphysics, which is a problem since its subject, being, is predicated in many ways *(pollachōs)* and not univocally *(kath' hen)*; nevertheless, the unity of metaphysics can be preserved if the meanings of being are predicated according to something common, and in fact Aristotle finds that in those meanings of being there is a reduction *(anagōgē)* to something one and common,[49] for "all being is said in many ways *(pollachōs)* but is also predicated according to something one and common *(kath' hen ti kai koinon)*."[50] In the space of one chapter, then, *kath' hen* is first opposed to *pollachōs* and then associated with it, but in association with *pollachōs* it can no longer retain the same meaning it had when it was opposed to it, for it can be associated with analogy's multiplicity of meaning only when the "one" no longer refers to meaning as such but to "something one."

Thomas follows Aristotle and repeats that being is said in many ways "according to something common" *(secundum aliquid commune,* a literal translation of *kata ti koinon)*, giving the medical and health examples as

---

48. *Meta.* 7.4.1337; same: *ST* 1-2.20.3 ad3. Wippel detects, between the *De principiis naturae* and the Commentary on the *Metaphysics*, a slight development in Thomas' thought about how to describe the sameness and difference in the meanings of an analogical term *(Metaphysical Thought*, pp. 81–82).

49. Aristotle, *Metaphysics* 11.3.1060b31–36, 1061a10–11.

50. Ibid., 11.3.1061b11–12.

instances of this type of predication (*Meta.* 11.3.2195–96). In analogy the same name is predicated of different things according to "a meaning partly the same and partly different: different as regards the different modes of relation, the same as regards that to which the relation is directed"; for example, to be significative of health and to be productive of health are different ways of being related to health, but the health itself is one; and the varied meanings of being have something common, substance, to which all the meanings are reduced (*Meta.* 11.3.2197). Indeed, analogy's "partially same meaning" *would* eventually draw analogy back to a common core of univocity if that "partially same meaning" were on the same conceptual level as univocal meanings; but it is not, for what Thomas is attempting to show is that the moment of identity in an analogical term's various meanings is not a meaning at all but an individual reality to which all the different meanings necessarily refer.

Aquinas is stretching language in these texts from his commentary on the *Metaphysics.* Even though he implies that a partially unified *ratio* still obtains in analogical terms, the *ratio* is no longer, as it continues to be in univocal predication, a conceptual, logical unity, but a reference to concrete, individual natures or realities. Paradoxically, he is conceptualizing analogy as something quite distinct from univocity and yet still discussing analogy in terms of *ratio,* whose natural home remains the realm of univocity. In effect, he is adding a new analogous sense to the word *ratio,* creating a new analogous meaning for *meaning,* in order to do justice to the nuances of analogy as a way of understanding and signifying—all of which also stretches our semantics and exercises our understanding.[51]

In conclusion, Aquinas did not entirely cease using *ratio communis* after his early works, although its last explicit mention with respect to God and creatures seems to have been *DP* 2.5 ad6. Nevertheless, he sometimes avoided the phrase in later texts in which it might be expected to appear and, inspired as he was by his reading of Aristotle's *Metaphysics,* came to

---

51. Given Aquinas' sometimes confusing terminology, it is understandable that Cajetan and others have tried to explain the nature of analogy by recourse to a thinned-out conceptualism with its "imperfect abstraction" and partially unified concepts. But exiguous univocity will not work for analogy. Ironically, such misinterpreters do not get Aquinas on analogy right because they cannot appreciate his moves as he analogizes analogy's *ratio.*

stress more and more the different meanings of the analogical term as opposed to its single meaning, even though he still implicitly recognized a valid sense for *ratio* in analogy, as we can see when he describes the analogical term as having a *ratio* partly the same and partly different. However, *ratio* itself had to be liberated from its natural milieu in univocity and extended analogically before it could serve Aquinas in his explanation of analogy, even though he never adverts to the fact that the extension is occurring.[52]

However, given that Thomas did use *una ratio communis* in several texts and implied it in others, how are we to interpret it? What does it actually mean for him in the context of analogy? From the ensuing texts we may gather that he uses the following four terms to refer to the same reality: *ratio perfecta, ratio completa, ratio propria,* and *ratio communis.* Analogical terms are predicated *per prius et posterius,* so that only one of them has the *ratio perfecta,* the others possessing a *ratio imperfecta.*[53] Another text states the same thought, equating *imperfecta* and *secundum quid* (*SS* 2.42.1.3). That in which the *ratio completa* of a common analogical term is found receives the primary predication of that term (*DV* 1.2.51–54). In an analogical term's predications, the *ratio communis* "is perfectly found in one," but in the other predications it is retained relatively and secondarily (*DM* 7.1 ad1). Finally, when something is said of many analogically, "it is found according to its proper meaning *(propria ratio)* in only one of them, from which the others are named" (*ST* 1.16.6). In other words, the *ratio communis* of an analogical term is really the *same reality* as the term's "perfect," "complete," and "proper" meanings, but its signification differs insofar as it refers to their capacity to be included within a whole range of analogical

52. Klubertanz states that in three early texts from the *Sentences,* Thomas explains analogy in terms of a *una ratio,* while he describes it in terms of *diversae rationes* in all his later texts (*Aquinas on Analogy,* pp. 23–24). Although Wippel has shown that in all three texts Thomas qualifies the *ratio* as possessing an analogical rather than univocal unity (*Metaphysical Thought,* p. 570, n. 238; cf. Montagnes, *Doctrine,* p. 103, n. 70; Ralph McInerny, *Studies in Analogy* [The Hague: Nijhoff, 1968], p. 2, n. 2), there can be no doubt that the phrase *diversae rationes* takes on, in Thomas' later writings, a larger share of the explanatory burden with respect to analogy.

53. *ST* 1.5.6 ad3; 1-2.88.1 ad1.

predications. The *ratio communis* is directly found in only one predication, namely, that predication in which the subject is capable of receiving the full force and meaning of the predicate, whereas in all other predications it is signified not directly but secondarily or relatively, insofar as the secondary, analogically extended meanings of the common term somehow refer to it (e.g., calling food healthy, which happens by a secondary or analogically extended meaning of *healthy*, makes sense to us only if that secondary meaning is related back to the primary, proper, and yet common meaning of *healthy*, which occurs in predications where the subject is a living, organic body).[54] *Community* and *unity*, then, as pertaining to both univocity and analogy, are themselves highly analogical terms.[55]

54. McInerny (*Studies*, p. 63) writes: "The notion which is analogically common is none other than the *ratio propria* of the name. . . . The *ratio communis* of the analogous name is not obtained by picking out the minimal content of all the meanings of the name, but is rather the most proper meaning of the term in question, a meaning which is not properly saved by all the things to which it is considered to be common." *Communis* as used of univocals and analogicals is itself quite analogical (ibid., pp. 65–66). Cf. Edward Schillebeeckx, *Revelation and Theology*, trans. N. D. Smith, 2 vols. (New York: Sheed and Ward, 1968), 2:198–201. For David Burrell, Thomas' *ratio communis* is not the pure idea or *res significata* shorn of its modes, but a metalinguistic notion that calls attention to the fact that certain concepts are able to be predicated transempirically; it is not something we possess, but use, in our judgments ("Aquinas on Naming God," *TS* 24 [1963]: 201–2, and n. 68). In Burrell's own account, the *ratio communis* of analogous predication is the *way* the scheme works, not something common to its different uses; the *ratio communis* is the *fact* that we use certain terms the way we do (*Analogy and Philosophical Language* [New Haven: Yale, 1973], pp. 225–26).

55. Wippel cautions against seeing Thomas' analogy as containing a core of univocity: "According to Thomas's thinking we should not view an analogical intelligible content as something we grasp simply by abstracting it from the participated way it is realized in creatures so as to view it in itself, as it were, and then predicate it of God according to his mode of being. Such an approach would subordinate both created beings and God himself to this abstracted absolute perfection in itself. And it would in effect reduce such abstracted analogical concepts to univocal concepts" (*Metaphysical Thought*, p. 572).

7. Analogy as Judgment in Aquinas

Chapter 6 has discussed the interpretation of Aquinas' analogy of referential multivocity as a web of predication always maintaining a relation to an individual reality, rather than as an isolated, abstract, and self-contained concept. This chapter will extend this idea by showing that for him every predication is a judgment seeking and bespeaking the truth, and that therefore theological analogy also subsists in an enveloping web of true judgments or discernments about God and creation. We will first treat the nature of judgment in Aquinas' thought insofar as it relates to truth and concept, then explain how his transcendental analogy between God and creation arises from and is justified by a series of mutually supportive first-order judgments about God and creatures, and finally discuss his idea of the graced judgment of faith.

Before turning to the subject of judgment and truth in Thomas, however, it would be helpful to offer a short though representative survey of the range of opinions during the last half-century concerning the epistemological status of Thomistic analogy. Even as Cajetan's interpretation of Thomistic analogy began to show stress fractures, some scholars continued to favor a Cajetan-inspired epistemology of analogy that focuses on the representational nature of the concept, even while sometimes disagreeing with him about other aspects of his interpretation of Thomistic analogy.

For Hampus Lyttkens, the analogous concept as applied to God and creatures can differ only in degree since we cannot conceive God's wisdom as entirely different from human wisdom. Because he thinks Aquinas supports a Neoplatonic ontology placing God at the zenith of a connected linkage going all the way down to the lowest point in creation[1]—thus making the difference between God and creatures only a matter of degree—he also discerns a similar condition in Aquinas' analogous statements about God: "When 'the thing' is said to exist in God in a higher way, this can only be understood as a difference in degree: a stronger difference in its existence in creation and in God may well be expressed, but not conceived. If such a stronger difference is stressed, the statement may lose its meaning. Analogy must, therefore, presuppose a connexion between God and creation."[2] James Ross also defends a common *res significata* in analogous terms and says that to reject it is "tantamount to rejecting the entire theory of St. Thomas."[3] J. H. Nicolas speaks, in Cajetanian terms, of the analogical concept's "proportional unity" and "imperfect abstraction."[4] Battista Mondin also speaks in a conceptualist manner of the intrinsically analogous concept as "incompletely abstracted," as representing one of the analogates perfectly and the others imperfectly, and as formed by a "vague intuition."[5]

Averse to explaining the epistemological status of analogy by a Scotistic or Cajetanian abstract conceptual unity, however, the early Schillebeeckx was one of the first to use "tendential" language to describe the epistemic

1. Hampus Lyttkens, *The Analogy between God and the World,* trans. A. Poignant (Uppsala: Almqvist and Wiksells, 1952), pp. 390, 413–14.

2. Ibid., p. 390. For other texts indicating Lyttkens' conceptualism, see pp. 246–66, 310–50.

3. James Ross, "Reply of Professor Ross," *IPQ* 2 (1962): 661.

4. J. H. Nicolas, "Affirmation de Dieu et connaissance," *RT* 64 (1964): 202, 214. He also remarks that "the analogical process in general consists in an extension of the concept" (*Dieu connu comme inconnu* [Paris: Desclée, 1966], p. 267). Robert Meagher writes: "The problem is that of forming a 'ratio communis' that will include God and creature alike, that is, the problem of extending man's meanings and concepts to infinite or transcendent proportions without their becoming inapplicable to the finite and the concrete" ("Thomas Aquinas and Analogy: A Textual Analysis," *Thomist* 34 [1970]: 251).

5. Battista Mondin, *The Principle of Analogy in Protestant and Catholic Theology,* 2nd ed. (The Hague: Nijhoff, 1968), pp. 83–84.

awareness of analogy, which provides us with an "objective perspective onto God."[6] "The typically noetic value of our knowledge of God is therefore situated in a projective act, in which we reach out for God, but do not grasp him in understanding, although we are well aware that he is to be found in the precise direction in which we are reaching."[7] In the direct line of concepts, then, Schillebeeckx argues, we "tend towards God."[8] Thus the basis of our knowledge of God is neither a Cajetanian concept nor a Maréchalian subjective dynamism of spirit but rather the "*objective* dynamism of the content of being" that occurs in an "intellectual tending or projection."[9]

William Hill desired to keep to the middle road between Cajetanian conceptualism on the one hand and theological symbolism or implicit intuitionalism on the other. Concerning Cajetan's "intrinsically analogous concept," he writes: "The question is whether this does not bestow upon the concept an intelligible content where God is concerned, that it cannot have. There is surely some concept of God—He cannot be humanly known otherwise. But does that concept 'represent' Him (in virtue of proportions intrinsic to the concept) or does it merely 'designate' Him in a totally referential manner?"[10] Hill wanted to avoid any conceptual representationalism. Still, "what remains of enduring value in the tradition is its insistence upon taking the very signification of the concept seriously, so that any employment of analogy as a projective act cannot be seen as reducing the concept to a mere symbol or as only functional and of subjective value. Rather the cognitive value of analogy is one deriving from the objective contents of the concept."[11] In analogy, for Hill, an act of judg-

6. Edward Schillebeeckx, *Revelation and Theology,* trans. N. D. Smith, 2 vols. (New York: Sheed and Ward, 1968), 2:167.

7. Ibid., 2:175.

8. Ibid., 2:177.

9. Ibid., 2:205–6. Early in his career, when the articles that comprise *Revelation and Theology* were written, Schillebeeckx was a proponent of Dominic de Petter's epistemological theory of implicit intuition, but he later abandoned this position in favor of hermeneutics and the historical method (*Jesus,* trans. H. Hoskins [New York: Seabury, 1979], p. 618), though he never entirely relinquished a metaphysical realism.

10. William Hill, *Knowing the Unknown God* (New York: Philosophical Library, 1971), p. 28.

11. Ibid.

ment "projects" the *ratio* or concept onto God and understands God "as lying in the direction of the pure perfection [the *ratio*] bespeaks."[12] Judgment "affirms God as an infinitely removed and unconceptualizable term, but within a perspective opened up by the intelligible contents of a concept."[13] "All human awareness of the divine then is without any proper conception of God and at the same time totally by way of a concept. Such ideas are not representational but they do allow for a consciousness of God that, while partial, is nonetheless cognitive, objective, non-metaphorical, and non-symbolic."[14]

A few other thinkers, like Hill, have also found it appropriate to emphasize the judgmental nature of analogy. Étienne Gilson is one of the earliest to have explicitly linked analogy and judgment in Aquinas. While Scotus' view of analogy is conceptual, "the Thomist doctrine of analogy is above all a doctrine of the *judgment* of analogy. It is in effect thanks to the judgment of proportion that, without changing its nature, one can use the concept sometimes equivocally, sometimes analogically, sometimes univocally."[15]

Henri Bouillard remarks that in Cajetan and Suarez analogy is a property of the concept itself insofar as it is representational. Instead of Scotus' univocity of the concept of being they both speak of the analogous nature of the concept of being, but this latter is imperfectly abstracted and tends ultimately to a sort of confused univocity. But for Aquinas, who never employs Cajetan's phrase "analogous concept," analogy is a matter of making true predications about God, of using concepts in judgments.[16]

---

12. Ibid., pp. 142, 259, n. 69.

13. Ibid., p. 143.

14. Ibid., p. 144. Following Hill's lead, Thomas Guarino states that analogical language "allows revelation to offer a genuine 'vision' of God, while remaining respectful of all the restraints that a simple representationalism tends to ignore" (*Revelation and Truth: Unity and Plurality in Contemporary Theology* [Scranton/London: University of Scranton/Associated University Presses, 1993], p. 136).

15. Étienne Gilson, *Jean Duns Scot* (Paris: Vrin, 1952), p. 101. For the same opinion, see George Klubertanz, *St. Thomas Aquinas on Analogy: A Textual Analysis and Systematic Synthesis* (Chicago: Loyola, 1960), pp. 115–20, 147–55; Henri de Lubac, *The Discovery of God*, trans. A. Dru from 3rd French ed. (Chicago: Regnery, 1967), p. 201.

16. Henri Bouillard, *The Knowledge of God*, trans. S. D. Femiano (New York: Herder and Herder, 1968), pp. 105–7.

David Burrell, relying heavily on Wittgenstein and the tradition of linguistic philosophy, considers analogy to be the semantic expression of the judgments philosophers make. Analogy is usage based on judgment, and the facts of philosophical inquiry are correlative with the contours of analogy. Responsible analogous language depends totally on the "level of reflective awareness regarding the realities."[17] Only analogy as the lived use of language escapes the Scotistic "univocal core" of conceptualistic formalism. Analogy thus fulfills a need demanded by insight into reality and is the result of how language must work in order to do justice to insight, which is a matter of judgment.[18] Furthermore, Burrell also discerns in Aquinas a view of analogy as semantic usage based on judgment.[19]

For Colman O'Neill, analogy occurs when a predicate is transferred from its normal linguistic context to a new one, and thus theological analogy is a judgment of faith or theology that carries a positive significance bearing on the very reality of God. To speak of "analogical *concepts*," he says, is a "disastrous misunderstanding" that conduces to rationalism. Still, judgments use concepts, and thus we have the paradox of all theological discourse—that theological judgment "affirms transcendence, even though

17. David Burrell, *Analogy and Philosophical Language* (New Haven: Yale, 1973), p. 169.

18. Ibid., chaps. 1–2, 9. Burrell speaks of these judgments in another way as "a style of argumentation that is self-involving and that directs inquirers into an inevitably analogous use of language to express the conclusions at which they hope to arrive" ("Analogy, Creation, and Theological Language," *PACPA* 74 [2000]: 50). Heidegger remarks that univocal concepts cannot do justice to the "basic structure of real reality," in which "homogeneity and heterogeneity interlace in a peculiar manner" (*Frühe Schriften* [Frankfurt, 1972], p. 199, cited in Rüdiger Safranski, *Martin Heidegger: Between Good and Evil*, trans. E. Osers [Cambridge, MA: Harvard, 1998], p. 63).

19. Ibid., chaps. 6–7. In "A Note on Analogy" (*NS* 36 [1962]: 225–32), Burrell mentions that an article by Yves Simon ("On Order in Analogical Sets," *NS* 34 [1960]: 1–42) helped stimulate him to view analogy as a matter of judgment. Burrell mentions the "incommensurability of apprehension and judgment" ("Religious Language and the Logic of Analogy: Apropos of McInerny's Book and Ross' Review," *IPQ* 2 [1962]: 657), and shows the importance of judgment in Aquinas' naming of God ("Aquinas on Naming God," *TS* 24 [1963]: 183–212). Elizabeth Johnson also links analogy with judgment in *She Who Is: The Mystery of God in Feminist Theological Discourse* (New York: Crossroad, 1992), p. 114; and John Wippel shows how Aquinas' analogy of being, which is at the core of his considered judgment about the true nature of the real, is his properly nuanced response to Parmenides' aporia about the one and the many (*The Metaphysical Thought of Thomas Aquinas: From Finite Being to Uncreated Being* [Washington, DC: CUA, 2000], pp. 65–93).

by means of a limited concept."[20] In all theological judgments, therefore, our concepts "direct our thought towards God" by "aiming" at God.[21]

With this survey as a backdrop for what follows, we now turn to judgment and truth in Aquinas.

1. Judgment and Truth

Aquinas' epistemology of judgment is a rich theme able to be treated from several perspectives, but in our present context we will limit ourselves to the relationship between judgment, truth, and concept. He notes that while the original denotation of *judgment (judicium)* is the judge's just decision in a court proceeding, the term can be extended to mean any correct determination about any matter whatsoever, practical or speculative.[22] Indeed, after an exhaustive investigation, Benoit Garceau discovers that there are three main extended senses of *judicium* in Aquinas.[23] The primary and most basic sense, which he received from Bonaventure's reading of Aristotle, is "discerning the truth with certitude," and in this manner

20. Colman O'Neill, "La prédication analogique: l'élément négatif," in *Analogie et dialectique*, ed. P. Gisel and P. Secretan (Geneva: Labor et Fides, 1982), pp. 82, 87–89; cf. idem, "Analogy, Dialectic, and Inter-Confessional Theology," *Thomist* 47 (1983): 52, 57.

21. O'Neill, "Prédication analogique," pp. 88–89. Other writers have also used similar tendential or directional language reminiscent of Schillebeeckx. Gilson remarks that true analogical judgments orient us toward a goal, "the direction of which is known to us but which, because it is at infinity, is beyond the reach of our natural forces" (*The Christian Philosophy of St. Thomas Aquinas*, trans. L. K. Shook [New York: Random, 1956], p. 110). For W. Norris Clarke, analogy is based not on concepts but on our ability to make the judgments we do ("Analogy and the Meaningfulness of Language about God: A Reply to Kai Nielsen," *Thomist* 40 [1976]: 64–72). Through the mediation (not representation) of the analogous concept, God is situated at an "invisible apex" in an upward direction, and a "positive knowledge-through-love" is thereby gained, "obscure, vector-like, indirect, non-conceptual," based on the dynamic thrust of the human spirit, so that God *must* be affirmed and yet is still beyond representation (ibid., pp. 93–95). Cf. idem, *The Philosophical Approach to God* (Winston-Salem, NC: Wake Forest University, 1979), pp. 59–61.

22. *ST* 2-2.60.1; for Aquinas, *judicium* is the proper act of the judge (*judex*), and he breaks down both words etymologically into *ius dicens* (saying what is just). Cf. Robert Ashmore, "The Analogical Notion of Judgment in St. Thomas Aquinas" (Ph.D. dissertation, University of Notre Dame, 1966); Benoit Garceau, *Judicium: vocabulaire, sources, doctrine de saint Thomas d'Aquin* (Montreal/Paris: Institute of Medieval Studies/Vrin, 1968), pp. 224–34.

23. *Judicium*, pp. 13–14, 76–95, 98, 150–51, 221–23, 251–55.

judicium can be used to signify any cognitive power's discernment of its proper object, whether the power is one of the external senses, the common cerebral locus for all sensation, the instinctive faculty of animals and humans, or the intellect.[24] The second sense, based on Augustine, is the appreciation of the meaning and value of things. The third sense, foreshadowed by Peter of Spain's assimilation of judgment with Avicennian assent and Aristotelian composition/division, is the intellect's act of declaring its conformity with reality, which takes place in the mind's second operation of forming propositions. It is this last sense of judgment in Aquinas that interests us most in this and the next section.

In his early works Thomas associates truth, real existence, and the mind's act of composing and dividing, but judgment in the sense of knowing truth as the correspondence between thought and thing does not yet appear. "Truth is based more on a thing's being than on its essence . . . and the relation of correspondence, in which the nature of truth consists, occurs in the very operation of the intellect's understanding the being of a thing as it is, by means of a certain assimilation to it."[25] Similarly, "the nature of truth consists in two things: in a thing's being, and in the apprehension of a cognitive power proportioned to a thing's being" (*SS* 1.19.5.2). The first operation of the mind looks to a thing's essence, whereas the second looks to its being, and since truth is based on being and not on essence, truth is found properly in that operation of the mind which involves the affirmation or denial of a proposition (*SS* 1.19.5.1 ad7). The mind's composing act is directly related to the being of the composite realities it knows, for the double operation of the intellect corresponds to the two components in every reality—being and essence: while the first operation apprehends essences, "the other comprehends a thing's being by com-

24. Garceau, *Judicium*, pp. 241–51. For examples of *judicium* as used of the various cognitive powers lower than intellect, see: *SS* 2.1.1.4; 3.23.2.2.1; *DV* 1.9; *SCG* 2.48.1246; *DP* 3.7; *ST* 1.17.2; 1.78.4 ad2; *DSC* 10 ad8; *Phys.* 8.6.1018; *Rom.* 12.1.967; *1 Cor.* 2.3.118; *Anima* 2.27.28–44; 2.28.30–31; 2.28.196–98, 282–84; 3.6.45–61; *Sensu* 16.173; 18.217–19; *DA* 13; *Meta.* 1.1.6; 1.1.30; 4.11.670; 4.12.673; 4.14.692, 695; 11.6.2231; *Ethic.* 6.9.243–46. Cf. Ashmore, "Analogical Notion," *passim*; André Hayen, *L'intentionnel selon saint Thomas*, 2nd ed., preface by J. Maréchal, Museum Lessianum (section philosophique), 25, (Brussels/Paris: Desclée, 1954), pp. 127–32.

25. *SS* 1.19.5.1, p. 486. "The very being of a thing is the cause of truth, according as it is in the intellect's knowledge" (ibid.).

posing an affirmation, since the being of a reality composed of matter and form . . . also consists in a certain composition of form to matter or of accident to subject" (SS 1.38.1.3). The being of a composite reality results from the joining of the reality's principles (BDT 5.3), and thus our intellect, whose knowledge originally comes from realities that possess a composite being, "does not apprehend that being except by composing and dividing" (SS 1.38.1.3 ad2). Thomas is arguing that since truth is based on being, and since the beings we naturally come into contact with are composite realities, the mind knows being only by forming various positive or negative propositions. He is suggesting an isomorphism or parallelism between the mind's composing act and the composite being which that act apprehends.

While some of his later texts still continue to note the parallelism between composition in reality and composition in the mind,[26] in other passages Thomas explains truth as a recognition of the correspondence or conformity between thought and reality, and situates truth in the mind's composing act, not now because of an isomorphism between this act and reality but because this act is something proper to mind and only occurs in the mind.

The nature of the true consists in a correspondence (adaequatio) of reality and intellect. A reality does not correspond to itself, however, but correspondence occurs between different things. Hence the nature of truth is first found in the intellect when the intellect begins to have something proper to itself that is not possessed by the reality outside the soul, yet something corresponding to that reality, so that between intellect and reality a correspondence may be recognized. When the intellect apprehends the essence of a reality, however, it only possesses the likeness of the reality existing outside the soul, just as a sense power does when it receives the form of a material reality. But when the intellect begins to judge about the reality apprehended, then its very judgment is something proper to it which is not found in the reality outside the soul; and this judgment is said to be true when it corresponds to the external reality. Moreover, the intellect judges about the reality apprehended at that very instant when it says that something is or is not . . . and thus truth is found primarily in the composition and division of the intellect.[27]

Judgment here names that act which is proper to intellect and not found in external reality. In ST 1.16.2 he defines truth as the "conformity between

---

26. Meta. 9.11.1898; ST 1.13.12; 1.85.5 ad3.   27. DV 1.3; same: DV 1.11.

intellect and reality" and says that to know the truth is to know that conformity through the formation of positive or negative propositions; neither a sense power nor the intellect's simple understanding of an essence
can know that conformity, for neither knows the relation *(comparatio)* between the reality sensed or understood and the sense's or intellect's apprehension of it.[28]

The positive composition or negative division of a proposition that occurs in judgment is also the simultaneous assertion of the corresponding
positive or negative truth.

> When we say that something is, we signify that the proposition is true; and when
> we say that it is not, we signify that the proposition is not true. This holds both for
> affirmation and negation: for affirmation, as when we say that Socrates is white,
> since this is true; for negation, as when we say that Socrates is not white, because
> this is true, namely, that he is not white. (*Meta.* 5.9.895)

Further, "in judging, the intellect has two acts: affirmation, by which it assents to the true, and negation, by which it dissents from the false."[29]
Aquinas regards the second operation of the intellect, which he sometimes
identifies with judgment based on reflection, as a propositional composition or division that either assents to truth or dissents from falsity.

Aquinas' late commentary on Aristotle's *On Interpretation* (1270–71)
synthesizes many of the themes we have been discussing.[30] Truth and falsity are found in the intellect only insofar as it composes a proposition by
comparing one simple concept to another;[31] and only the addition of *to be*

28. Truth and falsity reside in the intellect's act of forming enunciations, for there "not
only does the intellect possess the likeness of the reality understood but it also reflects on
that very likeness, by knowing and judging it" (*Meta.* 6.4.1236).

29. *Ethic.* 6.2.65–67. Aquinas uses *affirmatio* and *compositio,* and *negatio* and *divisio,* as
synonyms (cf. *Meta.* 6.4.1229, 1232, 1241–43). In this late text from his commentary on Aristotle's *Nicomachean Ethics* (1271–72), assent and dissent are considered as intrinsic to affirmation and negation as such: to affirm *is* to assent to truth, and to negate *is* to dissent from
falsity. In an earlier text from the *Sentences* (1254–55), however, assent and dissent referred to
the fact that the enunciation formed by composition or division is either conceded as true
or denied as false, thus requiring a second act beyond that of forming the enunciation in the
first place (*SS* 3.23.2.2.1). The later text reveals a more integral view of assent and dissent.

30. See also *Meta.* 9.11.1897–1900.

31. *Herm.* 1.3.26. Cf. *Herm.* 1.3.25, 35; *Anima* 3.5.222–29; *SCG* 1.59.496; *Meta.* 6.4.1229, 1241.
Herm. 1.3.26 also explains that since the intellect's concepts are the likenesses of realities,
they can be considered and named in two ways—in themselves, and according to the nature

or *not to be* to names and verbs can make the true or false happen,[32] for "enunciations are related to truth just as things are to being or nonbeing" (*Herm.* 1.15.203). The intellect alone can be true since it alone can know how its own state is conformed or not to the thing in reality. To know this "relation of conformity," moreover,

is nothing other than to judge that a thing is or is not such in reality, which is to compose and divide, and thus the intellect does not know truth except by composing or dividing through its judgment. If the judgment accords with reality it will be true (as when the intellect judges a thing to be which actually is, or a thing not to be which actually is not), but the judgment will be false when it is not in accord with reality (as when it judges a thing not to be which actually is, or a thing to be which actually is not).[33]

A judgment is a knowing and claiming of the truth by means of the mind's act of forming positive or negative enunciations, which compare one concept to another through the positive or negative copulas.

Further, it is because composition or affirmation, and division or negation, signify being or nonbeing[34] that there is no truth or falsity unless "*to be* or *not to be* is added, through which the judgment of the intellect is expressed."[35] As early as *SS* 1.33.1.1 ad1 Thomas had recognized that *to be (esse)* could mean three things: the essence or nature of a thing, which the definition signifies; the primary act of any essence, as for example, to live

---

of the realities of which they are the likenesses. He offers the example of a statue of Hercules, which in itself is made of and called bronze, but insofar as it is the likeness of Hercules is called a man. Truth or falsity in the intellect always involves a composition in the sense that the intellect compares, as mental entities in their own right, one simple concept to another, and this entitative comparison of concepts is always a composition and never a division; but if this process of comparing concepts as entities in their own right is also referred to reality, then sometimes it is called a composition and sometimes a division: "composition, when the intellect compares one concept to another and thereby apprehends the conjunction or identity of the realities whose concepts they are; division, when the intellect so compares one concept to another that it apprehends the realities to be separate." Cf. Paul Durbin, "Unity and Composition in Judgment," *Thomist* 31 (1967): 113–17.

32. *Herm.* 1.3.33; cf. 1.3.35.

33. Ibid., 1.3.31; cf. 1.3.32; 1.7.85.

34. "To signify being is proper to affirmation, and to signify nonbeing is proper to negation" (*Herm.* 1.8.108); same: 1.1.10; 1.8.90; 1.9.110.

35. *Herm.* 1.3.35. Truth or falsity applies to the intellect's composing act, "insofar as it judges something to be or not to be" (*DM* 16.6, ad1 of 2nd series).

is the being of living things; and the truth of the composition or division in propositions, inasmuch as the verb *to be* is a copula; moreover, while this last sense of *to be* is found in the composing and dividing intellect, "it is based on the thing's being, which is the act of the essence." *Herm.* 1.5.73 also explains that the finite form of the verbal copula, *is (est)*,

signifies that which is first recognized by the intellect *(cadere in intellectu)* in the mode of absolute actuality, for *is*, predicated absolutely, signifies actual being and thus signifies in the mode of a verb. But because actuality, which this verb *is* principally signifies, is generally the actuality of every form or act, whether substantial or accidental, it happens that when we wish to signify that any form or act is actually in some subject, we signify it through this verb *is* . . . and thus this verb *is* signifies composition as a consequence.

The finite verbal copula *is* denotes composition as a consequence of signifying the act of being. In his commentary on Aristotle's *Metaphysics*, Thomas also notes that as a general rule the verbal copula of most propositions signifies both the actuality of real being and the truth of the proposition by way of composition or division, the former causing the latter. For *is* signifies a substance in the sentence "the human is an animal," whereas it signifies a quality in the sentence "the man is white"; but *is* as a verbal copula also signifies the truth of a proposition, which is based upon the way things are in reality.[36] As an exception to the rule, *is* merely means the truth of the proposition, and not any actual being, only when some nonbeing or privation is affirmed of a subject (e.g., when we call a sky cloudless or a horse lame).

Thus, while Thomas never forsakes the parallelism between being and truth so heavily underscored in the *Sentences,* in some of his later works one can also detect his concern to bestow upon the mind a proper, unique act of comparison and reflection in the process of coming to know the truth—the moment of judgment which nonintellectual reality does not possess. However, the actuality of the real, which the verb *to be* primarily signifies, is always presented throughout his works as the foundation and cause of the secondary meaning of *to be,* the truth of the proposition.

---

36. *Meta.* 5.9.890, 895–96; same: 6.4.1223–26.

ii. Judgment and Concept

In Aquinas' *ex professo* treatment of how judgment forms and asserts a positive or negative enunciation, we receive a fairly straightforward view: the mind's second operation compares and combines into a logical or mental synthesis, by means of the copula, the simple concepts acquired from its first operation of apprehensive abstraction. The first operation of the mind, also known as the "understanding of indivisibles," forms the simple concept of something by apprehending its essence,[37] and the second operation "composes and divides simple concepts of this sort" (*Herm.* 1.3.25), "conjoins or divides its concepts," and "unites or divides . . . some incomplex" (*Meta.* 6.4.1241). Thus, "the knowledge of simples precedes the knowledge of composites" (*Post.* 1.2.14), and the first operation is necessary for the second, "since composition and division cannot take place except with respect to things simply apprehended."[38] When the intellect's first operation apprehends the essences of human and animal, for example, as two individual realities, it understands them successively one after the other by two separate simple concepts; but when the intellect forms from these simple concepts a composition or division, it now understands them as one, insofar as it makes a single enunciation from them and understands the subject and predicate simultaneously.[39]

In these texts, many of which come from his logic and psychology of knowledge, Thomas portrays the formation of affirmative or negative propositions as a simple matter of the judgment's comparing and combining the simple, atomic concepts that are the products of the mind's simple apprehension of essences, so that concepts always precede judgments and furnish the components out of which judgments are constructed.[40] But

37. *Meta.* 6.4.1232; *Herm.* 1.3.25.

38. *Herm.*, preface, no. 1. The human intellect either composes one apprehension with another or divides one apprehension from another (*ST* 1.85.5); and the intellect's second operation of composition and division is ultimately reduced to that first operation by which it considers the simple essence (*SS* 3.24.1.1.2 ad2).

39. *Meta.* 6.4.1229. *Anima* 3.5.37–39: "The intellect composes many incomplexes that were separate previously and makes out of them a single understanding."

40. For variants on this traditional view of Aquinas' epistemology of judgment, with much textual support from Aquinas himself, see Peter Hoenen, *Reality and Judgment*

this may be too simplistic a picture of the relationship between concept and judgment, for there are also other indications that Thomas is able to take a view different from the one presented in his explicit treatments of the mind's second operation.[41]

The fact that Aquinas can bestow upon the terms *apprehensio* and *conceptio* both a narrow and a broad meaning is one of the indications that these terms need not be so restricted to describing only the mind's first operation, that the simple mental concepts they refer to would always have to be anterior to judgmental composition or division—which at least opens the possibility that the concept might be the fruit as well as the root of judgment.

The narrow signification of *apprehensio* refers to a sense power's or to the intellect's simple, direct, and immediate grasp of its proper object, without any complex process or discourse of reason; this meaning is especially evident in those places where Thomas describes the twofold or threefold operation of the intellect.[42] In an early text he writes that the intellect has two operations: one that consists in the "apprehension of a

according to St. Thomas, trans. H. F. Tiblier (Chicago: Regnery, 1952), pp. 1–14, 29–35; Durbin, "Unity and Composition," pp. 83–120; Ambrose McNicholl, "On Judging," *Thomist* 38 (1974): 768–825, especially nn. 113–21.

41. Various voices have questioned the more traditional Thomist view that the conceptual products of apprehensive abstraction are always primary and prior to the act of judgment. Étienne Gilson speaks disapprovingly of the outlook that would see in judgments only "correlations of essences apprehended by way of concepts" (*Being and Some Philosophers,* 2nd ed. [Toronto: PIMS, 1952], p. 222). For Ambrose McNicholl, judgment cannot be merely a mental synthesis of concepts, for it is a "simple and original act" ("On Judging Existence," *Thomist* 43 [1979]: 578). Joseph Owens claims that for Aquinas the process of judgment is more primary than the process of conceptualization, for the synthesizing actuality of existence, which only the synthesizing judgment grasps, has the primacy over essence in every reality; and although in logical contexts Thomas portrays the incomplex concepts gained through simple apprehension as prior to the judgment's subsequent combining of them, in actuality conceptualization can never occur without concomitant judgment, and vice versa, just as essence and existence, their respective objects, are also necessarily concomitant in reality (*St. Thomas Aquinas on the Existence of God,* ed. J. R. Catan [Albany: SUNY, 1980], pp. 29, 46).

42. For the loci in Thomas that speak of the mind's operations, see Francis Cunningham, "The Second Operation and the Assent vs. the Judgment in St. Thomas," *NS* 31 (1957): 1–33. More often Thomas follows Aristotle and delineates two operations of the intellect, but sometimes on his own authority he adds the process of reasoning as a third.

simple essence" and is variously named the conception of the intellect *(imaginatio intellectus)*, the understanding of indivisibles *(intelligentia indivisibilium)*, or a fashioning *(formatio)*; and a second that consists in the composition or division of a proposition and is also called an assurance *(fides)*.[43] Later, when he describes the twofold operation of the mind in his commentary on Aristotle's *On the Soul*, we find the first operation described as a simple understanding, an understanding of indivisible or simple things, and an apprehension; and the second operation described as a composition or division of things understood, a judging or saying, and a knowing or being wise.[44] Thus, *apprehensio* in its strict sense is synonymous with the mind's first act of simple understanding, which grasps a thing's essence or definition and is prior to and ingredient in the mind's complex second act of composing and dividing.[45]

However, Thomas is also familiar with a broader meaning of *apprehen-*

---

43. *SS* 1.19.5.1 ad7; cf. *SS* 3.23.2.2.1; 3.24.1.1.2; 1.38.1.3; *DV* 14.1; *DSC* 9 ad6. We also find the first operation called an informing *(informatio—Post.,* preface, 4), and the second called a kind of belief *(credulitas—DSC* 9 ad6). *Intelligentia indivisibilium* is used throughout Thomas' writings, but the other terminology tends to be restricted to his earlier works. In a few early texts the double operation is keyed to the two components of reality, being and essence *(SS* 1.38.1.3; *BDT* 5.3). M.-D. Chenu ("Un vestige du stoicisme," *RSPT* 27 [1938]: 63–68) has shown how the Aristotelian distinction between the understanding of indivisibles (translated into Latin as *intelligentia indivisibilium*) and composition/division was— under the influence of the Stoic distinction between representation and assent, which was then taken up by the Arab philosophers—transmitted to the Latin medievals in a tradition peripheral to the direct Aristotelian one originating from Boethius (who used *simplex intelligentia*), with the following terminology derived from the Latin translations of Avicenna and Averroes: the mind's first act is called *formatio* (Averroes) and *imaginatio* (Avicenna), and the second act is called *fides* (Averroes) and *credulitas* (Avicenna). See Garceau, *Judicium*, pp. 104–12, 117–26, 130–31; for the Arabic and Greek origins of *formatio* and *imaginatio*, see Owens, *Existence of God*, p. 242, n. 21. Garceau *(Judicium*, pp. 131–34, 141–42) maintains that Thomas never uses *simplex apprehensio* to designate the mind's first operation, which is not true (see *Anima* 1.10.255–56, and *Meta.* 1.2.46); in any case, Thomas certainly possesses the idea of simple apprehension as any cognitive grasp, sensate or intellectual, in which no discursive process is involved.

44. *Anima* 1.8.244; 2.29.48–52; 3.1.34–38; 3.5.7–17; 3.6.45–52. In *ST* 2-2.45.2 ad3, the intellect's two acts are "to perceive" and "to judge."

45. The first sentence of Thomas' preface to his Commentary on Aristotle's *On Interpretation* states that the intellect's first operation "apprehends the essence of anything." Apprehension and understanding also grasp the definition of a thing *(Anima* 1.8.166–67; 2.29.48–49). For the equivalence of simple apprehension and simple understanding, see *Anima* 1.4.178–79; 1.8.244; 1.10.255–56. Other examples of the strict meaning of *apprehensio*:

sio, which can signify any act of cognition whatsoever, as we may gather from the times he uses the term in contexts dealing with composition/division, judgment, and truth. Thus, truth is said to consist in a thing's being and in the cognitive power's apprehension that is proportioned to that being,[46] which by implication associates *apprehensio* with composition and division, since it is by these latter that we know truth; in the context of speaking of faith as a "thinking with assent," he states that the "intellect apprehends the truth" (*Heb.* 11.1.554); and the mind's act of composition is said to be the means by which the intellect apprehends the identity or diversity of things (*Herm.* 1.3.26). Sometimes the narrow and broad meanings are even placed side by side: *apprehendere* may be used to describe both the first and second operations of the mind;[47] the soul is said to have four different ways of apprehending beings (broad meaning), and yet the act of understanding is also said to "apprehend one thing by one apprehension" (narrow meaning).[48]

Moreover, *conceptio* can also carry a narrow or broad meaning for Aquinas, the former referring to the characteristic activity of the mind's first operation, which is said to "conceive *(concipere)* what a thing is."[49] This "simple conception" or idea is equivalent to a thing's meaning or definition (*Herm.* 1.2.20), and is thus what the name signifies (*DP* 7.6); it is the likeness of the thing (*Herm.* 1.3.27) and, as a definitional apprehension of it, assimilates the mind to the external reality and represents it.[50]

The broader signification of *conceptio* carries beyond the bounds of the intellect's first operation. Thomas speaks of our intellect conceiving the proposition that God exists (*DP* 7.2 ad1), and asserts that "the sentence signifies a composite conception."[51] The "mind's concept" *(conceptus mentis)*

BDT 6.2; *SCG* 1.59.496–97; *Post.*, preface, 4; *Herm.*, preface, 1; *ST* 2-2.83.1 obj.3. Cf. *Post.* 1.1.9; 1.44.405; 2.20.596; *Meta.* 4.6.605; 6.4.1232.

46. *SS* 1.19.5 ad2; *DV* 1.8 ad3.

47. *ST* 2-2.83.1 obj. 3.

48. *Anima* 1.4.173–91. Other examples: *SS* 1.19.5.1; 1.19.5.3 ad3; 1.38.1.3; 3.35.2.2.1. Cf. *DV* 11.1.266–72; 21.4 ad4.

49. *Post.*, preface, 4.

50. *R 108*, prologue, p. 279:1–24. The mental word as conceived "is a certain likeness of the thing" (*Col.* 1.4.31).

51. *Herm.* 1.4.44; cf. 1.6.76; 1.7.85.

may comprise several individual ideas somehow linked together, which is evident from the possibility of an internal contradiction between them (*Quod.* 5.2.1 ad1), which could not happen if such a concept were only one idea. He also recognizes the so-called "common conceptions of the soul," which are various general principles of knowledge immediately and intuitively recognized by all people, such as the principle of noncontradiction or the principle that equals taken from equals leave equals;[52] and since cognitive principles of this sort are enunciations formed by the acts of composition and division, the "common conception" refers to a product of the mind's second operation of judgment.[53]

This brief terminological prelude leads to the supposition that, for Aquinas, just as the concept strictly understood is the product of apprehension strictly understood, so might the concept broadly understood be the fruit of apprehension broadly understood—which is confirmed by what follows.

In Aquinas' eyes it is through its understanding that the intellect forms its interior word or concept: "the intellect by understanding conceives and forms the intention or understood meaning which is the interior word" (*SCG* 4.11.3473); and "the concept is the product of the act of understanding."[54] Further, it takes careful thinking and inquiry to bring about under-

52. *Post.* 1.5.50–51; 1.18.155; 1.19.159–62; 1.36.314; *Meta.* 7.17.1652, 1654. In *BDH* 1.140–46 he asserts that the "common conception" is known to every intellect and agrees with Boethius in defining it as "an enunciation which anyone accepts upon hearing it." *Meta.* 11.4.2210 refers instead to "common propositions"; cf. *BDH* 2.9–13; *Heb.* 11.2.565.

53. *Post.* 1.2.15, 19. In *DV* 11.1.266–72 the "first conceptions of the intellect" may refer either to complex propositions *(dignitates)* or to simple ideas *(incomplexa)* such as the "meaning of being."

54. *DV* 4.2; cf. *ST* 1.34.1 ad3; *SCG* 4.14.3499. Bernard Lonergan speaks of the "rational character of conceptualization" and abstraction in Aquinas, wherein there occurs "the elimination by the understanding of the intellectually irrelevant because it is understood to be irrelevant" (*Verbum: Word and Idea in Aquinas*, ed. David Burrell [Notre Dame: UND, 1967], p. 39). For Lonergan, then, Aquinas is not a proponent of conceptualism, which "consists precisely in the affirmation that concepts proceed not from intellectual knowledge and so intelligibly but, on the contrary, with the same natural spontaneity as images from imagination" (ibid., p. 217). In similar fashion, Peter Geach sees concepts as products of the mind's making and criticizes the view that would consider the process of abstractive conceptualization as simply a matter of acquaintance or intuitive recognition, calling that position abstractionism and absolving the Thomas of the *Summa theologiae* from it (*Mental Acts*

standing, for only after discursive reasoning are we able to come up with a synthetic understanding and viewpoint,[55] and before we actually understand something in the mental concept or word we are said "to think in order to understand."[56] Thus, when the intellect understands something, it forms for itself an interior word or concept.[57] This concept, moreover, may be either simple or complex, for Aquinas claims that the concept which our intellectual operations generate may be signified either through a "simple word" (*vox incomplexa*), which occurs when the intellect "forms definitions," or through a "complex word" (*vox complexa*), which takes place when the intellect forms a proposition or enunciation.[58]

Finally, one may choose examples from Thomas' works showing that he acknowledges, either implicitly or explicitly, that at least some concepts are the fruit of judgment and other rational processes. Three are offered here. First, he says that if we want to understand anything, even the nature of a stone, we arrive at the word or concept, which is the product of our understanding, only after much reasoning and thinking, all of which amounts to a disciplined discourse of questioning (*discursus inquisitionis* —*John* 1.1.26).

Second, Thomas contends that it is not of the very nature of essence in general that it should be either exclusively complex or exclusively simple: for if it were exclusively complex then there could never exist a simple essence, which we know is not the case since God is a simple nature; and if

---

[London: Routledge and Kegan Paul, n.d.], pp. 40–41, 130–31). For a defense of Geach's position, see Anthony Lisska, "Deely and Geach on Abstractionism in Thomistic Epistemology," *Thomist* 37 (1973): 548–68.

55. *ST* 1.14.7. See Julien Peghaire, *Intellectus et ratio selon saint Thomas d'Aquin* (Ottawa: Institut d'Études Médiévales, 1936), pp. 247ff.

56. *DP* 9.9. Lonergan sees Aquinas as holding that "the inner word of the human mind emerges at the end of a process of thoughtful inquiry" (*Verbum*, p. 9; see nn. 41–47 for relevant texts). Cf. Garceau, *Judicium*, p. 142, for a similar view.

57. This word can be called a *conceptio* (*ST* 1.27.1) or a *conceptus* (*ST* 1.34.1).

58. *DV* 4.2; *DP* 8.1; *John* 1.1.25. Cf. *DV* 3.2; *Quod.* 5.5.2; *DP* 9.5; *ST* 1.85.2 ad3. Gaston Rabeau shows that the concept is the product of all types of intellectual knowledge, arguing that later Thomists unwarrantably narrowed the scope of the concept so that it applied only to the mind's first operation of simple understanding (*Species. Verbum: L'activité intellectuelle élémentaire selon S. Thomas d'Aquin*, BibThom 22 [Paris: Vrin, 1938]). For Lonergan, "an account of the Thomist inner word has to be an account of judgments no less than of the formation of definitions" (*Verbum*, p. 4).

it were exclusively simple then no complex essence could ever be found, which again is false since humanity is a complex nature.[59] Even though it appears as if Thomas is arguing to conclusions on the grounds of a direct inspection of the nature of essence in general, the process is actually quite the reverse: for he can conceive the "nature" of essence in general and realize that it is not exclusively either simple or complex, *only insofar as his concept of essence is itself a conclusion* flowing from his previous judgments that human essence is complex and God's essence completely simple. Certainly, one would have every right to think, on the grounds of everyday experience, that essence as such must always be complex, and would have no reason to suppose that it might be otherwise, *unless one also already knew* that some simple essence (God or angel) did in fact exist, on the basis of which one could then modify one's normal everyday concept of essence.

Third, repeating a well-known Avicennian maxim, Thomas often invokes the principle that "being is the first concept of the intellect" or "being is what is first understood by the intellect."[60] Although the vocabulary with which the axiom is expressed *(apprehensio, conceptio,* and *concipere)* suggests the mind's first operation, and even though Thomas shares at times in some of the essentialistic strains that Avicenna's epistemology is noted for,[61] we should not suppose that Thomas's only view is that being is

---

59. *SS* 2.3.1.1, p. 87.

60. "Ens est prima conceptio intellectus" *(Post.* 1.5.50); "primum enim quod cadit in imaginatione intellectus est ens, sine quod nihil potest apprehendi ab intellectu" *(SS* 1.8.1.3); "illud autem quod primo intellectus concipit quasi notissimum et in quod conceptiones omnes resolvit est ens, ut Avicenna dicit" *(DV* 1.1.100–103); "illud quod primo cadit in apprehensione intellectus est ens" *(DV* 21.4 ad4). In the prologue to the *De ente et essentia* (lines 3–5), where the axiom first appears, we read that "ens autem et essentia sunt quae primo intellectu concipiuntur." Other texts in which the axiom appears: *SS* 1.38.1.4 obj. 4; *BDT* 1.3 obj. 3; *Meta.* 1.2.46; cf. *Meta.* 4.6.605. Amélie-Marie Goichon argues that the *De ente et essentia* is fundamentally inspired by Avicenna and that Thomas quotes him more often early in his career, the citations becoming rarer as time goes on ("Un chapitre de l'influence d'Ibn Sina en Occident: le *De ente et essentia* de S. Thomas d'Aquin," in *Le livre du Millénaire d'Avicenne,* vol. 4 [Tehran, 1956], pp. 118–31). See also John Wippel, "The Latin Avicenna as a Source of Thomas Aquinas' Metaphysics," *FZPT* 37 (1990): 51–90. The maxim is taken from Avicenna's *Metaphysics* 1.6 (Venice ed., 1508, 72rb–73ra; *Avicenna Latinus,* ed. S. Van Riet, 5 vols. [Louvain/Leiden: Peeters/Brill, 1968–83], 3:31–32): "Res et ens et necesse talia sunt quod statim imprimuntur in anima prima impressione, quae non acquiritur ex aliis notioribus se." The quote in the Van Riet edition is taken from chapter 5 instead of chapter 6.

61. See Goichon, *La distinction de l'essence et de l'existence d'après Ibn Sina (Avicenne)*

the primordial concept (in the narrow sense) of the mind's first operation, for there are other indications in his thought that the concept of being is to be broadly understood, that is, as the fruit of judgments, whether they be few or many, spontaneous or reasoned.

On the one hand, Thomas informs us that, as regards simple apprehension, more universal realities are known before less universal, for being is first known by the intellect, and then animal before human, and so on (*Meta.* 1.2.46); and both operations of the mind—the understanding of simple ideas and composition/division—possess something that they understand before all else: being is the primordial object of the mind's first act, is included in every subsequent act of simple understanding, and is that upon which the first principle of the mind's second act, the principle of noncontradiction, depends.[62] On the other hand, he notes that whereas the word *human* derives its meaning from human nature, and *thing (res)* from essence, the term *being (ens)* derives its meaning "from the act of being" *(ab actu essendi)*.[63] In this latter text he is clearly distinguishing being from nature or essence, and it is a well-known Thomistic commonplace that *esse* is not the object of simple understanding but rather of the judgmental acts of the mind's second operation. Thus, Thomas can be read both ways on the question of whether the concept of being is the root of all judgments or the fruit of some of them, that is, whether the concept of being is an independent, essentialist, and primal concept of the mind's first operation, or a quasi-essential concept that is the product and, as it were, the residue of even more primary existential judgments: he opts for the former in those texts where he is quoting Avicenna and allowing some

---

(Paris: Desclée, 1937). She mentions Avicenna's famous "flying man" example (pp. 13–15; the example is from his *De anima* 1.1 [2rb]), which is redolent of Descartes's *cogito* and indicates that for Avicenna the primal intuition of being does not absolutely depend on sensible experience: if a man were created instantaneously and perfectly, but with eyes veiled, hovering in a void so as to feel no resistance of air, and with his bodily members not touching or meeting, without doubt he could reflect and ask if he himself exists, and affirm that he does, despite being unable to experience his bodily members or even his brain or anything exterior—he could affirm his existence without knowing his own length, width, or depth.

62. *Meta.* 4.6.605.

63. *Meta.* 4.2.553. The word *being (ens)* signifies and receives its meaning from "the very act of to-be" (*ipsum esse*—ibid., 4.2.556, 558). See also *SS* 1.19.5.1.

of the Avicennian vocabulary's essentialistic themes to shape his own thought, but he implies the latter if we combine the texts that derive *ens* from *esse* with his understanding of judgment as the way to knowing *esse*.[64]

For Aquinas, then, the mind's concept in the broad sense can be a definition, a judgment, or anything at all in which the intellect speaks its interior word. Thoughtful inquiry and a process of reasoning often precede and prepare the way for that final concept in which the intellect understands whatever it understands. And if this is so, then Aquinas' theological or transcendental analogy[65] may also be seen as broadly conceptual, in the sense that the meanings of that analogy are themselves the fruit of a web of interwoven theological first-order judgments stretching out toward the truth.

III. Analogy as Judgment

Aquinas' theological analogy is rooted in and arises out of true judgments about God and creatures. This section will indicate how the thesis about the judgmental nature of analogy in Aquinas is substantiated by the way he portrays theological analogy as a mean between univocity and equivocity, and by the place he assigns transcendental analogy in his treatise on God.

A. Theological Analogy as the Mean between Univocity and Equivocity

Aquinas always argues, in his formal epistemological treatment of theological analogy, that true theological predication cannot possibly be a matter of univocity or equivocity,[66] and concludes that the only alternative

---

64. Wippel writes: "What one first discovers through original judgments of existence can be summed up, as it were, under the heading being, or reality, or something similar. Once the intellect makes this discovery, it expresses it in a *complex concept or notion*, as 'that which is'. This . . . is what Thomas has in mind when he refers to being *(ens)* as that which is first known" (*Metaphysical Thought*, p. 44, first set of italics added).

65. Unless otherwise specified, *analogy* in the remainder of the chapter refers to the analogy of referential multivocity.

66. For a table that schematizes the arguments Thomas uses against univocity and equivocity as regards the divine names, see Bernard Montagnes, *La doctrine de l'analogie de l'être d'après saint Thomas d'Aquin,* Philosophes Médiévaux 6 (Louvain/Paris: Publications

left is that of analogy. By a process of elimination, then, he determines that predicates can truly be said of God only by way of analogy.

First of all, he rejects univocal predication with respect to God and creature because of previous truths already known about God. In general, he either states a universal condition of univocal predication and then shows how such a condition cannot hold for God and creature or, conversely, lays down an impediment to univocal predication and then explains how such an impediment obtains whenever a predicate is commonly said of God and creature.

He offers five main reasons for his rejection of univocity. First, univocal names must have the same definition, but the definition of what is said of the creature is not the definition of what is said of God, and thus predicates said of God and creatures are not univocal (*CT* 1.27). The creaturely and divine definitions cannot be the same since we have no capacity to comprehend God by knowing the divine definition (*CT* 1.26). The incomprehensibility of God, therefore, precludes any definition of God and the univocal predication based upon it.

Second, even if, quite impossibly, a creaturely and divine predicate possessed an identical definition, there would still be no grounds to claim univocal predication, which does not occur unless the same form is received according to the same mode of being, for God and creature possess nothing according to the same manner of existence. He uses the example of the word *house,* which is said nonunivocally of an actually existing house and of a house existing in the artist's imagination, since the house in both instances has a different level of being; and such is the case with God and creatures, for even if they shared the same form they could not do so according to the same level of being *(modus essendi),* "for there is nothing in God which is not the divine being itself," which is not the case with creatures (*SCG* 1.32.285). Just as *house* cannot be predicated univocally

---

Universitaires/Béatrice-Nauwelaerts, 1963), appendix 2, pp. 181–83; also, pp. 67–70. See also Hampus Lyttkens, "Die Bedeutung der Gottesprädikate bei Thomas von Aquin," *NZST* 6 (1964): 280–83. For an enlightening treatment of Thomas' position on our analogical knowledge of God, see Wippel, *Metaphysical Thought,* pp. 543–72. Wippel notes that Thomas discusses our nonquidditative knowledge of God before taking up the issue of our analogical knowledge of God and that his epistemology of analogy is grounded in his ontology.

since a house exists materially in reality and immaterially in the builder's mind, so *goodness* cannot be predicated univocally of God and creature since even if it had the same meaning in both cases, it would still exist in God simply and in the creature in manifold and various ways.[67] For whatever exists in creatures in a multiple and deficient fashion exists in God unitedly and perfectly; for example, *wise* said of humans bespeaks a perfection distinct from all other perfections and from the human essence, faculties, and act of being, but we do not intend any of these connotations when we predicate *wise* of God; when said of humans, *wise* "circumscribes" and "comprehends" the reality signified, but when said of God it leaves God as incomprehensibly "exceeding" the meaning of the name (*ST* 1.13.5). Thomas' second reason argues then that even if the meaning of a name were the same for a creature and God, God's simplicity, perfection, incomprehensibility, and identity of being and essence would still prohibit any univocal predication of that name.

He bases his third argument, which is subtle and similar to the second, upon the identity of being and essence in God. Nothing can be predicated univocally of God and creature, for in all univocal predication a common meaning is shared equally among the subjects.

However much a creature imitates God, however, it can never reach the point where something would belong to it for the same reason that it belongs to God; for those predicates which have the same meaning in different subjects are common to those subjects as regards their substance or essence but are distinct according to their act of being; but whatever is in God is his own act of being, for just as essence and being are the same in him, so are knowledge and the act of actually knowing the same in him. Therefore, since the act of being which is proper to one reality cannot be communicated to another, it is impossible for a creature to reach the point where it could possess something in the same way as God possesses something, just as it is impossible for it to attain the same act of being as God has.[68]

Univocity can apply only to those realities in which essence and being differ, for two humans share their humanity, not their acts of being; but in God, whose "act of being is his nature," any form signified by a name is identical with the divine being itself, and thus nothing can be said univo-

---

67. *DP* 7.7, and ad5–6.
68. *DV* 2.11.103–18; cf. *SS* 1.prol.1.2 ad2; 1.19.5.2 ad1; *SCG* 1.32.285.

cally of God and creature, for any perfection said of God always implicates the divine act of being, which can never belong to the creature.[69]

The fourth reason is rooted in the truth that God does not participate in any nature or quality. Univocal predicates belong by participation to those subjects of which they are predicated; but nothing can be said of God by participation, for whatever participates in something possesses it in a partial fashion, whereas God has every mode and degree of perfection and is essentially whatever he is (*SCG* 1.32.288–89).

The fifth reason derives from the truth that God is not a univocal cause, for an effect that is not equal in nature or form to its cause cannot receive the univocal predication of that form; but the forms caused by God do not equal the divine power, since creatures "receive in a divided and partial fashion what in God is found simply and universally" (*SCG* 1.32.284). Univocal predication is impossible because the finite creature cannot equal the infinite power of God (*DP* 7.7 ad1).

The boundaries between these reasons are vague and fluid, and one reason easily shades into another. Together, they prove for Aquinas that nothing can be predicated univocally of God and creature. The conclusion is epistemological and semantic, but the reasons themselves are various ontological truths about God that Aquinas has previously established to his own satisfaction. Our awareness of certain truths about God demands that we acknowledge the nonunivocal character of any predication about God.[70]

As his second move, Thomas also adduces two fundamental reasons to demonstrate that nothing can possibly be said of God and creatures by means of pure equivocity either.[71] For if the predication of the divine names involved equivocity, then our knowledge of God would be destroyed (epistemological reason); and the order and likeness between creature and God precludes any equivocal predication of the divine names (ontological reason).

---

69. *SS* 1.35.1.4; cf. *DP* 7.7, and ad 2–3.

70. For some interesting thoughts on why the divine names are nonunivocal for Thomas, see Lawrence Dewan, "St. Thomas and the Divine Names," *SE* 32 (1980): 24–30.

71. Thomas is only arguing against pure or fortuitous equivocity (*SCG* 1.33.290), not the rationally intelligible equivocity that is the same as analogy.

The first, epistemological reason simply argues from the *fact* that we know some truth about God to the conclusion that the divine predicates cannot be equivocal. The structure of the argument is essentially a *modus tollens* conditional statement whose consequent, after being denied, also requires the antecedent to be denied: if the attributes commonly said of creatures and God were equivocal, then we would have no knowledge of God; but we do know some truths about God, and thus the attributes cannot be equivocal. Sometimes Thomas gives the bare bones of the argument: "Wisdom is not said equivocally of God and creature, otherwise created wisdom would not lead us to the knowledge of uncreated wisdom, and similarly with power and goodness";[72] one pure equivocal cannot lead to the knowledge of another, but "through our knowledge we arrive at a cognition of the divine knowledge" (*SS* 1.35.1.4). More bluntly, if the names we predicate of God are equivocal, then we can know nothing of God; but philosophers and Romans 1:20 witness to the fact that we do know things about God (*ST* 1.13.5). The inner workings of the way we know God would be hampered if the names and concepts we use were equivocal, for then all philosophical demonstrations and other theological reasoning about God would be liable to the fallacy of equivocation and would in fact be sophistical.[73] Since we know God from creatures, if there were only an equivocal agreement of names, "we would know nothing of God except empty names to which nothing corresponds in reality" (*DP* 7.7). Reasoning from creatures to God could not take place if the terms we use were equivocal, for knowledge does not depend "on vocal sounds but on the meaning of names," and in fact we do know God and do reason to God from creatures, which is clearly admitted by all those who speak of divine matters (*SCG* 1.33.293–94).

Another text offers a variation of the epistemological reason:

In vain is any name predicated of a subject unless through that name we understand something about the subject. If names are said of God and creatures in a purely equivocal fashion, then we understand nothing about God through those names, since the meanings of those names are known to us only inasmuch as they

72. *SS* 1.2.1.3, *sed contra*.
73. *DP* 7.7; *ST* 1.13.5.

are said of creatures. It would be in vain, then, to say or prove that God is a being, or good, or anything else of this sort. (*SCG* 1.33.295)

Thomas is reasoning that, since the only way we know God is through creatures, and since the meanings of the names we predicate of God are first known to us because of the way they are predicated of creatures, if we grant for the sake of argument that these names are said equivocally of God and creatures, then we can never really come to know anything about God when we predicate them of God—that is, though the physical sounds seem to be saying something of God, in reality the meanings remain creaturely and can have no application with respect to an uncreated being. If the meaning of *good* in "God is good" and "a creature is good" were known to us only through creatures, *and* if at the same time it were totally equivocal, then creatures would provide us no justifying fulcrum for levering creaturely meanings toward a divine subject. Thomas' theological epistemology is insistent that the only road to the knowledge of God passes through the realm of creatures, and this is why equivocity is such a death knell for that epistemology, for it sunders the only bond of intelligibility and meaning between creatures and God, leaving our knowledge and speech about God untethered to reality and subject to capricious custom.[74] He leaves the final steps of the *modus tollens* conditional up to us: but we *do* know and name God, and not vainly or capriciously; hence, names cannot be said equivocally of God and creatures.

The second, ontological reason is the likeness between creature and God, which precludes pure equivocity in divine predication. Sometimes Thomas gathers this reason from the texts of scripture,[75] sometimes he expresses it more philosophically by asserting that whatever is caused must bear some likeness to its cause,[76] and sometimes he takes both tacks (*SCG* 1.33.292). He also notes the order or relation between God and creatures: in names fortuitously equivocal, "we do not recognize any order or relation

---

74. "Nothing prohibits anything from being named equivocally by any name, if customary usage permits it" (*SCG* 1.42.344).

75. The most cited text, Genesis 1:26, says that humans are made to the image and likeness of God (*DV* 2.11, *sed contra*).

76. *DP* 7.7; cf. ad7 of the first series of objections, and ad3–5, 7 of the second series.

of one thing to another, but it is totally accidental that one name is attributed to different things"; but in the names said of God and creatures there
is the "order of cause and caused," which is not accidental and thus makes
equivocal predication impossible.[77]

Another text links both reasons against equivocity:

> It cannot be asserted that whatever is said of God and creatures is predicated in a
> purely equivocal fashion, because unless there were some correspondence *(conve-
> nientia)* between the creature and God in reality, God's essence would not be the
> likeness *(similitudo)* of creatures, and so by knowing his own essence he would not
> know creatures; similarly, we could not attain the knowledge of God from created
> realities, nor from among the names applied to creatures could we assert one
> name of God more than another; for in equivocal predication it does not matter
> which name is used, since no correspondence to reality is recognized anyway. (*DV*
> 2.11.122–34)

This argument is cast as a contrary to fact conditional, and so the implication is that we already in fact do know the two truths that, by denying the
twofold consequent, also lead us to deny the supposition of equivocity in
the antecedent: God knows creatures through their likeness to the divine
essence, and we know God through creatures.[78]

Aquinas ultimately bases his rejection of equivocity, therefore, on three
previously known truths which he now takes for granted: creatures bear
some likeness to God; God knows creatures through his essence, to which
creatures are likened; and we know God through creatures. Even the bare
fact of our knowing any truth *at all* about God prevents the possibility of
pure equivocity, whereas particular truths about the transcendence of God
are used to reject the possibility of univocity. In either case, his discussion
depends upon a reflex look at the truths garnered through the methods of
systematic theology. To our modern way of thinking, born of Cartesian introspection and Kantian criticism, this seems to beg the question: we

---

77. *SCG* 1.33.291. Cf. *CT* 1.27; and *DP* 7.7, where Thomas remarks that all the various
opinions about the divine names admit that divine predication is based on some relation.

78. I have described this text as a combination of the epistemological and ontological arguments against equivocity. Montagnes (*Doctrine,* p. 70) and Wippel (*Metaphysical
Thought,* pp. 551, 560) assert that Thomas does not use an (exclusively) ontological or metaphysical argument against equivocity until the *Summa contra gentiles.*

would automatically tend to place the epistemological questions of univocity and equivocity first, and only afterwards take up the ontological
concerns of theology. But Aquinas lived and thought long before the pro-
genitors of the modern age of philosophy, and he saw no problem in basing knowledge on being, epistemology on ontology. He does not beg the
question within his own system, for he does not formally or consciously
use epistemology as a prolegomenon (Heideggerian-style presuppositions
are of course another matter) to the task of establishing the ontological
truths of theology, and so he is free to work out the epistemology and semantics of divine predication by reflecting on the ramifications of the
truths he already knows about God.

Finally, then, Aquinas reasons that if the truths we already know about
God make it impossible to countenance either univocity or equivocity as
regards divine predication, then the process of elimination leaves analogy
as the only remaining possibility.[79] Analogy points to a relation between
creatures and God, by which we compare things to God as to their first
origin and thus attribute to God the names of perfections.[80] Analogy

is a mean between pure equivocity and simple univocity, for in those names which
are said analogically there is neither one meaning as in univocal names, nor totally diverse meanings as in equivocal names, but the name which is analogically
predicated in plural ways signifies different relations to something one. (ST 1.13.5)

Analogy is a mean between univocity and equivocity because it avoids the
strict sameness of meaning proper to univocity and the radical diversity of
meaning characteristic of equivocity, and it is the only remaining possibility precisely because the judgments of theology demand that between God
and creature there be difference without equivocity and likeness without
univocity.[81] In other words, analogy turns out to be the only epistemolog-

---

79. SCG 1.34.297; cf. SS 1.2.1.3, sed contra; 1.35.1.4; DP 7.7. Francis Ruello claims that Albert
the Great does not delineate univocity from analogy so clearly as Thomas (Les "noms divins"
et leur "raisons" selon saint Albert le Grand, commentateur du "De divinis nominibus,"
BibThom 35 [Paris: Vrin, 1963], pp. 51, 79, n. 32, 80, n. 33), but what Albert means by univocity is open to dispute.

80. DV 2.11.137–39; CT 1.27; ST 1.13.5.

81. For the International Theological Commission, analogy is also the mean between
an overly positivist and an excessively negativist understanding of theological knowledge
and language: "Analogy protects against an objectivist, reified and ultimately mysteryless

ical explanation capable of responding to the two principal presuppositions for there being any theological truth in the first place: for equivocity cannot account for the fact that some true knowledge of God actually exists, and by derogating from God's transcendence univocity disallows the requirement that our true theological judgments recognize God *as God*.

Therefore, Aquinas' doctrine of theological analogy arises out of his epistemological reflections upon what he sees as the necessary presuppositions and consequences of true theological judgments.

B. The Place of Theological Analogy in Aquinas' Treatise on God

The position of Aquinas' treatment of theological or transcendental analogy within the larger context of his treatise on the one God strengthens our contention that for him such a doctrine of analogy subsists in a second epistemological judgment reflecting back upon the primary judgments of theology. We shall inspect his placement of transcendental analogy in the *Summa contra Gentiles* and the *Summa theologiae*. Our only concern is to comprehend the formal structure of his treatise on the one God, to see how he arranges the various parts that make up the environment for his treatment of analogy.

Beginning with the *Summa contra Gentiles:* chapters 1–9 of the first book discuss matters introductory to the treatise on the one God, and chapters 10–13 offer various proofs for God's existence. Once these proofs have shown that a "first being we call God" exists, Thomas investigates God's attributes and properties, employing negative theology's "way of remotion" (*SCG* 1.14.116–17). The primary principle of this negative theology, which will serve as the basis for the rest of its conclusions, is "God is totally immobile," which Thomas sees as manifested directly by the proofs for God's existence and confirmed by scripture (*SCG* 1.14.119).

Chapters 15–27 treat the chief theses of Thomas' negative theology. God is eternal, immaterial, pure act without any passive potentiality, incorpore-

---

understanding of faith and dogma. But it protects as well against an overly negative theology, which regards dogmas as mere ciphers of an ultimately inconceivable Transcendence and consequently fails to recognize the historical concreteness of the Christian mystery of salvation" ("On the Interpretation of Dogmas," *Origins* 20 [17 May 1990]: 9).

al, and without any accident or external determination (15–17, 20, 23–24); God does not possess a complex being, is not subject to extrinsic violence, does not belong to any category of being, and is neither the substantial form of any body nor the formal being of all reality (18–19, 25–27); God is not different from the divine essence, and the divine essence is not different from the divine being (21–22).

Chapter 28 proves that God is the universally perfect being, and is based on chapters 13 (God as the first being and first efficient cause), 16 (God as pure act), and 22 (God as the One whose being and essence are not distinct). God is said to be perfect because he does not lack anything of being, which sounds deceptively like a proposition of negative theology ("does not lack") but in fact is not. For whereas all genuine statements of negative theology assert that God *does lack* something implying imperfection (body, accident, composition, time, etc.), "God is universally perfect" means that God *does not lack* anything implying perfection. In fact, "God is all-perfect" is actually the logical predecessor and epistemic progenitor of "God is not at all imperfect," which is the core contention of negative theology. Since, as chapter 28 suggests, to understand God as all-perfect is another way of interpreting God as pure act, and since in chapter 16 *actus purus* is Thomas' interpretation of God as the first cause and first being, which are themselves conclusions of the proofs for God's existence in chapter 13, then an affirmative theology, based on the positive fact of God's existence and seeing God as pure act and all-perfect, undergirds the arguments of Thomas' negative theology and is the necessary though unannounced foundation for it.[82]

Basing itself on scriptural quotes and on the fact that in creation God gives all things their perfection and also transcends them, chapter 29 explains how there is a real though deficient likeness of creatures to God.

---

82. Even God's immobility, which *SCG* 1.14.119 expressly announces as the primary proposition of negative theology, flows from the proofs that posit the fact of God's existence. David Burrell (*Aquinas: God and Action* [Notre Dame: UND, 1979], chaps. 2–4; *Knowing the Unknowable God: Ibn-Sina, Maimonides, Aquinas* [Notre Dame: UND, 1986], chaps. 3–4) discusses Thomas' treatment of God's simplicity, infinity, immutability, and eternity, and notes that Thomas' path to these theological negations begins from *esse* as positive actuality (*Knowing*, p. 50).

Moreover, the absolute perfection of God and the likeness of creatures to God are the requisite ontological underpinnings for the ensuing epistemological discussion of chapters 30–36, which consider questions about the predication of the divine names, including the problem of analogy. These seven chapters are an example of theology reflexively and formally assessing its own epistemological status, and all of them depend in the final analysis upon theological truths known by the methods of systematic theology.[83]

We now turn to the *Summa theologiae*. The treatise on the one God in the first part displays the following order of questions: an introduction about the science of theology; proofs for the existence of God; treatments of God's simplicity, perfection, goodness, infinity, immanence, immutability, eternity, and unity; two questions on how God is known and named by us; and then treatments of God's own knowledge, ideas, truth, life, will, love, justice and mercy, providence, decree of predestination, power, and beatitude. Question four on God's perfection also includes an article on the creature's likeness to God, which is the analogue to chapter 29 of the *Summa contra Gentiles*, and as is also the case with the earlier Summa, the two epistemological questions are placed in the middle of the treatise.[84]

Question two on God's existence is of central importance, just as it is in the *Summa contra Gentiles*.[85] First of all, nowhere does Thomas say or im-

---

83. Chapter 30 is based on chapter 28; 31 on 23 and 29; 32 on 21–25 and 28–29; 33 on 29 and 32; and 35 on 29 and 31.

84. Colman O'Neill asserts that in the first part of the *Summa theologiae* analogy has two ontological presuppositions: the existence of God (*ST* 1.2.3) and the participation of creatures in God, which establishes their similarity to God (*ST* 1.4.3), a similarity Thomas sees as taught by Genesis 1:26 and 1 John 3:2 ("Prédication analogique," pp. 84–86). These two biblical passages portray the human as the image of God both protologically and eschatologically, the first taking us back to the beginning, and the second looking forward to when we shall be like God in the blessed vision of heaven; our likeness to God is dynamic, imperfect, and still in a pilgrim state (idem, "Analogy," pp. 51–53).

85. For the Greek, Arabic, and Jewish sources of Thomas' proofs for God's existence, see René Arnou, *De quinque viis Sancti Thomae ad demonstrandum Dei existentiam apud antiquos Graecos et Arabes et Iudaeos praeformatis vel adumbratis* (Rome: Gregorian, 1932); a few additional sources relating to the third and fifth ways may be found in *BT* 4 (1934), no. 233. See also Jules Baisnée, "St. Thomas Aquinas' Proofs of the Existence of God Presented in Their Chronological Order," in *Philosophical Studies in Honor of the Very Reverend Ignatius Smith, O.P.*, ed. J. K. Ryan (Westminster, MD: Newman, 1952), pp. 29–64. For a complete

ply that we prove God's existence by means of analogy, as some have claimed.[86] "God exists" does not employ an already existing analogy but actually generates one in order to know and express its own truth—that is, "God exists" is itself an analogical judgment of enormous epistemological complexity that transfers *exists* from its normal worldly uses to God.[87]

Second, depending on whether we see the proofs as theological or philosophical exercises, either they strengthen and elucidate the meaning given to the noun *God* by the theological environment or they generate that meaning themselves. It is generally admitted that the proofs in the *Summa theologiae* are theologically motivated and inspired, using philosophy as a handmaiden to theology. They serve as a theological reflection on the significance of faith's confession that God exists, in order to make this confession thinkable and to understand it better, and so that the basic affirmation of God's existence may serve to ground the science of theology and help systematize all else that follows in the treatise on the one God.[88] When the proofs for God's existence are essayed (and assayed) within a theologically oriented culture, *God* already carries an accepted meaning (Thomas says at the conclusion of each proof, "This we call God"), one that can function as a nominal definition within each proof.[89]

---

inventory and critical appraisal of these same proofs, see Fernand van Steenberghen, *Le problème de l'existence de Dieu dans les écrits de S. Thomas d'Aquin*, Philosophes Médiévaux 23 (Louvain-la-Neuve: Editions de l'Institut Supérieur de philosophie, 1980). John Wippel gives a more positive philosophical assessment of the proofs in *Metaphysical Thought*, pp. 379–500.

86. George Klubertanz states that God is known to exist, first by an indeterminate analogy of causality, and finally by analogy of participation ("The Problem of the Analogy of Being," *RM* 10 [1957]: 569–73). Lyttkens also claims that Thomas uses the causal analogy in his natural theology (*Analogy*, pp. 395–414), whereas it is truer to say that the "causal analogy" is really the logical, second-order reflection on what happens epistemologically when the causal *principle* is at work in theology.

87. O'Neill, "Prédication analogique," p. 87; and Battista Mondin, "Triplice analisi dell'analogia e suo uso in teologia," *DTP* 34 (1957): 418–21.

88. Victor White, *God the Unknown* (New York: Harper, 1956), pp. 49–60; Thomas O'Brien, *Metaphysics and the Existence of God* (Washington, DC: Thomist Press, 1960), pp. 179–84; Wayne Hankey, "The Place of the Proof for God's Existence in the *Summa theologiae* of Thomas Aquinas," *Thomist* 46 (1982): 375; O'Neill, "Prédication analogique," pp. 84–86; idem, "Analogy," pp. 51–53.

89. Van Steenberghen thinks that Thomas uses "the provident creator of the universe" as

In this situation, the meaning of *God* is further enhanced and illumined by the proofs, insofar as they first reason from the facts of experience to the ultimate cause of all things and then identify that cause, via the nominal definition, with God, and in so doing clarify and justify the meanings faith and theology have given to *God*. If the proofs are interpreted as functioning within a theologal culture and context, then, at least part of the meaning of *God* arises out of them.[90] If they are viewed as pure philosophical demonstrations, however, then the very meaning of *God* is derived from the truth about God: the meaning of *God* in this case is not a necessary presupposition to the demonstration of God's existence but is what comes to light as philosophical reason searches out and attempts to understand the world's intelligibility.[91]

Third, Aquinas frequently invokes the conclusions of the proofs for

---

the nominal definition for God (*Le problème*, pp. 288–96). O'Brien admits that the nominal definition may have a place in theology but not in any metaphysical proof of God's existence (*Metaphysics*, pp. 190–214).

90. "The meaning of divinity, no less than its reality, is . . . precisely that to which the five ways lead" (White, *God*, p. 60). Gordon Kaufman takes the opposite view, that the meaning of *God* must precede the proof of God, that proving God's existence is a matter of showing that *God* has a real referent (*God the Problem* [Cambridge: Harvard, 1972], p. 44, n. 6).

91. W. Norris Clarke writes that God cannot be defined or meant before discovering him, at least philosophically: "The *philosophical* meaning of God should be exclusively a function of the *way by which He is discovered*" ("Analogy," p. 84, n. 9). Without special reference to Aquinas, other authors make similar points: C. J. F. Williams shows how the meaning of *God* is a function of the way we know God ("Existence and the Meaning of the Word *God*," *DR* 77 [1959]: 53–71); James McWilliams asserts that we must first judge God to exist before we can specify the meaning of the word *God* ("Judgmental Knowledge," *MSch* 39 [1962]: 378); similarly, Michael Levine holds that the judgment of God's existence is necessary for any literal or analogical talk about God ("'Can We Speak Literally of God?'" *RS* 21 [1985]: 53–54); more generally, Richard Swinburne argues that the analogical meaning and coherence of any words or thoughts about God depend on the prior truth of certain statements about God (*The Coherence of Theism* [Oxford: Clarendon, 1977], pp. 1–5, 48–49, 70–71, 278–80, 294–96). With reference to Aquinas, Burrell states that in talk about God, meaning is not so much presupposed as it is constituted by judgment ("Aquinas on Naming God," p. 202). Even more generally, Lonergan contends that for Thomas knowledge always measures meaning and that there is a "clear reduction of meaning to knowledge" (*Verbum*, pp. 152–53). K. Surin realizes that he disagrees with Thomas on this point: Thomas "needs a theory of theological *truth* on which to hinge his theory of theological *meaning*"; but "this is incongruous: it is a philosophical commonplace that a statement has to be meaningful before it can be assigned a truth-value" ("Creation, Revelation, and the Analogy Theory," *JTS* 32 [1981]: 405, n. 1, 408).

God's existence in many of the subsequent questions of his treatise on the one God, as we also showed for the *Summa contra Gentiles*.[92]

What, then, does the arrangement and order of chapters and questions in the two works reveal about analogy? If we distinguish questions dealing directly with God's essence (God's goodness, perfection, simplicity, infinity, unity, etc.) from those dealing with the divine operations (intelligence, will, free choice, life, blessedness, etc.), then only the *Summa theologiae* completes the treatment of God's essence before the epistemological questions are broached, for the *Summa contra Gentiles* discusses God's goodness, unity, and infinity after the questions about our knowing and naming of God. In both works, however, the questions about God's operations are treated after the epistemological questions. The two works, moreover, both discuss the following subjects prior to the questions about our knowledge and naming of God: God's existence, simplicity, perfection, eternity, and immutability. The conclusions of the questions on eternity and immutability, however, are never used in the epistemological questions. While the *Summa contra Gentiles* concerns itself with God's perfection and the likeness of creatures to God in the two questions immediately preceding the questions about the knowing and naming of God, the *Summa theologiae* places early in its first part the treatment of God's perfection and the likeness of creatures to God. In this latter work, then, the questions on God's existence, simplicity, and perfection are all linked together at the very commencement of the treatise on the one God and thus demonstrate more clearly the pure positivity—God as pure act and subsistent act of being—that undergirds Thomas' negative theology.

For both summas, then, the questions about our knowing and naming of God always precede the questions about God's operations and always follow at least some of the discussions about God's essence. The treatments of God's essence that in both works precede and most heavily influence the subsequent epistemological questions are those dealing with God's existence, simplicity, and perfection, and with the likeness of crea-

---

92. Consult Leo Elders on how the various proofs influence the subsequent series of attributes in the *Summa theologiae* ("L'ordre des attributs divins dans la *Somme théologique*," *DTP* 56 [1979]: 225–32). See also Hankey, "Place of the Proof," p. 393.

tures to God. This suggests that for Aquinas, therefore, the truth about God that must be known before the epistemological issues can be fruitfully considered is that there exists a God who is the subsistent act of being itself, who is universally perfect, and to whom creatures bear some likeness.

IV. *The Graced Judgment of Faith*

Our contention is that Aquinas' theological analogy originates in judgments about God, and since we will also need to ask in future chapters whether those judgments are rooted mainly in reason or in faith, it will be helpful to say a word concerning his view of faith as a graced judgment about God.[93]

For Aquinas, the goal or object of the theological virtue of faith is God as First Truth and everything else that exists insofar as it is touched by the truth-full mystery of God.[94] *DV* 14.8 ad9 identifies God as both the primary witness *for* faith and the principal goal *of* faith, for First Truth "testifies principally about itself." This means that God's truth and testimony are self-justifying,[95] for God testifies to God, but this self-referentiality is no cause for alarm, for God's testimony cannot fail to proclaim the truth.[96]

93. Works that may be consulted with profit for discussions of Aquinas' treatment of faith: Roger Aubert, *Le problème de l'acte de foi*, 3rd ed. (Louvain: Warny, 1958), part 1, chap. 2; Juan Alfaro, "Supernaturalitas fidei iuxta S. Thomam," *Gregorianum* 44 (1963): 501–42, 731–87 (an abstract appears in *TD* 14 [1966]: 111–16); Benoit Duroux, *La psychologie de la foi chez saint Thomas d'Aquin* (Tournai: Desclée, 1963); Tad Guzie, "The Act of Faith according to St. Thomas: A Study in Theological Methodology," *Thomist* 29 (1965): 239–80; Peter Riga, "The Act of Faith in Augustine and Aquinas," *Thomist* 35 (1971): 143–74. More recently, John Jenkins has given a good description of how grace and the light of faith figure in Aquinas' account of the act of faith (*Knowledge and Faith in Thomas Aquinas* [Cambridge: Cambridge University, 1997], pp. 141–210).

94. *SS* 3.24.1.1.1; *DV* 14.8; *ST* 2-2.1.1. Although in the first two works Thomas opens his treatise on faith with the question about faith as a virtue, in the article from the *Summa* he commences his discussion with an article on first truth as the object of faith, which is unique among his contemporaries, though the phrase "first truth" had been current since William of Auxerre (d. 1231—William Vander Marck, "Faith: What It Is Depends on What It Relates To," *RTAM* 43 [1976]: 134–48).

95. For more on this point, see Duroux, *Psychologie*, pp. 21–29.

96. Although human testimony can fail in truthfulness, God's cannot, for it is based on the "divine judgment," which is "most true and most solid since it derives from truth itself, which can neither deceive nor be deceived" (*Heb.* 6.1.281). Nevertheless, the divine truth is

Somehow, deep within our spirits, we encounter God as the "first believable truth" (*SS* 3.24.1.1.1) and decide whether or not to believe in God-testifying-to-God, for "faith is nothing else than a participation in or adhesion to the truth" (2 *Tim.* 2.2.57), and the light of faith is "a certain sealing of the First Truth in our mind" (*BDT* 3.1 ad4).

If the divine truth is the object of faith, and if for Aquinas judgment is the normal path to truth, then it should not surprise us to find him talking of faith in terms of judgments and propositions. Indeed, while the God who is believed in is simple, the believer's act of faith involves a complex judgment, for since the mind always forms propositions in order to know reality, even faith can assent to the divine truth only by forming a complex proposition. Nevertheless, the judgment of faith is a means rather than an end: it aims at faith's ultimate goal, the mysterious reality and truth of God.[97]

The will's special role in the judgment of faith is clear from Aquinas' interpretation of the Augustinian definition of faith as a "thinking with assent."[98] This definition allows him to distinguish the act of faith or belief from all other acts of the human intellect. *SS* 3.23.2.2.1 distinguishes belief as a "thinking with assent" from vision, scientific knowledge, opinion, doubt, and ignorance: vision occurs when the intellect immediately sees and understands the first principles of any problem, and thus it is an "assent without thinking"; scientific knowledge occurs when the intellect gains its certitude by a process of reasoning, by resolving various conclusions into their immediately understood principles, and thus it is "a thinking before assent, since reason leads to understanding by means of resolu-

---

still the guarantor of the divine truth, which is not a concern for Thomas since in his eyes faith cannot avoid this veracious circle.

97. *SS* 3.24.1.1.2; *DV* 14.8 ad5; *ST* 2-2.1.2. M.-D. Chenu describes the historical context for *ST* 2-2.1.2 in *La parole de Dieu*, vol. 1: *La foi dans l'intelligence* (Paris: Cerf, 1964), pp. 31–50. Aquinas avoids the oversubtle distinctions of some of his predecessors, who sought to protect the unity of faith across different salvific epochs by denying that faith is a temporally dependent judgment: he resolutely holds that faith is such a judgment but protects its unity by asserting that its ultimate goal and object is the one God.

98. *SS* 3.23.2.2.1; *DV* 14.1; *Heb.* 11.1.553–54, 558–59; *ST* 2-2.2.1. For the views of Aquinas' predecessors and contemporaries on the Augustinian formula, see Candido Aniz, "Definición agustiniano-tomista del acto de fe," *La ciencia tomista* 80 (1953): 25–74; also Duroux, *Psychologie*, pp. 61–66.

tion"; opinion is a "thinking without perfect assent" since it does not gain certitude but inclines to one side of an issue with a realization that the other side may be true; doubt is a "thinking without assent" since it finds various alternative solutions to a problem equally persuasive; ignorance is neither thinking nor assent. Belief, however, is a thinking with assent, for it occurs when the intellect judges it right to cling to a truth of faith "on account of some reason for which it seems good" to cling to that truth, although the reason in question, due to our intellect's weakness, does not permit us to see or understand God. For while faith judges with certitude that assent ought to be given to the truth of God, it does so without being able to peer directly into the depths of God or deduce the mystery of God from other intuitively known principles.[99]

The will is what coaxes the intellect, in belief, to assent with conviction to what it does not fully understand. Faith captivates the intellect "according to the will's command," and the "mediating will" is always involved in the believer's reasoning.[100] Faith assents with certitude to the truth "through a certain voluntary choice which the divine authority brings about and through which the intellect . . . clings firmly to the things of faith and assents to them with every assurance."[101] Faith is a "thinking with assent" precisely because the will as an exterior agent, and not the interior evidence, brings the intellect to assent; and since the mind is not at rest through having seen the interior necessity of the truth, it continues to think, even though it already has, prematurely as it were, given its full assent under the influence of the will (SS 3.23.2.2.1 ad2). Faith is thinking and

99. Faith is a mean between understanding and scientific knowledge on the one hand—with which it agrees because of its firm conviction—and doubt, suspicion, and opinion on the other, with which it agrees in not grasping its object on the grounds of internal evidence (ST 2-2.2.1; cf. DV 14.1.195–200; Rom. 1.6.105; Heb. 11.1.559; ST 2-2.1.4; 2-2.4.1). Faith is a cross, therefore, between the type of knowledge that assents firmly on grounds of cogent intrinsic warrants and the type that cannot so assent because such grounds are lacking, for faith produces a vigorous assent but without the inner intuitive evidence to support it (Heb. 11.1.558). Even the Holy Spirit's gifts of understanding and wisdom, which illumine, clarify, deepen, and extend the judgment of faith to all reality (SS 3.35.2.1.1–2; 3.35.2.2.1; ST 2-2.8.1–3; 2-2.45.1–3), cannot make up for the lack of inner intuitive evidence, which remains faith's lot until the blessed vision of God.

100. SS 3.23.2.2.1. Faith is "subject to the command of the will" (DV 14.4.129–30).

101. Heb. 11.1.558; cf. Rom. 1.6.105; 10.2.831.

assenting simultaneously, for "thinking leads to assent, and assent quiets thinking; but in faith, assent and thinking stand on an equal footing, for the assent is not caused by the thinking but by the will" (*DV* 14.1.175–79). The person of faith continues ceaselessly to ponder and question, for faith demands the inquiry of thought as part of its own nature.[102]

For Aquinas, moreover, faith is a gift of divine grace involving both inner and outer elements. The outer elements are the preaching of faith and the external invitation to faith, together with miracles as signs of God's approbation of the preacher's message; the internal element is variously described as an interior light, a sanctifying grace, or a divine instinct to believe. The inner and outer elements collaborate in bringing forth the act of faith: the outer elements give form and content to the interior grace,[103] which itself in turn strengthens the will and illumines the mind to hear the message and accept the invitation to believe.[104] The outer elements can help motivate the act of faith but also require the inner grace of God, for faith's principal act of assent "is from God who moves inwardly through grace" (*ST* 2–2.6.1).

Against the Pelagians, Thomas always held that faith was a product of God's interior grace, but the way in which he understood and described that grace underwent some development. *BDT* 3.1 ad4 describes that grace

102. See Chenu, *Foi*, pp. 77–104, for the historical context of *ST* 2-2.2.1 on the will's role in faith. He mentions the "audacious originality" (p. 78) of this article, since Thomas manages to combine at the heart of faith both the intellectualism of Aristotle and the religious feeling of Augustine, for whom adhesion, intellectual obscurity, and the intervention of the will are all essential elements of faith's assent. Thomas follows and breaks with Aristotle simultaneously, since he makes faith an act of speculative intellect and yet also asserts that its certitude is caused not by evidence but by the will, a synthesis of opposites that neither Hugh of St. Victor nor Albert the Great could envisage. Contrary to Albert, Thomas also makes Augustine's "thinking" an inner element of faith, which is always restless and inquiring since it does not see.

103. *Rom.* 10.2.844 remarks that the Cornelius of Acts 10, whose heart was inclined to believe, still needed to have Peter come and preach to him in order that he might know what he was to believe.

104. See Max Seckler, *Instinkt und Glaubenswille nach Thomas von Aquin* (Mainz, 1961), and the review by Edward Schillebeeckx in *Revelation and Theology*, vol. 2, chap. 2. For a good treatment of *instinctus* and *inspiratio* in Thomas, see the McGraw-Hill Latin-English edition of the *Summa theologiae* (1964–76), vol. 24, appendix 5. Cf. also Duroux, *Psychologie*, pp. 100–108.

as an "interior light which induces one to believe,"[105] and *SCG* 3.151–52 implies that this interior light is a matter of sanctifying grace: wanting to set aside the Pelagian error that places the beginning of faith in and from ourselves, Thomas argues that if sanctifying grace causes the love of God in us, then it must also cause faith in us, since we cannot be directed to charity's goal of the vision of God unless we first possess faith's knowledge of that goal. At this stage, Thomas is content to counter Pelagianism with the sanctifying grace that is the root of both faith and charity.

In Thomas' later works, however, the interior grace of faith is identified with that divine instinct or actual grace by which God moves the soul and prepares it to receive the gift of sanctifying grace. As his commentaries indicate, his close reading of scripture is one of the main foundations for his later view.[106] Christ is the author of faith in two ways: by teaching the faith verbally and by impressing it on our hearts (*Heb.* 12.1.664). Christ draws and attracts us by word and visible signs, and "by moving and stimulating *(instigare)* our hearts interiorly" with invisible signs (*John* 15.5.2055). Since our hearts cannot be converted unless God draws us, St. Paul mentions, as the first step in God's fulfillment of the decree of predestination, the "interior calling," which Thomas defines as a "certain instinct *(instinctus)* of the mind by which the human heart is moved by God to assent to the things that belong to faith or virtue."[107] By this instinct God interiorly moves and

105. *DV* 18.3 distinguishes the exterior from the interior speaking of God that leads to faith: the exterior speaking is that of preachers, and the interior type is called an *inspiratio* by which God bestows a sign of his essence or a likeness of his wisdom; prophets and apostles were instructed in faith by the interior speaking, but faith arises in the hearts of others by the exterior speaking. This *inspiratio* is evidently not the same as the interior light of *BDT* 3.1 ad4, for it is special to prophets and apostles and not a general characteristic required for every act of faith, for even prophets and apostles need the interior light in order to generate an act of faith, even though they receive the content of that faith from inspiration rather than from preaching. In this text *inspiratio* is an interior teaching or instruction, whereas the grace of interior light is rather a force or inducement to belief.

106. Other influences are his reading of the Council of Orange's condemnation of Semi-Pelagianism and its emphasis on God's transient, actual graces, and a passage from the *Eudemian Ethics* (7.14.1248a15–30), which he uses to support his contention that the will needs to be moved by God (*ST* 1-2.9.4; 1-2.68.1). See Jan Walgrave, *Selected Writings*, ed. G. de Schrijver and J. Kelly, Bibliotheca Ephemeridum Theologicarum Lovaniensium 57 (Louvain: University Press, 1982), chaps. 8–9.

107. *Rom.* 8.6.707. This interior calling is an instinct "by which God touches the heart

stimulates us to do good (*Rom.* 9.3.781); quoting Philippians 2:13, "it is God who works in us, both to will and to accomplish," he states that the divine operation working within our hearts produces an instinct that moves and impels *(impellere)* us to believe (*John* 6.5.935). Christ also produces an interior instinct in us to do well (*John* 15.5.2055), and the Holy Spirit teaches us in an inward fashion, inclining *(inclinare)* our affections and impressing our heart (*Heb.* 8.2.404). The divine instinct is an active and impulsive grace—moving, impelling, inclining, calling, instigating, attracting, and instructing.[108]

Indeed, in Thomas' later works *instinctus* can even become a technical term for the initiating and instigating actual grace *(gratia operans)* of the Holy Spirit, which moves the will to command the intellect to assent to faith. The instinct of the Holy Spirit moves the will to influence the intellect to apprehend God's First Truth as the person's own sovereign and eternally salvific good. Thomas makes sure to reject even Semi-Pelagianism, for he places the divine instinct of actual grace, which is the "gratuitous help of God who moves the soul inwardly," at the absolute beginning of the genesis of faith, both in the process of preparing for faith and in the act of faith itself (*ST* 1–2.109.6).

v. Conclusion

Aquinas does not hesitate to assert that the names we employ in divine predication are known to us only insofar as they are used of creatures. For some, such a claim would immediately raise the specter of cryptic univocity: for if the meanings are inherently creaturely, then are we not simply saying something creaturely of God whenever we predicate of God names taken from creatures? How could a divine name really mean anything different when predicated of God? And if it could not, then we are faced once

---

through grace" (*Gal.* 1.4.42; cf. *Rom.* 1.4.68). *Quod.* 2.4.1 ad1–2 identifies the interior instinct and interior calling.

108. Although the interior instinct is not the same as prophetic inspiration, it can still be called an *inspiratio* in a general sense (*Rom.* 1.4.68), insofar as First Truth teaches and illumines us inwardly (*Quod.* 2.4.1 ad3).

again with the univocity that blurs the uniqueness and transcendence of God.

Aquinas' path around the obstacle of univocity is to recognize a judgment that both uses and produces concepts, all the while transcending them. He does not expatiate upon such a judgment explicitly, however, for his express formal teaching makes judgment a synthesis of already fully established concepts—which *would* render divine names taken from creatures incapable of signifying the divine reality—and yet his actual practice of theology and other indications in his thought implicitly reveal that his transcendental analogy is a matter of judgments that transcend their concepts. We have already seen in this chapter that he has texts suggesting that certain concepts, broadly understood, may be the fruit of judgment, and we have also concluded that analogical meanings are examples of such concepts. We have interpreted Aquinas as grounding transcendental analogy in theological judgments because of two warrants: the description of our knowing and naming of God as analogical, since the only other possibilities—univocity and equivocity—cannot do justice to the truths we already know about God; and the carefully chosen placement of the epistemological questions about analogy within his treatise on the one God. This interpretation of Aquinas is no less valid for the fact that he does not realize that what is implicit elsewhere in his thought and practice transgresses the confines of his explicit doctrine of judgment.

Inspired by Aquinas' example, therefore, we may distinguish essentialist apprehension from judgmental understanding. Whereas all judgments dealing with a reality that can be bodily experienced are comprised of terms whose objects, in principle at least, are able to be apprehended by direct insight, judgments about God use creaturely names in the very act of claiming something beyond their mundane referents, without at the same time ever having any direct apprehension or insight into the divine reality now meant by the divine name. The divine name is always tied to its source in creatures, can be understood only in relation to our knowledge and naming of creatures, and can never gain one iota more of intuitive content (since we cannot see or define God). But if we understand concept broadly, then the divine name can be conceived in a way that transcends its creaturely meaning, *but only on the grounds of and by constant reference to the truth of the judgments in which it is used of God*. Analogy as judgment, therefore, which is analogy-in-the-act rather than analogy-after-the-fact, uses and abuses concepts by claiming in their very employment to refer to a Transcendent that is not open to conceptual insight. Theological analogy, paradoxically, in its truth-claim sans intuitive apprehension, asserts what *cannot* be fully conceived or defined, and yet makes its assertion with concepts inextricably bound to creaturely modes.[109]

Aquinas' theological analogy subsists in the judgments he makes about God, judgments that necessarily transcend the very concepts that comprise them.[110] The basic unit of theological analogy is the complete statement, and the meanings of discrete concepts must be referred back to the truth-claim of the whole proposition.[111] Moreover, while analogy-in-the-act arises in the judgments themselves, his formal doctrine of analogy is only established once he takes a reflexive look at his original theological judgments and analyzes what must be the case epistemologically in order for them to be true.[112] If we tend automatically to think of judgments as

109. Subtle and perceptive expositors of Aquinas may disagree with this interpretation. James Ross, for example, argues that the term *good,* as used in "God is good" and "Socrates is good," would be equivocal, and in fact "God is good" would be meaningless, "not quixotically by having no conceptual but only a judgmental meaning, but quite literally," unless *good* possessed a common meaning ("Reply of Professor Ross," p. 662).

110. O'Brien (*Metaphysics*, pp. 232–35) remarks that the proofs for God's existence necessarily lead to an analogical cause outside their own order, for in each proof "the effect as such is transcended in assigning a cause in which the same formality is not found" (p. 234). Clarke ("Analogy," pp. 82–84) contends that in the same moment of thought God is affirmed as the real condition of all intelligibility, and *God* is affirmed as necessarily analogous. Ian Ramsey expresses the same view for the empirical tradition in philosophy: a qualifier "works" a model in a progressive direction toward God, until the "penny drops" and a characteristically different situation is evoked; the language expressing that situation is on the one hand normal or "empirical," and on the other strange or different, and in the ultimate instance, the qualifier even reverses the meaning of the model—for example, from the model of matter to God's property of immateriality (*Religious Language: An Empirical Placing of Theological Phrases* [London: SCM, 1957]).

111. "The theological theory of proper analogical predication deals with the very complex phenomenon of complete statements which express judgments inspired by faith about the reality of God. . . . It is false to place this theory on the same footing as those which deal only with concepts" (O'Neill, "Analogy," p. 57).

112. Theological analogy "has to do with the linguistic expression of a knowledge about God that is held, whether rightly or wrongly, to be *already acquired* and to be *true,* even

built up out of concepts, so that truth is meaning-dependent, in the case of theological analogy we must also reverse the direction and think of the meaning of the divine names as truth-dependent.[113]

Looking ahead: Part Three will investigate in more detail those crucial theological truths undergirding Aquinas' understanding of theological epistemology, especially its element of theological or transcendental analogy, and inquire whether those truths are primarily judgments of reason or of faith.

---

though necessarily imperfect. Those who speak in this way of analogical predication take it as given that there are judgments about God, whether of faith or reason, in which, by means of concepts drawn from the created world, the human person attains the reality of God himself. All that the theory of analogy is meant to do is to account for the oddities of linguistic expression which result from this conviction" (O'Neill, "Analogy," p. 45).

113. Cf. Roger White, "Notes on Analogical Predication and Speaking about God," in *The Philosophical Frontiers of Christian Theology*, ed. B. Hebblethwaite and S. Sutherland (Cambridge: Cambridge University, 1982), pp. 208, 210, 225.

Part Three. Crucial Truths about God

8. Aquinas and the Existence of God the Creator

The main focus of this chapter is on the question whether Aquinas' reason or faith has pride of place in his understanding of what is no doubt the primary supportive pillar of his theological epistemology—the existence of God the Creator. The answer to this question amounts to an interpretation of an interpretation, for it aims, first, to discern how Aquinas interprets his philosophical predecessors, how he sees his own thought in relation to them, and how he disentangles the interwoven threads of faith and reason in the problem of God the Creator; and it aims, second, to appraise the presuppositions of Aquinas' own self-understanding and determine whether his view of God the Creator derives more from reason or from faith. Since his various tractates on the one Creator God invariably begin with the proof from motion for God's existence, which he ascribes to Aristotle, we will first of all examine the context and content of Aristotle's proof, along with Aquinas' exegesis of it, keeping in mind that the goal is to search out Aquinas' theological presuppositions that will be revealed in his interpretation of Aristotle. And since it is often difficult to establish "what St. Thomas thought from what St. Thomas thought Aristotle thought from what Aristotle himself did think,"[1] in order to avoid vapid

---

1. Walter Turner, "St. Thomas' Exposition of Aristotle: A Rejoinder," *NS* 35 (1961): 224. Cf. Joseph Owens, *St. Thomas Aquinas on the Existence of God,* ed. J. R. Catan (Albany: SUNY, 1980), pp. 1–19.

generalities our investigation will have to go into enough detail to catch the critical nuances of Aquinas' reading of Aristotle.

1. Aquinas' View of Aristotle's First Principles

A. The Unmoved Mover of Aristotle's Physics

For our purposes here we need to scrutinize three central topics from book eight of Aristotle's *Physics:* the eternity of motion in chapter 1, which is the crucial and overarching context for the rest of the book; Aristotle's cosmic *Weltanschauung* in chapters 3 through 6, which includes the proof of the unmoved mover; and the nature and location of the unmoved mover in chapter 10.[2]

As to the first topic, chapter 1 argues for the eternity of motion, which is absolutely essential for Aristotle's view of the physical world and the role of the unmoved mover within it. His first argument for the eternity of motion depends on the nature of motion as the actualization of what is movable. He observes that what is movable must either have come into existence or have been in existence eternally. If it has come into existence, then it required some previous motion by which it has come into being; and if it was in existence eternally, but at rest, then it would again need some previous motion in order to remove the hindrance to its motion that had kept it at rest up to that point. In both cases, a previous motion is required, and one previous to that one, and so forth to infinity, so that there never was a time without motion (8.1.251a8–b10). His second argument is based on the nature of time, which is always divided by the "now" or moment, which itself always has time on either side of it, before and after. Since there is always time before and after any moment of time, and since for Aristotle time is a necessary consequence of motion, motion must be eternal in both directions (8.1.251b10–28). His third argument reasons that motion is also required to destroy things, so that even after a destroyer moves in order to destroy something, the destroyer will still need another mover to destroy it in turn, and so on to infinity, so that motion will always contin-

---

2. The Aristotelian references end with the standard Bekker citations, and the translations are the author's with consultation of the McKeon edition of Aristotle's works.

ue into the future. He remarks that any other view of the matter is simply a figment of one's imagination (*plasma*—8.1.251b28–252a5). After a review of competing theories, he concludes that motion always was and always will be (8.1.252a5–b6). Note how his first and third arguments simply accept as givens both the fact of motion and the involvement of motion in the various types of efficient causality.

Regarding the second topic, chapters 3 through 6 portray Aristotle's integrated view of the universe, including the unmoved mover of chapters 4 through 6. On the grounds of what is immediately apparent to our senses, chapter 3 rejects the positions that all things in the universe are always at rest or always in motion, and that the things in motion are always in motion while the things at rest are always at rest. But sense knowledge alone cannot adjudicate between the two remaining options: that all things are so constituted as to be capable of both motion and rest; and that some beings are always unmoved, some always in motion, and yet others sometimes in motion and sometimes at rest (8.3.253a22–254b6). By disciplined reasoning, however, Aristotle will attempt to demonstrate that the only possible position is the latter, for "this holds the solution of all the difficulties that were raised and is the concluding position of our investigation" (8.3.253a30–32).

Chapter 4 (8.4.254b7–256a3) commences Aristotle's investigation of the first and most crucial entity upon which the eternal motion of his cosmos depends—the unmoved mover. By a complicated and subtle argument whose details need not detain us for our present purposes, he proves that "all things in motion are moved by something" (8.4.256a3).

Chapter 5 begins by proving that no infinite regress is possible in things moved by another, otherwise there would be no first term to begin the series (with the implied false consequence that nothing would be moving now). Therefore, Aristotle deduces a mover that moves itself and is not moved by something else (8.5.256a4–21). He strengthens his first conclusion by acknowledging that each mover in the series may be in motion either essentially (through itself) or accidentally (through another, as the soul moves accidentally when the body to which it is united moves). But the motion of the unmoved mover cannot be accidental, for the accidental is not necessary, and what is not necessary may fail, so that there might be a time when there is no motion; but there must always be motion, as he has proved in chapter 1 (8.5.256b3–13). He also shows that there cannot be an infinite regress in essential motions either, for consequences contrary to the principle of noncontradiction follow upon the supposition of an infinite regress. His intermediate conclusion is more complex: the first entity in motion *either* derives its motion from something at rest *or* moves itself; and if we had to choose, we would probably pick the latter, for that which moves itself independently is more a cause than that which depends for its causality upon something else (8.5.256b27–257a31). He now scrutinizes the self-moved mover more closely (8.5.257a33–258b9). "If it is necessary that there be eternal motion, then it is also necessary that there be a mover that is either unmoved or moved by itself" (8.5.257b24–25). But the only way a mover can move itself is when one part moves without itself being moved, and another part is moved by the first part. His final conclusion states it is clear that the first mover is unmoved: for whether the series progresses through various moved movers to the unmoved mover, or whether we arrive at that which moves and stops itself, in both cases the result is that in all motion there is a first mover that is unmoved (8.5.258b4–9).

Chapter 6 shows that the unmoved mover is one, eternal, and exempt from any kind of change, and that it is responsible for one, continuous, eternal motion. Since there is eternal motion, there must be at least one eternal[3] unmoved mover, though at this stage Aristotle is still willing to grant that there may be more than one unmoved mover (8.6.258b10–16). He contrasts his eternal, separate, and universal unmoved mover with those particular and transitory self-movers that are soul-body composites. Although animating souls come into and go out of existence without a process of change (for they have no parts with which to change), not every unmoved mover can be so transitory, for then there would be no first cause of the entire process of generation and corruption as a whole. Neither singly nor together can such particular unmoved movers be the cause of such a necessary and eternal process, for their number is without limit

---

3. The Cornford text (Loeb), not Bekker, has *aidion* (eternal) at 258b11.

(and thus liable to an infinite regress) and not simultaneous (8.6.258b16–259a6). He concludes, therefore, that beyond the individual unmoved principles of motion, which come and go, there must be something that embraces *(periechein)* the whole process of generation and corruption, is separate from each of the individual causes, and is itself the cause of their coming into and going out of existence, and of the whole process of continuous change (8.6.259a3–5). Employing an early prototype of Occam's razor, he also now argues that the economy of nature and reason would have us choose one unmoved mover rather than many, if one will do as well as many—which it will—for the determinate is better than the unlimited. Moreover, the continuity of eternal motion is one and thus demands a single mover (8.6.259a6–20). However, it is necessary to posit an unmoved mover that does not move even accidentally, "if there is going to be among things an unceasing and undying motion, and if being is going to remain selfsame and within its limits, for if the principle perdures, the universe will also be permanent, since it is in continuous relation with the principle" (8.6.259b24–28).

In the concluding paragraphs of chapter 6 we can see how the unmoved mover functions as an integral foundational element within Aristotle's cosmic worldview (8.6.259b32–260a19). His picture of the universe, which must account for the regularity of celestial motion and the perpetuity of the processes of generation and corruption, as well as various changes in the sublunary sphere, comprises four elements: (1) the eternal, unmoved mover, which causes eternal, continuous motion; (2) the thing first moved by the unmoved mover (the outer celestial sphere together with the fixed stars), which moves eternally and continuously since the motion derived from the unmoved mover is one and the same and always imparted in the same way; (3) that which is moved by (2) above (planets, sun, moon, and other heavenly bodies), which are subject to change of place and discontinuous motion; (4) the things ultimately moved by (3), which sometimes move, sometimes rest, and are subject to changes of various sorts (all of which are sublunary bodies). This schema can account for both perpetuity and change, which is why Aristotle picked the option he did in chapter 3 as the only possible way to view the universe:

Because some things are moved by an eternal unmoved mover and therefore are always in motion, whereas other things are moved by an agent that is itself in motion and changing, with the result that they also necessarily change. But the unmoved mover, as has been said, since it remains simple and unvarying and in the same condition, will give rise to a motion that is one and simple. (8.6.260a14–19)[4]

Concerning the third topic, chapter 10 demonstrates that the unmoved mover is indivisible and without physical size, and resides at the circumference of the universe (8.10.267b17–26). The unmoved mover cannot have any physical magnitude, for such magnitude would have to be either finite or infinite: but it has already been proved in chapter 5 of book three that there cannot be such a thing as an infinite magnitude; and a limited magnitude cannot have unlimited power, nor can a limited agent keep anything going for an infinite time. "But the first mover does cause eternal motion during an infinite time. It is clear, therefore, that the first mover is indivisible and without parts and has no magnitude" (8.10.267b24–26). He is content to conclude his *Physics* with a kind of negative arche-ology that opens up vistas onto his *Metaphysics:* the first principle of all matter and motion is an unmoved mover without material magnitude.

One more point should be mentioned before leaving the *Physics.* Aristotle writes that the first mover "must reside either at the center or the circumference [of the heavens], for these are its principles.[5] But the things nearest the mover are those that move most quickly, and [in the case of the heavens] the motion of the circumference is quickest, and so the mover is there" (8.10.267b6–9). Debate has centered on the meaning of *there (ekei)*,

---

4. Aristotle gives us another glimpse of his worldview in *On Generation and Corruption,* 2.10. The eternal circular motion of the heavens causes the perpetuity and continuity of the processes of generation and corruption. However, the eternal motion, which is one, cannot cause the duality of generation and corruption but instead causes the generator, the sun, to approach and retire along the ecliptic, or zodiac circle. And since this ecliptic motion is ceaseless but also possesses a dualism, it causes both the perpetuity and the dualism of generation and corruption. Together, then, the one eternal motion of the heavens and the duality of the sun's continuous motion are the efficient causes of the ceaseless alternation of generation and corruption within the sublunary world. Likewise, *Metaphysics* 12.6.1072a17 also states: "Clearly, both together are the cause of eternal variety."

5. The center and circumference are what define and generate a circle or sphere, and so the first mover must be at one of them in order to exercise its influence over the universal, heavenly orb.

which is ambiguous (does it mean "in" or "at" the circumference?), and on the problem generated if one considers the first mover to be *in* the circumference of the heavens as a sphere-soul, for this seems to imply that the first mover would move accidentally as the entire heavenly sphere moves, but such accidental movement would make it incapable of fulfilling its role, in Aristotle's eyes, of producing the eternal motion of the heavens.[6]

We now turn to Thomas' *Sententia super Physicam*, his most extensive

6. In his commentary on the *Physics*, Simplicius of Cilicia (ca. 530 A.D.) relates his own opinion on this matter and instructs us about the views of two earlier commentators, Eudemos of Rhodes, a pupil of Aristotle, and Alexander of Aphrodisias (ca. 200 A.D.—the text is taken from Bekker's edition of Aristotle's works, 3:453a6–b11, and is supplemented by two passages from the 1526 Venice edition of the commentary, pp. 319b–320a [microfilm copy made in 1961 of the original, which is in the Vatican Library, List 27, no. 30], which supply two lacunae in the Bekker text [lacuna at Bekker 453a28, supplied by Venice 319b45–53; lacuna at Bekker 453a48, supplied by Venice 320a13–23]). The Pythagoreans had taught that the first mover is at the center of the sphere, but Eudemos thought it was in the great sphere that embraces the poles of the universe. Alexander claimed, however, that it was in the total circumference beyond the sphere, which he thought protected the first mover from any accidental motion since the heavenly periphery as a whole neither moves nor changes but abides eternally in the selfsame state. Simplicius contests Alexander's position and claims like Eudemos that the first mover is in the entire universe and not merely at its outer superficies, but in a transcendent fashion. The first unmoved mover is a perfect bodiless essence that is unrelated to the cosmos, moves without touching what it moves, and embraces the whole cosmos with its unlimited power. Simplicius protects the first mover from accidental motion by reason of its heightened transcendence, and his thought was probably influenced by Neoplatonic or Christian ideas stressing God's transcendence. In *Phys.* 8.23.1169 Aquinas would seem to agree with this "transcendent" interpretation of Simplicius. Some modern opinions on the problem: Marcel de Corte asserts that the unmoved mover of the *Physics* is an efficient cause moving by contact at the extreme limit of the world's circumference ("La causalité du premier moteur dans la philosophie aristotélicienne," *Revue d'histoire de la philosophie* 5 [1931]: 105–47); for Jean Paulus, the unmoved mover is the *physically* unmoved *part* of the self-moved mover, that is, the soul of the outer heaven, which resides at its surface, moves by contact as an agent, is not absolutely separate, and is immobile only physically, insofar as it is not subject to material generation ("La théorie du premier moteur chez Aristote," *RP* 33 [1933]: 283); Joseph Owens (*The Doctrine of Being in the Aristotelian "Metaphysics*," 3rd ed. [Toronto: PIMS, 1978], p. 439, n. 10) and Fernand van Steenberghen (*Le problème de l'existence de Dieu dans les écrits de S. Thomas d'Aquin*, Philosophes Médiévaux 23 [Louvain-la-Neuve: Editions de l'Institut Supérieur de philosophie, 1980], p. 257) also see the prime mover as an immanent sphere-soul; but Anton Pegis considers it to be the same god Aristotle treats of in *Metaphysics* 12.7–10 ("St. Thomas and the Coherence of the Aristotelian Theology," *MS* 35 [1973]: 74–78); cf. Harry Wolfson, *Studies in the History of Philosophy and Religion*, ed. I. Twersky and G. H. Williams, 2 vols. (Cambridge: Harvard, 1973–77), vol. 1, chap. 2.

commentary on book eight of the *Physics,* where we are most interested in those passages that may reveal Thomas altering Aristotle's meaning in order to accommodate his own interpretation. He acknowledges the importance of eternal motion in Aristotle's procedure, for in *Physics* 8.6 and *Metaphysics* 12.6 "he uses the eternity of motion to prove a first principle." But then Thomas adds an explanation for why Aristotle employs such a proof:

This is the most efficacious way of proving the existence of a first principle, which cannot be denied. For if it is necessary to posit a single first principle, granted that the world and motion exist eternally, how much more must we posit such a principle if their eternity is denied. For it is clear every new beginning requires an innovating principle, and the only thing that might seem to militate against the necessity of positing a first principle is if things exist from eternity. Hence, if even when eternity is granted it follows that the first principle exists, then it will be shown it is totally necessary that a first principle exist. (*Phys.* 8.1.970)[7]

Thomas is interpreting Aristotle as desiring to prove that his first principle is an innovating cause, one that brings existence out of nonexistence and bestows an absolute beginning upon things. The most "efficacious" way to do this is to grant the hypothesis that the world and motion are eternal, for if one can show the innovating cause at work even in the midst of an eternal series where every individual appears to have another before it, then one has accomplished the proof under the most adverse conditions possible. Notice, however, how Aquinas has undermined the Aristotelian proof's direct and absolute dependence on eternal motion, which Aristotle can eliminate neither from his worldview nor from his proof. Whereas Aristotle proves that the world is necessarily eternal and then on that basis shows the need for an unmoved mover, Thomas does not posit eternity as a necessary presupposition but sees it as a suppositional concession to a possible state of affairs, from which a first principle can nevertheless be

---

7. A parallel text, *SCG* 1.13.110, displays the same sequence of thought. The proof commencing with the world's eternity is the most efficacious precisely because, when eternity is granted, God's existence is less manifest. "For if the world and motion begin for the first time, some cause must clearly be posited that produces the world and its motion in the beginning, since whatever comes into existence anew must have its origin in some innovating cause, for nothing brings itself from potency to act or from nonbeing to being."

proved if the proof is "efficacious" enough.[8] Moreover, Aristotle is unaware of the distinction Thomas later makes between existential innovation and temporal beginning.

Thomas also critiques Aristotle's first argument for the eternity of motion by having recourse to book two of his *Metaphysics* in order to challenge that premise of the argument which perceives motion and its subject as the necessary vehicles for every process of coming into being. Thomas is clashing with Averroes, who defends Aristotle's argument and at the same time rejects creation from nothing, on the grounds that every motion, including the motion that is creation, presupposes a subject that must preexist the motion (*Phys.* 8.2.973). Thomas counters by saying that Aristotle proves in *Metaphysics* 2 that what is most true and most being is the cause of being for all existing things, so that even matter is produced, not presupposed, by what Aristotle calls "being in the highest degree." And precisely because every motion does in fact need a subject, "it follows that the production of universal being by God is neither a motion nor a change but a kind of simple emanation" (*Phys.* 8.2.974). Indeed, Aristotle's proofs in book eight against the beginning of motion are meant to refer only to individual instances of becoming, not to the universal production of being (*Phys.* 8.2.987), for "although Aristotle posited an eternal world, he did not nevertheless believe that God is the cause only of that world's motion and not also the cause of its being" (*Phys.* 8.3.996).[9] He has found in Aristotle a

8. Jean Paulus claims that Thomas borrows from Maimonides the artifice by which he justifies Aristotle's commencing his proof of the unmoved mover with the eternity of the world ("Le caractère métaphysique des preuves thomistes de l'existence de Dieu," *AHDLMA* 9 [1934]: 150, n. 1).

9. In *Phys.* 8.2.975 Thomas also sees Aristotle as teaching the universal production of being in *Physics* 1.8.191b19–26. But in that passage, while Aristotle *agrees* with his opponents that nothing can come from absolute nonbeing *(haplōs ek mē ontos)*, he contends that something can come from being and nonbeing in a qualified sense *(kata symbebēkos)*, for everything comes to be from the qualified being of matter and the qualified nonbeing of privation. It appears Aristotle cannot conceive of a universal production of being out of absolute nonbeing. Indeed, in book one of the *Physics* (1.9.192a25–34) he also holds that matter is eternal, utilizing an argument whose structure is similar to the one by which he proves motion to be eternal: since everything comes from matter and is resolved back into matter, if matter were not eternal it would have to exist in order to become and would still exist after having been corrupted, both of which are impossible.

God who is the cause of being as well as the first mover. However, he turns Aristotle's reasoning on its head, for he reads him to be arguing (1) that motion presupposes a subject and (2) that creation cannot presuppose a subject, which together establish (3) that creation cannot be a motion; however, while (1) is in the *Physics*, (2) is assumed by Thomas to be Aristotle's position on the strength of *Metaphysics* 2; but Aristotle's actual minor premise in the text is "every process of coming to be is a motion," which together with the major premise yields the conclusion that "every process of coming to be presupposes a subject." Thomas substitutes another proposition for Aristotle's actual minor premise and fashions an inference quite foreign to the thought of the *Physics*.

In conclusion, Aristotle proves from the very beginning of book eight the eternity and necessity of the world and its motion, and this conclusion is indispensable as a premise in the proof of the unmoved mover. Like other Greeks, Aristotle equates eternity and necessity, and opposes both to chance and contingency. He is looking to explain particular, contingent acts of motion, generation, and corruption, as well as the eternal motion of the entire heavenly firmament, but he takes the existence of the whole universe and its motion as a given that requires no further explanation. Thus, he betrays no inkling of contingent created existence at the heart of the universe—existence that would still cry out for explanation even in a necessary world whose motion is eternal. The very manner in which he proves motion's eternity is a clear indication that he never even suspects a motionless, creative origination of being.

For Aquinas, however, only God is eternal and necessary, while everything else is contingent and in need of explanation. The Creator God, by a motionless act of mind and will, originates the whole of creation whose being is absolutely contingent. Aquinas knows that, even if the world were not eternal, the contingency at the heart of a temporal creation would still demand an eternal Creator. He attempts to harmonize this Christian view of the cosmos with Aristotle's *Weltanschauung*, which leads him to downplay the crucially central role the eternity of motion plays in Aristotle's proof by ironically asserting that Aristotle only puts it there in order to make his argument even stronger than it would be without it. Aquinas also criticizes Aristotle's proof of motion's eternity by introducing the notion of a motionless innovation of being, which Aristotle's philosophy cannot fathom.

B. The Primary Substance of Aristotle's Metaphysics

We now turn to book twelve of Aristotle's *Metaphysics.* Chapter 6, in a brief reprise of the *Physics,* argues for an eternal and immovable substance on the grounds of the unquestioned eternal necessity of motion and time (12.6.1071b4–19). "There must, therefore, be such a principle whose substance *(ousia)* is actuality *(energeia).* Furthermore, these substances must be without matter, for they must be eternal if anything is eternal; they are in act, then" (12.6.1071b19–22). For Aristotle, actuality is opposed to temporality and matter, for matter is the principle of potency, and potency opens up the possibility that something might not exist eternally.

Chapter 7 meditates on how an eternal actual substance can move without being moved and discovers that "the primary objects of desire and thought move while not being moved" (12.7.1072a26–27) and that "the final cause produces motion by being desired, but all the others move by being moved" (12.7.1072b3–4). Whereas the *Physics* had considered the unmoved mover to be an efficient cause, Aristotle here has a new intuition leading him to realize that an efficient cause cannot move without also being somehow moved and that the only genuinely unmoved mover is the final cause because it can remain separate from what it moves.[10] He then declares that the first mover/substance exists of necessity and that upon it the heavens and all of nature depend (12.7.1072b13–14). Its actuality is pleasant, and since thought is divine, and contemplation the most pleasant and best kind of thought, god is always in that good state of contemplation that we only sometimes possess. Indeed, god is in a better state:

Life belongs to god, for the actuality of mind is life, and god is that actuality. God's autonomous actuality is life most good and eternal. We say that god is a living be-

---

10. The fact that Aristotle switches to final causality, probably under pressure from his own theory about how efficient causality works, is yet another indication that he possessed no notion of a motionless efficient causality, for if he had possessed such a concept he could have answered his own reservations without turning to final causality.

ing, eternal and most good, so that life and an unbroken eternal span of existence belong to god; for god is this. (12.7.1072b26–30)

Here Aristotle moves beyond the *Physics* by investing the first princi- ple/mover with religious and mystical overtones, identifying it with god.[11] To conclude chapter 7, he asserts that there is a substance that is eternal, unmovable, separate from material reality, without magnitude or parts, indivisible, impassive, and unalterable.

One can easily detect the influence of book eight of the *Physics* in these two chapters from book twelve of the *Metaphysics:* both works reason to an eternal and unmovable first mover/substance, whose immateriality means it is without parts or magnitude and makes it incapable of suffering change and whose task it is to keep the universe eternally moving. In three ways, however, the *Metaphysics* steps beyond the *Physics:* it identifies the first principle and unmoved mover of the *Physics* with activity and god; it expresses more forcefully and clearly the first principle's absolute separa- bility from the material realm; and it focuses on the primary substance as a final rather than efficient cause.[12]

Metaphysics 12.8 introduces us to the polytheistic and somewhat pan- theistic elements of Aristotle's *Gottwelt,* which is a multilayered divine realm environing and enveloping the universe. By a complicated celestial

11. The *Physics* never calls the first mover god, nor does the *Metaphysics* until 12.7.1072b23–25.

12. "The supreme source of motion was for Aristotle a final cause in which efficient causality originated: finality was the first instance of a moving cause because in a world in which being itself had no origin the only thing that did have an origin and needed to be ex- plained was the intelligibility and continuity that the heavens and nature maintained. . . . If being has no origin, then there is no universal efficient cause. There is a universal efficient- less final cause, the order of separate entities, and chief among them the supreme entity who moves as a supreme desirable" (Pegis, "Coherence," pp. 116–17). Leo Elders thinks he detects efficient causality at 12.8.1073a28 and 12.8.1074a37 (*Aristotle's Theology: A Commentary on Book Lambda of the Metaphysics* [Assen: Van Gorcum, 1972], p. 239), but this opinion lacks solid foundation in the text. Edward Booth also shows how Aristotle's *Metaphysics,* which ultimately identifies the individual existing substance with form (9.8.1050b) and presuppos- es that all natural forms have always existed, bequeathed to all subsequent metaphysicians the aporia of trying to explain the origin of existence by recourse to form alone (*Aristotelian Aporetic Ontology in Islamic and Christian Thinkers* [Cambridge: Cambridge University, 1983]). David Burrell remarks that it took "the revelation of a free creator to alert readers of Aristotle's *Metaphysics* . . . to his failure to ask why there might be anything at all" ("Analo- gy, Creation, and Theological Language," *PACPA* 74 [2000]: 38).

arithmetic, the chapter multiplies unmoved divine substances (either 55 or 47), whose ordinal position and prestige are determined by the order of the heavenly bodies' motions, which it is their task as final causes to produce and at whose apex is a chief substance whose job it is to generate the motion and order of the whole universe (12.8.1073a26–b3). Aristotle can speak of the "divine bodies that move through the heaven" (12.8.1074a30–31); and when he resorts to the ancient tradition about the divine, it is only to separate from later mythic accretions its original philosophical kernel of truth and to note with approval that the ancients thought "the divine to embrace the whole of nature"[13] and "the first substances to be gods" (12.8.1074a38–b14).

Aristotle's polytheism is also evident elsewhere in his corpus.[14] He reports the common human feeling that the gods dwell in the highest heaven, where immortal is linked with immortal, and locates up near the gods the primary heavenly body, which is composed of a superterrestrial fifth element not subject to decay, associating it with immortality and calling it "something divine."[15] In his view, then, the divine realm includes the heavenly bodies, which he calls "the visible aspects of the divine,"[16] along with whatever it is that causes them to move, which may be singular or plural.[17] Aristotle's divine world is a layered, hierarchical one, where diverse beings share more or less in a common quality of divinity and are bound together into a whole by mutual ties of necessity and finality.[18]

13. Aristotle's quasi-pantheism, according to which the divine embraces the whole of nature, is rooted in his view of the form as "something divine" (ti theion—Physics 1.9.192a16–17), since form in itself carries the divine qualities of permanence and actuality. Thomas explains that the form is divine insofar as it participates in the likeness of divine being (Phys. 1.15.135; Herm. 1.3.30) but does not suspect the implicit pantheism of Aristotle's physical morphology and metaphysical ousiology.

14. Regarding the Greek penchant for juxtaposing the one divine realm or theion with the many theoi, see Werner Jaeger, The Theology of the Early Greek Philosophers, trans. E. S. Robinson, Gifford Lectures of 1936 (Oxford: Clarendon, 1947), chap. 2.

15. On the Heavens 1.3.270b5–25; cf. ibid., 2.3.286a8–12.

16. Tois phanerois tōn theiōn (Metaphysics 6.1.1026a17–18).

17. Metaphysics 6.1.1026a10–29, where tis and ti (a singular someone or something) and tauta (these) can alternately refer to the divine. For other texts where Aristotle switches between the singular and plural while discussing the divine realm, see Owens, Doctrine of Being, p. 445, n. 38.

18. Metaphysics 12.6–10 (together with Physics 8.6.259a6–20) is a crucial text for the

question of whether Aristotle was a monotheist or a polytheist. The difficulty is that *Metaphysics* 12.6–7 and 9–10 are prima facie monotheistic, whereas chapter 8, with its question about one or many movers, seems an alien polytheistic addition; compounding the issue is the monotheistic fragment about one mover and one heaven within chapter 8 itself (12.8.1074a31–38). The problem, then, is twofold: how to situate chapter 8 within its larger context, and whether to understand it in its own right as an integral, unified whole or to see the monotheistic passage as an interpolation taken from Aristotle's earlier or later writings. Philip Merlan ("Aristotle's Unmoved Movers," *Traditio* 4 [1946]: 1–30) holds that *Metaphysics* 12.8 and *Physics* 8.6 are both authentic and integral, and concludes that Aristotle is a consistent polytheist, his first movers forming a graded series within a general sphere of divinity. Merlan describes Jaeger's position: Aristotle was originally a monotheist (*Metaphysics* 6–7 and 9–10), then later veered toward polytheism in order to adjust his views to contemporary astronomy (chapter 8), but finally reconsidered his position and wrote an independent reflection leaning toward monotheism that was later added to chapter 8 ("Movers," p. 2, n. 8). (Elders complicates the question even further by holding that none of *Metaphysics* 12.8 is from Aristotle's hand [*Aristotle's Theology*, pp. 57–68].) For Merlan, however, Aristotle wrote chapters 6–7 and 9–10 in order to prove the existence and investigate the nature of separate entity; but entity *(ousia)* simply means "sphere or kind of being" ("Movers," n. 31). So Aristotle's question at the beginning of chapter 8 about whether there is one or more than one separate entity is tantamount to asking whether within the one sphere of separate, divine entity there is only one or more than one individual. And his conclusion of 55 or 47 unmoved movers rests on two premises: the number of movers must match the number of heavenly motions, for an otiose separate substance is unthinkable (12.8.1074a17–31); and there is only one universe, matched by the one sphere of separate, divine entity (12.8.1074a31–38). Thus, the question about individuals within the divine realm appropriately situates chapter 8 within the whole context of *Metaphysics* 12.6–10; and 12.8.1074a31–38 is a key premise (rather than an alien addition) for chapter 8's determination of 47 or 55 as the number of separate entities, for with more than one universe there could be an untold number. Merlan writes that the doctrine of *Metaphysics* 12 "is consistently polykinetic (or 'polytheistic') rather than inconsistently monokinetic (or 'monotheistic')—although certainly not anthropomorphic. Generally, it is true, we are inclined to think of the transition from polytheism to monotheism as being at the same time a transition from crude anthropomorphism to a purer notion of God. A middle stage, a de-anthropomorphisized polytheism, appears as a logical construction rather than a living reality. But it seems that Aristotle (and, perhaps, Plato, too) represents just this intermediary stage. It was the anthropomorphism or anthropopathism of the popular religion by which they were repelled, not its plurality of gods. . . . Aristotle's unmoved movers are gods certainly not resembling men; but still they are many" ("Movers," p. 28). Owens supports Merlan's interpretation (*Doctrine of Being*, pp. 447–50, and n. 50). It does seem that Aristotle applies the terms *god* and *divine* in an orderly, gradated fashion, first to the separate substance that moves the whole universe (a substance that *Metaphysics* 12.8.1074a31–38 says is one in meaning [*logos*] and number), then to the separate substances that initiate each celestial motion within the whole, and finally to the outer celestial sphere or other heavenly bodies moved by these separate substances. Owens remarks that the Greek notion of the divine is "independent of its unity or plurality. The fundamental unity of things becomes a problem of *order*, not of derivation" (*Doctrine of Being*, p. 445).

Aristotle wraps up book twelve by plumbing the nature of the divine primary substance, which chapter 9 establishes is the act of thinking, not merely the faculty of thought. And since the object of the divine substance's thought can only be the most excellent of things—itself—his god turns out to be self-thinking thought, a thinking on thinking whose activity and object are the same (12.9.1074b15–1075a12).[19] However, this self-thinking thought, which contemplates itself in solitary splendor, nevertheless exists for the sake of the whole universe, for it is the absolutely first principle, which, by being loved and desired, inspires all the eternal processes of motion and life. Chapter 10 explains how the universe is good in all its parts but even more so as regards its first principle, and makes plain once again the central role of the world's eternity in the investigation of the first cause (12.10.1075b30–34). Favoring a unified administration of the universe over the chaos of multiple governing principles, Aristotle ends book twelve with a line from the *Iliad* (2.204): "The governance of many is not good; let there be one ruler" (12.10.1076a4).

We now turn to Aquinas' *Sententia super Metaphysicam*, his extensive commentary on Aristotle's *Metaphysics*, and once again we are most interested in how Aquinas' presuppositions guide his interpretation of certain passages from book twelve, where pagan philosophy and Christian theology display converging interests. He realizes that Aristotle has grounded his inquiry into immaterial substances upon the world's eternity but also states that only probable reasons are available for proving it (*Meta.* 12.5.2496–98). Of course, in order to know that Aristotle's reasons for the world's eternity are merely probable, Aquinas must presuppose the latent premise that God can accomplish a motionless and timeless act of creation, or else he could not answer Aristotle's contention that any new motion in time always implies a previous motion in time.

Realizing that Aristotle's primary substance moves the heavens and all nature "as an end," Aquinas also gently coaxes Aristotle into saying that the necessity of the outer sphere's motion is not absolute but conditioned on

19. Van Steenberghen (*Problème*, pp. 272–73) says that Aristotle's god is neither provident nor cognizant of inferior realities, but Elders (*Aristotle's Theology*, p. 257) claims that *Metaphysics* 12.9 is compatible with the view that God knows all things.

that final end, God, so that "the entire necessity of the first motion is subject to the will of God" (*Meta.* 12.7.2534–35).[20] Aquinas is adverting to the intrinsic relation between an end or goal and the intellectual faculty of will, which he here identifies with God's will choosing when to actuate the first motion of the universe; but Aristotle only meant that the outer sphere and the heavenly bodies *necessarily* move by desiring the primary substance as an end, not that the first principle itself may decide *voluntarily* whether and when to move the heavens. Aquinas also balks at calling the many first substances and movers god (*Meta.* 12.10.2597), and like other Christian thinkers dedeifies the pagan divinities.[21]

Aquinas takes pains to show that the utter simplicity and separability of Aristotle's God as self-thinking thought does not derogate from divine providence or from God's knowledge of things in the world.[22] God knows things other than himself, for by knowing himself he also knows all the other things that are contained in himself as in a causal principle (*Meta.* 12.11.2614–15).[23] This explanation of the primary substance's omniscience rests squarely upon that substance's being the productive cause of every-

20. Since "it depends on the divine will" whether the heavens are moved eternally or not (*Caelo* 2.4.334), Aquinas' God, by freely deciding whether and when to bestow being and motion, upends and overturns Aristotle's divine world of necessary connections. In *DP* 7.1 ad1, Aquinas interprets Aristotle's god as acting not by natural necessity but by reason and will.

21. For the plurality of immovable movers in Aristotle, Averroes and Aquinas, see Wolfson, *Studies*, vol. 1, chap. 1. Throughout his writings Aquinas explains that pagan polytheism may call separate intelligences, souls, and heavenly bodies divine insofar as they bear a close likeness to the divine substance (*Caelo* 1.7.75; 1.20.199; 2.1.290–92; *Phys.* 3.6.335; 8.16.1106; *Pater* 1037) and participate in God the First Cause (*Caelo* 2.4.334; 2.19.475; *Ethic.* 8.7.130–31; *SDC* 19.351–52; 32.464). But such terminology can be used without admitting to a "multitude of deity" (*SDC* 3.72–75). Instead of seeing the Aristotelian theosphere as a polytheistic realm where different levels and planes of divinity nonetheless share a common divine status, Aquinas first purifies the notion of divinity by applying it to the true God alone (Aristotle's primary substance and first mover) and then grants the divine appellation to lower creatures only in an etiolated, weakened sense.

22. In *SCG* 1.63–71, he responds to some of Aristotle's commentators who, referring to *On the Soul* 3.6.430b21–26 and *Metaphysics* 12.9, denied that God knows singulars (Avicenna), futures, infinites, and evils (Averroes).

23. Aquinas interprets *Metaphysics* 12.9 to mean that God is the principal though not sole object of the divine intellect (*SCG* 1.70.600), and sees Aristotle as holding that God understands in himself those things that exist outside himself (*DP* 3.16 ad23).

thing in the world. A little later, Aquinas also sees Aristotle's God as both an efficient and a final cause, arguing in effect that an ultimate final cause cannot exercise its causality unless it has first produced as an efficient cause the realities that are directed back to it as a final cause.

> The nature of those realities that exist for an end is derived from that end, as for example, when an army's order exists not only for the sake of its commander but also must be from its commander, since it exists for his sake. Likewise, the separate good which is the first mover is a better good than the good of order which is in the universe. For the whole order of the universe exists on account of the first mover, so that whatever is in the first mover's intellect and will is unfolded in the ordered universe. And so the whole disposition of the universe must be from the first mover. (*Meta.* 12.12.2631)

However, if the primary substance of *Metaphysics* 12.9 is an entity upon which other things depend only as a final cause, then it need not actively produce any effects and thus have to know them beforehand. A primary substance that is only a final cause could function quite well by knowing only itself, for it would still exert its final causality when other entities desire it, but without its having to know or actively cause them. Aquinas is surely reading into Aristotle his Christian notion of God as the knowing, willing, loving, and active agent of creation.

Believing that Aristotle ends book twelve as an advocate of monotheism, Aquinas finishes his own commentary on it by accenting the unity of the universe and the oneness of God.

> The whole universe is as one principality and one kingdom, and so it must be administered by one governor. And so [Aristotle] concludes that there is one ruler of the entire universe, the first mover, which is the first intelligible and first good, and which above he called God, who is blessed forever and ever. (*Meta.* 12.12.2663)

Two further texts from books two and seven of the *Metaphysics*, along with Thomas' commentary on them, may be usefully discussed at this point, as their examination will show how easily and effortlessly Thomas mines from Aristotle two of his most influential philosophical concepts: the existential intensity of being and the agent cause. The first text from book two[24] (2.1.993b23–31) reasons that whatever causes derivative truths

---

24. Book two is most likely a genuine Aristotelian fragment that was added late to the

to be true is true in the highest degree, for a thing has a certain trait in the highest degree *(malista)* if it is the cause of that same trait in other things (e.g., fire is hottest since it is the cause of heat for other things). Hence, the principles of eternal things are always most true, for they are not merely sometimes true, nor does anything cause their existence *(to einai),* but they rather cause the existence of other things, so that as each thing is in respect of existence, so it is in respect of truth. *To einai* seems to mean, in the context of the whole passage, the fact that something exists with some quality or trait: the existence of hot things, for example, refers to the fact that some things really become and are hot. But how do the principles of eternal realities cause the existence of other things? In the context of what we already know about Aristotle's doctrine in book twelve, the principles of eternal realities—the immaterial, primary substances— cause the eternal revolution of the heavens as final causes, and through the subsequent efficient causality of the heavens and their celestial bodies are also the ultimate causes of all sublunar substantial generation and cor- ruption, through which sublunar entities come into and pass out of exis- tence.

Aquinas begins by repeating Aristotle on the maximal possession of traits: something maximally *(maxime,* which translates *malista)* possesses a trait whenever it causes that trait in other things (*Meta.* 2.2.292). For Aquinas, Aristotle's "eternal realities" are the celestial bodies, and his "principles of eternal realities" are the separate substances (*Meta.* 2.2.295– 96). Following Aristotle exactly, he remarks that these latter have no cause but are themselves the "cause of being" *(causa essendi)* for other things (*Meta.* 2.2.295). The separate substances transcend even the celestial bod- ies since, although the latter are incorruptible, "they still have a cause, not only with respect to their motion, as some have thought, but also with re- spect to their being, as the philosopher expressly states here" (*Meta.* 2.2.295). Moreover, the fourth proof for God's existence found in *ST* 1.2.3 utilizes this text to prove the existence of a God who, as "a being in the

final redaction of the main work, since it betrays no connection to the rest of the *Meta- physics,* or vice versa, and is given the name alpha minor, the sequence of the other books having already been set (Owens, *Doctrine of Being,* pp. 89–90).

highest degree" *(maxime ens)*, is "the cause of being, goodness and every perfection." Aquinas has evidently turned Aristotle's final causality into efficient causality, has interpreted the prosaic, factual sense of Aristotle's *to einai* as the intensive internal being of entities, and has discovered, in Aristotle's name, that God as *maxime ens* is the productive cause of that being.[25]

In the course of a discussion about the nature of essence, the second text from book seven (7.17.1041a26–32) asks why bricks and stones are a house, remarking that in "why" questions we are looking for the cause, and that while in the case of certain things, such as a house or a bed, we are seeking the final cause, in the case of others we are looking for "what began the process of motion" *(ti ekinēse prōton)*. Aristotle then generalizes, asserting that we search for the moving cause in the case of generation or corruption, but that we also *(kai)* search for the final cause "in the case of existence" *(epi tou einai)*. The *kai* is instructive, for what he intends to say is that whereas the moving cause is sought only in the case of generation and corruption, the final cause is sought both in that case *and also* in the case of existence. In the context of book seven he apparently means that in instances of generation or corruption we look for the moving cause that brings the process of generation or corruption about, whereas in those instances where the process is complete and the final product is in its settled state of existence, we also look for the final cause that explains why the thing is the way it is. The moving cause explains becoming, which is the product of motion (e.g., the carpenter is the moving cause of the house's being built); and the final cause explains existence (e.g., the purpose for which the house is built is the reason why it takes the form it does and is made from certain kinds of materials). In terms of his worldview, Aristotle would look to explain sublunar generation and corruption by invoking the moving cause, for motion is the primary form of change and causes the becoming of things, but he would explain the existence of the heavenly bodies, which simply move locally but are not generated or corrupted,

25. Another text decries the opinion of those "who supposed that Aristotle had thought that God is not the cause of the substance of the heavens but only of their motion" *(Meta.* 6.1.1164).

by reference to the final cause. In short, Aristotle's moving, efficient cause, the only kind of productive cause he knows, is adduced as the reason for becoming, not for being.

With great exactitude and precision, and by utilizing the house example, Thomas correctly explains this text in the context of book seven, but he also calls Aristotle's moving cause the "agent cause"—*causa agens* (*Meta.* 7.17.1659–60). Nevertheless, he adds that here Aristotle is speaking only about material substances and "the natural agent that acts through motion; for the divine agent that produces *(influere)* being without motion is a cause not only of becoming but also of being" (*Meta.* 7.17.1661). "Moving cause" will not do in the case of God, since God's creative existential causality cannot be subsumed under a notion that requires motion; and so Thomas renames the moving cause the agent cause, which he then subdivides into the natural agent that causes becoming by means of motion and the divine agent that without motion produces being.[26] Since in Thomas' eyes Aristotle is aware of the divine agent cause, he asserts that in this passage Aristotle must be restricting his discussion to the natural agent alone. More eisegetically than exegetically, Thomas manages to turn Aristotle's quite generic notion of efficient causality into a specific one, which at the same time protects the putative Aristotelian notion of a divine and motionless origination of being.

One final question of a comparative nature remains, whose resolution will also provide a fitting conclusion to section I. Is Aristotle's arche-ology, or theory of the first principles, consistent in the causalities it assigns to the first mover of *Physics* 8/*Metaphysics* 12.6 and the primary substance of *Metaphysics* 12.7–10? Do his efficient and final causality in their most primordial instantiations ultimately cohere in these texts? From what we have

---

26. Étienne Gilson ("Notes pour l'histoire de la cause efficiente," *AHDLMA* 29 [1962]: 7–31) shows how Peter of Auvergne, relying on Avicenna, distinguishes the moving cause from the efficient cause of being and comes up with a fivefold instead of fourfold division of causes. Thomas, also following Avicenna, subdivides what he calls the agent cause into the natural agent, which acts through motion, and the divine agent, who "gives being" (*SS* 2.1.1.2 ad1). The *causa agens* is a flexible tool, as Thomas slides from the natural to the divine agent in his interpretation of Aristotle. Avicenna, a philosopher conversant with the Islamic faith in the one Creator God, was among the earliest proponents of the distinction between the moving cause of becoming and the efficient cause of being.

already seen it is clear no easy harmonization is possible, and a scholarly consensus on this issue is lacking.[27]

Aristotle faces a dilemma: since efficient causality is for him a matter of motion, which in his eyes necessitates that things be somehow in contact with one another, the first mover must always be in contact with the entity it moves. Moreover, since his theory of efficient causality also demands that whatever moves another be itself simultaneously moving, at least accidentally, then whatever moves is also itself moving and so is not entirely unmoved. The completely unmoved entity, then, can no longer be an efficient cause at all but only a final cause. The unmoved principle of the whole order of efficient causes cannot be an efficient cause itself, for a *moving* cause cannot be ultimate. Aristotle must have felt the impact of the quandary forced upon him by his own theory of efficient causality, which no doubt accounts for the saltation from efficient to final causality in *Metaphysics* 12.6–7, for which the reader is unprepared, and yet he never developed a higher-order theory to harmonize and reconcile the first mover's efficient causality with the primary principle's final causality.

Thomas breaks the impasse, however, the inner unconnectedness between Aristotle's efficient and final causality, by reading into his thought a notion of efficient causality that permits the bestowal of being in a motionless productive act that causes without moving, and by assigning this

27. Simplicius of Cilicia disagrees with Alexander of Aphrodisias, who taught that the first mover of the *Physics* is only a final cause, whereas it is clear to Simplicius that Aristotle thought it to be a productive cause as well (Bekker ed. of Aristotle, 3:453a28–48); Simplicius' problem is to make sure that the first mover is not moved even accidentally while it exercises its productive causality, a problem handled by his transcendent view of the first mover. While Marcel de Corte ("Causalité," pp. 105–47) claims that Aristotle's theology is not coherent and sees the reason in the fact that Aristotle was not able to transcend the astronomy of his day, Jean Paulus ("Théorie," pp. 283, 400–403) unifies Aristotle's thought by subordinating the god of the *Physics* to the god of the *Metaphysics*. Owens supports Paulus (*Doctrine of Being*, p. 438, n. 10; cf. "Aquinas and the Proof from the *Physics*," *MS* 28 [1966]: 119–50). Helen Lang thinks that while *Physics* 8 does not decide what kind of causality the first mover possesses, *Metaphysics* 12 makes the further determination that the causality in question is final ("Aristotle's First Movers and the Relation of Physics to Theology," *NS* 52 [1978]: 500–517), but such a harmonization strategy is highly dubious. Pegis wonders how the same first mover's efficient causality of *Physics* 7–8 and *Metaphysics* 12.6 can become, without warning, the final causality of *Metaphysics* 12.7, with *kinein* (to move) changing its meaning drastically from 12.6 to 12.7 ("Coherence," pp. 74–78, 86–107).

bestowal of being to the first mover/primary substance now understood as a divine principle. Thomas can glide over Aristotle's predicament because he has cut the link between efficient causality and motion and is able to see in Aristotle's first principle the divine initiator of being. Because Aristotle cannot dissociate existence and its origination from the phenomenon of motion, he cannot imagine an absolute beginning to things and must let stand, in the end, the final dichotomy between the unmoved mover of *Physics* 8/*Metaphysics* 12.6 and the telic god(s) of *Metaphysics* 12.7–10. How was Thomas able to accomplish what Aristotle could never even dream?

The deeper truth that Aquinas possesses is the knowledge of God as creative pure act and subsistent being,[28] as the infinitely perfect Creator and absolute initiator, out of nothing, of all being, motion, and time.[29] Because he reads this truth into Aristotle he minimizes the necessity of the premise of eternal motion in Aristotle's proof for the first mover, whereas this premise is absolutely necessary for Aristotle since for him there is no absolute contingency in things (for time and motion and existence cannot *not* be), and since his divine principle is not transcendent and free but securely ensconced within the universe (if perhaps at its edge) and implicated in its eternal doings by bonds of necessity. How did Aquinas obtain his deeper knowledge of God?

II. The Richness of God's Existence in Aquinas' Theology

By several different proofs Aquinas claims to demonstrate the existence of God by reason alone, and the fact that in those proofs he relies so much upon his mentor Aristotle, who was not privy to the Christian faith, bolsters that claim. But the situation is more complicated than that. First, Aquinas so metaphysicizes[30] the proofs that the first principle of Aristotle's

28. From here on "subsistent being" will be commonly used to translate Aquinas' *ipsum esse subsistens,* though more literal renditions may also be used, such as "subsistent being itself," "subsistent to-be itself," "act of subsistent being," or "subsistent act of being."
29. For Aristotle, the concept of "origination out of nothing" is philosophical nihilism and suicide.
30. Gilson sees Aquinas as existentially transposing the Aristotelian essentialist proofs of God (*The Christian Philosophy of St. Thomas Aquinas,* trans. L. K. Shook [New York:

Physics and *Metaphysics* can be construed as the absolute initiator of be-ing.[31] Further, as we observed at the end of the last chapter, the proofs are usually constructed within an overarching context of theological faith and systematic theology. Finally, as we have just seen in some detail, Aquinas delicately and unobtrusively inserts themes into the Aristotelian argu-ments that are quite foreign to the Stagirite's thought—creation as a mo-tionless activity, God's transcendence and freedom, and the one God as bestower of being—and thoroughly transform his worldview.[32] One can-not escape the feeling that even the proofs for God's existence, which form the foundation for the whole edifice of Aquinas' systematic theology, are not hermetically sealed against the influence of truths that Aristotle was unaware of. *De facto,* Aristotle did not know these truths, but *could* he have known them, *de iure,* before the Judeo-Christian revelation? Moreover, how does Aquinas know them?

To help answer these queries, we shall now examine how Thomas draws out of the apparent philosophical proof for God's existence his most fun-damental truth that God is subsistent being. We will look at how this pro-cess develops in some early chapters from the first book of his *Compendi-um theologiae,* since it develops its systematic conclusions on the sole foundation of the first proof from motion and so allows us to avoid in those conclusions a possible contamination from the other proofs for God that do not so clearly derive from Aristotle.

Chapter 3 is a very simple statement of the first proof for God based on

Random, 1956], pp. 77–83). Owens also argues forcefully and at length that Thomas' proofs for God's existence work only when taken existentially (*Existence of God,* the last six essays; idem, "Proof from the *Physics,*" pp. 119–50). For a critique of Owens, see John Yardan, "Some Remarks on Metaphysics and the Existence of God," *NS* 37 (1963): 213–19.

31. For Aristotle, act is equated with form, which is opposed to the potentiality of matter and temporality and as such is eternal. For Aquinas, being as created act is still different from the form, which is itself potential with respect to being. Cf. James Doig, *Aquinas on Metaphysics* (The Hague: Nijhoff, 1972), pp. 323–32.

32. Cf. G. Ducoin, "Saint Thomas, commentateur d'Aristote. Étude sur le commentaire thomiste du livre lambda des *Métaphysiques* d'Aristote," *AP* 20 (1957): 78–117, 240–71, 392–445; George Kuykendall, "Thomas' Proofs as *Fides Quaerens Intellectum:* Towards a Trinitarian *Analogia,*" *SJT* 31 (1978): 114, 127; Michael Dodds, *The Unchanging God of Love,* Studia Friburgensia, N.S. 66 (Fribourg, Switzerland: University of Fribourg, 1986), pp. 177–91.

our observation of things in motion, concluding with the first mover that is above all things, whom we call God. Chapter 4 massages this conclusion to yield the further assertion about God's immobility, which as a statement of negative theology simply denies of God the kinds of movement with which the proof in chapter 3 began—locomotion, growth, alteration, generation, and corruption—and which Aquinas below will also see as tantamount to God's immutability.

Chapter 6 shows the necessity of God's existence:

Everything that may possibly be and not be *(possibile esse et non esse)* is mutable. But God is totally immutable, as was shown. Therefore, it is not possible for God to be and not be. Everything that exists in such a manner, however, that it is not possible for it not to be, necessarily exists; for to be necessary signifies the same thing as to be impossible not to be. It is necessary, therefore, that God exist.

The first three sentences reveal an ambiguity that Aquinas will not exploit until later chapters. What does he mean by *possibile esse et non esse?* He may mean what Aristotle would mean by such a phrase: that the possible is what may come into or go out of existence, by a process of motion and change. If Thomas means this, then the possible is the physically mutable, and the denial of such mutability to God means that God is not such a possible being in a physical sense. But the argument's metaphysical tenor reveals that Thomas probably has in mind a much deeper significance: the possible is what is subject, in its own inner being, to an absolute beginning by creation and an absolute termination by annihilation. In this case, the possible is mutable in the sense that it cannot explain its own origins or assure its own continuation. However, the denial of mutability to God in chapter 4 (which was really a denial of God's mobility) can have had in mind only the motions and changes on whose level the original proof proceeded—*unless* motion has already taken on in that proof a metaphysical sheen, and the unmoved mover has already been invested with a subsistent act of being, which would mean that when chapter 4 ostensibly denies physical mobility and mutability of God, what it is really rejecting, in Thomas' eyes, is any metaphysical potency in God. After introducing the notion of metaphysical contingency and possibility, then, chapter 6 goes on to integrate the physical immobility of God into an argument that is now being cast on the metaphysical level of being and existence.[33]

Chapter 9 establishes the simplicity of God. For any composite being contains two factors that are related to each other as potency to act; but the first mover, as immobile, can have no such combination, for whatever is potential is ipso facto movable. Hence God cannot be composite and must be simple. Thomas again transcends Aristotle: while the latter equates potency with matter, and form with act, teaches that all composites are made from form and matter, and sees mobility as rooted in the potency of matter, the former intimates, but does not state, a deeper kind of composition in this passage, one in which form and essence as metaphysical potency are distinguished from being as metaphysical act, and in which mobility is seen as something's metaphysical potency to receive actuality.

In the course of demonstrating that God is his own essence, chapter 10 argues that since in God there is no combination of potency and act (from chapter 9), God must be pure act. God as pure act, therefore, is an immediate consequence of God's simplicity, which is based on God's (metaphysical) immobility, which is itself a consequence of Thomas' immensely fruitful understanding of the proof for God's existence.

Chapter 11 proves that God is being itself *(ipsum esse)*, on the grounds that God is simple and pure act (from chapters 9 and 10). The *ipsum esse* hidden in Thomas' understanding of God's existence and immobility now comes to light explicitly.[34]

33. We might note that the argument of chapter 6 is similar in structure to the third proof for God's existence in *ST* 1.2.3 and to *SCG* 1.15.124, which on grounds of contingency attempt to demonstrate a necessary God. But Aristotle has no such argument. The only necessity he knows is the type opposed to the physical contingency of the generable and corruptible composites of nature, not to the metaphysical contingency of created being.

34. Van Steenberghen shows, in a discussion of how Thomas in the *Compendium theologiae* derives the attributes of God from the proof based on motion, that he passes without comment from the pure act of Aristotle (no potency to further change or determination) to the pure act of God who is infinite and without any limiting potency or essence (*Problème*, pp. 312–23; for a valuable exposition of Thomas' Aristotle-inspired proof for God based on motion, see Scott MacDonald, "Aquinas' Parasitic Cosmological Argument," *Medieval Philosophy and Theology* 1 [1991]: 119–55; for detailed expositions of the second proof from motion in *SCG* 1.13, and of an implicit proof from contingency at 1.15.124, see Norman Kretzmann, *The Metaphysics of Theism: Aquinas' Natural Theology in "Summa contra gentiles" I*

In conclusion, pure act and subsistent being seem to be elements of Thomas' very concept of God, and so he quite naturally interprets in their light the proof for God's existence. As interpretive concepts that were not really part of the original Aristotelian proof, they lie hidden in Aquinas' exegesis, only to emerge categorically when Thomas needs them for his deeper forays into God's nature. Their correlative concept of an inner contingency of created being also makes an early debut in chapter 4 because Thomas requires the premise of metaphysical possibility in order to prove God's metaphysical necessity. In the *Compendium theologiae* we have seen how Aquinas invests the proof for God's existence based on motion with a metaphysical richness and density unimaginable to Aristotle. In general, Aquinas fashions the proofs for God's existence into formidable theological tools: they are indisputably foundational for his systematic theology because he seeds within their premises and harvests in their conclusions the monotheistically revolutionary truth that God is the pure, infinite, subsistent act of being. This Ur-truth will continue to propagate other truths throughout his systematic theology and theological epistemology.

III. *Aquinas and the Philosophers on God the Creator*

As we continue to search out Aquinas' philosophical and theological presuppositions, another question raises its hand: Does Aquinas recognize God the Creator by reason or by faith? As a step toward an answer, this section will discuss whether he thinks the Greek philosophers acknowledged the Creator God,[35] while the next will examine his own position on how creation and its cause are known.

Before the Christian era no Greek philosopher teaches a transcendent

---

[Oxford: Clarendon, 1997], pp. 54–112). A similar process is pursued in *SCG* 1.13–28 and *ST* 1.2–11, but in these texts Thomas has recourse to the second proof based on efficient causality (which concludes to God as the cause of being) or to the fourth proof based on degrees of participation (which arrives at God as the greatest being)—neither of which really originate with Aristotle.

35. For a good treatment about which truths Thomas thinks philosophers can know about God, see John Wippel, "Thomas Aquinas on What Philosophers Can Know about God," *ACPQ* 66 (1992): 279–97.

God freely creating *ex nihilo*. Whereas the Judeo-Christian Creator God is stationed outside the world and brings it into existence by personal fiat, the Greek gods are inside the world, identified either with anthropomorphic beings (as in Homer and Hesiod) or with Mind, Eros, Form, Being, or the Infinite (as in the Presocratic philosophers).[36] Neither Plato's Form of the Good nor the demiurge of the *Timaeus* is a genuine Creator God, nor is Aristotle's first principle a Creator.[37] The certainly post-Christian and probably post-Islamic Neoplatonic work *Liber de causis* calls the causal activity of the first cause a creation, which suggests that its author was a monotheist.[38] And when other Neoplatonic works emphasize the univer-

---

36. Jaeger, *Theology*, pp. 16–17. Roy Hack writes against the then-common view that the Presocratic philosophers were thoroughgoing naturalists in reaction against the theogonies and cosmogonies of Homer and Hesiod; philosophy from Thales onward was really concerned with describing how the cosmos came to be and with settling on where the divine dwelt (*God in Greek Philosophy to the Time of Socrates* (Princeton: Princeton University, 1931). See also Lloyd Gerson, *God and Greek Philosophy: Studies in the Early History of Natural Theology* (London/New York: Routledge, 1990), especially pp. 82–141 on "Aristotle's God of Motion."

37. The Good in Itself is an object of thought and desire but not a productive agent of being. "Aquinas goes further than Plato in making Essence, in its supreme form, the active cause of everything" (John Findlay, *Plato: The Written and Unwritten Doctrines* [London: Routledge and Kegan Paul, 1974], pp. 394–95). The demiurge cannot be a genuine Creator, in the Christian sense, because it is embedded in the universe and acts according to eternal patterns and ideas that are not of its own choosing or making. Anton-Hermann Chroust claims that Aristotle's lost dialogue *On Philosophy* argues for the uncreatedness and indestructibility of the universe, in reaction to Plato's mitigated creationistic thesis in the *Timaeus* ("Aristotle's Doctrine of the Uncreatedness and Indestructibility of the Universe," *NS* 52 [1978]: 268–79). See also Joseph Owens, "Aristotle and God," in *God in Contemporary Thought: A Philosophical Perspective*, ed. S. A. Matczak (New York: Learned Publications, 1977), pp. 436–38; idem, "The Relation of God to World in the *Metaphysics*," in *Études sur la "Métaphysique" d'Aristote*, Actes du VIe Symposium Aristotelicum (Paris: Vrin, 1979), pp. 207–28.

38. E.g., see propositions 16 and 18. The work upon which the *Liber* is heavily based, Proclus' *Elements of Theology* (fifth century A.D.), does not describe the supreme One as a being and proclaims a host of subordinate gods, whereas the *Liber* eliminates the plurality of gods and calls the first cause "being." Leo Sweeney notes that in the *Liber* a word for "create" occurs some 45 times and that creation is defined as a giving of being to all things ("Doctrine of Creation in *Liber de causis*," in *An Étienne Gilson Tribute*, ed. C. J. O'Neil [Milwaukee: Marquette, 1959], pp. 274–89). While the *Liber* does imitate good Neoplatonic form by having the First Principle diffuse its fullness and goodness to all things through the instrumentality and mediation of a hierarchical series of hypostases, it has the First Principle give being to all by a direct creation, not by a mediated overflow or emanation. Proclus, for whom being is a secondary hypostasis, takes existence for granted and seeks to explain how

sality and immediacy of their first causes, they probably do so in constructive reaction to the by then widespread belief in an almighty Creator.[39]

In a position that had both advocates and critics among the theologians of his own time, Aquinas claims that Aristotle and a few others were cognizant of creation but erred in certain details that accompanied their notion of it.[40] Whether explicitly or implicitly, he can remark that Plato and

things become united and informed; for the author of the *Liber*, the First Principle is being and must give being before any *informatio* can take place. "The impact of divine revelation upon our author has been strong enough to break through an otherwise rather rigid Neoplatonism and his Supreme Cause becomes the 'First Creative *Being*'" (ibid., p. 289, and n. 77).

39. Cornelia de Vogel, "*Deus Creator Omnium:* Plato and Aristotle in Aquinas' Doctrine of God," in *Graceful Reason*, ed. L. P. Gerson (Toronto: PIMS, 1983), pp. 222–23.

40. According to Faustinus Prezioso, Alexander of Hales grants to the philosophers a knowledge of creation; Bonaventure declares himself unsure on the issue but leans toward thinking Aristotle did not know creation, and some of his followers—including Matthew of Aquasparta and Roger Marston—follow suit; those who agree with Thomas include Roger Bacon and Duns Scotus; those who disagree with him and deny a knowledge of creation to Aristotle include William of Auvergne, Robert Grosseteste, Giles of Rome, and Henry of Ghent, the first two revealing some pique as they refute those who would try to "excuse" Aristotle in this matter (*De Aristotelis creationismo secundum S. Bonaventuram et secundum S. Thomam* [Rome: Officium Libri Catholici, 1942], pp. 12–26; see pp. 64–83 for how Bonaventure and Aquinas disagree on whether the eternity of the world in Aristotle is contrary to creation). See also Zachary Hayes, *The General Doctrine of Creation in the Thirteenth Century: With Special Emphasis on Matthew of Aquasparta* (Munich: Schöningh, 1964). Albert's position is nuanced: Gilson says that in his eyes the philosophers neither affirmed nor denied the strict notion of creation *ex nihilo* (*History of Christian Philosophy in the Middle Ages* [New York: Random, 1955], p. 672, n. 13); Lawrence Dewan finds Albert discovering creation among the Peripatetics as to production of form but not as to production of matter *ex nihilo* ("St. Albert, Creation, and the Philosophers," *LTP* 40 [1984]: 295–307); see also the texts in Anton Pegis, *St. Thomas and the Greeks*, The Aquinas Lecture, 1939 (Milwaukee: Marquette, 1939), p. 107, n. 72. In his *De universo* (1-2.27), William of Auvergne contends that the Greeks (Aristotle is meant) erred on the fundamental point of creation, since they did not realize the power and freedom of God the Creator (text quoted in Owens, *Doctrine*, p. 4, n. 19). Giles of Rome's *Errores philosophorum* is a good example of how Thomas' benign interpretation of Aristotle was tenaciously opposed by the opponents of Aristotelianism in the thirteenth century. Giles claims that Aristotle's misunderstanding of creation is the "mainstay of his errors" and begins chapter 3 by writing: "Anyone who carefully investigates the matter can see that all his errors flow from the supposition that nothing new comes forth into being except through a preceding motion" (ed. J. Koch [Milwaukee: Marquette, 1944], p. 14). Giles will not excuse Aristotle, as Thomas does, by saying that he requires a preceding motion only for the processes of becoming but not for the absolute genesis of all reality by creation. For Siger of Brabant, creation can be affirmed only by revelation (Gilson,

Aristotle recognize a universal cause of the world,[41] though he also mentions Aristotle's error in asserting the eternity of the world, noting that such a position is against the Catholic faith and cannot be demonstrated apodictically.[42]

Frequently, Aquinas makes a complicated dual assertion, stating that while Aristotle and others do posit creation, they also fall into error over certain issues relevant to its proper understanding. Plato and Aristotle did not deviate from the Catholic faith by claiming some eternal beings to be uncreated but by asserting some created beings to be eternal.[43] The complete notion of creation *ex nihilo* comprises three elements: nothing can be presupposed in the thing created, which makes creation different from all other processes of change; in the thing created, nonbeing has a priority of nature over being, such that if the creature were left to itself, nonbeing would result; and creation began in time after nothing had existed beforehand. Creation can be demonstrated according to the first two elements, "and thus the philosophers posited creation," but it cannot be proved by reason as regards the third element, "and it is not conceded by the

History, pp. 39, 719, n. 15). Maimonides sees the fact of creation as revealed by the Torah (*Guide of the Perplexed* 1.25–27; trans. with introduction and notes by S. Pines [Chicago: University of Chicago, 1963]). William Dunphy disagrees with those who assert that Maimonides rejects the demonstrability of creation *ex nihilo* because he identifies it with creation in time, which cannot be demonstrated; rather, neatly distinguishing creation in eternity from creation in time, he affirms that neither can be demonstrated, but does not seem ever to have explicitly posed the question about the rational demonstrability of creation from nothing ("Maimonides and Aquinas on Creation: A Critique of Their Historians," in *Graceful Reason*, ed. L. P. Gerson [Toronto: PIMS, 1983], pp. 361–79).

41. DP 3.5; DSS 9.102–7; cf. *De aetern.*, lines 10–13. Aquinas speaks of the manifest falsity of the opinion of those who suppose Aristotle's God does not cause the substance of the heavens but only their motion (*Meta.* 6.1.1164); Aristotle's God is the "maker *(factor)* of the heavenly bodies" and not merely their final cause, and Plato's God in the *Timaeus* is the "establisher *(conditor)* of the world" (*Caelo* 1.8.91; 2.1.291). ST 1.44.2 and SCG 2.37.1130, which are parallel to the first two passages above, omit the names of Plato and Aristotle.

42. *Meteor.* 1.17.138; 2.4.160; *Credo* 1.880 states the error without mentioning any names; cf. *Phys.* 1.15.139; *Gener.* 7.57; SS 2.1.1.5; SCG 2.81.1622.

43. DSS 9.215–22. The same point is made about Aristotle alone in *Decretalem* 1.432–37 and *Phys.* 8.3.996. Speaking of philosophers in general, Aquinas writes that "they confess that God is the cause of the world's substance, although they think it eternal, saying that the eternal God exists as the cause of an everlasting world in the same way as a foot would have been the eternal cause of a footprint if it had been impressed in the dust from eternity" (SCG 1.43.368). For more on the "foot eternally in the dust," see SCG, vol. 2, p. 54, n. 1.

philosophers but accepted through faith."[44] He even argues that in order to counter certain philosophers who taught that a created world existed from eternity, the Nicene Creed replaced the Apostles' Creed's *creator* with the word *factor* (maker), "which shows more clearly a beginning of the world's duration" (*SS* 3.25.1.2 ad9). Certain philosophers also had a faulty notion in that they posited mediators in the process of creation, so that higher intelligences help produce lower ones, and so on;[45] the same error is detected in those who, not fully appreciating that creation demands an infinite power, surmised that creatures can create.[46] Aquinas, therefore, grants to Plato, Aristotle, and other unnamed philosophers a genuine knowledge of creation *ex nihilo*, though their knowledge is imperfect since they do not realize that creation cannot occur through the mediation of creatures or that the world is not eternal.[47] In Aquinas' view, apparently, error on these two points did not substantially compromise their knowledge of the core meaning of creation.

This view is also indicated by the special place Thomas reserves for a few enlightened philosophers in each of three texts where he provides a thumbnail sketch of the progress of philosophy in three stages. The texts, with different emphases and terminology, all chart the philosophical advance from particular to universal causes. *SCG* 2.37.1130 finds that philosophers first detected the cause of accidental productions (e.g., the making of a bed), which presupposes a being in act; then the cause of substantial but particular productions (e.g., the making of a horse), which presupposes matter's potential being; and finally the cause of the totality of created

---

44. *SS* 2.1.1.2; cf. *SS* 3.25.1.2 ad2.   45. *SS* 2.1.1.3, and ad1.
46. *SS* 4.5.1.3.3 ad1, 4, 5.

47. After an even more exhaustive review of the pertinent texts than that attempted here, Mark Johnson confirms the conclusion that it is beyond dispute that Thomas throughout his career attributed a doctrine of creation to Aristotle ("Did St. Thomas Attribute a Doctrine of Creation to Aristotle?" *NS* 63 [1989]: 129–55), even in a passage from the *De articulis fidei* that used to appear inconsistent with Thomas' other treatments of the subject, but that the recent Leonine critical edition now shows has added a spurious *non* that makes Thomas seem to criticize Aristotle for not teaching creation (ibid., pp. 138–40). Johnson also proves that while Thomas early in his career thought Plato taught that matter was uncreated, he later changed his mind and attributed to Plato a doctrine of eternal creation ("Aquinas' Changing Evaluation of Plato on Creation," *ACPQ* 66 [1992]: 81–88).

being, which needs nothing presupposed to its causal action. *DP* 3.5 remarks that the earliest philosophers had no notion of an efficient cause, that later philosophers discovered the agent cause of specific beings, and that the philosophers of the third stage found the universal cause of being. *ST* 1.44.2 describes how philosophers first acknowledged the cause of accidental change, which produces a qualified being; then the cause of essential but particular change, which produces an individual substance; and finally the cause of being as such. In each work, philosophy's third stage discovers the universal cause of being, which Thomas clearly sees as the Creator God.[48]

Let us give a more detailed account of the third stage, which interests us most. *SCG* 2.37.1130 tells how the last group of philosophers, by entering even more profoundly into the origin of things, were finally led to consider the procession "of the whole of created being from one first cause," which pertains not to the natural philosopher but to the first philosopher or metaphysician, who treats of common being *(ens commune)*. *DP* 3.5

---

48. Cf. *Job* Prol., 1–29; *DP* 3.6, 16, 17; *ST* 1.49.3; *Phys.* 8.2.975; *Meta.* 6.1.1164; *DSS* 9.75–156. For texts and sources, see *SCG*, vol. 2, pp. 297–99, n. 1130; and Pegis, *Thomas and the Greeks*, pp. 101–4. Jan Aertsen writes: "Thomas can describe the history of philosophical reflection on the origin of reality as a continuous progression towards the idea of creation," which "appears as the result, yes the crowning of the *internal* development of the desire to know" (*Nature and Creature: Thomas Aquinas's Way of Thought*, trans. H. D. Morton [Leiden: Brill, 1988], pp. 201–2, 231). Lawrence Dewan justifies how Thomas might have arrived at his view of creation in Aristotle, by showing how various elements of their metaphysics of creature and Creator are not that far apart, especially their view of being as divided by act and potency ("St. Thomas, Aristotle, and Creation," *Dionysius* 15 [1991]: 81–96). As to the question whether Aristotle ever actually taught a philosophy of creation, a few scholars are willing to countenance the *de iure* possibility more than the *de facto* actuality. R. Jolivet asserted years ago that whereas Aristotle never in fact mentioned creation, in principle he possessed the philosophical premises that could have led to such a doctrine, though he was not able to draw from them the conclusions they implied ("Aristote et la notion de création," *RSPT* 19 [1930]: 5–50, 209–35). Anton Pegis holds that "Plato and Aristotle rose to the consideration of the First Cause of reality and yet did not assert creation," for they lacked the view of being possessed by Thomas ("A Note on St. Thomas, *Summa theologica*, I, 44, 1–2," *MS* 8 [1946]: 165, 168; see also his "St. Thomas and the Origin of Creation," in *Philosophy and the Modern Mind*, ed. F. X. Canfield [Detroit: Sacred Heart Seminary, 1961], pp. 49–65; and "Coherence," pp. 114–15 and nn. 141–43). In my opinion, Aristotle never taught a philosophy of creation, nor did he even possess the proper principles from which he might have deduced it. Instead, Thomas has completely transformed Aristotle's "principle of motion" into the "bestower of being."

says that the third group of philosophers (only this passage specifically mentions Plato and Aristotle) penetrated to the consideration "of universal being itself" *(ipsius esse universalis)*, so that they alone proposed a universal cause of the being of things, as is evident from Augustine.[49] *ST* 1.44.2 describes how some thinkers raised themselves to consider being insofar as it is being *(ens inquantum est ens)*; and thus they looked for a cause of beings insofar as they are being, and not merely insofar as they possess various qualitative modifications or are particular individual substances.

Aquinas links philosophers' recognition of the universal cause of being with their metaphysical consideration of being qua being. However, the different status of *commune ens* in Aristotle and Aquinas leads one to wonder whether Aquinas is not reading too much into the philosophic achievements of his third stage. As Joseph Owens has shown,[50] for Aristotle, being as such *(to on*—his *commune ens)* does not refer to a generalized concept but to a *pros hen* equivocal term (later called analogical by others) whose primary instance turns out to be divine entity acting as a final cause. This means that being as such can only be fully expressed by *first* expressing what divine entity means, and to understand being as such requires first understanding the primary entity to which all being is related. As Owens expresses it, because of this tight bond between the divine primary entity and being as such, Aristotle's brand of metaphysics may be called theological; but most Christian theologians, including Aquinas, advocate an ontological[51] conception of metaphysics, according to which metaphysics is viewed as *first* possessing an already constituted concept of *ens commune* as its subject, and as *then* searching for and finding the sufficient cause of its subject in the universal cause of being. This ontological view of metaphysics is what we encounter in the third stage of each text:[52] the third group of philosophers first hits upon the consideration of *ens commune* and then rises to its universal, creative cause.

The ontological conception of metaphysics preserves the transcendence

---

49. *De civitate Dei* 8.4 (PL 41:228); cf. *DSS* 9.102–7.

50. *Doctrine*, chaps. 1, 3, 7, 13, 18–19.

51. See *Doctrine*, chap. 1, for a discussion of the ontological versus the theological type of metaphysics.

52. This is explicitly the case in *DP* 3.5 and *ST* 1.44.2, and implied in *SCG* 2.37.1130.

of God, who exists outside the whole order of finite being and does not function merely as the primary instance of Form or Entity (unlike the primary substance in Aristotle's metaphysics), and who creatively causes the totality of being. The ontological conception also follows proper epistemological order, in which the contingency and potentiality of *commune ens* cry out for an explanation in God. Nevertheless, the ontological conception of metaphysics favored by Aquinas is not that of Aristotle, who was not simply looking for the sufficient cause of an already constituted *commune ens* but was discovering the very meaning of being by reference to the being of the primary substance. Paradoxically, the existential contingency of *commune ens* so plainly felt by Christian metaphysicians, which is precisely what prods them to look for an explanation in God, is exactly the opposite of what Aristotle the metaphysician thinks and feels, for to his mind the *very meaning* of being as such, his *commune ens*, is derived from what being means in the primary substance, and that entity's being is necessary and eternal and not in the least contingent.[53]

iv. *Creation and Creator*

This section will treat how Aquinas himself thinks creation and God the Creator are recognized by human beings. For him, everything pertaining to God not capable of rational demonstration, because it exceeds the power of *every* human intellect, is an essential truth of faith; but the truth about God that exceeds the intellect of only this or that person, but in principle is provable, is an accidental truth of faith (*SS* 3.24.1.2.2). Some

53. In an interesting article comparing Thomas' teaching in the second book of his Commentary on the *Sentences* with the position of his mid-thirteenth century contemporaries, Timothy Noone finds that the latter hold that the philosophers did not acknowledge a doctrine of creation from nothing—which was always thought to involve a creature's acquiring being after not being—since their eternal universe could not admit a temporal succession of being after nonbeing; Thomas is able to disagree with these writers, however, because he refocused the core meaning of creation on ontological dependence rather than temporal finitude, and read his own ideas about being into the philosophers' metaphysical theories ("The Originality of St. Thomas' Position on the Philosophers and Creation," *Thomist* 60 [1996]: 275–300). Noone notes, however, that Thomas is able to understand the philosophers' doctrines in terms of his own metaphysical *Weltanschauung* because he is "blessedly ignorant of the historical genesis of the philosophers' thought" (p. 300).

truths totally exceed the faculty of human reason (e.g., that God is three and one), whereas others can be reached by natural reason as well as by faith (e.g., that God exists, that God is one, and "other things of this sort"), and this second class of truths has been demonstratively proved by philosophers led by the light of natural reason (*SCG* 1.3.14). Aquinas calls those accidental truths of faith, which theology uses philosophy to prove, the "preambles of faith."[54]

Are the truths about creation and the Creator essential matters of faith, or can they also be reached by reason? According to *SCG* 4.1.3349, the essential truths of faith that must be believed are Trinity, Incarnation (which includes original sin and the sacraments), and eschatology (including resurrection and bodily glorification, last judgment, and eternal beatitude).[55] Creation and the Creator, however, are treated within the context of the first three books (especially the second) of the *Summa contra Gentiles,* which discuss the truths about God open to rational demonstration.[56]

For Aquinas, therefore, the truths about creation and the Creator are accidental matters of faith able in principle to be proved by the intellectually precocious and metaphysically astute, though in fact the vast majority of those who think that there exists a Creator God at the wellsprings of creation are able to do so only because of their faith. When we read Aquinas saying that creation is known by faith,[57] then, he should not be understood as talking about an essential matter of faith, for "not only faith

---

54. *BDT* 2.3. God's existence is not an essential matter of faith, for the truth that there is one God "does not fall under faith" (*Heb.* 11.2.577). He has some fine words on the difference between the essential and accidental truths of faith: "The knowledge of God gained through other sciences only illumines the intellect, showing that God is the first cause, one and wise, etc. But the knowledge of God gained through faith both illumines the intellect and delights the affections, since not only does it say that God is the first cause but also that he is our savior and redeemer, and loves us and became incarnate for us—all of which inflames the affections" (*2 Cor.* 2.3.73).

55. For the same, cf. *De unitate* 5.422–30; *1 Cor.* 15.1.894 mentions only Trinity and incarnation.

56. *SCG* 1.2–3; 1.9.

57. Faith "confesses that God is the Creator of all beings and that no other is Creator" (*SS* 1.43.2.1, *sed contra*). "The Christian faith primarily teaches humans about God, and through the light of divine revelation makes them able to recognize creatures" (*creaturarum cognitorem facit—SCG* 2.2.862). Cf. *SS* 1.37.1.1; 2.1.1.4; *SCG* 1.17.138; *Decretalem* 1.400–402, 410–18; *De articulis* 1.101–3.

holds that there is a creation, but reason also demonstrates it."[58] Moreover, he holds that since only articles essentially pertaining to faith are included in the creeds of Christendom, the rationally provable truths that are the preambles of faith can be included in a creed only if they also carry a meaning that is open solely to faith. For example, God's unity as demonstrated by philosophy is a preamble to faith, but the unity of the divine essence that is an article of faith refers to God's omnipotence and providence, which are not subject to proof (*DV* 14.9 ad8); and the article of faith is not that God simply exists, but that God exists as faith understands, namely, as exercising care for all things and as rewarding and punishing (*SS* 3.25.1.2 ad2). Similarly, the philosophers did not know creation as faith teaches it, namely, that after nothing was, things were produced in being (*SS* 3.35.1.2 ad2)—which implies that creation is included in the creed only insofar as it refers to the temporal beginning of the world. If, excepting the world's temporality, creation and the Creator God are rationally provable, then we might expect Aquinas to provide some proofs, which he does.

For this chapter's purposes we shall analyze the three types of proof for Creator and creation that depend on the nature of being: being as participated, being as accidental, and being as common. Once again, our main intention is to be attentive to any possible theological presuppositions or faith understandings on Thomas' part.

1. *Being as Participated.* In the arguments that depend on being as par-

---

58. *SS* 2.1.1.2; same. *DP* 3.5, *SDC* 18.345. "This conviction was relatively new in medieval thought. Thomas's teacher Albert the Great, for example, was of the opinion that this insight can be acquired not through philosophical reflection but only from Revelation" (Aertsen, *Nature and Creature,* p. 205). Aertsen sees both a philosophical and a Christian notion of creation in Aquinas, the former identified with the idea of absolute dependence in being, and the latter bound up with the concept of the temporal duration of that creaturely dependence (pp. 202–10). Aertsen's whole book is a massive and enlightening meditation, from many converging perspectives in Aquinas' thought, about the latter's philosophical attempt "to understand the intelligible structure of reality through an analysis that embraces both nature and creation" (p. 315; cf. pp. 275–78, 373–75). Aertsen agrees with Aquinas' own position concerning the rational demonstrability of the truth of creation. For two others who also explain how Aquinas argues philosophically for Creator and creation, see Norman Kretzmann, *The Metaphysics of Creation: Aquinas' Natural Theology in "Summa contra gentiles" II* (Oxford: Clarendon, 1999), pp. 56–100; John Wippel, *The Metaphysical Thought of Thomas Aquinas: From Finite Being to Uncreated Being* (Washington, DC: CUA, 2000), pp. 579–85.

ticipated, God is either explicitly or implicitly seen as Being itself, cause of being, or pure act. The first text is from *SS* 2.1.1.2. Anything imperfect in any category takes its origin from that in which the categorical nature is primarily and perfectly found, as is clear from the example of the heat in things, which fire brings about.

> Since, however, every thing (and whatever is in it) participates in being *(esse)* in some fashion and yet is also mixed with imperfection, it must take its origin, according to all that is in it, from the first and perfect being. But this is what "to create" means, namely, to produce a thing in being according to its entire substance. Hence all things must come about through creation by the first principle.

The second text is from *ST* 1.44.1. Whenever any perfection is participated in, it must be caused by that to which the perfection belongs essentially. But God is essentially being *(esse)* and necessarily one, so that all things other than God are not their own being and must participate in being. Their participation in being, then, is caused by the most perfect being—which proves, for Thomas, that every being is created by God.

The third text is from *DP* 3.5, whose argument is ascribed to Avicenna. It is necessary to reduce whatever is "through another" to whatever is "through itself," that is, to reduce what exists by participation to what does not. But God is pure act and his very own act of being, and so all beings come from God, for they are not their own being but have it by participation.[59]

In this type of proof, notice how participation appears to be a description of the situation that occurs when God is known to be the sole and unique act of being itself; for in that case, all else must exist by participation in God's being, which occurs through God's creative causality. Thus the proof has our knowledge of creation depending on our knowledge of participation. But how do we know the fact of participation? In the texts a general statement is made or implied that what exists by participa-

---

59. For other passages containing this type of argument, see *DE* 4.127–46; *SS* 2.37.1.2; *SCG* 2.6.881–84; 2.15.923, 926, 928–29; *CT* 1.68; *John* Prol., 5; *DSS* 9.102–18. Referring to the proof of creation based on participation in *ST* 1.44.1, Rudi te Velde admits that it and the proof for God's existence are circular, but is not very persuasive in attempting to explain why the circle is not a vicious one (*Participation and Substantiality in Thomas Aquinas* [Leiden: Brill, 1995], pp. 117–19).

tion is reduced to what exists essentially. This general statement appears to be a universal truth that we *first* come to know independently and then *later* apply to the case of God. In reality, however, we have no knowledge, *except in the case of God*, of any quality, perfection, or reality existing in a pristine, perfect, or "essential" state.[60] In Thomas' hands, then, the seemingly general and independent principle of participation is actually a more abstract, philosophical way of explicating the relationship between God and creation, and indeed depends for its own meaning upon the prior knowledge of God as pure subsistent being. Participation language is thus a settled terminology that serves to synthesize the insights of already garnered truths: it does not lead to recognizing God as Creator but rather expresses in a more philosophic fashion the religious truth about the God who creates.[61]

Further, the participation argument depends upon the distinction between a thing and its being, or equivalently, between what is imperfect and perfect in a thing. The example of fire and heat in the first text is easy enough to grasp: a thing can exist without being hot, and it is evident to the senses that fire causes heat. But then Thomas jumps from this example to the case of God as subsistent being causing all other things to participate in being. But how do we know that a thing's being is really (and not merely notionally) distinct from itself? For unlike the fire example, where a thing can exist without being hot, a thing cannot exist without *being* a thing. How are we to look for a cause of being as such, if we do not notice that a thing's being is different from its essence? Aristotle would consider existence the necessary accompaniment of the forms and natures of the universe, which perdures as long as they do, and not a contingent reality distinct from essence. For Aristotle, being and essence could at most be conceptually distinct, for since to know an essence is to know it here and now in its actual existence, being for him always remains part of the es-

---

60. Pace Thomas' medieval view, we know today that even the sun is not, as his favorite example would have it, the unique and "essential" instance of light and heat in the universe.

61. Even in Neoplatonism, where it finds its natural locus, the doctrine of participation is primarily a concise way of expressing the hierarchical status of things from the top down, of explicating how the One distributes all perfections in a gradated manner by emanating various hypostases from its own plenitude.

sential order. But for Aquinas, being, the gift from God that is at once most inner and most hidden, defies placement in the order of essence.

2. *Being as Accidental.* This proof, which is subtle and difficult and will require some explaining, appears in *DSS* 9.132–44. Thomas commences with the venerable Scholastic axiom that whatever is *per accidens* must be reduced to what is *per se,* that is, the mind cannot rest until the *per accidens* is explained by the *per se.* The *per accidens* can refer to what happens accidentally or contingently, to what occurs in an action outside the intention of the action's agent, or to what is not part of the essence or nature of something; the *per se,* conversely, can refer to what happens necessarily, to what occurs in an action as intended by the agent, and to what is part of the essence or nature of something. The context shows that Thomas is clearly using the third meaning of both phrases, and thus in this instance the axiom means that whatever is not part of the essence of any reality or process must eventually be explained by what is part of the essence of that reality or process.

The proof wants to distinguish the everyday process by which individual beings come into existence from the process by which "being universally understood" *(ens communiter sumptum)* comes into existence. In the first case, it states, an *individual* being comes into existence in a *per se* manner through a process of change involving motion. Here Thomas, following Aristotle, is referring to that type of change called substantial generation, and is saying that when an individual substance of a certain species comes into existence, *as an individual substance* it truly and really is generated as something new in the world and thus is *per se* a genuine example of the nature of substantial generation. For the nature of substantial generation as a process requires that the newly generated individual, qua individual, come from what was not already the individual[62] (or otherwise it would already be in existence and not be truly generated for the first time); in order to occur, the process also requires a primary matter as the potential principle, and an efficient cause that acts through motion.

---

62. The new (and to keep it simple, uncloned) ostrich chick, for example, derives ultimately from the genes of parents that share its species but differ from it as individuals within the species.

However, the proof continues, universal being as such cannot come into existence *per se* through the normal process of substantial generation but only *per accidens*, for it is not a genuine example of the nature of substantial generation inasmuch as *some* being or other is always already there at the beginning of the process: which means that being in general (and not just this or that being) can never really come into existence through the kind of motion known as substantial generation, except in the mitigated *per accidens* sense. But if the *per accidens* is reduced to the *per se*, then the *per accidens* origination of universal being through substantial generation must be explained by some *per se* origination of universal being. But creation out of nothing is the *per se* origination of universal being, an act that transcends motion and whose agent is the Creator.

The problem with this proof is that anyone who does not comprehend the radically contingent and accidental nature of universal being will not be able to assert its basic premises in such a way that they conclude to what Aquinas wants. If someone does not feel the need to explain the existence of being as such, but only the existence of this or that being, which can be accounted for by the normal processes of substantial generation, then the axiom that the *per accidens* must be reduced to the *per se* will be seen as holding in all cases except one, the case of being, for it will not be thought *necessary* to explain the genesis of being as such, since being simply *is*. Aristotle, for one, would find an absolute *per se* generation of being—which would require being to be generated out of absolute nothingness—impossible to accept. Based on his assumption of the eternity and necessity of being, he would in fact think that being as such can come into existence *only per accidens* and would feel no need to go any further in search of a more fundamental cause. Aquinas may respond to Aristotle that a motionless making *is* possible, but only *after* he knows the fact of creation, and not as some sort of metaphysical generalization arrived at independently of creation. It is beginning to look as if it is *because* Aquinas first knows a *creatio ex nihilo* that he is able to discern a more profound contingency at the heart of things, and not the other way around.

3. *Being as Common.* This argument appears in *DP* 3.5, which Thomas

attributes to Plato.[63] Whatever is common to many different things must be reduced to a unified, single cause. But being *(esse)* is commonly found in all things, however different. Thus, being must come from a single cause.

Thomas takes up the unity theme of Plato (and Neoplatonism) but interprets it according to his own understanding of being. The problem with this proof is that being cannot be recognized as common to all things unless it is recognized as a common reality that is *also really* different from the individualities and essences of things that differ among themselves. Otherwise, the common element in reality will be looked for on the level of essence, form, matter, or individuality—as is the case with Plato and Aristotle. This proof, then, actually rests on a knowledge of the real distinction between being and essence.

The proofs for God's existence are not the same as the proofs for the Creator God: neither *de facto,* for there have been real philosophers not conversant with monotheistic theology who never imagined creation and the Creator God and yet still posited a divine first principle of the world; nor *de iure,* since, as Thomas realizes, the word *God* can mean different things for different people, so that one may conclude to a God who is nevertheless not the Judeo-Christian Creator God.[64] In Thomas' arguments for the Creator God just discussed, one of the basic stratagems is to see being as a radically contingent component of reality in need of the Creator God as the profound explanation for it. But it has been suggested that Thomas' notion of radical ontological contingence may receive its very meaning *from* the truth of "creation from nothing" and thus should not function as a premise in an argument reasoning *to* that same truth. We will gain new insight into how Thomas relates God's freedom and creaturely

---

63. The argument also appears in *SCG* 2.15.925; *ST* 1.44.1; 1.65.1; *DSS* 9.119–31.

64. In a context where he wants to disavow the ontological proof for God's existence, Thomas notes that the word *God* can convey various meanings to different individuals: "It is not known to all, even to those who concede that God exists, that God is that than which a greater cannot be thought, for many ancients said that this very world is God" (*SCG* 1.11.67). In principle, the proofs for God's existence and God's creative causality are not necessarily identical, since we are not justified in assuming without further study that in the former the term *God* refers to the cause of universal being, which is what it must mean in the latter. Cf. Martin Lee, "Something Rather Than Nothing," *HJ* 27 (1986): 137–50.

contingence, moreover, by briefly reviewing his discussion of the world's eternity.

v. The World's Eternity

There is no need to offer an exhaustive account of how Aquinas handles the problem of the world's eternity.[65] His subtle and nuanced position, which mediates between the viewpoints of the extreme Aristotelians and extreme Augustinians,[66] is that whereas we can know the temporal beginning of the universe only by faith, reason alone can prove that even an eternal universe had to be created from nothing.[67] He uses three interlock-

---

65. That he considered it an extremely important issue is indicated by the numerous times he treated it: *SS* 2.1.1.5; *SCG* 2.31–38; 2.81.1622; *Decretalem* 1.432–37; *De articulis* 1.100–139; *CT* 1.98–99; *DP* 3.5; 3.14; 3.17; *ST* 1.44.2; 1.46.1–2; *Quod.* 3.14.2; 12.5.1; *Phys.* 8.2; *Meta.* 12.5.2492–99; 12.6.2508–18; 12.10.2597–98; *DSS* 9.55–64, 180–253; 18.108–37; *De aeternitate mundi; SDC* 11.264–72; *Gener.* 7.52, 57; *Cuelo* 1.6.64–66; 1.29.279–87; 2.4.334; 3.8.596–98; *Credo* 1.880. For some of the major texts in translation, along with some texts from Bonaventure and Siger of Brabant, see *On the Eternity of the World*, trans. and introduced by C. Vollert, L. Kendzierski, and P. Byrne (Milwaukee: Marquette, 1964). For the patristic arguments against the eternity of the world, see Wolfson, *Studies*, vol. 1, chap. 10. See also Anton Antweiler, *Die Anfangslosigkeit der Welt nach Thomas von Aquin und Kant* (Trier: Paulinus, 1961); John Wippel, *Metaphysical Themes in Thomas Aquinas* (Washington, DC: CUA, 1984), pp. 191–214; H. A. Davidson, *Proofs for Eternity, Creation, and the Existence of God in Medieval Islamic and Jewish Philosophy* (New York: Oxford, 1987); J. B. M. Wissink, ed., *The Eternity of the World in the Thought of Thomas Aquinas and His Contemporaries* (Leiden: Brill, 1990); Richard Dales, *Medieval Discussions of the Eternity of the World* (Leiden: Brill, 1990); Richard Dales and Omar Argerami, eds., *Medieval Latin Texts on the Eternity of the World* (Leiden: Brill, 1991). For an analysis of Thomas' treatment of the world's eternity in the *Summa contra Gentiles*, see Kretzmann, *The Metaphysics of Creation*, pp. 142–82. For background on Thomas' *De aeternitate mundi*, see James Weisheipl, "The Date and Context of Aquinas' *De aeternitate mundi*," in *Graceful Reason*, ed. L. P. Gerson (Toronto: PIMS, 1983), pp. 239–71; cf. William Wallace, "Aquinas on Creation: Science, Theology, and Matters of Fact," *Thomist* 38 (1974): 485–523.

66. "[Aquinas'] view was opposed to that of the extreme Aristotelians and Averroists, for whom the universe always existed in time and needed no creation. It was also opposed to the Ultra-Augustinists, like John Pecham and other Franciscans, for whom creation had to exist in time, from which creation itself could be demonstrated" (James Weisheipl, *Friar Thomas d'Aquino: His Life, Thought and Work* [New York: Doubleday, 1974; repr. Washington, DC: CUA, 1983], p. 200).

67. Wippel is even more exact: Aquinas taught from the beginning of his career that no one had ever successfully demonstrated that the world began to be, and at times even more strongly, that this could not in principle be demonstrated; but it was not until the *De*

ing reasons to defend his stance against both extremes: God creates by free will, not from necessity; creation implies radical contingence in the creature; and creation occurs *ex nihilo,* that is, without any presupposed matter, motion, or time. The fact that God creates freely out of nothing subverts the outlook of those who would try to prove the world's eternity on the grounds that nothing can come into existence except by way of matter in motion. The profound existential contingence of every creature, even a possibly eternal one, renders untenable the opinion of those who would posit a necessarily temporal creation on the grounds that creaturehood and eternity are incompatible.

On the issues of God's freedom and creaturely contingence, *SCG* 2.31 shows that from God's standpoint no creature is absolutely necessary at all. But if it is not necessary for a creature to be *at all,* then a fortiori it cannot be necessary for it to be *always.* God does not act from necessity or fulfill a debt in creating but brings forth every creature freely. Necessity between creatures, whether this be between different individuals or between a creature's substance and its properties, results from the relations between creatures or between a creature and its properties, though none of the entities or properties, in themselves, are intrinsically necessary; creaturely necessity (let us call it relational necessity), then, does not entail that a creature have necessary existence in its own right (absolute necessity). Creaturely contingence, therefore, which a creature possesses vis-à-vis God, is compatible with relational necessity.

An objection argues, in *SCG* 2.33.1097–98, that realities which have no potentiality to nonbeing cannot fail to exist, so that those which have no matter at all (purely intellectual beings) or at least a matter not subject to contraries (major heavenly bodies, for the medieval astronomer) possess a power of existing forever and so are incorruptible. If they cannot not exist, they must always exist. Thomas' answer mentions that the necessity referred to by the objection is the relational necessity of order, which does not entail absolute necessity.

---

aeternitate mundi (1271) that he took his most forceful position and asserted the possibility of an eternal creation, though he came close to the idea in *DP* 3.14 (*Metaphysical Themes,* pp. 213–14).

For although the heaven's substance has a necessity to exist, by dint of the fact that it lacks any potency to nonbeing, this necessity nonetheless is consequent upon its substance. Hence, once its substance is established in being, such necessity causes the impossibility of nonbeing; however, nothing makes it impossible for the heaven not to exist at all if we just consider the production of its substance. (*SCG* 2.36.1121)

Thomas is hinting that no amount of reasoning based on creaturely relational necessity can show that God creates the creature with absolute necessity. And if no creature is absolutely necessary, then every creature is contingent, that is, its existence does not well up from within its own essence but "happens"[68] to it from God.

Even an eternal world would not be absolutely necessary, for God does not create from necessity but by wisdom and will. Just as the infinite God made a finite world according to the divine wisdom, so can the eternal God produce a world with a temporal beginning according to that same wisdom (*SDC* 11.272). The world's finite temporal duration comes from the divine intellect that prescribes it, "since the total duration of things is included under God's intellect and power so that he may determine from eternity the measure of duration that he wishes for things."[69] No reasons can be given for the disposition of the universe as a whole since this depends "on the pure will of God," for which there are no reasons outside the divine nature itself.[70]

According to the Catholic faith we assert that the world began to exist, certainly not through natural generation but by flowing forth from the first principle, whose power was not bound to give it being in an infinite time but as it willed, after the world had not existed previously, in order that the excellence of its power over all being might be manifested—which is that the totality of being depends on it alone and that its power is not bound or determined to produce such being.[71]

Moreover, responding to the radical Aristotelians who claim that an eternal world is necessary, and using the doctrine of creation *ex nihilo*,

68. *Contingere* means "to happen."
69. *DSS* 9.55–64; cf. *SCG* 2.36.1123.
70. *DP* 3.17; cf. ad1, 3, 4, 6–9, 14.
71. *Caelo* 1.29.287. For other texts treating divine freedom and creaturely contingence, see *SS* 3.25.1.2 ad9; *CT* 1.98; *ST* 1.46.1, and ad6, 9–10; *Meta.* 9.9.1879; *SDC* 11.264–72; *Caelo* 1.6.64–66.

which accents the nothingness at the heart of every creature (SS 2.1.1.2), Thomas asserts that God needs no preexistent reality—no matter, motion, or time—in order to create,[72] since creation transcends the processes of matter in motion. He can also use creation *ex nihilo* against the conservative Augustinians who claim that an eternal creation is impossible, for the concept "to be from another" is not contradictory to the concept "to be always," "except when something proceeds from another through motion, which does not happen in the procession of things from God."[73] His reasoning seems to be this: if, as his opponents claim, God did create by a temporally indexed motion, then that motion would necessarily precede in time whatever it caused, which in turn would have a temporal beginning; but asserting a motionless act of creation short-circuits this line of reasoning. From the beginning to the end of his career, Thomas had recourse to his understanding of God as the free and transcendent Creator in order to answer the contrary putative proofs of both conservative Augustinians and liberal Aristotelians:[74] God's freedom makes a temporal or an eternal world equally possible, especially since the radical contingency of creation is compatible with an eternal world; and God's transcendence in creating out of nothing subverts both sets of objections against Thomas' position.

In conclusion, Aquinas views everything other than God as absolutely unnecessary and thus radically contingent in being, for creatures hang suspended from the good pleasure of God. Distinguishing absolute from relational necessity, which also implies, conversely, a distinction between radical and merely temporal contingency, he shows how radical contingence is compatible with relational necessity, which means that the former can exist even in eternal realities, since an eternity of time is incompatible only with temporal contingency. Of course Aristotle would not distinguish between the two necessities or between the two kinds of contingency: for

72. *CT* 1.99; *DP* 3.17, and ad15–18, 24; *ST* 1.46.1 ad1, 3, 5. God does not even need the eternal ideas so emphasized in Platonic and process philosophy.

73. *DP* 3.14; cf. ad8 of the first series of objections, and ad7–8 of the second; *ST* 1.46.1 ad1.

74. In *SS* 2.1.1.5 he thus argues against those who want to prove either the necessity (ad1, 3, 8, 10, 11, 13–14 of the first series) or the impossibility (ad1 of the second series) of the world's eternity, and does the same in *De aeternitate*, lines 90–94.

when he speaks of a thing's possibility for nonbeing, he means the temporal contingency of what Aquinas calls the (relational) necessity of order,
not the absolute contingence of an entity that God created from nothing
and could allow to decline into nonexistence; and what Aristotle considers
an absolutely necessary universe (for that the universe as a whole might
not have existed or might cease to exist is unthinkable to him) is in
Aquinas' eyes only relationally necessary. From the profound perspective
of his faith, Thomas makes the divine freedom responsible for the relational necessities of creation and pushes absolute necessity further back
into the deep, secret abysses of God.

This section and section III have argued that the ancient philosophers
did not know the essentials of the doctrine of creation, despite Aquinas'
opinion, for reason bereft of revelation naturally and instinctively limits its
endeavors to the world's relational necessities and thus experiences no
need to explain radical contingency. Ultimately, we must be *told* that our
existence is the decision of a God who loves without need and that all creation is suspended from the free and gracious will of God. Indeed, it is
only because he has heard and believed such things, and thinks that God is
transcendent, creative Will, that Aquinas can so confidently propose a motionless *creatio ex nihilo*, distinguish eternity from absolute necessity, and
claim the possibility of an eternal creation on the grounds of divine freedom.

VI. *God the Creator Philosophically Interpreted as Subsistent Being*

How does Aquinas come to know that God is *ipsum esse subsistens*, a
truth that, as we saw above in section II, is implicit in his interpretation of
the proof from motion for God's existence and comes to explicit awareness in the demonstration that God's being and essence are the same?[75]
Gilson's well-known thesis is that Aquinas considers what he calls "this

75. The main texts for this demonstration are *DE* 4; *SS* 1.8.1.1; *SCG* 1.22; *DP* 7.2; *ST* 1.3.4;
CT 1.11. In *ST* 1.3.4 the proof that God's being and essence are identical comes in the question immediately following the proofs for God's existence.

sublime truth" to be knowable both by reason, and by faith in the revelation of God's name in Exodus 3:14 as "I am who am," which would make it an accidental truth of faith.[76] Some claim that the identification of God's essence and being had already been made in Greek philosophy working without the benefit of faith.[77] However, mere material identity of words in a predication ("God is being") does not necessarily mean that the thoughts expressed flow from the same contextual worldview within which words and ideas find their natural niche. Greek philosophy's *ipsum*

76. In *SCG* 1.22.211 Thomas sees "this sublime truth" as having been revealed to Moses when he asks for the Lord's name and is told "I am Who Am" (Ex. 3:14). Gilson writes: "This pure act-of-being which St. Thomas the philosopher met at the end of metaphysics, St. Thomas the theologian had met too in Holy Scripture. It was no longer the conclusion of rational dialectic but a revelation from God Himself to all men that they might accept it by faith. There is no doubt that St. Thomas thought that God had revealed to men that His essence was to exist. . . . Thomistic existentialism concerned not merely natural theology, but theology in the strict sense. It is here indeed a question of a literal interpretation of the word of God. . . . Neither the identity of essence and existence in God nor the distinction between essence and existence in creatures belongs to the *revelatum*, properly so-called, since neither of these truths is beyond the range of natural reason considered as a judging faculty. Both are, nevertheless, for St. Thomas part of the revealable, and even of the revealable which has been revealed" (*Christian Philosophy of St. Thomas Aquinas*, pp. 93–94). Gilson also speaks of Thomas' reason and faith as "two beams of light so converging that they fused into each other" and of "the overwhelming truth blazing forth from their point of fusion." Émilie Zum Brunn follows Gilson's thesis on the "Christian metaphysics" stemming from the passage in Exodus ("L'exégèse augustinienne de *Ego sum qui sum* et la 'métaphysique de l'Exode,'" and "La 'Métaphysique de l'Exode' selon Thomas d'Aquin," in *Dieu et l'être: exégèses d'Exode 3:14 et de Coran 20:11–24*, ed. P. Vignaux et al. [Paris: Études Augustiniennes, 1978], pp. 141–64, 245–69).

77. Cornelia de Vogel thinks Exodus 3:14 was not a radical new point of departure for Christian theologians but an opportunity for encountering and recognizing an identification that had already been made and taught to them by the Greeks ("*Ego sum qui sum* et sa signification pour une philosophie chrétienne," *RevSR* 35 [1961]: 337–55). Agreeing with de Vogel, Pierre Hadot contests Gilson's affirmation that the identification of God and being is peculiarly Christian—an Exodus metaphysics ("Dieu comme acte d'être dans le néoplatonisme. A propos des théories d'É. Gilson sur la métaphysique de l'Exode," in *Dieu et l'être: exégèses d'Exode 3:14 et de Coran 20:11–24*, ed. P. Vignaux et al. [Paris: Études Augustiniennes, 1978], pp. 57–63). This identification, rather, is "the result of an interior evolution of Platonism" (p. 63). He gives indications of how Neoplatonism was able to conceive of the One as an infinitival "to be," focusing on a text comprising fragments from an anonymous commentary on Plato's *Parmenides* he thinks is from Porphyry. This text, realizing that the first hypostasis of Essence (*ousia*) cannot participate in some higher Essence, has it instead participate in Being (*einai*, the infinitive "to be"), which the One is said to be; and since the text identifies God and the One, it also equates God and Being.

esse subsistens, even if it exists, is certainly not that infinite divine synthesis of freedom, love, and graciousness that creates an absolutely contingent creation from nothing—which is the phrase's fully contextualized meaning for the theology of someone like Aquinas.[78] Moreover, we cannot be sure that later Greek thinkers, especially the Neoplatonists, have not been influenced by currents of thought originating in Christian circles.[79]

Gilson is correct when he claims that Thomas sees this "sublime truth" as an accidental truth of faith, and is also partially correct when he sees him as reaping this truth from his reading of Exodus 3:14. But if it is the case that Greek philosophy never discovered the monotheistic version of the truth that God is *ipsum esse subsistens,* one wonders if Thomas' philosophy all on its own could ever have attained to such a truth, or if one verse from scripture could have provided the context necessary for his theological assessment and appreciation of it. The position taken here is that God as *ipsum esse subsistens* is really Thomas' philosophical manner of interpreting and expressing a truth that is actually an *essential* object of his faith, namely, that God is the free and gracious Creator of the universe. Faith in the Creator God provides a fuller context and deeper inspiration than Exodus 3:14

---

78. What did Hadot's Neoplatonic author mean by his equation of God and being, an identification that Hadot admits found little echo in later Greek philosophy, which always places the One over the supreme being, God? He also thinks Boethius' *De hebdomadibus* received from the Neoplatonists, and then passed on to the medievals, the distinction between *esse* and *id quod est* (that which is) in everything other than God. But in an interesting display of how words can mean different things for different authors, Boethius' *esse* seems to mean substantial form (not being, as with Aquinas) as opposed to the *id quod est,* which is the individual existent substance (PL 64:1311B–D; this is also indicated at 1318C, where Gilbert de la Porrée, commenting on the terminology, understands the *esse* as *subsistentia* ["that by which something subsists": the examples given are bodiliness and humanity], and the *id quod est* as *subsistens* ["the subsisting thing": the examples are a body and a human]; cf. M.-D. Roland-Gosselin, *Le "De ente et essentia" de saint Thomas d'Aquin,* BibThom 8 [Paris: Vrin, 1926; repr. 1948], pp. 142–45). What Boethius seems to mean by this terminology is the distinction between the essence of an entity and the individual entity existing with that essence, not the distinction between being and essence.

79. Hadot admits that his text is unique even among Neoplatonists and is at odds with the more common Plotinian view that places the One over God. If the author is Porphyry, why would he disagree with Plotinus, his master, on such an important point? Whoever the author is, do not the identifications of God with the One and with Being, which were to have no reverberations in later Greek philosophy, point to either Jewish or Christian influence upon the author, as happened in similar fashion with the author of the *Liber de causis?*

alone can for his distinctive retrieval and reworking of the themes about God and being that came to him from Greek philosophy. While it is certainly true that it is his philosophical insight, as the hermeneutics of his faith, that distinguishes him from other theologians who shared his faith and yet did not see what he saw in the "I am who am" of Exodus 3:14 (Augustine, for example), it is his faith in God as Creator that inspires and impels him to search his philosophy for an expression and interpretation worthy of that profound truth. Faith in a free and transcendent Creator *can* imply that God is *ipsum esse subsistens,* if one has the philosophical acumen of Thomas, since such a Creator must be infinitely full of perfection in order to bestow being freely (not in response to an inner need) and transcendently (not to fulfill some role in a world process larger than divinity itself). If, as Aquinas holds, *esse* is the perfection of perfections, then the Christian God, in order to remain distinct from and not in need of creation, must *be* the simple, absolute, and infinite realization of *esse.* The polytheism, pantheism, and necessitarian emanationism that, either singly or collectively, are inherent in every ancient Greek conception of the divine cannot induce one to see God as being itself, for they either break God up into parts, insert God as a part of a larger whole, or make the divine action dependent upon necessities it did not create—all of which destroys the freedom, graciousness, and transcendence of *Ipsum Esse Subsistens.*

VII. *The Radical Contingence of Creatures Philosophically Interpreted as the Real Distinction between Being and Essence*

To speak of the real distinction between being and essence in creatures is another way of saying that their existence is not essential but accidental, that it arrives contingently from outside their essence instead of flowing necessarily from within it.[80] Since Aquinas demonstrates the real distinc-

---

80. On the radical contingence of being for Christian thinkers, a concept the Greeks did not have, see Gilson, *The Spirit of Medieval Philosophy,* trans. A. H. C. Downes, Gifford Lectures of 1931–32 (New York: Scribner's, 1940), chap. 4. Owens writes: "Nothing prompts [Aristotle] to ask how *existence* can be given to the new individuals by their efficient cause. The fact is taken for granted. The problem is ignored" (*Doctrine,* p. 359; cf. pp. 406; 460–69, and nn. 44–45).

tion on the basis of God as the subsistent act of being, as we will contend below (though this is controverted, as we shall see), and since, as we have argued above, he knows God as subsistent being primarily through his faith, then his proofs for the real distinction are an indication that it is his faith in the Christian Creator God that allows him to recognize the contingent creaturehood of the creature.[81]

Although Aristotle certainly taught a logical distinction between essence and existence, he did not recognize a real distinction: for all immaterial beings, in essence and existence, are necessary.[82] Even Boethius' celebrated distinction between *esse* and *id quod est* is not a plea for the real distinction, for he only means by it the difference between substantial form and concrete substance.[83] For Avicenna, the real distinction expresses his religious conviction about the uniqueness of God and explains the composition of all created being by comparison to the simplicity of the First Cause.[84] Averroes strenuously opposes Avicenna, insisting that the

81. Gilson asks: "Is it St. Thomas the theologian who, reading in *Exodus* the identity of essence and existence in God, taught St. Thomas the philosopher the distinction between essence and existence in creatures? Or is it St. Thomas the philosopher who, pushing his analysis of the metaphysical structure of the concrete even as far as the distinction between essence and existence, taught St. Thomas the theologian that *He Who Is* in *Exodus* means the *Act-of-Being*?" (*Christian Philosophy of St. Thomas Aquinas*, p. 94). Not providing a clear answer, Gilson contents himself with stating that Thomas' philosophy and theology cannot be easily separated. Josef Pieper writes: "The notion of creation determines and characterizes the interior structure of nearly all the basic concepts in St. Thomas' philosophy of Being" (*The Silence of Saint Thomas*, trans. J. Murray and D. O'Connor [South Bend, IN: St. Augustine's Press, 1999], p. 48). See also Bernardo Cantens, "The Interdependency between Aquinas' Doctrine of Creation and His Metaphysical Principle of the Limitation of Act by Potency," *PACPA* 74 (2000): 121–40.

82. Roland-Gosselin, "*De ente et essentia*," pp. 137–41. "For the Stagirite, 'to be a definite abiding something' is simply *to be*" (Owens, *Doctrine*, p. 376).

83. Roland-Gosselin, "*De ente et essentia*," pp. 142–45 (for Thomas' misunderstanding of the Boethian *esse*, see p. 186 and n. 3). See also n. 78 above. But Ralph McInerny takes a different view in "Boethius and St. Thomas Aquinas," *RFNS* 66 (1974): 219–45; see also his *Boethius and Aquinas* (Washington, DC: CUA, 1990).

84. Amélie-Marie Goichon shows how, for Avicenna, essence is related to existence as creatures are to Allah, and describes how he explains essences as hollows or cavities that are filled with existence by divine liberality (*La distinction de l'essence et de l'existence d'après Ibn Sina (Avicenne)* [Paris: Desclée, 1937], pp. 147–48). "In Avicenna's philosophy, the concepts of essence and existence result in the final analysis in the distinction between created and uncreated being" (ibid., p. 151). Cf. Roland-Gosselin, "*De ente et essentia*," pp. 150–56. David

distinction is only a logical one and accusing him of contaminating Aristotle with the alien thought of existence as accidental to essence because of his theological theories of creation's contingency.[85] In the first two chapters of his *De Trinitate,* William of Auvergne shows himself the heir of Avicenna in that the real distinction is based both on creation and to a certain degree on logical considerations.[86] Aquinas himself depends on Avicenna and William of Auvergne in his own exposition of the real distinction.[87] But Aquinas distances himself from Avicenna's interpretation of how being is accidental to essence: he thinks Avicenna taught that being is a predicamental or categorical accident, while he himself considers it to be a predicable accident in the sense that being is not part of the definition of essence.[88]

How does Aquinas prove the real distinction? This is a controverted is-

---

Burrell states that Avicenna, with some help from Alfarabi, was led by the Qur'an more than anything else to formulate the distinction between essence *(mahiyya)* and existence *(wujud)* ("Analogy," pp. 38–39; see also his "Essence and Existence: Avicenna and Greek Philosophy," *Mélanges Institut Dominicain d'Etudes Orientales* 17 [1986]: 53–66; *Knowing the Unknowable God: Ibn-Sina, Maimonides, Aquinas* [Notre Dame: UND Press, 1986], pp. 39–41).

85. Roland-Gosselin, *"De ente et essentia,"* pp. 157–59; Gilson, *History,* pp. 191; 220; 643, n. 18; Albert Judy, "Avicenna's *Metaphysics* in the *Summa contra gentiles,"* *Angelicum* 53 (1976): 209–10.

86. Roland-Gosselin, *"De ente et essentia,"* pp. 160–63; Gilson, "La notion d'existence chez Guillaume d'Auvergne," *AHDLMA* 15 (1946): 55–91, especially pp. 83–84. Armand Maurer holds, however, that the "at least in understanding" *(saltem intellectu)* of William's first main argument denotes only a conceptual distinction (*On Being and Essence,* trans. with introduction and notes by A. Maurer, 2nd ed. [Toronto: PIMS, 1968], pp. 23–25).

87. Roland-Gosselin sees Avicenna behind *SS* 1.8.4.2 and William as the inspiration for such texts as *SS* 1.8.5.2, 2.3.1.1, and *DE* 4 (*"De ente et essentia,"* pp. 185–99). Bonaventure, apparently, did not admit the real distinction (George Klubertanz, "*Esse* and *Existere* in St. Bonaventure," *MS* 8 [1946]: 169–88).

88. *Quod.* 2.2.1; 12.4.1. Thomas O'Shaughnessy ("St. Thomas' Changing Estimate of Avicenna's Teaching on Existence as an Accident," *MSch* 36 [1959]: 245–60) shows how Thomas' judgment, after 1265, becomes more negative concerning Avicenna's teaching that existence is an accident; influenced by Averroes' misinterpretation of Avicenna, Thomas from that date thinks Avicenna is speaking of a predicamental accident (i.e., one of the nine categories other than substance), whereas actually he, like Thomas himself, has a predicable accident in mind (i.e., one of the five ways—the other four are genus, species, difference, and property—in which a predicate can be related to a subject in an enunciation). Owens explains how Aquinas, by considering being as both essential and accidental, is a mean between Aristotle and Avicenna, since the former thought of being as only essential and the latter thought of it as only accidental (*Existence of God,* pp. 52–96).

sue. He uses two arguments that are logical/metaphysical in character and are to be found almost exclusively in his earlier works: one is based on how essence is understood, and the other on the nature of a genus. His later works betray a strong preference for an argument based on God as subsistent being, which may appear in either a simple or complex form, the latter including the notion of participation.[89] The controversy centers on two questions: Does Aquinas intend the logical/metaphysical arguments to conclude to a real or merely to a conceptual distinction between being and essence? And if the former, do they actually prove a real distinction between being and essence?[90] Let us turn first to Aquinas' argument based on God as subsistent being.

89. Mary Keating, "The Relation between the Proofs for the Existence of God and the Real Distinction of Essence and Existence in St. Thomas Aquinas" (Ph.D. dissertation, Fordham University, 1962); Leo Sweeney, "Existence/Essence in Thomas Aquinas' Early Writings," *PACPA* 37 (1963): 97–131. Cf. Joseph de Finance, *Être et agir dans le philosophie de saint Thomas* (Paris: Beauchesne, 1945), pp. 81–110. Cornelio Fabro thinks Thomas' ultimate proof is the one that makes use of participation, so that the real distinction is a metaphysical implication of transcendental participation (*La nozione metafisica di partecipazione secondo S. Tommaso d'Aquino,* 2nd ed. [Turin: Società editrice internazionale, 1950], pp. 212–44, 327–29); cf. Hampus Lyttkens, *The Analogy between God and the World,* trans. A. Poignant (Uppsala: Almqvist and Wiksells, 1952), pp. 342–47. However, Kretzmann argues that in the first book of the *Summa contra Gentiles,* chapter 22 on the real distinction is grounded in what he considers an argument for God's existence based on contingency found at 15.124 (*Metaphysics of Theism,* pp. 121–29).

90. Joseph Owens and John Wippel have been the chief opponents on this issue. Owens thinks Thomas only intends a conceptual distinction by the two logical proofs, and tries to prove a real distinction only on the basis of God as *ipsum esse subsistens* ("Quiddity and Real Distinction in St. Thomas Aquinas," *MS* 27 [1965]: 1–22; "Stages and Distinction in De ente: A Rejoinder," *Thomist* 45 [1981]: 99–123; "Aquinas' Distinction at De ente et essentia 4.119–123," *MS* 48 [1986]: 264–87). Maurer advocates this position also (*On Being and Essence,* pp. 20–27), as does Gilson: "The distinction of essence and existence presupposes the very notion of the pure act of being which its alleged demonstrations are supposed to justify" (*Christian Philosophy of St. Thomas Aquinas,* p. 82). Wippel asserts that Thomas sometimes both intends and succeeds in his attempt to prove the real distinction on the basis of logical and metaphysical analysis alone, without recourse to God ("Aquinas' Route to the Real Distinction: A Note on De ente et essentia c. 4," *Thomist* 43 [1979]: 279–95; *Metaphysical Themes,* chaps. 5–6; *Metaphysical Thought,* pp. 132–76, especially pp. 132–50, and nn. 8, 9, 11, and 39), though he also shows how Thomas sometimes bases his proof of the real distinction on the nature of God (*Metaphysical Thought,* pp. 585–90). James Doig (*Aquinas on Metaphysics,* pp. 272–73) and Leo Elders ("Les cinq voies et leur place dans la philosophie de saint Thomas," in *Quinque Sunt Viae* [Vatican City, 1980], p. 140) would support Wippel's view. Leo Sweeney ("Existence/Essence") thinks that Thomas by his logical proofs wants to

In the course of demonstrating that no creature is without composition, he uses the simple form of the argument:

For since in God alone is being identical with essence, in every creature, whether corporeal or spiritual, there must be found its essence or nature on the one hand, and its being on the other, which it acquires from God whose essence is his being; and so a creature is composed from being *(esse)*—or that by which it is—and what it is.[91]

Sometimes he employs the more complex form, which includes participation:

Being *(ens)* is predicated essentially of God alone, because the divine act of being *(esse)* is a subsistent and absolute act of being; being is predicated of every creature through participation, for no creature is its own act of being but is something that has an act of being. Whenever, however, something is predicated of another through participation, something else must also exist there besides that which is participated; and so in every creature, the creature itself which has an act of being is one thing, and its act of being is another.[92]

By adding a fourth step, Thomas can also prove that every created substance is composed of act and potency: (1) God is his own subsistent act of being; (2) since there can be only one such subsistent act of being, everything other than God participates in the act of being; (3) but this requires that the participator be other than the participated; (4) and since the participator is related to the participated as potency to act, every creature is composed of potency and act.[93] Both participation and the real distinction are equally dependent on the truth that God is the absolutely unique case of *ipsum esse subsistens*,[94] which is why Thomas, without mentioning participation, can sometimes use the simple form of the argument.

---

conclude to the real distinction but cannot justifiably do so. As will become clear, I favor the position of Owens and his supporters.

91. *SS* 1.8.5.1; the same basic argument is found in *SCG* 2.52.1277–80; *Quod.* 9.4.1; *DSC* 1; *DP* 3.5 ad1; *DSS* 3.26–30; 8.164–98. "Since God is subsistent being, nothing except God is its own being" (*SCG* 2.52.1275).

92. *Quod.* 2.2.1; same: *DP* 6.6 ad5; *CT* 1.68; *ST* 1.44.1.

93. *Quod.* 3.8.1; same: *Phys.* 8.21.1153; *ST* 1.75.5 ad4.

94. Every creature participates in "the nature of being *(natura essendi),* since God alone is his own being" (*ST* 1.45.5 ad1). Essence and being are the same only in the first principle of being, which is essentially being *(ens);* but being and essence differ in all other things, which are "beings through participation" *(entia per participationem—Post.* 2.6.462).

The most famous instance of the logical/metaphysical argument, based on the understanding of essence, is undoubtedly from chapter 4 of Thomas' youthful *De ente et essentia*. After showing that souls and angelic intelligences are pure forms, he takes care to prove that they are nevertheless not absolutely simple, pure act (*DE* 4.90–146):

Every essence or quiddity can be understood without knowing (*intelligere*) anything about its existence (*esse*): for I can understand what a human or a phoenix is and still not know (*ignorare*) whether it has existence in the nature of things. Thus, it is clear that existence is something other than essence or quiddity, unless perhaps there is something whose essence is its own being (*esse*); this thing must be unique and primary (*una et prima*). (*DE* 4.98–105)

If some reality is posited that is its own subsistent being, therefore, and if such a reality must be unique, then everything else's being must be other than its essence, and the being of the angelic intelligences must be something different than their form (*DE* 4.113–26). He concludes: "It is clear, therefore, that an intelligence is form and act of being (*esse*), and that it has its act of being from the first being (*ens*) which is the act of being only, and this is the first cause which is God" (*DE* 4.143–46).[95]

What are we to think of this proof? Is Thomas only trying to establish a conceptual distinction between being and essence?[96] It seems his proof, on the basis of a logical consideration about the understanding of essence,

---

Interestingly, Thomas in this last text is discussing Aristotle's assertion (*Posterior Analytics* 2.7.92b4–5) that it is one thing to know "what a thing is" (*to ti estin*) and another to know "that it exists" (*hoti estin*); when, a bit later, Aristotle slightly alters his terminology and speaks of human "nature" (*to ti estin*) being different from human "existence" (*to einai*—ibid., b10–11), it is clear the *to einai* means the same as the *hoti estin*. That is, Aristotle is referring to the *fact* that something exists and is known to exist, but Thomas transposes Aristotle's *einai* to the more profound level of the *interior act* of being, which can be known as different from essence in creatures only on the basis of recognizing God as the unique case of subsistent being. Thomas reads a real distinction of ontological import into what Aristotle had evidently meant to be taken only in an epistemological sense.

95. For other examples of the logical/metaphysical argument, based on either essence or genus, see *SS* 1.8.4.2; 1.8.5.2; 2.1.1.1; 2.3.1.1; *DV* 10.12.

96. Referring to *DE* 4, Maurer writes: "Nowhere in the treatise are we told that there is a *real* composition in creatures between their being and their essence, or that these two are *really* distinct" (*On Being and Essence*, p. 10; reasons given at pp. 22–25). To the texts Maurer adduces to show that for Aquinas different concepts may still express the same reality, one may add *Meta.* 4.2.550–53, 556–58; *BDH* 2.36–195.

may desire to establish a real distinction between being and essence, concerning which two points may be made.

First, he abandons the logical/metaphysical type of argument after the early *De ente et essentia* and *Sentences*, in which he is still under the heavy influence of Avicenna's essentialist metaphysics.[97] Further, in his maturity he is much more Aristotelian in his position about how the questions concerning a thing's existence and essence are to be related, such that he rejects the stronger, negative sense of *ignorare* in the early texts[98] and holds,

97. For background on Avicenna's influence in the West, see Amélie-Marie Goichon, *La philosophie d'Avicenne et son influence en Europe médiévale,* 2nd ed. (Paris: Adrien-Maisonneuve, 1951); Gilson, "Avicenne en occident au moyen âge," *AHDLMA* 36 (1969): 89–121; Albert Judy, "Avicenna's *Metaphysics* in the *Summa contra gentiles,*" *Angelicum* 52 (1975): 340–84. For Avicenna's influence on Thomas, see Goichon, "Un chapitre de l'influence d'Ibn Sina en Occident: le *De ente et essentia* de S. Thomas d'Aquin," in *Le livre du Millénaire d'Avicenne,* vol. 4 (Tehran, 1956), pp. 118–31; Georges C. Anawati, "Saint Thomas d'Aquin et la *Métaphysique* d'Avicenne," in *St. Thomas Aquinas, 1274–1974: Commemorative Studies,* 2 vols. (Toronto: PIMS, 1974), 1:449–65 (see pp. 449–53 and nn. 1–24 for a bibliographic survey); John Wippel, "The Latin Avicenna as a Source of Thomas Aquinas' Metaphysics," *FZPT* 37 (1990): 51–90. In the *De ente et essentia,* "the influence of Avicenna is preponderant" (Anawati, "Saint Thomas," p. 450). Citations of Avicenna are numerous in Thomas' early works but much rarer in his middle and later works: see C. Vansteenkiste, "Avicenna-Citaten bij S. Thomas," *TP* 15 (1953): 457–507 (450 citations); Aimé Forest, *La structure métaphysique du concret selon saint Thomas d'Aquin,* 2nd ed. (Paris: Vrin, 1956), appendix (250 citations); Anawati, "St. Thomas," pp. 456–65 (47 ideas from Avicenna's *Metaphysics* approved by Aquinas, and nine ideas that Thomas disagrees with). Van Steenberghen claims that Thomas in the *De ente et essentia* was excessively influenced by Avicenna's terminology and manner of thought and passed unjustifiably from being as a logical accident to being as an ontological coprinciple with essence (*Problème,* pp. 41–44, 334). In *Quod.* 8.1.1, unique in his writings, Thomas shows that in certain contexts he is willing to follow Avicenna in making the abstract essence superior to the existent individual: "Socrates is rational because the human is rational, not vice versa; hence, even if Socrates and Plato were not in existence, rationality would still belong to human nature." However, although it is true that if Socrates and Plato had never existed, rationality would still belong to human nature, this is so only because *other* human individuals have existed or are existing. Socrates is rational, then, because he is an existing human individual participating in rationality, which is universal in the sense of not being *bound* to any one existing human individual but *not* in the sense of having a real content of its own that would precede any and all existing human individuals.

98. The *ignorare* of *DE* 4 finds an echo in *SS* 2.3.1.1: "There is a certain nature whose being is not part of its understanding, which is clear from the fact that it can be understood though it is unknown (*ignorare*) whether it exists, as a phoenix or an eclipse or something of this sort." The stronger sense of *ignorare,* which the argument needs, refers to a total ignorance; cf. Ralph Masiello, "A Note on Essence and Existence," *NS* 45 (1971): 491–94; and Joseph Owens, "'Ignorare' and Existence," *NS* 46 (1972): 210–19. When Thomas later in his

in favor of Aristotle and against Avicenna, that our knowledge of a thing's essence always follows our knowledge of its existence.[99]

Second, the logical argument of *DE* 4 cannot justifiably conclude to a real distinction between being and essence. Some see a begging of the question lurking in the proof.[100] Even more tellingly, as the second sentence from the last paragraph suggests, the primary premise of the logical argument is false, for if we understand the essence of some real entity, and do not merely grasp the meaning of a name, then we cannot *not* know that some individual with that essence either has existed in the past or does exist now. And if this is the case, then the premise has given us no reason to conclude that essence is different from existence. The proof cannot get off the ground if Thomas cannot establish, by logical analysis alone, the *prima facie case* that being is not the same as essence.

Therefore, as the type of argument appearing in his middle and later works would have it, it is because we first know God as *ipsum esse subsistens* that we can conclude to the real distinction in creatures between being and essence, just as we also recognize the contingency of creation because we have heard of and believed in the voluntary act of God that

---

career learns of Aristotle's frequent use of the eclipse example in his logical works, he will also imitate him in tethering the question of an eclipse's nature to the question of its existence, and not leave its essence unconnected to its existence, as in this passage.

99. "It is useless to ask what something is if someone does not know *(nescire)* that it exists" (*Post.* 2.7.476). "Knowing that something exists simply, we can ask what that thing is" (*Post.* 2.1.411; cf. *Meta.* 7.17.1651). "Before knowing whether something exists we cannot properly know what it is, since there are no definitions of nonbeings. Hence the question whether something exists precedes the question what something is. But we cannot show whether something exists unless we first understand what is signified by the name" (*Post.* 1.2.17; cf. 2.6.465–69; 2.8.484; *ST* 1.2.2 ad2). One may know what the name *goat-stag* means, "but it is impossible to know the essence of a goat-stag, since nothing like it exists in the nature of things" (*Post.* 2.6.461; cf. *Meta.* 7.17.1655); and one must always ask whether the thing nominally defined (e.g., a brass mountain) actually exists (*Post.* 2.6.464). The definition is obviously not the same as the mere meaning of a name. From Thomas' later perspective, then, his earlier putative knowledge of the fictional phoenix's essence in *DE* 4 is actually just the meaning of a name, a *nominal* definition, for no essence can be *really* defined unless it is first anchored in some existing individual.

100. Sweeney states that the logical argument works only by bringing in other elements of Thomas' metaphysics of being that beg the question ("Existence/Essence," pp. 108–12, 127–31). "One realizes that *esse*/essence are act/potency not by what they are in themselves but by the relationship the existent has to God" (p. 127).

spawns it. Indeed, the real distinction between being and essence serves Aquinas as a philosophical interpretation of the theological truth about the radical contingence of creatures.

VIII. *Conclusion*

This chapter has investigated Aquinas' interpretation of the Aristotelian proof for God's existence based on motion and has seen his rich theologizing of that proof in the *Compendium theologiae;* it has looked at how Aquinas thinks creation and the Creator can be recognized by pure reason as well as by faith, both in his views about the philosophers' knowledge of the Creator and in some of his own proofs for the Creator; and it has studied how he responds to those who would contend, in contrary directions, that an eternal creation is either necessary or impossible. The chapter has found that various presuppositions of Aquinas' faith reside, often subtly and unobtrusively, at the heart of his discussions about God's existence, creation and the Creator, and the world's eternity. This analysis of his self-understanding, of how he thinks he has come to recognize some of his most crucial ideas about God and creation, has attempted to show that it is more by his faith than by his reason that he acknowledges the transcendent and free Creator as well as the radical contingence of creatures. Because of his faith Aquinas knows that creation, finite and fragile, temporal and conditional, depends solely upon the gracious and voluntary will of God; and at the heart of that faith, now philosophically interpreted, are the twin truths about God as subsistent being itself and about creatures as possessing a real distinction between their being and their essence, which together are his philosophical ways of signifying the infinite and unspeakable gratuity of the Creator and the profound provisionality at creation's core. And since these are among the great first-order truths about Creator and creation, to be examined in the next chapter, which are the indispensable theological and ontological supports for Aquinas' reflective, second-order transcendental analogy and theological epistemology of the divine names, in the end we conclude it is his faith more than his reason that inspires and justifies that analogy and epistemology.

9. Aquinas' Crucial Theological Truths

This chapter discusses the fundamental theological truths underlying Aquinas' theological epistemology—that God is the pure, perfect and infinite act of subsistent being, the transcendent, immanent, and free Creator to whom all creation bears a likeness.[1] We need not go into comprehensive

1. See Wayne Hankey, *God in Himself: Aquinas' Doctrine of God as Expounded in the "Summa Theologiae"* (Oxford: Oxford University, 1987), for a good treatment of how Aquinas' theology of God is indebted to many sources and is not simply an elucidation of Aristotle's metaphysics. As to the nature and purpose of the *Summa theologiae*, it should be noted there are different interpretations as to its intended audience. The customary view has been that it was written for beginners in theology at the University of Paris. Leonard Boyle has argued, however, that Aquinas wrote it not for sophisticated elites at the university but for ordinary Dominican friars, the *fratres communes*, who lived in the prioral houses of study of the various Dominican provinces, and who were preparing for or already working in the Dominican Order's characteristic ministry of preaching and hearing confessions (*The Setting of the "Summa theologiae" of Saint Thomas* [Toronto: PIMS, 1982]). John Jenkins, opposing the notion of the *Summa theologiae* as an introductory text, contends it was written as a comprehensive and synthesizing treatment of sacred doctrine for advanced theological students, whether they matriculated at one of the universities or not (*Knowledge and Faith in Thomas Aquinas* [Cambridge: Cambridge University, 1997], pp. 78–98). The question of the relationship between Aquinas' theology and philosophy—and the degree to which either is indebted to the other—must be raised when considering the first three books of his *Summa contra Gentiles*, which he himself says are based on reason rather than revelation. Norman Kretzmann calls these books Aquinas' *Summa philosophica*, which at the same time is his attempt at a systematic natural theology (*The Metaphysics of Theism: Aquinas' Natural Theology in "Summa contra gentiles" I* [Oxford: Clarendon, 1997], pp. 43–53). Thomas Hibbs, on the other hand, argues that these three books do not constitute an autonomous

detail about the history of his thought on each of these items but will explain them with a scope sufficient to display how they provide the ontological supports for his positive theology of the divine names in Part Four.

1. God Is the Infinite, Pure, and Perfect Act of Subsistent Being

It amounts to the same thing in reality for Thomas to call God subsistent being, pure act, universally perfect, and infinite; but the first two characteristics are the foundation for the latter two, either of which, moreover, can prove the other.[2] Having already discussed in the last chapter his view of God as subsistent being and pure act, we will look here at his treatment of the divine perfection and infinity.

A. A Perfect God

God, "who is not distinct from his own act of being *(esse)*, is the universally perfect being *(ens)*"; and Thomas means by *universally perfect* "that which does not lack any excellence *(nobilitas)* of any generic category."[3] Because God is the most positive and absolute act of being imaginable, the divine perfection extends to every categorical quality compatible with the divine nature.[4] Sometimes he says that God is "perfect in all ways"

---

philosophy, even though Aquinas is generally careful not to sow their arguments with revealed theological premises, for the philosophy in them is considered under the light of revelation, and Aquinas rearranges the normal order of philosophical questions in order to better serve his theological goals (*Dialectic and Narrative in Aquinas: An Interpretation of the "Summa contra gentiles"* [Notre Dame: UND, 1995], pp. 37, 63, 181–84).

2. God as subsistent being and pure act proves the divine perfection in *SCG* 1.28.264 and *ST* 1.4.2; and the divine infinity in *SCG* 1.43.362 and *ST* 1.7.1. The divine infinity proves the divine perfection in *CT* 1.21, and vice versa in *SCG* 1.43.359. On the basis of God's subsistent act of being, *ST* 1.7.1 concludes that God is both "infinite and perfect." As early as *SS* 1.8.2.1 these themes are intertwined: "That which does not have an absolute [i.e., infinite] act of being but whose being is terminated in something which receives it, does not have a perfect act of being, but only that which is its own act of being."

3. *SCG* 1.28.259. Cf. *DE* 5; *SCG* 2.2.861; *CT* 1.21; *DDN* 13.1.960–68; *ST* 1.4.2.

4. God's perfection is one of the pillars of Thomas' positive theology. Nevertheless, his negative theology is brought to bear upon how we comprehend the divine perfection: God is not *per-fectus* as having had to pass first through *(per)* a state of potency before being made *(factus)* perfect (*DV* 2.3 ad13; same: *DDN* 2.1.114; *ST* 1.4.1 ad1; *SDC* 22.382; cf. *DDN*

(modus), which may appear to imply that God's perfection is simply the total aggregate of all creaturely ways of perfection,[5] but the situation is more complex than that. A creature possesses its special kind of excellence insofar as its being is limited to some "specific type," but if something were to possess the whole "power of being" *(virtus essendi)* it could not lack any excellence accruing to any other thing; but God, who is his own act of being, possesses the whole power of being and thus cannot lack any excellence.[6] This means that God, beyond every creaturely mode of excellence, is modelessly perfect. Thomas utilizes a favorite quote from Dionysius to underscore this modelessness: "God does not exist by any particular mode

---

13.1.962, 964). Kretzmann (*Metaphysics of Theism,* pp. 131–42) and John Wippel (*The Metaphysical Thought of Thomas Aquinas: From Finite Being to Uncreated Being* [Washington, DC: CUA, 2000], pp. 516, 530–32) explain how Thomas, in his *Summa contra Gentiles* and *Summa theologiae,* uses a pattern of successive qualitative negations in order to demonstrate that God is absolutely perfect. Kretzmann stresses that *SCG* 1.15–28 removes individual imperfections from God (whom at this point Kretzmann still calls Alpha), culminating in the last chapter's global removal of any possible imperfection from God, with the result that God is established as supremely perfect, both intensively and extensively, or universally. Whereas Wippel holds, however, that the very notion of divine perfection is also negative in content—and thus he distinguishes the idea of divine perfection from the positive notion of divine goodness—Kretzmann sees Thomas in *SCG* 1.28 as starting something new, for while chapters 15–27 have eliminated individual imperfections from God, chapter 28, with its title "On Divine Perfection" (a title supplied by Thomas himself in this autograph portion of *SCG* 1), "emphasizes the affirmative version of the conclusion over the denial of imperfection" (p. 131). I agree with Kretzmann, for the idea of God's perfection seems to harbor more divine positivity than the mere denial of imperfection would allow, at both the morphological and the semantic levels. Moreover, according to Thomas' general view about the nature of demonstrative proof, if the demonstrations of successive qualitative negations are ever to eventuate in the proof of some positive attribute of God—whether perfection, goodness, or something else—then we must have known something positive about God somewhere else in the process. In *ST* 1.4.1, which asks whether God is perfect, the divine positivity at the basis of the proof is the supreme divine actuality unmixed with any potentiality, which is the same reason Thomas uses in *ST* 1.3.4 to show that essence and existence are the same in God (which is tantamount to recognizing God as *ipsum esse subsistens*). The placement of the question about divine perfection so early in the *Summa theologiae*'s treatise on God, as compared to its relatively late placement in *SCG* 1.28 after a whole series of qualitative negations, is a strong signal that Thomas acknowledges the pure divine positivity at the heart of God's perfection, and does not regard our knowledge of that perfection as merely the culminating and synthesizing moment of negative theology.

5. *SS* 1.2.1.3, p. 69; he also speaks of God's perfection as full and "encompassing all modes" (*omnimoda*—ibid., p. 70); cf. *Meta.* 5.18.1038–41.

6. *SCG* 1.28.260; cf. 3.1.1862.

but has absolutely and without limit comprehended and precomprehend-
ed in himself the totality of being."[7]

B. An Infinite God

Greek philosophy oscillates in its evaluation of the infinite *(apeiron)*
and indefinite *(aoriston)*. After some early philosophers began by regarding the cosmological principle of the infinite in a positive light, Plato and
Aristotle, following the lead of Parmenides and others who added the
principle of limit to the infinite, identified infinity with imperfection and
finitude with perfection, so that their divine principle is never an infinite
entity.[8] Plotinus, however, continued and deepened the dialectic by considering his ultimate principle, the One, to be infinite.[9] Among Greek theologians, Gregory of Nyssa was the first to teach the divine infinity, which
was also acknowledged by Dionysius and John Damascene.[10] In the West,

7. "Deus non quodam modo est existens, sed simpliciter et incircumscriptive totum esse
in seipso accepit et praeaccepit" (*SCG* 1.28.267); cf. *CT* 1.21–22; *DDN* 13.1.967; *ST* 1.4.2.

8. This is Leo Sweeney's main contention in *Infinity in the Presocratics: A Bibliographical
and Philosophical Study* (The Hague: Nijhoff, 1972); the work reacts to the more traditional
view of infinity's fate in Greek philosophy, such as may be found in A. H. Armstrong and R.
A. Markus, *Christian Faith and Greek Philosophy* (New York: Sheed and Ward, 1964), pp.
11–15. Sweeney counts Anaximander, Anaxagoras, and Democritus among those who identified infinity with perfection; for Anaximander's *apeiron*, see Werner Jaeger, *The Theology of
the Early Greek Philosophers*, trans. E. S. Robinson, Gifford Lectures of 1936 (Oxford: Clarendon, 1947), chap. 2. For Plato's view of the *apeiron*, see Cornelia de Vogel, "La théorie de
l'apeiron chez Platon et dans la tradition platonicienne," *Revue philosophique de la France et
de l'étranger* 149 (1959): 21–39. *Physics* 3.6.207a8–14 is an example of how Aristotle lines up
infinity with imperfection. Maurice Corvez shows that the God of Plato is not the infinite
God of Christianity ("Le Dieu de Platon," *RPL* 65 [1967]: 5–35). "The Aristotelian separate
substance called God in the *Metaphysics* is beyond doubt a finite being" (Joseph Owens,
"Aristotle and God," in *God in Contemporary Thought: A Philosophical Perspective*, ed. S. A.
Matczak [New York: Learned Publications, 1977], p. 433).

9. A dialogue between Sweeney and W. Norris Clarke clarified the issue of infinity in
Plotinus, with Sweeney eventually admitting that the One's intrinsic infinity is implied
whenever Plotinus speaks of the One as transcendent or formless, or as nonbeing (Sweeney,
"Infinity in Plotinus," *Gregorianum* 38 [1957]: 515–35, 713–32; Clarke, "Infinity and Plotinus:
A Reply," *Gregorianum* 40 [1959]: 75–98; Sweeney, "Plotinus Revisited," *Gregorianum* 40
[1959]: 327–31; Sweeney, "Another Interpretation of *Enneads* VI, 7, 32," *MSch* 38 [1961]:
298–303).

10. See Ekkehard Mühlenberg, *Die Unendlichkeit Gottes bei Gregor von Nyssa* (Göttingen:
Vandenhoeck and Ruprecht, 1966). The occasion for the breakthrough was Gregory's debate
with the Arian Eunomius, in which Gregory asserts God's ontological infinity and makes

however, the intrinsic infinity of the divine essence became an accepted notion only after 1250.[11] Aquinas argues for such a position himself, though in the years just before the commencement of his teaching career it was still contested.[12]

Aquinas affirms the ontological infinity of the divine essence, and on that basis, the infinite power of God.[13] God, who is subsistent being and

God's incomprehensibility (the crux of the debate with Eunomius) flow from it (ibid., pp. 100–147). Cf. Charles Kannengiesser, "L'infinité divine chez Grégoire de Nysse," RSR 55 (1967): 55–65. According to Salvatore Lilla's reading of Dionysius, God is infinite because he comprehends all things in himself, has a generative power that knows no limit, and is completely incomprehensible to the human mind—the first two reasons coming to him from Neoplatonism and the last from Gregory of Nyssa ("The Notion of Infinitude in Pseudo-Dionysius Areopagita," JTS 31 [1980]: 93–103). See Leo Sweeney, "John Damascene and Divine Infinity," NS 35 (1961): 76–106. In his De fide orthodoxa 1.9 (PG 94:836B), Damascene writes that God's proper name of Being (ho ōn) shows that he has existence "like some infinite and indeterminate ocean of essence" (hoion ti pelagos ousias apeiron kai aoriston). For a person like Damascene living in Syria, the word pelagos would connote the utter mystery of God, not in terms of the circumscribed confines of the Mediterranean Sea (thalassa), but with reference to the unfathomable pelagic depths of the Atlantic. Thomas cites this text as quoddam pelagus substantiae infinitum et indeterminatum (ST 1.13.11; also cited in SS 1.8.1.1 ad4; 1.22.1.4 obj. 4; DP 7.5; 10.1 ad9). Cf. Sweeney, "John Damascene's 'Infinite Sea of Essence,'" SP 4 (1962): 294–309.

11. See Sweeney, "Divine Infinity: 1150–1250," MSch 35 (1957): 38–51. In his commentary on the Sentences around 1245, Richard Fishacre was perhaps the first Western theologian to predicate infinity as a perfection of the divine reality itself (Leo Sweeney and Charles Ermatinger, "Divine Infinity according to Richard Fishacre," MSch 35 [1958]: 191–212). For a brief but packed account, replete with bibliography, of the history of infinity as a divine attribute, see David Balas, "A Thomist View on Divine Infinity," PACPA 55 (1981): 91–93. For a general appreciation of the whole philosophical enterprise to grasp infinity, see Sweeney, "Surprises in the History of Infinity from Anaximander to George Cantor," PACPA 55 (1981); 3–23.

12. Sweeney shows why, in the years 1235–50, certain theologians denied the essential infinity of God, and how Aquinas answers their objections ("Some Medieval Opponents of Divine Infinity," MS 19 [1957]: 233–45). For differing positions on Albert the Great's view of divine infinity, see Francis Catania, "Divine Infinity in Albert the Great's Commentary on the Sentences of Peter Lombard," MS 22 (1960): 27–42; and Francis Kovach, "The Infinity of the Divine Essence and Power in the Works of St. Albert the Great," Miscellanea Mediaevalia (Berlin/New York: de Gruyter, 1981), 14:24–40.

13. SS 1.43.1.1; DV 2.2 ad5; 29.3; SCG 1.43; DP 1.2; CT 1.18–20; ST 1.7.1. Cf. SS 4.49.2.1 ad2; DDN 5.1.629; ST 1.75.5 ad4; Meta. 2.4.329; 11.10. Sweeney shows how Bonaventure deems God's essence to be infinite because of its unity with God's power, which can make an infinite number of creatures and is omnipresent to all creatures. For Aquinas, however, God's power is infinite because of its unity with the divine essence, which is infinite in itself and not simply by its omnipresence in creatures ("Bonaventure and Aquinas on the Divine

possesses an absolute being not inherent in anything else, is absolutely infinite, for the divine being is not limited or contracted by being received in another finite nature.[14] "Every act mixed with potency has a limit to its perfection, but the act unmixed with potency is without limit to its perfection, and God is pure act without any potency" (*SCG* 1.43.362). The argument for God's essential infinity thus rests solidly on the truth that God is pure act, which is ipso facto infinite. Consider the following text:

Considered absolutely, being itself is infinite, for it can be participated in infinite ways by an infinite number of things. If, then, the being of something is finite, that being must be limited by something else which is its cause in some way. But there can be no cause of the divine being, since God is necessary in himself. Therefore, God's being and God himself are infinite. (*SCG* 1.43.363)

Given that "being itself" is infinite, then, God can be shown to be infinite on the grounds that there is no conceivable way in which God can be limited or made finite, for that would require God to have a cause, which is impossible. Moreover, "the first cause is above being *(ens)* insofar as it is the infinite act of being itself *(ipsum esse infinitum)*. That entity, further, is called a being *(ens)* which finitely participates in the act of being" (*SDC* 6.175). A creature's being, then, is made finite and limited by participating in the infinite act of be-ing, which God *is* absolutely.[15] The following text describes the two ways in which the act of being is made finite, and con-

---

Being as Infinite," in *Bonaventure and Aquinas: Enduring Philosophers*, ed. R. W. Shahan and F. J. Kovach [Norman: University of Oklahoma, 1976], pp. 133–53). Aquinas' God is one whose infinity "permeates his very entity" (ibid., p. 153). Aquinas' view of divine infinity sharply differentiates his doctrine of God from that of process theology, for which the act of being is finite and determinate (see David Schindler, "Creativity as Ultimate: Reflections on Actuality in Whitehead, Aristotle, Aquinas," *IPQ* 13 [1973]: 161–71; idem, "Whitehead's Challenge to Thomism on God and Creation: The Metaphysical issues," *IPQ* 19 [1979]: 285–99; William Hill, "In What Sense Is God Infinite? A Thomistic Perspective," *Thomist* 42 [1978]: 14–27).

14. *SS* 1.43.1.1; *DV* 2.2 ad5; *SCG* 1.43.360; *ST* 1.7.1.

15. According to Clarke ("The Limitation of Act by Potency: Aristotelianism or Neoplatonism," *NS* 26 [1952]: 167–94), Aquinas' principle that act is limited by potency is an original fusion of Aristotle and the Neoplatonists. It was the latter who, inspired by the Oriental mystery religions, began to look upon infinity as a matter of perfection instead of imperfection. The limitation principle has its origin in Neoplatonism and was widely accepted in the medieval universe of thought. Not until the *Summa contra Gentiles*, however, does Aquinas synthesize the limitation principle with Aristotelian act and potency, thereby deepening the

cludes by a process of elimination that God must be infinite, since the only two possible ways in which limitation and finitude can come about cannot apply to the divine being.

Act is finitized *(finire)* in only two ways: first, by its agent, as a beautiful home's size and appearance are received from the builder's will; second, by its recipient, as firewood's heat has a certain temperature because of the firewood's condition. However, the divine act itself is not finitized by any agent, because it is not from another but from itself; nor is it finitized by being received into another, for since no passive potency is mixed with it, it is pure act not received in another: for God is his own act of being not received in anything else. Hence it is clear that God is infinite; . . . For human being is limited to the human species since it is received in a specific human nature; and the case is similar for a horse's being or the being of any creature whatever. The being of God, however, since it is not received in anything but is pure being, is not limited to some particular mode of the perfection of being *(essendi)* but possesses in itself the totality of being *(totum esse)*. (*DP* 1.2)[16]

Thomas unambiguously delineates God's absolute infinity from other types of infinity found among creatures. He says that a created immaterial form, for example, such as an angel, is relatively infinite, for while its form is not received in matter, its form is not its own being but has been limited to a determinate nature (*ST* 1.7.2). Again,

Every creature is absolutely finite inasmuch as its being does not subsist absolutely but is limited to a certain nature in which it inheres. But nothing prohibits a creature from being relatively infinite. . . . Created immaterial substances are finite according to their being but infinite insofar as their forms are not received in something else, as if we were to call a separately existing whiteness infinite with respect to the nature of whiteness, since it is not contracted to some subject, though its being would still be finite since it is limited to some specific nature. (*ST* 1.50.2 ad4)

---

meaning of act and potency, which had only served to explain change for Aristotle. But Aquinas also transcends Plotinus by identifying God with subsistent Being, for Plotinus, still identifying being with limited essence, places his One above being.

16. "As far as the nature of being *(ratio essendi)* goes, the infinite can only be that which includes every perfection of being, which in different realities is able to be varied in infinite ways. In this manner, God alone is essentially infinite, since his essence is not limited to some determinate perfection but includes in itself every mode of perfection to which the nature of entity can be extended, and so God is essentially infinite. This sort of infinity cannot belong to any creature, for the being of any creature whatever is limited to the perfection of its own species" (*DV* 29.3). Divine infinity means that God's being is modeless and lacks the limits proper to a natural species.

After claiming that being is finitized by being received in essences, and form by being received in matter, Thomas continues:

A material substance is finite in two ways—on the part of the form which is received in matter, and on the part of the very being which it participates in according to its own mode—and so it exists finitely both from above and from below. A spiritual substance is finite from above inasmuch as it participates in being from the first principle according to its own mode, but is infinite from below inasmuch as it is not participated in by a subject. But the first principle, which is God, is infinite in all ways.[17]

One of the problems with an infinite God is how to understand the divine being as a concrete individual distinct from others while still preserving the divine transcendence. How can the infinite God be distinct from others without at the same time becoming limited and finite? The very fact that no being can be added to God distinguishes God from every other entity (*SCG* 1.26.247), and the divine purity of being delineates God from every other being (*DE* 5.20–21). God, precisely as the infinite act of being not received in anything else, is already individualized and distinct from all other individuals, though all other individuations occur when being is received by essence, or form by matter (*SDC* 9.233–35). To the objection that the infinite God cannot be a single, discrete object for the mind since God is the highest of beings and therefore of greatest generality, Aquinas responds that God does not possess a definite determination by way of limitation but by way of distinction: by the *very fact* that God is not defined or determined by limitation, as are all other realities, the divine being is distinguished from all other beings, and thus "the divine essence is something general, not in being *(essendo)*, since it is distinct from all other things, but only in causing."[18] Aquinas ingeniously answers that God is a distinct individual precisely *through,* not despite, the divine infinity, which distinguishes and individualizes the divine nature without limiting or finitizing it.

---

17. *DSS* 8.253–73; same: *ST* 1.50.2 ad4; *Quod.* 12.2.2; *SDC* 16.321–23. Cf. *DE* 5; *DV* 20.4 ad1; *R36* 7; *R43* 16; *DDN* 13.3.989; *Quod.* 3.2.1.

18. *Quod.* 7.1.1 ad1; also: *DV* 10.11 ad10; *Quod.* 7.3.1; *DP* 1.2 ad7; 7.2 ad4–5.

II. God Is the Creator and Conserver of the Universe

A. A Transcendent Creator

God is transcendent, most fundamentally, because the divine nature is the universally perfect, infinite, and subsistent act of being. Creation, which bestows being, is God's "proper action," while other agents do not cause being absolutely but rather the particularizations and individualizations of being; only an infinite first cause, which "comprehends the likeness of every being," can cause individuals to subsist as distinct from one another, whereas finite agents can only cause things to have certain determinations, since they themselves are limited by generic, specific, and accidental determinations.[19]

Aquinas does not tolerate the position, which he often ascribes to Avicenna, of a creation mediated by heavenly bodies or angelic substances, for faith teaches that the natures of all things are established immediately by God.[20] He sees the "Platonic" and Avicennian position as holding that the first cause immediately produces being and the highest of the intellectual substances, and afterward creates other inferior creatures and their qualities through the instrumentality of superior creatures. Several times he also ascribes the erroneous opinion of a mediated creation to the *Liber de causis*,[21] but in his own commentary on the work he writes that those are in error who think its author teaches that angelic intelligences are creators of souls (*SDC* 3.79). Nevertheless, in order to enlist the *Liber* in his own

---

19. *SCG* 2.21.971–72, 977. Also: *SS* 2.18.2.2; *DV* 5.9; *Decretalem* 1.410–18; *DP* 3.4; *CT* 1.70; *ST* 1.45.5; 1.65.3; 1.90.3; *Quod.* 3.3.1; *DSS* 10; *SDC* 3.79–85; 18.344–48; *Credo* 1.878. For some fine commentary on God's creative act in the *Summa contra Gentiles*, see Norman Kretzmann, *The Metaphysics of Creation: Aquinas' Natural Theology in "Summa contra Gentiles" II* (Oxford: Clarendon, 1999), pp. 30–100.

20. *DV* 5.9; same: *SS* 4.5.1.3.3 ad1; *Decretalem* 1.410–18; *DDN* 11.4.931–33. The heavenly bodies are mediators "in the work of governance but not in the work of creation" (*DV* 5.9). For Avicenna's views on emanation and on a creation mediated by successively lower levels of intellect, see Amélie-Marie Goichon, *La distinction de l'essence et de l'existence d'après Ibn Sina (Avicenne)* (Paris: Desclée, 1937), pp. 201–334. Much of what Aquinas says against Avicenna's mediated creation was adumbrated by William of Auvergne (Goichon, *La philosophie d'Avicenne et son influence en Europe médiévale*, 2nd ed. [Paris: Adrien-Maisonneuve, 1951], pp. 99–101).

21. *SS* 2.18.2.2 ad1; *DP* 3.4 ad10–11; *Meta.* 12.9.2559–60; *DSS* 10.25–27.

camp he practices some interpretive legerdemain in his reading of certain propositions and has Dionysius speak against the Platonizers, so that in Aquinas' view the *Liber* posits God as the sole creative cause of both existence and essential determinations but permits creatures to collaborate with God by being secondary causes of individuals and their operations within *already* constituted species.[22]

Except for an early passage from his commentary on the *Sentences*, Thomas is also adamant that God's power to create is not communicable to any creature. In this text, which is hidden in a larger article dealing with Peter Lombard's view about the power of the ministers of the sacraments, Thomas states that creatures, especially angels, can exercise a genuine ministerial, if subsidiary, role in creation, because creation does not require an absolutely but only a relatively infinite power.[23] However, he quietly but firmly rejects this notion of a ministerial creation in all his other *ex professo* treatments of the subject, arguing that no creature can help in creation, even instrumentally or "ministerially," since anything to do with creation demands an infinite power, which no creature possesses.[24] In *ST* 1.45.5 he

22. Aquinas interprets the *Liber*'s proposition three, which speaks of the first cause creating souls through the mediation of angelic intelligences, to mean that while the first cause produces the soul's essence, the angelic intelligence is responsible for its intellectuality; however, since intellectuality belongs to the essence of soul, the first cause, which gives the soul its essence, also gives it its intellectuality ("if all immaterial substances have their existence immediately from God, they have immediately from him the fact that they live and are intellectual" [*DSS* 11]), while the angelic intelligence does not give the soul its intellectual nature but produces intelligible forms in it through its operation (*SDC* 3.79–85; 18.344–48). He also uses Dionysius as an authority against the "Platonic" worldview because he deems him to consider God the unitary and immediate cause of all being and essential determinations, and to posit as one and the same in God what the Platonists divide up among various primary hypostases—such as First Being, First Life, First Intelligence, etc. (*DDN* 1.3.100; 5.1.612–13, 634; 11.4.931–34, 938; *SDC* 3.72–75, 84; 4.99–101, 121; 18.344–45). Robert Henle writes: "It is impressive—and almost amusing—to find the Platonizing Dionysius selected to speak for St. Thomas against the Platonizers" (*Saint Thomas and Platonism* [The Hague: Nijhoff, 1956], p. 424); cf. Pierre Faucon, *Aspects néoplatoniciens de la doctrine de saint Thomas d'Aquin* (Paris/Lille: Champion/University III, 1975), pp. 210–18.

23. *SS* 4.5.1.3.3 ad4–5, 7. The vocabulary reveals Lombard's original concern with how God's "authority" and the minister's "ministry" work together in the sacraments. *SS* 2.1.1.3 is also somewhat ambivalent on the question whether God can delegate the power to create, and both texts evince Thomas' respect for Peter Lombard's authority.

24. *DP* 3.4; cf. *SS* 2.18.2.2; *SCG* 2.43.1193; *DSS* 10. *DP* 3.4 ad2, 14–16 furnish a point by point repudiation of what he had countenanced in *SS* 4.5.1.3.3 ad4–5, 7. Granted that sacra-

associates Lombard's opinion with Avicenna's position and calls it impossible: since an instrumental cause requires some being upon which to exercise its secondary causality, and since being, the proper effect of creation, is itself presupposed to all other effects, the act of creation has nothing to offer any creature upon which it may exercise its instrumental causality, which means that no instrumental cause could ever have anything to *do*, any role, in the act of creation. Thomas' toying with the notion of a creation mediated by creatures, an idea urged upon him by the words of the respected Peter Lombard, is but a momentary divagation from his customary emphasis upon the unique and transcendent creative causality of God.[25]

Moreover, the fact that God conserves every entity in being[26] also accents the transcendence of God as Creator. God must conserve the universe since the divine power is directly responsible for its most basic principles—being, form, and matter (*SCG* 3.65). All existence would cease if God ceased acting, just as the process of becoming ceases when the efficient cause ceases its action.[27] God's conservative causality is dynamic and ongoing, for the creature's being is never a settled issue but rather a project that requires constant care and concern. Not privy to our modern

---

mental ministers do act as instruments of God's power in order to justify humans, one may not push the analogy to argue that creatures can help in God's creative act (*DP* 3.4 ad7–8).

25. Thomas is quick to repudiate fideistic occasionalism as well as Neoplatonic emanationism, for since God does not produce everything immediately, the secondary causes of nature retain their own proper activity and causality. Still, they cannot produce being itself or any of those realities whose production transcends the processes of motion and substantial generation, such as angels, human souls, matter, and the heavenly bodies (*SS* 2.18.2.2; *Quod.* 3.3.1; *DSS* 10.93–101, 193–99. Cf. *SCG* 3.66.2412; *CT* 1.130; *ST* 1.45.5 ad1; *SDC* 1.28; 23.384). God causes being absolutely, whereas natural agents are the causes of becoming, which begins the process leading toward being (*DP* 3.7; 5.1 ad4–5; 7.2 ad10). If Thomas sometimes speaks loosely of creatures as "giving being" (*DV* 5.9 ad7; *SCG* 3.66.2407; *DP* 3.7; *SDC* 1.23–29), we should understand him as referring to how creatures can prepare the way for the production of a being or modify a being in some way subsequent to its absolute production.

26. *Job* 11.150–55; 25.21–25; *SCG* 3.65; *DP* 5.1–2; *CT* 1.130; *ST* 1.104.1–2; *John* 1.5.135; *SDC* 4.

27. *DP* 5.1. "Things are conserved in being by God and . . . would be reduced instantly to nothingness if they were abandoned by God" (ibid.). If God did not conserve the world, as Augustine says, it would disappear in the blink of an eye (*SCG* 3.65). Cf. *Col.* 1.4.44; *John* 5.2.738–40; *DDN* 1.3.100; *Phys.* 2.6.195.

knowledge about the finite speed of light, Thomas asserts that every creature is related to God as the air is to the shining sun, for the air does not
continue for one moment to be lit once the sun ceases to illuminate it (*ST*
1.104.1). Creatures are compared to God, who "incessantly imparts being"
to them, as a thing being made is to that which is making it, for the maker
and the thing it is making must exist simultaneously.[28] God conserves all
reality because creatures are needy and require a constant divine care and
unceasing influx of divine energy.

B. An Immanent Creator

God is everywhere and in all things, for since the infinite divine power
causes the totality of being, the divine presence must be everywhere that
being can be found.[29] God does not occupy places bodily but is said to be
everywhere by dint of bestowing being upon the material creatures that
are located in all places.[30] Ubiquity is proper to God since only the divine
infinity is able to be in an infinite number of places simultaneously.[31] And,
although all beings are said to be distant from God because of the dis-
similitude between created natures and the divine essence, nevertheless
God is in all things as causing their being and acting in them intimately,
and thus nothing is distant from God as if it could exist without God within it.[32]

Although Thomas, inspired by Dionysius, can write that "God is the locus, foundation and chain that connects all things together" (*DDN*
10.1.851), he does not permit a pantheistic interpretation of this or any other expression of the divine immanence, which would see God as intrinsically bound up with worldly processes. God is essentially in things but is
not mingled with them as one of their material, formal or accidental ele-

28. *CT* 1.130; same: *Heb.* 1.2.31.
29. *SCG* 3.68; cf. *SS* 1.37.1.1–2; 1.37.2.1–2; *DDN* 3.1.234–36; 9.1.811; *Quod.* 11.1.1; *CT* 1.135; *ST*
1.8.1–4; 1.52.2.
30. *ST* 1.8.2; same: *SS* 1.37.2.1.
31. *ST* 1.8.4; *SS* 1.37.2.2. "God is ubiquitous since he is uncircumscribed" (*Quod.* 11.1.1
ad4). However, though an angel is also not in a place as circumscribed by it (as a body is), it
is still there in a restricted or limited fashion *(definitive)*, for not being infinite in essence or
power, it only operates in one place at a time (*ST* 1.52.2); cf. *DDN* 3.1.234–36; 9.1.811.
32. *ST* 1.8.1 ad1, 3; cf. *DV* 4.4 ad5.

ments;[33] rather, God is in things "in the manner of an agent cause" (*SCG* 3.68.2430) since every created being flows from God as its efficient and exemplar cause.[34]

God is immanent in all reality by essence, power, and presence:

Through essence, inasmuch as anything's being is a certain participation of the divine being, and so the divine essence is present to every existing reality insofar as it has being, as a cause is present to its proper effect; through power, inasmuch as all realities act by the power of God; and through presence, insofar as God immediately ordains and disposes all realities.[35]

God also operates intimately in all secondary agents by bestowing and conserving their power of action and by moving them to their acts.[36] Indeed, God's immanence in creatures is the most profound instance of one reality's presence in another. Since God originates and continues to uphold the being of things,[37] and since a thing's being is at its innermost and deepest core, God is most intimately present and acting in all reality.[38]

C. A God Who Freely Creates from Nothing

For Aquinas, God creates out of nothing, *ex nihilo*, since nothing whatsoever is presupposed to the divine creative act.[39] He argues that God can

33. *SS* 1.37.1.1; *SCG* 3.68.2430; *DP* 3.7; *ST* 1.8.1. God cannot be the material cause for in God there is no matter (*DE* 4–5; *SS* 1.35.1.1; *DV* 21.4; *SCG* 1.17; *R108* 49; *ST* 1.3.8), and God is not a body (*SCG* 1.20; 2.3.865; *DDN* 4.3; 9.1; *CT* 1.16–17; *ST* 1.3.1; *Phys.* 8.21; *Meta.* 12.8.2548–50; *SDC* 22); God is not the form of any body (*SCG* 1.27; *CT* 1.17; *Rom.* 1.7.143–45; *ST* 1.3.8; 2-2.94.1) or the formal being of any created reality (*DE* 5; *SS* 1.8.1.2; *DV* 21.4; *SCG* 1.26; *R108* 16; *DDN* 1.2.52; 2.3.165; 7.4.731; *ST* 1.3.8; *SDC* 9; 20).

34. *SS* 1.8.1.2; cf. *SS* 1.38.1.1; *DV* 7.1 ad13; *SCG* 4.21.3576. In *DDN* 5.1.630–31, Thomas interprets Dionysius' calling God the "being for the beings" (*esse existentibus*) in a causal rather than formal, pantheistic sense.

35. *CT* 1.135; same: *SS* 1.37.1.2; *DP* 3.7, *sed contra; John* 1.5.133–34; 13.4.1810.

36. *DP* 3.7; *ST* 1.105.5; *SS* 2.1.1.4; *SCG* 3.67.

37. God is within each reality and "holds it in being" (*DP* 3.7); God "is giving being to things" (*est dans esse rebus*, the present periphrasis connoting God's *continuing* action—*SS* 2.1.1.4; cf. *ST* 1.105.5).

38. *SS* 1.37.1.1; 2.1.1.4; *DP* 3.7; *CT* 1.130; *ST* 1.8.1; 1.105.5; *Pater* 1041.

39. *SS* 2.1.1.2; *SCG* 2.16; *Decretalem* 1.437–43; *De articulis* 1.100–139; *DP* 3.1; *CT* 1.69; *Rom.* 11.5.943; *ST* 1.44.2; 1.45.1–2; *Phys.* 8.2; *SDC* 18; *Credo* 1.881. For patristic historical background relating to the doctrine of *creatio ex nihilo*, see Harry Wolfson, *Studies in the History of Philosophy and Religion*, ed. I. Twersky and G. H. Williams, 2 vols. (Cambridge: Harvard, 1973–77), vol. 1, chaps. 9, 11 and 12.

create from nothing because God causes all being, even prime matter.[40] A natural agent's activity, which is confined to a limited and specific realm, occurs by some type of motion and requires a preexistent matter, but since God is "totally act" and "pure act," the divine activity is universal, presupposing nothing.[41] Since creation presupposes nothing and produces a reality's total being and substance, it cannot be a process of motion or change,[42] which requires a preexistent subject potentially able to move or change (SCG 2.17.949). And because creation is not a process of motion or change, it happens in an instant: "At the same time something is being created, it has been created."[43]

God does not create from any interior need or necessity but from the divine wisdom and the divine will's free choice.[44] God wills the divine goodness necessarily, but since that goodness is perfect and incapable of having any further perfection added to it from any creature, God does not ever have to will anything other than himself in order to fulfill and procure his own goodness.[45] Combating Neoplatonists and others who would limit God's freedom by asserting that God cannot do other than what he does because he can do only what he ought to do, Thomas denies that God fulfills any "duty of justice" in the production of creatures, for creation does not presuppose anything in creatures on the basis of which such a duty could be imposed on God.[46] Acting by the divine will, which is in con-

---

40. SCG 2.16.934, 943–45.

41. DP 3.1; "At the same time as bestowing being, God produces that which receives the being" (ibid., ad17).

42. SS 2.1.1.2 ad2; SCG 2.17; DP 3.2–3; CT 1.99; R108 94–95; ST 1.45.1 ad2; 1.45.2 ad2; 1.45.3. Cf. Antonin Sertillanges, Les grandes thèses de la philosophie thomiste (Paris: Bloud, 1928), pp. 81–120; idem, La philosophie de saint Thomas d'Aquin (Paris: Aubier, 1940), pp. 251–65.

43. "Simul aliquid, dum creatur, creatum est" (SCG 2.19.960); R108 100; ST 1.45.2 ad3; 1.46.3; 1.63.5; 1.74.1 ad1.

44. By treating of God's supreme happiness just before discussing creation, SCG 1.100–102 shows that God does not need to create in order to augment the divine blessedness (ST 1.26 on God's happiness also comes before ST 1.44 on creation, questions 27–43 on the Trinity intervening). See also SS 1.38.1.1 ad6; 1.43.2.1; 1.45.1.3; Job 36.322; 38.143; SCG 2.23; 2.28; DP 1.5; 3.15; CT 1.96; DDN 1.3.88; 4.1.271; ST 1.14.8; 1.19.3–4; 1.25.5.

45. ST 1.19.3; cf. DP 3.15 ad10, 14, 16. The divine will "has no necessary relation to any creature" (ibid., ad18).

46. SCG 2.28.1047,1052. God "produced things in being not from any duty but from pure liberality" (SCG 2.44.1217).

formity with the divine wisdom, God does not necessarily produce just one effect but freely creates many things.[47] Thus, the world's order and harmonious internal connections do not prove the necessity of its creation but only that the divine will "loves this order" (SS 1.43.2.1). There is a great gulf between Aquinas' voluntaristic creationism and the necessitarian emanationism characteristic of Neoplatonism.[48]

Aquinas employs various arguments to show that God creates not by natural necessity but by free will. One argument is similar to the *Summa theologiae*'s "fifth way" of proving God's existence and concludes to a divine intelligence working by will.[49] A second reasons that if creatures pre-exist in God's intelligence, and if things proceed from intelligence by means of will, then creatures have come from God's will.[50] A third ingeniously bases itself on the infinity of the divine being: natural agents with a fixed, determinate being produce determinate effects by natural necessity;

47. DV 2.14; 23.6; SCG 2.23–24; DDN 7.2; ST 1.25.5; 1.46.3.

48. Cf. SCG 3.65.2404; DSS 9.185–86. Klaus Kremer, after showing how Thomas' doctrine of creation is indebted to Neoplatonism as well as to Aristotelianism ("Die Creatio nach Thomas von Aquin und dem *Liber de Causis*," in *Ekklesia: Festschrift für Bischof Dr. Matthias Wehr* [Trier: Paulinus, 1962], pp. 321–44), in two later works ("Das 'Warum' der Schöpfung: *quia bonus vel/et quia voluit? Ein Beitrag zum Verhältnis von Neuplatonismus und Christentum an Hand des Prinzips bonum est diffusivum sui*," in *Parusia: Festgabe für Johannes Hirschberger* [Frankfurt: Minerva, 1965], pp. 241–64; *Die neuplatonische Seinsphilosophie und ihre Wirkung auf Thomas von Aquin*, 2nd ed. [Leiden: Brill, 1971]) tries to harmonize Plotinian emanationism with Christian/Thomistic creationism by arguing that since in both schemes of thought God's necessity, goodness, and freedom are mutually inclusive, the Christian concept of creation and the Neoplatonic concept of the demiurge's activity can be taken up into a higher unity that outshines all differences. Friedo Ricken ("Emanation und Schöpfung," ThPh 49 [1974]: 483–86) critiques such an attempt at harmonization. The ultimate question is whether Plotinus sees the One as free in relation to the hypostases emanating from it. Although Kremer adduces texts from Plotinus that speak of the One as free, and interprets those texts that speak of a necessary emanation as referring only to a moral necessity he deems compatible with the Christian/Thomistic theory of creation, Ricken shows that none of the Plotinian texts really speak of a radical freedom in the One and that Plotinus' "moral necessity" is still incompatible with the radical freedom of Thomas' Creator God, since for that God it would not be "morally" possible, in Plotinus' view, not to will the world. For an excellent treatment of the relation between freedom and creation in God, with special reference to Aquinas, see David Burrell, *Freedom and Creation in Three Traditions* (Notre Dame: UND, 1993).

49. DP 3.15, first proof; ST 1.19.4, first proof.

50. DP 3.15, third proof; ST 1.19.4, third proof.

but the divine being is indeterminate and infinite, and so, if the divine being were to produce only one natural, necessary effect, this effect would
have to be indeterminate and infinite in being; but there can be no essentially infinite entity other than God, and so the infinite God can produce
distinct and definite effects only through the determination of the divine
intellect and will—there is no other way to obtain a determinate effect
from an infinite and indeterminate cause.[51]

The cause of all things is to be found in the love and liberty of God's
free will. "When [God's] hand was opened by the key of love, creatures
came forth."[52] Aquinas takes a view pitting him against Neoplatonists and
others who would deny that the God who is supremely one can be responsible for the plurality of beings and their differences, because he sees
such multiplicity and inequality as originating not from chance, matter,
secondary causes, or the free choices of creatures,[53] but solely from the
gracious will of God. He argues especially against their worldview, which
can account for diversity only by recourse to secondary agents, which, as
their effects are multiplied and recede ever farther from the One's actuality and simplicity, bring about the diversity of the universe (SCG 2.42.1181);
and he counters their position by showing that God is not an emanating
nature but a creating intellect and will. Because God creates by acts of un-

51. ST 1.19.4, second proof; a cognate but not identical argument is found in DP 3.15, second proof.

52. SS 2, Prologue; cf. SS 1.45.1.3. God has made all things "through mere will" (SCG
2.29.1060). "The will of God is the principle of the totality of being (ens)" (Quod. 12.3.1 ad1).
For Aquinas on God as free, gratuitous love, see William Hill, "Two Gods of Love: Aquinas
and Whitehead," Listening 14 (1979): 49–64; for Aquinas' view of God as immutable love, see
Michael Dodds, The Unchanging God of Love, Studia Friburgensia, N.S. 66 (Fribourg,
Switzerland: University of Fribourg, 1986), chap. 4; both of these writers distinguish
Aquinas' outlook from that of the process theologians. On the freedom of God the Creator
in Aquinas, see Anton Pegis, St. Thomas and the Greeks, The Aquinas Lecture, 1939 (Milwau-
kee: Marquette, 1939), pp. 50–65; idem, "Necessity and Liberty: An Historical Note on St.
Thomas Aquinas," NS 15 (1941): 18–45. Cf. Florestano Centore, "Lovejoy and Aquinas on
God's 'Need' to Create," Angelicum 59 (1982): 23–36.

53. Chance: SCG 2.39; DP 3.16; CT 1.102; ST 1.47.1; Meta. 1.7.113–14; 8.2.1692; Gener. 1.1.5–6,
9; 1.3.21; 1.5.40; DSS 1.1–33. Matter: SCG 2.40; DP 3.1 ad9; 3.16; CT 1.71; 1.102; ST 1.47.1; Meta.
12.2.2440. Secondary causes: SS 2.1.1.1; 2.1.1.3–4; 2.7.3.1; 2.18.2.2; SCG 2.41–43; DP 3.6; ST
1.47.1; 1.49.3; 1.65.4; Meta. 1.9.142–48; DSS 10; 17.63–93; SDC 3; 18; Gener. 1.1.8; 1.2.16–17. Creatures' free choices: SCG 2.44; DP 3.16; ST 1.47.2; 1.65.2; DSS 12.131–54.

derstanding and intending, which are not fixed on one object or effect, even in his unity and simplicity God can be immediately responsible for a multitude of diverse effects without needing a plurality of mediators.[54] The forms of different realities are in the divine intellect, and since God creates according to those forms, the plural and diverse realities of the world can be caused immediately by God, the divine simplicity notwithstanding (*SCG* 2.42.1186). The wisdom and free will of God, therefore, are the primary cause of the world's plurality and diversity,[55] for it is God who originally intends to give each creature as much perfection as it can possess (*SCG* 2.45.1227). God creates the multiplicity and diversity of reality in order that the variety of the whole universe may be a more perfect likeness of the divine goodness than any one creature ever could be.[56]

Creation *ex nihilo*, God's creating in absolute freedom "out of the non-being which is nothing" (*ST* 1.45.1), is the root of the creature's profound

54. *SCG* 2.42.1187–88. Aquinas preserves the Christian God's voluntary immediacy to creation from an overly naturalistic and transcendent Neoplatonic First Cause. To do so, however, he must ignore the insistence of Dionysius that God's causality is like that of the sun, which, without thinking or choosing, by the very fact of its existence automatically shines upon all bodies according to the degree of their receptivity (*DDN* 4.1.269–71; 4.9.409; 4.16.502–3). The sun example derives from the more general Neoplatonic maxim, which Aquinas also refers to Dionysius, that goodness spreads itself out, automatically and naturally, into other beings and instantiations of goodness *(bonum diffusivum sui)*. Although he admits that Aquinas explicitly rejects necessitarian explanations of God's creative act, Kretzmann, betraying the philosopher's penchant for necessary causes, cites texts such as *SCG* 1.37.307 and *ST* 1.19.2 to show that Aquinas also at times derives from the Dionysian maxim the opposite idea that God creates from natural necessity. Kretzmann tries to harmonize Aquinas by asserting that while God's will is necessitated as regards *whether* to create, God voluntarily chooses *what* to create (*Metaphysics of Theism*, pp. 223–25; see also his *Metaphysics of Creation*, pp. 120–36). In these texts and elsewhere, however, it is clear that Aquinas' faith and theology lead the way, for though he cites the Neoplatonic axiom of the natural diffusiveness of goodness, he also reinterprets it, with help from his belief in the inner-Trinitarian communications of goodness, so that it does not threaten God's absolute freedom to create. In *DV* 21.1 ad4, he also reinterprets the maxim so that it refers not to efficient but to final causality. Cf. Julien Péghaire, "L'axiome *Bonum est diffusivum sui* dans le néoplatonisme et le thomisme," *RUO* 1 (1932): 5–30; Bernhard-Thomas Blankenhorn, "The Good as Self-Diffusive in Thomas Aquinas," *Angelicum* 79 (2002): 803–37; John F. X. Knasas, "*Contra* Spinoza: Aquinas on God's Free Will," *ACPQ* 76 (2002): 417–29.

55. *DE* 5; *Job* 26.177–79; *SCG* 2.45; 3.97; *DDN* 8.5.794–96; *DP* 3.16; *CT* 1.72–73; 1.102; *Eph.* 1.1.12; *ST* 1.47.1–2; 1.65.2; *Meta.* 12.2.2440; *SDC* 24.

56. *SCG* 2.45.1220–22; *ST* 1.47.1.

contingence. *Ex nihilo* means that the creature left to itself amounts to nothingness. "The creature does not possess being except from another; considered as left to itself, moreover, it is nothing, and hence its nature is first nothingness rather than being."[57] It is not until we recognize the transcendent God who creates in absolute freedom that we can know ourselves as existing in absolute contingency, dependent on the free choice of a loving God.[58]

III. *Creation Is a Likeness to God*

A. *Creatures Are Both Like and Unlike God*

If the words *likeness* or *similarity* (translations of *similitudo*) possessed only their normal philosophical significations, then one could not claim truthfully that creatures are like or similar to God. According to Aquinas, Aristotle teaches that things are said to be alike or similar because they experience the same reality, suffer something together, resemble one another in figure or proportion, or share in various forms and qualities that admit of difference of degree.[59] But in none of these ways can God and creatures be similar. So it is not surprising that Aquinas argues for the creature's likeness to God by relying on the protology of Genesis 1:26 ("Let us make the human in our image and likeness") and the eschatology of 1 John 3:2 ("We shall be like [God]"), as well as by recourse to God's transcendent creative causality.[60] Creatures are similar to God—not as equals, or as possessing different degrees of the same form, or as partaking of the same specific or generic category—"according to a certain analogy, as being itself is common to all"; and all creatures are "likened" to God as "to the first and universal principle of all being" (*ST* 1.4.3),[61] who "imparts all perfections

---

57. *De aetern.*, lines 192–95.

58. For Aquinas on God's creative liberty and the contingency of creation, see Faucon, *Aspects néoplatoniciens*, pp. 487–99.

59. *Meta.* 5.12.918–19; 10.4.2006–12.

60. *SCG* 1.29.270–71 and *ST* 1.4.3. Cf. *SCG* 1.54; 1.80.680; 1.93.786; *DP* 3.16 ad12–13; *ST* 1.47.1 ad2; *DSS* 12.100–119. Note how *SCG* 1.29, coming immediately before the epistemological and linguistic discussions of chapters 30–36, is for Aquinas the last of the ontological underpinnings for that discussion.

61. *ST* 1.44.3 speaks of the "the analogy of a certain imitation," and *DP* 3.4 ad9 of a

to things" (*SCG* 1.29.270). Moreover, as the caused is similar to the cause but not vice versa (e.g., the picture is like the person but not conversely), for similarity denotes dependence on the exemplar, so the creature is similar to God but not vice versa.[62]

Although the theological truths about the Creator and creation lead the way in showing that creatures are similar to God, Aquinas also uses the philosophical maxim that effects are similar to their causes, which is itself reduced to the metaphysical axiom that "every agent produces something like itself" *(omne agens agit simile sibi).*[63] This axiom holds only for principal causes, however, not for instrumental or accidental causes. Further, an effect may be unlike its cause due to matter or the influence of other causes: for example, clay is hardened into a brick by fire, but the hardness is due to the matter, not to the fire, and so fire cannot be called hard except metaphorically (*DP* 7.5 ad8). Again, there is a difference in the way univocal and equivocal causes bring about what is similar to themselves.[64] Despite the restrictions one must keep in mind in order to employ the axiom properly, its generality allows Aquinas the opportunity to express and justify his crucial theological thesis about God's creative act in a more universal and philosophical manner.[65]

"certain likeness of analogy"; *SS* 1.2.1.3 (pp. 68–69) says that all things "are made similar [to God] through analogy." Ontological analogy and likeness to God go hand in hand.

62. *DV* 4.4 ad2; *SCG* 1.29.273; *DP* 7.7, ad3 of 2nd series; *DDN* 9.3.832; *ST* 1.4.3 ad4.

63. "Since every agent insofar as it is an agent brings about something similar to itself, and since everything acts according to its form, the likeness of the agent's form must be in the effect" (*ST* 1.4.3). "The cause is somehow in the effect through a participated likeness of itself" (*DSS* 14.74–75). Other instances of the axiom: *SS* 3.23.3.1.1; 3.33.1.2; *DV* 21.4.205–8; *DM* 1.3; *DP* 2.2; 7.5; *CT* 1.101; *DDN* 2.4.185; 3.1.227; *ST* 1.5.3; 1.19.2; 1.45.6. In the *Summa contra Gentiles*, the majority of instances are from book two, where the axiom is often used to express the bond between creation and Creator (11.907; 16.937; 20.964; 21.977; 22.986; 23.992; 24.1004; 30.1067; 33.1100; 40.1162; 41.1173, 1176; 43.1201; 45.1220, 1225; 46.1233; 53.1286; 76.1562; 89.1736; 98.1830). Cf. Battista Mondin, "Il principio *omne agens agit simile sibi* e l'analogia dei nomi divini nel pensiero di S. Tommaso d'Aquino," *DTP* 37 (1960): 336–48; Henry Chavannes, *L'Analogie entre Dieu et la monde selon Thomas d'Aquin et selon Karl Barth* (Paris: Cerf, 1969), pp. 30–32; Rolf Schönberger, *Nomina divina: zur theologischen Semantik bei Thomas von Aquin* (Frankfurt/Bern: Lang, 1981), pp. 14–22.

64. For these last few points, see Mondin, *The Principle of Analogy in Protestant and Catholic Theology,* 2nd ed. (The Hague: Nijhoff, 1968), pp. 85–93.

65. John Wippel, studying how Thomas tries to justify the axiom philosophically, finds that the deductive proof from the nature of causal action as such is the most promising

However, creatures are also unlike God, for they are similar to God only "distantly" and "deficiently" (*ST* 1.6.4), inasmuch as God's essence is the "supereminent and unequaled likeness of things" (*DP* 7.7 ad5). The forms of creatures are found in God, but in a higher and different way, since God is a transcendent cause, and thus all reality is at once similar and dissimilar to God (*SCG* 1.29.270). While scripture always denies that God is similar to any creature, it both concedes (Gen. 1:26) and denies (Isa. 40:18 and Ps. 83:1) that the creature is similar to God, which Dionysius explains by saying that creatures are like God insofar as they imitate and represent as far as possible the one who is not perfectly imitable, but are unlike God insofar as they are less perfect than him and fail to represent him perfectly.[66] Lest anyone think that the creature's perfection falls short of God's by a definite amount, as would occur in a comparison of two things belonging to the same category of being, Dionysius adds that creatures are less than God and dissimilar to him not by some determinate measure but "infinitely" and "incomparably."[67] Commenting on Lateran IV's decree *Damnamus* concerning the errors of Joachim of Fiore, Thomas repeats one part of it almost verbatim—"we cannot observe however great a likeness between Creator and creature without having to note an even greater unlikeness between them"—and adds that the reason for the statement is to be found in the fact that "the creature is infinitely distant from God."[68] Creatures are dissimilar to God because they are not equal to God, because they possess only by participation what God is essentially, and because they are "incomparably deficient" with respect to God;[69] nevertheless, they are likened to God, not because they share a category with God, but because God is the "principle of every category."[70] Thomas' positive and negative theology and his interpretation of the Dionysian threefold way find

---

method, although he notes it needs further strengthening if it is to succeed as a proof ("Thomas Aquinas on Our Knowledge of God and the Axiom That Every Agent Produces Something Like Itself," *PACPA* 74 [2000]: 81–101).

66. *DV* 2.11 ad1; 3.2; *SCG* 1.29.271–72.
67. *DDN* 9.3.834; cf. *ST* 1.4.3 ad1.
68. *Decretalem* 2.273–76. The text of the decree is in *DS* 806.
69. *DP* 7.7, ad4 of 2nd series; cf. ad3 of 1st series.
70. *DP* 7.7, ad7 of 2nd series.

their ontological moorings in the theological truth of God's transcendent creativity, for divine creation posits in the creature a real though deficient likeness to God.

B. God's Essence and God's Ideas

The being of creatures is derived from God as from an exemplar (*exemplariter*—SCG 1.66.552), such that "whatever is in us from God imitates God in some way."[71] God's *essence*, "although it is one and simple, is the exemplar for all the multiplicity and complexity of reality" (*SCG* 1.58.492), "for the entity whose substance is its being is the pattern for all existents."[72] But God's *knowledge* is also the exemplar for all creatures, for the mind's internal model is what allows the artisan to produce various objects with definite forms, and since all natural realities are also endowed with such determinate forms, they must be rooted in the divine knowledge that thought out the universe in all its different parts.[73]

A word is in order about the distinction and interconnection, for Aquinas, between the divine *ratio, idea,* and *exemplar.* For intellectual creatures, the technical term *idea* refers to "a certain form understood by an agent according to whose likeness the agent intends to produce an exterior work" (*Quod.* 4.1.1). In God's case, however, there are two kinds of *idea:* one that is the practical "principle for the making of things" and is often called the *exemplar* or model, and another that is the speculative "principle of knowledge" for things and is usually known as the *ratio* or archetypal reason (*ST* 1.15.3). Thus, the divine mind contains the *rationes* for all possible realities, even those archetypal reasons that will never become the exemplary models for the production of things (*ST* 1.15.3 ad2). The divine intellect, by considering the divine essence, "discovers, so to speak, the different ways of imitating that essence, in which the plurality of ideas consists" (*DV* 3.2 ad6). Multiplicity originates from God "insofar as he has un-

---

71. *SCG* 4.21.3576; cf. *DV* 21.4.206–12. "The being of creatures is derived from the divine being according to a certain deficient assimilation" (*DDN* 1.1.29; cf. 1.2.51).

72. *DDN* 11.4.932; cf. 7.4.729; *ST* 1.44.3. The Son of God is the primordial archetype insofar as all creatures imitate him as the true and perfect image of the Father (*1 Cor.* 11.1.583).

73. *ST* 1.44.3; cf. *Meta.* 1.15.233.

derstood himself as the idea for many things, i.e., as participable by different kinds of imitation" (*SS* 2.18.2.2).

There is one thing which is the exemplar of all, the divine essence, which all things imitate inasmuch as they exist and are good. But there is plurality according to the [divine] intelligence's archetypal reason *(secundum intelligentiae rationem)*, and according to this there are many ideas. For although all things imitate the divine essence inasmuch as they exist, they do not all imitate it in one and the same way, but in different ways and according to different grades. The divine essence, therefore, insofar as it is imitable in this way by this creature, is the proper reason *(ratio)* and idea for this sort of creature, and similarly for other creatures.[74]

Early in his career Thomas distinguishes a double exemplary causality in God, with a corresponding double likeness in the creature to God. Creaturely perfections participate directly in the divine nature and bear a likeness to it, so that the divine nature is the exemplar of the perfection; but materiality, and creaturely limitations, defects, imperfections, and determinate grades of being only bear a likeness to the divine ideas, which are their exemplars.[75] The former similarity is called a "likeness according to participation" and the latter a "likeness according to proportion," and metaphorical predicates applied to God are based on the second type.[76]

---

74. *Quod.* 4.1.1; cf. *DDN* 5.3.663–68. Aquinas has pushed back into the relationship between God's essence and the divine ideas the old problem of how to get multiple and finite creatures from the one and infinite Creator. For treatments of the divine ideas in Aquinas and of the problems concerning their ontology and coherence in his thought, see Vincent Branick, "The Unity of the Divine Ideas," *NS* 42 (1968): 171–201; Louis-B. Geiger, "Les idées divines dans l'oeuvre de S. Thomas," in *St. Thomas Aquinas, 1274–1974: Commemorative Studies*, 2 vols. (Toronto: PIMS, 1974), 1:175–209; Mark Jordan, "The Intelligibility of the World and the Divine Ideas in Aquinas," *RM* 38 (1984): 17–32; John Farthing, "The Problem of Divine Exemplarity in St. Thomas," *Thomist* 49 (1985): 183–222; John Wippel, *Thomas Aquinas on the Divine Ideas*, Étienne Gilson Series 16 (Toronto: PIMS, 1993); Vivian Boland, *Ideas in God according to Saint Thomas Aquinas: Sources and Synthesis* (Leiden: Brill, 1996).

75. *SS* 1.2.1.2; 1.42.2.1; 3.32.1.1 ad5; *DV* 2.3 ad9; 3.2. Whereas even material things can be images of the divine ideas, the intellectual nature alone can be an image of God (*SS* 2.16.1.2 ad2; cf. *SS* 1.36.2.3; 1.38.1.1). God is not the exemplar of color and of truth in the same way, for truth bears a likeness to God's nature but color only to the divine idea of it (*SS* 1.19.5.2 ad4). Thomas follows Dionysius and Augustine, respectively, by having all things preexist in the divine essence and by placing ideas in the divine intelligence (Faucon, *Aspects néoplatoniciens*, pp. 218–27, 293–301).

76. *SS* 1.34.3.1 ad2; 3.2.1.1.1 ad3. Cf. Bernard Montagnes, *La doctrine de l'analogie de l'être d'après saint Thomas d'Aquin*, Philosophes Médiévaux 6 (Louvain/Paris: Publications Universitaires/Béatrice-Nauwelaerts, 1963), pp. 50–53; J. M. Artola, *Creación y participación: La*

This second type of exemplarity attempts to account for how God can be the source of limitation and materiality for creatures without implicating the divine essence itself in such limitation and materiality.

Thomas' later works, while trying to sort out which qualities belong intrinsically to the divine essence and which do not, also sometimes mention God's double exemplarity.[77] Although there cannot be a likeness of genus or species between God and creature, there can be "a certain likeness of analogy," as occurs between potency and act, or substance and accident; this likeness of analogy occurs "in one way, inasmuch as created realities imitate in their own manner the idea of the divine mind, as artifacts imitate the form which is in the mind of the artisan, and in another way, insofar as created realities are likened somehow to the divine nature itself, as from the first being other things are beings, and from the first good other things are good, etc."[78] However, "the likeness of all things preexists in the divine essence not with the same nature but in a more eminent fashion" (*DDN* 1.3.90), as effects preexist in their transcendent cause (*SCG* 1.29.270), for creatures do not attain a specific likeness as regards God's essence, though they do attain a specific likeness as regards their "representation of the archetypal reason *(ratio)* understood by God" (*ST* 1.44.3 ad1). Further, it is the creature's likeness to the divine essence that accounts for the fact "that the good and things of this sort are predicated commonly of God and creatures," for the reason we say "God is good" is not simply because God understands the goodness of the creature (*DP* 7.7 ad6).

Therefore, no creature can bear a specific likeness to God's essence but only an analogous one, and God's essence is the supereminent exemplar of

---

participación de la naturaleza divina en las criaturas según la filosofía de Santo Tomás de Aquino (Madrid: Publicaciones de la Institución Aquinas, 1963).

77. *SCG* 1.93.790 distinguishes between the human virtues God properly possesses and those virtues that, because of certain imperfections, cannot properly be said of God, so that they do not have an exemplar in the divine nature but only in the divine wisdom, "which includes the proper reasons for all beings, as is the case with other corporeal realities." *ST* 1.93.2 ad4 recognizes that any creature can be called an image of the exemplary idea in the divine mind, but wants to discuss only the image that implies a likeness to the divine essence—as, for example, all beings are like the first being, all living entities like the first life, and all intelligent creatures like the supreme wisdom.

78. *DP* 3.4 ad9; cf. *ST* 1.93.2 ad4. *ST* 1.15.1 ad3 states that God's essence is the similitude of all things.

creatures, so that the particular likeness in the creature is possessed by God in an absolute and infinite fashion. However, the exemplary idea of every creature is found in the divine mind according to the same specific likeness but with a different mode of existence. All creatures and creaturely qualities are contained in God's creative power which works by means of the divine ideas, but whereas some created realities, because of their generality and perfection, also bear an analogical likeness to the divine essence, others, due to their materiality or some other imperfection, are likened only to the divine ideas.[79] Literal divine predications referring to God's substance (e.g., "God is good") are based on essential likeness, whereas metaphorical predications are based on ideal likeness, which permits us to predicate things only of God's power, not of God's very essence (e.g., we can say that God makes a body but not that God is a body). There is no automatic formula by which Thomas decides whether a given nature or quality is an essential or merely ideal likeness to God, and by extension, whether a given predicate is said of God's essence or only of God's power. The decision arises in the context of his whole theology, where the truths he knows about God mold and form his assessment of the divine perfection and of what is compatible or not compatible with it.

C. Vestige, Image, Similarity

For Aquinas, as we have seen, the word *similitudo* carries the generic meaning of likeness, which is predicated of all creation vis-à-vis God. *Imitatio* is a synonym for *similitudo,* and both words may have either a static or a dynamic meaning.[80] However, *similitudo* more narrowly understood may also signify the third and most perfect level of *similitudo* generically understood. Thus, generic *similitudo* possesses three traditional subclasses, which Aquinas, taking his cues from scripture and Augustine, calls *vestigium, imago,* and *similitudo.*

A vestige is a "certain representation of the divine likeness" (*DDN*

---

79. *ST* 1.105.1 ad1 and *SCG* 1.93.790.

80. The static meaning denotes a creature's likeness to God simply by reason of its grade of being in the hierarchical scheme of things, whereas the dynamic sense refers to a creature's likeness to God by dint of its activity and operation (*SCG* 2.45–46; 3.20–21; *CT* 1.101; 1.103; *Quod.* 11.1.1 ad5).

9.3.833) in the creature insofar as the creature imitates the divine perfection.[81] The Latin *vestigium* originally refers to an animal's track, spoor, or
footprint, which leads to only an imperfect knowledge of the animal since
the vestige cannot represent the animal's actual shape or form.[82] When an
effect, then, represents its cause without possessing the cause's specific
likeness, that is, when it represents the causality of its cause but not the
cause's form of being—as happens when smoke and ashes represent a fire,
or a land's desolation represents a hostile army—then the effect possesses
the cause's vestige, which is able to point out that something has passed or
happened but not exactly who or what that something is.[83] In all creatures
there is found both a vestige of the divine nature—for some only insofar
as they exist but for others also insofar as they live—and a vestige of the
Trinity, inasmuch as every creature possesses a finite nature (Father), a
form or species (Son), and a grade or order within the universe (Holy
Spirit).[84] The vestigial representation of God in creatures is a distant and
obscure likeness, which permits only a confused knowledge of God.[85]

Thomas' doctrine of humans and angels as images of God is based primarily on Genesis 1:26 and Augustine's Trinitarian analogies, with some
collateral help from a few patristic theologians.[86] He tries to distinguish in-

---

81. *SS* 1.3.2.2; cf. 2.16.1.2 ad1; *SCG* 1.8.48; *Job* 11.110–14; *CT* 2.8.38–43; *Eph.* 3.3.149. Individuals in the genus of substance are especially vestiges of God (*SS* 1.3.2.3).

82. *SS* 1.3.2.1; 1.3.3.1.

83. *ST* 1.45.7; 1.93.6; *DP* 9.9.

84. *SS* 1.3.2.1; *Decretalem* 1.66–78; *DP* 9.9; *ST* 1.45.7; 1.93.2; 1.93.6.

85. *SCG* 4.26.3633; *SS* 1.3.2.1.

86. T. Camelot ("La theologie de l'image de Dieu," *RSPT* 40 [1956]: 443–71), discusses the
Greek patristic dossier on the theology of the image of God. John Sullivan shows how Augustine is the most significant source for Thomas' doctrine of the human as the image of the
Trinity, though he also uses Hilary of Poitiers and John Damascene (*The Image of God*
[Dubuque, IA: Priory Press, 1963], pp. 216–72). Cf. Olegario Gonzalez de Cardedal, *Teología
y antropología: El hombre "imagen de Dios" en el pensamiento de Santo Tomás* (Madrid: Editorial Moneda y Credito, 1967); and Battista Mondin, "La dottrina della *imago Dei* nel commento alle Sentenze," in Studi Tomistici, vol. 2, *San Tommaso e l'odierna problematica teologica* (Rome: Pontificia Accademia Romana di S. Tommaso d'Aquino, 1974), pp. 230–47.
According to Jaroslav Pelikan, Thomas' doctrine of the image of God "formed the fundamental presupposition for natural theology in his thought" ("*Imago Dei*: An Explication of
Summa theologiae, Part 1, Question 93," in *Calgary Aquinas Studies*, ed. A. Parel [Toronto:
PIMS, 1978], p. 28).

tellectual creatures as images of God from all other creatures as vestiges of God, by stressing the image as a specific copy that in some way imitates the imaged reality. The concept of image adds to the concept of mere likeness the notion of being copied from another, of being produced in imitation of another (thus one egg is not the image of another since the first is not copied from the second). However, not just any likeness copied from another suffices, for the nature of image requires that the copy express something of the essence or at least the external shape of the imaged reality.[87] Thus prepared linguistically, and with Genesis 1.26 as his justifying standard, Thomas argues that intellectual creatures are closest to God in that they alone know and love and experience the felicity that springs from intellectual contemplation, in which the divine happiness is also to be found; and thus only intellectual creatures, which constitute the ultimate grade of divine imitation, are said to be made in the image of God.[88] As images of God, intellectual creatures represent not only God's causality (like the vestiges of God) but also God's specific divine form.[89]

However, in order to protect God's transcendence while at the same time differentiating image from vestige, Thomas makes a distinction between the perfect and the imperfect image. The perfect image imitates both the specific nature of some reality and the external sign of the specific nature, as a son imitates his father both in his human species and in his outer shape, which is the external sign of the human species. The imperfect image imitates only the external sign of the specific nature and not its true inner being, as a stone statue imitates the external human figure. The image of God in intellectual creatures is an imperfect one, for such creatures do not share God's specific nature though they do really participate

87. SS 2.16.1.1; ST 1.93.1. Whereas the vestige is an imperfect likeness of something, "the image represents a reality more exactly according to all its parts and dispositions of parts, by which one may perceive even some aspects of the reality's interior qualities" (SS 1.3.3.1). Image "gets its name from imitating" (Col. 1.4.31) and "denotes an exact representation" (SS 1.3.4.4).

88. SS 2.16.1.2; DV 10.1 ad5; ST 1.93.2. Only those creatures are the image of God that "on account of their excellence imitate and represent God more perfectly" (SS 1.3.3.1). The image of God in the human is said to be copied from God as from a model (ST 1.93.1).

89. DP 9.9; ST 1.45.7.

in God's being.[90] Thomas remarks that the imperfect nature of the divine image in humans is implied by the nuanced language of Genesis 1:26, which states that humans are made "toward the image of God" (*ad imaginem Dei*), for the *ad* implies approach from a distance.[91] While he depends upon the notion of specific likeness in order to distinguish image from mere vestige, it turns out that the specific likeness in the case of God and intellectual creatures must be imperfect rather than perfect, analogical rather than univocal and formal, for in other texts he is quick to point out that no creature shares a generic or specific likeness with God but only a "likeness of analogy."[92] All creatures, then, however Thomas tries to differentiate the vestige from the image of God in them, possess an analogical likeness to God.

Aquinas' discussion of the various deepening levels of the human image of God reveals dynamic, eschatological, and Trinitarian motifs at the heart of his outlook about the *imago Dei*, which is heavily indebted to Augustine's *De Trinitate*. *ST* 1.93.4 notes three stages by which humans bear an intensifying image of God. First, there is the "image of creation" found in all humans, which is identified with the human capacity to know and love God and consists in the very nature of the mind itself. Second, there is the "image of re-creation" found only in the justified, which occurs through grace and by which the justified, either actually or habitually, know and love God, however imperfectly. Finally, there is the "image of similarity" found only in the blessed, which takes place through the "likeness of glory" and by which the saints in beatitude know and love God actually and perfectly. Aquinas repeats Augustine by asserting that the human image of the Trinity occurs primarily in actual instances of knowing and loving, and only secondarily in the habits and powers of the mind.[93] Moreover, the increasingly actualized human image of God also turns toward ever more

---

90. *SS* 2.16.1.1. *SCG* 4.26.3632 says the divine likeness in humans is like a stone sculpture of Hercules, which represents the external shape but not the true inner nature of the hero. *ST* 1.35.2 ad3 notes the difference between a king's image found in something of the same nature (his child) and in something of a different nature (a coin).

91. *SS* 1.3.3.1ad5; *1 Cor.* 11.2.604; *ST* 1.35.2 ad3; 1.93.1. Cf. *SS* 2.16.1.1 ad2; *SCG* 3.19.2007.

92. *DP* 3.4 ad9; *ST* 1.4.3. Cf. *SS* 1.2.1.3 (pp. 68–69); *ST* 1.44.3.

93. *ST* 1.93.7; cf. *DV* 10.3.

exalted objects for its acts of thinking and loving: first we know and love objects outside ourselves, then we bear an even deeper image of God as we know and love ourselves, and finally the image of God exists most profoundly within us as we behold and love, in an eternity of intense actuality, the Trinitarian God.[94]

iv. Participation: Aquinas' Christian View of the Universe

Aquinas teaches a doctrine of participation, either categorical or transcendental, whose philosophic provenance is the Platonic Ideas, Neoplatonic emanationism, and the Aristotelian distinction between act and potency.[95] His thought, which fuses the Platonic/Neoplatonic and Aris-

---

94. *ST* 1.93.8. Cf. *SS* 1.3.4.4; *DV* 10.7. See A. N. Williams for an emphasis about how Aquinas' theology of the *imago Dei* is heavily influenced by his conviction that union with God is humanity's eschatological destiny (*The Ground of Union: Deification in Aquinas and Palamas* [New York: Oxford, 1999], pp. 68–72).

95. Louis-B. Geiger, *La participation dans la philosophie de S. Thomas d'Aquin*, BibThom 23 (Paris: Vrin, 1942); Cornelio Fabro, *La nozione metafisica di partecipazione secondo S. Tommaso d'Aquino*, 2nd ed. (Turin: Società editrice internazionale, 1950); idem, *Participation et causalité selon S. Thomas d'Aquin* (Paris/Louvain: Béatrice-Nauwelaerts, Publications Universitaires, 1961); idem, "The Intensive Hermeneutics of Thomistic Philosophy: The Notion of Participation," *RM* 27 (1974): 449–91; W. Norris Clarke, "The Limitation of Act by Potency: Aristotelianism or Neoplatonism," *NS* 26 (1952): 167–94; idem, "The Meaning of Participation in St. Thomas," *PACPA* 26 (1952): 147–57; Rudi te Velde, *Participation and Substantiality in Thomas Aquinas* (Leiden: Brill, 1995); John Wippel, "Thomas Aquinas and Participation," in *Studies in Medieval Philosophy*, ed. John Wippel (Washington, DC: CUA, 1987), pp. 117–58; idem, *Metaphysical Thought*, pp. 94–131, 590–92. Geiger thinks there are two separate systems of participation in Aquinas: participation by composition and participation by similitude in the hierarchy of beings (pp. 77–217, 223–307), but Fabro thinks Aquinas only teaches the former kind, which is based on the distinction between essence and existence in creatures (*Nozione*, pp. 20–23; *Participation*, pp. 63–73). Te Velde leans to Fabro's more unitary view but criticizes his theory of participation by composition because it invariably implies an essence that must "exist" somehow before it is composed with *esse*; referring to Aquinas' account of God's seamless creative act, te Velde argues for just one type of participation in Aquinas, which is grounded in the real distinction between being and essence in creatures (pp. 76–116, 184–206). Montagnes (*Doctrine*, pp. 45–60) confirms Geiger's view: Aquinas teaches both a participation by way of formal likeness based on God's exemplary formal causality and a participation by way of composition based on God's efficient causality, but the former is underscored in the *Sentences*, while the latter is accentuated beginning with the *Summa contra Gentiles*. Wippel agrees that Aquinas teaches two types of participation—by composition and by assimilation or imitation—and argues

totelian streams that had remained independent for centuries, combines and changes what it extracts from these sources, disengaging participation from its matrices in the Platonic Forms and Neoplatonic One, and radicating act and potency—beyond every imagining of Aristotle—in being as the act of essence.[96]

"To participate is, as it were, to 'take a part', and so when something receives in a partial fashion *(particulariter)* that which belongs wholly *(universaliter)* to another, it is said to participate in it": the human participates in animality since the human does not possess the nature of animal according to its whole extension; for the same reason, Socrates participates in humanity, the subject in its accident, matter in its form, and the effect in its cause—in each case, the first member of each pair restricts, determines, or lessens in some way the universality or power of the second member (*BDH* 2.24). Possessing something by participation is opposed to possessing it essentially or totally. Thomas notes that Plato considered material reality to participate in the Forms or Ideas. The Form or Idea, being simply the specific nature itself, is thus the nature essentially and is called "human-in-itself," and so on. But the individual material substance also possesses, in addition to the nature, an individuating matter, and so it is said to participate in the Form (*Meta.* 1.10.153–56). "For whatever is totally something does not participate in it but is essentially *(per essentiam)* the same as it. But whatever is not totally something, because it has another thing added to it, is properly said to participate"; fire, for example, since it also has something other than heat, participates in heat, but a heat existing essentially all on its own would not participate in heat, since nothing but heat would be in it.[97] To totally possess a form or perfection means that the subject has all of it there is to have and has nothing else but it, and to essentially possess a form or perfection is really the same as possessing it to-

---

against te Velde that participation by composition does not imply that a creaturely essence must possess some sort of actual reality in itself before it is created with its corresponding act of being in an actual creature (*Metaphysical Thought*, pp. 129–31). Jan Aertsen concurs with Montagnes and Wippel (*Nature and Creature: Thomas Aquinas's Way of Thought*, trans. H. D. Morton [Leiden: Brill, 1988], pp. 182–90).

96. Fabro, *Nozione*, pp. 338–62; and both articles by Clarke.

97. *Meta.* 1.10.154; cf. *Heb.* 1.3.47; *SDC* 4.114.

tally, in the sense that a subject possesses totally and exclusively the essence of some perfection.[98] In this sense, however, only God and angels can possess anything totally and essentially, for only they can possess some perfection infinitely and in such a fashion that it exists in them unmixed with anything else (God absolutely and angels relatively).[99] But this suggests that Thomas' doctrine of participation is another way of asserting from a philosophical perspective the crucial theological truths that God is the infinite and perfect act of subsistent being, and that the being and essence of creatures are really distinct.

Everything participates in the being derived from God the first being, but God can participate in nothing,[100] for God as the subsistent act of being is most actual, but the participating subject is always potential; and since nothing is more formal or simple than being, which is the ultimate act participable by all creatures, God as the very nature of being cannot participate in anything more actual than himself, but the creature as "that which exists" is able to participate in something more actual than itself.[101]

98. Fabro capsulizes Thomas' view of participation: a subject is said to participate in some form or act when it possesses that form or act, but not in an exclusive and total way, and when some relationship exists between the subject participating in the form and that which is the form essentially (*Nozione*, p. 322). Clarke mentions three elements in Thomas' theory of participation: a source possessing some perfection unrestrictedly; a participating subject possessing the same perfection in a partial manner; and a dependence of the participating subject upon the unparticipating source, in order to obtain the perfection ("Meaning," p. 152). When Thomas speaks about divine predication, he usually distinguishes predication through participation (as when Socrates is called human because he possesses humanity) from essential predication (as when God is called good not as merely possessing goodness but as being goodness itself), which is the strong sense of essential predication (*SCG* 1.32.289; *DDN* 12.1.949; *DP* 7.7 ad2–3). In a few cases, however, where essential predication cannot be understood in its strong sense to mean the total and exclusive possession of some perfection, he asserts that a species or genus is never predicated according to participation but always essentially, since, for example, a human is truly and essentially an animal, "and not only something participating in animal" (*Meta.* 7.3.1327–28).

99. Perhaps Thomas thought the sun was a pure substantiation of fire and light unmixed with anything else, and the only individual of its kind in all the universe—though we know otherwise today. All his other illustrations of unparticipated material perfections (e.g., essentially subsisting heat or whiteness) are mere hypotheticals. The only genuine examples of unparticipating subjects are God, who is the totally simple act of absolutely infinite being, and angels, whose relatively simple essences are relatively infinite, in the sense that they are not constricted or determined by any material component of their being.

100. *SCG* 1.22.210; same: *SCG* 2.52.1280; *Quod.* 2.2.1.

101. *SCG* 1.23.214; 1.38.313; 3.19.2006; *DA* 6 ad2; *DP* 7.2 ad8; *ST* 1.3.4.

Since nothing participated in is held as one's natural possession (*DV* 15.1), creatures are not their own being but possess their being as something clinging to their substance.[102] The participating subject is compared to the participated perfection as potency to act, and every creature is composed of such participating and participated elements.[103] Thomas proves that everything other than God exists by participation since whatever exists essentially causes whatever exists by participation; but God is the unique case of essential being, and thus everything else exists by participation.[104] "Every created being *(ens)* participates, so to speak, the nature of being *(essendi)*, since God alone is his own being *(esse)*."[105] For Aquinas, participation is another way of expressing the truth that God as the subsistent act of being causes the creature whose being is distinct from its essence. Moreover, knowing God as the very act of unparticipating being allows one to know the creature as the participating complexus of act and potency. Participation is not so much a way to God as it is a way from God, that is, a philosophical device Thomas borrows in order to explain and elucidate the theological connection between Creator and creation.[106]

While God has every mode of perfection, the creature, which does not "possess being according to its total power," participates in being and every other perfection in a partial, limited, and imperfect fashion.[107] "A being *(ens)* is said to be that which finitely participates in the act of being *(esse)*" (*SDC* 6.175), and "the participated act of being is finitized to the capacity of the participating subject" (*ST* 1.75.5 ad4), for "whatever is participated is not received in the participating subject according to its total infinity but in a particularized manner."[108]

The creature's participation *in* God is linked to the theme of the crea-

---

102. *Quod.* 2.2.1; *SCG* 1.29.273.

103. *SCG* 2.53.1285; *ST* 1.75.5 ad4; *Quod* 3.8.1; *Phys.* 8.21.1153.

104. *SCG* 2.15.926; 3.66.2413; *SDC* 9.231.

105. *ST* 1.45.5 ad1; cf. *DP* 6.6 ad5.

106. Participation "is a condensed technical way of expressing the complexus of relations involved in any structure of dependence of a lower multiplicity on a higher source for similarity of nature" (Clarke, "Meaning," p. 152).

107. *SCG* 1.28.262; 1.32.288. Cf. *DDN* 11.4.934; *DSS* 8.109–16, 199–218; *Ethic.* 10.11.160; *SDC* 12.279; *Caelo* 2.18.463.

108. *SDC* 4.109; cf. *SDC* 5.145–46; *DV* 2.3 ad16.

ture as the dependent likeness *of* God. The fact that creatures have only through participation what God *is* essentially means that the likeness of creatures to God is not generic or specific but analogical (*ST* 1.4.3 ad3). Aquinas can express the relationship between participation and likeness in different ways. Sometimes he places them side by side: "Created being is a certain participation and likeness of God" (*DDN* 5.2.660). Sometimes he says that the creature's imitation of God is according to participation,[109] or speaks of the "participation of the divine likeness" (*John* 17.3.2214). Elsewhere, he says that the creature participates in God through imitation (*DV* 23.7 ad10), or speaks of "participation according to likeness."[110] "Creatures are not said to participate in the divine goodness as if they were a part of God's essence but because they are constituted in being through the likeness of the divine goodness, according to which they imitate the divine goodness not perfectly but partially."[111]

Finally, Thomas' doctrine of participation, indebted to the Neoplatonism of Dionysius, is a kind of shorthand for his Christian outlook on how God is the cause and goal of the hierarchical structure and order of the universe. "The goal of the world's governance is the essential Good, and all things tend toward participating in and becoming likened to that Good" (*ST* 1.103.4). Without actually mentioning the word, the following quote shows how participation is at the heart of Thomas' view of the universe:

The order of reality means that higher beings are more perfect than lower beings, and that what is contained in lower beings deficiently, partially and in a multiple fashion is contained in higher beings eminently and through a certain totality and simplicity. And so in God, as in the highest summit of reality, all things exist supersubstantially according to his own simple act of being. (*ST* 1.57.1)

v. Truth and Epistemology

Aquinas' theology of the divine names—to be discussed in the next chapter—especially the positive theology at its center, rests squarely on the

109. *SS* 1.2.1.3, *sed contra*.
110. *SCG* 1.75.642. A creature actually exists insofar as it "participates through likeness in the first and pure act" (*Quod.* 12.4.1).
111. *SS* 2.17.1.1 ad6; same: *SS* 3.27.2.4.3 ad1.

paramount truths of his systematic theological ontology, in which his faith leads the way. That theological ontology—God as the infinite and pure act of subsistent being, God as the transcendent and immanent Creator who freely chooses to create finite creatures with all their perfections, creatures as the likeness and image of God, and the doctrine of participation—both underscores his faith conviction that creation is intimately connected to its Creator and grounds his epistemology and semantics of transcendental analogy.[112] As Fabro has neatly expressed it, participation is the special ontology of analogy, and analogy the special semantics of participation.[113] Furthermore, although Aquinas never explicitly adverts to it, the crucial truths of his theological ontology also require that transcendental analogy, the epistemological heart of his positive theology, have at its own core something like the Dionysian paths of cause, negation and eminence, for even the causal positivity at the nucleus of analogy must be corrected by negation and transcended by eminence if our analogical judgments are to do justice to the incomprehensible mystery of God.[114]

112. Robert Meagher writes that for Aquinas, "the analogy of divine names . . . is rooted in the analogous causation of God as creator" ("Thomas Aquinas and Analogy: A Textual Analysis," *Thomist* 34 [1970]: 252). For Faucon (*Aspects néoplatoniciens*, pp. 674–75), Aquinas situated analogy in the context of creative causality, in which "analogy expressed the paradox of a creature radically dependent upon and absolutely different from God. . . . Such was the conviction Thomas Aquinas strove to explicate by elaborating a new doctrine of analogy conformed to the etiological norms of the Mosaic revelation." K. Surin holds that Aquinas' theory of analogy is based on a revealed theology of creation, which "must take the form of an ontology for the *imago Dei* if the analogy theory is to be an adequate theory of statements *about* God" ("Creation, Revelation, and the Analogy Theory," *ITS* 32 [1981]: 412).

113. Fabro, *Participation*, pp. 634–40; pp. 509–622 treat of the connections between causality, participation, and analogy. Agreeing with Fabro, Montagnes sees analogy and participation as rigorously parallel, since they are, respectively, the conceptual and real aspects of the unity of being (*Doctrine*, p. 114). For Clarke, Thomas bases analogy on causal participation and similarity ("Analogy and the Meaningfulness of Language about God: A Reply to Kai Nielsen," *Thomist* 40 [1976]: 81–88; cf. idem, *The Philosophical Approach to God* [Winston-Salem, NC: Wake Forest University, 1979], pp. 51–61).

114. A few writers have interpreted analogy within a Thomistic perspective as involving the Dionysian ways, but without ascribing the notion to Aquinas. Henri Bouillard notes that analogy has all three moments since "it is a synthesis of a thesis and an antithesis," where the way of eminence is the synthesis (*The Knowledge of God*, trans. S. D. Femiano [New York: Herder and Herder, 1968], p. 109). Ralph McInerny asserts that even affirmative divine names have moments of negation and eminence ("Can God Be Named by Us? Prolegomena to Thomistic Philosophy of Religion," *RM* 32 [1978]: 53–73). Colman O'Neill considers

Part Four, then, will examine Aquinas' theology of the divine names, which is how he invariably casts his discussion of theological epistemology and its related issues.

---

the threefold way within analogy and positive theology as a dialectic of mutually correcting judgments, not of contrary concepts that could then result in some "higher" concept of God ("Analogy, Dialectic, and Inter-Confessional Theology," *Thomist* 47 [1983]: 52–53, 59–60); even the judgment "God exists" displays moments of negation and eminence (idem, "La prédication analogique: l'élément négatif," in *Analogie et dialectique,* ed. P. Gisel and P. Secretan [Geneva: Labor et Fides, 1982], pp. 85–88).

Part Four. The Divine Names

10. Aquinas' Positive Theology of the Divine Names

1. Divine Names

The introduction, in the twelfth and thirteenth centuries, of grammar, dialectic, and the logic of language into the bosom of theological speculation on God's nature helped to create and sustain the tract "On the Divine Names" as an addition to the treatise on the divine essence.[1] Aquinas is the heir and continuator of this tradition. To understand his doctrine of the divine names we must first grasp his general theory of names.

---

1. For some informative pages on the gradual formation of the treatise on the divine names, from the Alexandrians up to the immediate precursors of Alexander of Hales, see the historical introduction in Ernst Schlenker, *Die Lehre von der göttlichen Namen in der Summa Alexanders von Hales* (Freiburg: Herder, 1938). According to Schlenker, the treatise makes use of the grammar, logic, and dialectic found in Aristotle, the Boethian commentaries, Abelard, the *logici moderni*, the School of Chartres, and theologians such as Praepositinus of Cremona and William of Auxerre. For a comparison of Lombard's and Aquinas' treatises on the divine names, see Cornelio Fabro, "Teologia dei nomi divini nel Lombardo e in Tommaso," *Pier Lombardo* 4 (1960): 77–93. Francis Catania ("'Knowable' and 'Namable' in Albert the Great's Commentary on the *Divine Names*," in *Albert the Great: Commemorative Essays*, ed. F. J. Kovach and R. W. Shahan [Norman: University of Oklahoma, 1980], pp. 97–128) finds Albert the Great more agnostic than Francis Ruello does on our ability to know and name God (*Les "noms divins" et leur "raisons" selon saint Albert le Grand, commentateur du "De divinis nominibus,"* BibThom 35 [Paris: Vrin, 1963]).

A. Theory of Names

What does Aquinas understand by the phrase *ratio nominis*? *DDN* 7.5.735 remarks that the word *ratio* can mean four things: a cognitive power; the cause of something; a process of reckoning; or "something simple abstracted from many, e.g., that which is abstracted from singulars through [intellectual] consideration, and pertains to human nature, is called the *ratio hominis*."[2] This last sense of *ratio* concerns a mental concept or meaning expressing the nature of something existing in many singulars. *Ratio hominis*, then, signifies human nature as understood, that is, the concept or meaning of humanity.[3] This is also the pertinent sense for the expression *ratio nominis*, which refers to the concept or meaning of a name.[4] *Nomen* (name), broadly understood to include both noun and verb, denotes a word used to signify "one simple understanding" or "a simple concept," whereas the sentence signifies a composite understanding.[5] Moreover, "the meaning *(ratio)* which the name signifies is the definition of the thing," and thus the *ratio nominis* signifies the definition meant by a name.[6]

Following a venerable tradition, Thomas distinguishes between a name's etymology (*id a quo imponitur nomen*: the linguistic component from which a name is derived) and its actual meaning (*id ad quod imponitur nomen*: that which a name signifies).[7] He likes to use the example of the noun *lapis* (stone): although *lapis* is derived etymologically from

2. *Ratio* is one of those brimmingly polysemic words. For its various meanings in Aquinas, see Julien Péghaire, *Intellectus et ratio selon saint Thomas d'Aquin* (Ottawa: Institut d'Études Médiévales, 1936), pp. 14–18.

3. As denoting the formal cause, *ratio* signifies the nature or form of something (cf. *SS* 2.13.1.2; *Phys.* 1.13.118; *DSS* 9.69–72). In terms of *ratio*'s fourth meaning mentioned in the text, then, the phrase *ratio hominis* can be taken objectively to signify the form of human nature as abstracted from individual humans; the phrase, however, by reference to the objective reality of human nature, can also quite easily and naturally signify the meaning of *human* as a concept.

4. The meaning of a name is distinguished from its mere external sound *(vox)*, and *ratio nominis* is equivalent to the "meaning *(significatio)* of a name" (*SCG* 1.33.293, 295).

5. *Herm.* 1.4.44; 1.6.75. Cf. *Herm.* 1.3.35; 1.4.45; 1.5.66; 1.6.79; 2.2.214.

6. *Meta.*, 4.16.733; same: *John* 1.1.25; *ST* 1.13.1; 1.85.2 ad3; *Herm.* 1.2.20.

7. *SS* 1.23.1.2 ad1; 1.24.2.2 ad2; *ST* 1.13.8; *Herm.* 1.4.44–45. The distinction between *impositio ab* and *impositio ad* was well known in the Middle Ages and goes back at least to Varro (d. 27 B.C.) in his *De lingua latina* (5.2), where he speaks of a word's being used *(imponere)*

laedere pedem ("to injure the foot," which stones tend to do), it does not *mean* a foot injury but signifies rather the concept of a stone.[8] Furthermore, in texts worthy of a medieval Frege, he also recognizes the distinction between a name's meaning and its range of reference.[9] The process of naming, therefore, comprises three components: the etymological derivation of a name, the actual meaning of a name, and the name's referential extension.

The name signifies reality[10] through the mediation of the intellect, for "the exterior word is a sign of [the intellect's] understanding, and such an understanding is the sign of reality" (*Herm.* 1.8.90); again, "by convention, the name is a word signifying a simple understanding, which is the likeness of reality" (*Herm.* 1.10.119); and thus the meaning of a name is "the intellect's conception of the reality signified through the name" (*ST* 1.13.4). The intellect mediates the process of naming, for "according to the Philosopher, words are signs of intellectual understandings, and such understandings are likenesses of things; and so it is clear that words are used to signify things by the mediating conception of the intellect."[11]

Thomas closely relates the intelligible meaning of a name to the reality signified by the name, but also distinguishes them:

---

both *a qua re* and *in qua re*, noting that the Greeks called the former *etymologia* and the latter *peri sēmainomenōn* (concerning the signified).

8. *Herm.* 1.4.44–45; same: *SS* 1.23.1.2 ad1; *DP* 9.3 ad1; *ST* 1.13.2 ad2; 1.13.8; 2-2.92.1 ad2. The *lapis* example is well-worn: Peter Helias had already used it around 1140 (cf. Charles Thurot, *Extraits de divers manuscrits latins pour servir a l'histoire des doctrines grammaticales au moyen âge* [Frankfurt: Minerva, 1964; repr. from *Notices et extraits des manuscrits de la Bibliothèque Impériale*, vol. 22/2, Paris, 1868], pp. 146–47).

9. *SS* 1.2.1.3; 1.4.1.1; 2.9.1.4; 3.6.1.3; *Herm.* 1.8.96. In his *Instituto Grammatica* 2.5 (ca. 500), Priscian asserts that the *nomen* signifies *substantia cum qualitate*, i.e., a subject under the determination of some form or quality. Following Priscian, medieval grammarians and logicians drew a distinction between a name's *substantia* and *ratio* (also known as the *forma* or *qualitas*). The *substantia* is the name's reference or material supposition, and the *ratio* is its formal meaning. Cf. See M.-D. Chenu, *La théologie au douzième siècle* (Paris: Vrin, 1957), pp. 100–107; Ralph McInerny, *The Logic of Analogy: An Interpretation of St. Thomas* (The Hague: Nijhoff, 1961), pp. 54–57; Ruello, *Les "noms divins,"* pp. 33–35. The medieval contrast between *ratio* and *substantia* is equivalent to Frege's famous distinction between *Sinn* and *Bedeutung*, sense and reference.

10. "Every name is used to signify the nature or essence of some reality" (*SCG* 1.22.211).

11. *ST* 1.13.1; same: 1.13.4 ad1; *Herm.* 1.10.121. Cf. McInerny, *Logic of Analogy,* pp. 61–64.

The meaning of anything is what its name signifies . . . but names are signs of intellectual concepts, and hence the meaning of anything signified through a name is the intellect's concept which the name signifies. This concept of the intellect is certainly in the intellect as in a subject, but it is also in the reality understood as in something represented, for intellectual concepts are certain likenesses of understood realities. . . . Therefore, the meaning of *stone* is certainly in the intellect as in a subject, but it is also in the stone as in that which causes the truth of the intellect's concept, which understands the stone to be such as it is.[12]

SS 1.2.1.3 also states that the meaning of a name exists in reality "insofar as in the reality outside the soul there is something that answers to the soul's concept, as the signified to the sign." But the intellect's concept is related in three ways to what exists in reality outside the soul: the concept may be the likeness of the thing existing in reality, and then it has "an immediate foundation in the thing, insofar as the thing itself, because of its conformity to the intellect, brings it about that the intellect's understanding is true and that the name signifying that understanding is properly predicated of the thing"; the concept may be a product of the human manner of understanding what is outside the soul in reality (e.g., the concept of genus), and such a concept has its immediate foundation in the intellect itself and its remote foundation in reality; and the concept may be a chimerical one without foundation in reality and thus in fact false. When the intellect's concept is a likeness of the thing, however, then the meaning of the name signifying that concept is said to be in reality insofar as "the thing signified by the name . . . exists in reality." Moreover, the article also asserts that for those realities possessing a definition, the meaning of a name is the definition of the reality, though this cannot be the case for those realities lacking a strict definition. Thus, the meaning of the word *quality*—which cannot be strictly defined in terms of genus and specific difference since it is already one of the ten highest genera of being—is "that which is signified by the name of quality, which is that by which quality is quality"; further, "the meaning of the wisdom which is predicated of God is whatever is conceived of this name's meaning, though the divine wisdom itself cannot be defined."

12. *R108*, Prologue, p. 279, lines 1–17; cf. *SCG* 1.34.298.

Aquinas teaches, therefore, that the name's meaning is the mind's concept, which is a likeness of the reality. The meaning of a name is subjective in the sense that it immediately refers to the concept within the mind, but it is also objective since it ultimately refers to the reality that causes the truth of the concept whose sign the name is. Normally the name's meaning refers to the definition, unless the reality in question has no definition. Crucial to Aquinas' explanation are the notions of likeness and representation, and the idea of the mind's concept as the product of the intellect's understanding.

B. On Naming God

Since we know God by reason or faith, and since whatever is known can be signified linguistically, it is clear that God is nameable by humans, although because naming follows knowing and because we know God only imperfectly, we can only name God haltingly, "as if by stammering"; indeed, only God can name God perfectly, "by generating a word equal to himself."[13] God can be named only to the degree that God can be understood: God cannot be named by us with a name expressing the divine essence (as *human being* expresses the human essence) but can be known and named from creatures according to the Dionysian threefold way of cause, eminence, and negation.[14] When faced with citations from scripture or other sources remarking on our inability to name God, Thomas tempers any radical negative theology lurking in them and interprets them to mean not that we cannot know or name God in any way at all, but that the divine essence is above all our knowing and naming. For example, when Dionysius says that of God there is neither sense, nor imagination, nor opinion, nor name, nor word, nor touch, nor knowledge, Thomas understands this to mean that no name expresses God perfectly (*SS* 1.22.1.1 ad1). Augustine's statement that God is not accessible to our intellect means that it is not possible to comprehend God perfectly.[15]

---

13. *SS* 1.22.1.1, *sed contra* and body of article.

14. *ST* 1.13.1. "Names which belong to creatures are attributed to God inasmuch as God's likeness is somehow represented in creatures" (*DV* 2.1 ad11); cf. *DP* 7.10 ad8.

15. *SS* 1.22.1.1 ad2; cf. *ST* 1.13.1 ad1. For Aquinas on the divine names, see Jan Walgrave, *Selected Writings*, ed. G. de Schrijver and J. Kelly (Louvain: University Press, 1982), chap. 3;

Sometimes Aquinas adverts to the distinction between a name's etymology and its actual meaning when discussing how a particular name may be predicated of God. He notes, for example, that the word *person*, whatever its etymology, actually signifies a complete substance and thus can be used properly of God (*SS* 1.23.1.2 ad1). He implies that although *person* may be traced etymologically to the mask through *(per)* which an actor speaks *(sonare)*, what the word actually *means* is a complete substance of a rational nature. Invested with such a proper meaning even among humans, *person* can also be used properly of God, bearing in mind the cautioning caveats of negative theology. Elsewhere he holds that while God is entirely perfect, perfection could not be attributed to God if we were only to consider the etymological origin of the word *perfect*, which comes from *per* (an intensifying preposition meaning "thoroughly") and *factus* ("made"), so that a creature is said to be perfect when it has been "thoroughly made"; for *perfect* in the sense just mentioned cannot be predicated of God since God is not made at all. Nevertheless, by a certain extension of the name, *perfect* may be said not only of that which reaches its completion by a process of making but also of that which "exists in complete act without any making."[16] In another text Aquinas relies on the distinction between a name's formal meaning and its referential extension (*SS* 1.2.1.3). Asserting that the meaning of a name is more a matter of its proper signification than of its range of reference, he claims that creaturely names can be applied to God if we consider their actual meanings but

---

David Burrell, "Aquinas on Naming God," *TS* 24 (1963): 183–212; idem, *Aquinas: God and Action* (Notre Dame: UND Press, 1979); idem, *Knowing the Unknowable God: Ibn-Sina, Maimonides, Aquinas* (Notre Dame: UND Press, 1986); John Wippel, *The Metaphysical Thought of Thomas Aquinas: From Finite Being to Uncreated Being* (Washington, DC: CUA, 2000), pp. 502–43. Rolf Schönberger's work, *Nomina divina: zur theologischen Semantik bei Thomas von Aquin* (Frankfurt/Bern: Lang, 1981), is written from a linguistic perspective. Mark Jordan notes that the predication of the divine names in Aquinas, while valid, ultimately fails linguistically to make God present, but that this negation is paradoxically the surest approach to God ("The Names of God and the Being of Names," in *The Existence and Nature of God*, ed. A. J. Freddoso [Notre Dame: UND Press, 1983], pp. 161–90). For a feminist perspective on the divine names and God-language in general, see Gail Ramshaw, "*De Divinis Nominibus:* The Gender of God," *Worship* 56 (1982): 117–31; idem, *God beyond Gender: Feminist Christian God-Language* (Minneapolis: Fortress, 1995).
    16. *SCG* 1.28.268; cf. *DDN* 2.1.114.

not if we focus on what they are applied to: for example, if we think of the name *wisdom* as "applied to a certain quality," then wisdom must be denied of God since God has no accidental qualities. The implication is that we can separate the deficient modes of predication that occur when wisdom is attributed to an accidental quality, and simply focus on the actual meaning of the name.[17]

At certain points, then, Aquinas' explicit treatment of the divine names seems to be based on three presuppositions: the name signifies the concept, which is the product of the intellect's act of simple understanding; names are discrete units of meaning within propositional wholes; and a name can be extended, from within the name itself, to signify a pure perfection that can then be predicated of God. However, other areas of Aquinas' thought, including his practice of basing theological epistemology on the truths of theological ontology, allow the interpreter to discover an epistemology in Aquinas that is more contextual and wholistic, as we have seen at some length in parts two and three of this book. For there we found that the concept can be the fruit of judgment and carry a contextual sense within the whole proposition,[18] and that creaturely names denoting perfections are analogically extended to God not prior to but simultaneous with our knowing a truth about God.

II. Aquinas' Positive Theology

In addition to the negative theology we investigated in chapters 2 and 3, Aquinas strongly subscribes to a positive theology[19] that acknowledges the

17. However, what permits Aquinas to predicate wisdom essentially rather than accidentally of God is not the distinction between actual meaning and referential extension but rather his recognition of the truth that everything in God is to be identified with the divine essence. Thus, although his explanation appears to presuppose an a priori grasp of the pure meaning of some perfection untethered as such to deficient creaturely modes, in actuality his interpretation bases itself on his prior recognition of certain fundamental truths about God.

18. Burrell writes that Aquinas' empirical theory of meaning is one where the "unit of meaning is the statement and not the word and whose attention is directed to use as well as structure" (*Analogy and Philosophical Language* [New Haven: Yale, 1973], p. 139).

19. The English adjective *positive* comes from the Latin verb *ponere*, meaning to place or

affirmative, proper, and substantial predication of God's divine attributes. We shall examine nine of the most prominent texts, in their chronological order, where he describes and justifies his positive theology.

1. *SS* 1.2.1.3. In this article Thomas argues against the negative and causal interpretations of divine predication. He asks whether the realities signified by the divine attributes exist in God, noting two opinions in this matter. The first, which he assigns to Avicenna and Maimonides, is that since God is subsistent being without an essence, the divine attributes can be true only by way of negation or causality, inasmuch as they either remove defects from God (negative interpretation) or give God a name because he causes the creaturely reality signified by the name (causal interpretation).[20]

---

posit. In terms of theological epistemology, positive theology posits various attributes as really and truly existing in God, which is not what positive theology means in the context of historical or systematic theology.

20. For Maimonides' position on the predication of the divine names, see *The Guide of the Perplexed* 1.50–60 (trans. with introduction and notes by S. Pines [Chicago: University of Chicago, 1963]). According to *Guide* 1.58, terms that are perfections for us (e.g., *living*) are necessarily predicated of God in affirmative propositions with predicates that are positive in form ("God is living"), but logically these propositions *mean* the negation of the opposite ("God is not mortal"); but terms that are imperfections for us (e.g., *mortal*) must be predicated of God either in negative propositions ("God is not mortal") or in affirmative propositions that use predicates negative in form ("God is immortal"). Harry Wolfson discusses Maimonides' negative interpretation of the divine attributes in *Studies in the History of Philosophy and Religion,* ed. I. Twersky and G. H. Williams, 2 vols. (Cambridge: Harvard, 1973–77), vol. 2, chap. 5; in vol. 1, chap. 8, Wolfson shows that Avicenna, Algazali, and Averroes also sometimes used the negative interpretation of divine attributes positive in form. For the profound religiosity that undergirds Maimonides' negative theology, see Diana Lobel, "'Silence Is Praise to You': Maimonides on Negative Theology, Looseness of Expression, and Religious Experience," *ACPQ* 76 (2002): 25–49; and Kenneth Seeskin, "Sanctity and Silence: The Religious Significance of Maimonides' Negative Theology," *ACPQ* 76 (2002): 7–24. *SS* 1.2.1.3 is Thomas' most detailed treatment of Maimonides' position. C. Vansteenkiste lists the texts where Thomas mentions Maimonides explicitly ("Autori Arabi e Giudei nell'opera di San Tommaso," *Angelicum* 37 [1960]: nos. 98–174 on pp. 374–93; for Thomas' view of Maimonides' negative theology, see nos. 100, 131, 167–71). For comparisons of Maimonides and Aquinas, see Jacob Dienstag, ed., *Studies in Maimonides and St. Thomas Aquinas* (New York: KTAV, 1975); C. L. Miller, "Maimonides and Aquinas on Naming God," *JJS* 28 (1977): 65–71; Alexander Broadie, "Maimonides and Aquinas on the Names of God," *RS* 23 (1987): 157–70; Avital Wohlmann, *Thomas d'Aquin et Maïmonide: Un dialogue exemplaire* (Paris: Cerf, 1988); Neil Stubbens, "Naming God: Moses Maimonides and Thomas Aquinas," *Thomist* 54 (1990): 229–67; David Burrell, "Maimonides, Aquinas, and Ghazali on Naming God," in *The Return to Scripture in Judaism and Christianity: Essays in Postcritical Scriptural Interpretation,* ed. Peter Ochs (New York: Paulist, 1993), pp. 238–46; also see his

But it follows from this opinion, Thomas states, that all names said of God and creatures would be predicated equivocally (he notes that Maimonides expressly says this),[21] and that there would be no likeness of the creature to the Creator. For according to such an opinion,

> whatever is conceived about the names of the attributes is not referred to God so that it may be a likeness of something which is in God. Thus it follows that what is meant by those names is not in God so that they might have a proximate foundation in him. . . . According to this opinion, the things meant by these attributes are only in the intellect and not in the reality which God is.

Others, like Dionysius and Anselm, propound the second opinion, that "whatever perfection is in creatures exists in God preeminently." Perfections exist in God preeminently since God has all perfections at once, since each of the divine perfections is complete and without defect, and since all of them are one in God. According to this opinion, "the concepts which our intellect conceives of the names of the attributes are true—though deficient and partial—likenesses of the reality which God is." The attributes also have a "proximate foundation in the reality which God is," and thus they belong to God truly *(recte)* and properly *(proprie)*.

Thomas then offers an ingenious argument whose aim is to show that these two opinions are different only superficially and actually agree if one looks to the reasons for which they are asserted. The first opinion, looking to created realities and realizing that among creatures, for example, wisdom is an accidental quality and essence a nonsubsisting principle, denies wisdom and essence as proper attributes of God since everything in God subsists and nothing in God is an accidental quality. But the second opinion considers the modes of perfection from which the divine names are taken, and "since God according to one simple being is perfect in all

---

Knowing the Unknowable God, pp. 51–65; Stephen Lahey, "Maimonides and Analogy," *ACPQ* 67 (1993): 219–32; Idit Dobbs-Weinstein, *Maimonides and St. Thomas on the Limits of Reason* (New York: SUNY, 1995).

21. Maimonides teaches that terms signifying God's attributes can be neither univocal nor ambiguous *(amphibola)* but must be equivocal *(Guide,* 1.56). "No other philosopher before him, whether writing in Greek or Latin or Arabic or Hebrew, has explicitly interpreted divine attributes as equivocal terms" (Wolfson, *Studies,* 2:231). Wolfson adds that by calling the divine names equivocal Maimonides refers to the fact that they are negative in meaning.

modes, which are signified by names of this sort," this opinion claims that the divine names "are appropriate for God positively *(positive)*," that is, are appropriately posited of the divine being. Neither opinion denies what the other says: the first would not claim that any mode of perfection is lacking to God, nor would the second admit any quality or other nonsubsistent reality in God.[22] The conclusion must be that the realities signified by the divine attributes truly *(vere)* exist in God.

2. *SS* 1.22.1.2. Aquinas asks whether anything can be predicated properly of God, the *sed contra* showing that proper or literal predication is opposed to metaphorical predication *(symbolice* or *metaphorice* or *transumptive)*. Although every perfection in creatures comes from God, the creature's way of possessing the perfection fails to represent the divine model perfectly. Since the names we predicate of God always signify the divine perfections according to the way in which creatures participate in them, these names always fail to represent God perfectly in their manner of signifying them. If, however, we consider the reality signified by the name, we find that certain names are principally used to signify the absolute perfection itself that comes from God and do not refer to any particular mode as part of their meaning, whereas other names are meant to signify a perfection received according to some manner of participation. For example, all types of knowledge have their exemplar in God, but the term *sensation* is meant to signify knowledge through the mode of material reception in a bodily organ, while *cognition* does not signify any particular manner of participating as part of its principal meaning. The names that are meant to signify some absolute perfection are properly and literally predicated of God, names such as *wise* and *good,* which, as Anselm

22. C. L. Miller sees Aquinas and Maimonides as closer to one another in their views on the naming of God than is commonly thought ("Maimonides and Aquinas"). Wohlman accentuates Thomas' doctrine of analogy as the defining difference between him and Maimonides, and claims that Thomas is more original than Maimonides even in how he interprets the negative aspects of language about God (*Thomas d'Aquin et Maïmonide,* pp. 105–64). Dobbs-Weinstein advises us that Maimonides and Thomas use different theories of language and address different problems (*Maimonides and St. Thomas,* pp. 186–87), while Kenneth Seeskin, in a similar fashion, sees their differences as rooted in the divergent presuppositions and goals of their theories of the divine names (*Searching for a Distant God: The Legacy of Maimonides* [New York: Oxford, 2000], pp. 44–53).

says, "it is absolutely and totally better for something to be than not to be." But those names signifying perfection in such a way that their very meaning includes an imperfect manner of participating "are in no way predicated properly of God but still may be predicated metaphorically of God because of that perfection." Such metaphorical names—feeling, sensing, seeing, stone, lion, and the like—signify various physical realities according to a definite manner of participating in existence or life.

Aquinas assigns the imperfect and determinate way of participating in God's perfections to the realm of material reality. That is, he does not see this limited manner of participating as proper to creatures as such but only to physical creatures. Thus, he views absolute perfections as proper to spiritual creatures, and perfections that include an imperfect manner of participating as proper to material creation.[23] Moreover, he does not tell us how he knows that certain things are absolute perfections, though the quote from Anselm would seem to suggest that it is from our human experience that we come to know what sorts of things it is absolutely better for a subject to be than not to be.[24]

3. *SS* 1.35.1.1 ad2. This response in an article about the knowledge of God argues for the proper predication of the divine names against the dispositional, negative, and actional interpretations. There are three opinions as to how names such as *life, being,* and *knowledge* are said of God. The first opinion says that such names signify in God certain dispositions added to the divine essence (dispositional interpretation). But this would imply composition and potentiality in God, "which is totally absurd." The second opinion asserts that, except perhaps for *being,* these names predicate no positive reality of God and thus are not said literally of God. Nevertheless, for two reasons they are predicated of God: on account of negation, so that

---

23. A later theology will distinguish between pure and mixed perfections.

24. Aquinas often appraises the pure or mixed quality of perfection terms by reference to the fundamental truth that God is pure spirit, a truth he uses to combat the position that would want to literally ascribe to God those perfection terms based on human experiences involving a bodily component. In today's theological climate, where there is often no firm consensus on the basic truths to be held about God, what is or is not a pure perfection term is also frequently debated, since various emotional and cognitive acts involving a bodily component do appear as pure perfections (as better to have than not to have) *for human beings.*

when God is said to be knowing, for example, what is really meant is that he is not ignorant, as a stone is; and on account of a "similarity of works," whereby God is said to know because he performs the actions that a knowing subject performs (actional interpretation)—thus, just as God is said to be angry because he punishes like an angry person, not because anger is literally in him, so is he said to be knowing or living. Against the negative interpretation, Thomas argues that every negation is founded on something positive. Against the actional interpretation, he reasons that a particular action is the way it is because of the nature of the agent from which it proceeds; thus, if God performs the actions of a knower, then God must in some fashion *be* a knower. The third opinion, which Thomas favors, is that such names are properly and literally predicated of God as regards the reality they signify *(res significata)* but not as regards their manner of signifying it *(modus significandi)*.[25]

4. *DV* 2.1. This passage also deals with God's knowledge. After disposing of the dispositional and metaphorical interpretations of divine predication, Aquinas critiques the causal interpretation (e.g., that God is said to be a knower because he causes knowledge in creatures) on the grounds that we would then have to predicate of God whatever he causes—for example, God would have to move because he causes motion—which is not permitted. Moreover, those attributes predicated of both cause and effect are not said to be in the cause because of the effect, but vice versa. Thus, "from the fact that God has a cognitive nature he infuses knowledge in us, not conversely." Names such as *knowledge, life,* and *essence,* therefore, do signify some reality in God.

Our intellect, however, is not able to represent God through being assimilated to God, in the way it can represent creatures. For whenever our intellect understands some creature, it conceives a certain form which is a likeness of the thing according to its total perfection, and so the intellect defines the thing; but because God infinitely exceeds our understanding, the form conceived through our understanding cannot completely represent the divine essence but carries instead some slight imitation of it—as we also see is the case with entities existing outside the soul: namely, that everything imitates God in some way, but imperfectly.

---

25. The next chapter will be devoted to a detailed investigation of this crucial distinction.

Our concepts do not define but rather imitate God in some small way, just as extra-mental reality does. However, if a name can be properly applied to some object only by dint of signifying the object's definition, then no name we give to God is really proper to God since no name's meaning can ever define God. Thus, according to Aquinas, even those names that "signify some reality in God" cannot be proper names of God.

Whereas in the first three texts Aquinas argues for the proper predication of the divine names, here he denies it. It is interesting to note that the divine infinity of *DV* 2.1, which here helps preclude the proper predication of the divine names, is also a fundamental reason, as we saw in chapter 5, for Aquinas' short-lived preference in the same article for the analogy of proper proportionality.

5. *DP* 7.5. This article argues, against the actional and negative interpretations of Maimonides[26] and others, that divine names such as *good* and *wise* signify the divine substance. It counters the actional interpretation by reasoning that God, with equal reason, could then be called wise, angry, and fire, for when he punishes he acts like an angry person and when he purges he acts like fire. But this is contrary to the position of the saints and prophets, who want to assert certain things of God (living and wise) but deny others (that God has a body or is subject to passions). In the actional interpretation, however, "all things could with equal reason be predicated and denied of God."

For two other reasons the negative interpretation is not valid either. First, in that case any name could be used of God if all we mean by the name is to exclude some other trait. For example, *lion* means "four-footed" and thus excludes two-footed birds. If our predicates were meant only to exclude certain realities from God, therefore, we could assert that God is a lion on the grounds that he is not a two-footed bird. Secondly, every negation is ultimately based upon and proved through some affirmation. Thus, if we knew nothing affirmatively about God we could never truthfully deny anything of God.

26. Seymour Feldman contends that Thomas partly misunderstands Maimonides' theory of the actional attributes of God ("A Scholastic Misinterpretation of Maimonides' Doctrine of Divine Attributes," in *Studies in Maimonides and St. Thomas Aquinas*, ed. Dienstag, pp. 67–74).

Following the lead of Dionysius, Thomas announces his own position: the divine names "signify the divine substance, though deficiently and imperfectly . . . and not . . . as comprehending it."[27] Whereas univocal causes and their effects share the same form, the effect of an equivocal agent exists in that agent in a more eminent fashion. But no effect equals the power of God, and so no form can have in God the same nature it has in any of his effects, but the form exists in God in a higher way. All the diverse divine effects are united in God's power and likened to the simple divine essence. At this point, Thomas' theological ontology, built on God the transcendent Creator who makes creaturely perfections as likenesses of the divine essence, asserts itself in his theological epistemology:

Since our intellect receives its knowledge from created realities, it is informed by the likenesses of the perfections found in created realities, e.g., of wisdom, power, goodness, etc. Hence, just as created realities through their own perfections are somehow made similar to God, though deficiently so, so also our intellect is informed by the intelligible forms of these perfections.

Since "knowledge is a similarity of the intellect to the reality known," and since the intelligible form is that by which the intellect is enlightened and assimilated to the reality known, "those things which the intellect, informed by the perfections of these intelligible forms, thinks or enunciates about God must truly exist in God, who corresponds to each of the aforementioned forms as the entity to which all of them are similar." Note the priority of the ontology and the strict parallelism between ontology and epistemology: our intellect gains its knowledge from created perfections that are ontologically likened, in deficient fashion, to God, and so when it is enlightened by the intelligible forms of these perfections it is likewise made similar, in deficient fashion, to God.

Thomas concludes the body of the article by underscoring the imperfect way in which we know God through the divine names. The divine names signify "that which the divine substance is (id quod est divina sub-

27. John Wippel finds that not until the *De potentia* and after does Thomas *explicitly* claim that some names apply to God substantially or essentially, the occasion provided by his debate with Maimonides' and others' extreme agnosticism concerning the divine names (*Metaphysical Themes in Thomas Aquinas* [Washington, DC: CUA, 1984], pp. 229–40; *Metaphysical Thought*, pp. 527–40).

stantia) but do not perfectly signify it according to what it is *(secundum quod est)* but according to how it is understood by us *(secundum quod a nobis intelligitur).*" The care with which he expresses his thought demonstrates his concern to uphold a positive theology that predicates divine names of the divine substance *(id quod est)* while at the same time rejecting any intuitive knowledge of the divine substance *(secundum quod est)* unjustifiably hiding under the aegis of that positive theology. Thomas' position is a mean, then, between the sort of negative theology that so stresses God's incomprehensibility that the divine names cannot be literally predicated of God's substance, and the kind of positive theology that at worst is tantamount to an essentialist knowledge of God or at least sees the predicates applied to God and creatures as univocal. He is claiming in his positive theology a truth *about* God's substance and at the same time denying any insight *into* God's substance. Most paradoxically, he is at once claiming a knowledge *about* God and admitting an ignorance *of* God.[28]

In the answers to objections, Thomas reinterprets certain statements from respected authorities that might be taken as propounding an excessive negative theology, modulating their meaning so that they might be in-

28. Consider the subtle differences in the positions of two of Aquinas' most famous twentieth-century commentators, Jacques Maritain and Étienne Gilson. Maritain, interpreting Aquinas' statement that certain names signify "that which the divine substance is," writes that such names "do indeed tell in some manner what God is," and that we can "know what God is in a more-or-less imperfect, but always true, fashion" (*The Degrees of Knowledge,* trans. under the supervision of G. B. Phelan from 4th French ed. [New York: Scribner, 1959], p. 425). But Gilson contends that Aquinas is only assuring us that such names designate the divine substance "as actually being what the names signify," which can occur without any positive concept of the divine substance (*The Christian Philosophy of St. Thomas Aquinas,* trans. L. K. Shook [New York: Random, 1956], p. 458, n. 47). "To escape the 'agnosticism of quidditative concept' to which some are ill resigned where God is concerned, it is not necessary to seek refuge in a more or less imperfect concept of the divine essence, but in the positive character of affirmative judgments," which still leave God's essence totally unable to be conceptualized (ibid., n. 51). Gerard Hughes, referring to perfection terms in Aquinas' doctrine of God, writes similarly: "We know something about the truth-conditions for the application of such terms to God; for we know that those truth-conditions obtain. But we do not know what those truth-conditions consist in. In other words, we know something *about* the meanings of these terms used analogically of God, since we know that they are related to the meanings of the same words used of ourselves: but we do not know what they mean when used of him" ("Aquinas and the Limits of Agnosticism," in *The Philosophical Assessment of Theology* [Washington, DC: Georgetown University, 1987], p. 51).

tegrated into his positive theology. In general, he will view these statements as denying a perfect knowledge of God, not as disallowing any positive knowledge of God at all. One objection quotes John Damascene to the effect that the names we predicate of God do not signify what God is essentially but indicate rather what he is not or some kind of relationship with creatures; Thomas responds that Damascene simply means that these names do not signify what God is "as if by defining and comprehending his substance" (ad1).[29] When Augustine tells us that God "escapes" every form of our understanding, we hear from Thomas that "God escapes the form of our understanding by exceeding every form of our understanding, not in such a way, however, that our understanding is not made similar to God at all according to some intelligible form" (ad13).

6. *DP* 7.6. Here Aquinas marshals several arguments against the causal interpretation of the divine names, which understands "God is good" to mean "God exists and causes goodness." If the causal interpretation were true, then all the names of God's effects could be applied to God with equal reason—for example, the heavens could be predicated of God since God causes them (which is clearly untrue in Aquinas' eyes). Again, we could not say God was good from eternity unless he were actually causing goodness from eternity (but for Aquinas God has always been good, even without creation).[30] Further, a cause must be *X* before an effect can be *X*:

29. Same: *ST* 1.13.2 ad1. For John Damascene's theory of divine predication, see *De fide orthodoxa* 1.4; 1.9 (PG 94:798–800, 833–38; FC 37:170–72, 189–90). For Damascene, it is impossible to say what God is in essence, and so names do not signify God's essence (*kat' ousian*—this is the *secundum quod est* Thomas also rejects, but Damascene lacks anything corresponding to the *id quod est* Thomas allows) but show one of four other things: either what God is not *(ti ouk esti)*, or some relation *(schesis)* to something that is distinguished from him, or the things that accompany *(parepomenōn)* the divine nature, or the divine activity *(energeia)*. Names such as *without beginning* and *incorruptible* belong to the first type, *Lord* and *King* to the second type, and *good, just, holy,* and *wise* to the third or fourth types, for these latter do not show the nature or essence itself but the "things around the nature" (*ta peri tēn physin*—PG 94:800BC, 836A, 837AB; cf. *De fide* 1.12 [PG 94:848AB]). However, *being (ho ōn)* and *God (theos)* are different: the former name displays God's essence and existence, while the latter manifests his operation (PG 94:836B–837A). Thus, Damascene recognizes negative divine names and two positive divine names, *being* and *God*. All other seemingly positive names are to be interpreted either relationally, actionally, or as pertaining to the divine energies radiating from God's core essence.

30. "From eternity it was true to say that God is wise and good, even granting that creatures were not in existence then and would never exist in the future" (*SS* 1.2.1.2).

"God is not called wise, then, because he causes wisdom but it is because he is wise that he therefore causes wisdom."[31]

7. *ST* 1.13.2. This article asks whether any name can be predicated of God's substance. Thomas begins by noting that two classes of names do not place anything in God's substance—those said negatively of God and those expressing God's relation to creatures.[32] There are several opinions, however, as to the signification of the names predicated of God absolutely (rather than relatively) and affirmatively (rather than negatively)—such as *good, wise,* and so on. He then describes the negative and causal interpretations of these names that we have seen in earlier texts, associating Maimonides' name with the first but giving no names for the second.[33] Employing the same arguments (now focused on the question of whether God is a body or not) against these positions as we have seen above in *DV* 2.1 and *DP* 7.5–6, he shows them to be weak interpretations of God's affirmative and absolute names.

Thomas then states his own position that affirmative and absolute names are predicated of God substantially *(substantialiter)*,[34] though they fail to represent God perfectly, just as creatures only imperfectly represent God. Since our intellect knows and names God from creatures, it knows and names God to the degree that creatures can represent him. But Thomas notes he has already shown (in *ST* 1.4.2–3) that God already possesses all the perfections of creatures since he is absolutely and universally perfect.

31. "God is not called wise because wisdom is from him, but a created entity is called wise inasmuch as it imitates the divine wisdom" (*SS* 1.2.1.2); God is called wise because "insofar as we are wise we somehow imitate his power by which he makes us wise" (*SCG* 1.31.280). These two quotes and the one in the text are to be taken ontologically rather than gnosiologically, for "from the wisdom which God causes, our intellect is led to attribute supereminent wisdom to him" (DP 7.5 ad4). *SS* 1.2.1.3 ad1 reveals the distinction between ontological and epistemological priority in a trenchant sentence: "Although the cause's condition *(conditio)* is known from the effect's conditions, the cause's condition is not nevertheless confirmed in its reality and truth *(verificare)* on account of the effect's conditions, but vice versa."

32. Although he gives no examples, Thomas is undoubtedly thinking of qualitative negations such as *immortal* and relative names such as *Creator* (God cannot be Creator without a relationship to creatures).

33. He probably has Alan of Lille in mind. Wolfson (*Studies,* 2:504–6, 524) names others who also held the causal interpretation, including Maimonides (*Guide* 1.53).

34. For *substantialiter, ST* 1.13.6 substitutes the synonym *essentialiter.*

Any creature, therefore, represents and is similar to God to the degree that it has some perfection, not representing God as something of the same species or genus but as a transcendent principle whose effects fail to match its nature but whose likeness they nevertheless attain in some measure. . . . When, therefore, it is said that "God is good," the meaning is not "God is the cause of goodness" or "God is not evil," but "that which we call goodness in creatures preexists in God according to a higher mode." From all of this, then, it does not follow that to be good belongs to God insofar as he causes goodness, but rather the other way around, that because he is good he diffuses goodness to things.

Thomas' positive theology packs quite a lot into "God is good": the proposition means that the creaturely quality we call goodness preexists in God in a more excellent way than it exists in creatures.[35] His ontology grounds his epistemology, and the two are tied together by the notions of likeness and representation.[36]

The answer to objection three makes a crucial distinction, insisting that while we can know and name God's substance as it is represented in the perfections of creatures (which is equivalent to the *id quod est divina substantia* of *DP* 7.5), we cannot in this life possess an intuitive insight into God's essence as it is in itself (*secundum suam substantiam,* which is the same as the *secundum quod est* of *DP* 7.5).

At this juncture we need to forestall a possible cause of misunderstanding. Thomas does not consider the minimalist negative and causal interpretations of the affirmative divine names to be the same as the entirely valid denials of qualitative negative theology or the Dionysian ways of negation and causation, despite the fact that similar terminology is employed. *ST* 1.13.2 shows that his rejection of the negative interpretation of the divine names is not tantamount to denying qualitative negative theo-

35. *ST* 1.13.6 says that "God is good" means, besides the fact that God causes goodness, that goodness preexists in God "more eminently" than in creatures. Gerard Hughes states that for Aquinas, "God is wise" means "that God is whatever it takes to ground the fact that he is the explanation of all human wisdom" ("Aquinas," p. 52).

36. Klaus Riesenhuber sees similarity, representation, and the doctrine of participation at the heart of Thomas' positive theology ("Partizipation als Strukturprinzip der Namen Gottes bei Thomas von Aquin," in Miscellanea Mediaevalia, vol. 13/2, *Sprache und Erkenntnis im Mittelalter* [Berlin/New York: de Gruyter, 1981], pp. 969–82). Cf. Günther Pöltner, "Die Repräsentation als Grundlage analogen Sprechens von Gott im Denken des Thomas von Aquin," *SJP* 21–22 (1976–77): 23–43.

logy or Dionysius' *via negativa,* for the negative interpretation is presented as one of the possible ways of understanding the absolute and affirmative divine names, from which he has *already* distinguished the negative names of qualitative negative theology. Thomas accepts God's negative *names* but rejects the negative *interpretation* of God's affirmative names. He sees a similar difference between the causal interpretation of the affirmative names, which he does not think is adequate, and the Dionysian way of causality, which he supports and employs in his own theology. Whereas the causal interpretation is opposed to the substantial predication of the divine names, the way of causality is actually one of the means Thomas uses in order to establish the latter. The difference between the causal interpretation and the way of causality is evident in *DP* 7.5 ad4, where he is explaining Origen's contention that God is called wise because he fills us with wisdom. Origen does not mean to assert, writes Thomas, that when we say "God is wise" we merely mean that God is the cause of wisdom (the causal interpretation), but that because of the wisdom God causes, our intellect is led to ascribe supereminent wisdom to God (i.e., the way of causality leads us to predicate transcendent wisdom of God).[37]

8. *ST* 1.13.3. This passage seeks to demonstrate that some of God's names are predicated properly *(proprie)* of the divine being, where *proprie* means "truly and really" as opposed to metaphorically. The *sed contra* cites Ambrose to the effect that whereas some names "point to the real nature of divinity" *(proprietatem divinitatis ostendere)* and "express the clear truth of the divine majesty" *(perspicuam divinae maiestatis exprimere veritatem)*, others are said of God "metaphorically, through a likeness" *(translative per similitudinem)*. Aquinas informs us we may consider two elements in the names we attribute to God: the perfections themselves signified by names such as *good* and *living,* and our manner of signifying those perfections. With respect to what is signified, then, names such as these belong prop-

---

37. Thomas implicitly distinguishes the causal interpretation from the way of causality in *ST* 1.13.11 ad3 and *DDN* 1.2.45. Wolfson (*Studies* 1:125–26; 2:497–509, 522–23) conflates and confuses Thomas' understanding of the negative and causal interpretations of the affirmative divine names with Thomas' understanding of the Dionysian ways of negation and causality.

erly to God, but as regards our manner of signification they are not properly predicated of God since this manner belongs only to humans.

The response to objection one, highly reminiscent of *SS* 1.22.1.2 discussed above, explains the reason for the difference between proper and metaphorical predication.

Certain names signify perfections proceeding from God into created realities, but in such a way that the imperfect mode itself by which the divine perfection is participated in by the creature is included in the very meaning of the name, as *stone* signifies something that is a material being; and names of this sort can only be attributed to God metaphorically. But certain names signify the perfections themselves absolutely, without including some mode of participating in their very meaning—as *being, good, living,* etc.—and such names are properly predicated of God.[38]

Aquinas implies that the "imperfect mode" is not to be identified simply with creaturehood as such but with the condition of materiality.[39] The response to objection three adds a further nuance: whereas names predicated properly of God do connote physical conditions as regards their manner of signifying, names predicated metaphorically of God signify a physical condition as part of their very meaning.[40]

9. *ST* 1.13.12. This article takes up the paradoxical task, necessary for any positive theology, of showing that affirmative propositions, which involve

---

38. Cf. *SS* 1.4.1.1; 1.34.3.2 ad3.

39. When the principal signification of a name includes matter, which cannot be attributed to God, then that name can be predicated only symbolically *(symbolice)* of God; but names can be predicated nonsymbolically of God when their meanings contain no defect or dependence upon matter (*DV* 2.11). For example, neither the externally spoken word nor the word produced by the imagination can be said properly of God, but only the word of the heart produced by the intellect, for only this latter word "is wholly removed from materiality, bodiliness, and every defect" (*DV* 4.1.217–21). Since quantity results from matter, no type of quantity can be predicated of spiritual realities except metaphorically, but some qualities may be properly ascribed to spiritual realities since certain qualities may be entirely immaterial (*DP* 9.7). Since light is a physical quality perceivable by the senses, it can be said of spiritual realities only metaphorically (*SS* 2.13.1.2; *ST* 1.67.1).

40. *SS* 1.22.1.2 ad4 states that a physical condition in a name's principal meaning makes it false as a predicate of God, but imperfection in the manner of signifying renders a predication not "false or improper" but only "imperfect." We can speak of God from the physical realities of the world insofar as every creature represents the divine goodness in some measure, and thus names can be transferred metaphorically to God inasmuch as what is signified by them is a sign of the divine goodness (*DV* 23.3; cf. *DV* 7.2.66–74).

the complex combination of subject and predicate, can be truthfully formed about the simple, uncomplex God.[41] In every true affirmative proposition, subject and predicate must somehow signify the same thing in reality *(res)* while differing in their meaning *(ratio):* "the man is white," for example, means that the man and the white are identical in subject but differ in meaning, for the "meaning of man" and the "meaning of white" differ; again, "the human is an animal" means that the same reality that is a human is also an animal, for in the same subject both a sensate and a rational nature exist so that the subject is called both animal and human—the subject and predicate being identical in subject *(suppositum)* but different in meaning.

Even in propositions where the same thing is predicated of itself, the case is still in some way the same, inasmuch as what the intellect expresses by the subject pertains to the supposit and what it expresses by the predicate pertains to the nature of the form existing in the supposit, as it is said, "predicates are understood formally and subjects materially." The plurality of subject and predicate corresponds to the diversity of meaning, but the intellect signifies their identity in reality through their very composition. Considered in himself God is totally one and simple, but our intellect nevertheless knows him according to different concepts, since it cannot see him as he is in himself. However, although it understands him through different concepts, it nevertheless knows that what corresponds to all these concepts is one and the same absolute reality. The intellect represents this plurality in meaning through the plurality of predicate and subject, but represents the unity through the composition.

The human mind, according to Aquinas, knows the truth of God's unity and simplicity even as it expresses this truth through the propositional composition that it cannot avoid, for somehow its understanding of divine simplicity transcends the complex rational processes connatural to itself.

In conclusion, from the texts studied in this section one may construct an outline of Aquinas' theology of the divine names. He arranges all the attributes or names that can be predicated[42] of God into three general class-

---

41. Cf. *SS* 1.4.2.1; *SCG* 1.36.302.
42. Names that denote only imperfection, defect, or evil (e.g., *sinful*) should never in any way be predicated of God.

es: (1) the negative names of qualitative negative theology, which are usually negative in form and meaning (e.g., *incorporeal*) but can also be positive in morphology though negative in meaning (e.g., *simple*); (2) relative names (e.g., *Lord* or *Creator*), which denote some kind of connection between God and creatures; (3) absolute and affirmative names (e.g., *good* or *lion*). Aquinas discusses five different interpretations of the meaning of the names in this third class, only the last of which he considers to be fully adequate: the dispositional, actional, negative, causal, and substantial interpretations, the last of which views affirmative and absolute names as signifying a positive truth about God's essence. Insofar as his positive theology[43] refers to predications that posit some affirmative truth about God's substance, both metaphorical and proper predication belong to it, the former imperfectly and the latter perfectly. For Aquinas, then, positive theology refers, in its fullest and deepest sense, to the predication of those affirmative and absolute names that signify a proper truth about God's very being.[44]

Theological analogy serves Aquinas primarily as an explanatory device for positive theology in its most developed state, for analogy helps to explain what is taking place in the substantial and proper predication of the divine names; at the same time, by avoiding equivocity and univocity, analogy prevents the theologian from falling into agnosticism on the one hand or from depreciating God's infinite and transcendent mystery on the other. Moreover, the proper and substantial attributes and names of God

43. Though Aquinas does not actually use the phrase *positive theology*, he does mention predicates that are said *positive* of God (e.g., SS 1.2.1.3) and certainly recognizes the reality denoted by the phrase as used here.

44. Colman O'Neill distills the medieval analysis of divine names into two elements: the way in which the name as predicate is related to God as subject, which results in relative, negative, or substantial predication; and the reality that the divine predicate directly signifies, which produces either proper or metaphorical predication ("Analogy, Dialectic, and Inter-Confessional Theology," *Thomist* 47 [1983]: 46–47). In a summary statement, Wippel describes Aquinas as allowing us a knowledge of God that is proper, substantial, and analogical, but that also, while not purely negative, can never be comprehensive, and in this life must remain nonquidditative and always ready to deny the *modus significandi* we employ in any predication of a divine attribute (*Metaphysical Thought*, pp. 574–75). See also Thomas Guarino, "The Truth-Status of Theological Statements: Analogy Re-Visited," *ITQ* 55 (1988): 140–55.

are subject to the critique of qualitative negative theology, never allow us to intuitively grasp or comprehend God's essence, and even in their analogical predication must be denied according to the requirements of modal negative theology, whether objective or subjective. Since the affirmative and proper names of God are partly established through the way of causality, critiqued through the way of negation, and always predicated in a manner consonant with the way of eminence, it is clear that Aquinas has successfully managed to integrate the Dionysian threefold way into his theory and practice of positive theology, though it is also patent that in order to do so he has had to tone down the more extreme formulations of the *via negativa* found in Dionysius and others.

III. *Proper Name of Divinity*

Aquinas mentions three candidates for the most distinctive and proper name of divinity: *Deus, Qui est,* and *Tetragrammaton* (referring to the four Hebrew consonants of *Yahweh,* God's sacred name). We will follow the order of questions he provides for us in *ST* 1.13.8–9, 11.

ST 1.13.8 asks whether the noun *Deus* names the divine nature. Using the stone example discussed in section I above, Thomas first distinguishes between a name's etymology and its proper meaning. In general, while a substance is originally known through its properties and operations, its name is used to designate the substance itself, and such is the case with God: while the name *God* is etymologically derived from the act of providence—for those who speak of God intend to give the name *God* to the one who shows universal providence over all things—the name is used to signify the divine nature.[45]

45. Same: *SS* 1.18.1.5 ad6; *God* signifies the "ruler and provider *(provisor)* of all things" (*Credo* 869). In *ST* 1.13.8 (cf. *DDN* 12.1.939) Thomas quotes Dionysius as explaining the etymological genesis of *God* by reference to the notion of providence. Objection one mentions three etymological meanings taken from John Damascene (*De fide orthodoxa* 1.9 [PG 94:836B–837A]), who sees them as based on divine operations. First, Damascene notes that the Greek *theos* can be derived from *theein* ("to run"), which, he adds in explanation, is *periepein ta sympanta* ("to treat with the whole universe")—the idea, apparently, is of God running about at the edge of the universe so as to be able to take care of it as a whole; Thomas faithfully renders *theein* by "to run" (cf. *Caelo* 2.1.290) and understands Dama-

From its effects we cannot know the divine nature as it is in itself so that we might know its inner essence, but we can know it through the way of eminence, causality and negation. And so the name *God* signifies the divine nature. For this name is used to signify some reality existing above all things which is the principle of all and removed from all. For this is what those who name God intend to signify. (*ST* 1.13.8 ad2)

For Thomas, the threefold way by which we know God also shows up in the very meaning of the name *God,* which designates the reality that is above all things, removed from all things, and the principle of all things.

ST 1.13.9 asks whether the name *God* is able to be communicated to or shared with other entities, the *sed contra* quoting Wisdom 14:21 about the "incommunicable name." Aquinas first contrasts two ways in which a name may be shared by many. A name is truly and properly communicable to others when its total meaning can be shared by many, but it is only communicable by similitude or likeness if just a part of its meaning is shared by many. For example, the noun *lion* may be truthfully shared among all those entities actually possessing the nature signified by the name, but it is only communicable by similitude to those entities that merely share in certain leonine qualities such as courage and strength— and these latter are called lions metaphorically.

Aquinas next remarks that every nature able to exist in and be individuated by more than one subject (e.g., human nature) is common to many individuals. Those natures unable to really exist in more than one individual subject (e.g., the nature of the sun)[46] are not common to many individuals in reality, though they may be considered as common to many in the opinion of certain people, for any nature, qua universal nature, can always be imagined as existing in many individual subjects. But the singular,

---

scene's added explanation as "to foster all things." Second, *theos* may be derived from *aithein,* which means "to burn," for, as Thomas quotes Damascene, "our God is a fire consuming all evil" (cf. *DV* 4.1 ad11; *Psalm* 13.1). Third, *theos* can be derived from *theasthai,* which means "to consider all things" (cf. *SCG* 1.44.381; *DDN* 12.1.948; *CT* 1.35; *Praeceptis,* p. 230). In his response to objection one, Thomas unites all three meanings in the central notion of providence (cf. *SDC* 3.65; 9.213). Curiously, he elsewhere describes the Latin *Deus* as derived from the act of distributing, inasmuch as God is the "giver of things" (*dator rerum*—*Praeceptis,* p. 230).

46. According to Aquinas' antiquated astronomy, the solar nature truly exists only in the single sun of our solar system, the other stars of the universe not being thought of as suns.

qua singular, is separate and distinct from all other beings, and therefore
the name used to signify a unique individual cannot be communicated to
many in either reality or opinion, for a unique singular *cannot even be
thought of or imagined* as existing in many. No name signifying an individual, then, is able to be properly communicated to many, but only
metaphorically, as someone may be called *Achilles* metaphorically on account of courage.

Since *God* is meant to signify the divine nature, and since the divine nature is unique and cannot be multiplied, the name *God,* in reality, cannot
be communicated to many individuals, though it is communicable to
many in opinion, just as the word *sun* is communicable to many individuals in the opinion of those who posit many suns.[47] Nevertheless, *God* is
communicable to many metaphorically, as those are called gods who participate in something divine through some likeness, as Psalm 82:6 says, "I
said, 'You are gods.'" However, if there were a name used to signify, not
God's nature, but God's unique subjectivity *(suppositum)* insofar as it is
considered to be "this individual something" *(hoc aliquid),* that name
would be in all ways incommunicable to all other individuals, as is perhaps
the case with the name *Tetragrammaton (Yahweh)* among the Hebrews—
it would be as if someone were to use the word *sun* to designate "this individual subject" *(hoc individuum).*

ST 1.13.9 ad3 clarifies the special status of the word *God:*

Although the names *good, wise* and the like are certainly taken from perfections
proceeding from God to creatures, they are still not used to signify the divine nature but rather those perfections themselves. And thus in truth and reality such
names are able to be shared with many. But the name *God* is taken from the distinctive operation of God, which we continually experience, in order to signify the
divine nature.

God means the divine nature, which cannot be really shared with any other being, since God is absolutely unique. Although perfection terms are
predicated of God substantially, and even though God's perfections are really identical with the divine essence, as *names* these perfection terms are

47. Aquinas notes at this point, following Lombard's gloss, that the *gods* of Galatians 4:8
("You were slaves to things that by nature are not gods") are so only in human opinion.

used by us to signify those perfections that God *is* infinitely and that creatures participate in finitely, not to signify the divine nature as such. Thus, both creatures and God can be given the names of these perfections in truth and reality, but the name *God* can truthfully be said only of the one God. Nevertheless, as *ST* 1.13.9 ad2 is quick to point out, even though the name *God* is incommunicable to many individuals in reality and truth, the fact that it is not a proper name, but an appellative name that "signifies the divine nature as existing in one that possesses it," permits it to be communicable to many in the opinion of some people (presumably polytheists).

ST 1.13.11 asserts that *Qui Est* is the most proper name of God,[48] that is, the name that most perfectly and unambiguously signifies God's unique and matchless reality. The *sed contra* quotes Exodus 3:13–14 on the revelation of *Qui Est* as God's name to Moses,[49] followed by three arguments in the body of the article.

Qui Est is the most proper name of God, first, on account of its meaning, for it signifies not just any form but being itself; and since God's being is identical with the divine essence, which is not true of any creature, *Qui Est* is the most proper and unique name of God.[50]

48. Same: *SS* 1.8.1.1; 1.8.1.3; *DDN* 5.1.632–39; *DP* 2.1; 7.5; 10.1 ad9; *John* 8.3.1179. *Qui est* can be translated as "He Who Is" or simply "Who Is," and is a third person masculine singular form based on Thomas' understanding of the Mosaic revelation of God's name as "I am who am."

49. The *sed contra* of *SS* 1.8.1.1 also mentions John Damascene and Maimonides as authorities; cf. *SCG* 1.22.211. For places in Thomas' works where he uses or discusses Exodus 3:14, see Émilie Zum Brunn, "La 'Métaphysique de l'Exode' selon Thomas d'Aquin," in *Dieu et l'être: exégèses d'Exode 3:14 et de Coran 20:11–24*, ed. P. Vignaux et al. (Paris: Études Augustiniennes, 1978), pp. 245–69; cf. Luis Clavell, *El nombre proprio de Dios segun Santo Tomas de Aquino* (Pamplona: Universidad de Navarra, 1980), pp. 19–37. For the patristic evaluation of *Qui Est* (the Latin authors especially see it as meaning eternity), see Clavell, *Nombre*, pp. 42–52. Zum Brunn notes that Augustine, while not the first to have given the ontological cast to the name of Exodus 3:14, makes abundant use of it throughout his commentaries, identifying being and immutability; he is the first of the Latins to relate the name revealed to Moses with the "I am" of John 8, and John Chrysostom is the first among the Greeks to do so ("L'exégèse augustinienne de *Ego sum qui sum* et la 'métaphysique de l'Exode,'" in *Dieu et l'être*, ed. P. Vignaux et al., pp. 141–64).

50. Cf. *SCG* 1.22.211; *SS* 1.8.1.1. *Qui Est* is the proper name of God "since it is characteristic of God alone for his substance not to be different from his being" (*SCG* 2.52.1281). For Thomas' originality in explaining *Qui Est* by his metaphysics of being as act, see Clavell, *Nombre*, pp. 52–63; cf. Ruello, *Les "noms divins,"* pp. 182–84.

Second, *Qui Est* is the most proper name for God on account of its universality and manner of signifying. All other names either are less common than *being* or, if they are coextensive with it, at least restrict it in idea (the transcendentals); hence, all other names limit being and give it a form in some way. Now our intellect in this life cannot know God's essence as it is in itself but always limits in some way whatever it understands about God, and in so doing fails to understand the way in which God exists in himself. Therefore, we more properly predicate of God whatever names are less restricted and more common and absolute. This is why Damascene states that *Qui Est* refers to God as "an infinite and indeterminate ocean of essence,"[51] for every other name is restricted by some mode of an entity's essence, whereas *Qui Est* is limited to no specific form of being but is related indeterminately to all things. This reason rests on the ability of *Qui Est* to point especially to the infinite and indeterminate status of God's being, which is characteristic of God alone.

Third, *Qui Est* is the most proper name for God on account of its way of consignifying time,[52] for it signifies being in the present tense, which is especially proper to God since the divine being knows neither past nor future.[53] *ST* 1.13.11 ad1 puts all the pieces together:

The name *Qui Est* is a more proper name for God than the name *Deus*, with respect to that from which it is derived, namely from being, and with respect to its mode of signifying and consignifying. . . . But with respect to what it is meant to signify, *Deus* is more proper since it is used to signify the divine nature. And a still more proper name is *Tetragrammaton*, which is used to signify God's incommunicable and, so to speak, singular substance itself.[54]

51. Damascene's quote is from *De fide orthodoxa* 1.9 (PG 94:836AB), where God is said to be like *ti pelagos ousias apeiron kai aoriston;* the quote is also found in *SS* 1.8.1.1 ad4, 1.22.1.4, obj. 4; *DP* 7.5; 10.1 ad9.

52. Here Thomas is referring to the fact that a verb always connotes some temporal index along with the action it denotes.

53. There is a fourth reason given in Thomas' works, one based on Dionysius' idea that the most noble and universal of all the participations of God's goodness is being (*DDN* 5.1.632–39; *SS* 1.8.1.1).

54. Besides *ST* 1.13.9, the Tetragrammaton is also mentioned in *SCG* 4.7.3408. Armand Maurer lists Jerome, Alcuin, and the Venerable Bede as possible sources for Thomas' idea of the Tetragrammaton as God's most proper name, but the most evident source is Maimonides (*Guide* 1:60–62), who like Philo before him regards the names *Qui Est* and *Tetragrammaton* as quite distinct ("St. Thomas on the Sacred Name 'Tetragrammaton,'" *MS* 34

iv. *Proper versus Metaphorical Predication*

The divine names signify God's perfections, and Aquinas construes them as perfection terms.[55] God is "absolutely and simply perfect," the one "in whom are found all the excellences existing in all categories of being."[56] God is the superlative degree of every possible perfection and thus a *super* can be prefixed to every perfection as it is predicated of him: for example, God is simultaneously most beautiful and above beauty *(superpulcher)*.[57]

The distinction between proper and metaphorical predication is linked to the question whether a predicate signifies perfection only or perfection together with imperfection.

Since every perfection, and no imperfection, is in God, any perfection found in a creature can be said of God with respect to the perfection itself, if every imperfection is removed. If a name, however, is based on something imperfect, as *stone* or *lion*, then it is said of God symbolically or metaphorically; but if it is based on something perfect, then it is said properly, though in a more eminent fashion. (*SS* 1.4.1.1)

All the names meant to "signify some perfection absolutely" are literally (*proprie* is Thomas' term) said of God, but the names signifying some perfection in such a way that they include an imperfect mode of participation in their very meaning (e.g., *feel, sense, see, stone*) "are in no way said literally of God, but by reason of that perfection, can still be said of God metaphorically" (*SS* 1.22.1.2).

[1972]: 275–86; cf. idem, "The Sacred Tetragrammaton in Medieval Thought," in *Actas del V Congreso Internacional de filosofía medieval*, 2 vols. [Madrid: Editoria Nacional, 1979], 2:975–83). Maurer contends that only the *Summa theologiae* suggests *Tetragrammaton* as a more proper name for God than *He Who Is*. In a few places Thomas feels the need to justify the Dionysian opinion that *Good* is God's most proper name, even though he realizes this opinion follows the Platonic manner of subordinating being to goodness (*DDN* 3.1.225–28; 13.3.994; but cf. *ST* 1.13.11 ad2).

55. He refers to these perfections as God's attributes (*SS* 1.2.1.2) or excellences *(nobilitates)*, this latter term being especially prevalent in his earlier works (*SS* 1.2.1.1–2).

56. *SS* 1.2.1.2, *sed contra;* cf. *SS* 1.8.4.2 ad3.

57. *DDN* 4.5.343; cf. 13.1.962. Hampus Lyttkens' insistence on seeing divine predication in Thomas as God's "belonging to a class" is untrue to Thomas' studious denial of just such a notion ("Die Bedeutung der Gottesprädikate bei Thomas von Aquin," *NZST* 6 [1964]: 284–86).

How are we to know the difference between absolute and "imperfect" perfections? Sometimes Thomas quotes Anselm's answer: "Everything which it is absolutely better to be than not to be must be attributed to God."[58] Nevertheless, the overall context for Thomas' appraisal of whether perfections are "perfect" enough for God to possess them is his knowledge that certain truths obtain about God. For example, while the *sed contra* of *SS* 1.2.1.2 asserts that God possesses "whatever excellence there is in anything," *SS* 1.2.1.1 ad2 from the preceding article shows that the situation is not so simple as that. The objection reasons that since everything is perfect insofar as it can produce in nature something similar to itself, and since God is most perfect, then God must be able to produce another divine essence similar to himself so that there will be several divine essences. Thomas responds that the perfection of the divine essence, which is identified with pure act, requires that it be unique, for a second divine essence would have to be potential with respect to the first divine essence and would therefore not be pure act; moreover, it is not necessary that whatever belongs to the excellence of a creature should belong to the excellence of the Creator (which rejects the unnuanced *sed contra* of *SS* 1.2.1.2), who exceeds the creature infinitely, just as ferociousness, which is a positive quality in a dog, would not be a positive quality in a human. For the purposes of the present section, then, it is important to observe that however helpful it might be to use Anselm's axiom as a preliminary criterion for deciding which perfections are to be predicated properly of God, the ultimate judgment is also based on the truths we acknowledge about God; for although the ability to reproduce all spiritual perfections *would* be a perfection *for us*, we nevertheless can grasp that such an ability is not a pure perfection for God once we realize that pure act can never reproduce itself.

DP 7.5 ad8 is another indication that Thomas decides whether a perfection is absolute or imperfect in the context of other truths about God. In order to explain the difference between proper and metaphorical predicates, this response notes that an effect may be likened to its cause but may

58. *SS* 1.2.1.2, *sed contra* (Thomas mistakenly ascribes the quote to Augustine). Anselm says with respect to things such as essence, goodness, and wisdom, which are properly said of God, that it is "absolutely and entirely better for them to be than not to be" (*SS* 1.22.1.2). The idea is from chapter 5 of Anselm's *Proslogium* and chapter 15 of his *Monologium*.

also differ from its cause. The example is a brick hardened by fire. Insofar as clay is heated it is similar to the fire that heats it, but when, having been heated, it condenses and hardens into brick, it then differs from the fire, and this is due to its material condition. The quality by which the brick is likened to the fire may be properly predicated of the fire, because the fire is hot by nature and the brick is hot because it has been heated by the fire. But the quality by which the brick differs from the fire, its hardness, is falsely predicated of the fire if the intention is to do so literally, though it may be predicated metaphorically of the fire. Those aspects of creatures by which they are similar to God signify no imperfection and so are predicated properly of God (e.g., to exist, live, and understand).

But there are some characteristics by which the creature differs from God (potentiality, privation, motion, etc.) due to the fact that it exists from nothing, and these are falsely said of God.[59] Whatever names include in their very meaning conditions of this sort cannot be said of God except metaphorically (*lion, stone,* etc.), because they have matter in their definition. They are predicated metaphorically of God, however, on account of a likeness of effect.

It is because one *already* knows that nothing material can be predicated literally and truly of God that ones realizes certain positive predicates implying matter can be said only metaphorically of God.[60]

---

59. These imperfections are in creatures "inasmuch as creatures exist out of nothing" (*SS* 1.2.1.2).

60. Contemporary theology has paid much attention to the role of metaphor in theological statements. With Paul Ricoeur's writings often serving as inspiration and warrant (*The Rule of Metaphor,* trans. R. Czerny, K. McLaughlin, J. Costello [Toronto: University of Toronto, 1977]; "Naming God," trans. D. Pellauer, *USQR* 34 [1979]: 215–27), metaphor is seen not merely as linguistic ornamentation, which was the case for Aquinas and the rest of the classical theological tradition, but as a creative production of new meaning stemming from imagination and insight (David Tracy, *The Analogical Imagination* [New York: Crossroad, 1981], pp. 405–45; Sallie McFague, *Metaphorical Theology: Models of God in Religious Language* [Philadelphia: Fortress, 1982]; Janet Martin Soskice, *Metaphor and Religious Language* [Oxford: Clarendon, 1985]; Garrett Green, "The Gender of God and the Theology of Metaphor," in *Speaking the Christian God: The Holy Trinity and the Challenge of Feminism,* ed. Alvin Kimel Jr. [Grand Rapids: Eerdmans, 1992], pp. 44–64). For the biblical imagery of God, see Virginia Mollenkott, *The Divine Feminine: The Biblical Imagery of God as Female* (New York: Crossroad, 1983); cf. Sandra Schneiders, *Women and the Word: The Gender of God in the New Testament and the Spirituality of Women* (New York: Paulist, 1986). Scholars have also studied the relationship between analogy and metaphor, frequently with special reference to Aquinas (Tracy, *Analogical Imagination,* pp. 405–45; Roger Hazelton, "Theolog-

Finally, although Thomas nearly always connects divine metaphorical predication with the notion of materiality and offers terms referring to material beings as examples of metaphorical predicates, materiality as such is not always required in order for a divine predicate to be metaphorical. For it is also true that any name expressing a perfection "with a mode proper to creatures" can be predicated only metaphorically of God, and names expressing such a mode are those used to designate either the specific nature of a created entity (such as *human* or *stone*) or the properties

ical Analogy and Metaphor," *Semeia* 13 [1978]: 155–76; David Burrell, *Analogy and Philosophical Language,* chap. 10; Cornelius Ernst, "Metaphor and Ontology in *Sacra Doctrina*," *Thomist* 38 [1974]: 403–25; Richard Swinburne, "Analogy and Metaphor," in *The Philosophical Assessment of Theology,* ed. Gerard Hughes [Washington, DC: Georgetown University, 1987], pp. 65–84; Ralph McInerny, *Logic of Analogy,* pp. 144–52; idem, *Studies in Analogy,* [The Hague: Nijhoff, 1968], chaps. 2 and 3; idem, *Rhyme and Reason: St. Thomas and Modes of Discourse* [Milwaukee: Marquette, 1981], pp. 33–43; Gerard Hughes, "Aquinas," pp. 52–60). Some see no salient difference between analogy and metaphor in Aquinas: Catherine Mowry LaCugna mentions Aquinas' view that "all biblical names and forms of address to God are metaphors," and notes that McFague's metaphorical theology "has the merit of freeing the Christian imagination from the stranglehold of a deadly literalism" ("God in Communion with Us: The Trinity," in *Freeing Theology: The Essentials of Theology in Feminist Perspective,* ed. Catherine LaCugna [San Fransisco: HarperCollins, 1993], p. 101); while Susan Ross asserts that in *ST* 1.13 Aquinas argues for "the metaphorical nature of all religious expressions" ("God's Embodiment and Women: Sacraments," in *Freeing Theology,* p. 203), even though the third article of the question she refers to concludes that some names are said of God properly and not metaphorically. But other writers correctly note the distinction between analogy and metaphor in Aquinas' thought (see the works by McInerny cited above). Basing himself on Aquinas, J. A. DiNoia holds that the name *Father* is predicated metaphorically of the triune God (by appropriation of the first person of the Trinity) and is predicated literally and properly of the first person ("Knowing and Naming the Triune God: The Grammar of Trinitarian Confession," in *Speaking the Christian God,* ed. Alvin Kimel Jr., pp. 162–87). Elizabeth Johnson recognizes the difference between analogical and metaphorical language about God and speaks of "the nonliteral although still meaningful character of [analogy's] speech about God" (*She Who Is: The Mystery of God in Feminist Theological Discourse* [New York: Crossroad, 1992], pp. 114, 116). However, the word *literal* is ambiguous: it may mean "physically the case," which is what feminist theologians want to deny about masculine imagery and language as regards God, and for which, in their eyes, metaphor's nonliteral semantics is a good antidote; but *literal* may also mean "strictly and truly the case," which does not include connotations of physicality in the instance of God. What Aquinas calls the "proper" predication of the divine names is also a literal predication in the second but not the first sense, and is distinguished by him from metaphorical predication: God's proper predicates are also literal predicates, not because they connote physical characteristics in God but because they claim something strictly true about God, which is never the case with God's metaphorical predicates.

of a created entity deriving from its specific nature, "for a distinctive mode of perfection and being is appropriate to each species" (*SCG* 1.30.276). In every name designating a specific type of created entity, then, we understand "a distinct manner of being" according to which the specific type "is distinguished from God" (*SCG* 1.31.280). This means that even a nonmaterial specific name such as *angel* cannot be said of God except metaphorically. In order for a perfection term to be predicated properly of God, therefore, it must neither connote the imperfection of materiality nor signify a distinct kind of creature distinguishable from God. Names predicated truthfully and properly of the divine being must transcend both the potentiality of matter and the finite limits of creatures' specific natures.[61]

v. Taxonomy of the Divine Names

In different contexts Aquinas offers different classifications of the divine names. We have already seen above that divine predication may be negative, relative,[62] or substantial, and that substantial predication is either proper or metaphorical. Other texts help to fill out the taxonomy.

Names taken from creatures denoting deformity, defect, or fault, of none of which is God the author—such as *sinner* or *devil*—cannot be truthfully predicated of God in any way at all, not even metaphorically.[63]

SCG 1.30.276 lists three kinds of name predicated of God substantially: names designating an absolute perfection without any defect, which are also said of creatures; names expressing a perfection with a mode proper

---

61. W. Norris Clarke distinguishes between relatively and absolutely transcendent perfection terms ("Analogy and the Meaningfulness of Language about God: A Reply to Kai Nielsen," *Thomist* 40 [1976]: 73–75, 88–92). He offers an interesting image concerning the types of extension open to various terms: those with ceiling but no floor (chemical activity); those with ceiling and floor (sense knowledge); those with floor but no ceiling, which are relatively transcendent perfection terms (intellectual love); and those with neither ceiling nor floor, which are absolutely transcendent perfection terms (being and its transcendentals).

62. The relative names of God are predicated temporally ("God was not Lord until he had a creature subject to himself" [*ST* 1.13.7 ad6]), though they imply a foundation in the eternal God (*SS* 1.8.1.1 ad2; 1.8.4.1 ad3; 1.30.1.1–2; 1.37.2.3; *SCG* 2.11–12; *ST* 1.13.7; 1.34.3 ad2).

63. *SS* 1.22.1.3 ad3; 1.34.3.2 ad2.

to creatures, which are said of God according to likeness and metaphor; and names signifying a perfection with the mode of supereminence distinctive to God, which are said of God alone.[64]

Some texts distinguish within the proper names of God between those names expressing some simple perfection that can also be predicated of creatures (*power, goodness,* etc.) and those names signifying the perfection together with the superlative manner in which the perfection is found in God, so that they cannot be properly said of creatures (*omnipotent, highest good, highest wisdom, ubiquitous, first being,* etc.).[65]

Based on a composite schema indebted to Ambrose, Augustine, and Dionysius, *SS* 1.22.1.4 assigns the divine names to three ultimate categories. God is named either through a likeness taken from creatures or through a reality that exists properly and primarily in God and secondarily in creatures. The first type of name is metaphorically said of God and is studied in "symbolic theology" *(symbolica theologia).* The second type of name has two subgroups: those names signifying something common in God and pertaining to the unity of majesty, which are treated in "unitive theology" *(theologia unita);* and those names proper to a person of the Trinity, which are treated in "discriminative theology" *(theologia discreta).* Negative names are based on the affirmative names of unitive and discriminative theology (*SS* 1.22.1.4 ad2), and relative names always imply something absolute in God—for example, *Creator* implies *power* in unitive theology, and *incarnation* implies *second person* in discriminative theology (*SS* 1.22.1.4 ad3). The ultimate generic categories or philosophical modes of

64. For other ways to express God's supereminence, see *DDN* 12.1.949, 955. Aquinas must explain some Matthean texts (19:17; 23:8–10) that seem to imply that God alone is teacher or father or good. His own theory would naturally interpret such names as said properly of both creatures and God (though primarily of God), but the scriptural texts would lead one to interpret them as names of eminence, i.e., as predicated properly and exclusively of God. He contends that the scriptural way of talking is justified because such names are said of God essentially, naturally, and properly, whereas they are said of creatures by participation and instrumentally (*Matt.* 19.1581; 23.1848; *Rom.* 16.2.1227). Nevertheless, in his theory a name's proper and essential predication of God does not necessarily entail its exclusive predication, nor does a name's predication of the creature through participation exclude its proper predication.

65. *SS* 1.43.1.2 ad1; *DV* 5.8 ad3; *SCG* 1.30.276; *Quod.* 11.1.1.

predication appropriate for the divine names are the substantial and the relative,[66] the former being employed in the unitive theology of the one God and the latter in discriminative Trinitarian theology.

We conclude with a comprehensive synopsis of Aquinas' taxonomy of the names of God. Some names can never in any way be said of God since they denote only imperfection and defect.

Names can be said of God either because they remove imperfection from God (negative names), relate the divine effects to God (relative names), or place some positive perfection in God (substantial names). Aquinas defends a positive theology of the substantial names of God against various inadequate views, which we have termed the dispositional, actional, negative, and causal interpretations.

The substantial names of God are subdivided into metaphorical names and proper names, the latter positing some perfection as really and truly belonging to God.

The proper names of God are subdivided into absolute names and names of eminence.

Absolute names are analogous names proper both to God and to creatures, but they are said primarily of God and secondarily of creatures as regards the reality they signify; they are also said of God in an eminent fashion and are subject to the corrections and purifications of negative theology.

Names of eminence are said properly and exclusively of God.

Metaphorical substantial names belong to symbolic theology, whereas other divine names may belong to the unitive theology of the one God or to discriminative Trinitarian theology.[67]

---

66. *SS* 1.8.4.3; cf. 1.22.1.3 ad2.

67. Battista Mondin offers a fourfold classification of perfection attributes in Aquinas: simple perfections, mixed or specific perfections, negative perfections, and imperfections (*The Principle of Analogy in Protestant and Catholic Theology*, 2nd ed. [The Hague: Nijhoff, 1968], pp. 93–98).

VI. Primacy and Dependence in Divine Predication

Thomas speaks often about the distinction between what he calls priority and posteriority in divine predication, which applies only to those names predicated properly, absolutely, and analogically of God and creatures. He employs the terminology *per prius* ("primarily" or "with priority") and *per posterius* ("secondarily" or "with posteriority"). *Per prius* refers to the fact that something exists or is known/named *before* something else, which in turn exists or is known/named *per posterius,* that is, *after* the *per prius* reality. The *per posterius* reality is dependent either for its existence or for its knowledge/naming upon the *per prius* reality.[68]

Sometimes the discussion of primacy and dependence in divine predication is cast in terms of the distinction between the perfection signified by a name and the manner in which the name signifies it. All names signifying absolute perfections, as to the reality they signify, are said primarily of God and dependently of creatures, but are said primarily of creatures as to their manner of signifying those perfections.[69] For example, paternity, personhood, wisdom, and life belong primarily to God, flow from God to creatures, and are primarily predicated of God as to the realities they signify, but they are primarily predicated of creatures as to their manner of signification,[70] "as is the case with all the other names predicated of God and creatures analogically" (*SS* 1.25.1.2).

In a similar vein, while attempting to explain Ephesians 3:14–15, "I kneel before the Father from whom all fatherhood in heaven and on earth is named," *Eph.* 3.4.169 states that any divine name we use can be understood in two ways: insofar as it signifies the concept of the intellect, and in this way the name is said primarily of the creature; and insofar as it manifests the essence of the reality named, and in this way the name exists primari-

---

68. The language of primacy/dependence will be used instead of priority/posteriority, as it is more serviceable and less strange.

69. Cf. *SS* 1.22.1.2; *ST* 1.13.3; *DP* 7.5 ad8.

70. Paternity: *SS* 1.4.1.1; *ST* 1.33.2 ad4. Personhood: *SS* 1.25.1.2. Goodness and life: *ST* 1.13.3. Wisdom is primarily in God insofar as God by his wisdom makes us wise (*SS* 1.8.1.2). "All those things that do not denote some material or bodily disposition are truly in God and more truly than in other things" (*SS* 1.35.1.1 ad2).

ly in God. "Insofar as *fatherhood* signifies the concept of the intellect which names the reality, it is found in creatures before it is found in God, for the creature becomes known to us before God does; but insofar as *fatherhood* signifies the reality itself that is named, it exists in God before it exists in us, since every generative power in us is certainly from God." Names are used of creatures before they are used of God, because "by using names derived from creatures the intellect rises to God," but as regards the reality they signify these names are said primarily of God, "from whom perfections descend to other things."[71]

ST 1.13.6, a dense and difficult text weaving several threads of thought together, begins its treatment of primacy and dependence in divine predication by remarking that an analogical name is commonly predicated of many things only by reference to something one, which is always included in the extended meanings of the name. An analogical name is predicated primarily of that reality which is included in the meaning of the name as it is predicated of all other realities, and it is predicated in a dependent fashion as regards those other realities, inasmuch as its meaning in their case must make reference to that reality in which its primary meaning is verified. For example, *healthy* is predicated primarily of the animal since the healthy animal is necessarily included in the meaning of *healthy* as it is predicated of medicine, for medicine is called healthy only insofar as it fosters the health of the animal. All metaphorical names said of God signify the likeness of God to creatures—"God is a lion," for example, means that God acts as powerfully as a lion does—and are defined "through what is said of creatures," which means that they are said primarily of creatures. And even all nonmetaphorical names (Thomas is thinking of God's absolute and analogous names) would be said primarily of creatures if they were predicated of God only according to the causal interpretation, for in this interpretation "God is good" *means* "God causes the creature's goodness," and thus goodness as said of God would include in its meaning the goodness of the creature. But the situation is different if we consider such names to be predicated substantially of God, such that "God is good" and

---

71. *CT* 1.27; cf. *DM* 1.5 ad19; *Rom.* 13.1.1021. The name is primarily the creature's, for the concept signified by the name defines the creature, but no creaturely concept can define God (*DV* 2.1 ad11).

"God is wise" *mean* "these things pre-exist in God in a more eminent fashion":

> With respect to the reality signified through the name, such names are said pri-
> marily of God rather than of creatures since perfections of this sort flow from God
> to creatures. But with respect to the name's meaning, such names are primarily
> used by us for creatures, which we know first of all. Thus, such names also have a
> manner of signifying which belongs to creatures.

Thomas is trying to distinguish absolute analogical names from metaphorical names by the criterion of their primacy or dependence in divine
predication. But these names are not distinguished as regards their meaning or manner of signifying, since both types of name are originally used
to signify a reality first known among creatures. However, they are different with respect to the reality signified, insofar as the name's intelligible
meaning refers to the ultimate reality in God. The metaphorical name and
idea refer to God's reality insofar as it is a likeness to creaturely reality,
which makes *even the reality* in God something secondary to creaturely reality. Thomas emphasizes that we would have to say the same thing about
analogical names if they signified a reality about God in the way the causal
interpretation understands the situation: for then the reality itself in God,
as signified by the analogical name, would be in relation to the creature as
the cause of the creature, which means that the *reality as signified* would
exist in God dependently and not primarily. The substantial interpretation
of analogical names, however, preserves the priority of the reality signified
about God, for in such a view the predication of some perfection of God
means that the perfection really preexists in God in a higher fashion: that
is, the real perfection in God is not *directly signified* by means of any connection to creatures, however much it is also the case that the Dionysian
way of causality is used in order to arrive at the recognition that it is true
to predicate such a perfection of God.

Paradoxically, although the concept behind the perfection term is primarily and first of all predicated of the creature, it is later used in a judgment that claims the perfection to be absolutely and primarily in God,
even though we do not grasp the divine level of the perfection or its mode
of eminence in God, for our level of intuitive knowledge always remains

bound to the creatures of whom we first predicate the perfection. Our judgments of truth about God transcend our intuitive conceptual knowledge. *DDN* 1.3.101 attempts to describe one way in which the truth about God transcends the meaning of concepts:

When individual names signifying something clearly distinct from other things are used in divine predication, they do not signify that thing finitely but infinitely. For example, *wisdom* as understood among creatures signifies something distinct from justice since it signifies something as existing in a definite general and specific category, but as understood in divine predication it does not signify something determined to a general or specific category, nor does it signify something as distinct from other perfections, but rather something infinite.

Thomas is asserting that the predicate *wise* must connote that God's wisdom is infinite and simple—even though he is the first to admit that he does not comprehend the nature of divine wisdom—and he can say this only because he has already assented to the theological truth that every perfection in God is infinite and simple. His ruminations on the link between the meaning of a name and the reality it signifies amount to his assessment of the epistemological conditions of possibility for those true judgments about God that his systematic theology has already recognized.

SCG 1.34.298 shows how in divine predication what is prior and primary in reality is dependent and posterior in cognition. In analogical predications, sometimes something primary in reality is also primary in knowledge and meaning, as substance is primary as regards accident, both in reality (since it causes the accident) and meaning (since substance is included in the definition of accident). Sometimes, however, a thing that is primary in nature is dependent in knowledge and meaning, as the curative power of healing in certain entities is primary in reality as regards the health of the animal (since it causes the animal's health as its effect), but dependent and secondary in knowledge (since our ability to know and name the curative power depends on our knowing and naming that power's effects in the animal); and thus *health-giving* is predicated primarily of the entity's curative power as to its reality, but *healthy* is predicated primarily of the animal as to the meaning of the name.[72] "Therefore, since we ar-

72. There are some material problems with the two examples Aquinas uses. According to

rive at a knowledge of God from other things, the reality signified by the names said of God and other things exists primarily in God according to his own mode, but the meaning of the name exists in God in a dependent fashion. Thus God is said to be named from the things he causes."[73]

In conclusion, the substantial, proper, and analogical divine names are predicated primarily of God as regards the absolute perfection they signify, for God *is* the perfection in an infinite manner and causes the participated perfection in creatures. However, the metaphorical divine names are said primarily of creatures as regards the relative perfections they signify. Both metaphorical and analogical divine names are predicated primarily of the creature as regards their meaning and their manner of signification, because we know creatures first and then God through creatures.[74]

---

his usual teaching, phenomenal accidents are known to the senses before the intellect understands the nature of the substance underlying them. But here he is referring to a fully reflective philosophical knowledge, where substance is included in the definition of accident but not vice versa. Concerning the health example, there is no doubt that *healthy* is said primarily of animals as regards knowledge and meaning, but it is not clear that *health-giving* in reality is said primarily of the curative powers of various entities, since health-giving medicines, for example, are only instrumental causes of health, whereas the body itself is the principal cause of its own health. Aquinas chose an example focusing on an instrumental rather than a principal cause, though God is the principal cause of all perfections.

73. Although in reality all perfections exist beforehand in God, we *designate* God's perfections with names that first of all signify creaturely perfections, which are in reality, however, dependent upon and derived from God's prior and primary perfections (*DV* 4.1.157–69, and ad10).

74. Roger White offers a Barthian interpretation of *ST* 1.13.6, where Aquinas allegedly asserts that the analogical divine names are predicated primarily of God even as regards their meaning and manner of signification ("Notes on Analogical Predication and Speaking about God," in *The Philosophical Frontiers of Christian Theology*, ed. B. Hebblethwaite and S. Sutherland [Cambridge: Cambridge University, 1982], pp. 201, 207–8). But such a view is contrary to Aquinas' stated position. Hampus Lyttkens also thinks he discerns various Neoplatonic analogies in Aquinas in which *both* the name and the reality are derived from God, referring to the text where the creature "is not named a being except insofar as it imitates the first being" (*SS* Prologue, 1.2 ad2), and remarking that the analogy which refers to a cause on the basis of its effect "consists in designating the primary from the secondary analogate" (*The Analogy between God and the World*, trans. A. Poignant [Uppsala: Almqvist and Wiksells, 1952], pp. 342–47, 384). First, however, the text from the *Sentences* does not say creatures are named from God's being *named* but from God's being *imitated*, i.e., it only wants to claim that the real being of the creature, which is later known and named by us, is what it is because it imitates the being of God—only in this sense is the creature's being named from God, not in the sense Lyttkens imagines. McInerny concurs with this assessment: "God is

VII. Different Meanings of the Divine Names

The question of whether the divine names are synonymous is important in itself but also serves to show how Aquinas' theological epistemology accentuates the difference between the meaning of a name and the reality signified by a name. Faced with the general argument that if attribute X and attribute Y are really the same in God, then the names denoting them must be synonymous,[75] Aquinas throughout his career denies the conclusion, but does so for varying reasons.

One group of texts bases the nonsynonymy of the divine names on the reality of God's nature, which no one name can fully express but which each individual name can signify partially and differently. SS 1.2.1.2 remarks that because of God's absolute simplicity all the divine attributes are one in reality, but that their names are not synonymous since they do not signify, as synonyms do, "totally the same thing." And the meanings of the names are diverse, "not only on the side of human reason but from the nature of the reality itself." R108 1–3 bases the plurality and diversity of the divine names on the fact that our intellect cannot comprehend God in this life but knows him on the basis of his effects, which are partial though true likenesses of the divine nature. The meaning of the names is "founded" on the divine essence, which is the "support" for the truth of the names.[76]

---

named from creatures with regard to the *ratio nominis;* creatures can be said to be named from God in the sense that that from which the name is imposed to signify is an effect of God who is this perfection eminently and *essentialiter*" (*Logic of Analogy,* p. 164). Secondly, Lyttken's final quote is also misguided. For Aquinas, the secondary analogate, *as known,* is *always* based upon and designated from the primary analogate, though the analogate that is secondary in knowledge may be primary ontologically. Since God is always known on the basis of creatures, all analogical divine names are predicated primarily of creatures and secondarily of God as regards their conceptual meaning and manner of signification. No analogy recognized by Aquinas would designate the primary by the secondary analogate, since designation is a function of knowing. With respect to the meaning of the name, then, "the creature saves such names *per prius* and it remains true that the analogous name is said according to its proper notion of one alone" (McInerny, *Studies in Analogy,* p. 64).

75. Johannes Bauer argues in just this fashion: if in God the most perfect justice is the same as the most perfect mercy, then the expressions *divine mercy* and *divine justice* are synonymous ("Können die Namen Gottes Synonyme sein? Mit besonderer Bezugnahme auf Thomas von Aquin," *SJP* 19 [1974]: 86).

76. R108 2–3; also: R108 51.

SS 1.35.1.1 ad2 offers an imaginary example to help explain the nonsynonymy of the divine names. Suppose there are four men, each of the first three possessing a separate habitual knowledge dealing with physics, geometry, and grammar, respectively. The fourth man possesses a single habit that includes all three sciences. He can truly be called a physicist, geometer, and grammarian, and though he possesses only one habit, the names said of him are truly different since "each one of them expresses the reality imperfectly." Such is the case with God. While the perfections of creatures are different, the one simple being of God possesses all perfections in a unified fashion. And so, when God is called a being or is said to know or will, in each case a part of God's perfection is expressed, but not the total perfection. Thus, all these perfections are really one in God but differ in meaning; further, this difference "is not only in the understanding but is founded in the truth and perfection of the reality."[77] In Aquinas' view, since no one name can bespeak God's entire perfection, it must be that each name, with a different meaning, expresses a different part of that perfection.

Without denying the basic arguments of the first group of texts, a second group adds to the battery of reasons in favor of the nonsynonymy of the divine names the epistemic fact that a name's signification of reality is mediated through the intellect's understanding. *SCG* 1.35.300 notes that just as different realities are likened to the one simple God through diverse forms, so is our intellect likened to God through its different concepts, inasmuch as it is led to know God through the different perfections of creatures.[78] Each concept is a partial likeness of God's simple being, and we attribute different names to God on the basis of those different concepts. Although these names signify the divine reality that is totally one, they are not synonymous since they do not have the same meaning, and their meaning is different because "the name signifies the intellect's concept before the reality understood."[79]

---

77. Cf. *DV* 2.1; *Heb.* 11.2.565.

78. *SCG* 1.31.282 asserts that the names we give God are many and diverse because God's effects from which we take those names are also many and diverse. If we knew God's essence perfectly as it is in itself we could express it with only one name. Cf. *Rom.* 1.6.117; *CT* 1.24.

79. Cf. *CT* 1.25; 2.9.256–76.

SS 1.2.1.3 emphasizes our inability to comprehend God's perfection as well as the epistemic fact noted above.

Since God according to one and the same reality is perfect in all ways, we cannot by one concept apprehend his total perfection, and as a result neither can we name it. We must have different concepts of God, which are different meanings, and we must use different names to signify those meanings. Hence, those names are not synonymous inasmuch as they signify the different meanings.

God's unity, which is the focal point for the different meanings of the divine names, is like the mathematical point, which, though one in reality, is nevertheless also the reason for the truth of various considerations—for example, the point as the center of a circle or as the beginning of a line (SS 1.2.1.3 ad6).

DP 7.6 remarks that every divine name would be synonymous from the viewpoint of God as the ultimate reality signified by the name, for God is absolutely one; but the name does not signify the reality except through the mediation of the intellect's understanding, in which there exists "the meaning understood through the names." Nevertheless, something in God must correspond to the concepts and meanings of the intellect, otherwise "God is good" would simply mean that God is thus *understood* by us to be good, not that God *is* good.

All those many and diverse meanings have something corresponding to them in God himself, of whom all those concepts of the intellect are likenesses. . . . All the meanings are certainly in our intellect as in a subject but they are in God as in the basis that makes these concepts true (*ut in radice verificante has conceptiones*). For the intellect would not have true concepts of any reality unless that reality corresponded by way of likeness to those concepts.

ST 1.13.4 ad1 agrees that the name immediately signifies the concept of the intellect and does not signify the reality "except through the intellect's mediating concept."

Just as to the different perfections of creatures there corresponds one simple principle represented in many and various ways through those different perfections, so to the many and various concepts of our intellect there corresponds one totally simple reality imperfectly understood according to these concepts. And so, although the names attributed to God signify one reality, because they signify it by diverse and plural meanings they are not synonyms. (ST 1.13.4)[80]

80. SS 1.22.1.3 displays the same conclusion from early in Aquinas' career: "although all

In arguing for the different meanings of the divine names, therefore, many of the texts from both groups mention the partial and imperfect way in which humans know the total perfection of God, and they see the divine reality as the ontological root for the plurality and diversity of our concepts and names for God. But only the passages from the second group also rely on the epistemic fact that names signify realities through the mediation of intellectual meanings, and thus explain how the truth about the one and simple God is not opposed to the plural meanings of the divine names.

[the names of God's attributes] signify one reality, they do not nevertheless signify the one reality according to one meaning, and thus they are not synonyms."

11. The Distinction between the Reality Signified and the Manner of Signification

A few times in the last chapter we saw Aquinas refer to the distinction between the reality signified *(res significata)* by a name and the name's manner of signification *(modus significandi)*, and assert that while the absolute and analogical predicates of positive theology are affirmed of God as regards the reality they signify, they must be denied as regards their manner of signification.[1] For some scholars, however, the *res/modus* distinction ultimately leads back to the univocist camp of Duns Scotus, for it permits a latent core of univocity to reside in the *res significata*.[2] One

1. For brevity's sake we will refer to the *res/modus* distinction. A characteristic text: "In every name predicated by us [of God], imperfection is found with respect to the name's manner of signifying, which does not belong to God, though the reality signified is suitable to God in some eminent manner" (*SCG* 1.30.277). The same sentiment is found in other texts such as *SS* 1.35.1.1 ad2 and *ST* 1.13.3. Aquinas often explains a saying of Dionysius—that negations about God are true while affirmations are vague—by claiming that affirmations are true as regards the reality they signify but not as regards their manner of signification (*SS* 1.22.1.2 ad1; 1.4.2.1 ad2; *SCG* 1.30.277; *DP* 7.5 ad2; *ST* 1.13.12 ad1; *SDC* 6.161). However, Hampus Lyttkens thinks the distinction plays no essential role in Aquinas' theory of the divine names ("Die Bedeutung der Gottesprädikate bei Thomas von Aquin," *NZST* 6 [1964]: 277–80); and Klaus Müller claims the application of the *res/modus* distinction to the divine names "says really nothing at all" (*Thomas von Aquins Theorie und Praxis der Analogie: Der Streit um das rechte Vorurteil und die Analyse einer aufschlussreichen Diskrepanz in der "Summa theologiae"* [Frankfurt am Main/Bern/New York: Peter Lang, 1983], p. 100).

2. Richard Swinburne, *The Coherence of Theism* (Oxford: Clarendon, 1977), pp. 78–80.

writes that the predication involved in analogy of attribution is both univocal and equivocal: "It is univocal, insofar as it always denotes the same *proprietas rei;* it is equivocal since, through a different *modus significandi,* it 'connotes' a different existential mode of the denoted *proprietas.*"[3] Another writes, in similar fashion, that "the same property is signified, but the way in which the property inheres in the subject is different."[4] A third contends, more globally, that the *res/modus* distinction is a "bogus distinction between what words really mean and what they mean to us."[5] If the *res/modus* distinction is a surreptitious return to univocity, then Aquinas' claim that the absolute names of positive theology are predicated analogically of God cannot be upheld, and God's transcendence will be slighted by their predication. Section I looks at the historical genesis of the distinction's terminology.

1. Historical Background

Thanks to the combined efforts of several scholars, today we have a fairly good picture of the Western ancestry of the term *modus significandi,* which began its career in grammar, was later incorporated into logic and epistemology, and in its later contexts was distinguished from the *res significata.*[6]

3. Jan Pinborg, *Logik und Semantik im Mittelalter: Ein Überblick* (Stuttgart/Bad Cannstatt: Frommann-Holzboog, 1972), p. 101; but cf. G. Scheltens, "Die thomistische Analogielehre und die Univozitätslehre des Duns Skotus," *FSt* 47 (1965): 323.

4. Jonathan Kvanvig, "Divine Transcendence," *RS* 20 (1984): 378.

5. John Morreall, *Analogy and Talking about God: A Critique of the Thomistic Approach* (Washington, DC: University Press of America, 1978), p. 114. For Morreall, the reality signified is what the word *really* means, but we do not know what that is: for the reality signified is a "core meaning" that has picked up limited connotations by being applied to creatures for so long; supposedly, after stripping away the "encrustations" of the modes of signification, we are left with the "pure" meaning, the reality signified. But at this point no one can describe that pure meaning, and so it is no meaning at all.

6. Charles Thurot, *Extraits de divers manuscrits latins pour servir a l'histoire des doctrines grammaticales au moyen âge* (Frankfurt: Minerva, 1964; repr. from *Notices et extraits des manuscrits de la Bibliothèque Impériale,* vol. 22/2 [Paris, 1868]), especially pp. 148–60; Überweg-Geyer, *Die patristische und scholastische Philosophie,* vol. 2 in *Grundriss der Geschichte der Philosophie,* 11th ed. (Berlin: Mittler, 1928), section 37, especially pp. 455–60; Martin Grabmann, *Mittelalterliches Geistesleben,* 3 vols. (Munich: M. Hueber, 1926, 1936,

The remote foundations of the term are to be found in Aristotle, Boethius (480–525), and the Latin grammarian Priscian, a contemporary of Boethius. Chapters 2 and 3 of Aristotle's *On Interpretation* teach that the noun and verb "signify" *(sēmainein)* something, and that the verb "signifies time in addition" *(prossēmainein chronon):* for example, *health* is a noun and *is healthy* a verb, the latter signifying, in addition to what the noun signifies, that the health is *now* presently existing. In his commentary on Aristotle's *On Interpretation,* Boethius understands the Philosopher to mean that while the noun may signify *(significare)* time in one sense (in words such as *today* or *tomorrow*), only the verb necessarily and as part of its very nature consignifies *(consignificare)* time according to its "proper mode" *(proprius modus)*.[7] It is clear that Boethius' *consignificare* is very close to Aristotle's *prossēmainein,* and that the Boethian verb consignifies time according to a *modus*.[8] In his *Instituto grammatica* (2.4.17) Priscian refers to the "semantic properties" *(proprietates significationum)* of the various parts of discourse, which by the middle of the twelfth century will be discussed under the term *modi significandi.*

1956), vol. 1, chap. 4, and vol. 3, chaps. 3 and 12; M.-D. Chenu, "Grammaire et théologie aux XIIe et XIIIe siècles," *AHDLMA* 10 (1936): 5–28; idem, *La théologie au douzième siècle* (Paris: Vrin, 1957); Franz Manthey, *Die Sprachphilosophie des hl. Thomas von Aquin und ihre Anwendung auf Probleme der Theologie* (Paderborn: Schöningh, 1937); Brendan O'Mahoney, "A Medieval Semantic: The Scholastic *Tractatus de modis significandi,*" *Laurentianum* 5 (1964): 448–86; idem, "The Medieval Treatise on Modes of Meaning," *PS* 14 (1965): 117–38; Geoffrey Bursill-Hall, *Speculative Grammars of the Middle Ages* (The Hague/Paris: Mouton, 1971); Jan Pinborg, *Die Entwicklung der Sprachtheorie im Mittelalter* (Munster: Aschendorff, 1967); idem, *Logik und Semantik;* idem, "Speculative Grammar," in *The Cambridge History of Later Medieval Philosophy,* ed. A. Kenny, N. Kretzmann, J. Pinborg (Cambridge: Cambridge University, 1982), pp. 254–69; John Wippel, *Metaphysical Themes in Thomas Aquinas* (Washington, DC: CUA, 1984), pp. 224–26; idem, *The Metaphysical Thought of Thomas Aquinas: From Finite Being to Uncreated Being* (Washington, DC: CUA, 2000), pp. 506–8, 519–20, 536–38; E. J. Ashworth, "Signification and Modes of Signifying in Thirteenth-Century Logic: A Preface to Aquinas on Analogy," *Medieval Philosophy and Theology* 1 (1991): 39–67. For the old logic in the Middle Ages, see *The Cambridge History,* section three, pp. 101–57; and for the logic of the high Middle Ages, see section four. Other relevant literature may be found in Ashworth, *The Tradition of Medieval Logic and Speculative Grammar from Anselm to the End of the Seventeenth Century: A Bibliography from 1836 Onwards* (Toronto: PIMS, 1978).

7. *In librum Aristotelis De interpretatione,* 2nd ed., "De nomine" (PL 64:421D–422B); cf. idem, *De divisione* (PL 64:888D–889A).

8. Cf. Pinborg, *Entwicklung,* pp. 30–45.

In the early Middle Ages, from the eighth to the beginning of the twelfth century, grammar, in conjunction with dialectic and rhetoric, was taught in the cloister and cathedral schools, mainly as a commentary on Priscian and Donatus. In its middle third, however, the twelfth century experienced a logicizing of grammar under the influence of the translations of Aristotle's logical organon, especially as it was interpreted by the commentaries and logical treatises of Boethius and by other Arabic commentaries.[9] This logicizing took place especially at the hands of Peter Abelard (d. 1142) and Peter Helias, a professor at Paris around 1140 who is the founder of the medieval logic of language, and who explains Priscian's *Instituto grammatica* through Aristotle's *Categories* and *On Interpretation*.[10] He teaches that the parts of speech are distinguished from one another by their *modi significandi*, which is his interpretation of Priscian's *proprietates significationum*. A part of speech is a sound indicating the mind's concept; it is a way *(modus)* of signifying or consignifying something. He argues for seven parts of speech—noun, verb, participle, pronoun, adverb, preposition, and conjunction—on the grounds that there are only seven modes of signification. The "essential modes" are what pertain always and universally to the parts of speech, and the "accidental modes" are either species of the essential modes (e.g., a noun may be either appellative or proper) or something secondary to an essential mode (e.g., the single or plural number of a noun).[11]

The thirteenth century deepened this logicizing of grammar by treatises dealing with the sentence, the enunciation, the properties of terms (such as supposition and distribution), and the syncategorematicals, which are various connective, modal, or numeral terms (such as *every, to-*

9. For Boethius' influence on medieval logic, see Chenu, *Théologie*, chap. 6. The early period of medieval logic, which runs from the beginning of the twelfth century to about 1230, is sometimes called *logica antiqua* and is further subdivided into *logica vetus* and *logica nova*: the former is founded on Porphyry's *Isagoge*, Aristotle's *Categories* and *On Interpretation*, and Boethius' logical treatises; the latter is based on the remaining treatises of Aristotle's logical organon.

10. Abelard distinguishes the noun from the verb by the way *(modus)* each signifies time (Thurot, *Extraits*, p. 150). For the very early logic before Abelard and Peter Helias, see Grabmann, *Mittelalterliches Geistesleben*, 3:94–113.

11. See Thurot, *Extraits*, pp. 153–55, 170.

tal, not, and, necessary, etc.). The most famous treatise of this period is Peter of Spain's *Summulae logicales* (ca. 1240–45).[12]

From 1270 to 1350 a new genre flowered, known as "speculative grammar" *(grammatica speculativa),* whose works were commonly called treatises or summas on the modes of signification *(Tractatus de modis significandi* or *Summae modorum significandi),*[13] and whose authors were named "Mannerists" *(Modistae).* Relying on Aristotle's logical corpus (as interpreted by Boethius), Priscian, Donatus, and Peter Helias, the *Modistae* treatises merged grammar with logic and metaphysics, and attempted to construct a philosophy of language capable of describing a universal grammar isomorphic with and dependent upon reality. The *Modistae* take for granted a realistic epistemology, especially in their celebrated triad of *modus essendi, modus intelligendi,* and *modus significandi:* a physical noise *(vox)* becomes a word *(dictio)* and a part of speech *(pars orationis)* by possessing a determinate manner of signifying *(modus significandi)* within the language, but the manner of signifying is directly conditioned by the human manner of understanding *(modus intelligendi),* which is itself representative of the various categories and modes of real being *(modus essendi).*[14]

The *modus significandi* gradually became identified with a word's *consignificatio,*[15] which could mean two things: the syntactic meaning of a word, which is a word's semantic relationship with other words within the total statement; and the connotative meaning of a word as distinct from its denotative meaning (e.g., the verb consignifies tense, one of its accidental modes).[16] The *modus significandi* can be different even when the reality referred to remains the same, because the *modus intelligendi* on which the

12. This treatise is divided into seven smaller ones on enunciation, universals, predicamentals, syllogism, topics, fallacies, and properties of terms.

13. Cf. Grabmann, *Mittelalterliches Geistesleben,* 1:115–46. The *Modistae* tractates diminished with the rise of nominalism, which could not abide their realistic view of universals.

14. Cf. Boethius of Dacia, *Opera: Modi significandi sive quaestiones super Priscianum Maiorem* (written ca. 1270), ed. J. Pinborg, H. Roos, S. S. Jensen, vol. 4/1–2 of Corpus Philosophorum Danicorum Medii Aevi (Hauniae: Gad, 1969), pp. 4.15ff, 7.42ff, 27.36, 64.77ff, 81.25, 83.51, 262.83.

15. For the details of this process, see Pinborg, *Entwicklung,* pp. 30–45.

16. Bursill-Hall, *Speculative Grammars,* pp. 54–55; Thurot, *Extraits,* pp. 155–56.

modus significandi is based can also be different. A common example is that of pain: *dolor* (*pain,* a noun) and *doleo* (*I am in pain,* a verb) signify the same reality *(res significata),* some sort of pain, but the former does so "in the manner of something permanent" *(per modum permanentis)* and the latter "in the manner of a flowing or becoming" *(per modum fluxus vel fieri).*[17] Jan Pinborg offers a concise summary of the grammatical analysis distinctive of the *Modistae:*

> According to modistic analysis words consist of a phonological element *(vox)* and two levels of semantic components, one concerned with specific or lexical meanings *(significata specialia),* the other with more general meanings, called *modi significandi,* on which in turn the syntactical component depends. . . . By a first imposition the expression is connected with a referent, insofar as a name is instituted to refer to a definite object or attribute of an object. How this happens is almost never discussed in any detail. The relation holding between the expression and the object referred to is called the *ratio significandi.* It is often described as the "form" which turns a mere sound into a lexeme *(dictio).* . . . In a secondary imposition the lexeme receives a number of *modi significandi* which determine the grammatical categories of the word. . . . A given lexeme can be associated with different *modi,* so that the same lexeme may be realised as different parts of speech and as different grammatical forms. . . . Obviously then, the *modi* are a kind of semantic modifiers, further determining the lexical meaning of the *dictio,* thus preparing it for various syntactical functions.[18]

Aquinas certainly recognizes the triad of *modus essendi, modus intelligendi,* and *modus significandi* (*Herm.* 1.8.90); and he also knows how to employ the purely grammatical distinctions of the *Modistae* and other medieval grammarians, especially in his Trinitarian theology.[19] Nevertheless,

17. O'Mahoney, "Medieval Semantic," pp. 466–86; idem, "Medieval Treatise," pp. 124–28.

18. Jan Pinborg, "Speculative Grammar," pp. 257–58. For the plethora of *modi significandi* required by the *Modistae* in order to fully define each part of speech, see O'Mahoney, "Medieval Treatise," pp. 128–38; Bursill-Hall, *Speculative Grammars,* pp. 345–91.

19. For example, in *ST* 1.39.3. James Egan shows how Aquinas uses the grammatical distinction between the concrete and abstract modes of naming in his teaching on the Trinity ("Naming in St. Thomas' Theology of the Trinity," in *From an Abundant Spring,* ed. by *Thomist* staff [New York: P. J. Kenedy, 1952], pp. 152–71). For a commentary on *ST* 1.39 from a semantic perspective, see Michael-Thomas Liske, "Die sprachliche Richtigkeit bei Thomas von Aquin," *FZPT* 32 (1985): 373–90. Cf. Fernando Inciarte, "La importancia de la unión predicado-sujeto en la doctrina trinitaria de Tomás de Aquino," *Scripta Theologica* 12 (1980): 871–84; idem, "Zur Rolle der Prädikation in der Theologie des Thomas von Aquin: Am

he probably did not know any of the *Modistae* texts properly speaking, for he does not use the modal definition for the parts of speech, and the first real texts of the *Modistae* genre only appear about four years before his death, in 1270, with Martin and Boethius of Dacia.[20] Still, many of the ideas of the *grammatica speculativa* were no doubt known and discussed some time before they began to be formally published.

We conclude this section with three points. First, the *res/modus* distinction has its historical roots in the discipline of grammar, from Peter Helias to the *Modistae*. Aquinas, however, incorporates the distinction into his theological epistemology and justifies it by recourse to theological truth.[21] Second, while some of the *modi* are essential to the various parts of speech, they are accidental to the specific, lexical meanings of individual words.[22] This opens up the possibility of excising the *modi* in order to penetrate to the pure lexical meaning as such. But Aquinas will not allow this in his understanding of the *modi,* for as was observed in the last chapter, the meaning of any divine name is always rooted in creaturely reality, so that we can never cut away a creaturely mode in order to come up with a meaning for the name that applies purely and only to God. Third, the grammatical employment of the *res/modus* distinction has a propensity to support univocity to the degree that it refers to an inner-worldly reality that remains the same in itself even though the ways of understanding and signifying it may vary. Aquinas' use of *modus intelligendi* and *modus significandi,* however, as the next section will attempt to show, is more mysterious and difficult to

Beispiel der Trinitätslehre," in Miscellanea Mediaevalia 13/1, *Sprache und Erkenntnis im Mittelalter* (Berlin: de Gruyter, 1981), pp. 256–69.

20. Pinborg agrees with Manthey and O'Mahoney on this point (*Entwicklung,* p. 69, n. 19). For some background to the "modes of discourse" in Aquinas, see Mark Jordan, "Modes of Discourse in Aquinas' Metaphysics," NS 54 (1980): 401–16.

21. Pinborg sees Aquinas' use of the *modus significandi* as based on real existential differences, whereas the *Modistae* relied more on Avicenna's "existence-indifferent conception of being" (*Entwicklung,* pp. 38–39, 44–45, and n. 68). Keith Buersmeyer shows how Aquinas knows that the polysemy of the verb *is* depends on first knowing the truth about reality, and how he is more flexible than the *Modistae* in not attempting to make grammar adjudicate for metaphysics ("The Verb and Existence," NS 60 [1986]: 145–62).

22. It is interesting to note, in passing, that Aquinas holds, contrary to the opinion of the *Modistae,* that the verb's consignification of time is not accidental but essential to its very meaning (*DV* 1.5; *Quod.* 4.9.2); cf. Chenu, "Grammaire et théologie," pp. 9–22.

grasp: for the reality of the transcendent God is *not* the same as the reality of the finite creature, and yet in true theological judgments the same creaturely meaning of the name, with its attendant creaturely modes of understanding and signification, somehow reaches beyond the creature to posit a reality in the infinite God.

II. The Res/Modus *Distinction in Aquinas*

Every proper and positive divine name can be considered in three ways: in terms of the reality signified, which ultimately exists properly and primarily in God; in terms of the conceptual meaning of the name, which is predicated properly only of the creature; and in terms of the manner of signification, which is a consequence of our conceptual mode of understanding and is also predicated properly only of the creature.[23] By denying the *modus significandi* of God, Aquinas usually intends to reject anything composite in God—since the human mode of signification always entails composition—but rejecting composition also involves refusing anything accidental or anything finitely abstract or concrete in God. Moreover, his denial of the *modus significandi* ultimately rests upon two stanchions: the negative theological truth that God exists modelessly and the epistemological truth of the human creature's congenital mode of understanding.

A. *God's Modelessness and the Creature's Finite Mode*

We have already seen in chapter 9 that Thomas identifies God with the pure perfection of infinite and modeless being. "Nothing is said of God by participation, for whatever is participated in is determined to a particular mode and so is possessed in a partial way and not according to every mode of perfection" (*SCG* 1.32.288). As pure being, God "is not limited to some mode of the perfection of being but possesses the totality of being";[24] God "does not exist by any mode, i.e., according to some finite and limited mode, but has universally and infinitely encompassed in himself the totality of being" (*DDN* 5.1.629), for God "cannot be circumscribed" (*SCG*

---

23. *DV* 2.1 ad11; *SCG* 1.34.298; *ST* 1.13.3; 1.13.6.
24. *DP* 2.1. Cf. *SS* 1.43.1.1; 1.43.1.2 ad4; *DV* 29.3; *SCG* 1.43.360.

1.28.267). If God's mode is the divine essence,[25] and the divine essence is the divine being, which is infinite and without finite mode, then God is infinitely modeless and possesses no mode at all.[26] God's modeless infinity is perhaps the primary truth of Thomas' qualitative negative theology since it denies of God that which is at the root of the creature's creaturehood—limitation, determination, finitude, mode.

Correlatively, therefore, the creature's mode is the limited and determinate grade of being the creature enjoys,[27] for Thomas writes that "the different grades of beings are constituted from the different modes of being *(modi essendi),*"[28] and the mode proper to the creature is in fact its very own species (*SCG* 1.30.276), which is always finite.[29] All things are given their mode by God (*SS* 1.3.2.3 ad3), as no creature receives being according to its total power but has it restricted to its own special mode of excellence (*SCG* 1.28.260).

God's modelessness and the "moded" or limited way in which creatures possess their perfections are the basis for Thomas' rejection of the *modus significandi* of God, by which he usually intends to deny composition or accidents in God. But sometimes by denying the manner of signification he simply wants to note that while our names signify finite and definite forms distinct from one another, in God the perfections signified are infinite, indefinite, and not really distinct from one another.[30]

Thomas recognizes an isomorphism between modes of being, modes of understanding, and modes of signifying, the first causing the second and the second the third. Since creatures receive perfections from God in an imperfect manner, and since the signification of any name used by us depends on our knowledge, which is based on the imperfect manner in

25. "Any mode of God is the divine essence" (*John* 1.11.213); cf. *DV* 2.11.103–18; 8.2 ad2; *SCG* 1.32.285.

26. Thomas speaks loosely, then, when he talks of God as having a mode (*SS* 1.43.1.2 ad1; *BDH* 3.51; *DV* 5.8 ad3; *SCG* 1.29.270; *DP* 3.15 ad19), and speaks oxymoronically when he mentions God's "universal mode of being" (*DSS* 8.199–218, 253–61) or God's "mode of supereminence" (*SCG* 1.30.276), for God's mode is the mode of modelessness.

27. *SS* 1.19.2.1 ad3; *SCG* 1.31.280; *Quod.* 4.1.1; *ST* 1.44.2.

28. *SCG* 1.50.424; cf. *SS* 2.18.2.2; *SCG* 1.50.426; 1.69.579; 1.93.790.

29. *SS* 1.8.1.2, *sed contra* 2.

30. *DP* 7.5 ad2; *DDN* 1.3.101.

which creatures participate in God, any name can be denied of God with respect to its manner of signification (*SS* 1.22.1.2). Even in the case of terms denoting absolute perfections, there is always a creaturely connotation *(consignificatio)* insofar as our manner of understanding the perfection is necessarily influenced by our experience of material reality (*SS* 1.22.1.2 ad2). All three modes can be denied of God: "All the things affirmed of God can also be denied of him since they are not fitting to him in the way they are found in created things and as they are understood and signified by us" (*DDN* 5.3.673).

B. The Human Manner of Understanding

In general, "every knower has knowledge of the reality known, not through the mode of the known reality but through the mode of the one knowing" (*SS* 1.3.1.1). Our intellect is "informed by created realities" (*SS* 1.4.2.1 ad2), and more particularly, takes its proper manner of understanding *(modus intelligendi)* from material realities.[31] God transcends whatever we can know or say of the divine being on the basis of material and created reality, for God transcends that reality and the human manner of understanding founded on it.[32] But *DP* 7.2 ad7 also signals in a striking fashion our intellect's ability to transcend its own manner of understanding. The intellect naturally understands being in the way it is found in the realities from which the intellect receives its knowledge, and being is in these things not as subsisting essentially but as inhering concretely and accidentally in some substance.

Reason discovers, however, that there is some subsistent being; and so, although the word *being (esse)* signifies in a concrete fashion,[33] when the intellect attributes being to God it transcends its own manner of signifying, attributing to God that which is signified but not the mode of signifying.

---

31. *SS* 1.22.1.2 ad2; cf. *ST* 1.13.3 ad3.

32. See *SDC* 6.170–71 (cf. *DDN* 1.3.77), where Aquinas constructs an elaborate outline to show how we come to affirm attributes of God and harmonizes it with other outlines he has found in the *Liber De causis* and Dionysius' *On the Divine Names*.

33. The text's *per modum concreationis* must be a mistake for *per modum concretionis*.

The objection Aquinas is responding to claims we should not attribute being to God since God is simple and subsistent, whereas being is always attributed to something like a concrete accident inhering in it. But *if* we have
discovered a subsistent being, Aquinas reasons, then the truth that "God is
subsistent being" must be upheld even though the mind realizes in the assertion itself that its concepts and way of understanding cannot do justice
to the truth it affirms. Truth outstrips the way in which we ineluctably understand. Indeed, unless we already knew that God is subsistent being we
would never be able to affirm that our way of asserting *this very truth itself*
falls short of God, since we know it falls short only because, whereas it
necessarily connotes God's being as something concrete and accidental, we
know that God's being is really absolute and identified with God's essence.

To generalize, then, the human manner of understanding can be denied
of God because some already known divine truth contradicts what that
mode of understanding, left to itself, would connote or imply about God.
Aquinas' examples of denying the *modus intelligendi* of God follow this
pattern. For example, *SCG* 2.12 demonstrates that God cannot be really related to creation, since this would imply that God is dependent on something created; and then *SCG* 2.13.919–20 proceeds to argue that since such
relations are not really in God and yet are still predicated of him, they
must be attributed to him simply on account of our way of understanding,
"for when our intellect understands one thing as referred to a second it
also understands at the same time *(cointelligere)* a relation of the second to
the first even though the second is sometimes not really related to the
first."[34] Another example: although creation is not really a process of
change, it seems to be so according to our mode of understanding, for we
imagine and understand the same thing as existing both before and after
its creation; and since the manner of signification follows the manner of
understanding, we also signify creation as if it were a change.[35]

34. Cf. *DP* 7.11. The mind cannot escape its way of understanding *and yet also knows* that
it cannot escape and so judges its predications about God accordingly.

35. *SCG* 2.18.953; *ST* 1.45.2 ad2. *SCG* 2.10.903 states that power is attributed to God's immanent actions only according to the manner of understanding and "not according to the
truth of the matter."

For Aquinas, composition is the most salient feature of the human way of understanding that must always be denied in divine predication. Our intellect knows the simple in the mode of the complex, apprehending the simple form as a subject and attributing something to it (*ST* 1.13.12 ad2), for the intellect forms propositions according to the manner of the complex and composite realities from which it naturally receives its knowledge (*SS* 1.4.2.1). Nevertheless, the intellect rises above its natural way of knowing and does not attribute such composition to God, understanding that what corresponds to all its different concepts is one and simple: "For the intellect does not attribute to the realities it understands the way in which it understands them, as it does not attribute immateriality to the stone though it knows the stone immaterially" (*SCG* 1.36.302). The mind does not judge falsely when it understands the simple God in a complex fashion, for there is a double meaning to the proposition "the intellect which understands a thing otherwise than it is, is false":

The adverb *otherwise* can modify the verb *understand* in relation to the thing understood or to the one understanding. If the former, then the proposition is true, and the meaning is: any intellect is false which understands a thing to be otherwise than it actually is; but this is not the case here, for when our intellect forms a proposition about God it does not say that he is composite, but that he is simple. If the latter, however, then the proposition is false. For the intellect's mode of understanding is different than the thing's mode of being, and it is clear that our intellect understands in an immaterial fashion those material realities that exist on a level below itself, not that it understands them to be immaterial but that it possesses an immaterial mode of understanding. Similarly, when it understands simple realities above itself, it understands them according to its own mode, i.e., in a composite fashion, not nevertheless so that it understands them to be composite. (*ST* 1.13.12 ad3)

The manner of understanding, moreover, determines the manner of signifying, to which we now turn.

C. The Human Manner of Signification

When Thomas denies that the human manner of signification applies to divine predication, he primarily intends to bolster God's simplicity and ontological subsistence and thus to separate from God the inevitable connotations of composition, abstraction, and concretion that arise whenever

our mind forms and signifies any predication, as well as the related connotation that would imply anything accidental in God. Because he already
knows that nothing composite, concrete, abstract, or accidental really exists in God, he can reject what the human manner of signification would
seem indirectly to posit in God and can impute such connotations to the
characteristic fashion in which our mind signifies its meanings, rather
than to any reality in God.

He explains the different mode of being or "subsisting" of various substances by reference to their level of simplicity or complexity. Material
substances have a different mode of being than separate intellectual substances, and separate intellectual substances than God, for while God *is* the
divine being and nature, separate substances are not their own being but
are their own nature, and material substances are neither their own being
nor their own nature but subsist only as individuals.[36] But even though we
know these different modes of being exist, the mode of signification of
"God is good" and "that woman is good" is the same in both cases; in fact,
it is only because Thomas realizes God's mode of existence is not the same
as the mode implied and connoted when we say "God is good" that he tells
us we must deny this manner of signification when we predicate goodness
of God.[37] A similar situation obtains in the case of concrete and abstract
names:

36. *DA* 17 ad10. *DA* 17 argues that the essence of the human soul separated from its body
belongs to the genus of separate intellectual substances and has the same mode of subsisting, since both kinds of entity are subsistent forms. Material realities, however, do not belong to the same genus as separate essences and have a different mode of being (*DA* 16). Cf.
DP 7.7 on how a house has a different "mode of existing" in material reality and in the
builder's mind. Thomas can also refer to the ten Aristotelian categories of being as diverse
grades of material entity that give rise to diverse modes of being (*DV* 1.1.114–61). Being *(ens)*
is divided into the ten categories according to a different mode of being *(modus essendi)*,
and since the modes of being are proportional to the modes of predication, the ten most
universal genera are called the ten "predicaments" or categories of predication (*Phys.* 3.5.322;
cf. *SS* 1.8.4.3; 1.22.1.3 ad2).

37. It is not universally true, then, to say that, for Thomas, "a difference of *modus essendi*
of a referent corresponds to a difference of *modus significandi* of a predicate" (James Ross,
Portraying Analogy [Cambridge: Cambridge University, 1981], p. 165), though it is true in the
case of the ten Aristotelian categories, which are the ultimate modes of predication corresponding to the ten most fundamental modes of being among material realities (*Phys.*
3.5.322). It is precisely because the creaturely mode connoted by a predicate's mode of signi-

In all the reality that exists below the first cause, certain things are found that are complete and exist perfectly, while others are imperfect and incomplete. The perfect things are those that are per se subsistent in nature, which we signify through concrete names (*human, wise,* etc.); the imperfect things are those that do not subsist through themselves, as forms, which we signify by abstract names (*humanity, wisdom,* etc.). . . . . Every name we use either signifies a sharing in something complete, as concrete names do, or signifies something as an incomplete formal component, as abstract names do. Hence no name we use is worthy of the divine excellence.[38]

According to Thomas, the human manner of signification is directly dependent on the real combination of subsistent and concrete realities with nonsubsistent and abstract qualities and forms; it renders our every name unworthy of God since we know that God is neither concrete in a composite fashion nor abstract in an incomplete or imperfect fashion.

SCG 1.30.277 tells us more exactly why the human manner of signification renders every name we use unworthy of God's transcendent excellence:

With a name we express reality in the way that our intellect conceives it. Having the origin of its knowledge in the senses, our intellect does not transcend the mode found in material reality, in which, on account of the composition of form and matter, the form and that which possesses the form are different. A simple form is indeed found in material reality, but it is imperfect since it does not subsist; and a subsistent entity that possesses the form is also found in material reality, but it is composite *(concretio)* rather than simple. Whatever our intellect signifies as subsistent, therefore, it signifies as a composite being, and whatever it signifies as simple it signifies not as *that which is* but as that *by which* something is. And so, as regards the mode of signifying, every name we predicate has imperfection, which does not belong to God, though the reality signified is suitable to God in some eminent way. This is clearly the case in the names *goodness* and *good*: they signify something, respectively, as nonsubsistent and as concrete; in this respect no name is appropriately applied to God but only with respect to the reality that the name is used to signify.

fication does *not* correspond to God's mode of being as the predicate's referent that Thomas feels constrained to deny our human mode of signification in all divine predication.

38. *SDC* 22.378, 383. While *humanity* and *human being* both refer to the whole human essence, the former does so "in the manner of a part" and the latter "in the manner of a whole" (*SS* 1.23.1.1); *homo* signifies the human as a concrete whole and *humanitas* signifies that abstract form, human nature, by which a human is a human (*Meta.* 7.5.1379–80).

Theological truth tells us that our names cannot do justice to God, whose simplicity is perfectly subsistent rather than imperfectly abstract, and whose subsistence is totally simple rather than concretely composite.

> Every name fails to signify the divine being since no name signifies at the same time something perfect and simple, for abstract names do not signify a being subsisting through itself and concrete names signify a composite being; . . . rejecting whatever is imperfect, we use both kinds of name in divine predication, abstract names on account of their simplicity and concrete names because of their perfection.[39]

An individual substance existing with categorical accidents always entails a certain degree of composition, at least of the subject and its accidents.[40] For this reason alone we would have to deny any accidents in God, but we must also do so for two further reasons: an accident implies dependence, which cannot belong to God (*SS* 1.8.4.3); and, since God is his own being and therefore identified with pure actuality, no further perfection can accrue to him by way of an accident.[41] Because of the theological negation of accidents in God, Thomas holds that although we predicate of God certain perfection terms (such as *wisdom*) that signify accidents in creatures, we must not suppose they signify accidents in God (*ST* 1.3.6 ad1) and must therefore deny their manner of signification.[42] Once again, his reason for rejecting the mode of signification is its connotation of something in God that he already knows to be untrue. Since no divine name can be taken as implying an accident in God, any name that among humans would have as its highest genus one of the nine categorical accidents (such as quality) is said to be predicated according to its proper specific meaning but not according to its generic meaning (e.g., *wisdom* denotes the perfection of knowledge in God but not a quality), since that generic meaning always refers to a categorical accident.[43]

In conclusion, Aquinas acknowledges the traditional triad of mode of being, mode of understanding, and mode of signification, each item sup-

---

39. *SS* 1.4.1.2; same: *ST* 1.3.3 ad1; cf. *SS* 1.8.1.1 ad3; *SCG* 1.26.248; *DP* 8.2 ad7; *ST* 1.13.1 ad2.
40. *Meta.* 7.11.1533–36 and *SS* 1.8.4.3; cf. *Meta.* 7.5.1379–80.
41. *DP* 7.4 and *SCG* 1.23.
42. *SS* 1.9.1.2, and ad4.
43. *SS* 1.8.4.3 and *DP* 7.4 ad2, 9; cf. *SS* 1.4.1.1; 1.22.1.3 ad2; 1.35.1.1 ad2; 1.35.1.4 ad7.

porting the one after it.[44] His *res/modus* distinction is a shorthand way of pointing out how every proper predication signifying a reality in God inevitably falls short of God. The *res/modus* distinction refines our positive assertions about God by separating from God every composition, abstraction, concretion, and accident.[45] The denial of the mode of signification makes sense only in the context of previously known theological truths, for such truths justify our removing from God the imperfections implied by our human modes of understanding and linguistic expression. Upholding positive theology's affirmations of a reality in God and at the same time purifying its predications by recourse to theological truth, the *res/modus* distinction is a microcosm of how Aquinas' positive and negative theology work closely together.

III. *The* Res/Modus *Distinction and the Analogical Nature of Divine Predication*

Does Aquinas' use of the *res/modus* distinction veil a hidden univocity now secretly readmitted into divine predication? Three reasons respond in the negative.[46]

First, Aquinas' analysis discovers three essential elements to all divine predication: the reality signified, the manner of signification, and the meaning of the name predicated of God. The denial of the manner of signification does not leave us with a pure concept exactly fitted to God's transcendent perfection, for our concept of any perfection, which is the same as the name's meaning, is always and unavoidably bound up with creatures and primarily predicated of them. The mind uses the meaning of

44. W. Norris Clarke, "Analogy and the Meaningfulness of Language about God: A Reply to Kai Nielsen," *Thomist* 40 (1976): 75–80; Günther Pöltner, "Die Repräsentation als Grundlage analogen Sprechens von Gott im Denken des Thomas von Aquin," *SJP* 21–22 (1976–77): 26–37.

45. Ralph McInerny, *The Logic of Analogy: An Interpretation of St. Thomas* (The Hague: Nijhoff, 1961), pp. 59–60, 157–61.

46. David Burrell distinguishes Scotus' use of the distinction, which leads to univocity, from Aquinas' (*Analogy and Philosophical Language* [New Haven: Yale, 1973], pp. 117, 178–80). John Wippel absolves Aquinas of any "veiled univocity" in his use of the distinction (*Metaphysical Themes*, p. 238).

the name to signify some reality in God, all the while denying the human mode of signification, but the mind never sees or conceives anything more in the concept than the creature's perfection, which the concept innately signifies. There is no conceptual univocal core that has been abstracted from its finite and infinite modes, for the divine name's conceptual meaning is *always* referred to the creature as the focal point of semantic unity for the name's other analogical extensions within divine predication. Analogy comes to pass when the mind predicates the name and its meaning of God in an act of judgment claiming a truth about the holy darkness of God, which transcends anything the concept can intuitively grasp on its own.[47] The divine name does not become analogical by being reconceived in a deeper fashion with reference to a putatively purer divine meaning, but rather by being used in a true judgment that posits some reality in God. The truth of the judgment is what makes us realize that the concept, *as used but not as conceived,* has been extended beyond the creaturely realm. We never really know in a clear conceptual fashion what a divine name might mean for God, and whatever we do know about such a name is always a consequence of the judgments we have already made about God.

Second, the *res/modus* distinction is really an encapsulation of the whole expanse of Aquinas' positive and negative theology.[48] The *res/modus* distinction first posits a reality in God (positive theology) and then, on the basis of a qualitative negative theology that proclaims God's transcendent modelessness and refuses any conceptual insight into God's mysterious reality, rejects those connotations of divine predication that would place anything composite, abstract, concrete, or accidental in God (modal negative theology). Aquinas' theological epistemology teaches us that, while a true affirmation signifies a reality of God at the same time as the manner of signifying that reality is denied, we never understand the inner essence

47. Edward Schillebeeckx, *Revelation and Theology,* trans. N. D. Smith, 2 vols. (New York: Sheed and Ward, 1968), 2:170–78, 204. "The *act of signifying* goes further than the *ratio nominis*..." (ibid., p. 171).

48. Burrell interprets the *res/modus* distinction as an integral part of Aquinas' negative theology, which continually denies that any concept can represent God (*Analogy,* pp. 162–64).

of God's infinite and modeless being; and this means that one cannot use the *res/modus* distinction to distill a pure univocal concentrate of meaning out of a compound mixture of finite and infinite modes.[49] Thus, although it is true that a too wooden or clumsy interpretation of the distinction can draw one back to univocity,[50] Aquinas nevertheless employs the distinction as a kind of partial compendium of his theological epistemology, and thus its proper interpretation should evoke the interconnected combination of judgments that comprise his positive and negative theology and that together reject any univocity in our knowledge of God.

Third, since in Aquinas the analogical nature of divine predication and the use of the *res/modus* distinction are matters of judgment instead of concept formation, the danger of the "common core of univocity" is avoided. His theological analogy depends not on a more profound conceptualization but on a recognition of the truth about God. One author has written that Aquinas uses the distinction to remind us we have to consider two things any time we employ a perfection-expression for God: "the immediate context in which it applies, and the intention or scope latent within the term."[51] This "intention" within the term, however, is not a new level of concept but rather the fact that the term can be used to express true judgments about God. When Aquinas speaks of a statement's "intention to signify" *(intentio significare)*, the phrase first of all refers to the statement's objective design or tendency to express the truth.[52] In his the-

49. Bernard Montagnes, *La doctrine de l'analogie de l'être d'après saint Thomas d'Aquin* (Louvain/Paris: Publications Universitaires/Béatrice-Nauwelaerts, 1963), pp. 99–103; William Hill, *Knowing the Unknown God* (New York: Philosophical Library, 1971), pp. 141–42. For Burrell, the *res/modus* distinction "does not yield any privileged access to the *res*" (*Aquinas: God and Action* [Notre Dame: UND Press, 1979], p. 10).

50. Burrell, *Aquinas,* p. 10; Henri de Lubac, *The Discovery of God,* trans. A. Dru from 3rd French ed. (Chicago: Regnery, 1967), pp. 200–201.

51. Burrell, *Aquinas,* p. 10.

52. André Hayen describes how Aquinas uses *intentio/intendere* at the level of intellect and will to mean intensity, voluntary intention, voluntary attention, or the mind's knowledge of reality—this latter is the *intentio intellecta* or "understood intention" (*L'intentionnel selon saint Thomas,* 2nd ed. [Brussels/Paris: Desclée, 1954], pp. 47–51, 161–201). *Intentio significare,* therefore, could refer to voluntary intention (what the statement's author "means" or "wants" to say) or to the knowledge contained in the statement itself ("God is good" intends of itself to say something about God), but the former is reduced to the latter, since what the statement's author wants to say is always at least partially and sometimes predom-

ological epistemology of the divine names, the *res/modus* distinction serves to underline the absolutely central position he gives to the truth status of our theological judgments about God.

---

inantly determined by what the statement itself *does* say. In *DDN* 4.9.412, for example, the *intentio significare* is the intelligible meaning of a word or phrase as opposed to the mere physical sound or sight of syllables, words, or sentences; in *John* 1.1.25, the one using the noun *stone* is said to "intend to signify" the actual stone.

Conclusion. Speaking the Incomprehensible God

"Speaking the Incomprehensible God" is shorthand for the way in which, to quote from the Preface, "Thomas weaves his negative and positive theology together, precisely because *only that interweaving* can do justice to the fact that the church must speak and praise, must invoke and love and follow the God *who just is* the Mysterious and Incomprehensible One who ever escapes and is never caught by our ideational and conceptual schemes." Thomas' blend of positive and negative theology, however academic its form of expression and social location, is ultimately the servant of the church in its worship of the utterly mysterious God, and thus Thomas the academic also serves Thomas the spiritual guide. For despite Pannenberg's doxological equivocity, the church cannot *really worship* God unless it is somehow able to know that God and somehow able to speak to and about that God, while at the same time the church cannot worship the *real God* unless it worships the incomprehensible God. Thomas' interplay of positive and negative theology, therefore, enables the church's language about God and its worship of God to be truthfully iconic without becoming blasphemously idolatrous.

For at least three central reasons, moreover, Aquinas' nuanced combination of positive and negative theology, argued both philosophically and theologically, is a valuable resource for contemporary discussions among scholars about how we ought to think and speak about God: his practice (if not always his theory) of placing truth before meaning as the basis for

353

his theological epistemology and transcendental analogy; the fact that his faith more than his pure reason is the inspiration and foundation for the truths that undergird his theological epistemology; and the balanced, comprehensive nature of that theological epistemology, which acknowledges the tensioned nature of any truth about God.

First, the warrants for the major contours of Aquinas' theological epistemology are based firmly on the truths of his systematic theology, which support and justify the way he interprets the interplay of positive and negative theology. His theological epistemology, looking back reflexively at the original theological judgments of his systematic theology, searches for and announces the underlying epistemic conditions of possibility for the truth of those judgments. But the original truths themselves are a given, and Aquinas' epistemology never questions their validity. The necessary presupposition of Aquinas' search for epistemic and linguistic theological meaning is the context of the truths about God to which he already assents. The example of his theological epistemology can serve as a cogent reminder that often our debates about God-talk may not be so much over words or concepts or hermeneutical methods as over the truths about God we hold dear.

Second, in Aquinas the theologian, the truths of faith enjoy a primacy over the truths of reason, even though he himself may not always be aware of this. A central affirmation of his theology, upon which his theological epistemology rests, is the truth that God is the infinite act of subsistent being. On the basis of a detailed analysis of the relevant texts, it has been argued that Aquinas' faith is the primary motivation for this assertion, though his reason and philosophy support, defend, and give expression to what his faith has recognized: that God is the transcendent, gracious, and absolutely free Creator of a radically contingent universe. Aquinas' faith and religious mentality, nourished on a profound meditation of the word of God in scripture, lie at the basis of his doctrine of analogy and positive theology, which are not simply the progeny of Reason but also the children of Grace. The example of Aquinas would suggest that in the contemporary discussion about God-talk our own faith stance should be acknowledged as a deep and abiding presupposition intimately involved and vitally interested in the eventual outcome.

Third, Aquinas' theological epistemology is balanced and comprehensive. While his positive theology is the epistemological corollary to the truth that creatures have come forth from God as likenesses of God, his negative theology in turn is the consequence of knowing that those same creatures have been created from nothing and cannot be God. All the elements of his theological epistemology—God's dual incomprehensibility, qualitative and modal negative theology, the Dionysian threefold way, positive theology, transcendental analogy, and the *res/modus* distinction— must mutually invoke and modify one another in order to do justice to the full truth about God. His theological epistemology is moderate and equipoised, with an internal system of checks and balances. His negative theology is never so extreme that he denies any knowledge at all of God, which leads him deftly to moderate the radically negative statements of a Dionysius or a John Damascene. Nevertheless, looming over all knowledge is the mysterious incomprehensibility of God, from whom Aquinas' qualitative negative theology removes whole realms of discourse, and whose essence humans cannot intuit in this life or ever fathom comprehensively, even in the life to come.

Thomas' positive theology of the proper and substantial predication of the divine names is robust and unapologetic. He considers the proper predication of the divine names to be different from and deeper than the metaphorical predication of the divine names. Moreover, his analogy of referential multivocity, including the special case of theological analogy, does not suffer from a hidden core of univocity, for his analogy, taking its cue from Aristotle's *pros hen* equivocity, finds its unity not in an abstract concept but in a concrete reference to one reality; and his analogy is more a matter of judgment than of concept in the traditional narrow sense, for it arises out of those extensions of meaning that occur and must be understood in order for certain truths to be assertable. However, even his positive theology is still subject to the nuances, cautions, and purifications stemming from both types of modal negative theology, objective and subjective. Theological analogy clings to the mean, eschewing a too minimalist or too maximalist appraisal of our knowledge of God. Moreover, even analogy, that specially appointed guardian of positive theology, has its own internal moment of negation.

Aquinas is that most Catholic of thinkers in that he betrays a clear predilection for "both/and" over "either/or." Another title for this Conclusion could easily have been "Truth's Light and God's Darkness," which also would capsulize in a lapidary fashion the tensile equilibrium of his theological epistemology, which is a study in contrasts as it strives to interweave positive and negative theology and preserve their close relationship from unraveling. "Truth": this is judgment over simple abstractive concept, and positive knowledge about God's very being rather than global negative unknowing. "Light": this is the illumination our lives receive from faith and grace, and from our rational and linguistic faculties, as they search out the truth about the mystery of God. "God": truth's light, however feeble its beam, is aimed at the gracious, infinite, and creative mystery of God, not simply at our concepts or ideas about God. "Darkness": nevertheless, the searchlight of truth, with analogy and metaphor as its rays, can play only lightly upon the thick darkness of God enveloping Mt. Sinai, illumining its tenebrous presence but never penetrating and irradiating its core.

Aquinas' theological epistemology is vital as a contemporary resource because it permits no easy and unilateral slide into either purely positive or purely negative theology, into univocity or equivocity. It would encourage our theological dialogue to keep the tensioned truth of God in view and to remember that only a fruitful interplay of positive and negative theology can ever do justice to the Elusive One who always evades epistemic and linguistic capture, and yet who at the same time, as the Gracious and Free One, desires to be acknowledged and worshiped as our Creator and Sustainer.

Bibliography

1. Works by Thomas Aquinas

Note: For Aquinas' complete bibliography arranged topically and/or chrono-
logically, and for discussions of authenticity and of the dates and circumstances of
composition, see the following works: James Weisheipl, *Friar Thomas D'Aquino:
His Life, Thought, and Work,* rev. ed. (Washington, DC: CUA, 1983), pp. 355–405,
478–87; Simon Tugwell, *Albert and Thomas* (New York: Paulist, 1988), pp. 201–59;
Gilles Emery, "Brief Catalogue of the Works of Saint Thomas Aquinas," in Jean-
Pierre Torrell, *Saint Thomas Aquinas,* vol. 1: *The Person and His Work,* trans.
Robert Royal (Washington, DC: CUA, 1996), pp. 330–61; the prefaces of the vari-
ous volumes of the Leonine Commission.

The order of each entry below is as follows: first, the title of Aquinas' work; second, the Latin edition used (the Leonine Commission volumes are almost all critical editions, except for some of the very earliest—especially vols. 4–7 [*ST,* parts 1
and 1–2]); third, an English translation if one exists. The volumes of the Leonine
Commission (Rome/Paris, 1882–) are signified by LC, and Marietti is always understood as the publisher when Turin is referred to as the place of publication.

Collationes in decem praeceptis. Critical Latin edition by J.-P. Torrell, "Les *Collationes in decem preceptis* de saint Thomas d'Aquin," *RSPT* 69 (1985): 5–40,
227–63. *The Catechetical Instructions of St. Thomas Aquinas,* trans. J. B. Collins
(New York: Wagner, 1939), pp. 69–116; rev. ed., in *God's Greatest Gifts* (Manchester, NH: Sophia Institute, 1992).
Collationes super Ave Maria. Opuscula Theologica, ed. R. M. Spiazzi (Turin, 1954),
2:239–41. *The Catechetical Instructions of St. Thomas Aquinas,* trans. J. B. Collins
(New York: Wagner, 1939), pp. 173–80.

Collationes super Credo in Deum. Opuscula Theologica, ed. R. M. Spiazzi (Turin, 1954), 2:193–217. *The Sermon-Conferences of St. Thomas Aquinas on the Apostles' Creed,* ed. and trans. (from a critical Leonine text without the apparatus) Nicholas Ayo (UND, 1988).

Collationes super Pater Noster. Opuscula Theologica, ed. R. M. Spiazzi (Turin, 1954), 2:221–35. *The Catechetical Instructions of St. Thomas Aquinas,* trans. J. B. Collins (New York: Wagner, 1939), pp. 135–70.

Compendium theologiae ad fratrem Raynaldum. LC 42 (1979): 83–205. *Compendium of Theology,* trans. C. Vollert (St. Louis: B. Herder, 1947).

Contra errores Graecorum. LC 40 (1967): A71–A105.

De aeternitate mundi. LC 43 (1976): 85–89. *St. Thomas Aquinas, Siger of Brabant, St. Bonaventure: "On the Eternity of the World,"* trans. C. Vollert, L. A. Kendzierski, P. M. Byrne (Milwaukee: Marquette, 1964), pp. 19–25.

De articulis fidei et ecclesiae sacramentis ad Archiepiscopum Panormitanum. LC 42 (1979): 245–57. Translation of the second part on the sacraments in J. B. Collins, *Catechetical Instructions of St. Thomas Aquinas* (New York: Wagner, 1939), pp. 119–31; rev. ed., in *God's Greatest Gifts* (Manchester, NH: Sophia Institute, 1992).

De ente et essentia. LC 43 (1976): 369–81. *On Being and Essence,* trans. A. Maurer, 2nd ed. (Toronto: PIMS, 1968).

De perfectione spiritualis vitae. LC 41 (1970): B69–B111. *The Religious State, the Episcopate, and the Priestly Office,* trans. J. Procter (St. Louis: B. Herder, 1903).

De principiis naturae. LC 43 (1976): 39–47. *Selected Writings of St. Thomas Aquinas,* trans. R. P. Goodwin (Indianapolis: Bobbs-Merrill, 1965), pp. 7–28.

De rationibus fidei ad Cantorem Antiochenum. LC 40 (1968): B57–B73.

De substantiis separatis ad fratrem Raynaldum. LC 40 (1969): D41–D80. *Treatise on Separate Substances,* trans. F. J. Lescoe (West Hartford, CT: St. Joseph College, 1959).

De unitate intellectus contra Averroistas. LC 43 (1976): 291–314. *On the Unity of the Intellect against the Averroists,* trans. B. Zedler (Milwaukee: Marquette, 1968).

Expositio et Lectura super Epistolas Pauli Apostoli. Ed. R. Cai, 2 vols. (Turin, 1953). Four of the commentaries have been published by the same house, Magi, in Albany, NY: *Galatians,* trans. F. R. Larcher, 1966; *Ephesians,* trans. M. L. Lamb, 1966; *1 Thessalonians* and *Philippians,* trans. F. R. Larcher and M. Duffy, 1969.

Expositio libri Boetii De hebdomadibus. LC 50 (1992): 267–82.

Expositio libri Peri hermenias. Ed. R. M. Spiazzi (Turin, 1955), pp. 3–88 (citations from this edition, which reproduces LC 1 [1882], have been checked for accuracy against the critical text in LC 1*/1 [1989], which revises LC 1). *Aristotle on Interpretation: Commentary by St. Thomas and Cajetan,* trans. J. T. Oesterle (Milwaukee: Marquette, 1962).

Expositio libri Posteriorum. Ed. R. M. Spiazzi (Turin, 1955), pp. 146–404 (citations from this edition, which reproduces LC 1 [1882], have been checked for accuracy against the critical text in LC 1*/2 [1989] which revises LC 1). *Commentary on* *the Posterior Analytics of Aristotle,* trans. F. R. Larcher (Albany, NY: Magi, 1970).

Expositio super Isaiam ad litteram. LC 28 (1974).

Expositio super Job ad litteram. LC 26 (1965). *The Literal Exposition on Job: A Scriptural Commentary concerning Providence,* trans. A. Damico (Atlanta: Scholars, 1989).

Expositio super primam et secundam Decretalem ad Archidiaconum Tudertinum. LC 40 (1969): E29–E44.

Lectura super Joannem. Ed. R. Cai (Turin, 1952). *Commentary on the Gospel of St. John* Part I (chaps. 1–7), trans. J. A. Weisheipl and F. R. Larcher (Albany, NY: Magi, 1980).

Lectura super Matthaeum. Ed. R. Cai (Turin, 1951).

Postilla super Psalmos. Psalms 1–51 are found in the Parma (1852–73) reprint ed. (New York: Musurgia, 1948–50), 14:148–353; psalms 52–54 are found in P. Uccelli, ed., *S. Thomae Aquinatis in Isaiam prophetam, in tres psalmos David, in Boetium de Hebdomadibus et de Trinitate expositiones* (Rome, 1880), pp. 241–54.

Quaestio disputata De anima. LC 24/1 (1996). *Questions on the Soul,* trans. J. H. Robb (Milwaukee: Marquette, 1984).

Quaestio disputata De caritate. Quaestiones Disputatae, ed. P. A. Odetto (Turin, 1949), 2:753–91. *On Charity,* trans. L. H. Kendzierski (Milwaukee: Marquette, 1960).

Quaestio disputata De spe. Quaestiones Disputatae, ed. P. A. Odetto (Turin, 1949), 2:803–12.

Quaestio disputata De spiritualibus creaturis. Quaestiones disputatae, ed. M. Calcaterra and T. S. Centi (Turin, 1965), 2:367–415. *On Spiritual Creatures,* trans. M. C. Fitzpatrick and J. J. Wellmuth (Milwaukee: Marquette, 1949).

Quaestiones de quodlibet I–XII. LC 25, 2 vols. (1996). Partial translation in S. Edwards, *Quodlibetal Questions 1 and 2* (Toronto: PIMS, 1983).

Quaestiones disputatae De malo. LC 23 (1982). *Disputed Questions on Evil,* trans. John and Jean Oesterle (Notre Dame: UND, 1983).

Quaestiones disputatae De potentia. Quaestiones Disputatae, ed. P. M. Pession (Turin, 1949), 2:7–276. *On the Power of God,* trans. English Dominicans (Westminster, MD: Newman, 1952).

Quaestiones disputatae De veritate. LC 22, 3 vols. (1970–76). *The Disputed Questions on Truth,* trans. R. W. Mulligan, J. V. McGlynn, R. W. Schmidt, 3 vols. (Chicago: Regnery, 1952–54).

Responsio ad Lectorem Venetum de 36 articulis. LC 42 (1979): 339–46.

Responsio ad Magistrum Joannem de Vercellis de 43 articulis. LC 42 (1979): 327–35.

Responsio ad Magistrum Joannem de Vercellis de 108 articulis. LC 42 (1979): 279–94.

Scriptum super libros Sententiarum. Books 1–2 ed. P. Mandonnet, *Scriptum super Sententiis,* vols. 1–2 (Paris: Lethielleux, 1929); books 3–4 ed. M. F. Moos, vols. 3–4 (Paris: Lethielleux, 1933, 1947); vol. 4 of the *Moos* edition only has distinctions 1–22 of book four, but Parma (1852–73) volume 7/2 has distinctions 23–50.

Sententia libri De anima. LC 45/1 (1984). *Aristotle's "De Anima" with the Commentary of St. Thomas Aquinas,* trans. K. Foster and S. Humphries (New Haven: Yale, 1951); repr. Dumb Ox Books, UND, 1994.

Sententia libri Ethicorum. LC 47, 2 vols. (1969). *Commentary on the Nicomachean Ethics,* trans. C. I. Litzinger, 2 vols. (Chicago: Regnery, 1964); repr. Dumb Ox Books, UND, 1993.

Sententia libri De memoria et reminiscentia. LC 45/2 (1985): 103–33.

Sententia libri De sensu et sensato. LC 45/2 (1985): 1–101.

Sententia super libros De caelo et mundo. Ed. R. M. Spiazzi (Turin, 1952), pp. 1–311, which is a reproduction of LC 3 (1886) without variants or notes.

Sententia super libros De generatione et corruptione. Ed. R. M. Spiazzi (Turin, 1952), pp. 315–85, which is a reproduction of LC 3 (1886) without variants or notes.

Sententia super Metaphysicam. Ed. M.-R. Cathala and R. M. Spiazzi (Turin, 1950). *Commentary on the Metaphysics of Aristotle,* trans. J. P. Rowan, 2 vols. (Chicago: Regnery, 1961); repr. Dumb Ox Books, UND, 1995.

Sententia super Meteora. Ed. R. M. Spiazzi (Turin, 1952), pp. 389–510, which is a reproduction of LC 3 (1886) without variants or notes.

Sententia super Physicam. Ed. P. M. Maggiólo (Turin, 1965), which is a reproduction of LC 2 (1884) without variants or notes. *Commentary on Aristotle's Physics,* trans. R. J. Blackwell et al. (New Haven: Yale, 1963).

Summa contra Gentiles. LC 13–15 (1918–30) is published in *Liber de veritate catholicae fidei contra errores infidelium,* vols. 2–3 (Turin, 1961), with some corrections and a full annotation. *On the Truth of the Catholic Faith,* trans. A. C. Pegis, J. F. Anderson, V. J. Bourke, C. J. O'Neil, 5 vols. (Garden City, NY: Doubleday, 1955–57).

Summa theologiae. LC 4–12 (1888–1906); this text has been published, without critical apparatus but with good bibliographies and extensive notes, in *Summa theologiae* (Alba/Rome: Editiones Paulinae, 1962). A lively translation can be found in the Latin-English bilingual edition by various editors/translators in 60 vols. (New York/London: McGraw-Hill/Eyre and Spottiswoode, 1964–76); vol. 61 is the general index (London: Eyre and Spottiswoode, 1981).

Super Boetium De Trinitate. LC 50 (1992): 75–171. Translation of questions 1–4: *Faith, Reason and Theology,* trans. with introduction and notes by A. Maurer, Medieval Sources in Translation 32 (Toronto: PIMS, 1987); translation of questions 5–6: *The Division and Methods of the Sciences,* trans. with introduction and notes by A. Maurer, 4th ed., Medieval Sources in Translation 3 (Toronto: PIMS, 1986).

Super librum De causis. Ed. C. Pera (Turin, 1955), which makes use of H.-D. Saffrey's critical text (Fribourg, 1954). *Commentary on the Book of Causes,* trans. and annotated by V. Guagliardo, C. Hess, R. Taylor, with an introduction by V. Guagliardo (Washington, DC: CUA, 1996).

Super librum Dionysii De divinis nominibus. Ed. C. Pera (Turin, 1950).

11. Other Primary Sources

Aristotle. *Aristotelis Opera*. In the recension of I. Bekker, 5 vols. Berlin: de Gruyter, 1960–61.

———. *The Basic Works of Aristotle*. Ed. with an introduction by Richard McKeon. New York: Random, 1941.

Avicenna. *Avicenna Latinus*. Ed. S. Van Riet, introductions by G. Verbeke, 5 vols. to date. Louvain/Leiden: Peeters/Brill, 1968–83.

Boethius of Dacia. *Opera: Modi significandi sive quaestiones super Priscianum Maiorem*. Ed. J. Pinborg, H. Roos, S. S. Jensen; Corpus Philosophorum Danicorum Medii Aevi, 4/1–2. Hauniae: Gad, 1969.

Busa, Robert, ed. *Index Thomisticus: Sancti Thomae Aquinatis Operum Omnium Indices et Concordantiae*. 41 vols. Stuttgart: Frommann-Holzboog, 1975.

Cajetan, Cardinal Tommaso de Vio. *De nominum analogia et de conceptu entis*. Ed. P. N. Zammit. Rome: Angelicum, 1934.

———. *The Analogy of Names and the Concept of Being*. Trans. E. A. Bushinski and H. J. Koren, with annotations. Duquesne Studies, Philosophical Series, no. 4. Pittsburgh: Duquesne University, 1953.

Fathers of the Church. Various translators and editors. Vols. 1–. Washington, DC: CUA, 1947–.

Maimonides, Moses. *The Guide of the Perplexed*. Trans. with introduction and notes by S. Pines, introductory essay by L. Strauss. Chicago: University of Chicago, 1963.

Migne, J.-P., ed. Patrologia latina (PL). 221 vols. Paris, 1844–64.

———. Patrologia graeca (PG). 161 vols. Paris, 1857–66.

Peter of Bergamo, comp. *Tabula aurea: In opera sancti Thomae Aquinatis, index*. Rome: Editiones Paulinae, 1960.

Plato. *The Dialogues of Plato*. Trans. B. Jowett, introduction by R. Demas, 2 vols. New York: Random, 1937.

Pseudo-Dionysius. *The Divine Names and Mystical Theology*. Trans. with introduction by John D. Jones. Milwaukee: Marquette, 1980.

———. *The Complete Works*. Trans. Colm Luibheid; foreword, notes, and translation collaboration by Paul Rorem; preface by Rene Roques; introductions by Jaroslav Pelikan, Jean Leclercq, and Karlfried Froelich. Classics of Western Spirituality. New York: Paulist, 1987.

Simplicius of Cilicia. *Hypomnmata eis ta okt Aristotelous physiks akroases biblia meta/tou hypokeimenou tou Aristotelous*. Microfilm copy (1961) of the original Venice edition (1526), which is in the Vatican library (List 27, no. 30).

III. *Secondary Literature*

Adler, Mortimer J. "The Equivocal Use of the Word 'Analogical.'" *NS* 48 (1974): 4–18.

Aertsen, Jan. *Nature and Creature: Thomas Aquinas's Way of Thought.* Trans. H. D. Morton. Leiden: Brill, 1988.

Alès, Adhémar d'. "De Incomprehensibili." *RSR* 23 (1933): 306–20.

Alfaro, Juan. "Supernaturalitas fidei iuxta S. Thomam." *Gregorianum* 44 (1963): 501–42; 731–87.

Alpern, Barbara D. "The Logic of Doxological Language: A Reinterpretation of Aquinas and Pannenberg on Analogy and Doxology." Ph.D. dissertation, University of Pittsburgh, 1980.

Alston, William. "Aquinas on Theological Predication: A Look Backward and a Look Forward." In *Reasoned Faith: Essays in Philosophical Theology in Honor of Norman Kretzmann,* ed. Eleonore Stump, pp. 145–78. Ithaca: Cornell, 1993.

Anawati, Georges C. "Chronique avicennienne 1951–1960." *RT* 60 (1960): 614–34.

Anderson, James. *The Bond of Being.* St. Louis: Herder, 1949.

———. "Analogy in Plato." *RM* 4 (1950): 111–28.

Aniz, Candido. "Definicion agustiniano-tomista del acto de fe." *La ciencia tomista* 80 (1953): 25–74.

Antilla, Raimo, and Warren Brewer. *Analogy: A Basic Bibliography.* The Hague/Berlin: Mouton/de Gruyter, 1977.

Antweiler, Anton. *Die Anfangslosigkeit der Welt nach Thomas von Aquin und Kant.* Trier: Paulinus, 1961.

Armstrong, A. H., and R. A. Markus. *Christian Faith and Greek Philosophy.* New York: Sheed and Ward, 1964.

Arnou, René. *De quinque viis Sancti Thomae ad demonstrandum Dei existentiam apud antiquos Graecos et Arabes et Iudaeos praeformatis vel adumbratis.* Rome: Gregorian, 1932.

Artola, J. M. *Creación y participación. La participación de la naturaleza divina en las criaturas según la filosofía de Santo Tomas de Aquino.* Madrid: Publicaciones de la Institución Aquinas, 1963.

Ashmore, Robert B. "The Analogical Notion of Judgment in St. Thomas Aquinas." Ph.D. dissertation, University of Notre Dame, 1966.

Ashworth, E. J. *The Tradition of Medieval Logic and Speculative Grammar from Anselm to the End of the Seventeenth Century: A Bibliography from 1836 Onwards.* Toronto: PIMS, 1978.

———. "Signification and Modes of Signifying in Thirteenth-Century Logic: A Preface to Aquinas on Analogy." *Medieval Philosophy and Theology* 1 (1991): 39–67.

———. "Analogy and Equivocation in Thirteenth-Century Logic: Aquinas in Context." *MS* 54 (1992): 94–135.

Aubert, Roger. *Le problème de l'acte de foi.* 3rd ed. Louvain: Warny, 1958.
———. "Saint Thomas d'Aquin et la *Métaphysique* d'Avicenne." In *St. Thomas Aquinas, 1274–1974: Commemorative Studies*, 2 vols., 1:449–65. Toronto: PIMS, 1974.
Baisnée, Jules A. "St. Thomas Aquinas' Proofs of the Existence of God Presented in Their Chronological Order." In *Philosophical Studies in Honor of the Very Reverend Ignatius Smith, O.P.*, ed. J. K. Ryan, pp. 29–64. Westminster, MD: Newman, 1952.
Balas, David L. "A Thomist View on Divine Infinity." *PACPA* 55 (1981): 91–98.
Balthasar, Hans Urs von. *The Theology of Karl Barth.* Trans. J. Drury. New York: Holt, Rinehart and Winston, 1971.
Barth, Karl. *Church Dogmatics.* Trans. G. T. Thompson et al., 5 vols. Edinburgh: T. and T. Clark, 1936–77.
Bauer, Johannes. "Können die Namen Gottes Synonyme sein? Mit besonderer Bezugnahme auf Thomas von Aquin." *SJP* 19 (1974): 83–91.
Beaurecueil, M. J. de. "L'homme image de Dieu selon saint Thomas d'Aquin." *Études et recherches* 8 (1952): 45–82; 9 (1955): 37–96.
Blanchette, Oliva. *The Perfection of the Universe according to Aquinas: A Teleological Cosmology.* University Park: Pennsylvania State University, 1992.
Blankenhorn, Bernhard-Thomas. "The Good as Self-Diffusive in Thomas Aquinas." *Angelicum* 79 (2002): 803–37.
Boland, Vivian. *Ideas in God according to Saint Thomas Aquinas: Sources and Synthesis.* Leiden: Brill, 1996.
Bonansea, Bernardino. "The Human Mind and the Knowledge of God: Reflections on a Scholastic Controversy." *FS* 40 (1980): 5–17.
Bonhoeffer, T. *Die Gotteslehre des Thomas von Aquin als Sprachproblem.* Beiträge zur historischen Theologie 32. Tübingen: Mohr, 1961.
Booth, Edward. *Aristotelian Aporetic Ontology in Islamic and Christian Thinkers.* Cambridge: Cambridge University, 1983.
Bouillard, Henri. *The Knowledge of God.* Trans. S. D. Femiano. New York: Herder and Herder, 1968.
Boulanger, A.-B. "Le 'semi-agnosticisme' du P. Sertillanges et le thomisme du R. P. Romeyer." *RT* 35 (1930): 158–89.
Bourke, Vernon J., comp. *Thomistic Bibliography: 1920–1940.* St. Louis: *Modern Schoolman* (supplement to vol. 21), 1945.
Boyer, Charles. "The Meaning of a Text of St. Thomas: *De veritate*, Q.1, A.9." Appendix to *Reality and Judgment according to St. Thomas*, by Peter Hoenen, trans. H. F. Tiblier, pp. 295–309. Chicago: Regnery, 1952.
Boyle, Leonard. *The Setting of the "Summa theologiae" of Saint Thomas.* Étienne Gilson Series 5. Toronto: PIMS, 1982.
Bradley, Denis. "Thomistic Theology and the Hegelian Critique of Religious Imagination." *NS* 59 (1985): 60–78.

Branick, Vincent P. "The Unity of the Divine Ideas." *NS* 42 (1968): 171–201.

Broadie, Alexander. "Maimonides and Aquinas on the Names of God." *RS* 23 (1987): 157–70.

Brugger, Walter. "Sprachanalytische Überlegungen bei Thomas von Aquin." *ThPh* 49 (1974): 437–63.

Brunetti, Manlio. "La conoscenza *speculare* di Dio in S. Tommaso d'Aquino." *Divinitas* 1 (1957): 528–49.

Brunn, Émilie Zum. "La 'Métaphysique de l'Exode' selon Thomas d'Aquin." In *Dieu et l'être: exégèses d'Exode 3:14 et de Coran 20:11–24*, ed. P. Vignaux et al., pp. 245–69. Paris: Études Augustiniennes, 1978.

———. "L'exégèse augustinienne de *Ego sum qui sum* et la 'métaphysique de l'Exode.'" In *Dieu et l'être: exégèses d'Exode 3:14 et de Coran 20:11–24*, ed. P. Vignaux et al., pp. 141–64. Paris: Études Augustiniennes, 1978.

Buersmeyer, Keith. "The Verb and Existence." *NS* 60 (1986): 145–62.

Bulletin thomiste. Vols. 1–12. Paris: Le Saulchoir, 1924–65.

Bultmann, Rudolf. "What Sense Is There to Speak of God?" In *Religious Language and the Problem of Religious Knowledge*, ed. R. Santoni, pp. 186–97. Bloomington: Indiana University, 1968.

Burrell, David. "A Note on Analogy." *NS* 36 (1962): 225–32.

———. "Religious Language and the Logic of Analogy: Apropos of McInerny's Book and Ross' Review." *IPQ* 2 (1962): 643–58.

———. "Aquinas on Naming God." *TS* 24 (1963): 183–212.

———. "Beyond the Theory of Analogy." *PACPA* 46 (1972): 114–21.

———. *Analogy and Philosophical Language*. New Haven: Yale, 1973.

———. *Aquinas: God and Action*. Notre Dame: UND, 1979.

———. Review of *Portraying Analogy*, by James F. Ross. *NS* 59 (1985): 347–57.

———. "Essence and Existence: Avicenna and Greek Philosophy." *Mélanges Institut Dominicain d'Etudes Orientales* 17 (1986): 53–66.

———. *Knowing the Unknowable God: Ibn-Sina, Maimonides, Aquinas*. Notre Dame: UND, 1986.

———. *Freedom and Creation in Three Traditions*. Notre Dame: UND, 1993.

———. "Maimonides, Aquinas, and Ghazali on Naming God." In *The Return to Scripture in Judaism and Christianity: Essays in Postcritical Scriptural Interpretation*, ed. Peter Ochs, pp. 238–46. New York: Paulist, 1993.

———. "Analogy, Creation, and Theological Language." *PACPA* 74 (2000): 35–52.

———. "Creation, Metaphysics, and Ethics." *FP* 18 (2001): 204–21.

Bursill-Hall, Geoffrey L. *Speculative Grammars of the Middle Ages*. Approaches to Semiotics 11. The Hague/Paris: Mouton, 1971.

Cambridge History of Later Medieval Philosophy. Ed. N. Kretzmann, A. Kenny, J. Pinborg. Cambridge: Cambridge University, 1982.

Cantens, Bernardo. "The Interdependency between Aquinas' Doctrine of Creation and His Metaphysical Principle of the Limitation of Act by Potency." *PACPA* 74 (2000): 121–40.

Carabine, D. "Apophasis East and West." *RTAM* 55 (1988): 5–29.

Cataldo, Peter J. "Plato, Aristotle, and *pros hen* Equivocity." *MSch* 61 (1984): 237–47.

Catania, Francis J. "Divine Infinity in Albert the Great's Commentary on the *Sentences* of Peter Lombard." *MS* 22 (1960): 27–42.

———. "'Knowable' and 'Namable' in Albert the Great's Commentary on the *Divine Names.*" In *Albert the Great: Commemorative Essays,* ed. and with an introduction by F. J. Kovach and R. W. Shahan, pp. 97–128. Norman: University of Oklahoma, 1980.

Centore, Florestano. "Lovejoy and Aquinas on God's 'Need' to Create." *Angelicum* 59 (1982): 23–36.

Chapman, Tobias. "Analogy." *Thomist* 39 (1975): 127–41.

Chavannes, Henry. *L'Analogie entre Dieu et la monde selon Thomas d'Aquin et selon Karl Barth.* Paris: Cerf, 1969.

Chenu, M.-D. "Grammaire et théologie aux XIIe et XIIIe siècles." *AHDLMA* 10 (1936): 5–28.

———. "Un vestige du stoicisme." *RSPT* 27 (1938): 63–68.

———. *La théologie au douzième siècle.* Preface by É. Gilson. Études de philosophie médiévale 45. Paris: Vrin, 1957.

———. *La parole de Dieu.* Vol. 1: *La foi dans l'intelligence.* Paris: Cerf, 1964.

———. *Toward Understanding St. Thomas.* Trans. with authorized corrections and bibliographical additions by A.-M. Landry and D. Hughes. Chicago: Regnery, 1964.

Chevalier, J. "Aristote et S. Thomas d'Aquin, ou l'idée de création." *Lettres* 14 (1927): 427–47.

Chroust, Anton-Hermann. "Some Comments on Aristotle, *De caelo* 279a18–35." *DTP* 53 (1976): 255–64.

———. "Aristotle's Doctrine of the Uncreatedness and Indestructibility of the Universe." *NS* 52 (1978): 268–79.

Clarke, W. Norris. "The Limitation of Act by Potency: Aristotelianism or Neoplatonism." *NS* 26 (1952): 167–94.

———. "The Meaning of Participation in St. Thomas." *PACPA* 26 (1952): 147–57.

———. "Infinity and Plotinus: A Reply." *Gregorianum* 40 (1959): 75–98.

———. "Analogy and the Meaningfulness of Language about God: A Reply to Kai Nielsen." *Thomist* 40 (1976): 61–95.

———. *The Philosophical Approach to God.* Foreword by J. R. Scales, introduction by E. M. Adams. Winston-Salem, NC: Wake Forest University, 1979.

Clavell, Luis. *El nombre proprio de Dios segun Santo Tomas de Aquino.* Pamplona: Universidad de Navarra, 1980.

Collins, Mary. "Naming God in Public Prayer." *Worship* 59 (1985): 291–304.

Connell, Desmond. "St. Thomas on Reflection and Judgment." *ITQ* 45 (1978): 234–47.

Connolly, Thomas W. "The Attributes of God in the *Sentences* of St. Thomas." *PS* 4 (1954): 18–50.

Corbin, Michel. "Négation et transcendance dans l'oeuvre de Denys." *RSPT* 69 (1985): 41–76.

Corte, Marcel de. "La causalité du premier moteur dans la philosophie aristotélicienne." *Revue d'histoire de la philosophie* 5 (1931): 105–47.

Corvez, Maurice. "Le Dieu de Platon." *RPL* 65 (1967): 5–35.

Craig, William Lane. "The Eternal Present and Stump-Kretzmann Eternity." *ACPQ* 73 (1999): 521–36.

Craighead, Houston. "Rudolph Bultmann and the Impossibility of Godtalk." *FP* 1 (1984): 203–15.

Cunningham, Francis. "Judgment in St. Thomas." *MSch* 31 (1954): 185–212.

———. "The Second Operation and the Assent vs. the Judgment in St. Thomas." *NS* 31 (1957): 1–33.

Dales, Richard. *Medieval Discussions of the Eternity of the World*. Leiden: Brill, 1990.

Dales, Richard, and Omar Argerami, eds. *Medieval Latin Texts on the Eternity of the World*. Leiden; Brill, 1991.

Daniélou, Jean. "L'incompréhensibilité de Dieu d'après saint Jean Chrysostome." *RSR* 37 (1950): 176–94.

———. *A History of Early Christian Doctrine before the Council of Nicea*. Vol. 2: *Gospel Message and Hellenistic Culture*. Trans., ed., and with a postscript by J. A. Baker. London/Philadelphia: Westminster, 1973.

Davidson, H. A. *Proofs for Eternity, Creation, and the Existence of God in Medieval Islamic and Jewish Philosophy*. New York: Oxford, 1987.

Davies, Brian. *The Thought of Thomas Aquinas*. Oxford: Clarendon, 1992.

———. "Aquinas on What God Is Not." *Revue internationale de philosophie* 52 (1998): 207–25.

Dewan, Lawrence. "St. Thomas and the Divine Names." *SE* 32 (1980): 19–33.

———. "St. Albert, Creation, and the Philosophers." *LTP* 40 (1984): 295–307.

———. "St. Thomas, Aristotle, and Creation." *Dionysius* 15 (1991): 81–90.

Dienstag, Jacob I., ed. *Studies in Maimonides and St. Thomas Aquinas*. With introduction and bibliography. Bibliotheca Maimonidica 1. New York: KTAV, 1975.

DiNoia, J. A. "Knowing and Naming the Triune God: The Grammar of Trinitarian Confession." *Speaking the Christian God: The Holy Trinity and the Challenge of Feminism*, ed. Alvin Kimel Jr., pp. 162–87. Grand Rapids: Eerdmans, 1992.

Dobbs-Weinstein, Idit. *Maimonides and St. Thomas on the Limits of Reason*. New York: SUNY, 1995.

Dodds, Michael. *The Unchanging God of Love*. Studia Friburgensia, N.S. 66. Fribourg, Switzerland: University of Fribourg, 1986.

Doig, James C. *Aquinas on Metaphysics: A Historico-Doctrinal Study of the Commentary on the Metaphysics*. The Hague: Nijhoff, 1972.

Dondaine, Antoine. "Saint Thomas et la dispute des attributs divins (I *Sent.*, d. 2, a. 3)." *AFP* 8 (1938): 253–62.

Dondaine, H.-F. "Cognoscere de Deo 'quid est.'" *RTAM* 22 (1955): 72–78.

Duclow, Donald F. "Pseudo-Dionysius, John Scotus Erigena, Nicholas of Cusa: An Approach to the Hermeneutic of the Divine Names." *IPQ* 12 (1972): 260–78.

Ducoin, G. "Saint Thomas, commentateur d'Aristote. Étude sur le commentaire thomiste du livre lambda des *Métaphysiques* d'Aristote." *AP* 20 (1957): 78–117, 240–71, 392–445.

Dunphy, William. "Maimonides and Aquinas on Creation: A Critique of Their Historians." In *Graceful Reason: Essays in Ancient and Medieval Philosophy Presented to Joseph Owens, CSSR*, ed. L. P. Gerson, pp. 361–79. Toronto: PIMS, 1983.

Durbin, Paul R. "Unity and Composition in Judgment." *Thomist* 31 (1967): 83–120.

Duroux, Benoit. *La psychologie de la foi chez saint Thomas d'Aquin*. Tournai: Desclée, 1963.

Edwards, Denis. "Negative Theology and the Historical Jesus." *ACR* 60 (1983): 167–85.

Egan, Harvey D. "Christian Apophatic and Kataphatic Mysticisms." *TS* 39 (1978): 399–426.

Egan, James M. "Naming in St. Thomas' Theology of the Trinity." In *From an Abundant Spring*, ed. by *Thomist* staff, pp. 152–71. New York: P. J. Kenedy, 1952.

Ehrhardt, Arnold. *The Beginning: A Study in the Greek Philosophical Approach to the Concept of Creation from Anaximander to St. John*. New York: Barnes and Noble, 1968.

Elders, Leo. *Aristotle's Theology. A Commentary on Book Lambda of the Metaphysics*. Assen: Van Gorcum, 1972.

———. "L'ordre des attributs divins dans la *Somme théologique*." *DTP* 56 (1979): 225–32.

———. "Les cinq voies et leur place dans la philosophie de saint Thomas." In *Quinque Sunt Viae*, Studi Tomistici 9, pp. 133–46. Vatican City, 1980.

———. "St. Thomas Aquinas and the Problems of Speaking about God." *DC* 35 (1982): 305–16.

———. *The Philosophical Theology of St. Thomas Aquinas*. Leiden: Brill, 1990.

Emery, Gilles. "Brief Catalogue of the Works of Saint Thomas Aquinas." In Jean-Pierre Torrell, *Saint Thomas Aquinas*, vol. 1: *The Person and His Work*, trans. Robert Royal, pp. 330–61. Washington, DC: CUA, 1996.

Ernst, Cornelius. "Metaphor and Ontology in *Sacra Doctrina*." *Thomist* 38 (1974): 403–25.

Eschmann, I. T. "A Catalogue of St. Thomas' Works." In Étienne Gilson, *The Christian Philosophy of St. Thomas Aquinas*, trans. L. K. Shook, pp. 381–439. New York: Random, 1956.

Evans, Donald. "Preller's Analogy of 'Being.'" *NS* 45 (1971): 1–37.

Ewbank, Michael. "Diverse Orderings of Dionysius' *Triplex Via* by St. Thomas Aquinas." *MS* 52 (1990): 83–109.

Fabro, Cornelio. "Une itinéraire de S. Thomas: l'établissement de la distinction réelle entre essence et existence." *RP* 39 (1939): 285–310; repr. in his *Esegesi tomistica* (Rome, 1969), pp. 89–108.

———. *La nozione metafisica di partecipazione secondo S. Tommaso d'Aquino.* 2nd ed. Turin: Società editrice internazionale, 1950.

———. "Teologia dei nomi divini nel Lombardo e in Tommaso." *Pier Lombardo* 4 (1960): 77–93.

———. *Participation et causalité selon S. Thomas d'Aquin.* Preface by L. De Raeymaeker, Chaire Cardinal Mercier 2. Paris/Louvain: Béatrice-Nauwelaerts/ Publications Universitaires, 1961.

———. "The Intensive Hermeneutics of Thomistic Philosophy: The Notion of Participation." *RM* 27 (1974): 449–91.

Farthing, John L. "The Problem of Divine Exemplarity in St. Thomas." *Thomist* 49 (1985): 183–222.

Faucon, Pierre. *Aspects néoplatoniciens de la doctrine de saint Thomas d'Aquin.* Paris/Lille: Champion/University III, 1975.

Favre, André. "La philosophie de Przywara: métaphysique de créature." *RNP* 37 (1934): 65–87.

Feldman, Seymour. "A Scholastic Misinterpretation of Maimonides' Doctrine of Divine Attributes." In *Studies in Maimonides and St. Thomas Aquinas,* ed. J. I. Dienstag, Bibliotheca Maimonidica 1, pp. 58–74. New York: KTAV, 1975.

Ferré, Frederick. *Language, Logic, and God.* Chicago: University of Chicago, 1961.

Finance, Joseph de. *Etre et agir dans le philosophie de saint Thomas.* Paris: Beauchesne, 1945.

Findlay, John N. *Plato: The Written and Unwritten Doctrines.* London: Routledge and Kegan Paul, 1974.

Flanigan, Sister Thomas M. "The Use of Analogy in the *Summa contra gentiles.*" *MSch* 35 (1957): 21–37.

Forest, Aimé. *La structure métaphysique du concret selon saint Thomas d'Aquin.* 2nd ed. Foreword by É. Gilson, Études de philosophie médiévale 14. Paris: Vrin, 1956.

Franck, Isaac. "Maimonides and Aquinas on Man's Knowledge of God: A Twentieth Century Perspective." *RM* 38 (1985): 591–615.

Garceau, Benoit. *Judicium: vocabulaire, sources, doctrine de saint Thomas d'Aquin.* Montreal/Paris: Institute of Medieval Studies/Vrin, 1968.

Geach, Peter. *Mental Acts.* London: Routledge and Kegan Paul, n.d.

Geiger, Louis-B. *La participation dans la philosophie de S. Thomas d'Aquin.* BibThom 23. Paris: Vrin, 1942.

———. "Saint Thomas et la Métaphysique d'Aristote." In *Aristote et Saint Thom-*

as d'Aquin, ed. P. Moraux et al., pp. 175–220. Louvain: University of Louvain, 1957.

———. "Les idées divines dans l'oeuvre de S. Thomas." In *St. Thomas Aquinas, 1274–1974: Commemorative Studies*, 2 vols., 1:175–209. Toronto: PIMS, 1974.

Gerson, Lloyd. *God and Greek Philosophy: Studies in the Early History of Natural Theology*. London/New York: Routledge, 1990.

Gertz, B. *Glaubenswelt als Analogie: Die theologische Analogielehre Erich Przywaras und ihre Ort in der Auseinandersetzung um die Analogia fidei*. Düsseldorf: Patmos, 1968.

Ghisalberti, Alessandro. "La creazione nella filosofia di S. Tommaso d'Aquino." *RFNS* 61 (1969): 202–20.

Gilkey, Langdon. *Naming the Whirlwind: The Renewal of God-Language*. Indianapolis: Bobbs-Merrill, 1969.

Gilson, Étienne. "Avicenne et le point de départ de Duns Scot." *AHDLMA* 2 (1927): 89–149.

———. *The Spirit of Medieval Philosophy*. Trans. A. H. C. Downes, Gifford Lectures of 1931–32. New York: Scribner's, 1940.

———. "La notion d'existence chez Guillaume d'Auvergne." *AHDLMA* 15 (1946): 55–91.

———. "Maimonide et la philosophie de l'exode." *MS* 13 (1951): 223–25.

———. *Being and Some Philosophers*. 2nd ed. Toronto: PIMS, 1952.

———. *Jean Duns Scot*. Études de philosophie médiévale 42. Paris: Vrin, 1952.

———. *History of Christian Philosophy in the Middle Ages*. New York: Random, 1955.

———. *The Christian Philosophy of St. Thomas Aquinas*. Trans. L. K. Shook, with a catalogue of Thomas' works by I. T. Eschmann. New York: Random, 1956.

———. "Notes pour l'histoire de la cause efficiente." *AHDLMA* 29 (1962): 7–31.

———. *The Elements of Christian Philosophy*. New York: New American Library, 1963.

———. "Avicenne en occident au moyen âge." *AHDLMA* 36 (1969): 89–121.

Gisel, Pierre, and Secretan, Philibert, eds. *Analogie et dialectique*. Lieux Théologiques 3. Geneva: Labor et Fides, 1982.

Goichon, Amélie-Marie. *La distinction de l'essence et de l'existence d'après Ibn Sina (Avicenne)*. Paris: Desclée, 1937.

———. *La philosophie d'Avicenne et son influence en Europe médiévale*. 2nd ed. Paris: Adrien-Maisonneuve, 1951.

———. "Un chapitre de l'influence d'Ibn Sina en Occident: le *De ente et essentia* de S. Thomas d'Aquin." In *Le livre du Millénaire d'Avicenne*, vol. 4 (Tehran, 1956), pp. 118–31.

Gonzalez de Cardedal, Olegario. *Teologia y antropologia. El hombre "imagen de Dios" en el pensamiento de Santo Tomas*. Introduction by X. Zubiri. Madrid: Editorial Moneda y Credito, 1967.

Grabmann, Martin. *Mittelalterliches Geistesleben.* 3 vols. Munich: M. Hueber, 1926, 1936, 1956.

Green, Garrett. "The Gender of God and the Theology of Metaphor." *Speaking the Christian God: The Holy Trinity and the Challenge of Feminism,* ed. Alvin Kimel Jr., pp. 44–64. Grand Rapids: Eerdmans, 1992.

Grenet, Paul. *Les origins de l'analogie philosophique dans les dialogues de Platon.* Paris: Boivin, 1948.

Guarino, Thomas. "The Truth-Status of Theological Statements: Analogy Re-Visited." *ITQ* 55 (1988): 140–55.

———. *Revelation and Truth: Unity and Plurality in Contemporary Theology.* Scranton/London: University of Scranton/Associated University Presses, 1993.

Guérard, Christian. "La théologie négative dans l'apophatisme grec." *RSPT* 68 (1984): 183–200.

Guzie, Tad. "The Act of Faith according to St. Thomas: A Study in Theological Methodology." *Thomist* 29 (1965): 239–80.

Hack, Roy K. *God in Greek Philosophy to the Time of Socrates.* Princeton: Princeton University, 1931.

Hadot, Pierre. "Dieu comme acte d'être dans le néoplatonisme. A propos des théories d'É. Gilson sur la métaphysique de l'Exode." In *Dieu et l'être: exégèses d'Exode 3:14 et de Coran 20:11–24,* ed. P. Vignaux et al., pp. 57–63. Paris: Études Augustiniennes, 1978.

Hamlyn, D. W. "Aristotle's God." In *The Philosophical Assessment of Theology,* ed. Gerard Hughes, pp. 15–33. Washington, DC: Georgetown University, 1987.

Hankey, Wayne J. "The Place of the Proof for God's Existence in the *Summa theologiae* of Thomas Aquinas." *Thomist* 46 (1982): 370–93.

———. *God in Himself: Aquinas' Doctrine of God as Expounded in the "Summa Theologiae."* Oxford: Oxford University, 1987.

Hayen, André. *L'intentionnel selon saint Thomas.* 2nd ed. Preface by J. Maréchal, Museum Lessianum (section philosophique), 25. Brussels/Paris: Desclée, 1954.

———. *La communication de l'être d'après saint Thomas d'Aquin.* 2 vols., Museum Lessianum (section philosophique), 40–41. Louvain/Paris: Desclée, 1957–59.

Hayes, Zachary. *The General Doctrine of Creation in the Thirteenth Century: With Special Emphasis on Matthew of Aquasparta.* Munich: Schöningh, 1964.

Hazelton, Roger. "Theological Analogy and Metaphor." *Semeia* 13 (1978): 155–76.

Heath, Thomas R. "St. Thomas and the Aristotelian Metaphysics." *NS* 34 (1960): 438–60.

Heintel, Erich. "Transzendenz und Analogie." In *Wirklichkeit und Reflexion,* Festschrift Walter Schulz, ed. H. Fahrenbach, pp. 267–90. Pfüllingen: Neske, 1973.

Henle, Robert J. "Existentialism and the Judgment." *PACPA* 21 (1946): 40–53.

———. *Saint Thomas and Platonism.* The Hague: Nijhoff, 1956.

Hesse, Mary. "Analogy and Confirmation Theory." *Dialectica* 17 (1963): 284–95.

———. "Aristotle's Logic of Analogy." *PQ* 15 (1965): 328–40.

———. *Models and Analogies in Science.* Notre Dame: UND Press, 1966.

Hibbs, Thomas S. *Dialectic and Narrative in Aquinas: An Interpretation of the "Summa contra gentiles."* Notre Dame: UND, 1995.

Hill, William J. *Knowing the Unknown God.* New York: Philosophical Library, 1971.

———. "In What Sense Is God Infinite? A Thomistic Perspective." *Thomist* 42 (1978): 14–27.

———. "Two Gods of Love: Aquinas and Whitehead." *Listening* 14 (1979): 49–64.

———. "On *Knowing the Unknowable God:* A Review Discussion." *Thomist* 51 (1987): 699–709.

Hirschberger, Johannes. "Paronymie und Analogie bei Aristoteles." *PJ* 68 (1960): 191–203.

Hochstaffl, Josef. *Negative Theologie: Ein Versuch zur Vermittlung des patristischen Begriffs.* Munich: Kösel, 1976.

Hoenen, Peter. *Reality and Judgment according to St. Thomas.* Trans. H. F. Tiblier, with an appendix by Charles Boyer. Chicago: Regnery, 1952.

Holstein, Henri. "L'origine aristotélicienne de la *tertia via* de saint Thomas." *RPL* 48 (1950): 354–70.

Hughes, Gerard. "Aquinas and the Limits of Agnosticism." In *The Philosophical Assessment of Theology,* ed. Gerard Hughes, pp. 35–63. Washington, DC: Georgetown University, 1987.

Humbrecht, T.-D. "La théologie négative chez saint Thomas d'Aquin." *RT* 93 (1993): 535–66.

Inciarte, Fernando. "La importancia de la unión predicado-sujeto en la doctrina trinitaria de Tomás de Aquino." *Scripta Theologica* 12 (1980): 871–84.

———. "Zur Rolle der Prädikation in der Theologie des Thomas von Aquin: Am Beispiel der Trinitätslehre." In Miscellanea Mediaevalia 13/1, *Sprache und Erkenntnis im Mittelalter,* pp. 256–69. Berlin: de Gruyter, 1981

International Theological Commission. "On the Interpretation of Dogmas." *Origins* 20 (17 May 1990): 1–14.

Jaeger, Werner. *The Theology of the Early Greek Philosophers.* Trans. E. S. Robinson, Gifford Lectures of 1936. Oxford: Clarendon, 1947.

Jenkins, John. *Knowledge and Faith in Thomas Aquinas.* Cambridge: Cambridge University, 1997.

Johnson, Elizabeth. "The Right Way to Speak about God? Pannenberg on Analogy." *TS* 43 (1982): 673–92.

———. "The Incomprehensibility of God and the Image of God Male and Female." *TS* 45 (1984): 441–65.

———. "Mary and the Female Face of God." *TS* 50 (1989): 500–526.

———. *She Who Is: The Mystery of God in Feminist Theological Discourse.* New York: Crossroad, 1992.

Johnson, Mark. "Did St. Thomas Attribute a Doctrine of Creation to Aristotle?" *NS* 63 (1989): 129–55.

———. "*Alia lectura fratris thome:* A List of the New Texts of St. Thomas Aquinas Found in Lincoln College, Oxford, MS. Lat. 95." *RTAM* 57 (1990): 34–61.

———. "Aquinas's Changing Evaluation of Plato on Creation." *ACPQ* 66 (1992): 81–88.

———. "Apophatic Theology's Cataphatic Dependencies." *Thomist* 62 (1998): 519–31.

Jolivet, R. "Aristote et la notion de création." *RSPT* 19 (1930): 5–50, 209–35.

Jones, John D. "The Character of the Negative (Mystical) Theology for Pseudo-Dionysius Areopagite." *PACPA* 51 (1977): 66–74.

Jordan, Mark. "Modes of Discourse in Aquinas' Metaphysics." *NS* 54 (1980): 401–46.

———. "The Names of God and the Being of Names." In *The Existence and Nature of God,* ed. A. J. Freddoso, Studies in the Philosophy of Religion 3, pp. 161–90. Notre Dame: UND, 1983.

———. "The Intelligibility of the World and the Divine Ideas in Aquinas." *RM* 38 (1984): 17–32.

Journet, Charles. *The Dark Knowledge of God.* Trans. J. F. Anderson. London: Sheed and Ward, 1948.

———. "La portée des noms divins." *NV* 35 (1960): 150–54.

———. "Les noms de Dieu ineffable." *NV* 35 (1960): 291–309.

Judy, Albert. "Avicenna's *Metaphysics* in the *Summa contra gentiles.*" *Angelicum* 52 (1975): 340–84, 541–86; 53 (1976): 185–226.

Jüngel, Eberhard. *Zum Ursprung der Analogie bei Parmenides und Heraklit.* Berlin: de Gruyter, 1964.

———. *God as the Mystery of the World.* Trans. D. L. Guder. Grand Rapids: Eerdmans, 1983.

Kannengiesser, Charles. "L'infinité divine chez Grégoire de Nysse." *RSR* 55 (1967): 55–65.

Kasper, Walter. *The God of Jesus Christ.* Trans. M. J. O'Connell. New York: Crossroad, 1984.

Kaufman, Gordon. *God the Problem.* Cambridge: Harvard, 1972.

Keating, Mary W. "The Relation between the Proofs for the Existence of God and the Real Distinction of Essence and Existence in St. Thomas Aquinas." Ph.D. dissertation, Fordham University, 1962.

Keller, Albert. "Arbeiten zur Sprachphilosophie Thomas von Aquins." *ThPh* 49 (1974): 464–76.

Kelly, Bernard. *The Metaphysical Background of Analogy.* Aquinas Papers 29. London: Blackfriars, 1958.

Kimel, Alvin Jr., ed. *Speaking the Christian God: The Holy Trinity and the Challenge of Feminism.* Grand Rapids: Eerdmans, 1992.

Klubertanz, George B. "*Esse* and *Existere* in St. Bonaventure." *MS* 8 (1946): 169–88.

———. "The Problem of the Analogy of Being." *RM* 10 (1957): 553–79.

———. *St. Thomas Aquinas on Analogy: A Textual Analysis and Systematic Synthesis.* Chicago: Loyola, 1960.

———. "Analogy." *NCE* (1967): 1:461–65.

Knasas, John F. X. "Aquinas, Analogy, and the Divine Infinity." *DC* 40 (1987): 64–84.

———. "*Contra* Spinoza: Aquinas on God's Free Will." *ACPQ* 76 (2002): 417–29.

Kovach, Francis J. "The Infinity of the Divine Essence and Power in the Works of St. Albert the Great." Miscellanea Mediaevalia 14:24–40. Berlin/New York: de Gruyter, 1981.

Kremer, Klaus. "Die Creatio nach Thomas von Aquin und dem *Liber de Causis*." In *Ekklesia: Festschrift für Bischof Dr. Matthias Wehr,* pp. 321–44. Trier: Paulinus, 1962.

———. "Das 'Warum' der Schöpfung: *quia bonus vel/et quia voluit?* Ein Beitrag zum Verhältnis von Neuplatonismus und Christentum an Hand des Prinzips *bonum est diffusivum sui*." In *Parusia. Festgabe für Johannes Hirschberger,* pp. 241–64. Frankfurt: Minerva, 1965.

———. *Die neuplatonische Seinsphilosophie und ihre Wirkung auf Thomas von Aquin.* 2nd ed. Leiden: Brill, 1971.

Kretzmann, Norman. *The Metaphysics of Theism: Aquinas' Natural Theology in "Summa contra gentiles" I.* Oxford: Clarendon, 1997.

———. *The Metaphysics of Creation: Aquinas' Natural Theology in "Summa contra gentiles" II.* Oxford: Clarendon, 1999.

Kuntz, Paul. "The Analogy of Degrees of Being: A Critique of Cajetan's *Analogy of Names*." *NS* 56 (1982): 51–79.

Kuykendall, George. "Thomas' Proofs as *Fides Quaerens Intellectum*: Towards a Trinitarian *Analogia*." *SJT* 31 (1978): 113–31.

Kvanvig, Jonathan. "Divine Transcendence." *RS* 20 (1984): 377–87.

LaCugna, Catherine Mowry. "God in Communion with Us: The Trinity." In *Freeing Theology: The Essentials of Theology in Feminist Perspective,* ed. C. LaCugna, pp. 83–114. San Francisco: HarperCollins, 1993.

Lagrange, M.-J. "Comment s'est transformée la pensée religieuse d'Aristote." *RT* 31 (1926): 285–329.

Lahey, Stephen. "Maimonides and Analogy." *ACPQ* 67 (1993): 219–32.

Lakebrink, Bernhard. "Analektik und Dialektik: Zur Methode des Thomistischen und Hegelschen Denkens." In *St. Thomas Aquinas, 1274–1974: Commemorative Studies,* foreword by E. Gilson, 2 vols., 2:459–87. Toronto: PIMS, 1974.

Lang, Helen S. "Aristotle's First Movers and the Relation of Physics to Theology." *NS* 52 (1978): 500–517.

Lebacqz, Joseph. "Apprehension or Assent?" *HJ* 5 (1964): 36–57.

Lee, Martin J. "Something Rather Than Nothing." *HJ* 27 (1986): 137–50.

Lee, Patrick. "Language about God and the Theory of Analogy." *NS* 58 (1984): 40–66.

———. "Aquinas on Knowledge of Truth and Existence." *NS* 60 (1986): 46–71.

———. "Existential Propositions in the Thought of St. Thomas Aquinas." *Thomist* 52 (1988): 605–26.

Lemaigre, Bernard M. "Perfection de Dieu et multiplicité des attributs divins." *RSPT* 50 (1966): 198–227.

Levine, Michael P. "'Can We Speak Literally of God?'" *RS* 21 (1985): 53–59.

Liccaro, Vincenzo. "Conoscenza e inconoscibilità di Dio nel pensiero di Alano di Lilla." *Medioevo* 2 (1976): 1–20.

Lilla, Salvatore. "The Notion of Infinitude in Pseudo-Dionysius Areopagita." *JTS* 31 (1980): 93–103.

Liske, Michael-Thomas. "Die Perspektive des Sprechers und ihre logische Bedeutung." *ThPh* 56 (1981): 111–18.

———. "Die sprachliche Richtigkeit bei Thomas von Aquin." *FZPT* 32 (1985): 373–90.

Lisska, Anthony J. "Deely and Geach on Abstractionism in Thomistic Epistemology." *Thomist* 37 (1973): 548–68.

Lobel, Diana. "'Silence Is Praise to You': Maimonides on Negative Theology, Looseness of Expression, and Religious Experience." *ACPQ* 76 (2002): 25–49.

Lonergan, Bernard. *Verbum: Word and Idea in Aquinas.* Ed. D. B. Burrell. Notre Dame: UND, 1967.

Lossky, Vladimir. "La notion des 'Analogies' chez Denys le Pseudo-Aréopagite." *AHDLMA* 5 (1930): 279–309.

———. "La théologie négative dans la doctrine de Denys l'Aréopagite." *RSPT* 28 (1939): 204–21.

———. "Elements of 'Negative Theology' in the Thought of St. Augustine." Trans. T. E. Bird. *SVTQ* 21 (1977): 67–75.

Louth, Andrew. *The Origins of the Christian Mystical Tradition.* London: Oxford, 1981.

———. *Denys the Areopagite.* London/Wilton, CT: Chapman/Morehouse-Barlow, 1989.

Lubac, Henri de. *The Discovery of God.* Trans. A. Dru from 3rd French ed. Chicago: Regnery, 1967.

Lyttkens, Hampus. *The Analogy between God and the World: An Investigation of Its Background and Interpretation of Its Use by Thomas of Aquino.* Trans. A. Poignant. Uppsala: Almqvist and Wiksells, 1952.

———. "Die Bedeutung der Gottesprädikate bei Thomas von Aquin." *NZST* 6 (1964): 274–89.

MacDonald, Scott. "Aquinas's Parasitic Cosmological Argument." *Medieval Philosophy and Theology* 1 (1991): 119–55.

Macquarrie, John. *God-Talk: An Examination of the Language and Logic of Theology.* New York: Seabury, 1979.

———. *In Search of Deity.* The Gifford Lectures, 1983. New York: Crossroad, 1985.

Mandonnet, Pierre, and J. Destrez, comps. *Bibliographie thomiste.* BibThom 1. Paris, 1921. Rev. ed. M.-D. Chenu; Paris: Vrin, 1960.

Manthey, Franz. *Die Sprachphilosophie des hl. Thomas von Aquin und ihre Anwendung auf Probleme der Theologie.* Paderborn: Schöningh, 1937.

Marcus, Wolfgang. "Zur religiösen philosophischen Analogie in der frühen Patristik." *PJ* 67 (1959): 143–70.

Maritain, Jacques. *The Degrees of Knowledge.* Trans. under the supervision of G. B. Phelan from 4th French ed. New York: Scribner, 1959.

Mascall, Eric. *Existence and Analogy.* London: Longmans, 1949.

Masiello, Ralph. "The Analogy of Proportion according to the Metaphysics of St. Thomas." *MSch* 35 (1958): 91–105.

———. "A Note on Essence and Existence." *NS* 45 (1971): 491–94.

Masson, Robert. "Analogy and Metaphoric Process." *TS* 62 (2001): 571–96.

Maurer, Armand. "St. Thomas and the Analogy of Genus." *NS* 29 (1955): 127–44.

———. *Thomas Aquinas, On Being and Essence.* Trans. with introduction and notes, 2nd ed. Toronto: PIMS, 1968.

———. "St. Thomas on the Sacred Name 'Tetragrammaton.'" *MS* 34 (1972): 275–86.

———. "The Sacred Tetragrammaton in Medieval Thought." In *Actas del V Congreso Internacional de filosofia medieval,* 2 vols., pp. 975–83. Madrid: Editoria Nacional, 1979.

McFague, Sallie. *Metaphorical Theology: Models of God in Religious Language.* Philadelphia: Fortress, 1982.

———. *Models of God: Theology for an Ecological, Nuclear Age.* Philadelphia: Fortress, 1987.

McInerny, Ralph. *The Logic of Analogy: An Interpretation of St. Thomas.* The Hague: Nijhoff, 1961.

———. *Studies in Analogy.* The Hague: Nijhoff, 1968.

———. "Boethius and St. Thomas Aquinas." *RFNS* 66 (1974): 219–45.

———. "Can God Be Named by Us? Prolegomena to Thomistic Philosophy of Religion." *RM* 32 (1978): 53–73.

———. *Rhyme and Reason: St. Thomas and Modes of Discourse.* The Aquinas Lecture, 1981. Milwaukee: Marquette, 1981.

———. *Boethius and Aquinas.* Washington, DC: CUA, 1990.

———. *Aquinas and Analogy.* Washington, DC: CUA, 1996.

McLelland, Joseph C. *God the Anonymous: A Study in Alexandrian Philosophical Theology.* Patristic Monograph Series 4. Cambridge, MA: Philadelphia Patristic Foundation, 1976.

McNicholl, Ambrose. "On Judging." *Thomist* 38 (1974): 768–825.

———. "On Judging Existence." *Thomist* 43 (1979): 507–80.

McWilliams, James A. "Judgmental Knowledge." *MSch* 39 (1962): 372–78.

Meagher, Robert E. "Thomas Aquinas and Analogy: A Textual Analysis." *Thomist* 34 (1970): 230–53.

Meissner, William. "Some Notes on a Figure in St. Thomas." *NS* 31 (1957): 68–84.

Merlan, Philip. "Aristotle's Unmoved Movers." *Traditio* 4 (1946): 1–30.

Miethe, Terry, and Vernon Bourke, comps. *Thomistic Bibliography, 1940–1978.* Westport, CT: Greenwood, 1980.

Miller, C. L. "Maimonides and Aquinas on Naming God." *JJS* 28 (1977): 65–71.

Mollenkott, Virginia. *The Divine Feminine: The Biblical Imagery of God as Female.* New York: Crossroad, 1983.

Moltmann, Jürgen. *The Crucified God.* Trans. R. A. Wilson and J. Bowden. New York: Harper and Row, 1974.

Mondin, Battista. "Triplice analisi dell'analogia e suo uso in teologia." *DTP* 34 (1957): 411–21.

———. "Il principio *omne agens agit simile sibi* e l'analogia dei nomi divini nel pensiero di S. Tommaso d'Aquino." *DTP* 37 (1960): 336–48.

———. *The Principle of Analogy in Protestant and Catholic Theology.* 2nd ed. The Hague: Nijhoff, 1968.

———. "L'analogia di proporzione e di proporzionalità nel Commento alle Sentenze." *RFNS* 66 (1974): 571–89.

———. "La dottrina della *imago Dei* nel commento alle Sentenze." In Studi Tomistici, vol. 2, *San Tommaso e l'odierna problematica teologica,* pp. 230–47. Rome: Pontificia Accademia Romana di S. Tommaso d'Aquino, 1974.

Montagnes, Bernard. *La doctrine de l'analogie de l'être d'après saint Thomas d'Aquin.* Philosophes Médiévaux 6. Louvain/Paris: Publications Universitaires/Béatrice-Nauwelaerts, 1963.

Morreall, John S. *Analogy and Talking about God: A Critique of the Thomistic Approach.* Washington, DC: University Press of America, 1978.

Mortley, Raoul. "*Analogia* chez Clément d'Alexandrie." *Revue des études grecques* 84 (1971): 80–93.

———. "Negative Theology and Abstraction in Plotinus." *AJP* 96 (1975): 363–77.

———. "The Fundamentals of the *Via Negativa.*" *AJP* 103 (1982): 429–39.

———. *From Word to Silence.* 2 vols. Bonn, 1986.

Mortley, Raoul, and David Dockrill, eds. *The Via Negativa.* Papers from the *Via Negativa* conference held at the University of Sydney in 1981. N.P.: *Prudentia* (supplementary number), 1981.

Mühlenberg, Ekkehard. *Die Unendlichkeit Gottes bei Gregor von Nyssa.* Göttingen: Vandenhoeck and Ruprecht, 1966.

Müller, Klaus. *Thomas von Aquins Theorie und Praxis der Analogie. Der Streit um das rechte Vorurteil und die Analyse einer aufschlussreichen Diskrepanz in der* "*Summa theologiae.*" Regensburger Studien zur Theologie 29. Frankfurt am Main/Bern/New York: Peter Lang, 1983.

Muskens, G. L. *De vocis analogias significatione ac usu apud Aristotelem.* Groningen: Wolters, 1943.

Neidl, Walter M. *Thearchia. Die Frage nach dem Sinn von Gott bei Pseudo-Dionysius Areopagita und Thomas von Aquin.* Regensburg: Habbel, 1976.

Nicolas, Jean H. "Affirmation de Dieu et connaissance." *RT* 64 (1964): 200–222.

———. *Dieu connu comme inconnu.* Paris: Desclée, 1966.

Noone, Timothy. "The Originality of St. Thomas' Position on the Philosophers and Creation." *Thomist* 60 (1996): 275–300.

O'Brien, Thomas C. *Metaphysics and the Existence of God.* Washington, DC: Thomist Press, 1960.

Olshewsky, Thomas M. "Aristotle's Use of *Analogia.*" *Apeiron* 2 (1968): 1–10.

O'Mahoney, Brendan. "A Medieval Semantic: The Scholastic *Tractatus de modis significandi.*" *Laurentianum* 5 (1964): 448–86.

———. "The Medieval Treatise on Modes of Meaning." *PS* 14 (1965): 117–38.

O'Meara, Thomas. *Thomas Aquinas: Theologian.* Notre Dame: UND, 1997.

———. *Erich Przywara, S.J.: His Theology and His World.* Notre Dame: UND, 2002.

O'Neill, Colman. "La prédication analogique: l'élément négatif." In *Analogie et dialectique,* ed. P. Gisel and P. Secretan, pp. 81–91. Geneva: Labor et Fides, 1982.

———. "Analogy, Dialectic, and Inter-Confessional Theology." *Thomist* 47 (1983): 43–65.

O'Neill, M. S. "Some Remarks on the Analogy of God and Creatures in St. Thomas Aquinas." *MS* 23 (1961): 206–15.

O'Rourke, Fran. *Pseudo-Dionysius and the Metaphysics of Aquinas.* Leiden: Brill, 1992.

O'Shaughnessy, Thomas. "St. Thomas' Changing Estimate of Avicenna's Teaching on Existence as an Accident." *MSch* 36 (1959): 245–60.

———. "La théorie thomiste de la contingence chez Plotin et les penseurs arabes." *RPL* 65 (1967): 36–52.

Owens, Joseph. "Analogy as a Thomistic Approach to Being." *MS* 24 (1962): 303–22.

———. "Quiddity and Real Distinction in St. Thomas Aquinas." *MS* 27 (1965): 1–22.

———. "Aquinas and the Proof from the *Physics.*" *MS* 28 (1966): 119–50.

———. "'Ignorare' and Existence." *NS* 46 (1972): 210–19.

———. "Aquinas—'Darkness of Ignorance' in the Most Refined Notion of God." In *Bonaventure and Aquinas: Enduring Philosophers,* ed. R. W. Shahan and F. J. Kovach, pp. 69–86. Norman: University of Oklahoma, 1976.

———. "Aristotle and God." In *God in Contemporary Thought: A Philosophical*

Perspective, ed. S. A. Matczak, pp. 415–42. New York: Learned Publications, 1977.

———. *The Doctrine of Being in the Aristotelian "Metaphysics."* 3rd ed. Preface by E. Gilson. Toronto: PIMS, 1978.

———. "Existence as Predicated." *NS* 53 (1979): 480–85.

———. "The Relation of God to World in the *Metaphysics.*" In *Études sur la "Métaphysique" d'Aristote,* Actes du VIe Symposium Aristotelicum, pp. 207–28. Paris: Vrin, 1979.

———. *St. Thomas Aquinas on the Existence of God.* Ed. J. R. Catan. Albany, NY: SUNY, 1980.

———. "Stages and Distinction in *De ente*: A Rejoinder." *Thomist* 45 (1981): 99–123.

———. "Natures and Conceptualization." *NS* 56 (1982): 376–80.

———. "Aquinas' Distinction at *De ente et essentia* 4.119–123." *MS* 48 (1986): 264–87.

———. "Further Thoughts on Knowledge of Being and Truth." *NS* 60 (1986): 454–70.

Palmer, D. W. "Atheism, Apologetic, and Negative Theology in the Greek Apologists of the Second Century." *VC* 37 (1983): 234–59.

Pannenberg, Wolfhart. "Zur Bedeutung des Analogiegedankens bei Karl Barth." *TLZ* 78 (1953): 18–23.

———. "Analogie und Offenbarung: Eine kritische Untersuchung der Geschichte des Analogiebegriffs in der Gotteserkenntnis." Habilitationsschrift, Heidelberg, 1955.

———. "Möglichkeiten und Grenzen der Anwendung des Analogieprinzips in der evangelischen Theologie." *TLZ* 85 (1960): 225–28.

———. "Analogy and Doxology." In *Basic Questions in Theology,* trans. G. H. Kehm, 2 vols., 1:211–38. Philadelphia: Westminster, 1970.

Patfoort, Albert. "La place de l'analogie dans la pensée de S. Thomas d'Aquin." *RSPT* 76 (1992): 235–54.

Paulus, Jean. "La théorie du premier moteur chez Aristote." *RP* 33 (1933): 259–94, 394–424.

———. "Le caractère métaphysique des preuves thomistes de l'existence de Dieu." *AHDLMA* 9 (1934): 143–53.

Péghaire, Julien. "L'axiome *Bonum est diffusivum sui* dans le néoplatonisme et le thomisme." *RUO* 1 (1932): 5–30.

———. *Intellectus et ratio selon saint Thomas d'Aquin.* Ottawa: Institut d'Études Médiévales, 1936.

Pegis, Anton C. *St. Thomas and the Greeks.* The Aquinas Lecture, 1939. Milwaukee: Marquette, 1939.

———. "Necessity and Liberty: An Historical Note on St. Thomas Aquinas." *NS* 15 (1941): 18–45.

———. "A Note on St. Thomas, *Summa theologica,* I, 44, 1–2." *MS* 8 (1946): 159–68.

———. "St. Thomas and the Origin of Creation." In *Philosophy and the Modern Mind*, ed. F. X. Canfield, pp. 49–65. Detroit: Sacred Heart Seminary, 1961.

———. "*Penitus Manet Ignotum.*" MS 27 (1965): 212–26.

———. "St. Thomas and the Coherence of the Aristotelian Theology." MS 35 (1973): 67–117.

Pelikan, Jaroslav. "*Imago Dei*: An Explication of *Summa theologiae*, Part 1, Question 93." In *Calgary Aquinas Studies*, ed. A. Parel, pp. 27–48. Toronto: PIMS, 1978.

Penido, Maurilio. *Le rôle de l'analogie en théologie dogmatique*. BibThom 15. Paris: Vrin, 1931.

Phelan, Gerald B. *Saint Thomas and Analogy*. Aquinas Lecture, 1941. Milwaukee: Marquette, 1941.

Philippe, M.-Dominique. "*Analogon* and *Analogia* in the Philosophy of Aristotle." *Thomist* 33 (1969): 1–74.

Pieper, Josef. *The Silence of Saint Thomas*. Trans. J. Murray and D. O'Connor. South Bend, IN: St. Augustine's Press, 1999.

Pinborg, Jan. *Die Entwicklung der Sprachtheorie im Mittelalter*. Beiträge zur Geschichte der Philosophie und Theologie des Mittelalters 42/2. Munster: Aschendorff, 1967.

———. *Logik und Semantik im Mittelalter: Ein Überblick*. Afterword by H. Kohlenberger, Problemata 10. Stuttgart/Bad Cannstatt: Frommann-Holzboog, 1972.

———. "Speculative Grammar." In *The Cambridge History of Later Medieval Philosophy*, ed. A. Kenny, N. Kretzmann, J. Pinborg, pp. 254–69. Cambridge: Cambridge University, 1982.

Platzeck, Erhard. *Von der Analogie zum Syllogismus*. Paderborn: Schöningh, 1954.

Pöltner, Günther. "Die Repräsentation als Grundlage analogen Sprechens von Gott im Denken des Thomas von Aquin." SJP 21–22 (1976–77): 23–43.

Preller, Victor. *Divine Science and the Science of God: A Reformulation of Thomas Aquinas*. Princeton: Princeton University, 1967.

Prezioso, Faustinus. *De Aristotelis creationismo secundum S. Bonaventuram et secundum S. Thomam*. Rome: Officium Libri Catholici, 1942.

Przywara, Erich. *Analogia entis. Metaphysik, Ur-Struktur und All-Rhythmus. Schriften*, vol. 3. Einsiedeln: Johannes, 1962.

Rabeau, Gaston. *Species. Verbum: L'activité intellectuelle élémentaire selon S. Thomas d'Aquin*. BibThom 22. Paris: Vrin, 1938.

Rahner, Karl. "An Investigation of the Incomprehensibility of God in St. Thomas Aquinas." In *Theological Investigations*, trans. D. Morland, 16:244–54. New York: Seabury, 1979.

———. "The Experiences of a Catholic Theologian." Trans. P. Verhalen. *Communio* 11 (1984): 404–14.

Ramírez, Santiago M. *De analogia*. Vol. 2 (in four parts) of *Edición de las obras completas de Santiago Ramírez, O.P.*, ed. V. Rodriguez. Madrid: Instituto de Filosofía "Luis Vives," 1970–72.

Ramsey, Ian. *Religious Language: An Empirical Placing of Theological Phrases.* London: SCM, 1957.

————. *Models and Mystery.* London: Oxford, 1964.

Ramshaw, Gail. "*De Divinis Nominibus:* The Gender of God." *Worship* 56 (1982): 117–31.

————. *God beyond Gender: Feminist Christian God-Language.* Minneapolis: Fortress, 1995.

Rassegna di letteratura tomistica. Vols. 1–. Naples: Editrice Domenicana Italiana, 1966–.

Reale, Giovanni. *Aristotele, "La Metafisica."* Trans. in 2 vols., with introduction and commentary, Filosofi Antichi 1–2. Naples: Loffredo, 1968.

Reding, Marcel. "*Analogia entis* und *analogia nominum.*" *EvT* 23 (1963): 225–44.

Ricken, Friedo. "Emanation und Schöpfung." *ThPh* 49 (1974): 483–86.

Ricoeur, Paul. "The Specificity of Religious Language." *Semeia* 4 (1975): 107–48.

————. *Interpretation Theory: Discourse and the Surplus of Meaning.* Fort Worth, TX: Texas Christian University, 1976.

————. *The Rule of Metaphor.* Trans. R. Czerny, K. McLaughlin, J. Costello. Toronto: University of Toronto, 1977.

————. "Naming God." Trans. D. Pellauer. *USQR* 34 (1979): 215–27.

Riesenhuber, Klaus. "Partizipation als Strukturprinzip der Namen Gottes bei Thomas von Aquin." In Miscellanea Mediaevalia, vol. 13/2, *Sprache und Erkenntnis im Mittelalter,* pp. 969–82. Berlin/New York: de Gruyter, 1981.

Riga, Peter J. "The Act of Faith in Augustine and Aquinas." *Thomist* 35 (1971): 143–74.

Rocca, Gregory. "The Distinction between *Res Significata* and *Modus Significandi* in Aquinas' Theological Epistemology." *Thomist* 55 (1991): 173–97.

————. "Aquinas on God-Talk: Hovering over the Abyss." *TS* 54 (1993): 641–61.

Roig Gironella, Juan. "La analogia del ser en la metafisica de Aristoteles." *Espiritu* 28 (1979): 101–34.

Rogers, Eugene F., Jr. *Thomas Aquinas and Karl Barth: Sacred Doctrine and the Natural Knowledge of God.* Notre Dame: UND, 1995.

Roland-Gosselin, M.-D., ed. *Le "De ente et essentia" de saint Thomas d'Aquin.* With introduction, notes and études historiques, BibThom 8. Paris: Vrin, 1926; repr. 1948.

————. "De la connaissance affective." *RSPT* 27 (1938): 5–26.

Rolnick, Philip. *Analogical Possibilities: How Words Refer to God.* AAR Academy Series 81. Atlanta: Scholars, 1993.

Roques, René. *L'Univers Dionysien: Structure hiérarchique du monde selon pseudo-Denys.* Paris: Aubier, 1954.

————. *La "Hiérarchie Céleste."* Paris: Cerf, 1970.

Rorem, Paul. "The Place of the *Mystical Theology* in the Pseudo-Dionysian Corpus." *Dionysius* 4 (1980): 87–97.

———. *Biblical and Liturgical Symbols within the Pseudo-Dionysian Synthesis.* Toronto: PIMS, 1984.

———. *Pseudo-Dionysius: A Commentary on the Texts and an Introduction to Their Influence.* New York: Oxford, 1993.

Ross, James F. "A Critical Analysis of the Theory of Analogy of St. Thomas Aquinas." Ph.D. dissertation, Brown University, 1958.

———. "Analogy as a Rule of Meaning for Religious Language." *IPQ* 1 (1961): 468–502.

———. "Reply of Professor Ross." *IPQ* 2 (1962): 658–62.

———. Review of *The Logic of Analogy,* by Ralph McInerny. *IPQ* 2 (1962): 633–42.

———. "A New Theory of Analogy." *PACPA* 44 (1970): 70–85.

———. *Portraying Analogy.* Cambridge: Cambridge University, 1981.

Ross, Susan A. "God's Embodiment and Women: Sacraments." *Freeing Theology: The Essentials of Theology in Feminist Perspective,* ed. C. LaCugna, 185–209. San Francisco: HarperCollins, 1993.

Roy, Lucien. *Lumière et Sagesse.* Montreal: L'Immaculée Conception, 1948.

Ruello, Francis. *Les "noms divins" et leur "raisons" selon saint Albert le Grand, commentateur du "De divinis nominibus."* BibThom 35. Paris: Vrin, 1963.

———. "Le commentaire du *De divinis nominibus* de Denys par Albert le Grand. Problèmes de méthode." *AP* 43 (1980): 589–613.

Safranski, Rüdiger. *Martin Heidegger: Between Good and Evil.* Trans. E. Osers. Cambridge, MA: Harvard, 1998.

Schillebeeckx, Edward. "The Non-Conceptual Intellectual Dimension in Our Knowledge of God according to Aquinas." In *Revelation and Theology,* trans. N. D. Smith, 2 vols., 2:157–206. New York: Sheed and Ward, 1968.

———. "The Non-Conceptual Intellectual Element in the Act of Faith: A Reaction." In *Revelation and Theology,* trans. N. D. Smith, 2 vols., 2:30–75. New York: Sheed and Ward, 1968.

Schindler, David. "Creativity as Ultimate: Reflections on Actuality in Whitehead, Aristotle, Aquinas." *IPQ* 13 (1973): 161–71.

———. "Whitehead's Challenge to Thomism on God and Creation: The Metaphysical issues." *IPQ* 19 (1979): 285–99.

Schlenker, Ernst. *Die Lehre von der göttlichen Namen in der Summa Alexanders von Hales.* Freiburger theologischen Studien 46. Freiburg: Herder, 1938.

Schmid, J. *Im Ausstrahl der Schönheit Gottes: Die Bedeutung der Analogie in "Herrlichkeit" bei Hans Urs von Balthasar.* Münsterschwarzach: Vier-Türme, 1982.

Schneiders, Sandra. *Women and the Word: The Gender of God in the New Testament and the Spirituality of Women.* New York: Paulist, 1986.

Schönberger, Rolf. *Nomina divina: zur theologischen Semantik bei Thomas von Aquin.* Europäische Hochschulschriften XX/72. Frankfurt/Bern: Lang, 1981.

Schrijver, Georges de. *Le merveilleux accord de l'homme et de Dieu. Étude de l'analogie de l'être chez Hans Urs von Balthasar.* Bibliotheca Ephemeridum Theologicarum Lovaniensium 63. Louvain: University Press, 1983.

Schütz, Ludwig. *Thomas-Lexicon.* Paderborn: Schöningh, 1895. Repr.: New York: Musurgia, 1949; Stuttgart: Frommann-Holzboog, 1975.

Seckler, Max. *Instinkt und Glaubenswille nach Thomas von Aquin.* Mainz, 1961.

Secretan, Philibert. "De l'analogie." *FZPT* 28 (1981): 148–76.

Seeskin, Kenneth. *Searching for a Distant God: The Legacy of Maimonides.* New York: Oxford, 2000.

———. "Sanctity and Silence: The Religious Significance of Maimonides' Negative Theology." *ACPQ* 76 (2002): 7–24.

Sertillanges, Antonin. "Agnosticisme ou anthropomorphisme." *RP* 8 (1906): 129–65.

———. "L'idée de création dans saint Thomas d'Aquin." *RSPT* 1 (1907): 239–51.

———. "La création." *RT* 33 (1928): 97–115.

———. *Les grandes thèses de la philosophie thomiste.* Paris: Bloud, 1928.

———. "La notion de création." *RT* 35 (1930): 48–57.

———. *La philosophie de saint Thomas d'Aquin.* Paris: Aubier, 1940.

———. *Foundations of Thomistic Philosophy.* Trans. G. Anstruther. Springfield, IL: Templegate, n.d.

Shanley, Brian. *The Thomist Tradition.* Boston: Kluwer Academic, 2002.

Shibles, Warren A. *Metaphor: An Annotated Bibliography and History.* Whitewater, WI: Language Press, 1971.

Simon, Yves R. "On Order in Analogical Sets." *NS* 34 (1960): 1–42.

Simonin, H. D. "La notion d'*intentio* dans l'oeuvre de S. Thomas d'Aquin." *RSPT* 19 (1930): 445–63.

Sokolowski, Robert. *The God of Faith and Reason.* Notre Dame: UND Press, 1982.

Soskice, Janet Martin. *Metaphor and Religious Language.* Oxford: Clarendon, 1985.

Steenberghen, Fernand van. "La composition constitutive de l'être fini." *RNP* 41 (1938): 489–518.

———. *Le problème de l'existence de Dieu dans les écrits de S. Thomas d'Aquin.* Philosophes Médiévaux 23. Louvain-la-Neuve: Editions de l'Institut Supérieur de philosophie, 1980.

Stewart, David. "Aristotle's Doctrine of the Unmoved Mover." *Thomist* 37 (1973): 522–47.

Stubbens, Neil. "Naming God: Moses Maimonides and Thomas Aquinas." *Thomist* 54 (1990): 229–67.

Sullivan, John E. *The Image of God.* Dubuque, IA: Priory Press, 1963.

Surin, K. "Creation, Revelation, and the Analogy Theory." *JTS* 32 (1981): 401–22.

Sweeney, Leo. "Are *Apeiria* and *Aoristia* Synonyms?" *MSch* 33 (1956): 270–79.

———. "Divine Infinity: 1150–1250." *MSch* 35 (1957): 38–51.

———. "Infinity in Plotinus." *Gregorianum* 38 (1957): 515–35, 713–32.

———. "Some Medieval Opponents of Divine Infinity." *MS* 19 (1957): 233–45.

———. "Doctrine of Creation in *Liber de causis*." In *An Étienne Gilson Tribute*, ed. C. J. O'Neil, pp. 274–89. Milwaukee: Marquette, 1959.

———. "Plotinus Revisited." *Gregorianum* 40 (1959): 327–31.

———. "L'infini quantitatif chez Aristote." *RPL* 58 (1960): 505–28.

———. "Another Interpretation of *Enneads* VI, 7, 32." *MSch* 38 (1961): 289–303.

———. "John Damascene and Divine Infinity." *NS* 35 (1961): 76–106.

———. "John Damascene's 'Infinite Sea of Essence.'" *SP* 4 (1962): 294–309.

———. "Existence/Essence in Thomas Aquinas' Early Writings." *PACPA* 37 (1963): 97–131.

———. "Preller and Aquinas." *MSch* 48 (1971): 267–73.

———. *Infinity in the Presocratics: A Bibliographical and Philosophical Study.* Foreword by Joseph Owens. The Hague: Nijhoff, 1972.

———. "Bonaventure and Aquinas on the Divine Being as Infinite." In *Bonaventure and Aquinas: Enduring Philosophers*, ed. R. W. Shahan and F. J. Kovach, pp. 133–53. Norman: University of Oklahoma, 1976.

———. "Surprises in the History of Infinity from Anaximander to George Cantor." *PACPA* 55 (1981): 3–23.

———. *Divine Infinity in Greek and Medieval Thought.* New York: Lang, 1992.

Sweeney, Leo, and Charles Ermatinger. "Divine Infinity according to Richard Fishacre." *MSch* 35 (1958): 191–212.

Swinburne, Richard. *The Coherence of Theism.* Oxford: Clarendon, 1977.

———. "Analogy and Metaphor." In *The Philosophical Assessment of Theology*, ed. Gerard Hughes, pp. 65–84. Washington, DC: Georgetown University, 1987.

Teasdale, Wayne. "*Nihil* as the Name of God in John Scotus Eriugena." *CS* 19 (1984): 232–47.

Thibault, Herve. *Creation and Metaphysics: A Genetic Approach to Existential Act.* The Hague: Nijhoff, 1970.

Thomas, Janice. "Univocity and Understanding God's Nature." In *The Philosophical Assessment of Theology*, ed. Gerard Hughes, pp. 85–100. Washington, DC: Georgetown University, 1987.

Thurot, Charles. *Extraits de divers manuscrits latins pour servir a l'histoire des doctrines grammaticales au moyen âge.* Frankfurt: Minerva, 1964; repr. from *Notices et extraits des manuscrits de la Bibliothèque Impériale*, vol. 22/2; Paris, 1868.

Thyrion, Jacques. "La notion de création passive dans le thomisme." *RT* 34 (1929): 303–19.

Tirot, Paul. "Autour du debat sur l'analogie de proportionnalité propre chez saint Thomas d'Aquin." *Angelicum* 63 (1986): 90–125.

Torrell, Jean-Pierre. *Saint Thomas Aquinas.* Vol. 1: *The Person and His Work.* Trans. Robert Royal. Washington, DC: CUA, 1996.

Tracy, David. *The Analogical Imagination*. New York: Crossroad, 1981.

Tugwell, Simon. "The Incomprehensibility of God." *New Blackfriars* 60 (1979): 479–91.

———. Ed. and trans. *Albert and Thomas;* introductions by S. Tugwell. Classics of Western Spirituality. New York: Paulist, 1988.

Turner, Denys. *The Darkness of God: Negativity in Christian Mysticism*. Cambridge: Cambridge University, 1995.

———. "Apophaticism, Idolatry, and the Claims of Reason." In *Silence and the Word: Negative Theology and Incarnation,* ed. Oliver Davies and Denys Turner, pp. 11–34. Cambridge: Cambridge University, 2002.

Turner, Walter H. "St. Thomas' Exposition of Aristotle: A Rejoinder." *NS* 35 (1961): 210–24.

Tyrrell, Francis M. *The Role of Assent in Judgment: A Thomistic Study*. Washington, DC: CUA, 1948.

———. "Concerning the Nature and Function of the Act of Judgment." *NS* 26 (1952): 393–423.

Überweg-Geyer. *Die patristische und scholastische Philosophie*. Vol. 2 in *Grundriss der Geschichte der Philosophie,* 11th ed. Berlin: Mittler, 1928.

Vander Marck, William. "Faith: What It Is Depends on What It Relates To." *RTAM* 43 (1976): 121–66.

Vanneste, Jean. *Le mystère de Dieu: Essai sur la structure rationnelle de la doctrine mystique du pseudo-Denys l'Aréopagite*. Museum Lessianium, section philosophique, no. 45. Brussels: Desclée de Brouwer, 1959.

Vansteenkiste, C. "Avicenna-Citaten bij S. Thomas." *TP* 15 (1953): 457–507.

———. "Autori Arabi e Giudei nell'opera di San Tommaso." *Angelicum* 37 (1960): 336–401.

Velde, Rudi te. *Participation and Substantiality in Thomas Aquinas*. Leiden: Brill, 1995.

Vogel, Cornelia J. de. "La théorie de *l'apeiron* chez Platon et dans la tradition platonicienne." *Revue philosophique de la France et de l'étranger* 149 (1959): 21–39.

———. "*Ego sum qui sum* et sa signification pour une philosophie chrétienne." *RevSR* 35 (1961): 337–55.

———. "*Deus Creator Omnium:* Plato and Aristotle in Aquinas' Doctrine of God." In *Graceful Reason: Essays in Ancient and Medieval Philosophy Presented to Joseph Owens, CSSR,* ed. L. P. Gerson, pp. 203–27. Toronto: PIMS, 1983.

Völker, Walther. *Kontemplation und Ekstase bei Pseudo-Dionysius Areopagita*. Wiesbaden: Franz Steiner, 1958.

Waldmann, M. "Thomas von Aquin und die *Mystische Theologie* des Pseudodionysius." *Geist und Leben* 22 (1949): 121–45.

Walgrave, Jan H. *Selected Writings*. Ed. G. de Schrijver and J. Kelly, Bibliotheca Ephemeridum Theologicarum Lovaniensium 57. Louvain: University Press, 1982.

Wallace, William A. "Aquinas on Creation: Science, Theology, and Matters of Fact." *Thomist* 38 (1974): 485–523.

Wéber, E. "Langage et méthode négatifs chez Albert le Grand." *RSPT* 65 (1981): 75–99.

Webster, John. "Eberhard Jüngel on the Language of Faith." *Modern Theology* 1 (1985): 253–76.

Weisheipl, James. *Friar Thomas d'Aquino: His Life, Thought and Work.* Rev. ed. Washington, DC: CUA, 1983.

———. "The Date and Context of Aquinas' *De aeternitate mundi.*" In *Graceful Reason: Essays in Ancient and Medieval Philosophy Presented to Joseph Owens, CSSR,* ed. L. P. Gerson, pp. 239–71. Toronto: PIMS, 1983.

Wess, Paul. "Die Inkomprehensibilität Gottes und ihre Konsequenzen für die Gotteserkenntnis bei Thomas von Aquin und Karl Rahner." Doctoral dissertation, University of Innsbruck, 1969.

———. *Wie von Gott Sprechen? Eine Auseinandersetzung mit Karl Rahner.* Graz: Styria, 1970.

Westra, Laura. "The Soul's Noetic Ascent to the One in Plotinus and to God in Aquinas." *NS* 58 (1984): 99–126.

White, Roger. "Notes on Analogical Predication and Speaking about God." In *The Philosophical Frontiers of Christian Theology,* ed. B. Hebblethwaite and S. Sutherland, pp. 197–226. Cambridge: Cambridge University, 1982.

White, Victor. "Thomism and 'Affective Knowledge.'" *Blackfriars* 24 (1943): 8–16, 126–31; 25 (1944): 321–28.

———. *God the Unknown.* New York: Harper, 1956.

Wilhelmsen, Frederick D. "Existence and Esse." *NS* 50 (1976): 20–45.

———. "The Concept of Existence and the Structure of Judgment: A Thomistic Paradox." *Thomist* 41 (1977): 317–49.

Williams, A. N. *The Ground of Union: Deification in Aquinas and Palamas.* New York: Oxford, 1999.

Williams, C. J. F. "Existence and the Meaning of the Word *God.*" *DR* 77 (1959): 53–71.

Williams, Janet. "The Apophatic Theology of Dionysius the Pseudo-Areopagite." *DR* 117 (1999): 157–72, 235–50.

Williams, R. G. "The *Via Negativa* and the Foundations of Theology: An Introduction to the Thought of V. N. Lossky." In *New Studies in Theology,* no. 1, ed. S. Sykes and D. Holmes, pp. 95–117. London: Duckworth, 1980.

Winance, Eleuthère. "L'essence divine et la connaissance humaine dans le *Commentaire sur les Sentences* de saint Thomas." *RPL* 55 (1957): 171–215.

Wippel, John F. "Aquinas' Route to the Real Distinction: A Note on *De ente et essentia* c. 4." *Thomist* 43 (1979): 279–95.

———. *Metaphysical Themes in Thomas Aquinas.* Studies in Philosophy and the History of Philosophy 10. Washington, DC: CUA, 1984.

———. "Thomas Aquinas and Participation." In *Studies in Medieval Philosophy,* ed. John Wippel, pp. 117–58. Washington, DC: CUA, 1987.

———. "The Latin Avicenna as a Source of Thomas Aquinas' Metaphysics." *FZPT* 37 (1990): 51–90.

———. "Thomas Aquinas on What Philosophers Can Know about God." *ACPQ* 66 (1992): 279–97.

———. *Thomas Aquinas on the Divine Ideas.* Étienne Gilson Series 16. Toronto: PIMS, 1993.

———. *The Metaphysical Thought of Thomas Aquinas: From Finite Being to Uncreated Being.* Monographs of the Society for Medieval and Renaissance Philosophy 1. Washington, DC: CUA, 2000.

———. "Thomas Aquinas on Our Knowledge of God and the Axiom That Every Agent Produces Something Like Itself." *PACPA* 74 (2000): 81–101.

Wissink, J. B. M. "Aquinas: The Theologian of Negative Theology—A Reading of *ST* I, qq. 14–26." *Jaarboek 1993* (Utrecht: Thomas Instituut, 1994): 15–83.

———, ed. *The Eternity of the World in the Thought of Thomas Aquinas and His Contemporaries.* Leiden: Brill, 1990.

Wohlman, Avital. *Thomas d'Aquin et Maïmonide: Un dialogue exemplaire.* Paris: Cerf, 1988.

Wolfson, Harry A. *Philo.* 2 vols. Cambridge: Harvard, 1947.

———. *Studies in the History of Philosophy and Religion.* Ed. I. Twersky and G. H. Williams, 2 vols. Cambridge: Harvard, 1973–77.

Yardan, John L. "Some Remarks on Metaphysics and the Existence of God." *NS* 37 (1963): 213–19.

Zeitz, James V. "Erich Przywara: Visionary Theologian." *Thought* 58 (1983): 145–57.

———. "Reflections on Erich Przywara and Eberhard Jüngel." *Communio* 12 (1985): 158–72.

———. "Przywara and Von Balthasar on Analogy." *Thomist* 52 (1988): 473–98.

Index of Texts of Aquinas

Anima (Sententia libri De anima)

BDH (Expositio libri Boetii De hebdomadibus)

BDT (Super Boetium De Trinitate)

Caelo (Sententia super libros De caelo et mundo)

Col. (Expositio et Lectura super Epistolas Pauli Apostoli)

DE (De ente et essentia)

De aetern. (De aeternitate mundi), 239

De articulis (De articulis fidei et ecclesiae sacramentis ad Archiepiscopum Panormitanum)

Decretalem (Expositio super primam et secundam Decretalem ad Archidiaconum Tudertinum)

De perfec. (De perfectione spiritualis vitae)

De prin. (De principiis naturae)

De ration. (De rationibus fidei ad Cantorem Antiochenum)

R36 (Responsio ad Lectorem Venetum de 36 articulis)

R43 (Responsio ad Magistrum Joannem de Vercellis de 43 articulis)

R108 (Responsio ad Magistrum Joannem de Vercellis de 108 articulis)

Rom. (Expositio et Lectura super Epistolas Pauli Apostoli)

SCG (Summa contra Gentiles), 181–83, 186, 232

1 Tim. (Expositio et Lectura super Epistolas Pauli Apostoli)

2 Tim. (Expositio et Lectura super Epistolas Pauli Apostoli)

Index of Names

Index of Subjects

Speaking the Incomprehensible God: Thomas Aquinas on the Interplay of Positive and Negative Theology was designed and composed in Minion by Kachergis Book Design, Pittsboro, North Carolina; and printed by Lightning Source, Inc., La Vergne, Tennessee.

Breinigsville, PA USA
02 August 2010
242869BV00001B/14/P